Foundations of Lodging Management

Foundations of Lodging Management

David K. Hayes, Ph.D.

Jack D. Ninemeier, Ph.D.

PEARSON

Prentice
Hall

Upper Saddle River, New Jersey 07458

Library of Congress Cataloging-in-Publication Data

Hayes, David K.
　Foundations of lodging management / David K. Hayes, Jack D. Ninemeier.
　　p. cm.
　　ISBN 0-13-170055-3
　1.　Hospitality industry—Management.　I. Ninemeier, Jack D. II. Title.
　TX911.3.M27H3879 2006
　647.94′068—dc22

2005008365

Executive Editor: Vernon R. Anthony
Assistant Editor: Ann Brunner
Editorial Assistant: Beth Dyke
Executive Marketing Manager: Ryan DeGrote
Senior Marketing Coordinator: Elizabeth Farrell
Marketing Assistant: Les Roberts
Director of Manufacturing and Production: Bruce
　Johnson
Managing Editor: Mary Carnis
Production Liaison: Jane Bonnell
Production Editor: John Shannon/Pine Tree Composition

Manufacturing Manager: Ilene Sanford
Manufacturing Buyer: Cathleen Petersen
Creative Director: Cheryl Asherman
Senior Design Coordinator: Miguel Ortiz
Cover Designer: Anthony Gemmellaro
Cover Image: Neil Setchfield, Getty/Lonely Planet Images
Composition: Pine Tree Composition
Manager of Media Production: Amy Peltier
Media Production Project Manager: Lisa Rinaldi
Printer/Binder: Hamilton Printing
Cover Printer: Phoenix Color

Credits and acknowledgments borrowed from other sources and reproduced, with permission in this textbook appear on appropriate page within.

Pearson Education LTD.
Pearson Education Singapore, Pte. Ltd.
Pearson Education Canada, Ltd.
Pearson Education—Japan
Pearson Education Australia PTY, Limited
Pearson Education North Asia Ltd.
Pearson Educación de Mexico, S.A. de C.V.
Pearson Education Malaysia, Pte. Ltd.

10　9　8　7　6　5　4　3
ISBN 0-13-170055-3

To our parents:

M.D. and Pauline, whose support and encouragement
have been as greatly appreciated as they have
been unwavering.

Lorine and Ralph, who emphasized the importance
of education and purposeful endeavors balanced
with time to "smell the roses".

* * * * *

To Peggy and Lani, our partners in all we do.

Contents

Access this book's Companion Website at: www.prenhall.com/hayes

Preface   xi

1   INTRODUCTION TO LODGING AND TRAVEL INDUSTRIES   1

The Early Lodging Industry   3
United States Hotel Industry: 1900–2000   3
Segments of the Lodging Industry   3
Measuring Hotel Performance   10
Travelers and the Travel Industry   13
    Leisure Travelers   14
    Business Travelers   14
Partners in the Lodging Industry   14
    Transportation Services   15
    Travel Agents   18
    Tour Operators   19
    Web Site Operators   21
Trade Associations   22

2   THE STRUCTURE OF THE LODGING INDUSTRY   26

Hotel Owners   27
    Investors   28
    Owner/Operators   29
Management Companies   30
    The Role and Structure of Management
        Companies   30
    Management Contracts   35
    Management Company Advantages
        and Disadvantages   37

Franchising and the Lodging Industry   39
    Hotel Franchisors   39
    Hotel Franchisees   42
    Franchise Agreements   44
Ownership and Management
    Alternatives   48
Ownership and Operational Challenges   50

3   SERVICE AND HOTEL MANAGEMENT   54

Quality Impacts Service   55
    Service Concerns   56
    Service Expectations   57
Ingredients in a Quality Service System   57
    Consider the Guests Being Served   58
    Determine What the Guests Desire   58
    Develop Procedures to Deliver What Guests
        Want   60
    Train and Empower Staff   61
    Implement Revised Systems   62
    Evaluate and Modify Service Delivery
        Systems   62
Service and "Moments of Truth"   65
Service Delivery by Employees   68
Management Tactics for Effective
    Guest Service   70
    Recruit and Select Service-Minded Staff   70
    Provide Effective Orientation and Training   71
    Supervise with a Service Emphasis   71
    Empower Staff with Service Authority   72
    Emphasize Continuous Quality
        Improvement   72

LODGING PROPERTY STAFF ARE SERVICE
  PROFESSIONALS   73
BENCHMARK AGAINST THE BEST: THE
  RITZ-CARLTON HOTEL COMPANY   75

4   THE MANAGEMENT OF LODGING   81

THE ROLE OF MANAGERS   82
  Management Functions   82
  Management Principles   85
  Management Science and Art   87
HOTEL MANAGEMENT STRUCTURE   88
  Larger Hotels   89
  Smaller Hotels   89
THE ROLE OF THE HOTEL GENERAL
  MANAGER   91
  Owner Relations   92
  Staff Development   93
  Property Management   94
  Brand Affiliation Management   96
  Community Relations   98
THE ROLE OF THE GENERAL MANAGER'S
  SUPERVISOR   101
  Owner/Investor Supervision   101
  Management Company Supervision   104
  Brand Supervision   106

5   THE HOTEL TEAM: SUPERVISORS
AND ENTRY-LEVEL STAFF   110

IMPORTANCE OF TEAMWORK   111
ROLE OF SUPERVISORS   114
  Responsibilities   115
  Leadership Styles   116
SPECIAL SUPERVISORY CONCERNS   120
  Communication   120
  Motivation   122
  Training   126
  Coaching   130
  Effective Working Relationships   131
  Performance Appraisal Systems   133
  Employee Discipline   136
ROLE OF ENTRY-LEVEL EMPLOYEES   138
  Responsibilities   139
  Retention   140
  Career Tracks   143

6   THE HUMAN RESOURCES DEPARTMENT   147

IMPORTANCE OF HUMAN RESOURCES
  DEPARTMENT   148
  Background   149
  Human Resources Priorities   150

HUMAN RESOURCES ACTIVITIES   151
  Recruitment   151
  Selection   153
  Orientation   154
  Training   156
COMPENSATION   158
  Importance of Compensation   159
  Fringe Benefits   160
LEGAL ASPECTS OF HUMAN RESOURCES   161
  Employee Selection   162
  Employer-Employee Relationships   165
  Other Workplace Laws   165
EMPLOYEE SAFETY AND HEALTH   170
DIVERSITY AND LODGING INDUSTRY   171
HUMAN RESOURCES CHALLENGES   173

7   THE FRONT OFFICE DEPARTMENT   177

FRONT OFFICE RESPONSIBILITIES   178
  PMS Management   179
  Guest Services   180
  Accounting and Data Management   181
FORECASTING DEMAND   183
  The Effect of Demand on ADR   183
  Estimating Demand   185
  Use of the PMS in Forecasting Demand   185
ESTABLISHING ROOM RATES   188
  Yield Management   188
  Transient Rates   190
  Group Rates   192
RESERVATIONS   193
  Hotel Direct Inquiry   193
  Central Reservation System   195
  Internet Booking Sites   197
RECEPTION AND GUEST SERVICE   198
  Pre-arrival   199
  Arrival and Stay   200
  Departure   202
GUEST ACCOUNTING   203
  Data Management   204
  Night Audit   207

8   THE SALES AND MARKETING
DEPARTMENT   211

THE IMPORTANCE OF SALES
  AND MARKETING   212
SALES AND MARKETING ACTIVITIES   215
  On-Property Activities   218
  Off-Property Activities   222
HOTEL MARKETS   226
  Transient Travelers   226
  Group Travelers   229

SALES AND MARKETING TOOLS   231
  In-Person Sales Calls   231
  Print and Direct Mail   233
  Telephone   234
  E-mail   235
  Web Sites   236
  Client-Appreciation Activities   238
EVALUATION OF SALES AND MARKETING
  EFFORTS   239
  Performance to Sales and Marketing
    Plan   240
  STAR Report   241

9 THE ACCOUNTING DEPARTMENT   247

ON-PROPERTY HOTEL ACCOUNTING   248
  Centralized Accounting Systems   249
  Decentralized Accounting Systems   250
BUDGETING   251
  Long-Range Budgets   252
  Annual Budgets   253
  Monthly Budgets   254
INCOME CONTROL   255
  Operational Controls   255
  Cash Control   259
  Allowances and Adjustments   262
  Accounts Receivable Control   265
EXPENSE CONTROL   269
  Purchasing and Receiving   270
  Accounts Payable   271
FINANCIAL REPORTING   274
  The Income Statement   275
  Balance Sheet   277
  The Statement of Cash Flows   280

10 THE HOUSEKEEPING DEPARTMENT   283

THE ROLE OF HOUSEKEEPING   284
  Areas of Responsibility   284
  Interactions   286
MANAGING HOUSEKEEPING   289
  Staffing   290
  Managing Lost and Found   295
SAFETY TRAINING   297
CLEANING RESPONSIBILITIES   299
  Employee Scheduling   299
  Guest Room Cleaning   301
LAUNDRY OPERATIONS   307
  Laundry Processing   307
  Guest-Operated Laundry   312
  "Green" Hotels   314

11 THE MAINTENANCE DEPARTMENT   318

THE ROLE OF MAINTENANCE   319
  Areas of Responsibility   320
  Interactions   324
MANAGING MAINTENANCE   325
  Staffing   326
  Routine Maintenance   327
  Preventive Maintenance   330
  Emergency Maintenance   334
MANAGING UTILITIES   336
  Electricity   337
  Natural Gas   341
  Water   341
MANAGING WASTE   342

12 FOOD SERVICE AND MEETING
MANAGEMENT IN LIMITED-SERVICE
SETTINGS   346

RANGE OF FOOD SERVICES   348
  Breakfast Alternatives   349
  Other Food Services   351
MANAGEMENT OF LOBBY FOOD SERVICES   352
  Menu Planning   352
  Purchasing   356
  Receiving and Storing   358
  Setting Up Breakfast Service   359
  Maintaining Breakfast Service   360
  Cleaning Up   362
GUESTS AND LOBBY FOOD SERVICES   365
MANAGING MEETINGS   366
  Small Meetings Business   366
  Meeting Procedures   367
  Meeting Food Services   369

13 FOOD AND BEVERAGE OPERATIONS:
FULL-SERVICE HOTELS   373

FOOD AND BEVERAGE GUESTS   374
ORGANIZATION OF HOTEL FOOD
  AND BEVERAGE OPERATIONS   376
  Small Hotels   376
  Large Hotels   377
MENU PLANNING   378
  Guest Concerns   379
  Operating Concerns   381
FOOD SERVICE CONTROL POINTS   383
  Purchasing   383
  Receiving, Storing, and Issuing   386
  Serving and Service   387

À La Carte Dining   388
    Getting Ready for Service   388
    Service Procedures   391
Room Service   394
    Profitability   394
    Menu Planning   395
    Operating Issues   396
    In-Room Service   397
Banquet Operations   398
    Profitability   400
    Menu Planning   401
    Banquet Event Orders and Contracts   402
    Other Banquet Concerns   403

14 SAFETY AND SECURITY   409

The Importance of Safety   410
    Legal Liability for Guest and Employee
        Safety   410
    Hotel Responsibility for Guest Safety 412
Safety Resources   416
    Internal Resources   417
    External Resources   422
Special Safety-Related Threats   424
    Swimming Pools   424
    Spas   425
    Exercise Facilities   426
    Parking Areas   426
Protecting Property from Security
    Threats   427
    Internal Threats   429
    External Threats   432
    Area-Specific Threats   433
    Hotel Crisis-Management Plans   436

15 CAREERS IN THE LODGING INDUSTRY   441

Planning Precedes Career Decisions   442
    Career-Planning Steps   443
    Assess Personal Interests   443
Lodging Industry Career
    Alternatives   446
    Independent Hotel or Multi-Unit
        Organization?   446
    Large or Small Hotel Company?   450
    Franchisor or Operating Company?   451
    Profit or Non-Profit?   452
Obtaining the First Professional
    Position   454
    Collecting Information   454
    Important Concerns: Prospective
        Employers   456
    Important Concerns: Prospective
        Employees   457
Success in the First Professional
    Position   457
    Success Tactics   458
    First Days at Work   459
    Ongoing Professional Development   462
Entrepreneur or Intrapreneur?   466
    Definitions   466
    Why Hotels Fail   467
    Tactics of Successful Intrapreneurs   468
Domestic and Global Hotel Positions   470
    Working in Another Country   470
    Success Factors in Global Assignments 472

Glossary   479
Index   501

Preface

Lodging is one of the most exciting and rapidly changing segments of the hospitality industry. Given the interest in lodging, and its rapid growth (especially in the limited-service hotel segment), the authors wanted to provide students, instructors, and industry professionals a basic framework and structure for understanding the inner workings of this vitally important component of the larger travel industry. While many of the examples found in the text apply to the limited-service segment, hoteliers working in full-service hotels will find the text's content just as valuable. Our goal was to create a conceptual foundation that would teach readers about the fundamental hows and whys of management in the lodging industry. With the publication of *Foundations of Lodging Management* we believe we have met this goal.

Hoteliers operate hotels, and today's hoteliers face challenges unmatched in recent history. Changing consumer demands, the advent of the Internet as a major force in selling rooms, advanced operational technology at the front desk and in sales, and even the threat of global terrorism all have an impact on the day-to-day activities of those who work in and manage hotels.

Historically, if a hotelier wanted to know about how to manage a housekeeping, front office, or sales and marketing department, it was fairly easy to find a recently published book on these departmental specific topics. The same was true about all of the other individual operating departments in a hotel. If, however, the hotelier's goal was to understand the workings of the entire hotel, as well as how its component parts or departments interconnected, little published material was available. With the Prentice Hall publication, in 2003, of *Hotel Operations Management* (an operational guide for hotel general managers) the situation changed. The authors of the present text realized, however, that not all hoteliers are, or even aspire to be, general managers. In addition, and more importantly, the authors realize that in today's overwhelmingly limited-service hotel environment (defined in this text as a hotel with limited food and beverage offerings), many department heads will, at some point, perform a variety of roles traditionally performed by a hotel general manager. Because that is so, it is important for the executive housekeeper, the front office manager, and others in a hotel who may act as the manager on duty (MOD) to understand how the complete operation functions.

While limited-service hotels are typically smaller, and some might say less complicated to operate, than a full-service hotel, in many ways these hotels are very complex because individual hotel employees, supervisors, and managers are often required to multi-task. Therefore, each employee must be intensively trained and bring great flexibility and talent to his or her job. The cross-training of employees is a fundamental theme throughout this book, and readers will find that the information provided about one department is plainly enough presented that it can serve as an orientation to employees in other hotel departments. In fact, the authors believe that *Foundations of Lodging Management* should be required reading for all hoteliers regardless of their departmentally specific position because it will, in a simple manner, help them better understand the complexity of the entire hotel.

INTENDED AUDIENCES

Instructors

Instructors will find, for the first time, a basic yet comprehensive text that addresses, in simple language, all of the operating departments of a hotel. In addition, it contains information about the history of the hotel industry as well the role of hotels within the larger hospitality industry. It is appropriate both for those just beginning to study the hotel industry and for those currently working in the industry who seek to advance their careers by continuing their education.

The Supplemental Teaching materials developed for this text are vast and have been extensively reviewed and edited by the authors. The PowerPoints (available on the book's Companion Website at www.prenhall.com/hayes) enhance student learning by making the text material easy to understand and easy to remember.

Students

Serious hospitality students want to understand how an entity as large and complex as a hotel actually operates. *Foundations of Lodging Management* provides that information in an easy-to-read format. Regardless of their specific area of interest in the hotel industry, readers will soon learn how all of a hotel's departments (and employees!) can work together to ensure that guests are treated in a manner that consistently exceeds their expectations.

A basic understanding of the hotel industry is critical for those who are committed to hospitality as a career, as well as those who are simply considering such a career. The book's final chapter; "Careers in the Lodging Industry," will be of great interest to these students. In addition, readers working in related businesses, such as travel agencies, visitor and convention bureaus, and other travel-related areas, will benefit from understanding how the component parts of the lodging industry fit together.

In most cases, students who work in the lodging industry will start in one of the functional areas of a hotel. As their careers progress, they will gain added expertise and additional responsibilities. This book will be of immediate assistance because it will help these students understand now how what they are doing in a hotel affects the work of other employees and ultimately the guests' overall experience. Therefore it will be an important addition to any hotelier's professional library.

Industry Professionals

Many people are interested in how hoteliers do their jobs. Hotel investors need to understand what hoteliers can be expected to do to help ensure the quality and growth of their hotel investments. Employees look to the hotel's leadership to make decisions that benefit their short-term job goals and long-term employment interests. Guests, of course, rely upon professional hoteliers to ensure that they receive value and quality for their lodging expenditures. Finally, professional hoteliers, because they are professionals, seek to better understand how their own efforts complement those of the entire hotel staff. In any hotel, department heads, supervisors, and hourly employees all benefit when they understand how each meshes with the other. *Foundations of Lodging Management* is a valuable text for all of these readers.

CHAPTER ORDER AND CONTENT

To truly understand lodging, one must first understand its history (Chapter 1 in this text) as well as its structure (Chapter 2). Because hotels ultimately must provide exceptional service (Chapter 3), that topic is fully covered, then followed by a thorough discussion of management's role in the lodging operation (Chapter 4) as well as the role of supervisors and hourly staff (Chapter 5).

While there is no universal agreement on the best order in which to study the operational functions (not necessarily departments) of a lodging facility, the authors elected to begin with people. Thus, the hotel's human resources function (Chapter 6) begins the look at specific functional areas of a lodging facility. The human resources function is followed by the front office (Chapter 7), sales and marketing (Chapter 8), and accounting (Chapter 9) functions to illustrate the importance of sales to the long-term economic health of any lodging facility.

Housekeeping (Chapter 10) and Maintenance (Chapter 11) are included because they are so important to an understanding of how guests' needs are met by these critical functional areas. An examination of the food and beverage areas found in limited-service hotels (Chapter 12) as well as full-service hotels (Chapter 13) is included because of the unique role food and beverages play in a lodging facility. The last functional topics to be considered relate to the vitally critical areas of lodging safety and security (Chapter 14).

The final chapter (Chapter 15) allows readers to examine, in detail, the career opportunities available to those skilled in lodging management.

CHAPTER FUNDAMENTALS

The lodging industry is an exciting one, and the authors sought to convey its excitement through a text that would be, first and foremost, user-friendly. To that end, each chapter in *Foundations of Lodging Management* includes certain fundamental components.

Chapter Objectives

Each chapter begins with small number (five to seven) of specific learning objectives. These one-sentence objectives help students know exactly what they should learn by reading the chapter.

Chapter Outline

Each chapter's tiered outline has been carefully developed to provide the maximum ease in finding important information.

Chapter Overview

Each chapter begins with a one- or two-page narrative summary that describes what will be presented in the chapter, as well as why the information is important to know.

Lodging Language

As is true in many professional fields, hoteliers often speak their own unique language. Thus, for example, RevPar will be analyzed, the GDS will ensure reservation connectivity, DNDs will instruct housekeepers to clean a room at a later time of day, and a recodable lock will help ensure guest safety. When lodging-specific terms are used in the book (and they are used extensively), they are defined at the time of first usage, often with direct-use examples that help to further clarify their meaning. In fact, unique vocabulary is such an important part of this book and the industry that the glossary contains over 400 unique-to-lodging definitions.

Lodging On-line

In many cases, the amount of additional information a specific Web site could provide was significant and particularly useful. Where that was the case, the Web site was presented under the heading "Lodging On-line." In many cases, the addition of Web resources enhanced the book's own content. The Web references in this book are purposely extensive and are found in every chapter.

All in a Day's Work

Hoteliers routinely face unique problems and situations that require outstanding decision-making skills. The "All in a Day's Work" component of this text poses a true-to-life lodging problem as well as its solution. These vignettes can make for excellent classroom discussion topics.

Chapter Objectives Review

This section of the text reminds readers of the specific objectives presented at the beginning of the chapter. This enables readers who are uncertain whether they have achieved the chapter's stated objectives to return immediately to the section of text they should reread.

Lodging Language Glossary

At each chapter's end, a complete listing of the industry-specific terms defined in the chapter is presented. As a result, readers can quickly review these terms to ensure that they are understood and can be used in their proper context.

For Discussion

This extensive feature (ten discussion questions per chapter) encourages students to talk about specific issues related to the material they have mastered in each chapter. Many of these discussion questions can serve as excellent homework or writing assignments.

Team Activities

This chapter-concluding feature encourages students to work together to seek information, solve problems, or address lodging industry issues in a group setting.

The authors believe that *Foundations of Lodging Management* fills a need in the hospitality industry literature. Its up-to-date and comprehensive but plainly presented coverage of all areas of the lodging industry makes it an essential addition to the professional library of the serious hospitality student. It is our hope that students, instructors, and industry professionals will find it to be a significant contribution to the field of hospitality management. It has been our honor for a combined sixty-plus years to work in this exciting field and contribute, through the publication of learning materials such as this book, to the development of our fellow hoteliers and future industry leaders.

David K. Hayes, Ph.D.
Jack D. Ninemeier, Ph.D.

ACKNOWLEDGMENTS

The production of a book like this one is truly the culmination of the efforts of many. The authors' thanks go to Vernon Anthony, Executive Editor at Prentice Hall, for his belief in the project, Ann Brunner, our editor, for her outstanding assistance in text development, and the entire production staff at Pearson Education for their tireless efforts.

Photo identification, selection, and placement assistance were provided by Allisha Miller. Typing and manuscript editing services were provided by Debbie Ruff, a consistent contributor to all of our work. We appreciate her keen eye and outstanding efforts to improve the quality of our writing.

Also of tremendous assistance were our text reviewers, R. Thomas George, The Ohio State University; Tammie J. Kaufman, University of Central Florida; Jeffrey P. Ivory, St. Louis Community College; and James A. Chandler, East Carolina University, who added much to improve the structure and content of the text. For their efforts we are truly grateful.

The supplemental teaching materials developed for this text were created by Trishauna A. Hayes, special assistant (ESL) in the Ann Arbor, Michigan, public school system.

Photo Credits

Chapter 1

Page 2: Peter Correz/Getty Images Inc.—Stone Allstock. *Page 7:* David Murray and Jules Selmes © Dorling Kindersley. *Page 8:* © Dorling Kindersley. *Page 11:* Robin Smith/Photolibrary.Com. *Page 20:* Yellow Dog Productions/Getty Images Inc.—Image Bank.

Chapter 2

Page 29: Getty Images, Inc. *Page 33:* Alan Keohane © Dorling Kindersley. *Page 34:* Seth Kushner/Getty Images Inc.—Stone Allstock. *Page 42:* Jan Staller/Getty Images/Time Life Pictures.

Chapter 3

Page 59: Jeff Greenberg/PhotoEdit. *Page 61:* Steve Skjold/PhotoEdit. *Page 66:* EyeWire Collection/Getty Images—Photodisc. *Page 73:* Arthur Tilley/Getty Images, Inc.—Taxi. *Page 76:* Miro Vintoniv/Stock Boston.

Chapter 4

Page 91: Bluestone Productions/Getty Images, Inc.—Taxi. *Page 99:* EyeWire Collection/Getty Images—Photodisc. *Page 100:* David Weintraub/Stock Boston. *Page 104:* Giboux/Getty Images, Inc.—Liaison.

Chapter 5

Page 118: Jeff Zaruba/Zaruba Photography. *Page 124:* Stockbyte. *Page 131:* Photolibrary.Com. *Page 135:* Esbin/Anderson/Omni-Photo Communications, Inc.

Chapter 6

Page 157: Bob Daemmrich/The Image Works. *Page 162:* © Dennis MacDonald/PhotoEdit. *Page 169:* Stockbyte.

Chapter 7

Page 180: Myrleen Ferguson Cate/PhotoEdit. *Page 184:* Corbis Royalty Free. *Page 191:* Getty Images, Inc.—Taxi. *Page 193:* Laima Druskis/Stock Boston. *Page 194:* Farmhouse Productions/Getty Images Inc.—Image Bank. *Page 205:* Govin-Sorel/Getty Images Inc.—Stone Allstock.

Chapter 8

Page 219: Joseph Giannetti/Index Stock Imagery, Inc. *Page 223:* Pascal Quittemelle/Stock Boston. *Page 229:* Loven, Paul/Getty Images Inc.—Image Bank. *Page 234:* Lindy Powers/Index Stock Imagery, Inc. *Page 239:* Mark Richards/PhotoEdit.

Chapter 9

Page 251: Harry Bartlett/Getty Images, Inc.—Taxi. *Page 254:* Stewart Cohen/Getty Images Inc.—Stone Allstock. *Page 262:* Timothy Shonnard/Getty Images Inc.—Stone Allstock. *Page 270:* Brady/Pearson Education/PH College. *Page 278:* United States Steel Corporation.

Chapter 10

Page 289: Clarion Hotel and Conference Center, Lansing, MI. *Page 305a:* © Dorling Kindersley. *Page 305b:* Rob Melnychuk/Getty Images, Inc.—Photodisc. *Page 311:* Stockbyte.

Chapter 12

Page 350: Donovan Reese/Getty Images Inc.—Stone Allstock. *Page 362:* Steve Mason/Getty Images, Inc.- Photodisc. *Page 363:* Jeff Greenberg/PhotoEdit. *Page 365:* Stephen Whitehorn © Dorling Kindersley. *Page 368:* Getty Images, Inc.—Taxi.

Chapter 13

Page 381: Best Western International. *Page 388:* © Dorling Kindersley. *Page 389:* © Dorling Kindersley. *Page 398:* EyeWire Collection/Getty Images—Photodisc. *Page 400:* Silva, Juan/Getty Images Inc.—Image Bank.

Chapter 14

Page 418: Corbis Digital Stock.

Chapter 15

Page 444: Walter Bibikow /Index Stock Imagery, Inc. *Page 445:* David R. Frazier/David R. Frazier Photolibrary, Inc. *Page 459:* A. Ramey/Stock Boston. *Page 464:* Michael L. Abramson/Getty Images/Time Life Pictures. *Page 468:* Lonnie Duka/Getty Images Inc. —Stone Allstock.

1

Introduction to the Lodging and Travel Industries

Chapter Objectives

1. To tell you how the lodging industry has developed over its long history.
2. To provide highlights of the U.S. hotel industry.
3. To describe alternate ways to classify hotels.
4. To explain the hotel concepts of average daily rate and occupancy rate.
5. To identify the two major types of travelers.
6. To help you understand the roles of professionals in partner industries that assist hotels in meeting the needs of the traveling public.
7. To explain the importance of industry trade associations.

Chapter Outline

THE EARLY LODGING INDUSTRY
UNITED STATES HOTEL INDUSTRY:
1900–2000
SEGMENTS OF THE LODGING INDUSTRY
MEASURING HOTEL PERFORMANCE
TRAVELERS AND THE TRAVEL INDUSTRY
   Leisure Travelers
   Business Travelers
PARTNERS IN THE LODGING INDUSTRY

Transportation Services
   Airlines
   Bus Lines
   Trains
   Rental Cars
Travel Agents
Tour Operators
Web Site Operators
TRADE ASSOCIATIONS

Overview: Introduction to the Lodging and Travel Industry

The lodging industry has a long history. Travelers have always desired a safe and restful place to spend the night. Today, more and more people travel, and as a result, an entire industry has developed to meet their needs. There are many highlights in the United States hotel industry, and these two topics, a history of the industry in general and an overview of the evolution of the domestic lodging industry, are discussed in this chapter.

People travel for many reasons, including sightseeing, vacations, business, and personal trips. Numerous types of lodging properties are available to meet the different needs of those who travel. There are several ways to classify the wide range of hotel alternatives, and some of the most frequently used hotel classification systems are discussed in this chapter.

Details about numerous ways to assess hotel performance are explained in this text. You will learn about two methods, average daily rate and occupancy rate, in the present chapter. This discussion will help you to understand the types of concerns that hoteliers have as they manage their properties and will provide a preview of how they evaluate the performance of their properties.

The lodging industry is part of a much larger component in the world of business: the travel industry. People must be transported to the places where they will stay. The travel industry includes the airline, bus, train, and rental car businesses whose employees work with their lodging counterparts to help make travel safe, fast, and easy.

Travel agents are an important part of the travel industry because they assist people who desire travel-planning assistance. Tour operators also have a significant impact on travelers. For example, they work with travel agents to offer attractive packages that make it easy and cost-effective to travel. Web site operators are relatively new lodging industry partners who help travelers to reserve (book) hotel rooms and other travel services online. You will learn about these partners of the lodging industry in this chapter.

The final section of the chapter reviews the role of several associations that work to improve the lodging industry.

The travel industry is one of the world's largest.

THE EARLY LODGING INDUSTRY

The **lodging industry** consists of all the **hotels** and other businesses that provide overnight accommodations for guests. Many **hoteliers** also provide food, beverages, and even entertainment for their guests.

LODGING LANGUAGE

Lodging Industry: The total of all the businesses that provide overnight accommodations for guests.

Hotel: An establishment that provides sleeping rooms as well as various services to the traveling public.

Hotelier: The owner/manager of one or more hotels.

■

In the earliest days, people traveled for religious or business reasons. Inns could be found on the roads leading to religious shrines or temples as well as along significant trade routes. They were often operated by families that offered travelers very basic food and shelter in their homes. Sometimes they were operated by a church or other religious organization. As travel became more popular and less dangerous, people began to travel for more personal reasons, such as to see foreign lands or to experience foreign cultures.

The lodging industry in locations popular with travelers is usually large and well developed. Locations of this kind include areas near beaches and other tourist destinations and in cities with large populations. However, even rural settings and small communities that are less popular with **tourists** require a lodging industry large enough to meet the travel needs of people who visit for business, personal, or other reasons.

LODGING LANGUAGE

Tourist: An individual who travels for pleasure.

■

UNITED STATES HOTEL INDUSTRY: 1900–2000

The lodging industry has changed since its early beginnings and will probably continue to do so. This is one reason why it is an exciting and vibrant industry. To understand the modern hotel industry, it is helpful to examine hotels in the United States because they are, in many cases, worldwide leaders. American lodging facilities have evolved to include a tradition of innovation and orientation to guest service that is well worth noting. Highlights of the growth of the hotel industry in the United States since 1900 are shown in Figure 1.1.

SEGMENTS OF THE LODGING INDUSTRY

Today's lodging industry seeks to provide products and services to a variety of travelers. People seeking lodging accommodations almost all have several needs in common: safety, cleanliness, preferred location, and **value.** In addition, different types of travelers also desire specific features in their overnight accommodations. For

1900 Fewer than 10,000 hotels 750,000 to 850,000 rooms	**1900** A typical first-class hotel offers steam heat, gas burners, electric call bells, baths and toilet closets on all floors, billiard and sample rooms, barbershops and carrige houses. **1904** New York City's St. Regis Hotel provides individually controlled heating and cooling units in each guest room. **1908** The Hotel Statler chain begins in Buffalo. All guest rooms have private baths, full-length mirrors, and telephones, serving as the model for hotel construction for the next 40 years.
1910 10,000 hotels 1 million rooms 300,000 employees Average size: 60–75 rooms	**1910** Electricity is beginning to be installed in new hotels for cooking purposes, as well as for lighting. However, most hotels place candlesticks, new candles, and matches in every room— electric light bulb or not.
1920 Occupancy: 85 percent Hotel construction equipped reaches an all-timeof rooms are added along the new state and federal highways	**1920** Prohibition begins. **1922** The Treadway Company has some of the first management contracts on small college inns. **1925** The first roadside "motel" opens in San Luis Obispo, California, for $2.50 a night. **1927** The Hotel Statler in Boston becomes the first hotel with radio reception; rooms are with individual headsets to receive broadcasts from a central control room. **1929** The Oakland Airport Hotel becomes the first of its kind in the country.
1930 Occupancy: 65 percent AHA's *Hotel Red Book* lists 20,000 hotels Typical hotel: 46 rooms Average room rate: $5.60	**1930** Four out of five hotels in the United States go into receivership. **1933** Due to the Great Depression, hotels post the lowest average occupancy rate on record (51 percent). Construction grinds to a halt. **1934** The Hotel Statler in Detroit is the first to have a central system to "air-condition" every public room.
1940 Occupancy: 64 percent Average room rate: $3.21	**1940** Air-conditioning and "air-cooling" become prevalent. **1945** Sheraton is the first hotel corporation to be listed on the New York Stock Exchange. **1946** Westin debuts first guest credit card. The first casino hotel, the Flamingo, debuts in Las Vegas. **1947** Westin establishes Hoteltype, the first hotel reservation system. New York City's Roosevelt Hotel installs television sets in all guest rooms. **1949** Hilton becomes the first international hotel chain with the opening of the Caribe Hilton in San Juan, Puerto Rico.

FIGURE 1.1   Highlights in the Modern History of the United States Hotel Industry[1]

1950 Occupancy: 80 percent Typical hotel: 17 rooms Average room rate: $5.91	**1951** Hilton is the first chain to install television sets in all guest rooms. **1952** Kemmons Wilson opens his first Holiday Inn in Memphis, Tennessee. **1954** Howard Dearing Johnson initiates the first lodging franchise, a motor lodge in Savannah, Georgia. Conrad Hilton's purchase of the Statler Hotel Company for $111 million is the largest real-estate transaction in history. **Mid-1950s** Atlas Hotels develops the first in-room coffee concept. **1957** J.W. Marriott opens his first hotel, the Twin Bridge Marriott Motor Hotel, in Arlington, Virginia, and Jay Pritzker buys his first hotel, the Hyatt House, located outside the Los Angeles Airport. Hilton offers direct-dial telephone service. **1958** Sheraton introduces Reservation, the industry's first automated electronic reservation system, and the first toll-free reservation number.
1960 Occupancy: 67 percent $3 billion in sales Total hotel rooms: 2,400,450 Typical hotel: 39 rooms, independent and locally owned Average room rate: $9.99	**Early 1960s** Siegas introduces the first true minibar (a small refrigerator displaying products). **1964** Travelodge debuts wheelchair-accessible rooms. **1966** Inter-Continental introduces retractable drying lines in guest showers, business lounges, ice and vending machines in guest corridors, and street entrances to hotel restaurants. **1967** The Atlanta Hyatt Regency opens, featuring a 21-story atrium and changing the course of upscale hotel design. **1969** Westin is the first hotel chain to implement 24-hour room service.
1970 Occupancy: 65 percent $8 billion in sales Total hotel rooms: 1,627,473 Average room rate: $19.83	**1970** Hilton becomes the first billion-dollar lodging and food-service company and the first to enter the Las Vegas market. **1973** The Sheraton-Anaheim is the first to offer free in-room movies. **1974** The energy crisis hits the industry. Hotels dim exterior signs, cut heat to unoccupied rooms, and ask guests to conserve electricity. **1975** Four Seasons is the first hotel company to offer in-room amenities such as name-brand shampoo. Hyatt introduces an industry first when it opens a concierge club level that provides the ultimate in VIP (very important person) service. Cecil B. Day establishes the first seniors' program.
1980 Occupancy: 70 percent $25.9 billion in sales Total hotel rooms: 2,068,377 Average room rate: $45.44	**1983** Westin is the first major hotel company to offer reservations and checkout using major credit cards. VingCard invents the optical electronic key card. **1984** Holiday Inn is the first to offer a centralized travel and commission plan. Choice Hotels introduces the concept of market segmentation. Choice Hotels offers no-smoking rooms. Hampton Inns is the first to offer a set of amenities. **1986** Teledex Corporation introduces the first telephone designed specifically for hotel guest rooms. Days Inn provides an interactive reservation capability connecting all hotels. **1988** Extended-stay segment introduced with Marriott's Residence Inns and Holiday Corporation's Homewood Suites. **1989** Hyatt introduces a chainwide kids program for ages 3–12 and a business center at the Hyatt Regency Chicago. Hampton Inns is the first hotel chain to introduce the 100 percent satisfaction guarantee.

FIGURE 1.1 (continued)

1990	**1990** Loews Hotels' Good Neighbor Policy becomes the industry's first and most comprehensive community outreach program.
Occupancy: 64 percent	**1991** Westin is the first hotel chain to provide in-room voice mail. Industry sees record losses (61.8 percent).
$60.7 billion in sales	**1992** Industry breaks even financially after six consecutive years of losses.
Total hotel rooms: 3,065,685	**1993** Radisson Hotels Worldwide is the first to introduce business-class rooms.
45,020 properties	**1994** First on-line hotel catalog debuts—TravelWeb.com. Promus and Hyatt Hotels are the first chains to establish a site on the Internet.
Average room rate: $58.70	**1995** Choice Hotels International and Promus become the first companies to offer guests "real-time" access to their central reservations system. Choice and Holiday Inn are the first to introduce on-line booking capability.
	1999 Choice Hotels International is the first chain to test making in-room PCs a standard amenity for guests.
2000	**2000** Hilton unveils plans for the first luxury hotel in space.
Occupancy: 63 percent	**2001** September 11 destruction of the World Trade Center in New York causes city occupancy rates to plummet.
$97 billion in sales	**2002** Travel industry slowly recovers from terrorist attacks amid heightened airport security.
	2004 In-room high-speed Internet (HIS) access becomes a necessary amenity to attract business travelers.

[1] http://www.ahma.com/infocenter/lodging_history.asp

FIGURE 1.1   (continued)

example, affluent travelers frequently desire up-scale accommodations, long-term guests may want kitchen facilities, and business travelers may need a business center in their hotel.

LODGING LANGUAGE

Value (Lodging Accommodations): The price paid to rent a room relative to the quality of the room and services received.

■

There are more than 47,000 hotels in the United States with more than 4,400,000 sleeping rooms. Therefore, the "average" U.S. hotel has fewer than 100 rooms (4,400,000/47,000 = 93.6 rooms), and together these hotels achieve room revenues of more than $100 billion per year.

When most people think about "hotels," they think about a building with guest rooms suitable for sleeping. In its narrowest sense, this definition may be correct. However, there are several ways to classify hotels. For example, they can be classified by size. Small hotels (under 75 rooms) make up 52 percent of all hotels. Medium-sized hotels (75–150 rooms) make up 33 percent of all hotels. Large hotels (150–300 rooms) make up 10 percent of all hotels, and those larger than 300 rooms comprise 5 percent of all hotels. Using these definitions, approximately 85 percent of all U.S.

hotels are either small or medium-sized. For this reason, this book will examine smaller hotels very closely.

Another useful way to classify hotels relates to the services offered. Some travelers desire food and beverage services in addition to sleeping rooms. Properties that offer travelers food, beverages, and, in most cases, meeting space are classified as **full-service hotels.**

LODGING LANGUAGE

Full-Service Hotel: A lodging facility that offers complete food and beverage services.
■

A full service hotel has a restaurant and lounge. In addition, many offer **room service** to guests.

LODGING LANGUAGE

Room Service: Food and beverages are delivered to a hotel guest's sleeping room.
■

As the name implies, a **limited-service hotel** offers limited food and beverage service or, sometimes, none at all.

Most full-service hotels offer food and beverage service delivered to a guest's room (room service).

Full-service hotels offer food services that may rival the very best restaurants to be found in a city.

LODGING LANGUAGE

Limited-Service Hotel: A lodging facility that offers few, if any, food and beverage services.

Many limited-service hotels offer travelers a complimentary breakfast. They do not, however, operate restaurants, and they provide little, if any, space for group meetings. The majority of hotels in the United States are limited-service hotels. You will learn much about the operation of these properties in this book, including details about the limited food and meetings services they offer.

Figure 1.2 identifies many types of organizations that offer lodging accommodations for travelers. You will note that there are several types in addition to hotels that are emphasized in this book.

When reviewing Figure 1.2, note that lodging organizations are part of the **hospitality industry.** (The hospitality industry offers another component [food and beverage services] that is not addressed in this book.) As you will learn in the next section, the hospitality industry is itself part of a larger collection of organizations: the travel/tourism industry.

LODGING LANGUAGE

Hospitality Industry: Organizations that provide lodging accommodations and food services for people when they are away from their homes.

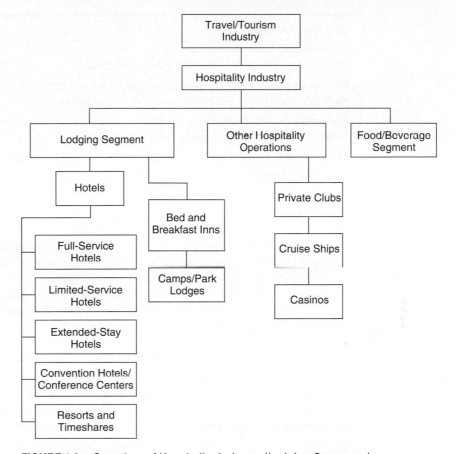

FIGURE 1.2 Overview of Hospitality Industry (Lodging Segments)

The lodging segment of the hospitality industry markets to travelers whose primary purpose for staying at a property is to secure lodging services. When you review Figure 1.2, note that the lodging segment of the hospitality industry includes hotels, **bed and breakfast inns** and **camps/park lodges.**

LODGING LANGUAGE

Bed and Breakfast Inns: Very small properties (one to several guest rooms) owned or managed by persons living on-site; these businesses typically offer one meal a day; also called B&B.

Camps/Park Lodges: Sleeping facilities in national, state, or other parks and recreational areas that accommodate visitors to these areas.

Figure 1.2 identifies five types of hotels. You have already learned something about full-service and limited-service hotels, so now we will define the other basic types of hotels in the lodging segment: **extended-stay hotels, convention hotels/ conference centers** and **resorts/timeshares.**

LODGING LANGUAGE

Extended-Stay Hotel: A mid-priced, limited-service hotel marketing to guests desiring accommodation for extended time periods (generally one week or longer).

Convention Hotel: A lodging property with extensive and flexible meeting and exhibition spaces that markets to associations, corporations, and other groups bringing people together for meetings.

Conference Center: A specialized hospitality operation specifically designed for and dedicated to the needs of small- and medium-sized meetings of 20 to 100 people.

Resort: A full-service hotel with additional attractions that make it a primary destination for travelers.

Timeshare: A lodging property that sells its rooms to guests for use during a specific time period each year; also called vacation ownership property.

■

Figure 1.2 also identifies other hospitality operations that offer sleeping accommodations. These operations, however, are not generally thought of as lodging properties because of the popularity of their other amenities. The organizations identified are **private clubs, cruise lines,** and **casinos.** They are examples of enterprises in the lodging industry that exist for reasons other than to provide sleeping accommodations, but which do so as a service to their members/passengers/guests.

LODGING LANGUAGE

Private Club: Membership organization not open to the public that exists for people enjoying common interests. Examples include country (golf) clubs, city clubs, university clubs, yacht clubs, and military clubs. Some private clubs offer sleeping rooms for members and guests.

Cruise Ship: A passenger vessel designed to provide leisure experiences for people on vacation.

Casino: A business operation that offers table and card games along with (usually) slot operations and other games of skill or chance and amenities that are marketed to customers seeking gaming activities and entertainment. Many casinos offer lodging accommodations for their visitors.

■

To this point we have been discussing lodging operations generally available to the traveling public. Other types of facilities offer sleeping accommodations for people away from their homes. These include non-commercial operations, such as schools, colleges, and universities offering residential services, health care (hospital and nursing homes) facilities, correctional institutions (prisons), and military bases.

This book was written for those who work in the hotel industry or are planning to do so, but the information it contains applies to many of the lodging facilities mentioned above.

MEASURING HOTEL PERFORMANCE

Room rental charges for guest rooms are based, in large measure, upon what guests are willing to pay. If a city (or an area within a city) has too few overnight accommodations for the number of people traveling to it, the prices charged for sleeping rooms will likely be high. Alternatively, if too many sleeping rooms are available, the prices charged for a room will likely be low.

Average Daily Rate (ADR) is the term used by hoteliers to indicate how expensive sleeping rooms are in a specific hotel or area.

Some hotel suites are so large and luxurious that they sell for several thousand dollars per day.

LODGING LANGUAGE

Average Daily Rate (ADR): The average (mean) selling price of all guest rooms in a hotel, city, or country for a specific period of time.

The computation of ADR is very simple:

$$\frac{\text{Total Revenue from Room Sales}}{\text{Total Number of Rooms Sold}}$$

If, for example, a hotel sells 150 rooms for one night, and if the total revenue from the room sales for that night is \$18,750.00, the hotel's ADR would be \$125.00:

$$\frac{\$18,750}{150 \text{ rooms}} = \$125.00 \text{ ADR}$$

Hotels can be classified by their rate structures. For example, some hotels are very elegant and can charge higher rates. Other hotels offer more modest accommodations for budget-minded travelers. As a result, hotels are sometimes classified as budget or economy (very low ADR), midscale (moderate ADR), or luxury (very high ADR).

You have now learned that an ADR can be calculated for a specific hotel. It can also be assessed for a town or other geographic area.

Assume that a town has several hotels with a total of 1,000 sleeping rooms available. Assume further that on a specific night, 750 rooms in the town were sold, and the revenue generated from these room sales was \$93,750.00. The ADR for the town on that date would also be \$125.00:

$$\frac{\$93,750}{750 \text{ rooms}} = \$125.00 \text{ ADR}$$

The ADR of a hotel, city, or region is one indicator of the strength of the hotel business in that location.

Another measure of hotel performance is also widely used by the managers: **occupancy rate.**

LODGING LANGUAGE

Occupancy Rate: The ratio of guest rooms sold (or given away) to the number of guest rooms available for sale in a given time period expressed as a percentage.

■

The computation of occupancy percentage rate is also simple:

$$\frac{\text{Total Rooms Sold}}{\text{Total Rooms Available}} = \text{Occupancy Rate}$$

If a hotel has 200 rooms and on a given night sells 150 rooms, the occupancy rate would be 75 percent.

$$\frac{150 \text{ rooms sold}}{200 \text{ rooms available}} = 75\%$$

One can compute the occupancy rate for a hotel, a city, or a larger region. It is also possible to compute an occupancy percentage for a period longer than one day. Assume that a town has several hotels with a total of 1,000 sleeping rooms available. During June (30 days in the month), the total number of rooms sold in the town was 18,000. The occupancy rate for that town in June would be 60 percent.

$$\frac{18,000 \text{ rooms sold in June}}{30,000 \text{ rooms } (30 \text{ days } [\times] \text{ 1,000 rooms})} = 60\%$$

Another measure of hotel performance—**revenue per available room (RevPar)**—combines both of these performance measures; it addresses room rate and room occupancy because it expresses the average revenue generated by each available guest room.

LODGING LANGUAGE

Revenue Per Available Room (RevPar): The average revenue generated by each guest room available during a given time period; the formula for RevPar is: occupancy percent ($\times$) ADR. Commonly referred to as "RevPar."

■

RevPar and the other two hotel performance measures just previewed will be discussed in greater depth in later chapters.

The ADR, occupancy rate, and RevPar are effective indicators of the strength of a specific hotel or a larger area's lodging business. When business is good, average room rates, occupancy percentages, and RevPars are high. When these indicators are low, knowledgeable hoteliers recognize that business is not as good as when they are higher. In a healthy and competitive lodging environment, the hotel industry offers travelers a variety of overnight accommodation options at a variety of prices.

TRAVELERS AND THE TRAVEL INDUSTRY

As you have learned, the lodging industry is part of the larger hospitality industry, which is, in turn, part of the travel industry.

The travel industry is sometimes called the travel and tourism industry or, simply, the tourism industry. Regardless of the term used, it refers to those businesses designed to serve the traveling public. Figure 1.3 illustrates the components of the tourism industry, including the lodging segment.

As can be seen in Figure 1.3, the tourism industry consists of:

- *Hospitality.* The food and beverage and lodging operations (including hotels) that house and feed travelers.
- *Retail (Shopping) Stores.* Stores and shops that appeal to travelers.
- *Transportation Services.* Businesses, such as bus lines, airlines, and rental car companies, that help move travelers from place to place.
- *Destination (Activity) Sites.* Locations offering activities and attractions enjoyed by travelers. Examples include amusement parks and ski resorts as well as other indoor and outdoor activities.

Tourism is the third-largest industry in the United States. It is surpassed in size only by the automotive and grocery industries. It is also one of the nation's largest employers and is the second- or third-largest employer in 30 of the 50 states. In 2002, leisure and business travelers spent a combined total of over $530 billion and helped provide more than 7 million jobs for American workers. Of these jobs, 2 million were in the hotel industry.

In its studies on travel, the American Hotel and Lodging Association (AH&LA) has found that of those who stay in hotels,

25 percent are attending a conference or group meeting

29 percent are business travelers

24 percent are on vacation

22 percent are traveling for other reasons (e.g., personal, family, or to attend a special event)

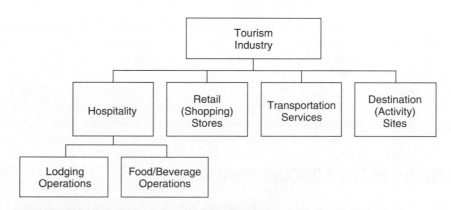

FIGURE 1.3   Components of the Tourism Industry

There are a variety of ways that travelers can be classified—for example, as male or female or as young or old. They can arrive by car or plane, be free-spending or thrifty, and can vary in any number of other ways. The most common distinction made in the lodging industry, however, is between those who are leisure travelers and those who are business travelers.

Leisure Travelers

Leisure travelers enjoy travel. In the hotel business, the term "leisure traveler" refers to persons who travel because they like the experience of visiting new places, are returning to places they have previously visited, or are participating in some leisure activity. Leisure travelers include vacationers and people traveling to shop, sightsee, attend concerts, and for a wide range of other activities. Leisure travelers may be families or individuals. They can be senior citizens riding a motor coach on a guided tour of historical sites and youngsters traveling with their families to participate in a regional soccer tournament. Leisure travelers often travel on the weekends, but, especially in the summer, they also travel through the week.

Depending upon its location, a hotel may find that the great majority of its guests are leisure travelers. A hotel on a Florida beach, for example, may attract guests primarily because of the beach. However, hotels that attract leisure travelers may still attract business travelers. The opposite is also true. Hotels primarily designed for business travelers may also host leisure travelers.

Business Travelers

Business travelers make up a large and extremely important portion of the travel business. As noted in the preceding section, people attending conferences/meetings (25 percent) or traveling or business reasons (29 percent) comprise more than half of travelers. Business travelers include those who attend work-related meetings, seminars, and conferences. Salespersons for business must travel to meet clients, demonstrate new products, and learn new skills.

Business travelers tend to spend more money for their overnight stays and also look for **amenities** and guest services not always offered at hotels geared toward leisure travelers.

LODGING LANGUAGE

Amenities: Hotel products and services designed to attract guests. Examples include Internet access and copying services, in-room hair dryers, irons, ironing boards, and microwave ovens, as well as indoor pools, exercise rooms, and in-room movies.

■

Much business travel involves trips to large cities; however, even the smallest of towns and the hotels located in those towns attract business travelers who are driving through a smaller town on the way to a larger town.

PARTNERS IN THE LODGING INDUSTRY

Many organizations, groups, and even entire industries assist hoteliers in serving overnight guests. The transportation industry helps guests travel to and from hotels. Travel agents assist travelers to select a mode of transportation and give advice about which hotels are best for a specific traveler's needs, and tour operators assist travel agents in their work. Increasingly, the World Wide Web (Internet) has influenced the way travel industry services are marketed and purchased, and the role of Web site operators is, therefore, of increasing importance.

Transportation Services

When a traveler decides to take a trip, one of the first and most important decisions concerns the kind of transportation to be used. Accessibility, speed, comfort, and cost all influence the choice. Generally, the fastest transportation methods also tend to be the most expensive. Historically, stagecoaches, steamships, and railroads developed travel routes that accommodated mail, freight, and passengers. Today, some businesses in the transportation industry, such as the United Parcel Service (UPS) and Federal Express (FedEx), specialize in transporting freight only. Others emphasize passenger transportation, and still others provide both. In the United States, the most popular forms of passenger transportation are airplanes, buses, trains, and automobiles, and these are the businesses most likely to work closely with hoteliers.

Airlines

Airline travel is the preferred method for the majority of leisure and business travelers whose destinations are far from their origination point. Airline travel is fast, and its popularity continues to grow. U.S. airlines carry well over 500 million passengers per year. In addition to the advantages of speed, airline ticket prices have, in the last three decades, become less expensive. This has resulted in yearly increases in the number of passengers who fly.

The airline industry is a partner with the hotel industry because many travelers fly into an airport, are picked up there by a hotel-owned and operated **hotel shuttle,** and are then driven to the hotel, where they can check in to their room. In these cases, the shuttle also returns the travelers to the airport when they are ready to depart.

LODGING LANGUAGE

Hotel Shuttle: A vehicle used by a hotel to transport guests to and from such destinations as airports, restaurants, and shopping.

∎

In the United States, there is a constant demand for air service, and the airline business is very competitive. This demand is met by airports of many sizes, including those large enough to serve as an airline **hub.**

LODGING LANGUAGE

Hub: Typically, a big-city airport within a short driving distance of a very large population center. These mega-airports are used to economically connect travelers with flights to their desired departure and arrival cities.

∎

Bus Lines

Buses are an important part of the travel industry and can have a substantial effect on a hotel's occupancy. Their use for long-distance transportation by individual travelers is much less than that of airplanes and automobiles. However, buses are used by

--- **ALL IN A DAY'S WORK** ---

The Situation

It was 4:00 o'clock in the afternoon. Dani, the general manager of the Day's Sleep Hotel, looked out her office window. "The snow is really coming down," she said.

"I know," replied her assistant manager. "We have already had a lot of travelers pulling off the Interstate to ask for rooms so they don't get stranded on the highway after dark. I think we will easily sell every room we have tonight."

"We need to call the airport and check flight status," said Dani, "or we could have some real problems tonight."

A Response

As this manager realizes, if the local airport closes because of the snowstorm, hotel occupancy for the area will be greatly affected. Hotel managers must know about industry partners who can help them make good business decisions when necessary. In this case, the closing of the airport would probably mean stranded airport travelers who will require accommodations (increased occupancy) and fewer incoming passengers who will not arrive if the airport is closed (decreased occupancy). The possible closure of the airport will have a big impact on this hotel manager's decision to sell (or not to sell) many rooms to highway travelers. Developing a personal contact at the local airport to help obtain up-to-date and accurate airport information is a good idea for hotel managers.

---

economy-minded travelers and by travelers being shuttled from airports, train stations, and parking areas. For many hoteliers, the most important role played by the bus lines is that of transporting **charter** travel groups.

LODGING LANGUAGE

Charter: A form of transportation rented exclusively for a specific group of travelers. Planes and buses are often chartered for group travel.

■

Charter buses often transport groups of travelers for less money than they would have to pay if they flew to the same destination. In some cases, chartered bus routes operating regularly between cities within 100 or 200 miles of each other may actually be faster than air travel, especially with new airport security measures. Therefore, bus travel can often be inexpensive and rapid.

The federal government defines a bus as a passenger-carrying vehicle designed to seat at least 16 people including the driver. While there are no universal definitions, bus industry professionals generally recognize the following bus types:

- *Economy.* School-type buses are the lowest-cost option for group travelers. These vehicles typically are arranged with bench (not individual) seating and contain no restroom facilities.
- *Deluxe Motor Coach.* This tour-type bus is the most selected for longer trips or for groups seeking more comfort than is available on an economy bus. The typical seating is 40 to 55 individual seats with VCR/DVD capability, multiple monitors, advanced sound systems, and restroom facilities.
- *Executive Motor Coach.* This top-of-the-line bus is chosen by those who prefer extra-luxurious bus travel. Executive coaches are custom-made. Options vary, but typically include full bedrooms, showers, kitchens, social and meeting spaces. The maximum capacity for buses of this type range from 5 to 20 persons.

Buses are generally welcomed by restaurant and hotel managers who want to attract bus operators for the increased business they can generate.

Trains

Passenger train transportation was critical to the early expansion and development of the United States. However, today the number of people who prefer to travel by train is much less than those who travel by airplane or automobile. In some areas, especially those that are densely populated, trains still play a major role in public transportation.

Historically, hotels were often built within a short distance of the train station. Today, while trains still move freight cost-effectively, it is generally unprofitable to operate trains for passenger transportation. Why? Public dollars are used to build airports, and airline companies utilize their profit from doing so. The automobile industry has benefited from the immense investment in public roads and highways as the federal government developed the Interstate highway system. Newly built hotels are often located near interchanges or exits on these highways. In addition, state, and local governments annually invest significant tax dollars in road construction and maintenance projects.

The average American citizen has been less enthusiastic, however, about using public dollars to purchase the land, track, and equipment needed for a reliable passenger rail system. An exception is the nationwide passenger rail routes operated by Amtrak.

The name "Amtrak" results from the blending of the words "American" and "Track." Its official name is the National Railroad Passenger Corporation. Amtrak is not a part of the federal government, but since its inception in 1971 has been dependent upon the federal government (and some state governments) for grants that allow it to continue operations.

The system carries over 65,000 passengers per day. New York, Philadelphia, and Washington are the areas where trains are most used and reflect the use of rail for large-city commuting rather than long-distance travel. Hotels located near train stations along these routes can generate substantial revenue volumes from these passengers.

LODGING ON-LINE

Amtrak works very hard to attract passenger travel. To see the passenger routes it operates, go to:

www.Amtrak.com

Does Amtrak service your town?

Rental Cars

Automobiles are the most popular method of travel in the United States, and the impact of their drivers and passengers on the hotel business is tremendous. Many American families own one or more cars, and use them extensively for short-distance travel. People who travel by air will frequently rent a car or other vehicle upon arrival at their destination.

The car rental business is an important part of the transportation industry and consists of all business that rent or lease passenger cars, vans, trucks, and utility trailers. In 2002, there were over 10,000 such operations in the United States, and they offered more than 1,640,000 vehicles available for rent. Some of these businesses offer only short-term rental, others only longer-term leases, and some provide both services.

California, Florida, and Texas have the greatest number of car rental outlets and the largest number of vehicles rented. Hoteliers that enjoy a close association with their local car rental businesses often find that travelers renting cars ask for advice about where to stay when they pick up their cars. Therefore, hotels can gain business from rental agency referrals.

Travel Agents

Assume that you were going to take an auto trip to a town 50 miles away. If you had previously driven there several times, you probably would not need help planning your trip. Now assume that even though you have never been there, you must plan a trip to Europe for 21 days for yourself and five other people. In this case, you are likely to want the services of an experienced **travel agent.**

LODGING LANGUAGE

Travel Agent: A professional who assists clients in planning and purchasing travel.

■

For many travelers, the knowledge and skill of professional travel planners are important to the success of the trip. Constantly changing airfares and schedules, thousands of available vacation packages, and the vast amount of information available on the Internet can make travel planning frustrating and time-consuming. To sort out their travel options, many leisure and business travelers seek the advice of a travel agent.

A 2002 survey reported that 26 percent of Americans (54 million adults) used a travel agent to book at least one business or leisure trip, flight, hotel room, rental car, or tour within the past three years. Historically, the number has been even higher; but travelers are increasingly using the Internet to learn about and purchase travel services, and as a result the use of travel agents has declined. Older consumers are more likely to use travel agents than younger ones. Four in ten travel agent users (43 percent) are Baby Boomer travelers (age 35 to 54), and one-third (33 percent) are Generation X and Y travelers (age 18 to 34). Travelers who use travel agents tend to be wealthier, take longer trips, and travel more frequently.

LODGING ON-LINE

The American Society of Travel Agents (ASTA) has over 20,000 members. Its mission is to enhance the professionalism and profitability of member agents through effective representation in industry and government affairs, education and training, and by identifying and meeting the needs of the traveling public.

To learn more about ASTA, go to:

www.astanet.com

When would you consider the use of a travel agent if you were planning a long trip?

Travel agents offer their clients individual tickets or **packages** and organize tailor-made travel on request.

LODGING LANGUAGE

Package: A group of travel services, such as hotel rooms, meals, and airfare, sold for one price. For example, a Valentine's Day Getaway package to Las Vegas suggested by a travel agent might include airfare, lodging, meals, and show tickets for two people at an all-inclusive price.

■

Travel agents generally advise about and sell vacation packages, air tickets, cruises, hotel bookings, car rentals, and other services. Many corporations have their own in-house travel agents. This is especially true when many members of the company do a lot of traveling to visit their own clients, make sales presentations, or attend meetings and conferences. The Association of Corporate Travel Executives was formed to meet the needs of this important group of travel professionals. Whether retained by individuals or working for corporate employers, travel agents inform and advise travelers about the best ways to maximize their experiences and minimize their expenses.

In the hospitality industry, hotel managers interact with travel agents on a daily basis because in most hotels a high percentage of the reservations will be made by travel agents using the **Global Distribution System (GDS),** which electronically links travel agents worldwide to individual hotel reservation systems.

LODGING LANGUAGE

Global Distribution System (GDS): Commonly referred to as the GDS, this computer system connects travel professionals worldwide who reserve rooms with hotels offering rooms for sale.

■

Travel agents have historically worked on a commission basis for the hotel room and airline services they sold. Recently, however, as airlines have reduced agent commissions (in some cases, no commission is paid), and as the Internet allows more travelers to make self-bookings, many travel agents have begun charging clients a fee for the services provided. However, hotels still generally pay a commission to travel agents who book rooms for clients. This commission may amount to 10 percent of the hotel room's price.

Regardless of how they are paid, travel agents contract for travel services on behalf of their clients. As a result, they have a legal responsibility to act in the best interests of their clients. Hoteliers should remember that while travel agents collect commissions from hotels, they actually work for the traveler. Wise hoteliers know that a good working relationship with local and national travel agents and the groups to which they belong is vital to their success.

Tour Operators

Tour operators are another important part of the travel industry. These travel professionals work closely with travel agencies but are, from a legal perspective, distinctly different.

LODGING LANGUAGE

Tour Operator: A company or individual that plans and markets travel packages.

■

While travel agents work directly for their clients and have a legal responsibility to act in their best interests, tour operators create packages that are designed to make a profit for the tour operator.

A tour operator can be any of a varied group of companies that purchase travel services in large quantities and then market the same services directly or through travel agents to individual travelers. A travel agent may recommend that a traveler buy a specific travel package. However, it is the tour operator who must develop the package, market it, and sell it to travel agency clients.

Assume that a tour operator wants to create a tour package of a trip to New Orleans. The tour operator would select an airline to provide transportation from various starting points to transport travelers to New Orleans. A charter bus would pick up the members of the tour group at the airport and transport them to the hotel preselected by the tour operator. Restaurants to be used and group activities to be undertaken would also be preplanned by the tour operator, as would the selection of tour guides to escort the travelers to the sites included in the package.

The tour operator would market the New Orleans package to travel agents throughout the country. They, in turn, might recommend the trip to their clients. If the package offered attractive prices and activities, clients might purchase it. The result: travelers from around the country will buy the tour operator's New Orleans package. If it is profitable, the tour operator might offer it again.

Since they purchase travel services in large quantities, tour operators can often obtain a significant discount, add a mark-up that represents their profit margin, and still offer lower prices than travelers could negotiate individually.

Large travel agencies may also assemble their own packages; however, when they do so, they take a risk because tour operators do not work on commission, as do travel agents. The tour operator's profit comes only from the sale of travel services previously purchased. Assume that a tour operator purchases 100 tickets to the

Tour operators create packages for small or large groups.

MTV Video Awards show with the intention of packaging them with airfare and overnight accommodations to create an "MTV Awards" travel package. The tour operator will have incurred the cost of the awards tickets regardless of whether the package sale is successful. Therefore, a travel agent may lose an unearned commission when a vacation package offered for sale does not sell. By contrast, the tour operator who has assembled the unsuccessful package is likely to face real, and sometimes substantial, monetary losses.

Tour operators can offer a variety of services. They may only sell self-guided trips, such as airline tickets to a large city, hotel reservations at a specific hotel, and tickets to the theater at a specific date and time. In this case, it is not a **guided tour**, nor is it directly managed by the tour operator. Any buyer could purchase the package, travel on the plane, stay in the hotel, and visit the theater.

LODGING LANGUAGE

Guided Tour: A group tour package that includes the services of one or more tour guides.

∎

Alternatively, a tour operator might decide to offer a full-service guided tour that includes transportation, hotel rooms, meals, activities, and the use of tour guides to serve as the travelers' escorts.

LODGING ON-LINE

The National Tour Association (NTA) has more than 4,000 members. Its membership includes tour operators, travel suppliers, and individuals representing many destinations and attractions.

To learn more about the NTA, go to:

www.ntaonline.com

What types of travelers do you think prefer guided tours? Which types would prefer self-guided tours?

Hoteliers interact with tour operators in several ways:

- Negotiating hotel rates offered to tour operators
- Hosting tour-package buyers within their hotels
- Assisting travelers who experience difficulties with one or more features of the tour related to the hotel's services
- Working with travel agents to market tours that include the hotelier's hotel(s)
- Providing hotel service at levels high enough to ensure a continued positive relationship between the tour operator and the hotel

Web Site Operators

People and companies operating Web sites that allow travelers to reserve (book) hotel rooms on-line are increasingly important partners to hoteliers. **On-line distribution** is the term used to describe this process of booking rooms.

LODGING LANGUAGE

On-line Distribution: The buying and selling of hotel rooms using the Internet.

∎

Hotel managers can create their own Web sites and sell their rooms directly to consumers who use the Internet to reserve rooms. Many hotels, however, also utilize intermediary Web site operators, such as Expedia and Travelocity, that sell hotel rooms on-line for numerous hotel companies. Consumers like to visit these sites to compare prices, hotel features, and locations before they make their hotel selections. Just as hotel companies have historically relied upon travel agents to "sell" hotel rooms, hoteliers now rely on Web site operators to do so. Rather than working for a commission as travel agents have traditionally done, Web site operators charge hotels a fee for each room sold. These fees are often negotiable. They are based upon the number of rooms the Web site operator books for the hotel, the hotel's room rates, and the favorable positioning of the hotel on the operator's Web site.

There are three types (models) of Web site operators that typically partner with hotels:

- *Traditional Direct-to-Guest Model.* Room rates are posted on a hotel's own Web site, and guests book their rooms directly with the hotel.
- *Opaque Rate Model.* Room rates are not seen by guests until after they have successfully "bid" for a room. Guests decide the amount they will pay. Then the Web site operator matches the guest's request with hotels willing to sell rooms at that price. Priceline.com is, perhaps, the most well-known Web site operator using this approach.
- *Merchant Model.* Room rates, (most often heavily discounted) are readily viewed on-line by potential guests. They book their rooms through the Web site operator, who then charges the hotel a fee for each reservation made. Examples include Hotels.com, Travelocity.com, and Expedia.com

On-line distribution is big business, and it is anticipated that it will continue to grow. Hotel industry experts predict that by 2008 more than 40 percent of all hotel bookings will be completed on the Internet. Therefore, the partnership between hoteliers and Web site operators is becoming increasingly critical to a hotel's success.

TRADE ASSOCIATIONS

You have learned that hoteliers work with other professionals in the travel industry to meet the needs of the traveling public. In many cases, hoteliers work with their peers to meet their own **professional development** needs and to communicate their viewpoints to the public, to government, and to other policy-making entities that affect the industry.

LODGING LANGUAGE

Professional Development: The process by which hoteliers continue to improve their knowledge and skills.

■

Trade associations typically hold monthly and annual gatherings and, in conjunction with these meetings, may offer educational seminars/workshops to improve the knowledge and skills of their members. As well, most trade associations invite companies that sell products and services of interest to the membership to participate in a **trade show** held in conjunction with their annual meeting. These shows attract **vendors** interested in showcasing their latest products and services. Trade shows are an extremely efficient way for show attendees to quickly learn about new products and services. Many associations also have both state- and local-level chapters, some of which also host their own trade shows.

LODGING LANGUAGE

Trade Show: An industry-specific event that allows suppliers to an industry to interact with, educate, and sell to individuals who are part of the industry; also called exhibition.

Vendors: Those who sell products and services to hoteliers.

∎

There are several associations that assist and represent the lodging industry:

- *American Hotel and Lodging Association (AH&LA).* Formerly known as the American Hotel and Motel Association, this is largest and oldest national hotel trade association in the country. Founded in 1910 and now based in Washington, D.C., it is a collection of state-level hotel associations working together to meet the educational, social, and legislative needs of its members.

  The organization is overseen by a board of directors consisting of a chairperson, vice-chairperson, secretary/treasurer, directors (elected by their respective states), an allied member, a corporate board director, and a representative from the National Restaurant Association. To learn more about this group and its goals, go to www.ahla.com

- *Asian American Hotel Owners Association (AAHOA).* The stated purpose of this group is to provide "an active forum in which Asian American Hotel Owners, through an exchange of ideas with a unified voice, can communicate, interact, and secure their proper position within the hospitality industry, and be a source of inspiration by promoting professionalism and excellence through education and community involvement." AAHOA is a rapidly growing group that strongly advocates the interests of individual hotel owners. To learn more about this group, go to www.aahoa.com

- *International Hotel and Restaurant Association (IH&RA).* This group, based in Paris, is an international association exclusively devoted to promoting and defending the interests of the worldwide hotel and restaurant industry. It is a non-profit membership organization that helps its members to achieve their business objectives and prepare for the future. To learn more about this association, go to www.ih-ra.com

- *Educational Institute (E.I.) of the American Hotel and Lodging Association.* While not technically a separate trade association, this group, located in Orlando, Florida, is affiliated with the American Hotel and Lodging Association. It creates and markets professional development and training programs for the hotel industry. The mission of E.I. is to help hotel owners and managers become better trained and to provide resources that allow them to upgrade the knowledge and job skills of their own hotel staff members.

  Hoteliers can "join" E.I. by becoming certified in a variety of specific hotel operating areas, including sales and marketing, food and beverage, and housekeeping and security. For more information, go to www.ei-ahla.org

─────────────── **ALL IN A DAY'S WORK** ───────────────

The Situation

It was early evening, and Joe was puzzled and frustrated. He was sorting through a pile of mailers he had received at his hotel within the past few weeks. Each mailer was from a company promising the "easiest" and "lowest-cost" installation of high-speed Internet access for guest rooms. His hotel had to install high-speed Internet access to remain competitive with the other hotels in the area that had already done so.

"Loni," called Joe to his assistant in the office next door, "do you know the difference between CAT 5 cable and CAT 3 cable . . . or maybe we should just go with wireless access?"

"Me?" replied Loni, "I don't know anything about cats."

"Be serious," said Joe, "I don't know much about cabling either, but one of us must learn about it, and about WiFi, Ethernets, and a whole lot more if we are going to make the right high-speed Internet access decision. It's a complicated area, and I don't want to make a mistake because it would be an expensive one!"

A Response

Change is a common part of every business including hotels. To remain current in their profession and to obtain new information needed to make good decisions, hoteliers must continually update their skills and knowledge. They must join associations that can provide up-to-date information, read monthly or weekly hotel publications, and take advantage of the resources offered by organizations like the Educational Institute of the AH&LA.

CHAPTER OBJECTIVES REVIEW

If you have successfully studied the material in this chapter, you should be prepared to:

1. Briefly trace the history of the hotel industry from its inception to today. (Objective 1)
2. Provide highlights of the U.S. hotel industry. (Objective 2)
3. Describe alternate ways to classify hotels. (Objective 3)
4. Compute the ADR and/or occupancy rates of a hotel, city, or area. (Objective 4)
5. Describe important and distinct characteristics of leisure and business travelers. (Objective 5)
6. Provide an overview of the transportation segment, travel agent, tour operator, and Web site operator partners who work with hotels to meet the needs of the traveling public. (Objective 6)
7. Explain the importance of industry trade associations in the professional development of a hotelier. (Objective 7)

LODGING LANGUAGE

Lodging Industry
Hotel
Hotelier
Tourist
Value (Lodging Accommodations)
Full-Service Hotel
Room Service
Limited-Service Hotel
Extended-Stay Hotel
Convention Hotel
Conference Center

Resort
Timeshare
Private Clubs
Cruise Ship
Casino
Camp/Park Lodge
Average Daily Rate (ADR)
Occupancy Rate
Revenue Per Available Room (RevPar)
Amenities
Hotel Shuttle

Hub
Charter
Travel Agent
Package
Global Distribution System (GDS)
Tour Operator
Guided Tour
On-Line Distribution
Professional Development
Vendors
Trade Show

FOR DISCUSSION

1. Think about the last time you spent the night in a hotel or other lodging facility. What were your specific reasons for selecting that property?
2. Make a list of several hotels in your area. What different types of travelers are each of these properties trying to attract? What might they be doing to attract these guests?
3. What are some factors that could cause a hotel's ADR to increase or decrease at various times of the year?
4. What are some factors that could cause the occupancy rate for a hotel in a specific city to increase or decrease at various times of the year? How could this variation be affected by ADR?
5. Think about your own hometown. Do you think the majority of visitors to its hotels are leisure or business travelers? List the reasons for your answer.
6. What is your favorite method of travel? How do you decide the method of transportation to use for a specific trip?
7. Have you ever used a travel agent? What types of trips do you think most require the help of a travel agent?
8. When you visit a Web site to reserve a hotel room, what Web site features are most important to you? How do you select the Web site that you visit?
9. Trade associations want to meet the needs of their members, including those that are social in nature. Identify some activities that you believe would be fun to do with others working in the same field as yourself. Do you believe socializing with business colleagues will help you in your own career? Why or why not?
10. In what ways do you think hotels will most change in the next ten years?

TEAM ACTIVITIES

Team Activity 1

List the most popular attractions within a 50-mile radius of your location. For each, describe the type of person(s) who are drawn to the attraction. How might hoteliers best market to these people to inform them of their hotel's features?

Team Activity 2

Go on-line and attempt to make a reservation at three different, but similarly priced, hotels in your local area. For each site selected, evaluate:

1. The attractiveness of the Web site
2. The ease with which a room reservation could be made
3. The quality of the information on the site for a:
   a. Leisure traveler
   b. Business traveler

2

The Structure of the Lodging Industry

Chapter Objectives

1. To inform you about the different types of investors who own hotels.
2. To tell how hotel management companies help hotel owners operate their hotels.
3. To describe the importance of management contracts in the operation of hotels.
4. To teach you about the impact of franchisors in the lodging industry.
5. To explain how franchisors and franchisees work within a franchise agreement to assist each other in promoting a hotel brand.

Chapter Outline

HOTEL OWNERS
    Investors
    Owner/Operators
MANAGEMENT COMPANIES
    The Role and Structure of Management
        Companies
    Management Contracts
    Management Company Advantages and
        Disadvantages

FRANCHISING AND THE LODGING INDUSTRY
    Hotel Franchisors
    Hotel Franchisees
    Franchise Agreements
OWNERSHIP AND MANAGEMENT ALTERNATIVES
OWNERSHIP AND OPERATIONAL CHALLENGES

Overview: The Structure of the Lodging Industry

The best way to understand how hotels operate is to start with an understanding of who owns them, who manages them, and finally, who franchises them. Many individuals and companies invest in hotels. Some investors are experienced in the ownership of hotels, while others are new to the business. An investor may own all or part of a hotel. Some individual investors own many hotels, and some hotels are owned by multiple investors. In some cases, investors plan to take an active role in how the hotels they own are managed. In other cases, investors purchase hotels strictly as a financial investment and have neither the interest nor the experience required to run a hotel. The latter owners need an individual or a company to operate their hotels for them.

Hotel management companies are businesses that operate hotels for owners who do not wish to manage their own properties. A hotel management company may consist of one, a few, or many individual hoteliers. Technically, a single hotel manager, operating a hotel for a single hotel owner, could be considered a hotel management company. In other cases, management companies can be extremely large, employ hundreds or thousands of people, and operate hundreds of hotels for many different owners. Knowing about the way hotel management companies actually run hotels for owners, as well as the management contracts both parties implement to set the rules for operating these hotels, is important in understanding the lodging industry.

Increasingly, franchise lodging companies, called franchisors, are playing a large role in the development, marketing, and operation of hotels. This is especially true in the United States. Knowing how franchisors and their franchisees work together to advance the standing of a hotel brand, and thus increase its value, is also critical to knowing how the lodging business operates. In this chapter, you will see how understanding franchise agreements, the legal document that defines the roles of the two partners in a franchise relationship, is essential to your knowledge of the lodging industry.

HOTEL OWNERS

Hotels are operated for two reasons. The first, as we saw in Chapter 1, is to meet the needs of the traveling public. Over the long run, however, this goal can only be achieved if the hotel also meets the hotel owner's **return on investment (ROI)** goal. Thus both serving guests and doing so profitably are important concerns for hotel owners.

LODGING LANGUAGE

Return on Investment (ROI): The percentage rate of return achieved on the money invested in a hotel property.

■

Different hotel owners may seek different ROIs depending upon their specific goals. In all cases, however, the ROI is computed using the following formula:

$$\frac{\text{Hotel income after taxes}}{\text{Total hotel investment}} = \text{ROI}\%$$

For example, for a hotel where the owner has invested $5 million and the after-tax income for one year is $600,000, the return on investment, in that year, would be computed as:

$$\frac{\$600,000.00}{\$5,000,000.00} = 12\%$$

Desired ROIs are generally not easy to achieve. They require wise hotel selection and investment, aggressive sales efforts, and professional hotel operations management. When the owner's ROI expectations are met, funds will be sufficient to maintain the hotel in a manner that appeals to guests and, as a result, helps ensure the continued success of the hotel.

It is important to understand that the owner of a hotel actually owns two distinctly different assets. The first asset is the real estate involved. This includes the land, building(s), and furnishings that make up the hotel. The second asset involved in owning a hotel is the operating business itself. For example, in a hotel that is currently operating, the value of the hotel consists of both its real estate value and the profits (if any) made by running the hotel. For a hotel that has yet to be built, the value of the real estate may be known and building costs can be estimated, but the value of the operating business must be projected. This means that it is usually easier to establish the worth and, as a result, the purchase price of a hotel that is operating than of one that has yet to be built. A hotel that is performing well will most likely have a sales price that reflects its performance. A hotel that is underperforming will generally be sold for less on a per-room basis because there is no guarantee, even with the proper investment and management, that it will be able to perform better than it does currently.

Individuals can own hotels, and so can legally formed partnerships and corporations. Real Estate Investment Trusts (REITS) are public, stock-issuing companies that can own and (since 1991) operate their own hotels. In some cases, hotel owners share ownership with their customers by "selling" the right to occupy a room for a specific amount of time each year (timeshare). Individuals and companies of many different kinds invest in (own) hotels. A convenient way to view this diverse group is by their participation in the actual operation of the hotel. Using this approach, hotel owners can be categorized either as investors or as owner/operators.

Investors

Those who invest in hotels do so for many reasons, including the favorable tax status resulting from the hotel's **depreciation**, the long-term effects of real estate **appreciation**, and the profits that can be made from the hotel's monthly operation.

LODGING LANGUAGE

Depreciation: The reduction in the value of an asset as it wears out. This non-cash expense is often termed a "tax write-off" because the decline in the value of the asset is tax deductible.

Appreciation: The increase, over time, in the value of an asset. The amount of the increased value is not taxed unless the asset changes hands (is sold).

Regardless of the motivation for buying a hotel, an investor, as defined here, is not typically active in the management of a hotel. The investor can be an individual, a corporation, or any other entity that seeks to acquire a hotel for its own purposes. Depending on the investment level, the investor may own all or part of the hotel. In some cases, several investors will pool their funds to purchase a hotel that is larger or more expensive than any one of them could have purchased individually.

Owner/Operators

Owner/operator: An individual or company that both owns and operates (manages) the hotel in which it has invested.

LODGING LANGUAGE

Owner/Operator: A hotel investor who also manages (operates) the hotel.

Owner/operators can be individuals and their family members, some of whom may work in the hotel every day, or very large multi-national hotel companies with offices all over the world. In both cases, the characteristic that distinguishes owner/operators from other hotel investors is their responsibility for the management of the hotel(s) they own.

Some hotels have a high real estate value because they are located in prime areas of a city.

MANAGEMENT COMPANIES

Because hotel investors, as defined in this chapter, do not typically operate the hotels they own, they must employ a manager to run the hotel. In such situations, if there is only one hotel to manage, a single **General Manager (GM)** could be hired and given the responsibility of operating the hotel.

LODGING LANGUAGE

General Manager (GM): The traditional title of the individual at a hotel property who is responsible for final decision-making regarding property-specific operating policies and procedures. Also, the leader of the hotel's management team.

■

An investor who owns many hotels, however, is likely to employ the services of a **management company**. A management company is an organization formed for the express purpose of managing one or more hotels.

LODGING LANGUAGE

Management Company: An organization that operates a hotel(s) for a fee. Also sometimes called a "contract company."

■

The Role and Structure of Management Companies

The financial success of any lodging facility is dependent, in large measure, upon the quality and skill of its on-site management. Before the mid-1950s, the owners of a hotel typically hired the best general manager they could find to operate the hotel(s) they owned. If they needed a manager with a specific level of skill or experience, they would try to find one. Even talented general managers, however, may not have had the experience in specific tasks that the owner sought. When that was the case, the result was often less than satisfactory for both the owner and the hotel's general manager.

In the 1950s and later, hotel owner groups began to purchase ever larger numbers of hotels. Their inability to actively recruit, train, and supervise the many general managers they required to manage their properties resulted in the growth of companies formed simply to manage hotels under ordinary as well as out-of-the-ordinary circumstances. Today, with the growth of large (and small) management companies, owners often find that a hotel management company, with its wide range of personnel, can provide managers with the exact experience they are looking for.

In many cases, owners face special problems in the operation of the hotels they own. Some of these special situations include:

- Managing/directing a major (complete) renovation of a hotel
- Operating a hotel in a severely **depressed market**
- Bankruptcy/repossession of the hotel
- Managing a hotel slated for permanent closing
- Managing a hotel because of the unexpected resignation of its general manager

- Managing a hotel for an extended period of time for owners who elect not to become directly involved in the day-to-day operation of the property

---

LODGING LANGUAGE

Depressed Market: A hotel market area where occupancy rates and/or ADRs are far below their historical levels.

■

Under the standard financial arrangement between a management company and a hotel's ownership, the management company receives a predetermined fee for its services. The fees charged by management companies to operate a hotel vary, but commonly range between 1 and 5 percent of the hotel's monthly revenue. Thus, regardless of the hotel's operating performance, the management company is paid the fee for its services and the hotel's owners receive the profits (if any) after all expenses are paid.

Sometimes, the hotel owner negotiates an agreement that ties the management company's compensation, at least to some degree, to the hotel's actual operating performance. In some cases this is acceptable, especially with hotels that are proven profitable. In other cases, however, it can take months or even years to turn an unprofitable hotel into a profitable one. Often, it is the owners of unprofitable or distressed market hotels that seek the assistance of management companies. Understandably, however, few hotel management companies are willing to enter into risky management agreements that may result in their financially subsidizing investors who own a hotel that either has been poorly managed in the past or is not likely to be profitable in its current condition.

As we have seen, some of the people who invest in hotels do not want to manage them. Many of these non-operating hotel owners choose to hire management companies because they have absolutely no interest in managing the property, or even in their continued ownership of it.

For example, assume that a bank has loaned money to a hotel investor to develop a property. The owner opens the hotel, but, over time, fails to make the required loan repayments. As a result, the bank is forced to repossess the hotel. In a case such as this, the bank, which is now the owner, will seek a management company that specializes in distressed properties to manage the hotel until it is put up for sale and purchased by a new owner.

The hospitality industry, because it is cyclical, sometimes experiences falling occupancy rates and ADRs. Sometimes these cycles result in properties that cannot pay back the money borrowed to purchase them, and the lenders then face the consequence of becoming involuntary owners through repossession. In such cases, effectively managing a hotel may simply mean optimizing the property's value while offering it for sale. Management companies that specialize in helping lenders maintain repossessed properties until they can be resold will:

- Secure and, if it has closed, reopen the hotel
- Implement sales and marketing plans to maximize the hotel's short- and long-term profitability
- Generate reliable financial data about the hotel
- Establish suitable staffing to maximize guest and employee satisfaction

• Show the hotel to prospective buyers
• Report regularly to the owners about the hotel's physical and financial condition

Clearly, in the situation above, a management company provides a vital service to the lender. While an individual general manager might be able to provide the same services (and usually at a lower initial cost), many hotel investors who unwillingly acquire control of a hotel hire management companies to operate their properties until they can be sold or closed.

Of course, management companies can also operate hotels for investors who want to keep their ownership in their hotels. The services of good management companies are always in demand because investors seek them out in an effort to maximize the ROIs of their hotels. Figure 2.1 is a list of the ten largest U.S. management companies based upon the total sales revenue of the hotels they manage.

The structure of hotel management companies can be examined from several different viewpoints. One way is to consider whether they are **first-tier,** or **second-tier**. The term "tier" refers simply to whose name is on the hotel the management company is operating. Tiering does not refer to the quality of the management of the management company or of the general managers working for it.

LODGING LANGUAGE

First-tier: Management companies that operate hotels for owners using the management company's trade name as the hotel brand. Hyatt, Hilton, and Sheraton are examples.

Second-tier: Management companies that operate hotels for owners and do not use the management company name as part of the hotel name. American General Hospitality, Summit Hotel Management, and Winegardner and Hammons are examples.

■

In a first-tier management company, the management company's name is also the name of the hotel. Examples include Hyatt, Sheraton, and Hilton. Second-tier management companies can operate many different brands of hotels because the management company's name is not the name used on the hotel.

Company	Properties	Gross Annual Revenues[*]
1. Interstate Hotels and Resorts	293	2,100.0
2. Tishman Hotel Corp.	22	584.1
3. Ocean Hospitalities	133	580.0
4. Destination Hotels & Resorts	27	515.7
5. Sunstone Hotels	57	476.9
6. John Q. Hammonds Hotels Inc.	59	431.2
7. Outrigger Enterprises Inc.	47	403.0
8. Lodgian Inc.	96	373.0
9. White Lodging Services Corp.	88	326.0
10. Rosewood Hotels and Resorts	12	269.1

[*]In millions of dollars.

Copyright HOTEL BUSINESS ® 2005 Green Book. May not be reprinted without express written permission.

FIGURE 2.1 Ten Largest Hotel Management Companies

Hilton is an example of a first-tier management company.

As we have seen in Figure 2.1, another way to examine management companies is by the number of hotels they operate or the annual revenues they earn. Because a hotel management company that operates one full-service resort hotel with 750 rooms is likely to employ more managers and have responsibility for higher revenue than another hotel management company that operates three limited-service hotels, each of which has 100 rooms, hotel management companies have historically been ranked (in size) by the number of rooms they manage rather than by the number of hotels they manage. The hospitality trade press periodically publishes rankings of the largest hotel management companies based upon the number of rooms managed.

While the size of a hotel management company may imply something about the company's successfulness, it is often more useful to segment hotel management companies by the manner in which they participate, or do not participate, in the actual risk and ownership of the hotels they manage. As a result, these companies can be examined based upon their participation in one (or more than one) of the following arrangements.

- *The management company is neither a partner in nor an owner of the hotels it manages.* In this situation, the hotel's investors hire the management company. This is common, for example, when lenders involuntarily take possession of a hotel. In other cases, the management company may, for its own business reasons, elect to concentrate only on managing properties and will not participate in hotel investment (ownership).

- *The management company is a partner (with others) in the ownership of the hotels it manages.* A common arrangement in the hotel community is that of a management company collaborating with an investor(s) to jointly own and manage one or more hotels. Frequently, in this situation, the management company

The ownership, by a single family, of a 50–100-room hotel like this one is very common in the hotel industry.

either buys or is given a share of hotel ownership (usually 1–20 percent) and then assumes the management of the property. Those hotel owners who prefer this arrangement feel that the partial ownership enjoyed by the management company will result in better performance. If the hotel experiences losses, they will be shared by the management company, and this can serve as a motivator for the management company to do well.

• *The management company only manages hotels it owns.* Some management companies are formed simply to manage the hotels it actually owns. These companies want to participate in the hotel industry as both investors and managers.

ALL IN A DAY'S WORK

The Situation

"You made the loan to Tillman," said Cynthia Pearson to John Gaylon, the vice president of Equity Bank.

"Yes, I know," replied John, "but I didn't know that two new hotels were going to open across the street from Tillman's within 24 months of granting the loan!"

"Well," said Cynthia, the president of Equity Bank, "Tillman is no longer making enough profit to repay his loan. And now that his company has filed bankruptcy, we have a problem."

A Response

Lenders to hotel owners may, for one reason or another, find themselves in a position where they must assume operational responsibility for a hotel. Rarely will the lender seek to run the hotel. Instead the lender will probably hire a management company to operate the asset (hotel) until its orderly sale can be arranged. The role of the management company is to protect the value of the asset while minimizing additional losses to the lender.

A clear advantage of this situation is that the management company will benefit from its own success if the hotels it manages are profitable. If the company is not successful, however, it will be responsible for any operating losses incurred by its hotels.

- *The management company owns some of the hotels it manages and none or only a part of others it manages.* Some management companies vary their ownership participation depending upon the hotel involved. Therefore, a given management company may:
  - Own all of a specific hotel as well as manage it
  - Manage and be an owning partner in another hotel
  - Manage, but not own any part of, yet another hotel property

Each of the above structures has advantages and disadvantages both for the management company and for those with whom it partners.

LODGING ON-LINE

Management companies concentrate on a variety of specialty areas. Swan Inc. is one of the most technologically advanced. To view its site and services, go to:

www.swanhost.com

Management Contracts

The management of a hotel by an entity that does not own the property can, for many reasons, become a very complex process. For example, assume that a guest slips and falls in the parking lot of a hotel owned by an investor but managed by a management company. Who might be held legally responsible for the guest's injuries? Similarly, if an employee of the hotel charges unfair treatment by management, will it be the management company or the owner who hired the management company that will be held **liable** for any resulting damages?

LODGING LANGUAGE

Liable: Legally bound to compensate for injury or loss.

■

To address these and numerous other issues, hotel owners and management companies sign **management contracts.** The contract clearly establishes the fees, operating responsibilities, and length of time for which the management company will operate the owner's hotel.

LODGING LANGUAGE

Management contract: An agreement between a hotel's owners and a hotel management company under which, for a fee, the management company operates the hotel. Also sometimes called a "management agreement," or an "operating agreement."

■

There are as many different contracts between hotel owners and the management companies they employ as there are hotels under management contract. Every hotel owner, depending upon the management company selected, will have a unique management contract for each hotel owned. In some cases, the contract may include pre-opening services that are provided even before the hotel is officially open. Pre-opening activities may include hiring and training staff, purchasing inventories, and other operational activities that must be done before the first overnight guest can be served.

In *Administration of Hotel and Restaurant Management Contracts,* James Eyster detailed many of the components typically included in a management agreement. This book, published in 1980, is considered a classic work in the field of hotel management contracts. It is an excellent addition to the serious hotelier's personal library, but finding a copy is getting more and more difficult.

LODGING ON-LINE

To order a copy of James Eyster's book *Administration of Hotel and Restaurant Management Contracts,* published by Cornell University Press, go to:

www.amazon.com

In the "Search" field, enter "Books", and then enter the author's name or the book's title.

While times have changed, and each specific management contract is different, many of the negotiable issues identified in Eyster's book must still be addressed by owners and prospective management companies when they are negotiating the details of a management agreement. Today, major elements of management agreements include:

- The length of the agreement
- Procedures for early termination by either party
- Procedures for extending the contract
- Contract terms in the event of the hotel's sale
- Base fees to be charged
- Incentive fees earned or penalties assessed related to operating performance
- Management company investment required or ownership attained
- Exclusivity (is the management contract company allowed to operate competing hotels in the area?)
- Reporting relationships and requirements (how much detail is required, and how frequently will reports be produced?)
- Insurance requirements of the management company (who must carry insurance and how much)
- Status of employees (are the hotel's employees employed by the owner or the management company?)
- The control, if any, that the owner has in the selection or removal of the general manager and other managers employed by the management company who work at the owner's hotel.

Management Company Advantages and Disadvantages

A variety of strengths and benefits can accrue to hotel owners who select a qualified management company to operate their hotels. Among these are:

- *Improved management quality.* In some cases, a management company is able to offer talented hotel professionals a better employment situation than an individual hotel owner. A hotelier's opportunities for advancement, increased training prospects, and employment security are frequently enhanced by working for a management company. As a result, owners benefit from the efforts of professional staff who are more highly skilled. In addition, a management company may have specialists on staff who can assist the property general manager in areas such as hospitality law, accounting, and food and beverage management. In many cases, the hotel's owners could not supply these additional resources.

- *Documented managerial effectiveness is available.* Banks, mortgage companies, and others who are asked to supply investment capital to owners want to know that the hotel for which loans are sought will, in fact, be operated with professional hotel managers. The selection of an experienced management company with documented evidence of past success in operating hotels similar to the one for which investment is requested adds credibility to a loan application submitted by the hotel's owners.

- *Payment for services can be tied to performance.* While most management companies charge a revenue-based fee to operate a hotel, owners can negotiate additional payment incentives that help ensure the very best management company performance possible. In this way, all of the resources of the company can be utilized in ways that benefit both the company and the hotel. Good management companies welcome such arrangements because they allow for above-average fees to be earned in exchange for above-average management performance.

- *Partnership opportunities are enhanced.* Many hotel owners are involved in multiple properties. When that is the case, an established management company and an ownership entity can work together in several different hotels. The management company will become knowledgeable about the owner's goals. The owner will become familiar with the abilities as well as the limitations of the management company. A long-term partnership can, in such cases, be helpful to both parties.

Despite the many advantages, hotel owners face some potential weaknesses or disadvantages inherent in the selection of a management company. These include:

- *The owner cannot generally control selection of the on-site general manager and other high-level managers.* When using a management company, the hotel's owner (even if allowed some input) will not typically select the hotel's general manager. As a result, the quality of the general manager may be related more to the choice of general managers available (currently employed by) the management company than to the quality needed by the hotel. Experienced owners know the importance of quality on-site management and insist upon the best general manager (as well as other managers) that the management company can provide.

- *Talented managers leave frequently.* Assume you were the owner of a hotel management company. You have contracts to operate large hotels (that pay you large fees) and smaller hotels (where the fees you earn are less). One of your general managers shows considerable talent operating a smaller hotel. The owner of the property is very happy with her. An opening for general manager arises at one of your larger hotels. Do you move the general manager? In many cases, the answer is probably yes. In such cases, the hotel owner may experience frequent turn-over of general managers, especially if the hotel owned is smaller, is in a less popular geographic location, or for some other reason is not viewed as desirable by general managers in the management company that operates it.

• *The interests of hotel owners and the management companies they employ sometimes conflict.* On the surface, it would seem that the interests of a hotel owner and the management company selected to operate the hotel would always coincide. Both are interested in operating a profitable hotel. In fact, disputes arise because hotel owners typically seek to minimize the fees they pay to management companies (because lower fees yield greater profits), whereas management companies seek to maximize their fees. As a result, hotel owners who hire management companies often have serious disagreements with them over whether the hotels are indeed operated in the best interest of the owners.

• *The costs of management company errors are borne by the owner.* Under most management contracts, the owner, not the management company, is responsible for all the costs associated with operating the hotel. As a result, any unnecessary costs incurred as a result of any errors in marketing or operating the hotel are borne not by the management company making the errors, but rather by the hotel's owner.

• *Transfer of ownership may be complicated.* The term (length) of a management contract, especially if the hotel is large, can be several years. As a result, if the owner decides to sell the hotel during the life of the contract, potential buyers who either operate their own hotels or use a different management

---

ALL IN A DAY'S WORK

The Situation

"You see," said Dan Segola, salesperson for Clarkson Foods, "since this hotel is managed by the Freeport Management Company, you qualify for our Breakfast Bonus program."

Dan was telling Shana Alexander, an employee of the Freeport Management Company, and the general manager of the Poplar Tree Hotel, about a special rebate program offered through Clarkson Foods.

"If you buy just five cases per month of Fruity brand orange juice for use on the Poplar Tree's continental breakfast bar, Fruity will write a monthly check to

your company. It's their way of rewarding high-volume customers like Freeport."

"But the Poplar Tree is a pretty small hotel," replied Shana. "We only have 70 rooms."

"That's O.K.," said Dave. "Because Freeport manages hotels all over the country, your hotel still qualifies for the volume discount."

If Shana participates in the program, who should receive the money paid by Fruity?

A Response

Despite the logic presented by the Clarkson Food salesperson, benefits such as rebates for purchases made by a hotel

should accrue to the hotel's owners, not the management company. The only exception would be if a specific section in the management contract allows the management company to accrue such benefits, and from the perspective of the hotel's investors, that is rarely, if ever, advisable. Shana should participate in the Breakfast Bonus program, accept the check, and deposit it in the hotel owner's bank account, but only when it is clear that doing so would be in the best interests of the hotel's investors, as well as the hotel's guests.

company may not be interested in buying. Even if the contract includes a **buy-out** clause, the cost of the buy-out may be so high that the owner can only sell to a buyer willing to pay the very highest price for the property, a fact that can limit the number of potential buyers.

LODGING LANGUAGE

Buy-out: An arrangement in which both parties to a contract agree to end the contract early as a result of one party paying the other the agreed-upon financial compensation.

■

FRANCHISING AND THE LODGING INDUSTRY

To truly understand the lodging industry in the United States, and in the rest of the world as well, you must first understand the **franchise** concept. In a franchise arrangement, one party (the **franchisor**) allows another party (the **franchisee**) to use, for a specific amount of time, the name, operating procedures, and systems developed by the franchisor. In exchange for the right to use these things, the franchisee pays a fee to the franchisor.

LODGING LANGUAGE

Franchise: An arrangement whereby one party (the franchisor) allows another party to use its logo, brand name, systems, and resources in exchange for a fee.

Franchisor: An organization that manages a brand and sells the right to use the brand name.

Franchisee: An individual or company that buys, under specific terms and conditions, the right to use a brand name for a fixed period of time and at an agreed-upon price.

■

Franchising allows one business entity to use the logo, trademarks, and operating systems developed by another business entity for the benefit of both. As a result, franchising creates a network of independent business owners sharing a **brand** name.

LODGING LANGUAGE:

Brand: The name of a specific hotel group. For example, Holiday Inn and Holiday Inn Express are two different brands. Additional examples of brands include Clarion, Comfort Inn, Hampton, Super 8, and Ramada.

■

Hotel Franchisors

To see the effect of franchising in the hotel industry, assume that a motorist is driving along a highway and sees the name of a popular hotel. The name is easily recognizable due, in part, to an extensive nationwide advertising campaign. In all probability, the driver will suppose that the hotel company purchased some land and built another hotel to operate in this location. In fact, that is not likely to be the case. It is much more likely that an independent investor has built the property and agreed to purchase a franchise from a hotel franchisor.

Many in the hotel industry believe that the first significant hotel franchising arrangements began in the 1950s with Kemmons Wilson and his Holiday Inn **chain**.

LODGING LANGUAGE

Chain: A group of franchisees who have all franchised the same hotel brand name. Also called "brand" or "flag."

◼

In a combination of what may well be part historical fact and part hotel lore, the story is told about how, in 1951, Wilson, a resident of Memphis, Tennessee, loaded his wife and five children into the family car and drove to Washington, D.C., for a vacation. He was quite unhappy with the motel accommodations he found along the way. The rooms he encountered were, he believed, too small, too expensive, and in many cases, not clean.

Wilson returned to Tennessee convinced that he could build a chain of hotels across the country that would operate under the same name and provide the traveling public with a lodging experience they could count on to be clean, comfortable, and moderately priced. He hired an architect to draw up the plans for a prototype hotel. The architect, according to legend, was watching an old Bing Crosby movie titled *Holiday Inn* while working, and sketched that name on the top of the plans he was drawing. Wilson, upon seeing the plans, liked them and the name at the top as well. As a result, the Holiday Inn chain was born.

The first Holiday Inn opened in Tennessee in 1952, and the four-hundreth Holiday Inn franchise began operation in December of 1962. Today, Holiday Inns franchises its name as part of the InterContinental Hotels group, which consists of over 1,500 hotels worldwide, including the brands Inter-Continental Hotels, Holiday Inn, Holiday Inn Select, Holiday Inn Express, Holiday Inn Crown Plaza, and Staybridge Suites.

LODGING ON-LINE

To see the Web site of the "new" Holiday Inn company, go to:

www.ichotels.com

In most cases today, a hotel franchisor has the ability to grant franchises for several different brands or flags. As a result, a hotel investor could, for example, elect to enter into a franchise relationship with Holiday Inn or Holiday Inn Express, two different brand names, both franchised by the InterContinental Hotels group. Alternatively, the investor could choose to franchise a Hilton Hotel, an Embassy Suite hotel, or a Hampton Hotel. The Hilton Hotels company franchises all three of these brands.

Today, hotel owners increasingly elect to affiliate their hotels with other hotels under a common brand name. Owners can choose the brand with which they wish to affiliate from a number of franchisors. For example, Choice Hotels International franchises the Clarion, Quality, Cambria Suites, Comfort Inn, Comfort Suites, Sleep Inn, MainStay Suites, Roadway Inn, and Econolodge brands. Cendant, the largest franchisor in the United States, manages the Amerihost, Day's Inn, Howard Johnson, Knights Inn, Ramada, Super Eight, Travelodge, and Wingate Inn brands, as well as other non-hotel franchised names, including Avis (car rental) and Century 21 (real estate sales). A variation of the franchise arrangement is that of "membership" hotels, (independent hotel owners who band together to create their own brand). Best Western is the largest of the membership groups, but from a guest's viewpoint, it operates essentially the same way as a chain.

While the actual brands managed by any single franchisor change as brands are bought and sold, the ten largest brands at the time of this writing are included as Figure 2.2.

Each brand will, depending upon the franchisor's structure, have a brand manager or president responsible for expanding the number of hotels in the brand and maintaining the quality standards established for it. In the overwhelming majority of cases, franchise companies do not actually own the hotels operating under their brand names. They only own the right to sell the brand name and to determine the standards that will be followed by the hotel owners who elect to affiliate with their brands.

The greatest advantage to a franchisor of entering into a franchise relationship with a hotel owner is the increase in fee payments to the brand that will result from the agreement. Like all businesses, franchise companies desire growth. In general, the greater the number of hotels that operate under a single brand name, the greater the value of the name and thus the fees that can be charged for using it. In addition, each additional hotel that affiliates with a hotel brand helps to pay for the expenses of operating that brand. Therefore, additional hotel properties operating under the same brand name typically mean greater profits for the franchise company. As a result, franchisors are aggressive in soliciting agreements with hotel owners who are already affiliated with another brand. In such cases, the franchisor is hoping that the hotel owner will agree to a **conversion** to a new brand name.

LODGING LANGUAGE

Conversion: The changing of a hotel from one brand to another. Also known as "re-flagging."
■

Conversions can be beneficial to a brand because they allow it to grow more quickly. They can be a detriment to the brand, however, if the converted properties

Brand	Properties	Rooms
1. Best Western International	4,107	309,385
2. Holiday Inn Hotels and Resorts	1,519	286,520
3. Marriott Hotels & Resorts	487	178,331
4. Days Inns Worldwide Inc.	1,898	157,025
5. Comfort Inns	2,021	150,570
6. Sheraton Hotels & Resorts	391	134,442
7. Hampton Inn/Suites	1,283	129,636
8. Super 8 Motels	2,079	125,754
9. Holiday Inn Express	1,497	124,523
10. Radisson Hotels & Resorts	436	102,574

Copyright HOTEL BUSINESS ® 2005 Green Book. May not be reprinted without express written permission.

FIGURE 2.2 Ten Largest Hotel Brands

Holiday Inn is one of the brands offered by InterContinental Hotels.

do not have the features and quality levels of the hotels already in the brand. Of course, franchisors also actively pursue owners developing new hotels who have not yet selected a franchise brand.

The franchise arrangement in the hotel industry is so popular, according to the American Hotel and Lodging Association (AH&LA), that over 75% of all U.S. hotels are involved in a franchise relationship.

Hotel Franchisees

Franchising has been of great benefit both to hotel investors and to the owners of brand names. The primary advantages to a hotel investor of buying a franchise are that doing so allows the hotel to acquire a brand name with regional or national recognition and connects the hotel to the Global Distribution System (GDS). As seen earlier, connectivity to the GDS is a necessity in today's hotel market. An independent hotel can also purchase this connectivity, but it is costly.

Affiliation with a strong brand will also typically increase the hotel's sales and therefore its profitability. The total fees paid by the hotel owner to the brand managers are related to the strength of the brand name and to the revenue the name will bring to the hotel. While the fees related to a franchise agreement are negotiable, they will, on average, equal from 3 to 15 percent of the revenue the hotel generates selling rooms.

In addition to increased revenue levels, affiliation with a brand often affects the ability of a hotel's owner to secure external financing. When owners seek financing from banks or other lending institutions, they most frequently find that these lenders, almost without exception, will require an affiliation with an established brand before they consider the loan request.

Additional advantages, depending upon the franchisor selected, may include assistance with on-site training, advice on purchasing hotel furnishings, reduced operating costs resulting from vendors who give brand operators preferred pricing, and free interior and exterior design assistance.

For a hotel's owners, purchasing a hotel franchise is actually very much like purchasing the long-term services of other professionals, such as attorneys or accountants, who help the owner maximize the value of an asset. For example, when selecting a franchise, there will be a number of companies (franchisors) offering the service. These service providers offer a variety of experience, skills, and knowledge. In addition, the prices they charge for their services will vary. Lastly, as is true in many relationships, the franchisor is likely to have a unique "style" of doing business that attracts (or repels) potential franchisees.

Factors that hotel franchisees look for prior to agreeing to affiliate with a specific hotel brand include:

- *The quality and experience of the brand managers.* Brand management, like hotel management, is complex. Brand managers who are experienced in their work will operate the brand better than those who are not. In addition, brand managers who are experienced, can show the hotel's owners a track record of their success (or failure). The relationship between a franchisor and a franchisee is not a true partnership, despite the claims of the franchisor, because the brand and its managers are not financially responsible for losses incurred by the hotel. In fact, no brand available today bases the fees it collects on the achieved profits. Fees, instead, are based upon achieved revenue. As a result, it is the hotel owners, not the brand managers, who bear the financial risk of poor brand management. This makes it critical for the brand managers to be experienced and talented and to demonstrate great integrity in dealings with their franchisees.

- *Perceived quality/service level of the brand.* Travelers associate some brands with higher quality, service levels, and costs than other brands. A Holiday Inn Crown Plaza, for example, will probably be perceived by most travelers as having more services (and charging a higher ADR) than a Holiday Inn Express. In most cases, franchisors, in an attempt to offer a franchise product that appeals to hotel owners at a variety of desired investment levels, will offer brands with a range of quality and guest services provided. Hotel owners who elect to operate the highest-quality brand offered by a franchisor will spend, on average, more to build or renovate each of their hotel rooms than if they selected a lower-quality level. In addition, total operating costs are likely to be higher with brands that offer guests more services (although ADRs are also likely to be higher in these cases). Of course, a well-managed, lower-cost limited-service brand can be more profitable for an owner than a poorly managed, limited-service brand property with a higher **system-wide** ADR. Hotel owners who seek to maximize their return on investment must select a brand that is both well managed and appropriate for the travelers to which the hotel is marketed.

LODGING LANGUAGE

System-wide: Term used to describe a characteristic of all hotels within a given brand. Used, for example, in: "Last year, the system-wide ADR for the brand was $99.50."
■

- *The amount of fees paid to the franchisor.* Far too many hotel owners, when evaluating alternative franchisors, focus only on the fees the hotel will pay to the brand. While the fees paid to a franchisor are certainly one factor to be considered, they are not the only factor, nor even the most important. Nearly all hotel owners feel that the franchise fees they pay are too high; conversely, nearly all franchisors feel that what their franchisees receive in exchange for their fee payments is a great value to the hotel. In fact, the fees paid to a franchisor are a negotiable part of the franchise arrangement and should be considered seriously only after the hotel owner has narrowed down the list of potential franchisors to those that meet other criteria the owner has established for selecting the brand.

- *Direction of the brand.* By far the most important factor in the long-term success of the franchisor/franchise relationship is the future direction of the brand. Obviously, it is impossible to predict the future, yet knowing how the public is likely to perceive a brand in five, ten, or twenty years is important when signing a franchise agreement for the same number of years. Hoteliers can detect clues to the future success of the brand if they examine:
  - The number of hotels currently operating under the brand name
  - The percentage of hotels that have elected to leave the brand in each of the past five years
  - The number of new properties currently being built under the brand's name
  - The number of existing hotels converting to the brand (if conversions are allowed)
  - The ADR trend for the last five years in comparison to the ADR trend for other hotels with which the brand competes
  - The occupancy rate trend for the last five years in comparison to the occupancy rate trend for hotels with which the brand competes
  - The percentage of total hotel room revenue contributed by the brand's reservation system and the percentage of hotels within the brand the achieve the average rate of contribution

LODGING ON-LINE

Lists of hotel franchisors, their mailing addresses, and the individual(s) responsible for each brand they manage can be quickly obtained on the Internet. For one source of hotel franchisor contact information, go to:

www.franchisehelp.com

Franchise Agreements

When a hotel owner decides to affiliate with a brand, the hotel owner and the brand managers sign a **franchise agreement**.

LODGING LANGUAGE

Franchise Agreement: Legal contract between a hotel's owners (the franchisee) and the brand managers (the franchisor) that describes the duties and responsibilities of each in the franchise relationship.

■

Unlike the practice in some other franchise industries, the majority of hotel brand managers (franchisors) do not operate hotels. They operate franchise companies. Hotel owners (the franchisees) are the operating entities in nearly all hotel franchise relationships. This is especially true of limited-service hotels.

With the ownership of a hotel vested in one business entity and the responsibility for brand management the responsibility of another business entity, it is not surprising that conflict can arise between the hotel's owners and the brand managers. For example, assume that the managers of a given brand decide that its logo, and therefore the exterior building signage identifying the brand to the traveling public, has become dated and is in need of modernization. The brand managers may have the authority to require franchisees to update their hotel signage. The owners, however, may resist because of the significant purchase and installation costs for replacing signs that are in perfectly good working order even if "dated." In fact, the hotel owners may disagree with the brand managers about numerous operating issues.

Conflicts between brand managers and owners are sometimes based on honest disagreements about how to advance the best interests of each party. On the other hand, franchisors have been known to promote their own interests more than those of their franchisees. Unlike what has happened in some other industries, the history of hotel franchising does not include widespread cases of franchisor fraud or deception. Nonetheless, hotel franchise relationships are subject to the same federal and state laws that protect franchisees from dishonest franchisors in all industries. The most important franchise-related law is the one enforced by the **Federal Trade Commission (FTC)**.

LODGING LANGUAGE

Federal Trade Commission (FTC): Government agency that enforces federal antitrust and consumer protection laws. It also seeks to ensure that the nation's business markets function competitively and are free of undue restrictions caused by acts or practices that are unfair or deceptive.

■

To ensure fairness in franchising, the FTC, in 1979, issued regulations with the full force of federal law. This set of laws is titled "Disclosure Requirements and Prohibitions Concerning Franchising and Business Opportunity Ventures." Commonly referred to as the "Franchise Rule," it spells out the obligations of franchisors when they attempt to sell franchises to potential franchisees.

LODGING ON-LINE

To review the entire Franchise Rule developed by the FTC and to learn about the requirements placed upon those who sell franchises, go to:

www.ftc.gov/bcp/franchise/16cfr436.htm

Essentially, the Franchise Rule requires that franchisors:

- Supply potential franchisees with a disclosure document at the first face-to-face meeting or 10 business days before any money is paid by the franchisee to the franchisor, whichever is earlier
- Provide evidence, in writing, of any profit forecasts made by the franchisor
- Disclose the number and percentage of franchisees achieving the profit levels advertised in any promotional ads that include profit claims
- Provide potential franchisees with copies of the basic franchise agreement used by the franchisor
- Refund promptly any deposit monies legally due to potential franchisees who elect not to sign a franchise agreement with the franchisor
- Not make claims orally or in writing that conflict with the written disclosure documents provided to the franchisee

In addition to federal laws and regulations, most states have franchise investment laws that require franchisors to provide a presale disclosure document known as an **FOC (Franchise Offering Circular)** to potential franchisees.

LODGING LANGUAGE

FOC (Franchise Offering Circular): Franchise disclosure document prepared by a franchisor and registered and filed with the state governmental agency responsible for administering franchise relationships.

■

These states prohibit the sale of a franchise inside their borders until the franchisor's FOC has been filed with the proper state authorities. Despite their disclosure requirements, neither the FTC not the states verifies the accuracy of the information in the disclosure documents. Verification of a franchisor's claims is the responsibility of the buyer (franchisee). For example, a hotel franchise company can claim that its franchisees make, on average, a 10 percent profit. This claim will *not* be verified as accurate by either the FTC or the state in which the franchisor files an FOC. Thus, owners considering a franchise should seek verification of any item in the FOC that is questionable prior to signing a franchise agreement.

LODGING ON-LINE

Owners of hotels can learn a great deal about buying and operating a franchise by joining the International Franchise Association (IFA). To review the type of information it provides to its members, go to:

www.franchise.org

Despite the relatively good relationships between franchisors and franchisees in the hotel industry, some owners feel that franchisors have too much power to set

brand standards and to control the terms and conditions of the franchise agreements.

LODGING LANGUAGE

Brand Standard: A hotel service or feature that must be offered by any property entering or remaining in a specific hotel brand. Used, for example, in: "The franchisor has determined that free local telephone calls will become a new brand standard effective January 1."

■

Groups of outspoken owners, led chiefly by the **Asian American Hotel Owner's Association (AAHOA),** have recently proposed, and actively campaigned for, fundamental changes in the basic franchise agreements that have long been in use. The proposed changes seek to give hotel owners more control over the content of franchise agreements and a more equal say in the operation of their hotels.

LODGING LANGUAGE

Asian American Hotel Owners Association (AAHOA): Association of hotel owners who, through an exchange of ideas, seek to promote professionalism and excellence in hotel ownership.

■

LODGING ON-LINE

The Asian American Hotel Owners Association (AAHOA) has been at the forefront of promoting fairness in hotel franchising. Its associate members interact with many brand-management companies. To learn more about AAHOA and to review its 12 Points of Fair Franchising, go to:

www.aahoa.com

ALL IN A DAY'S WORK

The Situation

"We had to make the change," said Jim Pratt to Andrew Haywood. "Today's business traveler is demanding it." Jim was one of the brand managers for the franchise company that Andrew had affiliated with when he purchased his first hotel.

"If I had known about this before, I might have chosen a different franchise company. This change will cost me thousands of dollars!" replied Andrew.

The two men were discussing the franchisor's recent decision to require the installation of high-speed Internet access in half of the rooms available in each of the hotels in the brand Andrew had selected.

A Response

In nearly all cases, franchise agreements give brand managers the right to modify brand standards as they see fit. In most cases, significant brand standard changes will be discussed in great detail with franchisees prior to implementation. It is unlikely, however, that any brand standard change proposed by a franchisor would be supported by every one of a brand's franchisees. In this case, despite the owner's objections, the hotel will, in fact, be required to comply with the new standard.

Franchise agreements are complex as well as increasingly important. Relatively few independently operated hotels can survive without a nationally recognized brand name. As a result, owners, management companies, and franchisors must all understand their roles in the hotel franchising environment and work together for the good of guests and the hotel industry.

OWNERSHIP AND MANAGEMENT ALTERNATIVES

As we have seen, owners of hotels may operate the properties themselves, hire a management company to operate them, and then, regardless of that decision, may elect to affiliate or not to affiliate with a hotel brand. Owners of both large and small hotels must make these same decisions. Figure 2.3 lists the world's largest hotels. Note that many are independent (not affiliated with a franchise brand) and others have an affiliation. Note also that most of the world's largest hotels are in Las Vegas, a very popular destination for leisure travelers and a major convention center.

Hotel investors have many options when considering the operation of the properties they own. This is true because there are a variety of ways that hotels can be owned and managed, including:

- *Single-unit property not affiliated with any brand.* Some single-unit properties have been in business for many years, are extremely successful, and may be the preeminent hotel in their community or area. This, however, is the exception. Single-unit properties have been historically capturing an ever-smaller **market share** in the lodging industry nationwide.

Size Hotel	City Location	Number of Rooms
1. MGM Grand	Las Vegas	5,034
2. Ambassador City Jomtlen	Thailand	4,631
3. Luxor	Las Vegas	4,476
4. Excalibur	Las Vegas	3,991
5. Circus Circus	Las Vegas	3,774
6. Mandalay Bay	Las Vegas	3,700
7. Flamingo Hilton	Las Vegas	3,642
8. Las Vegas Hilton	Las Vegas	3,174
9. Mirage	Las Vegas	3,049
10. The Venetian	Las Vegas	3,036
11. Monte Carlo	Las Vegas	3,014
12. Bellagio	Las Vegas	3,005
13. Hilton Hawaiian Village	Honolulu	2,998
14. Paris	Las Vegas	2,916
15. Treasure Island	Las Vegas	2,900
16. Opryland USA	Nashville	2,883
17. Bally's	Las Vegas	2,832
18. Imperial Palace	Las Vegas	2,635
19. Aladdin	Las Vegas	2,567
20. Harrah's	Las Vegas	2,559

FIGURE 2.3   World's Largest Hotels

LODGING LANGUAGE

Market Share: The percentage of the total market (typically in dollars spent) captured by a property. For example, a hotel generating $200,000 in business traveler guest room rental annually in a community where business travelers spend $1 million per year will have a 20 percent market share.

LODGING ON-LINE

The Roney Palace is an excellent example of a single-unit hotel that has elected not to affiliate with a brand. To see this unique property, go to:

www.roney-palace.com

- *Single-unit properties affiliated with a brand.* Individually owned properties that are part of a hotel chain are the most prevalent arrangement in the United States today. American brands are expanding rapidly internationally. Brand affiliation, whether international, nationwide, regional, or located within an even smaller area, is successful because of name recognition, and because it is often easier to obtain financing for businesses affiliated with a brand.

LODGING ON-LINE

While brands managed by U.S. companies such as Marriott and Hilton are most familiar to Americans, there are also very large brands operated by foreign companies. One of the largest of these manages the Sofitel, Novotel, Motel 6, and Red Roof Inns brands in the United States. To see the Web site of Accor, the French company that owns these brands, go to:

www.accor.com

Of course, some owners own more than one hotel. When they do, they have a variety of options available to them. These include:

- *Multi-unit properties affiliated with the same brand.* Some owners own several hotels and affiliate them all with the same brand. This often makes managing them easier because the expectations of the brand's owners are well known. In a large city, an individual owner could operate two (or more) hotels, with the same brand, in close proximity to each other. In a smaller city, of course, doing so would run the risk of the two properties competing directly for the same type of guest. In many cases, this model works well for owners who own multiple properties in multiple cities.

- *Multi-unit properties affiliated with different brands.* Some multi-property owners elect to affiliate with several brands. Sometimes they do this because they own more than one hotel in a market area and feel that two hotels with the same brand would not be best. In other cases, the owners may have some limited-service and some full-service hotels, and the same brand name would not fit both types of properties equally well.

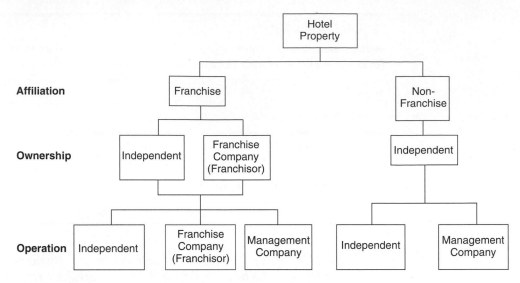

FIGURE 2.4   Hotel Ownership/Management Alternatives

- *Multi-unit properties operated by a management company or the brand.* We have seen how management companies will, for a fee, operate a hotel for an owner. Some brands will also, for a fee, offer management services to hotel owners.
- *Single or multi-unit properties owned by the brand.* Some brands actually own some of their own hotels. Independent (not owned by the brand) ownership and affiliation with a brand is, by far, the most common hotel arrangement in the United States.

Figure 2.4 is a summary of the possible ownership/management arrangements discussed above. It confirms that the ownership/management issues of a hotel can be complex because of the possible alternatives.

OWNERSHIP AND OPERATIONAL CHALLENGES

Understanding the specific ownership, management, and affiliation of a hotel is critical to understanding the decision-making involved in operating it. For example, in a hotel operated by a management company, the business interests of the owners of the hotel may sometimes conflict with the business interests of the management company. Consider the situation in which a contract for managing a hotel is up for renewal. Most unbiased observers would maintain that it is in the best interest of the hotel's owners to negotiate as short a contract length as possible and one that holds the management company responsible for financial results that are less than expected. The same observers would very likely state that it is in the best interest of the management company to negotiate as long a contract as possible and one that holds the hotel's owners, not the management company, financially responsible in the event that hotel operating performance does not meet anticipated levels. Likewise, hotel owners like to keep the fees they pay management companies low, while the management company, in most cases, would prefer higher fees.

It is a simple fact that hotel owners often find themselves in conflict or, at the very least, disagreement with brand managers about how to best operate the brand, as well as how to operate the individual hotels that make up the brand. Assume, for example, that the brand managers for a hotel have, as a brand standard, established breakfast hours for the hotel's complimentary continental breakfast to be from 6:00 a.m. to 9:00 a.m.

A hotel owner, however, may prefer to begin the breakfast at 7:00 a.m., rather than 6:00 a.m. on weekends to reduce labor costs. The change in starting times would violate the brand standard. When owners violate or ignore brand standards, the resulting influence on the hotel's relationship with the brand can be very negative and damaging.

In most cases, a hotel owner's relationship with a brand is developed with the brand's **franchise service director (FSD).**

LODGING LANGUAGE

Franchise Service Director (FSD): The representative of a franchise hotel brand who interacts directly with a hotel franchisee.

■

The job of the FSD is to monitor the franchisee's compliance with the franchise agreement. While the job title of this individual may vary from brand to brand, the position is always responsible for the day-to-day relationship between the franchisor and the franchisee. In some cases, the FSD may perform any inspections required by the franchisor. Other jobs include assisting the hotel with its PMS sales effort, monitoring and advising about the hotel's use of the franchise-provided sales tools, and advising the franchise on the availability and use of other franchisor resources.

Usually, the relationship between an FSD and a franchisee is very good. Sometimes, legitimate differences of opinion and conflicts can arise between a hotel franchisee and the franchisor's representative, and these issues, if not resolved, can negatively affect their relationship.

Management companies have their own brand challenges. Some management companies have excellent relations with the brands they manage for owners, but others do not. Sometimes, the wishes or directives of brand managers are in conflict with the management company. For example, a franchise company, in an effort to promote business, may send large, exterior banners to the hotel that advertise a special rate or hotel feature. Obviously, the brand would like these signs displayed on the property. The management company's sales philosophy, however, may not include hanging exterior banners because it believes they cheapen the image of the hotel. As a result, the banners are not displayed. It is likely that the FSD, upon learning the banners are not used, will see the management company as acting in a way that hurts the hotel, while the management company would feel the same way about the brand's directive that the banner be displayed.

Hotel owners, management companies, and franchisors must all work together to further the hotel industry. There are some areas of their relationship where hotel owners and brand managers (as well as owners and management companies) can honestly disagree about what is fair or what has, in fact, been agreed to. These differences of opinion can sometimes result in legal action by either party. Despite some areas of conflict, however, the relationships developed among these three major groups strongly and favorably affect today's lodging industry as well as the hoteliers working within it.

CHAPTER OBJECTIVES REVIEW

If you have successfully studied the material in this chapter, you should be prepared to:

1. Explain the differences between hotel investors, operators, and owner/operators. (Objective 1)
2. Understand the difference between first-tier and second-tier management companies. (Objective 2)
3. Explain the purpose of a management contract. (Objective 3)
4. Tell how hotel franchising began and how it affects today's lodging industry. (Objective 4)
5. Describe how franchisors and franchisees use a franchise agreement as a tool to help promote a hotel brand. (Objective 5)

LODGING LANGUAGE

Return On Investment (ROI)
Depreciation
Appreciation
Owner/Operator
General Manager (GM)
Management Company
Depressed Market
First-tier
Second-tier
Liable
Management Contract

Buy-out
Franchise
Franchisor
Franchisee
Brand
Chain
Conversion
System-wide
Franchise Agreement

Federal Trade Commission (FTC)
FOC (Franchise Offering circular)
Brand Standard
Asian American Hotel Owners Association (AAHOA)
Market Share
Franchise Service Director (FSD)

FOR DISCUSSION

1. Hotel investors seek strong ROIs through increases in the value of their hotel's real estate, operating profits, or both. What factors in a specific geographic area are likely to make the real estate value of a hotel increase? Decrease?
2. What advantages might a general manager who works for a management company have, compared to a general manager working for an individual hotel owner? What advantages might the general manager gain by working for the individual hotel investor?
3. Not all hotel owners enter into franchise agreements. Identify an independent hotel in your area. Why do you think the hotel's owners elected not to affiliate with a franchise brand?
4. Brand managers work hard to establish an image for their brand. Consider a hotel brand that is associated with rooms that sell for a high price. What factors might make a traveler want to choose that brand?
5. Brand managers for economy or budget hotels also work hard to establish their brand image. Consider a hotel brand that is associated with rooms that sell for a very low price. What factors other than price might make a traveler want to choose that brand?

6. Different brands have different brand standards. List some areas within a hotel where you believe standards could vary based upon variations in the system-wide ADR of a brand.
7. When you choose a hotel, does the brand influence your decision? Why?
8. Some observers of hotels believe there are now too many brands. Do you agree? How could the existence of too many brands be harmful to the hotel industry?
9. Many guests believe that brand managers actually own hotels when in almost all cases they do not. How does this affect the hoteliers who actually operate hotels?
10. In the past, low-cost brands had difficulty competing with higher-priced brands. The advent of the Internet has changed this somewhat. Go on-line and compare the Web sites of a high-priced hotel brand and a lower-priced brand. Do you agree that the Internet has helped lower-cost brands compete more equally for consumers?

TEAM ACTIVITIES

Team Activity 1

Identify the twenty-five hotels nearest to you. List their brand names and identify the corporations that own those brands. How many different brands were identified? How many different corporations that own the brands were identified?

Team Activity 2

Many students hoping to work for first-tier management companies believe that these companies own the hotels using their names. Identify five first-tier hotels in your area. Find out how many of them are *owned* and operated by the first-tier management company.

3 Service and Hotel Management

Chapter Objectives

1. To define quality and review its impact upon the level of service provided by a lodging property.
2. To discuss the six ingredients in a recipe to develop a quality service system.
3. To describe the concept of "moments of truth" in guest service.
4. To recognize the important role of employees in consistently delivering guest service.
5. To present management tactics that can be used to ensure effective guest service.
6. To explain that lodging employees are service professionals.
7. To present the basic guest service philosophy of the Ritz-Carlton Hotel Company.

Chapter Outline

QUALITY IMPACTS SERVICE
  Service Concerns
  Service Expectations
INGREDIENTS IN A QUALITY SERVICE SYSTEM
  Consider the Guests Being Served
  Determine What the Guests Desire
  Develop Procedures to Deliver What Guests Want
  Train and Empower Staff
  Implement Revised Systems
  Evaluate and Modify Service Delivery Systems
SERVICE AND "MOMENTS OF TRUTH"

SERVICE DELIVERY BY EMPLOYEES
MANAGEMENT TACTICS FOR EFFECTIVE GUEST SERVICE
  Recruit and Select Service-Minded Staff
  Provide Effective Orientation and Training
  Supervise with a Service Emphasis
  Empower Staff with Service Authority
  Emphasize Continuous Quality Improvement
LODGING PROPERTY STAFF ARE SERVICE PROFESSIONALS
BENCHMARK AGAINST THE BEST: THE RITZ-CARLTON HOTEL COMPANY

Overview: Service and Hotel Management

There are a wide range of organizations in the hospitality industry. Many offer lodging accommodations, and they are the focus of this book. Others offer food and beverage products. Still others are part of the recreation, leisure, or meetings segments of the industry. To be successful, all of these organizations have one thing in common; they must consistently provide quality guest service.

Lodging operations are sometimes said to be part of the "hospitality services" industry. A popular name for the segment offering food and beverage products is "food services." People purchasing lodging and food and beverages typically consider service to be a very important element in the experience they are buying. At its most basic level, every hospitality organization must focus on service. It is more often the service, not the product (food, beverage or sleeping room), that most influences the guests' perceptions about their experience and their interest in returning to the property or to another property in the chain.

How would you treat a special friend or a relative whom you invite into your home for a meal? The answer to this question can help to define how guests visiting a lodging operation should be treated. After all, the earliest travelers were offered meals and a safe night's rest by families living near trade routes and were invited into the family's home for today's equivalent of lodging and food services.

It is true that guests in your home would not be presented with a bill covering the charges at the end of their visit. By contrast, those visiting a hotel must pay before they leave. However, the policies and procedures, the training activities, and the basic vision and mission of the organization can be developed with an emphasis on serving guests just as you would host your friends and family.

Customers are guests. Do the terms "customer" and "guest" mean the same thing? Perhaps they do in a dictionary; however, in the real world of hospitality, the manager who treats a visitor as a guest will likely be more successful than competitors treating the visitor as a customer.

In this chapter, we will emphasize the principle that a service philosophy is important, and, as is true in so many other areas of lodging management, that "it all begins with the manager." We will define quality, review how it impacts the service provided by a hotel, and discuss what must be done to develop a quality priority and keep it going. A second major focus of the chapter will review the concept of "moments of truth," and we will discuss the procedures needed to maintain the vision that service must be an ongoing priority. A third major emphasis of the chapter focuses directly on employees. You will learn about your employees' role in delivering guest service and see that they are, indeed, service professionals. Finally, we will explain benchmarking, using, as an example, the Ritz-Carlton Hotel Company.

QUALITY IMPACTS SERVICE

The concept of **quality** is widely discussed in the world of hospitality management. Unfortunately, it is much easier to talk about quality than to effectively implement and consistently deliver it in a hospitality operation.

LODGING LANGUAGE

Quality: The consistent delivery of products and services according to expected standards.

■

For our purposes, quality is defined as "the consistent delivery of products and services according to expected standards." Note that **service**—the topic of this chapter—is specifically noted in the definition.

LODGING LANGUAGE

Service (Guest): The process of helping guests by addressing their wants and needs with respect and dignity and in a timely manner.

◼

This is important because the guest renting a room at a hotel or purchasing a meal at the hotel's restaurant is buying, and desires to obtain, an expected standard of service in exchange for the payment. Increasingly, guests are willing to pay more when they visit hospitality properties offering service that meets or exceeds their service expectations. The level of service quality is an important factor in the experience that guests receive during the visit to the lodging operation.

Service Concerns

Our definition of service focuses on basic concerns, and we must emphasize two important points. First, service is not the same as servility (to assist someone who is of a better social class). The Ritz-Carlton Hotel Company, which will be discussed later in this chapter, emphasizes this point in an exceptional way with its corporate mantra stating that all its employees are "Ladies and Gentlemen Serving Ladies and Gentlemen." This company knows that the best hospitality employees are those who genuinely enjoy working with others (employees on their team) and helping guests. They do so with respect and dignity.

Second, the definition of service emphasizes helping guests by addressing their wants and needs. What do guests want? A businessperson and a family are two very different types of guests, but at the most fundamental level they want the same things. Among these are basics like as a clean room in a safe environment and courteous, respectful treatment in their contacts with the property's staffs. All properties must, at the very least, meet these basic expectations at a charge that represents a **value** to the guests. Then, as guest expectations increase (for example, the desire for more luxurious guestrooms and public space and for more personalized service that may require a greater **employee-to-guest ratio**), the hotel can increase its charges to meet these higher-level expectations.

LODGING LANGUAGE

Value: The relationship between price paid and the quality of the products and services received.

Employee-to-Guest Ratio: The number of employees relative to the number of guests. In the lodging industry, this is typically expressed in terms of employees per room; a 500-room luxury, full-service property may have 500 employees: a 1:1 employee-to-guest ratio. A 100-room limited-service property may have 25 employees: a 1:4 employee-to-guest ratio.

◼

If you were a guest in a hotel, would you want a dirty room (as a result of the actions and inactions of management and staff who don't really care)? Would you want to be "greeted" by a front desk clerk making a personal telephone call while you waited to check in? Would you want to be told that problems in your room which could have been avoided (inoperative television and foul odors, for example) can't be fixed until tomorrow, and there are no other rooms available to which you can be moved? You would answer these questions with a no! Guests will answer the questions exactly the same way, will probably not return to the property, and will be quick to tell their friends and family about their unacceptable visit.

Service is critical to success, and, fortunately, it involves an attitude and philosophy that is within the control of the manager ("Let's Make It Right for the Guests") more than significant financial resources that may be beyond the manager's control.

Service Expectations

In the preceding section we asked whether you would be pleased if basic service concerns were not addressed during your visit to a hotel. Your response was probably no, and you realized that hotel guests encountering these levels of service would likewise be displeased.

It is often helpful to think about your own service expectations and use them to plan service experiences and to evaluate service procedures. Consider the guest check-in process. Guests will have formed some impressions about the property before they arrive to get their room. For example, they will have seen the building's exterior and some of its public space, and they may have had contact with representatives of the organization when reservations were made. However, first impressions about guest service are formed during the check-in process. What would you want to occur during check-in? Your responses probably include:

- No (or a short) wait time to check-in
- A friendly welcome, including eye contact, a smile, and acknowledgment of your name ("Welcome to our hotel, Ms. Gonzalez")
- Accurate reservation information
- The proper room available for you
- Answers to your questions
- Directions to your room
- Suggestions about where to park your car (if applicable)

Not surprisingly, your guests are likely to have the same expectations. Your own service desires can help you to determine your check-in procedures and the training required to check in guests according to your own standards. They will also suggest how evaluation of check-in service levels should be done. That is, you can use your own expectations to determine the extent to which your front desk staff demonstrates these service standards when guests check in.

INGREDIENTS IN A QUALITY SERVICE SYSTEM

The hospitality industry's emphasis on quality is not just a passing fad that will go away to be replaced by the next fad. Quality service is so important that entire books have been written about quality in the hospitality industry.[1] There are six ingredients

[1]See, for example, John King and Ronald Cichy, *Managing for Quality in the Hospitality Industry.* (Upper Saddle River, N.J.: Pearson Education, 2006.)

in a "recipe" that should be used to develop and implement a quality service system. These are shown in Figure 3.1.

We'll look at the "ingredients" in the recipe for quality guest service in this section.

Consider the Guests Being Served

Some lodging operations serve a narrow range of guests. Consider, for example, a small rooms-only lodging property with a strategic location at a busy interchange on an interstate highway. Most of its guests probably desire the same thing—a relatively inexpensive, safe, and clean sleeping room at a price representing a value to the traveler.

Other lodging properties may serve a more diverse range of guests. Consider, for example, an upscale restaurant in a hotel that is serving, at the same time, busy executives conducting business over dinner, a couple celebrating a wedding anniversary, a group of senior citizens enjoying their once-monthly dining-out social event, and a young couple on their first date.

What exactly do these seemingly diverse groups of diners have in common? (While it is up to the hotel's management team to determine this, a possible answer is: freshly prepared food delivered by servers who are attentive to their guests' unique needs in a special environment at a price that represents a value for the products purchased and the services received.)

Let's consider two other examples of hospitality properties serving diverse guest groups. First, a downtown hotel may serve business guests during the week and other guests visiting the downtown area for shopping and social reasons during the weekend. Second, a small hotel in a tourist destination may serve numerous groups of guests depending upon the convention and group meetings in the city at that specific time. For the first three days of the week, the hotel may be occupied primarily by a senior citizens group; during the next four days of the same week most of the guests are attending a high school sports tournament. It is important for managers to know as much as possible about all of the guests being served. They do this by using marketing tactics (see Chapter 7) and by recognizing that basic service expectations are integral to the guests' experiences.

Determine What the Guests Desire

A questioning process can be used to determine guests' wants and needs. Questions such as "What did you like about your visit?" and "What would make your visit more enjoyable?" can help a manager determine guests' needs. These and related

Ingredient 1:	Consider the guests being served.
Ingredient 2:	Determine what the guests desire.
Ingredient 3:	Develop procedures to deliver what guests want.
Ingredient 4:	Train and empower staff.
Ingredient 5:	Implement revised systems.
Ingredient 6:	Evaluate and modify service delivery systems.

FIGURE 3.1 Six Components of Quality in the Hospitality Industry

What special needs are required by families visiting hotels?

questions can be asked of guests by managers as they "manage by walking around" and/or by a simple questionnaire (comment card) given to guests as they check in as part of a packet of information received at that time. Alternatively, comment cards can be left in the guest rooms. In well-run properties, top-level managers routinely talk with guests as they check out to learn anything that can be helpful about what they liked and would have wanted during their visit.

Guest comment cards do not simply tell what guests want; the information helps managers to evaluate service systems. We will discuss this in greater detail later in this section. Increasingly, lodging properties of all sizes are implementing electronic surveys on the hotel's channel(s) in the guest room television to collect information about guest preferences.

Every lodging manager has another way to collect information about the guests—by asking the employees. It is ironic but true that line-level employees often know more about the likes and dislikes of guests than do their **supervisors** or even the property's **manager**. These staff members frequently have more extensive guest contact than any other employees in the property. Consider, for example, a guest complaining to a front desk clerk about the long line at time of check in or a food server receiving compliments (or complaints!) about the food in the hotel's dining room. When managers want to know about what their guests desire, they can simply ask the employees who provide the products and services to them.

LODGING LANGUAGE

Supervisor: A staff member who directs the work of line-level employees.

Manager: A staff member who directs the work of supervisors.

■

LODGING ON-LINE

Hoteliers can learn much about what guests think about their property by utilizing the services of a shopping service. To learn what a shopping service (also called "mystery shopper") does, and to see a sample of a great shopper's report form, go to:

www.satisfactionservicesinc.com

When you arrive, click on "Welcome to Satisfaction Services, Inc." and scroll down to the bottom of the screen. Click on "Client Demo" and scroll down the list of sample reports to "Hotel Evaluation." Click on this report and note the variety of information about almost every aspect of a guest's stay at the hotel.

Develop Procedures to Deliver What Guests Want

After the types of guests and their desires are known, the next ingredient in a quality service system is to develop procedures that will consistently deliver what guests want. Two of the best ways to make procedures more guest-friendly are to **benchmark** and to utilize **cross-functional teams** of employees. Benchmarking is the process of understanding exactly how your property does something and, additionally, determining how it is done by your competition. If, for example, guests desire fast check-in (and most, if not all, guests do!), it is important to know the property's current procedures to speed up the check-in process and, as well, to determine what other properties do to minimize guest check-in times. Studying available industry training resources, discussions with other hoteliers at professional meetings, reviewing articles in trade magazines, and careful observation when visiting other properties are among the benchmarking tactics that can be used.

LODGING LANGUAGE

Benchmark: The search for best practices and an understanding about how they are achieved in efforts to determine how well a hospitality organization is doing.

Cross-Functional Team: A group of employees from each department within the hospitality operation who work together to resolve operating problems.

■

Wise hospitality managers know the benefits of asking employees for advice about ways to improve work methods. Cross-functional teams are made up of staff members from each area in the hotel who meet, brainstorm, and consider ways to improve work methods. This contrasts with the more traditional alternative of utilizing employees from the same department to address a problem. The disadvantage of having only members of the same department meet is illustrated by a front office staff addressing a slow check-in problem and concluding that the problem doesn't rest with them because it is caused by the housekeepers who don't get rooms ready for reuse quickly enough. Alternatively, if employees from the front office, housekeeping, and even maintenance areas address the problem, all areas can work together to solve the problem. For example, a team may determine that the check-in process is slowed by guests asking about meeting room locations. A large map posted near the check-in area and/or small maps given to guests when they check in may reduce the need for busy front desk clerks to provide detailed and time-consuming information.

Cross-functional teams should consist of staff members from different hotel departments.

Train and Empower Staff

Hotel employees are critical to the consistent delivery of quality service. When new procedures are implemented to better meet the guests' service expectations, employees must learn new work methods. New or additional tools or equipment may also be necessary. After staff members are trained in revised work tasks, they can also be given the opportunity to make decisions about the unique needs, if any, of the guests they are helping. **Empowerment** is the act of granting authority to employees to make key decisions within their areas of responsibility. For example, service employees have a primary responsibility to please the guests. Empowered staff members are allowed to make decisions about how this is to be done as they interact with guests with differing wants, needs, and expectations.

LODGING LANGUAGE

Empowerment: The act of granting authority to employees to make key decisions within their areas of responsibility.

■

Before staff members can be empowered, they must be trained and provided with the tools and other resources needed to do their jobs. They must also be well aware that their primary responsibility is to serve the guests. Consider, for example, a limited-service property whose complimentary breakfast ends at 10:00 A.M. At 2:30 P.M. a couple with a young child check in to the hotel, and a parent asks if the child can have a glass of milk. If the first service request is answered by the front desk clerk with the comment, "I'm sorry; we have no food service available after 10:00 in the morning" (in other words, no), the guest's first request for service has been denied.

Contrast the above situation with another response: "I'll check to see if we have a carton of milk left over from breakfast. I am pretty sure we do, and I will get it for you now. Or we can bring it to your room if you would prefer that." This is the response of a front desk clerk who is empowered to make reasonable decisions that please the guests. In this situation, an inexpensive carton of milk is all that it will cost the hotel to begin delivering on its service promise. This, in turn, can yield a satisfied guest who knows that the hotel staff genuinely wants to help, and, as a result, the guest will return frequently to the property and to other units of the chain.

Implement Revised Systems

Implementation of revised procedures does not always need to be on an all-or-nothing basis. Assume that there are numerous guest complaints about room cleanliness. The hotel manager and the housekeepers may work together to develop revised room-cleaning procedures. The new work methods could be tried in selected rooms to test and further refine, if necessary, the more guest-friendly processes before they are rolled out to the entire property. Here's an example: Hotel guests desire a clean room, preferably one that looks as if they are the first person to ever sleep in it. With a traditional housekeeping model, a guest room is cleaned by a single housekeeper. Then, after the room is cleaned, it may be routinely (or randomly) checked by the head housekeeper according to a cleanliness checklist to make sure that it has been properly prepared for the next guest. What if, instead, a cross-functional team determined that a group of two housekeepers could clean a guest room together and do a self-inspection at the end of the cleaning process?

The manager might decide to try this approach and work with the team and the head housekeeper to study and plan how to do it. Then the new method could be used for several days with two housekeepers in rooms on a single floor or wing of the hotel. After close evaluation, the plan might then be expanded to other teams of housekeepers cleaning other rooms, with changes made in procedures, if necessary, as the process is rolled out.

Evaluate and Modify Service Delivery Systems

Over time, guest preferences are likely to change. In addition, technologies will evolve, and new and improved work methods may become useful. These can impact what guests desire and what products and services can be most effectively delivered. Problems can also arise in service delivery systems. These events provide examples of the need to evaluate and, if necessary, modify procedures in current use.

Hotel managers cannot address problems unless they are aware of them. While this is obvious, many hoteliers do not take advantage of a simple comment card system. It is much easier to retain existing guests than to continually find new ones.

Comment card systems can address the concerns of current guests with the goal of identifying problems and resolving them (hopefully while the guest is still at the property). Many hotels use a hard-copy guest comment card system to obtain this information. A sample comment card is shown in Figures 3.2a and 3.2b.

Note that the comment card asks guests to notify hotel staff about problems so they can be corrected before the guests depart. This is done because the hotel manager wants the guests to know about the hotel's sincere interest in addressing problems to their satisfaction. Prompt attention to problems dramatically increases the likelihood of **repeat business.**

LODGING LANGUAGE

Repeat Business: Guests who return to the property for additional visits after their first visit.

■

Increasingly, hoteliers are using technology to obtain guest comments and suggestions. In-room surveys using the television set are an example. Information generated by this method can be automatically tallied to enable managers to quickly and accurately determine guest opinions. Internet-related survey options are also possible. For example, guests can be invited to e-mail comments to a corporate Web site, and these sites may have a section dedicated to feedback from previous guests and other persons.

Careful analysis of comment card information helps to identify problems. Perhaps resolution will involve a new policy, training, purchase of tools or equipment, and/or changes in operating procedures. Perhaps the manager alone or all the property managers working together will decide what to do and other people on the team may be asked for advice. Will a cross-functional team be needed for careful study and analysis? An effective hotelier will know the best approach to address the

---

What Do You Think About Our Hotel?

Your time is very important and so are your thoughts about your stay at (name of hotel). We would

sincerely appreciate your thoughts about your visit. Will you please complete this survey and place

it in the Guest Comments box at the front desk or mail it to us?

While You Are Here

We want you to be 100% satisfied about every experience you have during your visit. If there is any-

thing we can do, please let us know. If you experience any problem, we **_guarantee_** to correct it.

Please call the hotel operator and tell the staff what we can do to make your stay with us more

enjoyable.

We are committed to making your visit enjoyable and hassle-free; please tell us how to do so.

Thank You!

FIGURE 3.2a   Guest Comment Card (Front Side)

	Exceeded Expectations	Met Expectations	Missed Expectations
Front Desk Staff	❏	❏	❏
Housekeeping Staff	❏	❏	❏
Restaurant/Lounge Staff	❏	❏	❏
Your Guest Room	❏	❏	❏
Restaurant and Lounges	❏	❏	❏

During your visit, did you have any problems? ❏ Yes ❏ No

If so, please tell us about them. . .
_____
_____
_____

Was the difficulty reported?
   ❏ Yes   ❏ No
To whom did you report it? _____
_____

Was it resolved to your complete satisfaction? ❏ Yes   ❏ No

If not, what could we have done differently to satisfy you?
_____
_____

Overall, did we exceed your expectations?   ❏ Yes   ❏ No

If not, what could we have done better?
_____
_____
_____

If you visited this area again, would you select our hotel?
   ❏ Yes   ❏ No   ❏ Undecided

How many times have you stayed at our hotel during the last year? _____

Date of this stay? _____

Your Room Number: _____

Name: _____

Address: _____
_____

City: _____

State: _____ Zip: _____

Telephone: _____

E-mail: _____

Would you like to be contacted about promotional offers?   ❏ Yes   ❏ No

Other Comments:
_____
_____
_____
_____

Was any specific employee(s) especially helpful to you?   ❏ Yes   ❏ No
If so, who: _____

Thank you for helping us to serve you better.

FIGURE 3.2b   Guest Comment Card (reverse side)

problem. Then, as problems are researched, no matter how small they may appear to be, the property will have taken another step on its journey toward consistently meeting required quality standards.

As you can see, the process of quality guest service is cyclical. It is driven by changes in (a) the guests being served, (b) their wants and needs, and (c) the work methods implemented to yield products/services meeting quality standards desired by the guests.

LODGING ON-LINE

Many limited-service lodging properties are owned/managed independently by families or small entre-preneurs who do not have access to the resources of large, multi-unit organizations. To learn about the many aspects of small-business management that must be understood by a hotel owner, go to:

www.toolkit.com

Click on "Small Business Guide" and review any of the numerous articles that will be available to you.

SERVICE AND "MOMENTS OF TRUTH"

"Moments of truth" are opportunities for guests to form an impression about a lodging organization. While a moment of truth may involve an employee (for example, excellent or rude service), there need not be any human interaction. Consider,

EVOLUTION OF SERVICE

Today's requirements for quality service have evolved from a past emphasis on commodities/products and are being incorporated into something that guests increasingly expect: an experience. This shift in expectations can be illustrated using something very basic: a place to sleep.

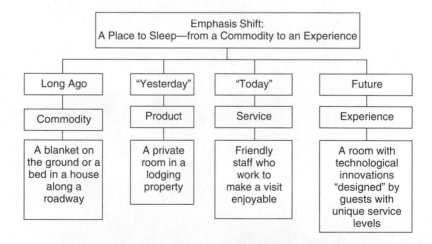

As seen above, long ago a traveler slept on a blanket on the ground or in a bed in a house along the road. "Yesterday" guests had access to a private room in a lodging property. "Today" the guest expects friendly service from the hotel's staff. In the future, lodging guests will enjoy an "experience." They will receive great service and will stay in a room which technology enables them to "design" for themselves. Do they want a certain "view" from the windows or the world's most famous paintings on the wall? (Plasma screen technology can provide them.) Do they want firm or soft pillows or black or blue ink in their pencils? What newspaper(s) do they prefer? This personal preference information will be available, and hotel staff will have their room ready for them at check-in time.

for example, the negative impressions formed by a guest who has to walk through a garbage-cluttered parking lot downwind from a foul-smelling garbage dumpster. Contrast this with the positive first impression created by the large vase of fresh, beautiful flowers at the check-in desk. Consider also the **wow factor** when one of these fresh flower stems is given to the guest as part of the registration process!

LODGING LANGUAGE

Moments of Truth: Any (and every) time a guest has an opportunity to form an impression about the hospitality organization. Moments of truth can be positive or negative.

Wow Factor: The feeling guests have when they receive or experience an unanticipated extra as they interact with the hospitality operation.

■

Hoteliers want their guests to have positive moments of truth. These occur through planning (for example, an efficient guest check-in process), but they can also be spontaneous, such as those that occur when an empowered staff member pleases a guest who has made an out-of-the-ordinary request. Unfortunately, negative moments of truth occur frequently in some hotels. Many of these can be anticipated (a manager who requires housekeepers to spend only a short time cleaning each room in order to reduce labor costs should not be surprised about guest room

This person may be forming an impression of the hotel just by walking down this corridor.

MANAGING THE MOMENTS OF TRUTH

Assume that a restaurant manager in a hotel determines that there are at least 42 moments when a guest can form an opinion of the operation. These include such things as when the guest enters the restaurant, receives the initial "meeting and greeting" by the receptionist, is escorted to the table, is seated, given a menu, and the lapsed time until the server's first visit to the table. Assume also that the restaurant is open for lunch (100 guests are typically served) and dinner (150 guests are served on an average shift). The number of *planned* moments of truth is significant:

Number of moments of truth per lunch period	= 100 guests (×) 42 moments of truth	= 4,200
Number of moments of truth per dinner shift	= 150 guests (×) 42 moments of truth	= 6,300
Number of moments of truth per day	= 4,200 + 6,300	= 10,700
Number of moments of truth per week	= 10,700 moments of truth (×) 6 days of weekly operation	= 64,200
Number of moments of truth per year	= 64,200 moments of truth per week (×) 52 weeks per year	= 3,338,400

The manager in this example has 3,338,400 formal (planned) opportunities each year to make a good impression. Unfortunately, there are also a (seemingly) infinite number of *informal* (unplanned) occasions when guest opinions can be formed. These include encounters with other employees, the perceived levels of cleanliness, and the guests' enjoyment of the food/ beverage products served in the hotel's restaurant.

cleanliness complaints). Others are unanticipated; consider, for example, a guest's reactions to a front desk clerk after a wake-up call is received one hour later than expected.

Lodging managers plan many aspects of a guest's experience at their properties. Through an organized planning process, they have a system in place for guest reservations and registration, for luggage transport to the room, for guest security and safety while guests are on-site, for guest check-out, and for other guest/property interactions. However, guests in these managers' hotels will probably encounter (sometimes by chance alone) other moments of truth which can be favorable or unfavorable and, in the process, influence their total perception of the visit.

Word of mouth advertising occurs when previous guests tell other others about their experiences during a visit to the property. Unfortunately, guests with negative impressions after a visit are likely to tell many more people about their problems than are guests who have just enjoyed a pleasing visit. To make matters worse, every time the negative experience is repeated, the extent of the problem is likely to be increased or exaggerated.

LODGING LANGUAGE

Word of Mouth Advertising: Favorable or unfavorable comments made when previous guests of a hospitality operation tell others about their experiences.

■

Our discussion so far shows that the simple definition of "quality" at the beginning of this chapter (the consistent delivery of products and services according to expected standards) can, in fact, be very difficult to attain. For example, if a lodging property serves 125 guests each day for several years, some guest-related problems

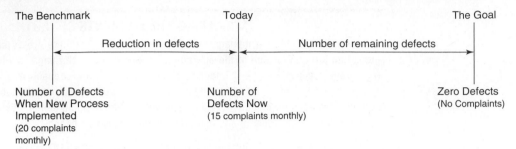

Assume that guest complaints are used to measure service defects. Process changes have reduced the number of defects from 20 complaints monthly (the benchmark) to 15 monthly complaints today. The measurement of success should focus on the reduction in complaints (5) rather than on the remaining number of existing complaints (15). Then revisions to systems and procedures can continue on the hotel's journey towards zero defects.

FIGURE 3.3 The March Toward Zero Defects

are to likely occur regardless of the extent to which a service attitude exists and guest-friendly processes are in place. However, the hotel's managers must make certain that effective plans are in place to minimize the number of service failures.

Some lodging managers establish a goal of **zero defects** when quality service processes are implemented. In other words, it is their hope that there will never be any guest-related complaints. However, goal of zero defects may be frustrating, because even with the best intentions and most effective processes in place, mistakes (defects) will occur. Figure 3.3 above illustrates how a decline in defects can be measured.

LODGING LANGUAGE

Zero Defects: A goal of no guest-related complaints established when guest service processes are implemented.

■

SERVICE DELIVERY BY EMPLOYEES

After viewing a video emphasizing quality service, one manager was heard saying to another, "I'd give anything to have service staff like those shown in the video." What the manager had seen was a series of situations in which a trained employee (a) provided a hospitable greeting, (b) practiced the "art and science" of suggestive upselling to provide a guest with a wider awareness of the property's products and services, (c) utilized product knowledge, (d) answered all guest questions, (e) helped other employees when they became especially busy during the work shift, and (f) met or exceeded the guests' service expectations.

Why couldn't (didn't) that manager employ, train, and enable staff members who consistently did these relatively simple and commonsense things? What kind of service was the manager's staff providing to guests if they did not do what was emphasized in the training video? Unfortunately, many people considering a recent

LODGING ON-LINE

Many lodging properties emphasize guest service in their Internet advertising. Select your favorite Web browser (e.g., Google, Excite) and type in "guest service and hotel." Numerous hotel Web sites will be displayed. Review several and note the types of service and amenities they advertise and offer to their guests.

experience in a lodging operation might also be asking, "What was wrong with the staff? What was wrong with their supervisor for allowing these things to happen? If I can see the negative impact a staff member's actions or inactions have on business, why can't the supervisor who works here everyday see it as well?"

The quality of service provided to guests in any type of hospitality operation is influenced most by the staff members providing the service and by the processes they use to provide the service. If this is true, and the employee is a key element in service delivery, what role, then, does the manager play?

It has been said that the vast majority of all problems in most lodging operations are caused by the manager. The observation runs contrary to the thinking of the manager who believes, "If only I could find good employees, my operating problems would be solved, my guests would be happy, and my business would be profitable!" In fact, it is the manager who effectively (or ineffectively) recruits, orients, trains, motivates, and empowers staff members to serve the guests. It is the manager who does (or does not)

ALL IN A DAY'S WORK

The Situation

"Well Cyndi, good luck," said Mr. Patel. "I know you will do a great job!"

Cyndi was the new general manager in a limited-service hotel that was not doing well. "Yesterday" it was very successful. Employee turnover was very low, and staff members gave a high priority to meeting and exceeding the expectations of the guests who stayed at the property. Sharon (the manager who had been there for many years) emphasized guest service as a key to success, and she was proven correct each year as business volume and profits increased. But Sharon retired. Alan, the manager who succeeded her, emphasized cutting costs instead of the philosophy of providing value for the guests. Staffing patterns were cut until employees had no extra time for even the

simplest interactions with guests' needs. The business suffered, and Mr. Patel, the hotel's owner, replaced Alan with Cyndi, who was instructed to "turn the business around." It was Cyndi's first job as a hotel general manager. With so many issues demanding her attention, she wasn't sure where to start.

A Response

Cyndi needs to understand that the hotel's greatest asset is its staff. They are the team that will yield success or failure. She should meet with all the staff members to obtain feedback about the operation: What do they like? Dislike? What do the guests like? Dislike? How do they respond to the guests' needs? The hotel's team should work together to formulate a mission statement that focuses on its role in serving the guests.

The team should define who the guests are and what they want, and should commit, as a team, to consistently move toward the goals expressed in the property's mission statement.

Cyndi can train the staff and empower them to be "ambassadors" to please the guests. They can be given the authority and power to respond to guests' needs in unique ways so as to meet the guests' expectations when the hotel falls short in some way. She must realize that these changes will not occur overnight because it will take time for the staff to begin to respect and trust her. Ultimately, employees who are satisfied and happy will provide quality products and services to the guests. Repeat business will result, and the financial performance sought by Mr. Patel will be achieved, and Cyndi will know she has been successful.[2]

[2]The authors acknowledge the assistance of Ms. Nancy Bacyinski, Regional Director of Operations, HDS Services, Ohio/Kentucky Market, for developing this solution.

serve as a role model to emphasize the importance of guest service in the hospitality organization. Managers cannot delegate the **accountability** which they receive from their own boss to their subordinates. Instead, managers are (and should be) held responsible for the extent to which the property is successful. In the next chapter, we will examine exactly how this is done. As emphasized throughout this chapter, service is an essential ingredient in the success of managers and lodging organizations.

LODGING LANGUAGE

Accountability: An obligation created when a person is delegated duties/responsibilities by higher levels of management.

■

MANAGEMENT TACTICS FOR EFFECTIVE GUEST SERVICE

How can managers ensure that their employees know and consistently practice effective guest service skills? What tactics can they implement to make service a top priority of all the staff members in a hotel operation? Some helpful tactics are listed in Figure 3.4.

Managers must understand their role in establishing and maintaining a service priority. They must recognize that what they do (and don't do) and what they say (and don't say) are the biggest factors in determining the extent to which service is emphasized in the operation.

Let's review the items on the service priority checklist.

Recruit and Select Service-Minded Staff

With proper management, a lodging property can be considered an **employer of choice** in the community. Its **turnover rate** can be relatively low, and experienced staff members can understand and consistently apply quality service principles. However, applicants will still need to be recruited and selected. One technique is hire applicants who give good answers to open-ended questions like "What would you do if a guest waiting behind other guests to check in came to the front of the check-in line to ask a question?" or "What would you do if a guest wants help with a specific item in the limited-service breakfast, and you are busy helping another guest at that moment?"

LODGING LANGUAGE

Employer of Choice: The concept that the hospitality operation is a preferred place of employment in the community for applicants who have alternative employment opportunities.

Turnover Rate: A measure of the proportion of a work force that is replaced during a designated time period (month, quarter, or year). It can be calculated as: Number of Employees Separated ÷ Number of Employees in the Workforce = Turnover Rate.

■

In addition to asking questions to learn about applicants' service initiatives, managers should emphasize the importance of service. They can, for example, discuss the property's **mission statement** with its service focus. They can also review how the position for which an applicant is applying relates to helping guests.

✓	Recruit and select service-minded staff.
✓	Provide effective orientation and training.
✓	Supervise with a service emphasis.
✓	Empower staff with decision-making authority for service.
✓	Emphasize continuous quality improvement.

FIGURE 3.4   Checklist to Maintain a Service Priority

LODGING LANGUAGE

Mission Statement: A planning tool that broadly identifies what a hospitality operation would like to accomplish and how it plans to accomplish it.

■

Provide Effective Orientation and Training

The manager's emphasis on quality guest service continues at the time of new employee orientation. Staff members should be reintroduced to the property's mission statement, which should emphasize the critical importance of guest service. They must be trained in guest-friendly procedures. That is, they must be given adequate time to obtain the required knowledge and skills before they have significant guest contact.

Since all employees must know the importance of guest service and how to deliver it, an extensive program on this topic should be presented as an integral part of the hotel's orientation program.

Many managers make at least two mistakes when planning and presenting training programs. First, they emphasize skills, such as how to check in a guest and how to a clean a room, and do not give enough attention to developing a service attitude and teaching how to effectively serve guests. They often shortchange the length of training because they believe that it is more important to get the staff member into the position quickly and/or that "Everything that must be learned can be taught on the job." In fact, providing effective guest relations training during the orientation process and taking the time to properly plan/deliver basic knowledge and skills training before new staff members have guest contact is very important.

Supervise with a Service Emphasis

Employees, like everyone else, normally do what they are rewarded to do. If service is important, lodging managers should emphasize this. They should thank staff members when exceptional guest service is rendered. (Note, for example, that the guest comment card illustrated in Figure 3.2 allows guests who complete a comment card to name a staff member who was especially helpful to them during their visit.) Managers should discuss service-related problems, if any, with the employees and mutually agree upon corrective actions during performance appraisals. Employee compensation decisions should be based, in part, upon the consistency of quality service delivery.

Effective lodging managers role-model service. In other words, they "walk the talk" and do what they tell their employees to do. Imagine the opportunity to role-model service when a lodging manager greets a guest at the hotel's front door and carries the luggage to the front desk. How about the manager who walks with guests

---

LODGING ON-LINE

Want to review some brief articles addressing customer (guest) service and training? If so, go to:

www.customerservicefocus.com

When you reach the site, you can click on articles addressing such topics as guest service training, phone skills training, service skills training, and customer focus. The articles you'll read relate to all retail industries and are not specific to the hospitality industry, but you'll learn many techniques that can be useful in developing and practicing guest service skills in the lodging industry.

---

to the front door as they leave, wishes them a safe journey, enthusiastically thanks them for their business, and asks them to return?

Empower Staff with Service Authority

The importance of employee empowerment has been noted throughout this chapter. Lodging managers should facilitate—not merely direct—the delivery of service. Staff members who are in contact with guests require the ability to make quick decisions that focus on guest needs as they arise.

Since it is not possible to anticipate what every guest wants all the time, it is not possible to develop and teach procedures that recognize how to consistently meet or exceed the expectations of every guest. Lodging managers empower their staff as they (a) share their service mission, (b) provide the training and other resources required to meet the needs of the majority of guests, and (c) encourage staff members to help guests with out-of-the-ordinary service requests.

Emphasize Continuous Quality Improvement

Guests and the lodging operations that serve them constantly change. Properties, then, typically either become better or worse. They rarely stay the same. Today's emphasis on "better, faster, cheaper" is important. However, the first two factors just noted (better and faster) should be developed with the guests' needs in mind. The third factor (cheaper) is also a meaningful goal as long as it involves taking error out of the products and service rather than reducing value from the guests' point of view.

The concept of **continuous quality improvement (CQI)** relates to the journey that the manager and staff take to reduce defects; or in other words, to get better. Whenever a problem is identified should be resolved and corrected in such a way

---

LODGING ON-LINE

To review articles about guest service that specifically focus on the hospitality/lodging industry, go to:

www.hospitalityexcellence.com/training/htm

When you arrive at the site, scroll down to the bottom and click on "articles." You'll note a wide range of articles focusing on such topics as "Check out the Bathroom as a Service Indicator" and "Employees Touch, Tarnish Memories."

Teamwork between staff in the front and back of the house is important.

that it cannot reoccur. CQI means that managers and their employees address both the largest problems (for example, guest complaints about service or value) and the smallest (for example, replacing a light bulb in a lobby lamp). In both cases, procedures are put in place to recognize and resolve problems, and defects are removed from the hotel's work methods. This is quality service improvement in action. As this happens, the improvement results in fewer defects. Another step has been taken on the lodging property's journey toward zero defects and excellence.

LODGING LANGUAGE

Continuous Quality Improvement (CQI): Ongoing efforts within a hospitality operation to better meet (or exceed) guest expectations and to define ways to perform work with better, less costly, and faster methods.

■

LODGING PROPERTY STAFF ARE SERVICE PROFESSIONALS

Professionals are people working in an occupation that requires extensive knowledge and skills. Medicine, law, accounting, and teaching are all occupations that satisfy this definition. People in these occupations have formal education in a specialized body of knowledge with a common base of information. In addition, membership in their profession is controlled by **licensing** or **registration** procedures that require the demonstration of effective knowledge and performance.

WHAT MAKES SERVICE SPECIAL?

Service is an attitude as much as or more than a skill. Lodging employees provide special service to their guests when they:

- acknowledge guests and thank them for visiting
- smile
- maintain eye contact
- reflect a genuine interest in providing quality service
- consider every guest to be unique
- create a warm environment of hospitality
- strive for excellence in guest service skills
- are courteous, polite, and attentive
- determine what guests *really* want and need, and then provide products/ services that address these wants and needs
- pay more attention to guests than to machines and co-workers
- invite guests to return

LODGING LANGUAGE

Professionals: People working in an occupation that requires extensive knowledge and skills in a specialized body of knowledge. Occupations typically involve a common base of information and often require licensing or registration.

Licensing: Formal authorization to practice a profession that is granted by a governmental agency.

Registration: Acceptance for one to work within a profession that is (typically) granted by a non-governmental agency such as an association.

■

Hospitality service personnel should also be thought of as professionals because they too must possess specialized knowledge and skills to be effective. Further, a common base of information relating to guest service is an integral part of every job in the hospitality industry. Certification rather than registration or licensing is available from professional associations serving the hospitality industry, including the American Hotel and Lodging Association and the National Restaurant Association.

Certification processes typically identify the competencies required for job success, make available training and/or resources that provide the knowledge/skills required for competency, and test to measure competencies. For example, the Educational Institute of the American Hotel & Lodging Association (EI of AHLA) offers two certification designations for managers of lodging properties: Certified Hotel Administrator (CHA) for those affiliated with full-service properties, and Certified Lodging Manager (CLM) for managers of limited-service hotels. In addition, it has several certification programs of interest to those with managerial responsibilities in limited-service properties. These include Certified Hospitality Housekeeping Executive (CHHE), Certified Hospitality Trainer (CHT), Certified Hospitality Supervisor (CHS), and Certified Lodging Security Supervisor (CLSS).

Entry-level personnel also have opportunities to obtain professional recognition from the EI of AHLA. There are programs available for front desk representative, bell attendant, guestroom attendant, laundry attendant, and security officer.

Each of the above designations requires experience and knowledge. The ability to consistently provide effective guest service is an important skill required for effec-

LODGING ON-LINE

To learn about the certification programs offered by the Educational Institute of the American Hotel & Lodging Association, go to:

www.ei-ahla.org

Click on "Certification."

tiveness in any hospitality position from those at the top of the organization to those with entry-level responsibilities.

BENCHMARK AGAINST THE BEST: THE RITZ-CARLTON HOTEL COMPANY, L.L.C.

There are many fine hotel companies, operating large and small hotels, that excel at providing quality service to their guests. The Ritz-Carlton Hotel Company, L.L.C. is widely known for its emphasis on quality. It has twice won the prestigious **Malcolm-Baldrige National Quality Award**, which is administered by the federal government (National Institute of Standards and Technology, Commerce Department). The Ritz-Carlton's Employee Promise, Credo and "Basics" establish a foundation of quality excellence that is an important part of the company's corporate culture.

LODGING LANGUAGE

Malcolm-Baldridge National Quality Award: Award granted to U.S. businesses that demonstrate successful quality-related strategies relating to leadership, information/analysis, strategic planning, human resource development/management, process management, business results, and customer focus/satisfaction.

While very few organizations receive the Malcolm-Baldridge Award, the philosophies emphasized in The Ritz-Carlton Hotel Company, L.L.C. Standards are useful benchmarking concepts for every organization in the hospitality industry. We end this chapter on service by presenting the Employee Promise, The Credo, and The Basics of the Ritz-Carlton Hotel Company, L.L.C. Hoteliers who benchmark against these statements of quality and service are benchmarking against some of the very best in the hospitality industry.

LODGING ON-LINE

Check out the Web site of The Ritz-Carlton Hotel Company, L.L.C. at:

www.Ritzcarlton.com

Go to "Leadership Center" and review the company's quality philosophy, history, awards, gold standards, and course outlines.

Hoteliers benchmark against one of the best when they learn about The Ritz-Carlton Hotel Company.

THE EMPLOYEE PROMISE

At the Ritz Carlton, our Ladies and Gentlemen are the most important resource in our service commitment to our guests. By applying the principles of trust, honesty, respect, integrity, and commitment, we nurture and maximize talent to the benefit of each individual and the company. The Ritz-Carlton fosters a work environment where diversity is valued, quality of life is enhanced, individual aspirations are fulfilled, and The Ritz-Carlton mystique is strengthened.

THE RITZ-CARLTON CREDO

The Ritz-Carlton Hotel is a place where the genuine care and comfort of our guests is our highest mission.

We pledge to provide the finest personal service and facilities for our guests who will always enjoy a warm, relaxed yet refined ambiance.

The Ritz-Carlton experience enlivens the senses, instills well-being, and fulfills even the unexpressed wishes and needs of our guests.

THE RITZ-CARLTON BASICS

1. The Credo is the principal belief of our company. It must be known, owned, and energized by all.
2. Our Motto is: "We are Ladies and Gentlemen serving Ladies and Gentlemen." As service professionals, we treat our guests and each other with respect and dignity.
3. The Three Steps of Service are the foundation of Ritz-Carlton hospitality. These steps must be used in every interaction to ensure satisfaction, retention, and loyalty.
4. The Employee Promise is the basis for our Ritz-Carlton work environment. It will be honored by all employees.
5. All employees will successfully complete annual Training Certification for their position.
6. Company objectives are communicated to all employees. It is everyone's responsibility to support them.
7. To create pride and joy in the workplace, all employees have the right to be involved in the planning of the work that affects them.
8. Each employee will continuously identify defects throughout the hotel.
9. It is the responsibility of each employee to create a work environment of teamwork and lateral service so that the needs of our guests and each other are met.
10. Each employee is empowered. For example, when a guest has a problem or needs something special you should break away from your regular duties, address and resolve the issue.
11. Uncompromising levels of cleanliness are the responsibility of every employee.
12. To provide the finest personal service for our guests, each employee is responsible for identifying and recording individual guest preferences.
13. Never lose a guest. Instant guest pacification is the responsibility of each employee. Whoever receives a complaint will own it, resolve it to the guest's satisfaction, and record it.
14. "Smile—We are on stage." Always maintain positive eye contact. Use the proper vocabulary with our guests and each other. (Use words like "Good morning," "Certainly," "I'll be happy to," and "My pleasure.")
15. Be an ambassador of your hotel in and outside of the workplace. Always speak positively. Communicate any concerns to the appropriate person.
16. Escort guests rather than point out directions to another area of the hotel.
17. Use Ritz Carlton telephone etiquette. Answer within three rings and with a "smile." Use the guest's name when possible. When necessary, ask the caller, "May I place you on hold?" Do not screen calls. Eliminate call transfers whenever possible.
18. Take pride in and care of your personal appearance. Everyone is responsible to convey a professional image by adhering to Ritz-Carlton clothing and grooming standards.
19. Think safety first. Each employee is responsible for creating a safe, secure, and accident-free environment for all guests and each other. Be aware of all fire and safety emergency procedures and report any security risks immediately.
20. Protecting the assets of a Ritz-Carlton hotel is the responsibility of every employee. Conserve energy, properly maintain our hotels, and protect the environment.

─────────────── **ALL IN A DAY'S WORK** ───────────────

The Situation

"Hey, Mr. Jamison, can I ask you something?" said Travis, a front desk clerk at the Seaside Hotel, when he saw Mr. Jamison crossing the lobby in front of the front desk. Mr. Jamison was the general manager of the 85-room limited-service property.

"Not right now, Travis; I'm very busy. I have three things to do in the next five minutes, and I am supposed to be at a Chamber of Commerce meeting at this very moment." With that, Mr. Jamison continued walking without allowing Travis time to ask his question.

"Well," thought Travis, "I guess Mr. Jamison remembers that there is a tour bus scheduled to stop here mid-afternoon with about 45 guests who will need to be checked in. The schedule shows that I am the only one here until 3:00 o'clock, when Latoya comes in. I'm sure he has scheduled an additional front

desk clerk but just didn't post the new shift on the schedule. That must be it. Or maybe he planned to work at the front desk himself."

At about 2:00 p.m., the tour bus arrived. Mr. Jamison had not returned from his lunch meeting, and there was no one available to help Travis with check-in so it went slowly. The tour operator was not pleased and demanded to speak to the manager.

A Response

Do managers ever create problems? Yes, they do, and the problem just described is an example. Perhaps Mr. Jamison was busy, but he should not be too busy to listen to his staff. Apparently he did forget to schedule additional front desk assistance. Perhaps he planned to work the front desk himself along with Travis. Regardless of the plan (if there was one), he forgot. Fortunately, Travis is an

excellent employee and wanted to remind him, but Mr. Jamison "doesn't have time to listen." As a result, the guests were delayed at check-in. Managers must always take the time to listen to staff members.

This is also important because of the image projected by the manager. Mr. Jamison would not want Travis or any other hotel employee to ignore guest's needs because they are "too busy." In fact, Mr. Jamison would expect staff members to give the highest priority to addressing guests' needs. Why should the employees expect anything less in their interactions with Mr. Jamison? If the hotel manager disregards employees' questions and concerns, staff members may feel it is O.K. to treat guests the same way. In this case, Mr. Jamison was too busy to do his job properly.

CHAPTER OBJECTIVES REVIEW

If you have successfully studied the material in this chapter, you should be prepared to:

1. Define quality and review its impact upon the level of service provided by a lodging property. (Objective 1)
2. Discuss the six "ingredients" in a "recipe" to develop a quality service system. (Objective 2)
3. Describe the concept of moments of truth in guest service. (Objective 3)
4. Recognize the important role of employees in consistently delivering guest service. (Objective 4)
5. Discuss management tactics that can be used to ensure effective guest service. (Objective 5)
6. Explain that lodging employees are service professionals. (Objective 6)
7. Present the basic guest service philosophy of the Ritz-Carlton Hotels. (Objective 7)

LODGING LANGUAGE

Quality	Supervisor	Empowerment
Service (Guest)	Manager	Repeat Business
Value	Benchmark	Moments of Truth
Employee-to-Guest Ratio	Cross-Functional Teams	Wow Factor

Word of Mouth Advertising
Zero Defects
Accountability
Employer of Choice
Turnover Rate

Mission Statement
Continuous Quality
   Improvement (CQI)
Professionals

Licensing
Registration
Malcolm-Baldridge National
   Quality Award

FOR DISCUSSION

1. What is the definition of excellent service at time of check-in (a) at a motel on the highway and (b) at a Ritz-Carlton hotel? Consider the market being served, the definition of acceptable service in each alternative, and the role of value from the guests' perspective in your analysis.

2. How do you personally define and evaluate service when you are a guest at a hotel? Do you think other guests have the same concerns about service as you do? Review the six ingredients necessary to develop a quality service system that were presented in this chapter. Assume you are the manager of a hotel property where guests must very frequently wait in line a long time to check in. Work through a potential solution to this problem utilizing the six-step method discussed in this chapter.

3. Think about the last time you visited a hotel or restaurant as a guest; what moments of truth do you recall? What impact did they have on your overall impression of the hospitality operation?

4. Discuss the following statement: "The vast majority of all problems in a lodging property are caused by the manager—not by the employees." Do you agree? Disagree? If you currently hold a job in the hospitality industry, what would your supervisor say about this statement?

5. Do you believe that line-level staff members in hospitality positions, such as front desk clerk and housekeeper, are professionals? Why or why not?

6. Review the components of the Ritz-Carlton Hotel Company's Quality Service Statement (Employee Promise, Ritz-Carlton Credo, and Ritz-Carlton Basics). What impact would they likely have on you if you were an employee of the Ritz-Carlton? Which of the concepts described in these statements would be applicable to employees working in *any* other lodging operation?

7. What three things are you learned in this chapter that will benefit you when you become a hospitality manager?

8. Assume that you are a hotel manager who is very concerned about providing quality guest service. List the topics you would discuss in a guest service training session presented to all new employees at the time of their orientation.

9. Sometimes even very good employees are reluctant to change. Assume, for example, that a specific housekeeping procedure had been utilized for many years at a property. A change is necessary because of numerous guest complaints. What tactics could you, as a manager, use to reduce the employees' resistance to change as new procedures are implemented?

10. Determining what guests want while they are staying at your lodging property and the extent to which they are satisfied during their visit are early steps in developing a quality service system. Several tactics to accomplish this were noted in the chapter. Assume you are a guest in a lodging property. Would you want to provide information to its manager(s) about your likes/dislikes? Why or why not? If you would, what method would you prefer be used to learn about your reactions to your experiences at the property?

TEAM ACTIVITIES

Team Activity 1

Make a list of things you would like and dislike if you were a guest in a limited-service property. What are some tactics which the property's manager could use to ensure that your likes were more consistently met and that your dislikes were more consistently avoided?

Team Activity 2

Review the Web sites of several multi-unit lodging organizations. To what extent do they emphasize service? What are examples of the ways this emphasis is made? What suggestions could you make to these organizations to improve their emphasis on service?

The Management of Lodging

Chapter Objectives

1. To explain the four major functions of management.
2. To show the organizational structure of different-size hotels.
3. To describe the five tasks for which all hotel managers are responsible.
4. To describe the task of brand affiliation management in detail.
5. To explain the various ways hotel managers are supervised.

Chapter Outline

THE ROLE OF MANAGERS
   Management Functions
     Planning
     Organizing
     Directing
     Controlling
   Management Principles
   Management Science and Art
HOTEL MANAGEMENT STRUCTURE
   Larger Hotels
   Smaller Hotels
THE ROLE OF THE HOTEL GENERAL
MANAGER

   Owner Relations
   Staff Development
   Property Management
   Brand Affiliation Management
   Community Relations
THE ROLE OF THE GENERAL
MANAGER'S SUPERVISOR
   Owner/Investor Supervision
   Management Company Supervision
   Brand Supervision
     Brand-Monitored Hotels
     Brand-Owned Hotels

Overview: The Management of Lodging

In every business, managers are responsible for providing the quality products and services customers or guests are looking for. The duties and responsibilities of managers can be viewed in several ways. One way to examine managers and their role in operating a business is to study the four major functions of management: planning, organizing, directing, and controlling. Planning involves setting goals and deciding what to do as well as when to do it. Proper organizing of the available resources can help managers reach the goals the business has established. Because most businesses rely upon employees to help accomplish organizational goals, these staff members must be directed, or led, in a way that ensures quality service. Finally, managers are responsible for monitoring and controlling the costs associated with operating a business.

Some hotels need only a few managers; others need a good many managers. In a large hotel, the organizational structure must accommodate many mangers, whereas in a smaller, limited-service hotel, there may be only one true manager. In hotels of all sizes, the managers will have certain tasks and responsibilities that must be accomplished. In this chapter, we will examine the five major responsibilities of a hotel's general manager in great detail.

Hotel managers are primarily responsible for the day-to-day activities of a hotel and report to their own bosses. In the hotel business, a manager's supervisor could be the owner of the hotel, a representative of a management company hired to run the hotel, or in some cases, the managers of the hotel's operating brand. All of these possibilities will be explored in this chapter.

THE ROLE OF MANAGERS

If you are reading this book, it is likely that you are now managing a hotel, or hope to manage one someday. Regardless of what they manage, all managers share some common responsibilities, and hotel managers are no exception. The word **management** itself gives clues to what managers actually do at work.

LODGING LANGUAGE

Management: The effective coordination of individual efforts to achieve established goals.

■

Management is the process of coordinating the many efforts required to achieve goals set by an organization. In the hotel business, the goals might include opening or remodeling a hotel, increasing an existing hotel's revenue levels, maintaining a swimming pool, or improving the overall quality of a guest's experience when visiting a hotel. It is important to understand that management is necessary anytime the goals of an organization require the efforts of more than one person. Certainly, that is the case in the hotel business.

Management Functions

Managers are the persons in an organization who are responsible for coordinating the efforts required to achieve goals. To see exactly how managers do their jobs, it is helpful to examine the four basic functions of management. While management has

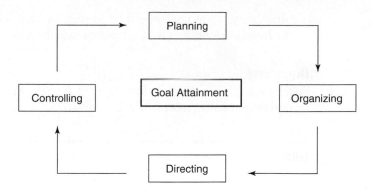

FIGURE 4.1   The Four Functions of Management

existed for centuries, Henri Fayol, a French manager in the mining industry, first identified these four management functions in 1916. As shown in Figure 4.1, these are:

- Planning
- Organizing
- Directing
- Controlling

While many modern writers and speakers on management have added to Fayol's original observations, his view that these four basic functions are the building blocks of management is still held to be true, and it is valuable to examine the individual functions in some detail.

Planning

Planning is the process of looking into the future in order to establish goals for an organization. Planning exists, to some degree, in every human activity. Whether you manage a factory, a church, a university, a hospital, an entire government, or a hotel, you must decide on the goals you want to achieve. When planning is done properly, it consists of an honest assessment of the current state of an organization as well as a realistic prediction of what the organization can achieve in the future. Planning consists of **short-range goals** and **long-range goals.**

LODGING LANGUAGE

Planning: The process of examining the future and establishing goals for an organization.

Short-Range Goals: Goals that are to be achieved in the very near future (usually less than one year). Sometimes called "short-term."

Long-Range Goals: Goals that are to be achieved over an extended period (usually longer than one year). Sometimes called "long-term."

■

In the hotel business, a short-range management goal might be to interview and select a local company to service the hotel's telephones when they are in need of repair. A long-term goal might be to plan for the eventual replacement and upgrade of the hotel's telephones and telephone system.

Organizing

After managerial planning has identified goals, managers must be concerned about **organizing** the resources of the organization to achieve these goals.

LODGING LANGUAGE

Organizing: Actions designed to bring together and arrange the resources of a group to help it achieve its goals.

■

The resources available to managers include people, facilities, material, equipment, and money. When management is effective, these resources are arranged in a way that maximizes the organization's chances of achieving its goals.

When managers organize resources, they answer questions such as:

- Who will be responsible for making organizing decisions?
- Which managers will be in charge of meeting specific goals?
- Who will determine the number of additional workers needed to achieve our goals?
- Who will identify other additional resources needed to achieve our goals?
- What organizational business structure will best help us meet our goals?

The organizational structure of a business is a very important factor in its ability to meet its goals. The specific structures commonly used in the hotel industry will be examined later in this chapter.

Directing

It is important to remember that management is an activity performed by people and with people. As a result, an important part of management is the creation of an environment that encourages workers to want to do their best work. **Directing** people in a way that results in their best work effort can be challenging. It involves leading and inspiring others, teaching new skills and attitudes, helping workers develop through their own efforts, and creating systems that compensate workers fairly.

LODGING LANGUAGE

Directing: The process of supervising staff members in the workplace.

■

It is wrong to see a manager as simply a taskmaster responsible for "making" others work. The best managers lead their organization's workers by "helping" them do their best work. Effective managers "lead" their workers in a direction that is good for the organization and for the workers. When this happens, guests, employees, and the business all benefit.

Controlling

Good managers know that it is necessary to check up or follow up on assigned tasks to ensure that the work of those managed is progressing toward the achievement of the organization's objectives. Even with proper planning, appropriate organizing, and good direction, some goals may not be achieved. This is so because misunderstandings, unexpected obstacles, or changes in the business environment can affect workers' efforts and thus result in unmet goals. The process of **controlling** is one of comparing actual results with planned results, comparing the progress of the organization in meeting its goals to original projections, and eliminating, if possible, the obstacles that hinder goal achievement.

LODGING LANGUAGE

Controlling: The process of comparing actual results to planned results and taking corrective action as needed.

■

Some managers think that accountants and other financial managers are the only ones responsible for the controlling function. In fact, all managers, when evaluating their own efforts as well as those of their own employees, can suggest and implement corrective actions that can lead to improved organizational performance and efficiency.

Figure 4.2 summarizes some of the major activities managers undertake when they perform the four functions of management.

Management Principles

The most important thing for managers to learn to manage is their own time. This is so because the effective use of your time, more than any other factor, is likely to lead to success in your management position. While education is important, there are many educated managers who do not consistently utilize what they know. Similarly, there are experienced and well-intentioned managers who have difficulty making the

Key Activities	Management Function			
	Planning	**Organizing**	**Directing**	**Controlling**
Activity 1	Determine objectives	Clarify workers' assignments	Communicate organizational objectives	Compare actual results with planned results
Activity 2	Identify the tasks to be completed to meet objectives	Select appropriate employees	Lead and challenge employees to do their best	Suggest corrective action where appropriate
Activity 3	Establish operating policies, procedures, and standards	Assign duties and authority for each employee	Reward workers by recognition and appropriate pay	Utilize information gained in the control process to improve the organization's planning process

FIGURE 4.2   Key Activities in Management Functions

most productive use of their time at work. The best managers know that "time is money"—for themselves and for their workers. As a result, effective managers look for methods and procedures designed to save time for their organization and themselves.

One concept that managers have found to be time-saving is that of identifying and following established managerial principles. These principles save time because they supply time-tested solutions to the questions and issues that often arise at work. For example, one managerial principle is that each worker should have one, and only one, immediate supervisor. Thus, if employees need to know where to obtain their daily work assignments, they will know exactly who will provide it. By the same token, the managers, in this situation, know exactly who they must supervise.

It is sometimes difficult to identify managerial principles that work in each and every situation. As a result, managers often use principles as a guide, and then determine, based upon specific circumstances, whether the principle appropriately applies. In most cases, however, managers will find that universal managerial principles can be identified and will be helpful in saving time for the organization as well as the manager.

Some managerial principles are considered to be universal; they apply to the management of any organization. Other managerial principles can be identified or created for a specific work group, hotel, or hotel company.

It is important to understand that a managerial principle is different from a company policy, but policies typically result from belief in a managerial principle. For example, a hotel manager might decide that new employees hired for a specific type of work are to be paid a predetermined starting wage. The hotel policy established the wage. The managerial principle this policy would be founded upon is:

Pay rates within an organization should be established fairly.

Consider two hotel organizations. In the first, the managers believe in the above principle and create pay policies based upon it. In the other organization, the managers either do not know or do not follow the principle. It is easy to see which organization will, in the long run, attract and retain better employees.

As your own career evolves, you will learn, discover, and develop your own set of managerial principles. These are statements about management that you believe to be true and on which you will base your own managerial policies. Some management principles that experienced managers have found to be true are included in Figure 4.3.

---

1. The good of the organization must be put before the good of the organization's individual members.
2. The responsibility to achieve organizational goals should be accompanied by the authority to do so.
3. Discipline in an organization is necessary but must be impartially applied.
4 A worker should have one (and only one) immediate supervisor.
5. Pay rates within an organization should be established fairly.
6. There should be clear lines of **authority** for use in achieving organizational goals.

FIGURE 4.3 Sample Management Principles

LODGING LANGUAGE

Authority: The power or right to direct the activities of others and to enforce compliance.

■

Your own list of managerial principles will develop as your career develops. It is important to remember that managerial principles such as these provide organizational direction and, as a result, free a manager's time to focus on the necessary management tasks of planning, organizing, directing, and controlling.

LODGING ON-LINE

Formerly known as the American Hotel and Motel Association, the American Hotel and Lodging Association (AH&LA) is the hotel industry's trade association. Its members utilize association resources to stay abreast of advances in hotel management that affect the hotels they manage and their own management careers. To learn about the educational services available through AH&LA, go to:

www.AH&MA.com

Management Science and Art

We have seen that management consists of certain processes and the application of certain principles. A question often considered by those who manage is simply this:

Is management a science or an art?

Those who believe that managers can only learn by doing wrongly believe that management is not a science. In their view, one cannot learn to manage by studying managerial processes and principles.

There is in fact a science of management, that is, a large body of knowledge and information about management. This information represents the best thinking on the process of management. The science of management, however, is not as comprehensive or accurate as mathematics or physics. The reason for this is simple. Management is a process that involves humans and human behavior. Humans are not always consistent. While the behavior of many people can be predicted to some degree, employees, supervisors, and managers often react differently when faced with the same situation. That is why that the art aspect of management is so important.

The art of management consists of an individual manager's creative power and personal skills. Creative power is evident when a manager contemplates problems, events, and possibilities. Some managers are very good at finding creative solutions to new problems. A manager's personal skill develops through practical experience and study. The best managers know that a life-long study of their management field and the continual updating of their knowledge base is an important part of maximizing their personal management skills.

While the science of management teachers a manager to know, the art of management teaches a manager to do. To illustrate the relationship in another area, consider the sailors of years gone by who used the stars to guide their ships. Astronomy was the science the sailors used, and navigation was the art they employed to sail the ships. In a similar manner, physicians will use their knowledge of the field of medicine (science) when treating a newly discovered disease (an art).

─────────────── **ALL IN A DAY'S WORK** ───────────────

The Situation

"But Beth told me to vacuum the third floor hallways right away," said Mark Bell, the hotel employee responsible for keeping the hotel's carpeted hallways neat and clean. "She is my boss, after all."

"Well, I'm telling you that I was just down to the second floor and its hallway is really dirty. It should be vacuumed first," said Walter, the man responsible for maintaining the hotel's plumbing, heating, and cooling systems. Walter was an important member of the hotel's

management team, and now Mark was not sure whether he should do as Beth, his immediate supervisor, had asked, or whether he should follow Walter's instructions. He certainly did not want to get into trouble with either one!

A Response

Some principles of management are so universally true that managers who violate them will nearly always find problems arising. In this case, the employee's frustration and confusion are the direct result of management's

violation of the unity of command principle. Despite his good intentions, Walter has placed Mark in a very unfortunate situation. If you were Walter's boss, you would need to explain to him the importance of involving Beth in any reassignment of her employee's tasks, with emphasis on the unity of command principle. This is not simply a matter of one manager being courteous to another; it is a critical managerial principle and necessary to follow if employees are to be clear about their duties and responsibilities.

A good manager, then, is both a scientist and an artist. Hospitality managers rely on both science and creative talent to do their jobs. In this book, you will discover information related to both the science and the art of hospitality management. Because the hospitality field continues to develop, you will sometimes face problems for which there is no "known" scientific solution. When that is the case, your personal problem-solving creativity will be utilized. Your creativity will be greatly influenced, however, by your knowledge of management science. When you apply the facts, principles, and rules of management to new situations, you will find that your managerial creativity is enhanced, and your skill as a management artist will continue to develop.

HOTEL MANAGEMENT STRUCTURE

If a hotel is to meet its service and profit goals, everyone in the organization must know the jobs for which they are responsible. **Organizational charts** help make those responsibilities clear.

───

LODGING LANGUAGE

Organizational Chart: A visual portrayal of the jobs and positions of authority within an organization.

■

Properly organizing a group's work efforts leads to the achievement of goals. A well-developed organizational chart is the result of management's thoughtful structuring of resources to meet its stated objectives.

Organizing work has always been an important part of management. Governments, businesses, armies, and institutions of higher education are all examples of organizations that carefully structure their human resources in a way that achieves maximum efficiency. This is also true in the hotel industry. Knowing the objectives of the hotel, breaking down work into its logical components, assigning qualified personnel, and informing each group member about their expected accomplishments enhances the hotel's ability to meet its objectives.

Larger Hotels

In a large hotel, the organizational chart will also be large because there are so many employees. From the guest's perspective, however, the primary functions of hotel personnel remain the same regardless of property size. Guests want to be checked into a safe and clean room and expect to be charged the correct amount upon departure. As the number of rooms in a hotel increases, so too does the number of staff employed, and the staff members work in increasingly more specialized positions. Figure 4.4, an organization chart for a larger, full-service hotel, illustrates the departments and functions found in such properties.

LODGING ON LINE

For a thorough examination of the activities and managerial responsibilities of hoteliers working in the full-service segment of the hotel industry, see the newest version of *Hotel Operations Management*. You can find it in a school's hospitality library or purchase it on-line at:

www.barnesandnoble.com

When you arrive, enter the book's title in the "Search" line.

Smaller Hotels

Smaller, limited-service hotels perform most of the same functions as larger properties, but must do so with fewer employees. Figure 4.5, an organization chart for a smaller, limited-service hotel, shows the most common organizational structure for a limited-service hotel of an approximately 75-room property, the most widespread type of hotel in operation today.

Note that the number of positions in this hotel is much smaller than in a full-service hotel (Figure 4.4). In fact, as we saw in Chapter 2, the owner of a limited-service hotel may even be its general manager. It is important to understand that in many ways the operation of a limited-service hotel is just as complex as that of a full-service property. This is because, with the exception of extensive food- and beverage-related services, all of the guest-related activities in a full-service hotel are also found in a limited-service hotel. As a result, most of the employees in a limited-service hotel must be multi-skilled and thus able to perform several tasks well.

A limited-service hotel, of necessity, will probably have an individual in charge of maintenance, as well as maintenance support staff, an executive housekeeper who supervises the hourly employees who clean the hotel's rooms and public spaces, and a front office manager who supervises the front desk staff.

Unlike a larger hotel, there may or may not be a designated individual specifically responsible for increasing the hotel's sales. A bookkeeper/accountant (typically part-time) is often retained to prepare financial reports and tax returns. Since the focus of this book is on limited-service properties and how they are operated, each of these specialty areas will be discussed in detail in the chapters that follow. We will begin by examining the role of the general manager, then follow with the additional tasks and responsibilities that must be assigned and appropriately performed if the hotel is to effectively serve its guests and meet its business objectives.

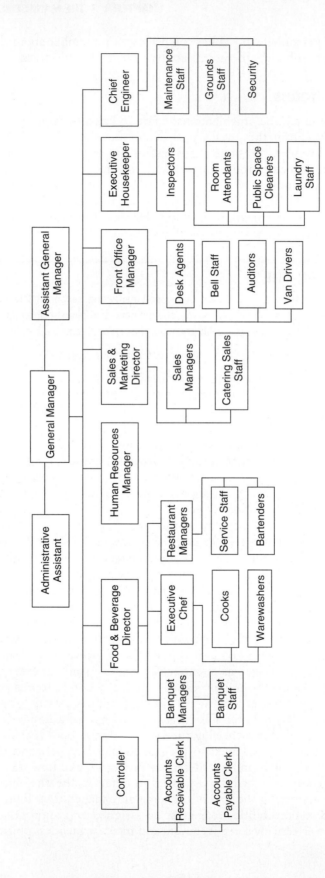

FIGURE 4.4 Organization Chart for Large (350-Room), Full-Service Hotel

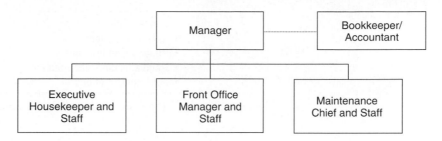

FIGURE 4.5 Organization Chart for Small (75-Room), Limited-Service Hotel

THE ROLE OF THE HOTEL GENERAL MANAGER

A limited-service hotel can be viewed from a variety of perspectives. Guests, of course, will see the hotel through their own eyes, as too will the hotel's employees, its owners, and its management team. To understand fully the operational requirements of such a hotel, it can be helpful to consider it from the perspective of its management team. This is not to imply that the managers and supervisors in a hotel are more important than the hotel's guests, other employees, or owners, but rather that those who operate the hotel on a day-to-day basis take the actions and make the managerial decisions that most directly affect all of these groups (and other groups as well).

Guests at limited-service hotels expect many of the same hotel features as do guests at full-service hotels.

> • Owner relations
> • Staff development
> • Property management
> • Brand affiliation management
> • Community relations

FIGURE 4.6   Key Responsibilities of a Hotel General Manager

Recall from Chapter 1 that the general manager is the leader of the on-site management team. In a limited-service hotel, the general manager is likely to be the single most important human variable affecting the hotel's short-term profitability and success. Hotel general managers "wear many hats" in the fulfillment of their duties. It is not possible to identify any one role that is most important, because the responsibilities involved in any specific general manager's position will vary based upon many factors, including the hotel's ownership structure, the location of the hotel, its size, and the services it offers to guests.

In some hotels, the general manager may be very guest-oriented and spend a great deal of time with them. In others, the general manager may be primarily a staff development specialist who guides the professional growth of other hotel employees. Still other general managers find that many of their duties take them away from the hotel itself. Figure 4.6 lists the five most important tasks for which the general manager of a hotel is typically responsible.

An examination of each of these activities can lead to a greater understanding of the general manager's role and, as a result, help clarify how a successful hotel operates.

Owner Relations

The general manager's role in owner relations is tremendously important. Investor relations include all communications between the general manager and those who own or invest in the property. As we have seen, property ownership can take many forms. A hotel may be owned and operated by a general manager. More often, however, the general manager is employed either directly by the hotel's owners or by a management company that operates the hotel for the owner.

Individuals or corporations who own or invest in a hotel property look to the general manager to have a positive influence on the hotel's standing in the market, its physical condition, and its profitability. As you learned in Chapter 2, a hotel really consists of two distinct components. The first is that of an operating hotel business. A hotel generates revenue, incurs expenses, and, hopefully, realizes a profit. However, a hotel is also a piece of real estate that has value. The land the hotel is located on and the hotel building itself will be worth a specific dollar amount. Some owners will view their hotel primarily in terms of its operating business success, whereas others will focus on the real estate value of the hotel. The general manager must continually inform ownership about the condition of both.

If the hotel requires additional investment in either the business, (such as additional employees or more spending on advertising) or in the real estate asset (such as new **FF&E**, roof repair, parking lot resurfacing, and the like), it is most often the general manager who will communicate that information to the hotel's ownership.

LODGING LANGUAGE

FF&E: The furniture, fixtures, and equipment used by a hotel to service its guests.

■

LODGING ON-LINE

The American Hotel Register Company is one of the world's largest suppliers of hotel FF&E products. To view its on-line catalog (click on the displayed book), go to:

www.americanhotel.com

Owners/investors are usually willing to make additional investments in a hotel property when doing so makes good economic sense. However, they generally must be presented with a persuasive case that additional investment is, in fact, a worthwhile course of action. It is an important part of the general manager's job to help make that case. If this is not done, the hotel building may deteriorate to the point that it results in a declining quality of service for guests, and ultimately, reduced business volume and profits.

The talents required to successfully manage the owner/investor relations portion of the general manager's job include financial analysis, proficiency in written communication, and effective public speaking/presentation skills. Owners want to know about the financial performance of their hotel properties. No one is likely to have a better idea of how the hotel is performing than general manager. The ability of a general manager to effectively inform investors and owners about the current performance and future needs of their hotels will be critical to the property's long-term success.

Staff Development

Regardless of a hotel's size, the general manager of a property will play a major role in the professional development of the hotel's key staff members. In this regard, general managers can be considered the teachers in a hotel. This is true even when the staff members to be taught by the general manager have greater technical expertise in a specific area of hotel operations, such as maintenance or accounting.

In today's world of rapid technological advances, it is unlikely that the general manager will be the most knowledgeable expert in very functional (departmental) area of the hotel. For example, the general manager will probably know less about how the electronic lock system operates than the person assigned to perform routine maintenance on the locks. However, the general manager is still the supervisor of this employee and as a result will be responsible for his or her growth and development as a hotel professional. In this example, the general manager is not the person who changes the batteries in the locking device, but may instruct the individual(s) who are responsible for doing this about the best way to replace the batteries with a minimum amount of disruption to guests. In addition, teaching supervisors and staff members how to establish systematic records (in this case, to record which lock batteries were changed as well as when they were changed) is another way general managers can help staff improve at their jobs.

Perhaps the best way for manager to teach those with whom they work is to serve as a **role model** for them.

LODGING LANGUAGE

Role Model: An individual who displays positive personal and professional characteristics that others find desirable.

◼

An effective role model consistently displays the guest-service-oriented characteristics needed for success in the hotel industry.

Managers sometimes complain, "My staff doesn't pay attention to me." This statement is typically made when an employee does not complete an assigned task, completes the task in a different manner than that which was recommended, or completes the work but does so poorly. In fact, the problem is typically *not* that employees pay too little attention to mangers but, rather, that they pay intensely close attention.

Every managerial action observed by an employee either adds to the manager's stature as a role model or detracts from it. When management, for example, simply insists that each guest room be cleaned perfectly every time, that is how the rooms will be cleaned. When management consistently greets each guest in a warm manner, employees will do the same. As role models, and leaders, general managers greatly influence those who look to them to set the standard of excellence for their hotels.

In some cases, you will find that you may even serve as a **mentor** for some of your staff.

LODGING LANGUAGE

Mentor: To serve as a personal teacher. Also: One who mentors.

◼

In a mentor relationship, the mentor (teacher) serves both as a role model and as a private tutor. In your own career, you are likely to have a mentor (as your career begins) and also to serve as a mentor (as your career advances and you begin to teach others).

Property Management

The actual operation of a hotel property is the activity most people think of when they consider the job of the hotel manager. It is true that there are a variety of jobs within the hotel that must be completed properly if guests are to have a satisfactory stay. It is also true that the ultimate completion of these tasks is the responsibility of the hotel's general manager working with the hotel's staff. On any given day, for example, a hotel general manager must be able to know:

- The number of guests that will be arriving
- The number of guests that will be departing
- The total number of rooms to be sold
- That a record of each arriving guest's name has been created and is readily available
- The room rate to be paid by each guest

- That all room amenities promised by the hotel will be provided
- That all services typically provided by the hotel will be available
- That each room to be used has been thoroughly cleaned
- That the hotel's physical plant will supply the necessary heating or cooling of air, water (at the proper temperature and in sufficient quantity), and power required by guests
- That the hotel's guests and their property will be safeguarded during the guest's stay
- That proper procedures are in place to record the daily financial activity of the hotel

Clearly, it is not possible for the hotel's general manager to personally complete all of these or the hundreds of other tasks that must be done daily. For example, the general manager of a limited-service hotel would not, on a daily basis, check each hotel room to be sold that night to ensure that cleanliness standards have been met. That is the job of the employees assigned the task of cleaning and inspecting guest rooms. What the general manager can and should know, however, is that the proper number of staff have been assigned to the job of cleaning rooms, that these staff have been thoroughly trained, that they have the necessary equipment and supplies to properly clean the rooms assigned to them, and that there is a qualified individual responsible for regularly checking the cleanliness of the rooms to be sold.

To effectively manage their hotels, general managers count on the help of the supervisory staff they have directly trained and developed, as well as the efforts of the **line-level** employees trained by the supervisory staff.

LODGING LANGUAGE

Line-Level: Employees whose jobs are most often non-supervisory. These are typically positions where the employee is paid a per-hour wage (not a salary) and performs a recurring and specific task for the hotel.

Sometimes referred to as an "hourly."

■

While successful hotel managers do not perform every routine task in their hotels, the best managers always know what needs to be done in their properties. As a result, they can identify needed improvements in the hotel's operation. For example, effective general managers, through observation, can identify that:

- cleaning procedures used in the breakfast area must be improved
- the maintenance-tool storage area should be reorganized
- room attendants must be better trained in the proper disposal of hypodermic needles found in guestrooms
- the guest room preferences of the hotel's best clients should be kept in a location easily accessible to the front desk staff
- **"comp"** room reports need to be submitted, with a justification for each comp, to the general manager's office on a daily basis if this is not currently being done

LODGING LANGUAGE

Comp: Short for "complimentary" or "no-charge" for products or services.

Rooms, food, beverages, or other services may be given to guests by management if, in their opinion, the "comp" is in the best interests of the hotel.

The term can be used either as an adjective (for example, "I gave them a comp room") or a verb (as in "I told the front desk agent to comp the room").

■

Knowing what needs to be done is actually an easy part of the management process. Knowing how to get the employees in each functional area to address the tasks in their respective areas of responsibility is the hard part. It is here that the general manager demonstrates real leadership and, often through sheer will power, motivates a hotel staff to achieve things that were never before considered possible.

Property management, while only one of the five major tasks of the general manager, is a task critical to the hotel's success. It is also one of the most exciting. The talents required to successfully handle this part of the job include organizational and coaching skills, analytical and financial analysis skills, the ability to anticipate guest needs, competitive spirit, and tremendous attention to detail. In addition, a truly effective general manager has the near-magical ability to inspire staff members to make guests feel truly welcome when they stay at the property.

General managers must be careful not to overmanage their properties. It may seem somewhat odd to warn an aspiring general manager about spending too much time managing the property, but this can happen. Remember, it is the manager's well-trained staff that provides guests with consistently excellent service. After all, no general manager can be on the property 24 hours a day, seven days a week.

General managers must do many things while they are at work. One important task that must be accomplished is that of managing the brand affiliation of the hotel.

Brand Affiliation Management

It would be difficult to overestimate the importance of brand affiliation in today's hotel environment or in the daily activities of a hotel general manager. This is especially true in the limited-service segment of the industry. Most guests are unaware of the fact that the great majority of hotels are not operated by the brand whose name is on the hotel, but rather by hoteliers employed by the hotel's owners or their chosen management company.

As a hotelier, it is important to understand that if you are operating a branded hotel, you have a responsibility to your employer, but you also have a responsibility to comply with the franchise agreement (see Chapter 2) signed by your hotel's owners. The agreement will always include a section that requires your best efforts in maintaining the established standards of the brand. In addition, the general manager of a branded property will be responsible for communicating effectively with franchise brand officials about marketing and sales programs offered by the brand that can improve the profitability of the hotel.

Conflicts can and do arise between hotel owners, hotel managers, and brand managers. For example, assume, that the brand managers for a hotel chain have established, as a brand standard, that three varieties of fresh fruit (apples, oranges, bananas, etc.), and two varieties of bread for toasting are to be offered on the hotel's complimentary continental breakfast buffet. The hotel's owners, however, as a cost-cutting measure, instruct the hotel manager to offer only two types of fruit and one type of bread for toasting anytime hotel occupancy falls below 25 percent.

A manager who follows the directive of the brand managers will violate the owner's wishes but following the instructions of the hotel's owner would be in violation of a brand standard. When owners instruct general managers to violate or ignore brand standards, this can adversely influence the hotel's relationship with the brand. When brand managers seek the general manager's compliance with acts that may be in the best interest of the brand managers but not the hotel's owners, difficulties may also arise. Issues always arise regarding loyalty to owners/employers and ethical standards for functioning as a professional general manager, but they take on extra complexity when a hotel is operated as part of a franchised chain.

For most general managers operating franchised properties, contact between themselves and the brand managers actually occurs through the hotel's franchise service director (see Chapter 2).

Legitimate differences of opinion and conflicts can arise between a hotel general manager and a franchisor's representative. The personal relationship, however, that ultimately develops between the franchise service director and the general manager is an important one. When the relationship is good, the franchise service director is seen as a valuable resource. When it is not good, conflicts between the franchise service director and the manager can escalate to the point where they negatively affect the manager's ability to effectively operate the hotel.

For example, assume that a hotel's owners elect to affiliate with a specific brand. Assume also that after one year of operation the hotel's sales revenues are not as high as the owners had projected. The owners complain to the brand managers that the brand is at fault for the lower-than-desired sales. In cases such as these, it is not unusual, (and in fact is most likely), that the brand managers and the franchise service director, will claim that the general manager, other managers in the hotel, or the hotel's operational methods are the cause of the sales shortfall. Not surprisingly, if you were the hotel's general manager, you would be unlikely to agree with this assessment. The potential for conflict is clear.

As a general manager, one of your chief responsibilities is to balance the legitimate interests of your hotel and the brand in a manner that reflects positively on your own professionalism. To illustrate one (of many) additional aspect of brand affiliation management, consider the **Quality Inspection Scores** (sometimes called Quality Assurance [QA] scores) regularly given to properties by the franchise brand.

LODGING LANGUAGE

Quality Inspection Scores: Sometimes called Quality Assurance (QA) scores, these scores are the result of annual (or more frequent) inspections conducted by a franchise company to ensure that franchisor-mandated standards are being met by the franchisee. In some cases, management companies or the property itself may also establish internal inspection systems. In general, however, it is the franchise company's quality inspection score that is used as a measure of the effectiveness of the general manager, the hotel's management team, and the owner's financial commitment to the property.

■

Quality Inspection Scores are the result of annual (or more frequent) inspections conducted by a franchise company to ensure that mandated standards are being met by the franchisee. In the typical case, a franchise brand inspector (sometimes the hotel's franchise service director) arrives at the hotel property (either with or without prior notification to the hotel) and, accompanied by the general manager, undertakes a complete property inspection. The property then receives a score or grade based on its compliance with established brand standards that have previously been communicated to the hotel.

If a property consistently scores too low on these inspections, it runs the risk of being dropped as a franchisee by the brand's managers. Properties that consistently score high on the inspections may be rewarded by the brand managers in a way that allows the hotel to use its high score in its promotion and advertising. Choice Hotels, for example, designates franchise partners that score very well as "Silver" award winners, those that score even better as "Gold" award winners, and the very highest scorers are designated as "Platinum" award winners. Other franchise companies employ similar awards for affiliated hotels scoring well on inspections.

LODGING ON-LINE

For an example of one company (United States Franchise System's Best Inn and Suites) that mandates the public reporting of the summary results of individual property Quality Inspection (Assurance) scores, go to:

www.bestinn.com

In some cases, management companies or the property itself may establish standards and inspection/rating systems in addition to, or in preparation for, the brand inspection. Often, the resulting scores of brand inspections are used in property ratings, marketing efforts, and even to partially determine the general manager and other hotel managers' compensation/bonuses. Therefore, Quality Inspection Scores become an important example of how the general manager interacts with franchisors and/or management companies. The talents required to successfully address the brand affiliation management portion of the general manager's job include well-developed interpersonal skills, persuasive ability, listening skills, and often the ability to write effectively.

General managers who have worked with various franchise companies will verify that different brands have differing "personalities." Some brands attempt to exert extreme influence on day-to-day property operations; others take a more hands-off approach. In either case, it is up to you as a general manager to manage the franchise relationship for the good of your investors, community, employees, and most important, your guests.

Community Relations

While it might at first appear that hotel managers have plenty to do simply contending with owner relations, staff development, property management, and brand affiliation issues, today's hotel managers have an additional and important role to play in their local communities.

In many communities, a hotel is more than merely another service business. In fact, the hotels in an area, collectively, can dictate in large measure how those outside the community view the area. There is no doubt, for example, that the hotels located in the French Quarter of New Orleans lend ambiance to the entire area. In a similar

Participation in long-range community planning is an important community relations role for hotel managers.

manner, the style of the hotels located along a specific stretch of beach will provide much of the character of that beach area. This is just as true of business-traveler-oriented hotels in non-tourist areas. Therefore, local government and community leaders often look to local hotel general managers to become leaders in efforts to attract new businesses, expand tourism opportunities, and provide input as to the needs of the local business community. All of these tasks are important because the financial health of any local hotel industry is partially dependent on the health of the entire local economy.

LODGING ON-LINE

One of the most famous tourism areas in the United States is the section of Miami, Florida, known as South Beach. It also provides an excellent example of how hotels help establish the ambiance of an area. To see a brief description of some Art-Deco limited-service and full-service SoBe (South Beach) hotels, go to:

www.sobenightsonline.com

When you arrive, click on "Hotels."

The opportunities for a general manager to assist the local community will be varied and significant. Consider, for example, the hotel general manager who gets a call from the local mayor asking if the hotel can assist in hosting a small gathering for the representatives of a manufacturing business that is considering building a new factory in the community. The manufacturer's decision to do so would mean many jobs for the local community (as well as the opportunity for increased guest

ALL IN A DAY'S WORK

The Situation

"I'm sorry Jim," said Sharon, the franchise service director for Better Stay Hotels. Sharon had just completed her bi-annual inspection of the Better Stay Hotel in which Jim was the manager. "Your quality assurance score went down from the last time I was here, and it actually went down quite a bit in the area of guest room cleanliness."

"We have a new person in charge of that," replied Jim. "She is just getting used to the job. It's only her second month at the hotel. I think that's why our scores were lower."

A Response

Despite knowing why his inspection scores were low, Jim has clearly neglected staff development: an important aspect of his job. When it is known that a key staff member (in this case the person in charge of guest room cleanliness) needs extra assistance or supervision, the manager's job is to provide that added attention. Jim obviously did not, and his hotel's quality inspection scores will reflect that fact. While a manager has many tasks, perhaps none are as important as developing an adequately trained staff to ensure the cleanliness of guest rooms.

room sales by the hotel). Obviously, the general manager would want to assist and, in fact, be a very visible host and community representative.

Additional community efforts that often involve a general manager include hosting and attending charity events, assisting with community fund-raisers held at your hotel, and interactions with community organizations seeking activity sponsorships from area businesses, including your hotel.

The talents required to successfully perform the community relations segment of the general manager's job include an outgoing personality, well-developed social skills, and, very often, effective public speaking and presentation skills.

Effective franchise service directors meet with hotel managers to discuss inspection results and scores after conducting a quality reassurance review.

THE ROLE OF THE GENERAL MANAGER'S SUPERVISOR

While the typical hotel organizational chart shows the general manager to be the highest-level on-property manager, all hotel managers have a person or group to whom they report. This reporting and the resulting supervision, if properly done, is critical to the long-term success of the hotel property as well as to the continued professional development of the general manager.

As the highest-level manager at the hotel property, the general manager is responsible to one or more of the following:

- The hotel's owners/ investors
- A management company
- The hotel's brand managers

Each of these important groups has its own view of adequate managerial performance. Therefore, it is helpful to examine each in the supervision of on-site managers.

Owner/Investor Supervision

In smaller, limited-service hotels, the general manager generally reports directly to the hotel's owner. In some cases, this may be a single individual. This is especially true with hotels consisting of 75 rooms or less because it is very possible for one individual or family to purchase such a property. The Small Business Administration is a division of the federal government that helps small business owners (such as those buying small hotels) to finance the purchase of their businesses. While many small owners serve as general manager of their hotel, the most successful of them will buy additional hotels and then seek professional managers to assist in the operation of these additional properties.

LODGING ON-LINE

The Small Business Administration helps individuals and small companies develop and expand. It has played a major role in assisting individual hotel owners in the purchase of their hotel properties. To review some of the many services offered by this agency, go to:

www.sba.gov

When you arrive, click on "About SBA."

When a general manager reports directly to the hotel's owner, there can be significant advantages and disadvantages. The advantages can include:

- *Better understanding of ownership goals and objectives.* As we discussed earlier in this chapter, owners can have different objectives for the operation of their properties. Some are most concerned about preserving the value of the hotel as a real estate asset, while others put more emphasis on the operational profitability of the hotel. A general manager who reports directly to the hotel's owner will be most familiar with the owner's goals and therefore can make better managerial decisions about how to achieve them.

- *Direct access.* Often it is important for a general manager to get a rapid answer to an important operational question. For example, assume that a general manager is considering the repair of a major piece of heating equipment in the hotel. The repair would cost $3,000, and a complete replacement of the equipment would be $10,000. Assume also that the piece of equipment provides the power to heat the hotel's hot water, and while it is out of service, the hotel will not have hot water. In this case the owner may decide to spend the additional money to completely replace the faulty piece of equipment. If the general manager reports directly to the owner, the owner can be asked quickly about a repair vs. replacement preference, and the proper management decision could be made promptly.

- *Clear lines of authority.* It might seem obvious that a general manager should perform in a way that serves the best interests of the hotel's owners. However, there are times, especially if the general manager is employed by a management company, when the interests of the owners can conflict with those of the management company or the brand with which the hotel is affiliated. When the general manager reports directly to the hotel's owners, these conflicts are most often reduced or eliminated because the **line of authority** is very clearly understood by both the general manager and the owners. In such a situation, the owner takes the role of superior, while the general manager will take a subordinate decision-making position.

LODGING LANGUAGE

Line of Authority: A direct superior-subordinate relationship in which one person (the superior) is completely responsible for directing (exercising control over) the actions of another (the subordinate).

Despite these advantages, working directly with the hotel's owners also has some disadvantages. These include:

- *Lack of owner experience in hotel operating methods.* For most hoteliers, the management of a hotel is their profession, whereas the owners of hotels are often in a different profession. The hotel owner's profession may be banking, real estate development, law, or any number of other occupations. Thus the owner may know very little about hotel operations but nonetheless, in most cases, will have a line of authority over the general manager. The result can sometimes be frustration and misunderstanding on both sides.

  For example, assume that Roger T., the owner of a hotel, also owns several restaurants. In the restaurant business, any charges incurred by a restaurant's guests are traditionally collected at the time of the guest's departure, and in line with this practice, Roger instructs his restaurant managers not to extend credit to any guests. In the hotel business, however, many guest charges, especially for the hotel's best customers, will be a **direct bill.** Unless Roger understands that there is a fundamental difference between the way hotels determine the creditworthiness of guests and the way restaurants approach the same issue, conflict could occur between Roger and his hotel management staff.

LODGING LANGUAGE

Direct Bill: A financial arrangement whereby a guest is allowed to purchase hotel services and products on credit terms.

■

- *Multiple lines of authority.* When a single individual owns a hotel, the line of authority between the owner and the general manager is typically quite clear. When the ownership of a hotel is held by two or more partners, however, or by a company with many owners, the question of precisely who the general manager reports to can be quite complex. For example, in a small company that owns a hotel, the hotel's general manager may report to the company's president regarding operational issues but to the company's chief financial officer on matters of money. Because operational issues and financial issues will often be interrelated, the potential for conflicting advice and direction in such cases is clear.

- *Issues of multiple loyalties.* Professional hoteliers have loyalties to their families, their vocation, their employees, their guests, and of course their immediate employers. In addition, general managers operating branded hotels have some responsibility to the brand's managers as well. When the owner of a hotel places demands on the general manager that cause any of these to get out of balance, conflict can result.

For example, assume that a hotel manager is operating a franchised property where the brand standard for light bulbs placed in the sleeping area of a guest room is a 100-watt bulb. The hotel owner, in an effort to reduce the property's utility costs, instructs the general manager to replace the 100-watt bulbs with 75-watt bulbs. In a situation such as this, the manager faces a direct conflict between the instructions of the owner and those of the brand managers. Unfortunately, the hotel manager may not be able to appeal the owner's directive to another authority figure, and thus the result is likely to be a violation of the brand standard as well as a reduction in guest satisfaction.

LODGING ON-LINE

Tharaldson Lodging Company, one of the country's largest direct owners (and operators) of limited-service hotels, is located in Fargo, North Dakota. It currently owns or manages over 350 hotels. To view the properties it owns or oversees as well as where they are located, go to;

www.tharaldson.com

When you arrive, click on "Locations."

Many hotel managers find that they prefer to work directly for, and be directly supervised by, the owners of a hotel. They cite the ease of accessibility to ownership and the clear lines of authority that generally result from such an arrangement. Other managers, however, prefer, for a variety of reasons, to work for a professional hotel management company or directly for a hotel brand.

Hyatt Hotels, a unique first-tier management company, manages both its brand and the hotels operating under the brand.

Management Company Supervision

As we saw in Chapter 2, sometimes a management company owns the hotel it operates. When that is the case, the property general manager works directly for the hotel's owners. Consider the following article from the January 5, 2004 issue of the on-line publication, *Hotel Business*.

Hilton Garden Inn Indianapolis Downtown Opens

Monday, January 05, 2004–9:44:25 A.M.

BEVERLY HILLS, CA— Hilton Hotels Corp. and First Hospitality Group announced the opening of the Hilton Garden Inn Indianapolis Downtown located in the landmark Fletcher Trust Building.

The hotel, located in the heart of the financial district, was built in 1915 and features a historically restored three-story atrium of marble floors and walls with classic columns.

First Hospitality Group owns and manages the newly constructed Hilton Garden Inn Indianapolis Downtown, under a franchise license agreement with Hilton Inns, Inc., the franchise subsidiary of Beverly Hills-based Hilton Hotels Corp.

As this article announces, the Beverly Hills Hilton Garden Inn is both owned and managed by First Hospitality Group; a hotel management company.

In many other cases, however, the management company does not own the hotel it operates. When that is so, the general manager is not supervised directly by the hotel's owners, but rather is employed and supervised by the management company.

A general manager who works for a management company advances in the organization by satisfying the desires of the company, which are not necessarily the same as the desires of the hotel's owners. One might think that a hotel management company and a hotel's owners would have identical goals, but that is not always the case. For example, assume you are the talented manager of a 75-room hotel. Your management company has just entered into a ten-year contract to operate a 150-room hotel in your hometown. That hotel needs a new general manager, and it is a position you would very much like to assume. However, the owners of your current hotel (located in another city) are adamant that they want you to remain and have even threatened the management company that they will not renew the management contract when it soon expires if you are allowed to transfer. This problem (and it is a good one for you!) as well as others like it can occur when long-term career advancement with your management company conflicts with the desires of the hotel owners for whom you are currently managing. In a situation such as this, your company will evaluate your long-term employment worth (just as you also must evaluate it) as well as the course of action that is best for the long-term growth of the management company. Clearly, however, it will not be possible to simultaneously satisfy your desire for promotion and your current hotel owner's desire for general manager stability.

When a management company operates a hotel, it can affect the supervision of a general manager, but it can also affect the supervision of other hoteliers in the hotel. Consider, for example, a hotel in which the owner is considering replacing a second-tier management company. If the change takes place, it is likely that the general manager, and, in a larger property, the person responsible for hotel sales, will be replaced. Other managers, such as the persons responsible for rooms cleaning and the maintenance of the facility, are much less likely to be replaced. This is true because a management company winning a new contract does not, as some believe, replace every employee at the hotel. In fact, to do so would disrupt the hotel tremendously. In this instance, a general manager may supervise some managers whose loyalty will be to the management company while other managers may be more loyal to a specific hotel and its owners.

Hotel general managers employed by a management company do not report to the hotel's owners, but rather to an area, district, or **regional manager.** While the specific title will vary by company, a regional manager is the person in a management company who has a direct line of authority over the general managers of the individual properties.

LODGING LANGUAGE

Regional Manager: The individual responsible for the operation of multiple hotels in a designated geographic area. In some companies, the person's title may be area or district manager.

■

Depending upon the size of the management company and the number of hotels it manages, the regional manager may supervise many individual general managers. It is the job of the regional manager to supervise the hotel general managers and to serve as the management company's contact with the hotels owners or investors.

LODGING ON-LINE

There are many fine management companies. One of the oldest and best-managed is Richfield. To view its Web site and review learn about its corporate evolution, go to:

www.Richfield.com

When you arrive, click on "History."

Brand Supervision

The brand with which a hotel affiliates will always exercise some control over the hotel and thus over its managers. While the brand managers of a franchised property will not typically have a line of authority over the hotel's general manager, they will determine, in many ways, how the general manager manages the hotel. This is the case when the brand manager's role is merely to monitor the hotel's operations, and it is especially true when, as sometimes happens, the brand managers are also the hotel's owners.

Brand-Monitored Hotels

When a hotel is merely monitored by its affiliated brand, the hotel's manager does not report directly to one of the brand's managers. At a franchised hotel, however, the franchise brand managers will make sure that the general manager performs certain specific tasks or assigns them to someone else on the hotel's staff. For example, many hotel chains have implemented a 100 percent satisfaction guarantee program. Essentially, these programs, which are mandated by the chains, require hotels that encounter a dissatisfied guest to either correct the guest's problem or comp the guest's stay. Understandably, there are times when a guest does not feel the problem was resolved (and thus would qualify for a free stay), but the hotel's management believes that the guest was accommodated fairly. In such a case, a complaint from the guest to the brand will be transmitted back to the hotel for final resolution. The resolution must take place within a reasonable time frame (typically 48–72 hours). In this situation, the brand managers are, in fact, directing the hotel general manager or the general manager's staff, to act on a specific matter and in a specific time frame. Technically this is not supervision, but it illustrates how brands, in many cases, exert some direct control over on-site property managers.

Brand-Owned Hotels

Historically, hotel brand managers saw the value of franchising as a way to rapidly increase the size of their chains. This was especially true with American hotel companies operating mid-sized and smaller limited-service hotels. Therefore, while a larger company like Marriott and Hyatt may in fact be the **sole investor** in one or more of the hotels affiliated with its brand, franchisors are not hotel owners in the great majority of cases.

LODGING LANGUAGE

Sole Investor: A single investor that owns 100 percent of a hotel. A sole investor may be an individual, a company, or someother financial entity.

■

Even though it is not typically the sole investor, a hotel brand may elect to be a partial investor in one or more of its branded hotels. Brand managers generally do not become hotel investors, but they may sometimes do so. There are several possible reasons, including:

- Serving as the hotel's management company at the request of an owner
- Serving as the hotel's management company at the request of a lending institution that has taken possession of the hotel (the brand may agree to this arrangement in exchange for a fee and partial hotel ownership)
- Serving as the hotel's management company while a hotel is being sold (the brand may also agree to this arrangement in exchange for a fee and partial hotel ownership)

In the above cases, the brand may agree to manage a hotel in exchange for a management fee and partial ownership. When a brand actually manages a hotel, the expectations are very high for the on-site hotel managers to maintain (or exceed) brand standards.

When a brand is assigned complete managerial responsibility for a hotel, the hotel's general manager will be supervised directly by one of the brand's managers. Regardless of whether the hotel's owners, a management company, or the hotel's brand managers supervise the general manager, there should always be a distinct line of authority in place, and the general manager should know and understand it.

─── **ALL IN A DAY'S WORK** ───

The Situation

"We'll just see about that!" said Mrs. Kaufield. "I've never heard of such a rule, and I stay in Best Sleep hotels all over the country. But I'll never stay at one again. I don't think your bosses at Best Sleep will be so happy with you when I tell them that! I want the telephone number to your company's headquarters right now!"

Brenda Kaufield was a guest at the Best Sleep Inn at the local city airport. She had been complaining loudly to Sylvia Johnston, the hotel's general manager, about the hotel's policy of requiring each guest to present a valid credit card at the time of check-in. Brenda Kaufield did not have such a

card. When the employee at the front desk refused to waive the policy and assign her a room, Brenda had demanded to see the hotel general manager. Sylvia had politely explained the hotel's policy but continued to adhere to it.

A Response

Hotel owners are free to set many of their own operational policies. It is the general manager's job to enforce these policies. Unless the policy violates a brand standard, this is also true in franchised hotels. In this case, a guest is unhappy with a locally instituted payment policy and wants to complain to the general manager's boss. The guest has

demanded the telephone number to company headquarters. In a franchised hotel, this would be a toll-free number directed to the hotel's brand managers, who would then relay the complaint back to the appropriate party at the hotel for resolution. As the general manager of a franchised hotel, Sylvia should, of course, provide the guest with the brand's complaint-line number if she cannot resolve the guest's issue. The hotel's owners may eventually decide to modify or eliminate the payment policy if enough guests complain about it. While it is in effect, however, it is the general manager's job to enforce it, despite the guest complaints that may result.

CHAPTER OBJECTIVES REVIEW

If you have successfully studied the material in this chapter, you should be prepared to:

1. Describe the four fundamental functions of management. (Objective 1)
2. Identify and read a hotel organizational chart. (Objective 2)
3. List the five tasks for which all hotel managers are responsible. (Objective 3)
4. Describe the manager's task of brand affiliation management. (Objective 4)
5. Explain various ways hotel managers are directly supervised. (Objective 5)

LODGING LANGUAGE

Management	Authority	Quality Inspection Scores
Planning	Organizational Chart	Line of Authority
Short-Range Goals	FF&E	Direct Bill
Long-Range Goals	Role Model	Regional Manager
Organizing	Mentor	Sole Investor
Directing	Line-Level	
Controlling	Comp	

FOR DISCUSSION

1. Some managers specialize in one of the four functional areas of management. In which functional area do you think you would do best? Why?
2. When managerial principles are violated, problems at work often result. Consider the last time you had a work-related problem. Was it the result of a managerial principle being violated? What principle do you think was violated?
3. Guests at limited-service hotels expect many of the same hotel features as guests of full-service hotels. List at least five features of a hotel room where limited-service guests would have the same expectations as guests staying in one of the world's largest full-service hotels.
4. Think about a skill you now have. Did you learn the skill by yourself, or did you have a teacher? Did that teacher serve as a role model, a mentor, or both?
5. Some managers believe it is important for all line-level employees to be proficient in English because they routinely come in contact with guests. Do you agree? What would you do if the number of qualified line-level employees who were able to speak English and were available for you to hire was less than the number you needed to help you properly operate your hotel?
6. Different brands have different standards, but each has a specific reputation it hopes to maintain. Consider your favorite hotel brand. Is it your favorite because of the specific brand standards it enforces or because of an experience you had at one of the brand's affiliated hotels? What are the implications for a hotel manager?
7. Good franchise service directors work hard to ensure that property general managers comply with brand standards. What specific skills do you believe would be needed to successfully perform the job of a franchise service director? How could you obtain those skills?

8. Some hotel owners manage the hotel they own. What are some advantages you would gain by operating a hotel you owned personally? Can you think of some possible disadvantages?

9. Hoteliers who work for a management company often find, as they advance in the company, that they are selected to be promoted to new hotels that are larger or more complex to operate than their current hotel. How do you think the management company would decide which hoteliers within the company are ready for such a promotion?

10. Many in the hotel industry believe that when a hotel is owned by the same organization that owns the hotel's brand, the managers of the hotel have extraordinary managerial responsibilities. Why do you think that is so?

TEAM ACTIVITIES

Team Activity 1

Assume that your team is in the beginning stages of establishing a new hotel brand. Identify three brand standards that you believe would make your brand unique in the market. What specific steps could your group take to ensure that the hotel owners and managers affiliating with your brand follow the standards you have established?

Team Activity 2

Some managers feel they are too busy managing their own properties to become active in their local business communities. Identify three areas in which community service could be good for a hotel's business. What are three potential pitfalls of such community activity?

5

The Hotel Team: Supervisors and Entry-Level Staff

Chapter Objectives

1. To show how teamwork is critical to a hotel's success and present tactics that supervisors can use to manage teams.
2. To explain what a lodging supervisor does.
3. To review special supervisory concerns: communication, motivation, training, effective working relationships, performance appraisal, and employee discipline.
4. To look closely at the role of entry-level employees with emphasis on their responsibilities, retention, and career tracks.

Chapter Outline

IMPORTANCE OF TEAMWORK
ROLE OF SUPERVISORS
    Responsibilities
    Leadership Styles
SPECIAL SUPERVISORY CONCERNS
    Communication
    Motivation
    Training
      Benefits of Training
      Individualized Training
    Coaching

Effective Working Relationships
Performance Appraisal Systems
Employee Discipline
ROLE OF ENTRY-LEVEL EMPLOYEES
    Responsibilities
    Retention
    Career Tracks

Overview: The Hotel Team: Supervisors and Entry-Level Staff

Chapter 4 discussed the role of the hotel's general manager, and you learned that it entailed many responsibilities and duties. However, the general manager cannot operate the hotel alone and must facilitate the work of a team of supervisors and entry-level employees. It is their work that will be discussed in this chapter.

We will begin by focusing on teamwork and show how it contributes to a hotel's success. Today's managers recognize the importance of every staff member and understand the benefits that can accrue from obtaining their suggestions about the best ways to please guests and to operate cost-effectively.

This chapter also explains the role of supervisors and presents several leadership styles that they may use. Much of a supervisor's work relates to human relations. We will discuss this concept as we review the tactics used by supervisors to effectively communicate with and motivate employees. Supervisors train, maintain effective working relationships, and manage teams. They must also conduct employee performance appraisals and implement positive and negative employee discipline tactics, and each of these responsibilities will be explained.

This chapter also focuses on entry-level employees. We will examine their roles and responsibilities, and review the factors that influence their relationships with the hotel's management team.

Many lodging properties suffer from high employee turnover rates. There are numerous common-sense tactics which can be utilized to reduce unwanted turnover, and many of these will be presented.

The final section focuses on career tracks for hotel employees. What opportunities are available for entry-level employees in small properties? In large organizations? In the lodging industry as a whole? We will answer these and related questions in the final section of the chapter.

Many employees indicate that they are "people-persons"; they enjoy serving guests and working with their fellow staff members. The topic of this chapter, then, should be of interest to anyone who aspires to a position in the lodging industry.

IMPORTANT OF TEAMWORK

Which member of the hotel's team is more important: the manager or the housekeeper? front desk clerks or maintenance employees? One does not have to think very long to realize these are ridiculous questions. The answer is simple: all staff members are integral to the property's success. Management and non-management staff must cooperate and work together as a **team** if the hotel and its staff members are to be successful.

LODGING LANGUAGE

Team: A group of individuals who work together and set the goals of the group above their own.

■

Effective work teams have a clear goal: their organization's success. Every member of the team is encouraged to participate in decisions that affect the team. When possible, decisions are made by agreement among the team members. Individual team members have a clear idea about their role and their work assignments, and if there is disagreement, it leads to discussions and consensus about the property's goals and/or the best ways to attain them.

At its most basic level, a hotel constitutes a formal group consisting of all its employees. At the same time, a hotel is organized into departments that include just part of the total group of employees. Within each department, work may be divided into smaller units. For example, large hotels may have employees in the front office department who only check-in/check-out guests; others in the same department are responsible for reservations. In smaller properties, one person may perform both of these front desk activities, but other employees must work in housekeeping, maintenance, and security functions.

In addition to formal work groups, informal groups may develop within a hotel for reasons including:

- common interests of group members
- the desire to be close to other employees in a similar situation
- economic concerns
- a desire to satisfy personal needs that are common to others

When the supervisor believes that the members of an informal group want to attain the hotel's goals, efforts can be made to work with the group. "Friendly" groups can be strengthened by increasing their status, reacting favorably to group members, and/or by ensuring that no obstacles hinder the group's continuation.

By contrast, supervisors confronted with an informal group that works against the hotel's goals must attempt to (a) modify the attitudes of group members, (b) redirect the group toward more useful goals, and/or (c) confront factors causing the group members' negative attitudes.

Effective supervisors use basic principles to effectively work with formal and informal groups. Fortunately, the same basic team-management tactics can be used with both types of groups.

Hotel managers build an effective team by using a **participative management** (shared leadership) style. The entire team (not just the manager) assists with problem-solving and decision-making tasks. Although the manager remains responsible for the effectiveness of the decision-making process, ideas are solicited as decisions are made, financial "numbers" are shared, and all employees are expected to be successful.

SUPERVISORS AND INFORMAL GROUP LEADERS SHARE LEADERSHIP TACTICS

Supervisors should pay special attention to how they interact with team leaders. The personnel who lead formal groups are hired by the hotel to perform this leadership role. The leaders of informal groups are not hired for this role but generally emerge through their interactions with members of their informal group. Many factors important to successful supervision (for example, the ability to respond differently to different people and being aware of the special needs of individuals) are also important in leading an informal group. Likewise, just as is true with supervisors, one's knowledge, skills, abilities, and contributions affect one's opportunity to become a group leader.

LODGING LANGUAGE

Participative Management: A leadership style that emphasizes the solicitation and use of employee input as managers make decisions.

Cross-functional teams are great examples of how a hotel team can be used to address and resolve defects on the property's journey toward higher quality levels.

Assume, for example, that there is a recurring problem with rooms being unavailable for guest check-in because they have not been cleaned after the previous night's occupancy. A meeting with front desk clerks might yield the opinion that housekeeping personnel should get the rooms ready earlier. A meeting of housekeepers might end with agreement that front desk staff shouldn't expect rooms to be available until mid-afternoon or later. By contrast, a more effective solution is likely to evolve from a meeting attended by both front desk clerks and housekeeping staff who can work together to find mutually agreeable ways to successfully address the problem.

Employee teams can form within departments and between departments in a lodging property. Department teams can:

- share a common identity
- have common goals and objectives
- share leadership
- cooperate with each other
- provide input to creative decisions that affect the department

Benefits to individual team members include less stressful work because responsibility is shared. Individuals will likely have a greater feeling of self-worth when they know they can influence another. Success that results from teamwork yields a sense of accomplishment.

Between-department (cross-functional) teams tend to work together because they have a common purpose. To be effective, a departmental or cross-functional team must operate within a culture that supports teamwork. The general manager must be committed to the team concept and must surrender to the team some of the formal control traditionally reserved for top management. Team members must be given the time required to completely and successfully undertake assignments, must know about alternative ways that decisions can be made (the general manager may need to provide this training), and all team members must be well aware of their responsibilities.

LODGING ON-LINE

There are numerous Web sites that will help you learn more about teamwork. One is:

www.ravenwerks.com/Teamwork/teamwork.htm

When you reach the site, you can click onto articles relating to global business, leadership, teamwork, best practices, marketing, customer service, and technology.

How can a hotel benefit from the broad-based use of teams? Higher productivity levels, increased quality and quantity of work outputs, and higher levels of employee morale can result. Moreover, operating costs can be reduced.

When general managers facilitate teamwork, they are practicing a different leadership style than the one traditionally used in the lodging industry. They have moved away from the philosophy that "I am the leader, and everyone must do things my way" to "We will all benefit when we work together as a team." Perhaps supervisors should be called "team leaders" or "team facilitators" to emphasize their ongoing interactions in the relationship with the staff members for whom they are responsible.

Several tactics are necessary for teamwork to be effective:

- Each member of the team must know the importance of the work to be done and must be given the training and other resources required to work effectively.
- Teams must know that they have the full support of upper management.
- Teams can be used in all areas of the lodging organization.
- Team members must have all the information necessary to understand the context of the situation and to make effective decisions.

Even in the smallest hotel, several people performing several different functions must work together to achieve the common goal of satisfying the guests. The future of the hotel and employment with it is tied to the ability of all its employees to perform as members of a team with guest-satisfaction goals. When this goal is understood and agreed upon, the hotel team can work together to plan the best way to achieve the goal. Then each team member can assume a specific responsibility as a part of the hotel's team to move toward that goal.

What role will teams play in hotel operations in the future? Can problems be assigned to teams for resolution? Can challenges, including development of policies and procedures, be assigned to teams? Should traditional employee performance-appraisal procedures be redesigned to solicit input from team members? Should teams be formed for specific purposes and then later be disassembled so that members' energies can be refocused on new issues? These are a few of the questions that, hopefully, will be raised as a result of this discussion. The answers will evolve as concerned hotel managers read and think about, and discuss with their peers, the increased role that teams can play in the operation of hotels.

ROLE OF SUPERVISORS

Before discussing the role of a supervisor, let's define three terms: **manager**, **supervisor**, and **entry-level employee**. Figure 5.1 can help us to do this.

Figure 5.1 indicates that the hotel general manager supervises the work of department heads (in large hotels) and managers (for example, in small, limited-service properties). Department heads direct the work of managers who (in both large and small hotels), direct the work of supervisors who are formally responsible for **entry-level employees**.

LODGING LANGUAGE

Entry-level Employees: Staff members working in positions that require little previous experience or knowledge of job tasks and who do not direct the work of other staff members.

∎

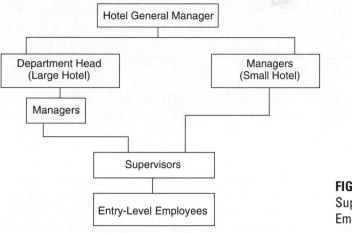

FIGURE 5.1 Hotel Managers, Supervisors, and Entry-Level Employees

Responsibilities

Supervisors have responsibilities to their own boss, to their management peers, and to their employees. Figure 5.2 reviews some of these.

When reviewing Figure 5.2, note that much of a supervisor's responsibility to superiors involves communication. For example, supervisors serve as a **linking pin**, to promote hotel goals and to provide proper reports and other information. Other responsibilities relate to the need to comply with operating requirements (operating within budget, complying with applicable policies and information) and to use the

To Superiors	To Peers	To Entry-Level Employees
• To respect them • To serve as a linking pin between higher and lower organizational levels • To help them be successful • To operate within budget restraints • To comply with applicable policies and procedures • To promote the hotel's goals • To provide proper reports and other information on a timely basis • To work effectively and efficiently • To use the hotel's limited resources as wisely as possible • To work with all staff as members of a team	• To respect them • To recognize them as individuals • To help them with job-related problems • To work with all staff as members of a team	• To respect them • To safeguard their health and well-being • To understand their problems and concerns • To help them be successful in their job • To support them • To treat them fairly • To recognize them as individuals • To help them find pride and joy in the workplace • To work with all entry-level employees as members of a team

FIGURE 5.2   A Supervisor's Responsibilities

hotel's resources wisely. Still other responsibilities relate to interpersonal aspects of the relationship (such as showing respect and working as a member of the team).

LODGING LANGUAGE

Linking Pin: The concept that the supervisor links upper levels of management with entry-level employees. Communication flows down and up the organization through the supervisor.

■

When reviewing the supervisor's responsibilities to peers in Figure 5.2, note that each responsibility relates to interpersonal issues (for example, to respect them, to recognize peers as individuals, and to work with them as members of a team).

Figure 5.2 also reviews the responsibilities of the supervisor to entry-level employees. Again there is more of an emphasis on interpersonal concerns (for example, respect, and providing help, support, and understanding) than on technical aspects of the job (for example, helping them to be successful).

Finally, when reviewing Figure 5.2, note the number of supervisors' responsibilities to superiors, peers, and entry-level employees that really focus on **human relations**.

LODGING LANGUAGE

Human Relations: Skills needed to understand and effectively interact with other people, including employees on the job.

■

Leadership Styles

Supervisors must practice effective **leadership** skills. They must combine their own knowledge, skills, attitudes, and abilities with those of their employees to accomplish work assignments. They know that leadership is an art that involves the use of common sense and abilities to interact with their staff and, at the same time, a science that uses proven managerial principles and procedures.

THE SUPERVISOR'S WORK DAY

What does a supervisor do during an "average" work day? Those with experience in the hospitality industry know there is no such thing as an average day. However, it is typical for lodging supervisors to be involved with the following tasks on a daily basis:

- Direct the work of employees
- Perform human resources duties, including those relating to selection, orientation, training, and compliance with applicable labor laws
- Evaluate employee performance
- Plan and schedule work
- Participate in meetings
- Manage machines and materials
- Interact with guests

LODGING LANGUAGE

Leadership: Accomplishing goals by working with others while, at the same time, gaining their respect, loyalty, competence, and enthusiastic cooperation.

To be an effective leader, supervisors must:

- have the knowledge and skill to do some of the technical aspects of the work done by those whom they supervise
- be confident about their own ability
- be concerned about those whom they supervise
- provide information to employees to help them participate in the decision-making process
- do what they expect employees to do
- consistently ensure that every task done by every staff member is understood, appropriately supervised, and accomplished on time
- train staff members to work as part of the hotel's team
- make appropriate and timely decisions
- help employees to develop an attitude of responsibility for the work they do
- seek responsibility (and take it) for their actions
- be involved in an ongoing professional-development program

Supervisors can utilize four basic styles of leadership that are identified in Figure 5.3.

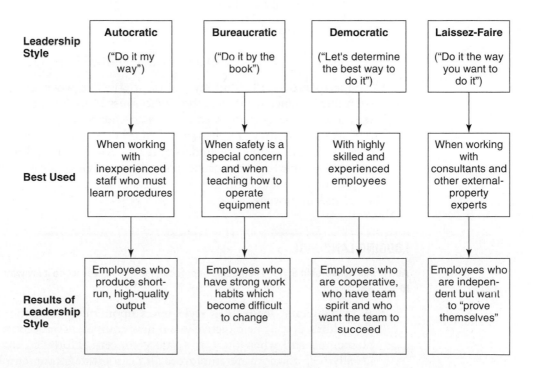

FIGURE 5.3 Styles of Supervisory Leadership

A well-trained supervisor will know which type of leadership style to adopt for any given situation.

Let's look at each of the leadership styles identified in Figure 5.3:

• The **autocratic leadership style** is most effective when a supervisor interacts with inexperienced staff members who must learn proper work procedures. It may also be appropriate when there is an emergency situation or little time to perform a task (for example, when a tour bus arrives earlier than expected because of a reservations misunderstanding). An autocratic leadership approach can yield employees who produce short-run, high-quality output. However, it is not likely to yield team players and can cause resentment between the supervisor and employees.

LODGING LANGUAGE

Autocratic Leadership Style: Leadership approach that emphasizes a "do it my way" philosophy.
■

• A **bureaucratic leadership style** relies upon rules, regulations, policies, and procedures. It may be effective when new equipment/procedures are being implemented and when there is a safety concern. However, the style does not usually help to motivate employees and can create strong employee resistance when future changes are required.

LODGING LANGUAGE

Bureaucratic Leadership Style: Leadership approach that emphasizes a "do it by the book" philosophy.

■

- The **democratic leadership style** is most effective when used with highly skilled and experienced employees. Time will be required to permit employee participation in the team decision-making process. Appropriate use of this style leads to cooperation and group spirit because the supervisor is centered on staff members rather than on the work to be done.

LODGING LANGUAGE

Democratic Leadership Style: Leadership approach that emphasizes a "let's determine the best way to do it" philosophy.

■

- The **laissez-faire leadership style** removes the supervisor from the decision-making process and is best used with very highly skilled, experienced, and educated employees and/or when working with outside experts, including consultants. The approach yields independent employees who, because they are on their own, may seek assurance that they are meeting performance expectations.

LODGING LANGUAGE

Laissez-faire Leadership Style: Leadership approach that emphasizes a "do it the way you want to do it" approach.

■

Which supervisory leadership style is best? Ideally, the supervisor would recognize the situation (employee, problem, or issue and its context) and adapt the leadership style most helpful for the specific circumstances. In fact, most supervisors subconsciously use one style in all situations with every employee (perhaps without even being aware of it). The reason: the approach best fits their personality and their beliefs about how employees should be managed. As well, they may be unaware of the benefits to the use of different styles in different situations or their thinking about the best leadership approach does not provide the necessary flexibility to do so.

In a typical limited-service hotel, there are two groups of employees: those who are interested in a long-term lodging career and those who are not. Effective supervisors might do well to use an autocratic leadership style with both groups as new employees learn how to do their jobs. Then, depending upon each staff member's own personality and abilities, a democratic or laissez-faire approach may be best for long-term staff members and an autocratic or bureaucratic approach might be best for those who are less interested in a long-term relationship with the property.

DO GOOD EMPLOYEES BECOME GOOD SUPERVISORS?

Entry-level staff members who are effective employees are often promoted to supervisory positions. However, the type of work done by supervisors is much different than that performed by their entry-level counterparts. For example, an entry-level front desk clerk can be very effective at checking in guests, making reservations, and dealing with guest-related problems. However, the front desk supervisor has to plan employee work schedules, forecast occupancy rates, work with the general manager on financial issues and training, and evaluate employees, among other tasks.

How does a new supervisor learn to do these management-related activities? It should be obvious that training is required. Hopefully, the manager making the promotion will accept the responsibility to help the new supervisor become successful and provide the necessary training. If this occurs, a good employee can become a good supervisor. If it does not, the good staff member will not become a good supervisor, and the responsibility for problems that arise rests with the manager, not with the new supervisor.

SPECIAL SUPERVISORY CONCERNS

What does a supervisor in a limited-service hotel do? Certain general activities are among the responsibilities of the supervisor of virtually any department. In this section, we will examine several of the most important.

Communication

Supervisors in any organization, including hotels, must be effective communicators. This point was emphasized earlier when we discussed the supervisor as a linking pin between entry-level employees and managers at higher organizational levels. Information flows through the hotel in a **communication** process in which the supervisor plays an important role.

LODGING LANGUAGE

Communication: The transmission of understandable information from one person to another by use of words, numbers, or other common symbols.

■

Have you even heard of a problem that was caused by a misunderstanding or a communication glitch? How can such problems occur so often when both the sender and receiver of the information speak the same language? What kinds of communication problems arise when, as is now often the case, employees in entry-level hotel positions do not use the same language as their supervisors?

Why is communication so frequently ineffective? Reasons include:

- Use of unfamiliar words or symbols. Terms such as "ADR" (average daily rate) and "RevPar" (revenue per available room) are unique to the hotel industry and must be explained when, for example, they are used to train new employees.
- Poor timing. For example, trying to communicate a very detailed message when the recipient is busy is not a good idea.
- Background disturbance. A supervisor trying to speak to an employee in a noisy area may have communication problems. Interviewing an applicant

while being interrupted with telephone calls or by staff members entering the office is not useful communication. (Nor is it a good managerial technique!)

- Personal considerations. The meaning of messages can be influenced by one's feelings about the other person. "I don't like him, and what he is saying is wrong or untrue" is an example. The opposite ("I like her; what she is saying must be true and correct") also occurs.
- Personal differences. Different educational levels, cultures, experiences, and perceptions impact the effectiveness of communication. Young supervisors attempting to direct the work of older employees, and college-educated supervisors interacting with high-school-aged employees, are examples.
- Other communication factors. Words are not the only way we communicate. Consider, for example, the message given by a smile or a frown. People also communicate with **body language.** For example, when their arms are at their side, they may be "saying" that they are receptive to a message, and conversely, when their arms are crossed, they do not welcome a message.

LODGING LANGUAGE

Body Language: The concept that one communicates by the way one's arms, hands, and/or legs are positioned during a conversation or presentation.

■

Effective supervisors spend much more time listening than talking. To listen effectively, supervisors must:

- Concentrate on what is being said. Try to determine what is—and is not—being said. A speaker's voice, appearance, and expressions all influence what one hears.
- Look directly at the speaker and don't let your ideas about the speaker or the subject influence what you hear.
- Ask questions; make the listening process active.
- Take notes, if applicable.
- Don't assume that you know what the speaker will tell you.
- Don't interrupt.

Supervisors in the hotel industry must be effective speakers, and this involves more than just knowing grammar (the proper usage of words). It may be necessary to talk to different employees in different ways as part of the leadership style being used. Effective speakers, who watch for facial expressions, give listeners the opportunity to ask questions, and they adapt their message to meet the needs of the listener(s). Words should be chosen carefully; the minimum number of words needed to make a point is best. Another tactic: use open-ended questions ("Why do you think we should do that?") instead of closed-ended questions ("Do you understand?").

Supervisors in the lodging industry must also know about the **grapevine.**

PLANNING FOR COMMUNICATION IN ONE SECOND (OR LESS)

Several thoughts typically arise just a moment or two before one decides to communicate, including:

- Is the communication necessary?
- What am I trying to accomplish?
- What am I going to say (or write)?
- What are the facts? Do I know how to express them?
- How will I organize my message?
- Have I thought about the people who will hear (read) my message? Why will they want to hear (read) it?
- Am I using the right words, numbers, or other symbols to ensure that the receiver understands the message?
- How should I inform the receiver? (Is person-to-person the best? Should it be a written or e-mail memo? How about a letter?)
- When should my message be communicated? (Now or at some other time?)
- Do I want to provide feedback opportunities to learn the receiver's perception about the message?

Have you ever thought about all of the factors that you consider just before you communicate a message? If so, you can begin to understand why communication problems occur all too frequently. Isn't it interesting that in a "people" business like the hotel industry, more attention isn't given to the communication process and how to communicate effectively?

LODGING LANGUAGE

Grapevine: Informal channels of communication that are not formally developed to disseminate information through an organization but are used for this purpose by employees.

Rumors and incorrect information can quickly spread through the grapevine. Should supervisors ignore it? No, because the information it provides can suggest clues about what employees are thinking and how they feel about their employer and their job. While the grapevine, then, should not be used to provide information, it can be useful input to the development of the information given to employees.

Motivation

The **attitudes** held by employees have a dramatic impact upon their job performance and their interest in remaining with the hotel.

LODGING LANGUAGE

Attitude: The way a person feels about objects, persons, or events.

An employee's attitude about many things, such as an interest in having a job, interacting with people, and living a healthy lifestyle, is formed long before the employee begins working at the hotel. Other attitudes, such as doing the best job possible, attempting to consistently meet the needs of guests, and following reasonable work procedures, may be formed or, at least, influenced by what does (and does not) happen in the workplace. Assume, for example, that a job applicant has no knowledge about the hotel as an employer. The new employee's experiences during the application and selection process and early job activities, including orientation and training, help establish an attitude that sets the stage for the staff member's relationship with the property.

Many supervisors believe they have responsibility to motivate their employees. Can this be done? If so, how?

To answer these questions, let's first define **motivation**: motivation is an internal force that drives employees to do something to reach a goal. Therefore, since motivation involves a force that must be developed within an employee, it is not possible for a supervisor to motivate an employee.

LODGING LANGUAGE

Motivation: An internal force that drives employees to do something to reach a goal.

■

How, then, can a supervisor motivate an employee? By providing job conditions to help employees attain the goals they have developed internally. In other words, the supervisor blends the employee's goals with those of the hotel.

It is important to maintain good employee **morale**, and this can be an objective of effective motivation strategies. Morale is a combination of all the feelings that an employee has about all aspects of the job. This includes the work to be done, the people with whom employees must interact, the hotel, and the work environment itself.

LODGING LANGUAGE

Morale: The feelings an employee has about all aspects of the job.

■

A hotel benefits from employees with high morale. Supervisors must attempt to consider an employee's personal goals so as to mesh them with those of the hotel.

DO EMPLOYEES HAVE BAD ATTITUDES?

You can probably imagine a hotel supervisor thinking about an employee: "I don't know why Chris has such a bad attitude about work, about helping out as a member of our team, and even about showing up on time." In fact, no one has an attitude (feeling about an object, person, or event) that is bad for them; the attitudes people hold are appropriate for themselves. Therefore, when we say that a person has a bad or negative attitude, what we are really saying is, "That person has an attitude which is different from mine. Since mine is right, an opposing attitude is wrong."

Effective supervisors recognize this most important point when interacting with employees. Human behavior is influenced by attitude. If an employee's behavior is incorrect, the supervisor must explain to the employee why it is inappropriate. The supervisor becomes a salesperson to explain, defend, and justify the reason(s) why the employee should modify specific feelings (attitudes). An effective supervisor can ascertain an employee attitude about something and the reasons for the attitude. With this understanding, the supervisor can implement change.

The proper motivation and training empower employees to give their best performance.

When an employee desires to accomplish the same things as does the department, work is more likely to be done according to required quality levels, and cooperation between staff is likely to improve. Staff members who feel good about their jobs may feel that way, at least in part, because of the opportunity to attain personal goals through work.

LODGING ON-LINE

Want to read some practical information about motivation and what makes people tick? Go to:

www.motivation-tools.com

Click on "Table of Contents." You can read articles relating to "elements of motivation," "motivation in the workplace," "youth motivation," "tall ships and motivation," and you can even learn about "self-discovery school."

A popular motivation theory dating to the 1950s defines five basic human needs and suggests that people must reach a self-determined level of satisfaction with a lower-level need before having a desire to attain higher-level needs.[1] While no need may ever be completely satisfied, the basic need most unfulfilled provides the strongest motivation at any given point in time.

[1]Abraham Maslow, *Motivation and Personality* (New York: Harper & Row, 1964).

Human Needs	How Met on the Job
• Physical Needs	• Rest breaks, increased compensation, work bonuses
• Safety and Security Needs	• Consistent application of work rules and policies, non-threatening work environment, availability of proper working equipment
• Social Needs	• Committee assignments, friendships with other employees, participation in social activities sponsored by the hotel, availability of an employee newspaper
• Ego (self-esteem)	• Awards such as employee of the month or year, service pins, paid attendance at external-property training sessions, recognition, personal letters from one's boss
• Self-fulfillment (Knowing that one is doing the very best one can do)	• Involvement in planning goals, objectives, and budgets and by participating in creative special projects

FIGURE 5.4   Basic Human Needs Can Be Met on the Job

Figure 5.4 reviews each of these needs and shows how they might be addressed on the job.

Another motivation theory was advanced by another researcher at about the same time as the theory just discussed.[2] It considers two sets of factors necessary in the workplace to promote employee motivation. One set is referred to as maintenance factors; the second set is called motivation factors. Details are listed in Figure 5.5.

According to the theory, maintenance factors do not motivate employees. However, if they are not present in the job/workplace, employee dissatisfaction will result. By contrast, the second set of factors identified in Figure 5.5 are called motivational factors, and they provide the conditions necessary to motivate employees. Note that the list of motivational factors is essentially common sense. It is, therefore, surprising, but true, that they are sometimes lacking on the job.

Experienced supervisors know that employees interested in their work are likely to have an internal drive (motivation) that will benefit the employee, the guest, and the hotel. They also understand that staff members who believe in the hotel's goals will be more willing to help the hotel than will other staff members motivated only by punishment and reward.

Many employees do not consciously know their own personal goals or needs. Motivation, then, can be a subconscious drive. Few people make an effort to objectively analyze themselves to consider "where they are going." Therefore, supervisors often have difficulty addressing issues about which the employee may not even be aware.

Is money a motivator? For some employees it may be; for others, it may not. Note, for example, that the list of motivational factors discussed above does not

[2]Frederick Herzberg et al., *The Motivation to Work.* (New York: Wiley, 1964).

Maintenance Factors	
Factor	Examples of Concerns
• Economics	• Wages, salaries, fringe benefits
• Security	• Procedures for handling grievances, reasonable work rules and policies, employee discipline programs
• Social	• Chance to interact with other employees on and off the job
• Working Conditions	• Proper levels of heat, light, ventilation, and number of working hours
• Status	• Job titles, work privileges, other signs of position or rank

Motivational Factors

- Challenging work
- Feelings of personal accomplishment
- Recognition of achievements
- Opportunities to participate in the decision-making process
- Increased job responsibilities
- Feeling important to the hotel
- Having access to information

FIGURE 5.5   Maintenance and Motivational Factors

include money. In fact, the motivational factors identified in Figure 5.5 will not cost hoteliers a significant amount of money to implement.

Training

Hotel supervisors have the very important responsibility of training their subordinates. All employees—both the newly hired and those with experience—benefit from effective training. Since the delivery of service is only as good as the employees who do it, training is critical to the task of meeting the hotel's goals.

WHAT DO EMPLOYEES WANT FROM THEIR JOBS?

There can be a wide difference of opinion between supervisors and their employees about what staff members most desire from their jobs. Sometimes, the concerns most important to employees are the last items considered by supervisors. Factors often judged most important by employees (for example, appreciation for work well done, a feeling of being in on things, help with personal problems) can be within the control of supervisors and do not cost money to provide. Contrast this with the view of many supervisors that their employees' concerns commonly center on financial issues, such as higher compensation and promotion. How is it possible that supervisors, working so closely with employees over long periods of time, frequently do not have a better idea about the needs and desires of their employees?

Benefits of Training

Experienced hoteliers know that training can positively influence:

- productivity
- quality
- guests' perceptions about the hotel
- attainment of financial goals
- improved job skills
- level of employee self-awareness
- employee job satisfaction
- help with employee recruitment efforts (applicants are more easily recruited to employers known for their emphasis on training)
- improvement in employee attitudes
- reduction in turnover
- improved teamwork

In spite of these and other benefits, some hotel supervisors and managers do not adequately develop and implement training programs. One reason may be their own lack of the knowledge and skills needed for developing and implementing training programs. Training is not difficult, but planning and delivering it take time, and the trainer has to make the necessary effort to ensure that it achieves the goals for which it is planned. Time correlates with money (costs), and training is, initially, more expensive than the alternative of not training. However, since trained employees are more productive, are better able to meet quality requirements, feel better about the work they do, and are more likely to remain with the hotel, it becomes easy to justify training time and expenditures.

Individualized Training

Staff members can be trained on an individualized (one-to-one) basis or in a group with other trainees. A four-step process can be used with either method, as outlined in Figure 5.6.

There are several advantages to an individualized training program:

- Training can focus on the specific needs of the individual trainee.

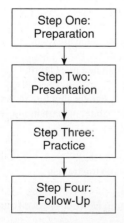

FIGURE 5.6 Four-Step Training Method

- The trainee can receive specific and immediate feedback about performance during the training.
- Training can progress at the speed most beneficial to the trainee.
- The trainer has a good opportunity to develop a more personalized working relationship with the trainee.

Let's look at how the Four-Step Training Method reviewed in Figure 5.6 can be used.

- *Step One—Preparation.* The techniques and strategies for developing individualized training are basically the same as those required to plan any other type of training activities. For example, the trainer must develop and consistently consider training objectives. Before teaching a **job task**, the trainer must know exactly how it should be done. Decisions about the time needed for training and its location along with the assembly and set-up of all necessary materials and equipment must occur before training begins. It is important to explain, from the trainee's point of view, why the training is important and how the trainee will benefit. Figure 5.7 reviews important details as a trainer prepares for the training.

LODGING LANGUAGE

Job Task: An activity that an employee working in a specific position must know how and be able to do. For example, a front desk clerk in a limited-service hotel must be able to properly check-in a guest.

◾

- *Step Two—Presentation.* After the training session is prepared, presentation issues become important. Specific work procedures become the foundation for presenting the training activity that should illustrate and emphasize the correct way to do each job task.

  After the trainer reviews how a task should be done, it is time to demonstrate the correct way to do the procedure. The demonstration can include repetition as necessary to make sure the trainee understands how each activity fits

---

To prepare for training the supervisor should:

1. Work out a time schedule indicating the sequence for and time allocated to training.
2. Break down the job by major tasks, procedures, and quality and quantity standards.
3. Have all necessary equipment, tools, and materials ready.
4. Select and properly arrange the training location.
5. Know how to begin the training process.
6. Identify the job tasks which the trainee must learn.
7. Put the trainee at ease.
8. Find out what the trainee already knows about each task.
9. Explain what the trainee should expect to learn in the session.
10. Set a good example for the trainee.
11. Tell "what's in it" for the trainee.
12. Consider the trainee's language level.
13. Share the training information with the trainee.

FIGURE 5.7   The Four-Step Training Method: Preparation

To present the training the supervisor should:

1. Explain and demonstrate job tasks to the trainee.
2. Maintain a patient and appropriate pace throughout the training.
3. Make sure the trainee understands each job task and procedure.
4. Encourage the trainee to ask questions.
5. Check for understanding by asking open-ended questions.
6. Take up only one point at a time.
7. Follow an orderly sequence by teaching tasks in the order they will be done on the job.
8. Provide only information or instruction that can be mastered at one session.
9. Make all instructions clear, concise, and complete.
10. Make the session interesting.
11. Have all equipment/tools available.
12. Show the trainee how to do the task correctly.
13. Remind the trainee to look at effectiveness from the point of view of guests and other employees.

FIGURE 5.8 The Four-Step Training Method: Presentation

into the entire job. Detailed steps in the presentation of the training are noted in Figure 5.8.

After the training has been presented it is time for the trainee to practice.

- *Step Three—Practice.* After the trainer has explained and demonstrated the basic job task, the trainee should perform the task alone. Repetition is an important way to be certain that the trainee knows how to do the work and can begin to acquire the necessary skills and speed. While the trainee practices, the trainer can make suggestions about ways to do the work better and, at the same time, compliment the trainee for acceptable performance. Figure 5.9 presents specific suggestions for this training step.

- *Step Four—Follow-Up.* At some point after the trainer has allowed the trainee to practice, the trainee should be able to do the work without constant supervision. The trainer should, however, observe the trainee just in case any problems arise. At this time, **reinforcement** and **feedback** become important. If

---

As the trainee practices the task alone, the supervisor should:

1. Test the trainee by asking him/her to perform the task in the required way within a specified time frame.
2. Ask the trainee to explain the hows and whys of the task on a point-by-point basis.
3. Carefully note and correct all incorrect and substandard performance.
4. Make sure the trainee understands requirements by asking questions such as: "Why is it best to do it this way?"
5. Continue questioning to be certain that the trainee understands.
6. Tell the trainee when he/she did well.
7. Correct errors during the training so the trainee can learn from mistakes.
8. Allow time for private (personal) practice.
9. Encourage the trainee to ask questions.

FIGURE 5.9 The Four-Step Training Method: Practice

To follow-up after training the supervisor should:

1. Allow the trainee to work independently in the appropriate work area.
2. Encourage the trainee to ask for help whenever it is needed.
3. Tell the trainee who to ask for help.
4. Check the trainee's performance frequently.
5. Let the trainee know how he/she is doing.
6. Help the trainee correct mistakes.
7. Make sure the trainee learns from mistakes.
8. Ask the trainee for suggestions about better ways to do the job and encourage him/her to improve on existing standards.
9. Reward good performance with feedback including a "thank you" and ongoing encouragement.

FIGURE 5.10   The Four-Step Training Method: Follow-Up

follow-up is effective, the trainee will develop a continued positive attitude about the training and, at the same time, will learn how to do the job correctly.

LODGING LANGUAGE

Reinforcement (Training): Use of words and actions that emphasize the proper way to do a job task.

Feedback (Training): The process by which a trainer informs a trainee about the extent to which a job task has been learned.

■

Figure 5.10 above presents specific follow-up training strategies.

LODGING ON-LINE

At the most basic level, the principles for training entry-level employees in the lodging/hospitality industry are the same as those for training staff members in other organizations in other industries. For a general trade resource focused on training, go to:

www.trainingmag.com

Review the information at this site, making special notice of generic training principles applicable to the hotel industry.

Coaching

The follow-up strategies just noted are part of the supervisor's ongoing **coaching** procedures. In effect, training never ends. The supervisor should discuss training results, job performance, and related matters with the trainee on an individual basis.

LODGING LANGUAGE

Coaching: The process by which a supervisor provides ongoing training and feedback to employees to help them reach their highest levels of performance.

■

The coaching process allows the supervisor to provide feedback and reinforce the trainee's basic skills. Even in the best of circumstances, employees may forget some of the information presented in training sessions. Coaching can be used to review basic information helpful in resolving problems as they occur. Typically, coaching focuses on problems and involves procedures that the supervisor believes will resolve them. Regardless of whether it is done informally, (for example, a simple conversation on the job) or by a more formalized process (for example, as part of a performance review process), coaching is a necessary and ongoing step in the process of training follow-up.

Effective Working Relationships

Neither the hotel nor its managers or supervisors can be successful unless entry-level employees perform according to expectations. This cannot occur without, at least in the long-term, an effective working relationship between supervisors and hotel employees.

Supervisors interact with their employees in several different ways to maintain this relationship: as a trainer, as a mentor, as a judge, and as the employees' representative. Let's review four of these roles:

- *Role as trainer.* It is typically the supervisor's responsibility to help new staff members acquire the knowledge and skills necessary for effective job performance. The supervisor's role as trainer, as just discussed, begins at this point. Effective supervisors also help employees plan professional development programs that provide knowledge and skills needed for different positions and even for promotion if employees desire these opportunities. (This topic will be reviewed later in the chapter.)

Supervisors play many roles when interacting with entry-level employees for an effective working environment.

- *Role as mentor.* Effective supervisors want to learn something about their employees as individuals so, that they can utilize the motivational tactics discussed earlier. To do so, they listen to their staff members, provide advice when requested, and offer potential solutions to work-related issues. *Note:* Since few supervisors are trained counselors, they should not normally discuss employees' personal or emotional problems. They can, however, refer employees to professionals who can provide assistance.

  Would you like a supervisor who was concerned about you and to whom you could talk and ask for help? Would you like a supervisor who listened to you and was willing to help you with problems that were within his/her control? The answers to these and related questions are probably yes, and this is the response most employees would give. Knowing this, therefore, suggests a great deal about the ideal relationship between the supervisor and employees.

- *Role as judge.* Supervisors must enforce hotel policies and rules fairly and consistently. To do so they must, first, be certain that employees are aware of and understand the rules and policies. This is best done at the time of new employee orientation and through employee meetings on an ongoing basis.

  The supervisor's role as judge extends to evaluating employee performance and resolving problems that may arise between individual staff members or employee groups. Sometimes these problems occur for reasons beyond the employees' control. (For example, how should employees know who is responsible for cleaning lobby floors after breakfast service has ended unless this task is included in job descriptions and/or discussed in training programs?) Problems between employee groups from different departments can frequently be resolved through the use of cross-functional teams facilitated by a supervisor who understands the need for the use of this type of team.

- *Role as employees' representative.* This aspect of a supervisor's role was discussed when we considered the concept of the supervisor as a linking pin. Supervisors must accurately present management information to employees and must defend and reinforce formal management actions. At the same time, they must represent their employees to top-level management and explain their views and perceptions.

CAN THE SUPERVISOR BE A FRIEND?

Friends are persons who share special interests and enjoy each other's company and willingly spend time together. Should supervisors have friends who are their employees on the job?

This is a difficult question to answer. After all, two employees may have worked together and become great friends before one was promoted to a supervisory position. Throughout this chapter we have discussed the need for supervisors to use human relations principles relating to respect, genuine concern, and even helping employees find assistance for non-work-related problems. These are things that friends would do for each other. However, can a supervisor be fair with two employees when one is a friend? Can a supervisor professionally discuss shortcomings with a friend during a performance appraisal interview? Will a supervisor assign difficult tasks to a friend? Will he/she enforce hotel policies and rules without making exceptions for friends? These are tough questions, because it is very difficult (impossible?) for most people to be friends off the job and have only a professional relationship while at work. Most human resources experts advise that supervisors should maintain professional, not personal (friendly), relationships with their employees.

ALL IN A DAY'S WORK

The Situation

"Hello, Venetta," said Lovi-Ann, "I haven't seen you since the graduation ceremony a year ago. How do you like your job in the hotel industry?"

"Hello, Lovi-Ann, it's really great to see you. Do you have time for a cup of coffee? Let's catch up on all the news."

The conversation over coffee presented a surprise for Venetta. "You know how excited I was about my new career at the Hilo Bay Hotel," said Lovi-Ann." When I began, the owners were just purchasing another property in town, and after training, I thought I could move into a management position very quickly and be on my way to a great career. Unfortunately, that didn't happen. For the first six months I was really just a vacation-relief worker filling in for entry-level employees who were gone. Then I became a dining room receptionist, and that's where I've been ever since."

After a moment Lovi-Ann continued, "I recognize the importance of all these jobs. I know I need to learn the basic knowledge and skills to be able to do them. However, after ten months on the job, I've still not done one single management task. When I ask about it, the bosses just say they are planning to do something. So now I'm just working there to earn money while I study for my real estate license."

"Wow," said Venetta, "You have gone from excitement to disappointment, and I can see why. My story is just the reverse, and so is that of others in our graduating class with whom I've spoken. We like the hotel industry and want to stay in it."

A Response

Did Venetta have a formal agreement with her new employer about a planned management-training program? What was the understanding about what she would do and how long she would do it after accepting employment at the hotel? We don't know the answers to these questions. But we can make an important point: before one accepts a position there should be a formal understanding between the applicant and the employer about the "what, where, and how long" of the initial employment (training) activities. Yes, the new employee must be flexible and recognize the need for reasonable deviations from the plan. Hopefully, there will be a schedule showing rotation through specific positions in defined departments, and there should be an understanding about the position that will be assumed after the training program is completed.

If no such agreement was in place, Lovi-Ann must accept some of the responsibility for the current situation.

Regardless, the hotel's management team must recognize that it is contributing to short- and long-term turnover at the property. They have lost Lovi-Ann and, probably, others like her who have become disillusioned with employment at the hotel. Over the longer term, they will have fewer applicants because people like Lovi-Ann will tell others to, in effect, stay away from the Hilo Bay Hotel.

The management team does not owe Lovi-Ann or other graduates a fast-track to the top in hotel management. They do, however, owe her and her peers access to a well-planned, high-quality initial orientation and training experience. They should also be truthful in informing applicants about what will and will not occur during training sessions and about the positions they can reasonably expect to attain after training is completed.

One might suspect that the same tactics used to interact with management trainees are used to manage other employees. If so, employee turnover and low morale are probably occurring and yielding a wide range of problems that could be prevented by managers who treated employees the way they would like to be treated.

Performance Appraisal Systems

Students in hospitality management programs like to know how well they are doing and are anxious for the faculty to evaluate their progress in class.[3] (For example, they want to learn their test scores as soon as possible!) In the same way, hotel employees want to know how well they are doing and desire their supervisors to assess their on-job efforts. A **performance appraisal** system should be in place to do this.

[3]This section and the one that follows are adapted from Jack Ninemeier and David Hayes, *Restaurant Operations Management.* (Upper Saddle River, N.J., Pearson Education, 2006).

LODGING LANGUAGE

Performance Appraisal: A periodic formal evaluation of an employee's job performance, including a discussion of professional development goals; also called "performance evaluation."

■

Well-designed performance appraisal systems help supervisors measure past employee performance, assist them to plan and develop activities for professional and personal improvement and establish goals and procedures to guide improvement efforts.

Although the goals of performance appraisal are so significant, many hotels do not have formal appraisal processes in place. Some of those that do, unfortunately, utilize programs that are flawed.

There are special concerns relating to performance appraisals about which hotel managers and supervisors should be aware:

- Some managers evaluate the employees themselves rather than their performance. For example, some formal evaluation systems require evaluators to compare employees against one another. As a result, some employees must be classified as "very good" and others must be "very bad," even though, in practice, all of them may be consistently meeting or exceeding job standards.

  Ideally, a performance appraisal answers two questions: How well does the staff member being evaluated perform each job task identified in the applicable job description? and If performance inadequacies exist, what corrective actions can be taken to improve the employee's performance in the job description task? (*Note:* hotel managers and supervisors must recognize their responsibility to identify job tasks, train the employees to meet quality/quantity standards, and provide the workplace tools and equipment necessary for the standards to be attained. Then they must assume the responsibility to provide leadership and, as applicable, an environment of empowerment that facilitates employee success.)

- Some evaluators do not like to confront employees and/or point out performance deficiencies. Thus they tend to rate all employees as "average," minimize the time spent on performance evaluations (perhaps, for example, they plan to do it "when they get around to it"), and are unwilling to share negative appraisal results with affected employees.

- Hotel managers and supervisors do not automatically know how to conduct performance appraisals. They must be trained in the process, they must know about standards of performance which are the benchmarks for performance appraisal, and they must provide proper documentation for the reviews.

Most, if not all, hotel performance appraisals are done by interview. Hopefully, the employee's immediate supervisor will conduct the appraisal or, at least, provide background information to the manager who conducts it. Sometimes, the employee is provided with a copy of the performance appraisal form in advance of the interview. The staff member can then do a personal assessment, and the interview can address areas in which the evaluator and employee disagree about performance. **Critical incidents** indicating positive and negative activities on the job are also helpful if they can be collected. Other concerns as the interview is prepared include considering performance goals to be reviewed and identifying suggestions for professional development opportunities.

Reviewing employee performance helps to improve problem areas.

LODGING LANGUAGE

Critical Incident: An activity (outcome) that results in unusual success or unusual failure in some aspect of a job.

■

The interview itself should be conducted in a relatively quiet place free of unnecessary interruptions. Some evaluators discuss areas of agreement first and then suggest areas for improvement. Feedback from employees should be solicited at every possible opportunity. The interviewer can inquire about the employee's perspectives about unsatisfactory performance, and, hopefully, they can work together to identify a resolution plan.

LODGING ON-LINE

There are numerous consulting organizations that offer employee performance appraisal solutions to users. To view the products and services offered by these organizations, use your favorite search engine and type in "performance evaluation." Many of the sites provide background information, review procedures used in performance appraisal systems, and even provide case studies of usage results.

The appraisal interview provides an excellent opportunity to review the hotel's vision and mission, emphasize the importance of guest service, and reinforce the contributions of the employee to the organization's success.

A final point: appraisals do not need to be done only when formally required by hotel policy. Instead, an informal follow-up conversation can occur at any time and, hopefully, will provide an opportunity for the manager or supervisor to reinforce performance changes made as a result of the appraisal session.

Performance appraisal forms and interview notes should be retained in the employees' personnel files. In some cases, employee compensation discussions take place at the same time as performance reviews. At other properties, these discussions occur at a second meeting. The amount, if any, of pay increase should be influenced by the performance reviews. When an employee's compensation has been adjusted, a written record of the adjustment should be placed in the employee's file. The record should include:

- employee name
- position
- old pay rate
- new pay rate
- effective date of change
- individual (manager) approving the change

At the time the document is prepared, the employee should be advised of the change as well as the reason(s) for it.

Employee Discipline

When some hotel supervisors think about employee **discipline**, they think of it in a negative way: punishment for wrongdoing. A better approach, however, is to view discipline as a method of encouraging employees to consistently meet performance standards. There are two ways to do this:

- **Positive discipline:** positive reinforcement for expected job performance
- **Negative discipline:** "punishment" for undesired job performance

---

LODGING LANGUAGE

Discipline: Activities designed to encourage employees to follow established policies, rules, and regulations.

Discipline (Positive): Reinforcement activities that encourage employees to continue to follow established policies, rules, and regulations.

Discipline (Negative): Punishment activities that encourage employees to follow established policies, rules, and regulations.

■

Many factors influence a hotel employee's job performance. Some are illustrated in Figure 5.11.

When reviewing Figure 5.11, note that the quality of hotel employee performance is influenced by:

- hotel-related factors, including the property's orientation and training programs, the leadership style(s) of the employee's supervisor, and the organization's policies and procedures

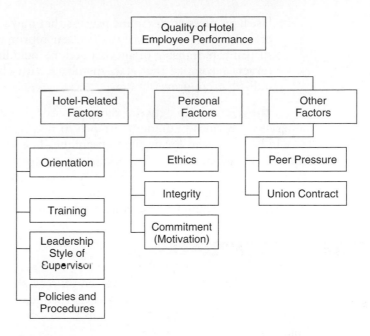

FIGURE 5.11   Factors Influencing Hotel Employee Performance

- personal factors, including ethics, integrity, and level of commitment to the hotel and its success
- other factors, including **peer pressure** and union contact, if any

---

LODGING LANGUAGE

Peer Pressure: Influence from fellow employees in the same position or organizational level to do (or not to do) something.

When there is a good relationship between the supervisor and the employees, the supervisor's instructions, suggestions, role-modeling, and other reinforcement tactics will encourage desired performance. It is only when this does not occur that negative discipline tactics become necessary.

Here are some suggestions to consider when negative discipline is required:

- Reprimands should be done in private.
- Negative discipline should only be utilized when initial positive discipline has been ineffective.
- All information leading to the decision should be available and factual.
- Discuss the employee's performance (behavior); do not attack the individual personally.
- Discipline as promptly as is practical.
- The severity of the punishment should be in line with the seriousness of the problem.
- Continue professional person-to-person contact with the employee after the disciplinary action.

- Use a progressive discipline process that may include, for example, one or more oral warnings followed by a written reprimand, followed, if appropriate, by suspension, transfer, or another action, including termination. (*Note:* many observers recognize that staff members with chronic disciplinary problems are unlikely to improve.)

If the relationship between the supervisor and employees is a good one, and the supervisor provides ongoing assistance to help employees become successful, there should be little need for negative discipline. The supervisor should use negative discipline only when the employee knows what to do but does not do it. The disciplinary action should then be immediate, consistent with the treatment of other employees, and impersonal. (Remember—it is the employee's behavior and performance, not the employee's personality, that must be addressed.)

ROLE OF ENTRY-LEVEL EMPLOYEES

You have learned that entry-level employees should be considered professionals. They deserve and desire this respect and will earn it when those above them in the hotel's organization utilize leadership tactics of the type discussed throughout this chapter.

ALL IN A DAY'S WORK

The Situation

"I guess I am doing okay," said Raoul, a front desk clerk at the Edgemont Inn, in response to a question posed by Nancy, a housekeeper at the property.

"Well," said Nancy in reply, "we housekeepers are not doing okay. In fact, we never do anything right! We never receive a sit-down evaluation from our supervisor." She continued, "Whenever there is a problem, we hear about it, and, of course, it's always our fault! The boss never accepts responsibility for lack of clear direction, never shares information with us, and never thanks us for showing up and doing a good job. No wonder another housekeeper quit this week, and you can be sure that I will be gone as soon as I find another job."

"I know that things must be bad," said Raoul. "The grapevine says that housekeeping is a tough place to work. That's interesting, because we at the front desk have the opposite problem: we

hear nothing from the boss and therefore don't know when there is a problem except when the guests tell us about issues that affect them. We don't have formal performance evaluations either, and even though our boss spends much of the day only a few feet from us, we really don't know how things are going."

A Response

Even though Raoul and Nancy are employed in two different departments with two different supervisors, they share some things in common: their supervisors are not utilizing proper leadership techniques. Their frustration affects their performance and, ultimately, their employment with the hotel. Both of their supervisors would do well to read about and practice the supervisory principles presented in this chapter. They should respect their staff members, provide input about employee performance, provide job-related information that

affects their staff, and recognize that they—not their staff members—are likely to be the root cause of the problems which are occurring.

When Raoul and Nancy were hired, they probably wanted to do a good job. They may have been open to a long-term employment relationship with the property. Unfortunately, that has now changed. The general manager should know about the turnover rates in these two departments and be concerned by it. The general manager should also recognize other problems that may indicate ineffective supervision. These can be dealt with by meeting with all the property managers to plan and implement an effective employee appraisal program. Along the way, the use of cross-functional teams to identify other problems and generate resolution alternatives can help to define where problems originate and what might be done to resolve them.

Professionals are proud, know the correct way to do their job, try to do it better, and make the profession better in the process. Professional entry-level employees "go the extra mile," are part of the hotel's team, try to put forth the best possible efforts to meet goals, and are genuinely interested in helping other employees and the guests.

Responsibilities

Entry-level employees have important jobs; if not, they would not be employed by the hotel. They know what is expected of them (because their supervisor tells and shows them!), and they consistently meet these standards. They have effective ways to communicate with their supervisor, and they do so often. Professional employees are courteous and are concerned about the problems that they and other staff members have on the job.

How employees get along with their supervisor will impact their success. In the best of circumstances there will be mutual respect and understanding between both parties. Perhaps a good relationship will arise naturally and will be easy to build upon. However, this may not be the case. Sometimes friction occurs between people. Then it is more difficult but even more important to work hard to develop, maintain, and improve the relationship. Good employees recognize that their boss will not be their personal friend. However, a professional relationship that considers both the job to be done and the human aspects of the best way to work is important.

Respect is necessary in every relationship, and it is necessary for success on the job. Employees who obtain promotions and pay raises usually have the respect of their peers and their supervisor. Respect is most likely to occur when the staff member:

- cooperates—complies with reasonable requests made by the supervisor
- consistently attains standards of quality and quantity output
- is dependable—actually does what he/she says will be done
- has good manners and is respectful of guests, co-workers, supervisors, and others
- works well with others
- shows an interest in the job and in the work to be done
- has ambition and is willing to work hard to be successful
- is loyal—supports the hotel, supervisor, co-workers, employees, and others
- is creative—generates ideas, does extra work if requested, and sets a good example for others

By doing these things, employees show respect for their peers and supervisors. In turn, they will gain the respect of others.

Supervisors of entry-level employees expect certain things of their staff members. Examples of reasonable expectations include:

- belief in and compliance with the hotel's policies and regulations
- assistance in providing the appropriate quality of products and services to guests
- suggestions about better ways to do assigned work

WHAT SHOULD EMPLOYEES EXPECT FROM THEIR SUPERVISOR?

The staff members of a hotel have a right to expect certain things from their supervisor. These expectations include:

- fair compensation for the job done
- safe working conditions
- training needed to perform the current job to standards and additional training to maintain performance and possibly advance
- help to ensure that all employees work well together
- an explanation of policies, rules, and regulations that affect them
- a fair evaluation of their work
- access to necessary information
- recognition for a job well done
- the use of a leadership style appropriate for the employee
- effective role-modeling; the supervisor sets a good example of professional behavior

---

- maturity—keeping promises, meeting work obligations, and a serious attitude about the job to be done
- speaking positively (or not all)
- a recognition that purposeful change is inevitable and cooperating with it rather than resisting it
- taking responsibility for on-the-job behavior
- consistently working to the best of one's abilities
- serving as a contributing member of the hotel's team

Many employees must work together to make a hotel successful. Supervisors must have the philosophy that work is accomplished with employees rather than in spite of them. Supervisors and their staff must work together in a cooperative, win-win relationship. As they do so, they help to serve the guests and also help to meet their own best interests.

LODGING ON-LINE

Some Internet Web sites provide a wide range of information about the management of people. For example, go to:

www.mapnt.org/library

When you arrive at the site, click on "employee performance," "communications (interpersonal)," "interviewing" (all kinds), or other management-related topics.

Retention

Hoteliers in all types of properties and in all areas of the country consistently complain about a labor shortage. Many cannot recruit all of the staff members they would ideally like to have. The solution to this challenge seems obvious but is more difficult to implement than to discuss: retain existing employees! It is not necessary to continually recruit, orient, and train new staff members if existing staff members remain with the organization. (*Note:* some **turnover** will always occur as, for example, staff members relocate, complete their education, or move on for other personal reasons. Some turnover, in fact, is good for the hotel because new employees with diverse attitudes and ideas are brought into the organization. However, the extensive turnover rates experienced by some properties seriously hinder their ability to maintain quality standards and meet financial goals.)

LODGING LANGUAGE

Turnover: The replacement of employees needed in an organization or a position as other staff members leave.

■

Earlier in this chapter we noted that supervisors can use different leadership styles and will, ideally, do so as necessary when interacting with individual employees. However, this is very difficult to do for at least three reasons:

- A hotel supervisor is very busy and does not have the time to get to know each employee.
- High turnover rates mean that the average employee's length of service is too short for a supervisor to learn details about each staff member.
- Employees are complex; the best style of leadership likely needs to be varied at different times even with the same individual.

Some hoteliers resign themselves to a belief that turnover is a cost of doing business. They believe that little or nothing can be done about it. Then their actions (and/or lack of actions) continue the cycle of recruitment–turnover–recruitment that causes significant problems for many hotels.

A better alternative: Become an employer-of-choice within the community. Many of the tactics to achieve this status really involve common sense. The supervisor should ask, "How would I like to be treated if I were an entry-level employee?" The answers to this basic question will suggest the tactics that can be utilized. The good news is that the implementation of tactics to achieve this goal is not expensive. They involve activities that recognize the worth and dignity of individual employees and allow them to find pride and joy in their jobs and in the workplace. Some of these tactics are noted below. Consider whether you would like it if your boss utilized them with you (and you probably would!). Therefore, consider using them when you become a hotel manager.[4]

Tactic 1: Be a Leader

- *Facilitate employees, don't manage them.* Select the best employees, train them adequately, provide the resources they need to be effective, and help them to resolve problems.
- *Consistently comply with all applicable employment laws.* Hotels usually employ young people. Sometimes employees work long hours; many receive tips. Employ only people who are legally allowed to work in the United States.

---

[4]This information is loosely adapted from: David Hayes and Jack Ninemeier *50 One-Minute Tips for Retaining Employees* (Menlo Park, Calif., Crisp Learning Systems, 2001).

- *Eliminate employees who don't contribute.* Entry-level employees who don't do the work increase the amount of work that must be done by their peers. Supervisors who are not effective leaders hinder the efforts of their subordinates.

- *Recognize that your guests are not always right.* Guests who abuse employees are not right. Employees need to be supported when interactions involving uncivil guests occur.

Tactic 2: Prepare Your Staff Members for Their Job

- Explain the total compensation package, including fringe benefits, to the employees.

- Inform employees about the monetary and other benefits they gain from working at the hotel.

- Share your vision about the hotel's future; let employees see the role they play in attaining its mission.

- Conduct an entrance interview. Discover information about each new employee's interests and goals. (Hopefully, you will find ways to address their concerns on the job.)

- Inform employees about professional development opportunities with the organization; take the responsibility to help them progress within their careers to the extent they wish to do so.

- Develop and consistently implement high-quality orientation and training programs.

- Be certain that employees with training responsibilities know how to effectively train.

- Conduct ongoing training for all employees; **pre-shift training** for a few minutes before the start of work each day is an example.

LODGING LANGUAGE

Pre-shift Training: Training sessions of employees in the same position (such as housekeepers) that last only several minutes and are conducted at the beginning of a work shift.

■

Tactic 3: Make the Hotel a Professional Place to Work

- Enforce zero-tolerance policy prohibiting sexual and other forms of harassment in the workplace.

- Enjoy the advantages of a culturally diverse workforce.

- Develop and implement programs and procedures that make employee safety a top priority.

- Comply with the Americans with Disability Act (ADA) and anti-discrimination laws relating to employees with disabilities.

Tactic 4: Supervise Consistently the Way You Would Want to Be Supervised

- Develop and enforce on-time policies for all employees.

- Provide employees with a personal copy of their work schedule.

- Know about and refer staff members to employee assistance programs if you become aware that they have personal problems.
- Invite fast-track staff members to attend management meetings; allow selected employees to begin supervisory training before they are promoted to a supervisory position.

Tactic 5: Create a Hospitable Workplace

- Conduct regularly scheduled meetings for all staff members.
- Solicit employee suggestions for useful ways to reduce turnover rates.
- Celebrate employees' birthdays and other special occasions.
- Utilize creative employee-recognition programs.
- Praise staff members when praise is due.
- Allow employees to share scheduling responsibilities, if applicable.
- Provide incentives for employees who work on non-scheduled shifts.
- Invite family members of new employees to visit the hotel.
- Solicit the employees' suggestions about ways to make working at the hotel fun.

Tactic 6: Celebrate Successful Employees

- *Reward success each time you see it.* Perhaps a "catch the employee doing something right" program would be helpful.
- Don't reward your best employees by giving them more work to do.
- Assist employees in meeting work responsibilities by identifying child-care and elder-care options. Identify public transportation system options for those needing these services.

LODGING ON-LINE

Want to learn more about managing turnover by retaining employees? If so, go to:

www.employeeretentionsurvey.com

This site lists some of the factors that impact the cost of turnover and provides a case study of turnover factors.

Career Tracks

Some entry-level employees working in hotels do not desire a career in the lodging or hospitality industry. They may be students working their way through school or older people working at a part-time job to supplement their income. By contrast, other staff members may have initially accepted a job at the property and are now interested in a career in the industry. Still others began working at a hotel already knowing that it was a first step in their lodging/hospitality career. There is a place for all of these staff members in the hotel, and the supervisor should interact with each type of employee in a consistent and fair manner.

Hotel employees, like everyone else, typically do what is best for them. If, for example, they perceive it to be in their best interest to remain at the property, they will do so. The reverse is also true, and they will leave for another opportunity that they believe to be better. It becomes the supervisor's challenge to make the hotel workplace compatible with their interests, and procedures to do so have been noted throughout this chapter.

There are many things that supervisors can do to promote careers in the hotel and the lodging industry:

- Show excitement—find opportunities to discuss the many benefits and rewards to working in the hotel industry
- Begin the emphasis on career rather than job at the time of new employee recruitment. ("There are lots of opportunities here; several of our managers began in the [entry-level] position for which you are applying; now they are managers.")
- Continue the career emphasis during orientation. ("Here is our hotel's organization chart. You are beginning in this entry-level position. Persons in these [upper-level] positions began where you are now, and they have advanced to positions of greater responsibility.")
- Provide opportunities for all employees who are proficient in their current job to receive training and professional development opportunities applicable to other positions if they wish to do so.
- Utilize time during performance evaluation sessions to discuss learning opportunities that can take place before the time of the next review.
- Serve as a mentor by making suggestions where appropriate and answering questions when asked.
- Serve as a role model; be positive and upbeat about the property and the lodging industry; actively participate in their personal development and training programs.
- Help interested employees plan a **career ladder**.

LODGING LANGUAGE

Career Ladder: A plan that projects successively more responsible positions within an organization or an industry. Career ladders allow one to plan and schedule developmental activities necessary to assume more responsible positions.

■

The hotel's organization chart is a simple career ladder and suggests successively more responsible positions in the property. For example, in a large hotel one may begin as a front desk clerk, advance to become a front desk supervisor, and then move to front desk manager. Alternatively, in a limited-service property, some staff members may wish to transfer between departments to gain a better understanding of how the entire hotel works. In both examples, the organization chart suggests advancement opportunities.

Employees working in large hotel organizations may have more opportunities for advancement than their counterparts in smaller hotels. (*Note:* Detailed information about the pros and cons of working for a large or a small hotel, a single or multi-unit organization, and an independent or franchisor's business is provided in Chapter 15. This information will be of interest to you as you plan your own career and will likewise be of interest to others in the hotel industry who are thinking about their own future.)

The challenge of every supervisor is to help employees find pride and joy in their work. For many this involves a future of more responsible challenges. Supervisors help their employees by encouraging this when applicable and by providing information that may not otherwise be available to them.

CHAPTER OBJECTIVES REVIEW

1. To show how teamwork is critical to a hotel's success and present tactics that supervisors can use to manage teams. (Objective 1)
2. To explain what a lodging supervisor does. (Objective 2)
3. To review special supervisory concerns: communication, motivation, training, effective working relationships, performance appraisal, and employee discipline. (Objective 3)
4. To look closely at the role of entry-level employees, with emphasis on their responsibilities, retention, and career tracks. (Objective 4)

LODGING LANGUAGE

Team	Communication	Performance Appraisal
Participative Management	Body Language	Critical Incident
Entry-level Employees	Grapevine	Discipline
Linking Pin	Attitude	Discipline (Positive)
Human Relations	Motivation	Discipline (Negative)
Leadership	Morale	Peer Pressure
Autocratic Leadership Style	Job Task	Turnover
Bureaucratic Leadership Style	Reinforcement (Training)	Pre-shift Training
Democratic Leadership Style	Feedback (Training)	Career Ladder
Laissez-faire Leadership Style	Coaching	

FOR DISCUSSION

1. Give an example of a time when teamwork by employees in different departments of a hotel can make a guest's experience more enjoyable.
2. Compose a response to an old-time supervisor who says, "I had to start at the bottom and do lots of things I didn't want to do because I was ordered to do so by my supervisor, who didn't care about me. This was a good experience (it taught me that the boss is always right), and now that I am the supervisor, my employees need to do what I tell them to do."
3. Assume that you are a supervisor and direct the work of several teen-aged employees who have worked for you for several months and, as well, several older employees who have been employed at the property for several years. What, if any, are examples of things you would permit the older workers to do that the young employees would not be allowed to do?
4. What are examples of messages that you as a supervisor would communicate to employees on a face-to-face basis? To a group of employees in a meeting?

5. Pretend that you are an entry-level employee in a hotel. What are some things that you would like your supervisor to do?

6. Develop a list of five topics that you as a hotel general manager would want all recently employed staff members to know about regardless of the department in which they work.

7. Assume you are a supervisor who has been asked to implement a new procedure in your department. How would you interact with leaders of affected formal groups to do so? Leaders of informal groups?

8. Compensation increases are of obvious interest to all employees. Should these be discussed during performance appraisal interviews or in a separate interview before the appraisal?

9. Review the list of entry-level employee retention tactics presented in this chapter that can be used to reduce turnover. Identify three tactics that you believe would be effective in your own situation. Why did you select these three?

10. Some people consider entry-level positions in the hotel and hospitality industry to be dead-end jobs. What is the difference between a dead-end job and an entry-level position in a well-managed hotel? How would you respond to someone who said that all beginning jobs in the hotel and hospitality industry are dead-end jobs?

TEAM ACTIVITIES

Team Activity 1

Assume that you and your team have been assigned a project by a hotel's general manager to develop a short training program for supervisors. Its objectives are to help them learn how to encourage their entry-level employees to consider a career in the industry. List the general topics you would include in your training program.

Team Activity 2

It is often said that the best employees are given a disincentive to do good work because, in return, they are given more work! If, for example, a new staff member must be trained, a good employee, not a bad one, will be assigned this task. What are some practical things you as a manager can do to reward rather than punish your good employees who assume training duties? Consider what can be done before, during, and after these good staff members undertake training responsibilities.

6

The Human Resources Department

Chapter Objectives

1. Explain the importance of the human resources department in a hotel.
2. Explain the tactics that should be used when recruiting, selecting, orienting, and training hotel employees.
3. Review the importance of fair and equitable compensation for hotel employees, explain how this goal can be achieved, and describe fringe benefits that may be available to hotel employees.
4. Review legal aspects of human resources as they relate to employee selection, employer-employee relationships, and other workplace laws.
5. Explain how a hotel's general manager can promote employee safety and health within the property.
6. Discuss five human resource challenges with which general managers must deal.

Chapter Outline

IMPORTANCE OF HUMAN RESOURCES DEPARTMENT
  Background
HUMAN RESOURCES ACTIVITIES
  Recruitment
  Selection
  Orientation
  Training
COMPENSATION
  Importance of Compensation
  Fringe Benefits
LEGAL ASPECTS OF HUMAN RESOURCES
  Employee Selection
  Employer-Employee Relationships

Other Workplace Laws
  Sexual Harassment
  Family and Medical Leave Act (FMLA)
  Compensation
  Employee Performance
  Unemployment Issues
  Employment Records
EMPLOYEE SAFETY AND HEALTH
DIVERSITY AND THE LODGING INDUSTRY
HUMAN RESOURCES CHALLENGES

Overview: The Human Resources Department

The hotel business needs people to produce and deliver the products and services that guests want. Employees, from top-level managers to entry-level personnel, must be recruited, selected, oriented, and trained to perform their jobs effectively. It is important to attract the most qualified applicants to fill vacant positions, and a variety of tactics can help with this effort. Selection tests can help managers assess the qualifications of applicants and identify the best ones. General information that must be understood by all staff members after they begin their employment can be presented during orientation sessions. Training in job-specific tasks is necessary and will benefit both the staff (because they will feel more comfortable doing their jobs) and the guests (who will benefit from employees doing the right things in the right ways).

Concerns relating to wages and benefits are also of obvious importance to employees. Compensation programs must be administered fairly, and there are legal issues which impact the hotel's salary, wage, and fringe-benefit decisions.

The workplace is also impacted by a broad range of other legal issues. Examples include zero tolerance policies for sexual harassment and the need to follow applicable provisions of the Family and Medical Leave Act. The assessment of employee performance must consider applicable laws and regulations, and there are even requirements relating to maintaining necessary employment records. A hotel must comply with these laws and regulations, and doing so must be the responsibility of one or more staff members in the property.

Employee safety and health concerns must also be addressed as part of the human resources function. Complying with and communicating information about Occupational Safety and Health Administration (OSHA) requirements and implementing a property-wide safety committee are important. Helping employees cope with violence in the workplace, AIDS, and issues relating to indoor environmental quality are examples of the wellness and health concerns with which today's hoteliers must deal.

The management of a hotel's human resources is a topic of critical importance to its success. This chapter addresses those concerns which are important regardless of property size.

IMPORTANCE OF HUMAN RESOURCES DEPARTMENT

Managers in every department in hotels of every size must be genuinely concerned about their employees. Large hotels typically have a **human resources department** that helps managers in each functional area to more effectively (and legally) manage its employees. Personnel in this **staff** department help other department managers to deal with human resources concerns, including recruitment, selection, orientation, training, compensation, legal, safety and health, and a wide range of other specialized tasks.

LODGING LANGUAGE

Human Resources Department: The functional area in a hotel with the responsibility to assist managers in other departments with human resources concerns, including recruitment, selection, orientation, training, compensation, legal, safety and health, and a wide range of other specialized tasks.

Staff (Hotel Department): A department in a hotel employing technical specialists who provide advice to managers and others with operating responsibilities. Large hotels typically have three departments with staff responsibilities: human resources, accounting, and purchasing.

■

Background

Historically, the term "personnel" or "personnel management" was used to describe supportive activities related to managing people. However, these terms are not really appropriate because the human resources function involves much more than just managing or directing employees at work. Many other behind-the-scenes activities that support the property's employees are part of the larger scope of human resources.

No hotel can be successful unless its human resource activities are effectively managed. In most limited-service and smaller full-service properties, there is neither a human resources department nor a full-time human resources director. These responsibilities may become part of the work of the general manager and, perhaps, a support person who performs clerical and record-keeping tasks related to human resources along with other job duties. Alternatively, some of the responsibilities for human resources may be decentralized. For example, the general manager may perform activities relating to property-wide concerns, such as ensuring that the application form complies with applicable legal concerns, and those responsible for specific hotel functions (front desk, for example) undertake other **HR**-related activities, including recruitment, selection, and orientation for their area of responsibility.

LODGING LANGUAGE

HR: Short for "human resources." Used for example in "When will the HR department complete the employee turnover study?"

■

Regardless of whether human resources activities are performed by a general manager with numerous other responsibilities, decentralized throughout the property, or undertaken by one or more human resource staff specialists, the same basic issues must be addressed if hotel employees are to be effectively (and legally) managed. There is an ever-increasing specialized body of knowledge that managers must know, understand, and apply. It is for this reason that many hotel owners and managers employ a trained technical HR expert as soon as it becomes cost-effective to do so.

An important managerial principle recognizes that one cannot delegate responsibility (accountability). In hotels with specialized human resources personnel, these staff members do not have hire and fire responsibilities. Their job is not to motivate employees, or to resolve problems that create high levels of turnover, or to recruit, select, orient, and train new staff members. This responsibility rests with **line department** employees. You can see, then, that the basic work responsibilities of hotel managers do not change even when HR specialists are available. **Line managers** are responsible for the success (or failure) of their own departments.

LODGING LANGUAGE

Line Department: Hotel divisions that are in the "chain of command" and are directly responsible for revenues (such as front office and food/beverage) or for property operations (such as housekeeping and maintenance and engineering).

Line Managers: Managers who work in line ("chain of command") departments within a hotel.

■

Human Resources Priorities

What do human resources personnel in large properties do? What activities undertaken by managers in smaller hotels relate to HR functions? Here are some examples:

- Implement policies and tactics to help to recruit, select, motivate, and retain the most qualified staff members.
- Develop and/or select and deliver orientation and supervisory training programs.
- Develop and communicate human resources policies that are fair to all employees and protect the hotel's rights.
- Interpret, implement, and enforce the ever-increasing body of laws and regulations that affect people at work.
- Maintain appropriate standards of work-life quality and ethical business policies and practices.

Figure 6.1 illustrates HR activities that help managers in line departments. As noted above, each of these activities becomes the responsibility of line department managers in smaller properties without HR departments.

The director of the HR department is typically a member of the hotel's **executive committee**, which consists of the manager(s) with property-wide responsibilities and department heads responsible for specific functions within the hotel. General managers in small properties without specialized human resources staff can also use an executive committee structure to centralize discussions and subsequent decision-making leading to policies and procedures affecting personnel-related issues in all departments.

LODGING LANGUAGE

Executive Committee: The group of top-level decision-makers within the hotel, including the manager(s) with property-wide managerial responsibilities and department heads (managers) responsible for specific functions.

■

- Recruits/screens applicants to fill vacancies.
- Interviews and evaluates (qualifies and classifies) applicants. Refers appropriate position candidates to line managers for their consideration.
- Meets with managers/supervisors on personnel-related matters, including hiring, retention, or release of probationary employees, transfers, demotions, and dismissals of permanent employees.
- Establishes and maintains an effective performance appraisal system; trains managers and supervisors who make employee evaluations.
- Maintains employee personnel files.
- Manages the compensation program within boundaries established by the hotel.
- Develops (selects) general training programs, such as for supervisors or employee safety, that are applicable to all hotel departments.
- Serves as an employee advocate within the hotel.

FIGURE 6.1   HR Activities to Support Line Department Managers

---

WHAT IS THE PREFERRED BACKGROUND FOR AN HR SPECIALIST?

Should a human resources specialist have a law degree so as to understand and react to the wide array of legal issues and the laws and regulations pertaining to employment? What about experience in human resources with increasingly more responsible positions in larger hotels? Does the best human resources director come up through the ranks by working in several operating departments? In fact, there is no one best way to begin and move ahead in a hotel human resources career. Many hotel chains have a preferred career progression track for this and other positions.

Suggestion: If you are interested in an HR career, discuss this during employment interviews and seek advice about initial and subsequent job positions which can lead to employment within a human resources department in the lodging organization of your preference.

HUMAN RESOURCES ACTIVITIES

In this section we will discuss some of the most important human resources functions, related to attracting the very best employees and properly preparing them for the work they will do.

Recruitment

The high turnover rate incurred by some hotels makes employee **recruitment** a seemingly never-ending and absolutely critical task.

LODGING LANGUAGE

Recruitment: Activities designed to attract qualified applicants for the hotel's vacant management and non-management positions.

Recruitment is especially difficult in locations where the **unemployment rate** is low and because of a common **stereotype** suggesting that entry-level positions in the hospitality industry are under-compensated with few opportunities for advancement. As the unemployment rate decreases (fewer people are looking for work), it becomes more difficult to attract job applicants. Employers must increasingly compete with other employers for the relatively few persons in the job market.

LODGING LANGUAGE

Unemployment Rate: The number of employable persons who are out of work and looking for jobs (usually expressed as a percentage of the total work force).

Stereotype: A common perception (true or untrue) about something; for example, a specific hotel may be perceived in the community as kind or unkind to its employees.

General managers must recognize that the need to recruit for vacant positions is directly related to the hotel's turnover rate; if few staff members terminate their employment, the need to recruit for vacant positions is lessened. There are many things that the hotel's executive committee and other managers can do to influence turnover rates. The development of policies, procedures, and standards to help make the hotel the employer of choice within the community (see Chapter 3) is a good place to start. If these succeed, the need for recruitment activities is reduced.

What are the best tactics to use when new staff members must be recruited? Human resources managers in large properties and department managers in smaller hotels can utilize the same methods. Often, a good mix of **internal recruiting** and **external recruiting** techniques is best. As the names imply, internal recruiting focuses on employees who are currently employed at the hotel (internal applicants); by contrast, external recruiting focuses on searching for applicants who are *not* currently employed at the hotel.

LODGING LANGUAGE

Internal Recruiting: Tactics to identify and attract staff members who are currently employed at the hotel for vacancies that represent promotions or transfers to other positions.

External Recruiting: Tactics designed to attract persons who are not current hotel employees for vacant positions at a property.

■

The human resources tool known as a **job description** is useful for both internal and external recruiting. People thinking about applying for a job want to know what the job involves. A job description identifies the tasks in a job. It is important that job descriptions be kept current so that there are no surprises after employees are hired.

LODGING LANGUAGE

Job Description: A list of tasks that an employee working in a specific position must be able to effectively perform.

■

Many hotels emphasize promotion from within, and this is an example of an internal recruiting technique. Managers in these properties look first to high-performing current staff members when higher-level managerial or supervisory positions become vacant. Promotional opportunities provide incentives for employees to remain with the hotel and to excel in their current positions. By contrast, other staff members may want to transfer to other positions at the same organizational level for professional development, personal interests, and/or other reasons. They should be allowed to do so if the transfer is in the best interest of the hotel.

Alerting friends and relatives of current employees about position vacancies is another example of internal recruiting. Sometimes, bonuses are paid to staff members who nominate applicants who are selected and then employed at the hotel for a specified time period. An advantage of this tactic is that current employees know what it is like to work at the hotel. If they like their job, they can be excellent recruiters within their circle of friends and families.

There are many external recruitment tactics that may be effective. The well-known ones include Internet job-posting sites, newspaper and other media advertisements, student job fairs, use of employment/executive search firms for managerial positions, recruiting at community schools/colleges, and the all-too-frequently-used "help wanted" signs outside/inside the hotel. It is important to consistently evaluate internal/external recruitment efforts to determine which are most effective.[1]

LODGING ON-LINE

One of the most popular job search sites for hourly and managerial positions is Hospitality Careers.com To view its Web site and jobs in your area, go to:

www.hcareers.com

All employees, by what they do or fail to do, make an impression on their fellow employees. This, in turn, affects the hotel's turnover rate. Employees can also influence the perceptions of applicants (who may, for example, talk with current employees about how great or terrible it is to work for the hotel).

Managers who seriously consider their recruitment strategies and solicit input from their staff members may discover tactics that will increase their hotel's market share of job applicants.

Selection

Selection is the process of evaluating applicants for positions in order to single out those most qualified and likely to be successful. Unfortunately, some hotels use the **warm body syndrome** and hire almost anyone who applies for a position.

LODGING LANGUAGE

Selection: The process of evaluating job applicants to determine who is most qualified for and likely to be successful in a vacant position.

Warm Body Syndrome: An often-used but ineffective selection tactic which involves hiring (almost) anyone who applies for a vacant position without regard to their qualifications for the job.

■

A **job specification** is a human resource tool that can help with employee selection. It identifies the personal qualities judged necessary for successful job performance. Within the limitations imposed by the law (see our discussion later in this chapter), examples of appropriate qualifications include experience, past performance, and physical abilities.

LODGING LANGUAGE

Job Specification: A list of personal qualities judged necessary for successful job performance.

■

Who makes selection decisions? Even in properties with human resources departments, the selection decision should be made by the appropriate manager in the line department.

---

[1]Readers interested in creative recruitment strategies are referred to David Hayes and Jack Ninemeier. *Fifty One-Minute Tips for Recruiting Employees: Finding the Right People for Your Organization* (Menlo Park, Calif.: Crisp Learning Systems Publications, 2001).

Information about each applicant's eligibility for a position must be gathered. This may be done by use of several selection tactics:

- Preliminary screening, including application form.
- Employment interview(s). If the hotel has a human resources department, a preliminary interview will probably be conducted by an HR staff member. Applicants successfully completing this screening interview will then be referred to a manager in the line department that needs them for a second interview. In smaller properties, the initial and follow-up interviews may be conducted in the line department by the individual who will be the immediate supervisor of the employee.

    Typically the interviewer should use a mix of open-ended questions (such as "How easy is it for you to interact with the strangers who are our guests?") and more structured questions (such as "What are the most important concerns when changing a filter on an air-conditioning unit?").
- Employment tests. Applicants are most frequently tested when experience or specific knowledge is required. For example, an applicant may be given a paper-and-pencil test that addresses the arithmetic involved in cashiering skills required for a front desk clerk.
- Reference checks and recommendations. After an applicant has given approval to do so, past employers may be contacted to confirm employment dates and positions held.
- Physical exams and drug testing. Physical exams may be useful for some positions (such as lifeguards) as long as they do not discriminate. Drug testing, while controversial, is legal under specialized situations in many states.[2]

Applicants judged by the screening process to be most qualified for and potentially successful in the vacant position will be offered a job with the property. If the applicant accepts the job offer, the next tasks involve helping the new employee prepare for success in the position.

Orientation

Orientation is the process of providing basic information about the hotel which must be known by all of its employees. Effective orientation is critical because it helps to establish the relationship between the hotel and its employees.

LODGING LANGUAGE

Orientation: The process of providing basic information about the hotel which must be known by all of its employees.

■

Orientation programs must be well thought out. They should not be done inconsistently and haphazardly, depending upon how busy the hotel staff is when a new employee begins work. The general manager shows a concern for the new em-

---

[2]An experienced, licensed attorney should be contacted for state/local regulations applicable to all selection tools.

ployees by seeing that the orientation program is organized, consistently comprehensive, and professionally well done.

Goals of orientation include:

- To reduce anxiety. New staff members are looking for reinforcement that their employment decision was a good one. Their initial impressions are likely to be positive learn about the hotel and observe the genuine respect and attention they receive from fellow employees.
- To improve morale and reduce turnover. Closely aligned with the preceding goal, orientation programs establish the foundation for the relationship between the new employees and the hotel.
- To provide consistency. An effective orientation process yields a team of employees who are more likely to be aware of and believe in the property's goals, who know what to do, for example, in case of a fire or other emergency, and who have a correct understanding of the hotel's personnel policies, including vacation, personal days, sick leave, and other benefits.
- To develop realistic expectations. New employees want to know what their managers expect of them. Orientation programs should provide this information.

Who conducts orientation programs? Since the orientation process involves informing employees about general information applicable to all hotel employees, human resources personnel in large properties normally perform this function. In smaller hotels, the general manager, department head, or supervisor should assume this responsibility. Sometimes it is helpful to make a distinction between orientation and **induction**. Induction refers to more specific information that employees in a department must understand or know how to do. For example, while every employee in the hotel must know about the importance of effective guest relations, only front desk personnel must know about uniform requirements applicable to employees in that department.

LODGING LANGUAGE

Induction: The process of informing new employees about matters related to the department in which they will work. This process follows the orientation process.

■

How does the orientation process work? This depends, in part, upon the number of new staff members to be involved in the orientation. In some large hotels with high turnover rates, there may be several new employees attending group orientation sessions every week. In smaller properties, one-on-one orientation is more common.

General topics to be covered in a comprehensive orientation program may include:

- Hotel overview, including its mission statement, the importance of effective guest service, and the emphasis on teamwork.
- Review of important policies and procedures.
- Detailed discussion of compensation, including fringe benefits.
- Safety/accident prevention concerns.

- Employee/union relations (if applicable).
- Physical facility, including a tour of all areas. A meal in the hotel's restaurant, if applicable, is often included as part of the tour.
- Other topics of priority to the hotel, such as its emphasis on quality, empowerment, and professional development opportunities.

Many hotels provide an **employee handbook**. Its purpose is to provide details of the basic subject-matter presented during orientation.

LODGING LANGUAGE

Employee Handbook: Written policies and procedures related to employment at the hotel; sometimes called an "employee manual."

■

In large properties, a personal introduction by the hotel's general manager can have a significant impact on the relationship between the employee and the hotel and its staff members. New employees will be impressed that the general manager cares enough to welcome them to the hotel's team.

The term **back-door marketing** refers to the tactic of treating employees just as you would guests. Guests may come in the front door, and employees may come in the back door (employee entrance); but hospitality tactics can be similar, if not the same, for both guests and staff members. Would hotel guests like to meet the general manager? Many would! Would new employees like to be greeted by the general manager? Yes, they would! Back-door marketing can show the hotel's hospitality to its employees.

LODGING LANGUAGE

Back-door Marketing: The tactic of treating employees, to the extent possible, just as guests would be treated by the hospitality operation.

■

In some hotels, a second follow-up orientation is held several weeks or months after the initial orientation session. This allows employees to provide input about their initial job experiences and to ask questions based upon their experience in the workplace. The session can also be used to reinforce the most important aspects of the orientation program.

Training

As you learned in Chapter 5, training is necessary to ensure that employees know how to do their job. It is necessary for all staff members regardless of how much experience they have in a position. New employees must be trained to perform all required job tasks so that quality and quantity standards can be consistently attained. However, even experienced staff members need training, as, for example, when new equipment is purchased or as revised work procedures are implemented. In fact, even general managers will require training as new operating techniques and managerial approaches evolve in response to advances in technology, modifications in company goals, and changes in the guests' requirements. Ongoing professional development opportunities can motivate individuals and help the hotel by preparing employees for advancement opportunities as position vacancies become available.

How do those with training responsibilities learn how to become effective trainers? In larger properties, HR personnel may develop programs designed to teach managers how to train. In smaller properties, the general manager may select a "train the trainer" program from among the many that are commercially available and/or employees with training responsibilities may attend off-site programs sponsored by the chamber of commerce or some professional association or group.

In some hotels, a departmental trainer may facilitate on-the-job training in all the tasks required for a new staff member in the department. Other hotels may utilize several trainers within a department, each of whom is responsible for conducting on-the-job training applicable to only selected tasks.

LODGING ON-LINE

The Educational Institute of the American Hotel & Lodging Association offers an extensive array of educational programs and independent learning formats for hoteliers and for hospitality management students. Go to:

www.ei-ahla.org

Note that courses of study are available for staff members working in almost any lodging department and position, and that programs are available for employees working in large and small lodging properties.

Many hoteliers believe that the best training comes from one-on-one interaction.

─────────────────── **ALL IN A DAY'S WORK** ───────────────────

The Situation

Sylva Cooper was the general manager of the Sunshine Springs Inn, a limited-service property with 65 rooms. She was facilitating the weekly meeting with her department managers. "You know," said Sylva, "I'm convinced that we can gain a competitive edge over the chain properties in this area if we can increase our emphasis on guest service. I think we already do a pretty good job. We occasionally get complaints about improper guest service, but we usually frequently receive positive feedback. What do you think about training all of our staff to excel in guest service, to consistently deliver quality service and then market our guest service attitude?"

"I think it's a good idea," said Jerome, the front desk manager.

"I agree also," said Vanessa, the housekeeping manager. "However, who is going to develop the training program? Who is going to present the training? When do we find time to bring our employees together for the training? After all, we're really busy now; maybe there will be more time to do this later in the year."

A Response

A small lodging property like the Sunshine Springs Inn does not have a human resources department to develop and deliver training programs. Even if it did, the department would be very busy with ongoing responsibilities and would also need to set priorities about the most important assignments. At the same time, no business organization can continue

doing what it has always done just because it lacks time, money, or other resources. Fortunately, off-the-shelf training programs are available. Some are specific to the hospitality industry; others are generic and can be used by any organization dealing with the public. In this case, Sylva and the department heads must recognize that their attitude about guest service is the most important factor in implementing a guest service emphasis and keeping it going. Creative scheduling can allow all staff members to participate in the training. Costs for wages paid to trainees and to purchase materials can be budgeted, and other hurdles can be overcome. It is really about attitude, and it all starts at the top of the lodging property.

COMPENSATION

Compensation is the total package of financial and non-financial rewards given to management and non-management employees in return for the work they do for the hotel.

LODGING LANGUAGE

Compensation: All the financial and non-financial rewards given to management and non-management employees in return for the work they do for the hotel.

■

When many staff members think of compensation, they often think about the **salaries** and **wages** they are paid. These are examples of direct financial compensation, which also includes bonuses and/or commissions. While these are typically the most significant forms of compensation, **fringe benefits** can also be significant.

LODGING LANGUAGE

Salary: Pay calculated at a weekly, monthly, or annual rate rather than at an hourly rate.

Wage: Pay calculated on an hourly basis.

Fringe Benefits: Indirect financial compensation, including employer-provided rewards and services other than wages and salaries. Examples include life and health insurance, paid vacation, and employer-provided meals. Sometimes simply called "benefits."

■

Importance of Compensation

Compensation is a necessity of life and the primary reason why most persons work. Of course, as we saw in Chapter 5, there are also non-financial rewards, such as praise and recognition, that can motivate employees.

Pay is important because employees require money to purchase food, shelter, clothing, and other necessities of life. It is also important because it indicates an individual's worth to the organization. In some cases, when employees compare their pay with what others in the organization are receiving (and most employees will do so), they are also comparing job difficulty levels and financial rewards.

Compensation is important to the hotel because the average hotel will pay approximately one-third (or more) of its total revenue to employees in the form of payroll and related costs. The level of pay attracts or detracts applicants and motivates (or alienates!) employees as managers attempt to attain higher work quality and quantity goals.

Compensation must be equitable from the perspectives of both the hotel and its employees. An effectively administered compensation program will be:

- *legal*—it will meet requirements imposed by governmental agencies
- *fair*—employees will all be paid relative to their contributions
- *balanced*—financial/non-financial rewards will represent a balanced part of the total reward package
- *cost-effective*—the hotel will receive reasonable productivity for the labor costs it incurs
- *reasonable (employees' view)*—staff members will perceive that their compensation is fair in relation to the work they do and comparable to what they would be paid by other employers for whom they could work.

It is difficult to administer a compensation program that adequately addresses every one of the preceding factors. This is an ongoing challenge for those who make compensation decisions.

When determining what is fair compensation for a particular position, three factors must be considered:

- What other employers trying to attract the same applicants pay for positions in their organizations. Salary and wage surveys can be used for this purpose.
- What employees working in different jobs within the hotel are paid. Differences between pay for different positions must be reasonable and defensible, and must be based upon the worth of each position to the hotel.
- What other employees working in the same position in the hotel are paid. This decision often considers the length of time the employee has worked for the hotel and the results of the employee's performance appraisals.

Overall hotel wages should be evaluated on a regular basis. When they are, compensation increases (raises) are also evaluated. In practice, decisions about raises are limited by each department's labor cost budget. For example, assume that the wages and salaries paid to front desk personnel are budgeted for a 3 percent increase next year. Some front desk employees will likely receive more than 3 percent, and other staff less; however, the total funds budgeted for pay increases can only be 3 percent more than what is paid by the department this year. It is helpful to learn about the compensation practices of competitive hotels, other organizations in the local hospitality industry, and other potential employers. Information about benefits programs offered by other employers in the community will also be of interest when compensation decisions are made.

Fringe Benefits

Different employees will receive different salaries and wages based upon such factors as position and length of time with the hotel. However, most benefits packages are available to all full-time employees as long as they have been employed by the hotel for a specified length of time.

As with other aspects of the compensation program, human resources personnel and line department managers work together to make benefits decisions in larger properties. In smaller hotels, decisions about benefits are made by the hotel's owner or general manager. In some cases, benefits programs are mandated by federal and state governments. These include unemployment insurance, Social Security and Medicare, and workers' compensation.

There are a wide range of voluntary benefits that hotels can offer in an effort to attract and retain qualified employees. Figure 6.2 shows examples.

The general manager, department heads, and human resources personnel, if applicable, have several responsibilities in managing a benefits program. They must:

- Determine objectives for the benefits programs. Most hotels want to match the benefits they offer with those of competing hotels. However, benefits offered by employers outside of the hospitality industry should be considered if they compete for employees.
- Facilitate discussions with employees about benefits desired through surveys and/or advisory committees.
- Communicate benefits. Many staff members think of their compensation as only their hourly pay or salary. The types and values of non-financial benefits should also be effectively and consistently communicated to staff members. These efforts should begin during orientation, be included in the employee handbook, and continue with presentations at employee meetings and in information provided in paycheck envelopes.
- Monitor costs. An aggressive assessment of labor costs and how they might be reduced or more effectively managed is an important ongoing activity of those responsible for compensation decisions. For example, the cost of medical insurance coverage is escalating, and negotiation, review of existing coverage, and cost-sharing with employees are examples of ongoing tactics often required to manage this benefit expense.

Historically, hotels and other hospitality organizations have been very conservative about offering voluntary benefits; few, if any, provided anything beyond vacation/holiday pay and, perhaps, medical coverage. Increasingly, however, hotels and other hospitality businesses are offering a wider range of benefits opportunities in efforts to attract and retain the very best employees.

Traditionally, hotels, and most other employers limit their full benefit packages to workers who are employed full-time. Part-time workers typically receive fewer benefits. It is important for hotel managers to make employees aware of the cost (to the hotel) of benefits. A full benefit package can easily constitute 30 percent or more of a full-time worker's total compensation. Thus, there is a big difference in cost to

Paid Leave Benefits
- Holidays
- Vacations
- Sick Leave
- Jury Duty
- Funerals
- Military
- Personal Leave
- Breaks
- Maternity
- Paternity

Unpaid Leave Benefits
- Maternity
- Paternity

Life Insurance Benefits
- Wholly employer-financed
- Partly employer-financed

Medical Care Benefits
- Employee Coverage:
  - Wholly employer-financed
  - Partly employer-financed
- Family Coverage:
  - Wholly employer-financed
  - Partly employer-financed

Dental Care
- Employee Coverage:
  - Wholly employer-financed
  - Partly employer-financed
- Family Coverage:
  - Wholly employer-financed
  - Partly employer-financed

Other Insurance Benefits
- Sickness/Accident:
  - Wholly employer-financed
  - Partly employer-financed
- Long-Term Disability:
  - Wholly employer-financed
  - Partly employer-financed

Retirement Benefits
- Defined Benefit Pensions:
  - Wholly employer-financed
  - Partly employer-financed
- Defined Contributions:
  - Savings and thrift
  - Deferred profit sharing
  - Employee stock ownership
  - Money purchase pension

Other
- Reimbursement Accounts
- Flexible Benefit Plans

Services
- Tuition Reimbursement
- Child Care
- Elder Care
- Financial Services
- Relocation Services
- Social/Recreational Programs

FIGURE 6.2 Examples of Employee Benefits Programs

the hotel of two workers, each making the same hourly wage, but one holding full-time employee status and thus receiving a complete benefit package, and the other holding part-time status.

LEGAL ASPECTS OF HUMAN RESOURCES

Many legal issues affect the interaction of hotel managers with employees. These impose significant restraints on what managers can do. Hotel managers who know about and keep current with information about legal aspects of employment can avoid costly and time-consuming disputes, grievances, and lawsuits. This section emphasizes some of these basics.

When orientation programs are effective, potential legal problems can be avoided.

Employee Selection

Job descriptions help to confirm that the requirements of the job were established before the employee selection decision was made. Job specifications driven by tasks identified in the job description should logically (not arbitrarily) identify qualifications needed by those employed for a position.

Job specifications must address **bonafide occupational qualifications (BOQs)**.

LODGING LANGUAGE

Bonafide Occupational Qualifications (BOQs): Qualifications to perform a job that are judged reasonably necessary to safely or adequately perform all the tasks required by the job.

Managers should carefully review job descriptions with the appropriate department managers to assess whether the tasks are necessary and whether they can be modified in a way that might accommodate a qualified worker. In all cases, BOQs should not unfairly or illegally eliminate otherwise qualified candidates. Legitimate BOQs might include language skills (for front desk clerks to communicate with guests) and minimum age requirements (for example, minors are not permitted to work during certain late-night hours).

Laws also affect the tools used to screen applicants during the selection process. For example:

- *Applications.* Applicants should only be required to provide their name, address, work experience, and other information directly related to the job for which they are applying. Proposed application forms should be reviewed by a

- Applicant's name, address, dates available for work, Social Security number
- Employment history
- Education and skills
- Criminal history and pending charges
- Employment status/authorization
- References
- Drug/background testing and authorizations

FIGURE 6.3   Permitted Employment Application Information

qualified attorney to see if they are in compliance with applicable federal and/or state laws. Figure 6.3 lists the types of information permitted on an application form.

- *Interviews.* Questions to be asked of job applicants should be written, so that all applicants are asked the same things. Questions should not screen out any class of applicants, should be directly related to judging the applicant's competence for effective job performance, and should only be asked if there is no alternative way to assess the applicant's qualifications. Questions about age, race, religion, and physical traits, including height and weight, should not be asked. Questions normally safe to ask relate to an applicant's present and former employment and job references.

- *Testing.* Some hotels typically use skill, psychological, and/or drug screening tests. While pre-employment drug testing is allowed in most states, there are typically strict guidelines which must be followed. If a hotel elects to drug test employees, its procedures should be first reviewed by a licensed attorney.

- *Background checks.* The information sought must be directly applicable to the position for which an applicant is applying. A consent form authorizing a background check should be signed by the applicant before the background check.

- *References.* As with background checks, the applicant's permission to check references should be obtained in writing. A hotel should never provide information about a former employee without having received a copy of that person's signed release.

There are numerous other laws that affect the employee selection process. The Civil Rights Act of 1964, among other things, one established the Equal Employment Opportunity Commission (EEOC), which administers civil laws relating to relationships between employers and employees. Hoteliers and other employers that have 15 or more staff members and are engaged in **interstate commerce** cannot discriminate against employees or others on the basis of race, color, religion, sex, or national origin. In addition to federal laws, many states have specific civil rights laws that address or prohibit discrimination. These may include such categories as marital status, arrest record, or sexual orientation.

LODGING LANGUAGE

Interstate Commerce: Commercial trading or transportation of people or property between/among states.

■

The Americans with Disabilities Act (ADA), enacted in 1990, prohibits discrimination in employment against people with disabilities. The ADA does not require hoteliers to employ an applicant who is not qualified to perform necessary work. It does, however, prohibit the elimination of applicants for no other reason except that they have certain covered disabilities. In some situations, the hotel may be required to make a reasonable accommodation to enable a disabled staff member to perform the job. For example, perhaps modifications could be easily made to a front desk area that would enable a front desk clerk in a wheelchair to perform necessary check-in/check-out duties.

The Age Discrimination in Employment Act (ADEA) applies to employers with 20 or more staff members and protects individuals 40 years of age or older from employment discrimination based on age.

Before qualified applicants can be selected, it is necessary to determine whether they are legally allowed to accept the position. This involves verification of work eligibility and compliance with applicable child labor laws. The Immigration Reform and Control Act (IRCA) of 1986 prohibits employers from knowingly hiring illegal persons to work in the United States. All employers, including hoteliers, must verify that anyone they hire is legally authorized to work in the United States. Form I-9 of the Department of Immigration and Naturalization Services (INS) must be completed. Applicants must have one or more of several approved documents to establish eligibility for employment:

- Social Security card
- original/certified copy of birth certificate
- unexpired INS employment authorization
- unexpired re-entry permit
- unexpired refugee travel document
- birth certificate issued by Department of State
- certificate of birth abroad issued by the Department of State
- United States citizen identification
- Native American tribal document
- identification used by resident citizens in United States

The Fair Labor Standards Act of 1938 protects young workers from employment that interferes with their education and/or is hazardous to their health/well-being. Persons age 16 and 17 can work for unlimited hours at any time if the Labor Department has declared that the job is not hazardous. Youths age 14–15 may work in selected jobs during non-school hours under specified conditions.

LODGING ON-LINE

The numerous regulations involved in the employment of minors are provided in the Fair Labor Standards Act (FLSA). To review basic information and learn answers to frequently asked questions, go to:

http://www.dol.gov/elaws/flsa.htm

As seen in the preceding discussion, there are many federal laws that affect how hoteliers make employee selection decisions. There are also state and/or local laws

and regulations, sometimes more strict than the federal laws. Because laws are constantly changing, it is a good idea to stay current by regularly seeking advice from experts on employment law. Hotel managers directly involved in employment must be certain that the employee selection procedures they use are legal and defensible.

Employer-Employee Relationships

Hoteliers have the basic right to hire or fire staff members because, in most states, their relationship with the employee is **at-will employment**. Assuming that no anti-discrimination laws are violated, this means that an employer can hire or dismiss an employee at any time if it is in the best interests of the business to do so.

LODGING LANGUAGE

At-Will Employment: The employment relationship that exists when employers can hire any employee they choose and dismiss an employee with or without cause at any time. Employees can also elect to work for the employer or to terminate the relationship anytime they desire to do so.

■

After an employee has been legally selected, an **employment agreement** should be drafted to specifically indicate the terms of the employment relationship. The employment agreement often takes the form of an official written **offer letter** which can help to prevent legal problems caused by misunderstandings.

LODGING LANGUAGE

Employment Agreement: Document specifying the terms of the relationship between the employer and the employee and indicating the rights/obligations of both parties.

Offer Letter: Document that specifies what the employer is going to give the employee if the job is accepted. Examples include position, compensation and benefits, start date, and employment location.

■

Other Workplace Laws

There are numerous other laws that can have a significant effect upon the management of staff members during their employment. Several of the most important are discussed in this section.

Sexual Harassment

A manager or supervisor cannot ask a subordinate for sexual favors in exchange for employment benefits; nor can an employee be punished if an offer is rejected. Sexual harassment includes the use of improper language or conduct. To protect against the liability that can result from allegations of discrimination or harassment, it is important that **zero tolerance** policies and procedures be in place. The best course is to issue appropriate policies, conduct applicable workshops, develop procedures that employees who allege harassment can use to obtain relief, and follow written procedures to report, investigate, and resolve incidences and grievances.

Zero Tolerance: The total absence of workplace behavior that is objectionable from the perspectives of discrimination or harassment.

■

Family and Medical Leave Act (FMLA)

Hotels that employ 50 or more personnel are required to provide up to 12 weeks of leave (unpaid) to an employee if the time is needed for the birth, adoption, or, in some cases, the foster care of a child. The act also applies when an employee or a member of an employee's immediate family has a serious illness. Immediate family, for the purpose of this law, has been defined as a parent, spouse, or child.

Compensation

The Fair Labor Standards Act (FLSA) was discussed earlier relative to the employment of minors. It also established a **minimum wage** to be paid to covered employees and pay rates for **overtime** work.

Minimum Wage: The lowest amount of compensation that an employer may pay to an employee covered by the FLSA or applicable state law. Most hotel employees are covered by minimum wage provisions; however, exceptions can include youthful employees being paid a training wage for the first 90 days of employment and tipped employees (if reported tips plus wages received at least equal the minimum wage).

Overtime: The number of hours of work after which an employee must receive a premium pay (generally one and one-half times the base hourly rate).

■

Another provision of the FLSA relates to equal pay: regardless of gender, employees holding essentially the same job must be equitably compensated with financial and non-financial rewards.

There are numerous laws relating to the taxes and credits employers must pay based upon the compensation paid to employees, and there are taxes that must be withheld from employees as well. Tax credits are sometimes granted to employers or employees. Examples of these taxes and tax credits include:

- *Income tax.* State, federal and, sometimes, local income taxes must be withheld from employee paychecks.

- *Federal Insurance Contribution Act (FICA)*—Taxes must be contributed by both employers and employees to fund the federal government's **Social Security** and **Medicare** programs.

Social Security: Retirement benefits paid to primary workers, survivor's benefits, and benefits for the retiree's spouse and children, and disability payments based upon contributions paid by the retiree and the retiree's employer(s).

Medicare: Hospital and medical insurance received by persons over 65 years of age who are eligible for Social Security benefits.

■

- *Federal Unemployment Tax Act (FUTA).* Employers must contribute a tax based on their total payroll to help care for persons who are out of work through no fault of their own.
- *Work Opportunity Tax Credit (WOTC).* Employers can receive tax credits for hiring disadvantaged workers.

Provisions relating to the above tax and credit programs are complicated and may change. In large properties, the human resource manager interacting with the personnel responsible for payroll is charged with seeing that the hotel fully complies with all the provisions of these laws. Managers in smaller properties must assume this responsibility themselves. They should seek advice from their accountants and other advisers who assist in the preparation of income and other tax documents, and from the agencies that administer the laws.

LODGING ON-LINE

State regulatory agencies increasingly use the Internet to provide information to businesses to help explain the laws and regulations they administer. To see an example, go to the Web site for the Hawaii Department of Labor and Industrial Relations (DLIR) at:

www.dlir.state.hi.us

At the site you can see how the department informs businesses in the state, including hotels, about the state's family leave laws, child labor laws, wage laws, and other regulatory topics discussed in this chapter.

Employee Performance

Hoteliers must comply with laws relating to the management of employee performance. These include:

- *Employee evaluation.* A hotel violates the law when its employee appraisal system is biased against a class of employees who are protected by the law. General managers should insist that evaluations in their hotels be based on work performance and nothing else.
- *Discipline.* Workplace rules and policies must not violate the law. They must be effectively communicated and consistently enforced. Some hotels use a **progressive discipline system** to encourage employees to comply with requirements. Figure 6.4 shows steps that may be included in a progressive discipline system. Each successive step yields more serious disciplinary action and requires proper documentation.

LODGING LANGUAGE

Progressive Discipline System: A process of negative discipline in which repeated infractions result in increasingly more severe penalties.

■

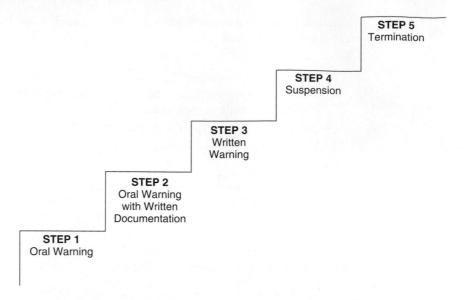

FIGURE 6.4   Common Steps in a Progressive Discipline Process

- *Termination.* The at-will employment relationship discussed earlier does *not* allow hoteliers to terminate employees in an illegal manner. *Unacceptable* reasons to terminate employees include:
  - Actions approved in the hotel's employee handbook
  - In an effort to deny benefits
  - For excused work absences
  - Because of attempts to unionize staff members
  - For reporting violations of the law
  - For being a member of a protected class of worker(s); for example, a specific race, sex, or religion
  - When an oral promise of continued employment has been made
  - In violation of a written employment contract

Unemployment Issues

Unemployment insurance programs are operated by federal and state governments and are expensive and difficult to administer. Each state requires employers, including hotels, to help maintain the public funds used to assist workers who have temporarily lost jobs.

LODGING LANGUAGE

Unemployment Insurance: Funds provided by employers to provide temporary financial benefits to employees who have involuntarily lost their jobs.

■

When an employee files an **unemployment claim**, a series of steps mandated by the individual state is used to determine whether the applicant is eligible and, if

The best performance appraisals allow an equal amount of input from employers and employees.

so, (a) for how much, (b) how long payments will be made, and (c) how long an employee must have worked for an employer to qualify for assistance.

LODGING LANGUAGE

Unemployment Claim: A claim made by an unemployed worker to the appropriate state agency asserting eligibility for unemployment benefits.
■

Employment Records

Federal and state agencies require that selected employee records be maintained. Examples include:

- Department of Labor records—The Fair Labor Standards Act requires that numerous records be maintained for each employee, including information about the employee's name, address, gender, job title, work schedule, hourly rate, regular/overtime earnings, wage additions/deductions, and dates of pay days.

- Records applicable to the Family and Medical Leave Act (FMLA) require information about dates that FMLA-eligible employees take a covered leave, the amount of leave, and other documentation.

- The Immigration Reform and Control Act requires that an Employment Eligibility Verification Form be completed and retained for each employee.

- The Age Discrimination and Employment Act requires that employers retain certain records, including those pertaining to personnel matters and benefit plans.

As you can see, than extensive body of laws and regulations impacts how hoteliers interact with applicants before employment and with employees after selection decisions are made. Someone on the hotel's staff must understand these laws and must keep up with them as they change. This staff member may be the human resources director in a large property and will usually be the general manager in smaller hotels. If the property employs an HR staff, the general manager should regularly ask its personnel for guidance about the hotel's policies/practices and when external legal assistance is warranted.

LODGING ON-LINE

Want to review an Internet source that provides lots of information about numerous topics, including employment laws that apply to hoteliers? If so, go to:

www.hospitalitylawyer.com

When you arrive at the site, review the large volume of information, all of which is written in everyday language (not "legalese").

EMPLOYEE SAFETY AND HEALTH

All hoteliers, including the general manager, department heads, and the employees themselves, must be concerned about **safety hazards** and **health hazards**. One may not generally think of a hotel's environment as unsafe or unhealthy, but problems can arise, especially when jobs are performed incorrectly.

LODGING LANGUAGE

Safety Hazards: Conditions in the workplace that can cause immediate harm. Examples include unsafe equipment, accidents, and the improper use of chemicals.

Health Hazards: Aspects of the workplace that can lead to a decline in an employee's health. Examples include stressful working conditions and exposure to toxic chemicals.

■

Many work-related accidents and illnesses in hotels relate to:

- The work that must be done. For example, housekeepers may need to use hazardous chemicals when cleaning guest rooms. Without proper training, very serious accidents can result.
- Working conditions. Slippery sidewalks or interior lobby floors can cause accidents for anyone who walks on them.

Managers in each department should be responsible for maintaining their workplaces and working conditions to minimize accidents. They should also be responsible for safety and other training for staff members. The general manager plays an important role by maintaining the philosophy that safety is the highest-priority concern. The manager can carefully observe the facility, equipment, and work procedures in use, note any problems, and follow up to ensure that they have been corrected. The manager is responsible for the budget; if funds for problem correction and training materials programs are needed, for example, they should be allocated.

Fortunately, hoteliers in properties of all sizes have access to **Occupational Safety and Health Administration (OSHA)** information and education materials.

LODGING LANGUAGE

Occupational Safety and Health Administration (OSHA): An agency of the U.S. Department of Labor which administers programs/regulations designed to provide a safe/healthful workplace for employees.

■

LODGING ON-LINE

The federal government's OSHA Web site provides valuable background information as well as updates about its efforts at safety regulation. To review this site, go to:

www.OSHA.gov

Hotels may have safety committees at two organizational levels: department groups concerned with issues applicable to their responsibilities, and a property-wide group concerned with issues that all affect all departments, such as fires and natural disasters. In larger properties, a member of the human resources department will likely serve on this committee.

A variety of health (wellness) issues can affect hotel employees. Examples include:

- Developing and selecting programs to help employees cope with stress.
- Developing procedures that address concerns about violence in the workplace.
- Communicating updated information about the human immunodeficiency virus (HIV; the virus that causes AIDS) in the workplace.
- Providing information about and helping to resolve problems relative to cumulative trauma disorders. These include repetitive motion injuries such as carpal tunnel syndrome suffered by some workers.

DIVERSITY AND THE LODGING INDUSTRY

The concept of **diversity** in the workforce receives much attention in the hospitality industry and especially in the hotel industry.

LODGING LANGUAGE

Diversity (Workforce): The range of differences in attitudes, values, and behaviors of employees relative to gender, race, age, ethnicity, physical ability, and other relevant characteristics.

■

The United States has historically been a "melting pot" of people from many different countries. The culture of the United States has always been diverse and is becoming even more so. One result is that the composition of the workforce, including employees in the hotel industry, is increasingly female, African-American, Hispanic, and Asian. The percentage of Anglo-American males who make up the hotel industry's workforce will likely continue to decrease in coming years.

You have learned that it is illegal for employers to discriminate against employees or others on the basis of race, color, religion, sex, or national origin. You also know that people with disabilities who are seeking employment cannot be discriminated against. Therefore, the hotel industry will have an increasingly diverse workforce—first, because the employee market itself is diverse, and second, because it is illegal to exclude people from employment consideration.

Historically, the hotel industry has employed many women and other minorities for entry-level positions. Some are promoted and assume very responsible and well-paying positions at the highest level of hotel properties and in multi-unit hotel organizations, including service on boards of directors. However, as a percentage of the total positions at these levels, the number of women is still relatively small. Increasingly, hotel organizations are developing and implementing diversity programs because it is the right thing to do, and because it makes good business sense.

What are the advantages to a lodging organization that actively recruits and promotes employees with diverse backgrounds? Research-based data on this question is scarce for the hospitality industry, but proponents of diversity initiatives frequently cite the following benefits:

- The organization's corporate culture is more open to change. It is, therefore, better able to recognize the need for changes required by the evolving marketplace and can implement them.
- A larger base of potential employees and more success in recruiting qualified applicants.
- Better relationships with guests and more opportunities for increased business—more guests of diverse backgrounds will be able to identify with employees, and staff members can more effectively interpret their needs and deliver a wider range of the products and services they desired.
- Higher retention rates for employees.
- Decreased guest complaints.
- Reduced possibilities of litigation.
- Greater ability to increase market share in emerging markets.
- Improved decision-making due to a more diverse range of creative alternatives generated to address operating challenges.
- Improved hotel reputation and image within the community and, for multi-unit organizations, within a region and/or the entire country.

Properly planned valuing-diversity efforts are not programs; rather, they are basic, ongoing changes in the hotel's organizational culture that are integrated into "the way things are done" at the property or company.

Strategies that can be useful in developing and implementing diversity initiatives include those relating to:

- Educational programs at all employee levels, including the highest in the organization, that address valuing-diversity issues.

- An emphasis on employing, training, and promoting the best employees from the diverse groups of staff members who work at the hotel.
- Emphasizing ownership by minority franchisees in multi-unit companies. This can include offering financial assistance to new minority franchisees and helping to match new franchisees with potential lenders.
- Advertising and marketing efforts directed toward minority markets.
- Interactions with minority vendors to increase the purchase of their products and services that meet the property's quality and cost requirements.
- Including minority organizations in the charitable activities of the hotel.

Diversity training activities are an integral part of a hotel's implementation efforts and must be developed for each specific organization. All employees at all organizational levels should participate in the training. For example, entry-level staff should know the basics of equality and develop respect for diverse cultures. Managers must know about diversity details when hiring employees and understand the basics of equal employment opportunity laws.

Hotels with a successful diversity emphasis do not merely have hiring quotas in place. Instead, they establish measurable goals, reward staff for attaining them, and continually improve their diversity implementation efforts because they know it is good for their business as well as their community.

HUMAN RESOURCES CHALLENGES

Near-term human resources activities in hotels of all sizes will probably continue to focus on staffing for currently vacant positions. However, managers should find ways to reduce employee turnover levels so that the need for ongoing and extensive recruitment and selection efforts will be lessened.

Over the longer term, numerous other human resources activities will become important and will become markers of the best-operated properties. These include:

- *Helping motivated employees to become more proficient in their jobs.* This occurs as managers emphasize empowerment. Employees who are informed about the hotel's goals and objectives can use their own decision-making abilities to best meet the needs of the hotel's guests.

- *Providing professional development opportunities.* Hotel managers should provide ongoing opportunities for their employees to gain additional job-related knowledge and skills which can lead to progressively more responsibilities, higher-level jobs, and the higher compensation that accompanies those jobs. Employees appreciate managers who provide them with the knowledge, skills, and resources necessary to be successful on the job. They will also have pride and joy in knowing that they are respected and trusted. Little things of this kind, in total, can enable the hotel to retain the best-possible employees available to meet the wants and needs of its guests.

- *Cultural diversity.* Managers and employees should be educated about the numerous professional, personal, and societal advantages that arise when the worth of all employees is recognized and rewarded without regard to gender or race.

ALL IN A DAY'S WORK

The Situation

Anita Fulton, the general manager of a 70-room limited-service hotel, was chatting with Phyllis Dewey, the human resources director of a large hotel in the city. They were both attending a conference sponsored by their state's lodging association.

"I am glad I graduated from law school and became an attorney," said Phyllis, "Seventy-five percent or more of my time is spent trying to understand, interpret, and communicate labor-related laws to my general manager and to our department heads. Also, I don't know what I would do if I didn't have access to the corporate-level human resources specialists in our chain. I am afraid I would be giving lots of wrong information to lots of people, and that would really put my hotel in jeopardy."

"Yes," said Anita, "work in the hotel industry can be fun, but it does have its challenges."

On the drive home from the conference, Anita thought to herself about her conversation with Phyllis. "Phyllis works full-time on human resources issues. She is an attorney and directs the work of several specialists. In addition, she has access to other experts in her corporate offices. By contrast, I am by myself. I don't have legal training. I have many other responsibilities besides those dealing with employment issues. If I want help, I need to pay for it. I really don't think I feel sorry for Phyllis!"

A Response

Anita is right. In small properties like hers, there are no staff specialists to assist in areas where technical expertise would be helpful. She runs a one-person operation and must be an expert on all areas of the hotel. How can Anita learn about and keep up with labor laws? How can she be confident that the procedures she uses for employee selection and workplace management are appropriate? How does she find time to train her staff in these techniques once she learns them herself? How does she get her managers to consistently follow policies and procedures designed to meet legal requirements? The answers to these tough questions involve the need for her to keep attending professional development sessions; her attendance at the lodging conference where she talked with Phyllis is an example. She must also keep current by reading trade magazines and by networking with her peers in other lodging properties. Knowing when to consult an expert (even though she must pay for it) is also important, and she should do so when, for example, application forms, employee handbooks, and policies relating to harassment and scheduling minors are developed.

Anita knows that the world of hotel management is exciting, in part, because it demands a significant amount of knowledge about a wide variety of concerns, including those relating to human resources. Her interest in and enthusiasm about all aspects of hotel operations help make her an effective manager.

- *Quality improvement.* Managers must plan and implement an ongoing total quality effort, including continuous quality improvement (CQI) to meet the property's goals and to become more competitive.
- *Employer of choice.* General managers must work with all the other managers to develop an organizational culture that helps the hotel become an employer of choice within the community. As this occurs, more and better applicants will be attracted to the hotel, retention rates will increase, and the resulting more highly motivated employees will contribute their ideas and efforts in an effort to make the hotel successful.

CHAPTER OBJECTIVES REVIEW

If you have successfully studied the material in this chapter, you should be prepared to:

1. Explain the importance of the human resources department in a hotel. (Objective 1)
2. Explain the tactics that should be used when recruiting, selecting, orienting, and training hotel employees. (Objective 2)

3. Review the importance of fair and equitable compensation for hotel employees, explain how this goal can be achieved, and describe the fringe benefits that may be available to hotel employees. (Objective 3)
4. Review the legal aspects of human resources as they relate to employee selection, employer-employee relationships, and other workplace laws. (Objective 4)
5. Explain how a hotel's general manager can promote employee safety and health within the property. (Objective 5)
6. Recall five human resource challenges with which general managers must deal. (Objective 6).

LODGING LANGUAGE

Human Resources Department
Staff (Hotel Departments)
HR
Line Departments
Line Managers
Executive Committee
Recruitment
Unemployment Rate
Stereotype
Internal Recruiting
External Recruiting
Job Description
Selection
Warm Body Syndrome

Job Specification
Orientation
Induction
Employee Handbook
Back-door Marketing
Compensation
Salary
Wage
Fringe Benefits
Bonafide Occupational
    Qualifications (BOQs)
Interstate Commerce
At-Will Employment
Employment Agreement

Offer Letter
Zero Tolerance
Minimum Wage
Overtime
Social Security
Medicare
Progressive Discipline System
Unemployment Insurance
Unemployment Claim
Safety Hazards
Health Hazards
Occupational Safety and Health
    Administration (OSHA)
Diversity (Workforce)

FOR DISCUSSION

1. Many hospitality students try not to start their careers at limited-service hotels. Why do you think that is the case?
2. The concept of "employer of choice" was addressed in this chapter. What are some things that you as a hotel manager could do to encourage your department heads to help establish an organizational culture that addresses your employees' wants and needs?
3. Staff members at all organizational levels are usually most concerned about their compensation (salaries, wages and fringe benefits). These costs are significant for the hotel. How exactly would you determine fair levels of salaries and wages from the perspectives of both the hotel and its employees?
4. There was extensive discussion about legal aspects of human resources in this chapter. What can you as a general manager do to help keep your hotel in compliance with all of the laws and regulations applicable to your property?
5. Assume you are the newly retained department head in a hotel that does not offer a property-wide train-the-trainer program for those who will conduct training. How would you sell the need for this program to the general manager?
6. Assume that the hotel general manager has given you, a department head in the property, a special project to identify all the topics that should be addressed in an orientation program for new employees. Make a list of the topics you would submit to the general manager.

7. Review the list of employee benefits found in Figure 6.2. Which ones would be important to you when you begin your professional career in a hotel? Which benefits would be important to you after you have 25 years of experience in the hotel industry? Are there any differences?

8. The chapter notes that general managers in small properties without human resources departments must still keep up with the ever-changing laws relating to employment. If you were the general manager in a small property, what tactics would you use to keep your property in compliance with current laws and regulations?

9. What are your views about the concept of at-will employment described in this chapter? Provide your responses from the perspectives of both an employer (the hotel manager) and an employee.

10. Name one policy that you as a hotel employee would like to have in a property where you worked. Name one that you would not want to have. (*Note:* If you recall your responses to this question when you are a manager, you will probably have an indication of policies/procedures that your staff members do and do not like.)

TEAM ACTIVITIES

Team Activity 1

Have teams develop procedures for a progressive discipline system that you would use in your hotel. What special concerns must be addressed to ensure that all the legal issues are considered? Discuss each team's response.

Team Activity 2

Have each team list ten creative tactics that a general manager or department head in a small limited-service property could use to recruit entry-level employees for a hotel. Contrast the effectiveness of each team's list.

7

The Front Office Department

Chapter Objectives

1. To explain the main activities that occur in a hotel's front office.
2. To describe the process of forecasting hotel demand and establishing room rates.
3. To review the major sources of hotel reservations.
4. To explain the role of the front desk before, during, and after a guest checks into the hotel.
5. To examine how the front office manages guest and hotel data, including the night audit.

Chapter Outline

FRONT OFFICE RESPONSIBILITIES
  PMS Management
  Guest Services
  Accounting and Data Management
FORECASTING DEMAND
  The Effect of Demand on ADR
  Estimating Demand
  Use of the PMS in Forecasting Demand
ESTABLISHING ROOM RATES
  Yield Management
  Transient Rates
  Group Rates
RESERVATIONS
  Hotel Direct Inquiry

Central Reservations System
Internet Booking Site
RECEPTION AND GUEST SERVICE
  Pre-arrival
  Arrival and Stay
  Departure
GUEST ACCOUNTING
  Data Management
    Movies
    Games
    Safes
    Internet Connections
  Night Audit

177

Overview: The Front Office Department

The front office area in a hotel includes a registration desk where guests check in and check out, but the managers and staff of the front office do much more than that. They assist in, or are responsible for, several important hotel functions, each of which is analyzed in detail in this chapter.

For many guests, the only person they will actually see when they check in or out of a hotel is a member of the front office. For that reason, the employees who work at the front office are critical to a hotel's long-term success.

Because the rooms sold by a hotel are extremely perishable (that is, a guest room left unsold on one night can never again be sold on that night), it is very important that hotels do the best job possible in matching guest room availability with guest room demand. In addition, since it is not possible to increase or decrease the number of rooms available to sell each day (because the hotel was constructed with a fixed number of rooms), an important responsibility of the front office is to sell rooms at an ADR that management feels will maximize total revenue. An aggressively managed and talented front office staff will do this well.

The making of guest reservations is often the first thing that comes to mind when one considers the main functions of a front office, and this is an essential and often complex aspect of its role. In addition to reservations, however, it is up to the front office to assign arriving guests to specific guest rooms and to respond to their special needs during their stay. These needs can include anything from transportation and information to medical assistance. In all of these situations and many others, the unwavering role of the front office is to make the guest's stay as comfortable and as welcoming as possible.

In addition to servicing guests, another essential task of the front office is its responsibility for collecting the money guests pay for their rooms. This means that the individual responsible for the front office must devise and administer revenue management systems that charge guests the right amount for the services they use, and that the hotel collects in full, and keeps secure, all the money it has earned.

When forecasting room demand, accommodating guests, and collecting monies for services rendered, the front office generates a large amount of information, much of which is critical for management decision-making. It is the role of the front office to collect, sort, and maintain this information and data in ways that assist in management decision-making. In this chapter, you will learn how that is done.

FRONT OFFICE RESPONSIBILITIES

The **front office** is sometimes referred to as the **front desk**, but it involves much more than just the activities occurring at the front desk. In a smaller, limited-service hotel, the front office may consist, physically, of only the area reserved for guest registration. In a larger property, the front office may include several staff members, each responsible for a portion of its management or operation.

LODGING LANGUAGE

Front Office: The area within the hotel responsible for guest reservations, registration, service, and payment.

Front Desk: The area within the hotel used for guest registration and payment.

■

The front desk in a hotel will be managed either directly by the general manager or, in a larger property, by an **FOM**.

LODGING LANGUAGE

FOM: The hotel industry term for a front office manager.

■

The front office is responsible for three very important duties:

- Management of the **PMS**
- Guest Services
- Accounting

LODGING LANGUAGE

PMS: The hotel industry term for a "property management system."

■

In smaller properties, these duties overlap. In fact, in a very small limited-service property, one person may perform all of these tasks and more. For the purpose of fully understanding these important responsibilities, however, it will be useful to take a brief look at each as illustrated in Figure 7.1. This will be followed by a more detailed examination of how these functions interrelate in a properly functioning front office.

PMS Management

The property management system is truly the heart of the front office. Its effective management is critical to a well-run property. The PMS is the computerized system used by a hotel to manage its rooms revenue, room rates, reservations and room assignments, guest histories, and accounting information as well as other selected guest service and management information functions. A simple PMS will have limited features, while more extensive (and expensive) systems offer hoteliers a wide range of management information features. Essentially, however, every PMS records (a) who is coming to the hotel, (b) what they spend when they are there, and (c) the form of payment used upon departure.

The management of a PMS entails understanding and using the system's preprogrammed features. The individual responsible for maintaining the PMS should be knowledgeable about all of its features. When a hotel is not affiliated with a franchisor, it selects and maintains its own PMS. In such cases, training on the system is often provided by the manufacturer of the PMS. When a hotel is franchised, the

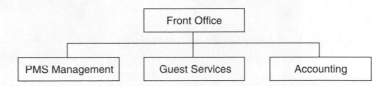

FIGURE 7.1 Three Functions of the Front Office

franchisor most often mandates the PMS to be used and conducts regular training sessions about its operation.

PMS systems, like any other piece of electronic equipment, require care and maintenance. Imagine for example, the problems that would occur if, one hour before many guests were to check in on a sold-out night, the PMS crashed, making it impossible for the front desk staff to ascertain the names of the guests who were coming to the hotel, the room types these guests had requested, and the room rates they were to pay. It happens but can often be avoided by proper PMS maintenance. Because a PMS consists of a hardware component and a software component, both must be of concern to the front office staff.

Management of the hardware requires that the front office staff keep the computer equipment clean and free of dust. Cables connecting PC workstations to the main computer should be examined periodically and replaced as needed. The source of power to the system should be managed and surge-protected so that unanticipated power surges do not affect the continued operation of the system. Any installed **back-up system** hardware related to the PMS should also be inspected and tested on a regular basis.

LODGING LANGUAGE

Back-up System: Redundant hardware and/or software operated in parallel to the system it serves. Used in times of failure or power outages, such systems are often operated on batteries. For example, a back-up system to the hotel's telephones would enable outside calling even if the main digital telephone system were to shut down.

The modern hotel PMS is a sophisticated and powerful management tool that can, in some cases, be accessed directly by guests.

While hardware problems sometimes occur, most frequently it is a software-related problem that causes PMS difficulties. Often, because the PMS is connected by a modem to the PMS's software support organization, repair can be achieved simply by calling PMS software support. In fact, one of the primary features separating outstanding PMS systems from less effective ones is the system's level and availability of software support.

Guest Services

The front office is responsible for a variety of guest services. These include the welcome guests receive when they arrive at the hotel to check in, as well as services related to their stay. Remember that for most guests the front office staff will be their only contact with hotel employees. The employees of the front office must be highly trained and ready to assist in a variety of guest-related requests for services. Some of these services can be:

- Transportation to and from an airport
- Handling luggage
- Providing directions to attractions within the local area
- Taking guest messages
- Routing mail
- Newspaper delivery
- Management of safety deposit boxes
- Arranging wake-up calls
- Providing for guest security by the careful dissemination of guest-related information
- Handling guests' concerns and disputes

Depending on the location of the hotel and the services it offers, these guest service functions may be attended to by any of the individuals employed at the front desk. In a larger property with more activity, some of these guest services may have a specific individual assigned only to that task. In all cases, guests will return to a hotel with a friendly helpful staff, but may not return to a hotel with poorly trained or indifferent front office staff.

Accounting and Data Management

The front desk is an important area within a hotel that is responsible for gathering and reporting financial information. In Chapter 9, we will examine hotel accounting functions in detail. In this chapter, we will review the front office responsibilities for managing important financial and personal data related to guests. This data includes reservations, charges, payments, and money due to be paid to the hotel. In addition, we will also look at the important role played by the **night audit** and the work of the hotel's **night auditor**.

LODGING LANGUAGE

Night Audit: The process of reviewing for accuracy and completeness the accounting transactions from one day to conclude, or "close," that day's sales information in preparation for recording the transactions of the next day.

Night Auditor: The individual who performs the daily review of all the financial transactions with hotel guests recorded by the front office.

■

Some hotels maintain a great deal of information (data) about their guests, while others do not. The nature of the hotel business, however, requires that the front office personnel be skilled in their work, because the intricacies of the financial transactions that must be recorded by the front office can be complex. For example, assume that four men traveling to a hotel to attend a softball tournament share a room for two nights. Upon departure, each wants to pay his share of the **folio**'s balance.

LODGING LANGUAGE

Folio: Detailed list of a hotel guest's room charges as well as other charges authorized by the guest or legally imposed by the hotel.

■

One man wishes to pay with cash, one with a check, one with a credit card, and another with a debit card. As can be seen, even the simplest of transactions can get complex, but the front office must ensure that all guest folios are properly processed and recorded. Additional accounting or data management tasks that must be completed by the front office include maintaining an accurate list, by room number, of guest room occupants, verifying the accuracy of the room rates charged to guests, and confirming checkout dates.

Data management is an extremely important front office function. Some of this data relates to guests, and some relates to the effective management of the hotel. The amount of data processed in a hotel is large and growing larger each year. An effective front office manager in a U.S. hotel in the pre-computer 1930s would, very likely, have kept a record of a specific guest's preferences for room location, type of bed (double or king-sized) preferred, and the like. This information would have been written down by hand and referred to when that specific guest reserved a room or checked into the hotel. Today's professionally managed front office would have such information, and much more, available through the features of the hotel's PMS. Today, even the smallest computerized hotel would know, at the very least:

- The date of the guest's last stay
- The guest's address, telephone number, and credit or debit card information
- The room rate paid and **room type** occupied by the guest during the last stay
- A history of the guest's prior folio charges
- The form of payment used by the guest to settle his or her account with the hotel
- The guest's membership in groups receiving a discount from the hotel
- The guest's company affiliation
- The guest's room-type preferences

Depending upon the sophistication of the PMS, even more data on individual guests may be secured and maintained by the front office staff.

LODGING LANGUAGE

Room Type: Specific configurations of guest rooms. For example, smoking vs. non-smoking, king-sized bed vs. double beds, or suite vs. regular sleeping room. Commonly abbreviated (K for king, NS for non-smoking, etc.), the hotel's reserving of the proper room type is often as important to guests as whether the hotel, in fact, has a room available for them.

■

In addition to maintaining data on individual guests, the front office collects and evaluates information related to the hotel's operation. Some guest-related examples include the tracking of guest telephone calls (including those that are complimentary and those for which the hotel imposes a charge), the viewing of in-room movies for which there is a charge, and updating the clean or dirty status of rooms. This is necessary to ensure that a guest checking into the hotel is assigned a room that has been cleaned.

FORECASTING DEMAND

One of the most important questions an effective front office must be able to answer is, upon first examination, very simple. That question is: *How many rooms will the hotel sell tonight?*

The question is much more complex than it appears. For example, a hotel with 100 rooms available to sell forecasts that 50 rooms will be sold on a given night. It would seem that this hotel is prepared to house the guests it anticipates. If, however, the hotel has only 25 rooms with king-sized beds, and if 30 rooms of this type have been reserved, the front office staff will not be able to accommodate all of the guests who reserved a room with a king-sized bed. Similarly, if the hotel has 25 rooms in which smoking is permitted, but 30 of them are reserved, the hotel would, again, be unable to meet the requests of all the guests.

Before any guest can be properly and profitably checked into a hotel, the front office staff will have accomplished a great many important tasks. The most critical of these, however, are forecasting the demand for guest rooms, establishing room rates, and making guest reservations.

The Effect of Demand on ADR

In Chapter 1, we examined briefly how the number of guests requesting hotel rooms affects a hotel's average daily rate (ADR). As the demand for guest rooms in a given area increases, you will recall, the ADR charged for rooms typically increases as well. As a result, one of the most important roles played by the front office is that of maximizing the hotel's revenue per available room (**RevPar**).

LODGING LANGUAGE

RevPar: "Revenue Per Available Room"; the average revenue generated by each of a hotel's guest rooms during a specific time period. The formula for RevPar is:

Occupancy % (x) ADR = RevPar

■

RevPar is a simple computation of A (×) B = C

Where:

A = Occupancy %

B = Average Daily Rate (ADR)

C = Revenue Per Available Room (RevPar)

Thus:

Occupancy % (×) Average Daily Rate = RevPar

For example, in a hotel with an occupancy rate of 70 percent, and an ADR of $90, RevPar would be:

$$(70 \text{ \%}) (\times) (\$90.00) = \$63.00$$

Put another way, each of the hotel's rooms generated, on average, $63 each day for the period being evaluated. RevPar can be computed on a daily, weekly, monthly, or even annual basis. Mathematically, when a hotel's occupancy rate increases, RevPar increases. In a similar manner, when ADR increases, RevPar also increases. Thus, to improve RevPar, the goal must be to increase the occupancy rate and/or the ADR. It is the job of the front office to help the hotel achieve one or both of these goals.

Properly forecasting guest demand for hotel rooms is important for two reasons. The first is that hotel rooms can be sold for a higher price when the hotel knows that demand for its rooms will be greater. Second, increased demand for rooms means that more rooms will be sold. As a result, both occupancy and ADR for a hotel will increase during a time of heavy demand for rooms. When this occurs, RevPar for the hotel will increase, as will the hotel's profitability.

Sporting events can have a major effect on demand for hotel rooms in the area where the event is held.

Estimating Demand

The daily demand for hotel rooms, even in the same geographic area, varies greatly. This is a reality and the challenge faced by all hotel managers. Imagine, for example, the difference in demand for hotel rooms in Indianapolis, on the day before the Indianapolis 500 race (traditionally a **sell-out** period for the entire Indianapolis area) and on the Wednesday night before Thanksgiving (traditionally a very slow day for business travel of all types).

LODGING LANGUAGE

Sell-out: (1) A situation in which all rooms are sold. A hotel, area, or entire city may, if demand is strong enough, sell out. (2) A period of time in which management must attempt to maximize ADR.

■

The point to remember is that a front office manager must know when there is strong demand for the hotel's rooms—that is, what special events, group activities, holidays, or other factors will influence room demand. To maximize RevPar, the hotel's management staff must attempt to drive (increase) ADR when the demand for rooms is high and to increase occupancy (by offering lower rates) when demand is low. Both of these strategies, if successfully implemented, will have the effect of increasing RevPar, and both strategies depend on the ability of the front office team to forecast room demand.

To illustrate the importance of forecasting demand, imagine a hotel in a college town. Five times per year, the college's football team plays a home game. Traditionally, attendance at the games enables all area hotels to sellout at a high ADR. The importance of knowing the dates of these games as far into the future as possible, so that sales-related hotel staff will not inadvertently sell rooms on those dates for a low rate, is evident.

Many hotels find that the demand for their rooms varies on a weekly basis, regardless of special events that may be held in the area. Hotels that primarily service business travelers, for example, generally find that Tuesday or Wednesday is the day when demand for their rooms is greatest. Hotels that service leisure travelers will likely find that weekends generate the most business. To summarize, the proper forecasting of demand requires that the front office:

- Keep accurate historical records to understand past demand and its possible impact on future demand
- Know about special events or circumstances that will affect future room demand

In all cases, the front office must be able to forecast the demand for rooms well enough to allow the hotel to effectively price its rooms and maximize its RevPar.

Use of the PMS in Forecasting Demand

Forecasting hotel demand is very difficult without the use of a properly functioning, up-to-date PMS. For some hotels, the date of an annual occasion such as a holiday, sporting event, graduation, or concert may be known well in advance. The staff of the front office, by reviewing past hotel records, can estimate the demand for guest rooms during these events. Details of past information, however, are only readily accessible by using a computerized PMS. As stated earlier in this text, most franchise companies mandate that the franchisee use the franchisor-approved PMS. For independent hoteliers, there are a variety of PMS systems on the market. If a PMS is effective:

1. *Information will be easily accessible.* This is an absolute necessity. It has been said that there are managers who know what happened in the past and others who know what is happening now. The best front office management staff, however, must also know what will happen in the future. The ability of a hotel to forecast is greatest when those responsible for the front office know about the past, present, and future demand for their rooms.

    To compete effectively in today's hotel environment, all front office staff members must have the ability to access rapidly the **historical data** they need to forecast properly. In addition, the **guest history** of individual guests must be easily accessible. When a PMS is too advanced or complicated for easy use by the hotel employees who will be using it, problems related to the inability to acquire timely data will occur.

LODGING LANGUAGE

Historical Data: Information related to the stays of past guests. Collectively, this information details the history of all past hotel guests.

Guest History: Information related to the past stay(s) of one guest.

■

The readily accessible historical data in a PMS should include:
- How many rooms were sold during a specific date or time period(s?)
- Who stayed at the hotel during that time?
- What room type did they occupy?
- What room rate were they charged?
- When did they make their reservation?

Unless front office staff members can rely on the PMS to supply answers readily to questions like these, the hotel's forecasting ability will be greatly diminished.

2. *It will be compatible with Windows office products.* This is related to the preceding item. Most of the computer-literate staff members employed by hotels today will be familiar only with the Microsoft Corporation's automated office products, including Word for word processing and Excel for the creation of spreadsheets. Because Microsoft commands 90 percent or more of the office products market, the use of a PMS that reports data to the front office in these familiar forms is essential.

    Most hotels today use Microsoft Word for mailing correspondence, including marketing letters, Microsoft Excel for financial and spreadsheet analysis, and Microsoft Access for data base management.

3. *Internet connectivity will be easy.* The ability to easily connect to the Internet, while not a standard in PMS equipment as recently as ten years ago, is now a critical requirement. There is so much data on the Internet, and its use is so pervasive, that all PMS equipment and software must provide access to it if a front office is to forecast room demand properly.

LODGING ON-LINE

Microsoft office products in the Windows format have become the standard in the hotel industry. To view the wide range of these business tools available to hoteliers, go to:

www.microsoft.com

When you arrive, click on "Office" listed under "Product Families."

---

4. *A strong revenue management component will be included.* An effective PMS will include an advanced **revenue management (RM)** program. This program is used to help the hotel forecast room demand because it will have been designed for that very purpose. Some systems have very sophisticated and detailed features that can readily be used by a **revenue manager**, while others take a less complex approach. While there is sometimes a fine line between having enough options and having too many, the revenue management component of a PMS must at least be equal to the forecasting abilities of the front office staff.

LODGING LANGUAGE

Revenue Management (RM): The process and procedures used to maximize RevPar. Sometimes referred to as RM for short.

Revenue Manager: An individual whose major task consists of forecasting room demand so that the hotel can maximize RevPar. In larger hotels, this will be a full-time position. In a smaller, limited-service property, the general manager or front office manager will have this responsibility.

∎

ALL IN A DAY'S WORK

The Situation

"I can't believe it!" said Mike Rice, the general manager of the hotel, as he reviewed the report.

"Believe it," replied Dani Pelley, front desk clerk on the a.m. shift.

It was 9:30 a.m. and Dani had printed, as she always did, a reservation activity report for the prior 24 hours. The PMS provided such reports easily, and upon further investigation Dani had discovered that Karl (a desk clerk working the night audit shift) had sold 75 of the hotel's 90 rooms to one guest, for a Saturday night date nine months in the future. Because the guest had wanted to buy so many rooms, Karl had given the guest a 20 percent discount on each room reserved.

"That's the day State University holds its graduation this year," said Mike.

"Right," replied Dani. "We've sold out the hotel every State University graduation for the past four years. And always at a rate higher than our normal ADR. This year, Karl has basically sold out the hotel already, but our ADR compared to last year will be awful!"

A Response

It is too late for Mike to do now what should clearly have been done earlier. As soon as management is aware that a specific future date is both a high-demand date and is available for staff members to sell, room rates for that date should be adjusted in the PMS to reflect the desired rate. In addition, during a high-demand date such as the one identified here, normally allowable discounts for room purchases should be eliminated or reduced. In this case, unfortunately, the hotel will be legally required to honor the guest's reservations, but in the future, it must improve the timeliness of its demand forecasting process.

ESTABLISHING ROOM RATES

Perhaps no task of the front office is more important than the timely establishment of room rates that help the hotel to maximize RevPar. In a larger hotel, this task may be assigned to a director of sales and marketing, a revenue manager, or some other staff person. In a limited service hotel, however, the task will generally fall to the general manager or the front office manager.

After a hotel has done a good job of identifying when demand for its rooms will be greatest, the general manager or the front office manager can implement yield management to establish both transient and group room rates.

Yield Management

Yield management is a revenue enhancement concept that originated in the airline industry. Today it is used by the car rental, cruise line, and lodging industries as well as other industries that sell a commodity, like a hotel room, that cannot be carried over in inventory if it remains unsold on a given day. The actual methods utilized to forecast demand and thus establish yield management strategies are many and are as varied as the individuals operating hotels.

To illustrate the yield management concept, assume that a hotel sells its rooms for $150 per night at **rack rate**.

LODGING LANGUAGE

Rack Rate: The price at which a hotel sells its rooms when no discounts of any kind are offered to the guest. Often shortened to "rack."

■

It is appropriate to sell at "rack" when the hotel is confident that the demand for hotel rooms will be greater than the supply. In other words, when the forecast says that all, or nearly all, rooms will be sold, it is not necessary to discount the rooms to help ensure their sale. When demand for rooms is less than the number of rooms available to sell, discounts are typically offered.

To illustrate, assume that a hotel with a $150 rack rate routinely offers discounts plans of 10 percent, 20 percent, and 30 percent off the rack rate based on forecasted demand. When demand is very light, discounts as high as 30 percent off rack are offered to maximize occupancy rates. When demand is stronger, the hotel only offers discounts of 20 percent, 10 percent, or, in cases where the demand for rooms equals or exceeds supply, no discount at all.

In a high demand period, guests requesting reservations carrying 30 percent discounts are told that such discounts are not available, and the hotel would not accept their reservation request. On another, lower-demand date, however, the same request for a reservation at the 30 percent discount rate would, indeed, be accepted. The opening and closing of discounted rates is the core activity of yield management, and a person who does it well is effective in this task. Figure 7.2 is an example of a strategy that might be employed by the hotel used in the above example to manage the yield from the sale of rooms on a given night:

Sophisticated users of this strategy are likely to employ highly advanced and often complex methods of managing yield. Some techniques for this purpose may be

Forecasted Room Demand	Rate Strategy
90–100 % occupancy	Offer no discounts
70–90 % occupancy	Offer discounts up to 10%
50–70% occupancy	Offer discounts up to 20%
Less than 50% occupancy	Offer discounts up to 30% or more

FIGURE 7.2   Yield Management Strategy Based on Room Demand

included in a property's PMS, but individuals operating a specific hotel may develop their own techniques.

Just as RevPar maximization is related to managing ADR, it is also related to managing occupancy percentage. Perhaps the most well known, but least understood method of managing occupancy is the practice of **overbooking** the hotel. Any discussion on over-booking must begin with a simple truth. That truth is: *No experienced hotelier would ever knowingly take a reservation for a room that is not going to be available for the guest upon arrival.*

LODGING LANGUAGE

Overbooking: A situation in which the hotel has more guest reservations for rooms than it has rooms available to lodge those guests. Sometimes referred to as "oversold."

■

There are at least two reasons this is true. First, in an overbooked situation, a guest with a reservation who arrives to find that the hotel has no room available is inevitably, and correctly so, angry. No professional hotelier wants to make guests angry! Second, from a financial point of view, it will be expensive to relocate the guest. This is true because, in most cases, the hotel that has **walked** a guest must pay for, at the least:

- Transportation to/from an alternative property
- Telephone calls made by the guest to inform those who need to know about the alternative lodging accommodations
- The cost of the first night's room charges at the alternative hotel

---

LODGING LANGUAGE

Walked: A situation in which a guest with a reservation is relocated from the reserved hotel to another hotel because no room was available at the reserved hotel.

■

Why then do hotels overbook? Sometimes it is an error on the part of the hotel. This would be the case, for example, if a guest reservation was made, but mistakenly not recorded in the PMS. Sometimes, however, an experienced manager, practicing yield management, intentionally accepts more reservations than the hotel can accommodate because the manager wants to completely fill the hotel and anticipates that one or more of the guests who have reservations will be a **no-show**.

LODGING LANGUAGE

No-show: A guest who makes a room reservation but fails to cancel it or does not arrive at the hotel on the date of the confirmed reservation (see Figure 7.3).

■

For example, in a 100-room hotel that experiences a typical 5 percent no-show rate, the sale of 101 rooms on a given night, while technically overbooking the hotel, is not likely to result in a guest being walked. This is so because on an average sold-out night, 5 percent (5 rooms) of the guests who were supposed to arrive will not do so.

Since the hotel only overbooked by 1 percent (1 room), the number of no-shows (5) will, on average, exceed the number of rooms overbooked (1).

LODGING ON-LINE

Each of the major credit/ debit card issuers helps businesses with issues like no-show charges. To review one such company's resources, go to:

www.mastercardmerchant.com

When you arrive, under "Quick Links," select "For Your Industry," then "Lodging," to see how these cards are utilized by businesses such as individual hotels.

No-shows are not unique to the hotel business. Restaurants, airlines, and rental car agencies are just a few of the businesses that must also manage their reservations while knowing that a certain percentage of those reserving will not show up to claim their product or service. If the hotel's total reservation management plan is too conservative (for example, it does not factor in no-shows), rooms will go unsold even on sell-out nights. If it is too aggressive (it factors in large numbers of no-shows), too many guests with confirmed reservations will arrive at the hotel. These guests will, inevitably, need to be walked and, just as inevitably, will be upset. Therefore, this situation must be avoided whenever possible.

Transient Rates

While much has been written about yield management, some of what is said is overly simplistic. It implies that hoteliers can eliminate discounts on rooms during busy periods with no long-term impact on the hotel's regular guests. That is simply

---

While PMS systems vary somewhat, front desk staff should be instructed on the proper procedure for billing a no-show guest. In general, the following steps are required:
- Create or select a "room" in the PMS called "No Show"
- Check the no-show guest into that room
- Charge one night's room charge to the room
- Charge the room payment to guest's credit or debit card
- Finalize payment and ensure that a zero balance is now due
- Check the guest out of the room
- Record the no-show charge

FIGURE 7.3   Charging a No-Show

not true. Consider, for example, the case of Hosea Gamez. Mr. Gamez stays every Tuesday through Thursday at the Sleep Well Hotel. His room rate is the hotel's normal **corporate rate**. One week, the hotel's staff forecasts great demand for its rooms and decides to eliminate all discount programs, (including corporate rates) and will sell its rooms only at rack rate for that week.

LODGING LANGUAGE

Corporate Rate: The rate a hotel charges to its typical business traveler. This rate is normally 5–20 percent below the hotel's rack rate.

Understandably, Mr. Gamez may be quite upset with the hotel's decision. In fact, if he is charged a higher than normal rate for his room during this busy week, he may decide to look elsewhere for a room in future weeks when the hotel is not forecasted to be so busy. If, in fact, he stays at another hotel and likes it, the Sleep Well may have lost a good customer. The lesson here is clear; hotels must practice yield management but must also be aware that there may be some individual, regular guests whose room rates must be considered on a case-by-case basis. While the rates for typical **transient** travelers can indeed be yield-managed, care must be taken when yield-managing the rates of corporate travelers as well as some other large-volume room buyers. This concept is so important that some franchisors do not allow hotels to eliminate the discounts offered to corporate travelers (and selected others) except in the rarest of cases.

Government employees are a large part of the transient market.

LODGING LANGUAGE

Transient: Individual guests who are not part of a group or tour booking. Transient guests can be further subdivided by traveler demographics to obtain more detailed information about the type of guest staying in the hotel (for example, corporate, leisure, and government).

■

Good front office employees are well-trained in knowing which of the hotel's transient travelers retain their regular, **non-yieldable** room rates even during very busy times for the hotel.

LODGING LANGUAGE

Non-yieldable: A discounted room rate that continues to be offered even when a hotel has implemented a yield management strategy. Examples may include corporate or government rates.

■

Group Rates

Perhaps the most important distinction to be made in the area of establishing demand forecasts, and thus rates, is that of transient rates vs. **group** rates. Many people who do not understand the hotel industry believe that the great majority of the rooms sold in a hotel are sold to individual transient travelers.

LODGING LANGUAGE

Group: Individual guests who are part of a larger, multiple traveler booking. For example, those in a leisure tour bus, wedding party, sports team, and the like.

■

This is certainly true in some hotels, but in others, such as convention properties, hotels located close to demand generators that attract groups, and hotels which actively seek group business, most rooms are sold to guests traveling as a group or attending a group function.

In the great majority of cases, group room rates are 100 percent yieldable; that is, the price to be charged the individual travelers within a group should be based solely on the hotel's forecasted demand for a given time period. This is true even in times of normal business volume. Consider the case of a hotel that has been invited to bid on a piece of tour group business consisting of one tour bus carrying 40 individual travelers. The week in which the tour bus has requested rooms is a very normal one for the hotel: demand is forecasted to be about the same as in any other typical week. In this case, however, if the tour bus is scheduled to arrive on Sunday (traditionally a very slow night for the hotel), a much lower room rate could be offered to attract the bus tour than if the same bus operator requested rooms on Tuesday night (consistently a very busy day for this hotel). This is so because the hotel is unlikely to sell the 40 rooms on Sunday night but is likely to sell all or some of them on Tuesday night. The point to remember, then, is that while a hotel should implement demand forecast systems that support yield management efforts, care must be taken to consider the total impact of yield management decisions on selected corporate or other

Those traveling by tour bus are viewed by many hotels as a very desirable segment of the group business market.

special transient rates while leaving group rates highly yieldable, even during periods of normal hotel occupancy.

RESERVATIONS

The effective management of guest reservations is one of the most complex tasks undertaken and achieved by a successful front office. This is so because the hotel's revenue is dependent, in large measure, on the front office's ability to effectively forecast demand, establish rates, and then take the proper number of reservations effectively. Reservations can be made for hotel rooms in a variety of ways, and the hotel front office must be trained to respond properly to each reservation source. For purposes of examining precisely how a hotel receives and records its guest reservations, reservations may be viewed as coming either from:

- Hotel Direct Inquiry
- Central Reservation System
- Internet Booking Site

Hotel Direct Inquiry

In many cases, guests who wish to stay at a hotel will simply place a telephone call directly to the hotel when they want a transient or even group reservation. The manner in which these calls are handled by the front office staff can make a tremendous difference in the success of the hotel. Compare, for example, the two alternative telephone greetings below that might be used by a front office staff member responsible

Senior citizens are an increasingly large segment of vacation travelers.

for simply answering the telephone. If you were a hotel owner, which response would you prefer to be in use at your hotel?

Front Desk Agent A: "Clarion Hotel."
Front Desk Agent B: "It's a great day at the Clarion Hotel!
This is Kimberly. How may I assist you today?"

Most hoteliers would agree that the greeting of front desk agent B would result in a better image for the hotel, and therefore that more room reservations will be made. It is important to realize that any telephone call made to the hotel could potentially be a guest requesting to make one, 100, or even 1,000 reservations! Therefore, every telephone call is important and should be answered professionally and promptly (before three rings).

To check the effectiveness of the telephone sales effort, some hotels use outside parties to "shop" the hotel. These individuals call the hotel for the purpose of making a reservation (later they will call back to evaluate how the hotel handles cancellations). How the hotel processes the reservation request is evaluated in detail, with a written summary provided to the hotel's management. These evaluations can identify areas of the front office that could use improvement.

The art of selling rooms by telephone is highly developed, and there are excellent tools available to hoteliers wanting to improve their own and their staff's effectiveness. Critical areas that should be examined for training include:

• Telephone etiquette
• Qualifying the guest
• Describing the property
• Presenting the rate

- Overcoming price resistance
- **Upselling**
- Closing the sale
- Recapping the sale

LODGING LANGUAGE

Upselling: Tactics used to increase the hotel's average daily rate (ADR) by encouraging guests to reserve higher-priced rooms with better or more amenities than are provided with lower-priced rooms (for example, view, complimentary breakfast and newspaper, increased square footage).

■

Those responsible for the management of the front office should know whether the individuals answering the telephone and selling rooms by phone are effective in that task. If they are not, sales will suffer until staff training improves. A periodic review of front office telephone skills and training methods is critical if this important area is to receive the attention it deserves.

In addition to telephone calls made directly to the hotel, in nearly all hotels **walk-in**s occur on a regular basis.

LODGING LANGUAGE

Walk-in: A guest seeking a room who arrives at the hotel without an advance reservation.

■

Many travelers, for any number of reasons, find themselves in need of a hotel room but without a reservation made in advance. Travelers whose plans are variable may not know where they will be at the end of the day. Other travelers find that their plans change during the day, and still others simply prefer not to make advance reservations. Walk-ins can very positively affect the overall profitability of a hotel. In some properties, particularly those in highway locations, walk-ins account for as much as 30 percent or more of total rooms sold. On bad-weather days, such as snowstorms or heavy rains, a highway hotel may completely sell out to drivers who elect to stop for the night until the weather improves. To sell rooms to walk-ins, excellent **curb appeal** as well as a friendly initial greeting from the front office staff is needed.

LODGING LANGUAGE

Curb Appeal: The initial visual impression the hotel's parking areas, grounds, and external buildings create for an arriving guest.

■

Central Reservation System

Franchised hotels of the type examined most closely in this text are entitled to use the services of the central reservation system operated by their franchisor. Generally, this central system is accessed by guests who call a toll-free number (no charge to the caller) when they want a hotel reservation. In most hotels, a very significant number of transient room reservations come from this toll-free number. In nearly all cases, the franchisor distributes a print and/or e-directory of affiliated hotels, and then staffs one or more reservation centers with individuals who answer calls and act as reservation agents for the hotels within the franchisee network. Potential guests simply dial the toll-free number, make their reservation request known to the individual answering the telephone, and receive rate and availability information about the desired hotel(s). After they complete the reservation process they are given a **confirmation number**, or if they are canceling a reservation, they are given a **cancellation number**. In some cases, group rooms are also sold by the toll-free number, but these sales usually account for a fairly small amount of the total rooms sold.

LODGING LANGUAGE

Confirmation Number: A series of numbers and/or letters that serve to identify a specific hotel reservation.

Cancellation Number: A series of numbers and/or letters that serve to identify the cancellation of a specific hotel reservation.

An effective franchise toll-free number delivers between 5 percent and 40 percent of the total transient **room nights** sold by a hotel, depending upon its location.

LODGING LANGUAGE

Room Nights: The number of rooms used times the number of nights they are sold. For example, a guest who reserves two rooms for five nights each has made a reservation for 10 ($2 \times 5 = 10$) room nights.

A transient hotel near a city may receive only 10–20 percent of its volume from the franchisor, but a resort location will be much higher. Generally, the better-known the franchisor, the larger the contribution of room nights sold by its toll-free number. Just as important, the better-known franchisors most often deliver reservations sold at rates higher than those achieved by the hotel's own front office reservationists.

Since the reservation agent accepting telephone calls in a national reservation toll-free call center is not likely to be familiar with each specific hotel in the franchise system, it is critical that the information available to the agent about the hotel is 100 percent accurate. In general, a toll-free number call center will request that the hotel supply as much information as possible on a variety of topics, including:

- Room availability
- **Black-out dates**
- Room rates
- Seasonality of rates
- Room types
- Distances to local attractions
- Hotel amenities and services offered
- Directions to the property
- Ratings and ranking information

LODGING LANGUAGE

Black-out Date: Specific day(s) when the hotel is sold out and/or is not accepting normal reservations.

■

In addition to taking telephone calls, central reservation system personnel will also manage the hotel's connection to the Global Distribution System (GDS). Was discussed in Chapter 1, the GDS is the vehicle by which travel agents and others reserve rooms by computer. This is much preferable to calling a hotel brand's central reservation system or calling the hotel directly because the GDS allows hotel room rates to be quickly compared between brands. For example, assume you are a travel agent. A client wants you to reserve a hotel room in Oklahoma City for a specific Friday evening. You could place calls to the central reservation systems of several different brands (if you knew which brands were represented in that city), compare rates, and then make the reservation. By connecting to the GDS, however, you would quickly be able to:

- Identify all the hotels located in the city
- Select those with rooms available on the desired night
- Compare room rates
- Evaluate each hotel's location and features
- Make the reservation
- Receive a confirmation number

The advantages of using the GDS are clear, and its popularity continues to increase even among those who are not full-time travel professionals. As a result, it is an important for the front office staff to make sure the information about the hotel used in the GDS is accurate and up-to-date.

Internet Booking Sites

The Internet has become a popular way for individual travelers to serve as their own travel agents and to book room reservations with hotels without having to call them directly. Today there are literally hundreds of Internet sites at which an individual can make a hotel room reservation. This is possible because these Internet booking sites are connected to the GDS. As a result, virtually anyone with a computer and Internet access is able to select an Internet booking site, enter dates on which a room reservation is desired, read (or view) information about the hotels that have availability on those dates, and then reserve a room on-line.

Hotel brands want individual consumers to use the Internet to make reservations because, unlike travel agents, individual travelers do not charge the hotel a fee for making the reservation. As a result, all hotel brand managers include an Internet booking site as part of their central reservation system. The result has been a large decline in the number of reservations made through the GDS by travel agents, but a tremendous increase in the number made by individual travelers. As more consumers use the Internet and as more hotel companies come to see the Internet as a significant marketing tool, this source of transient reservations is likely to grow from its current, industry-wide, single-digit percentage of all room nights sold to much larger proportions of total room sales.

LODGING ON-LINE

Navigating a hotel brand's Internet site to make reservations has become increasingly easy for consumers. To see what the traveler sees, select either of the following hotel sites:

http://www.choicehotels.com/

or

http://www.marriott.com

Find the rates and availability of rooms for your next birthday at the hotel nearest your hometown or school.

LODGING ON-LINE

An advantage to travelers of using a non brand-specific Internet booking site is that they can view competing hotel brands at the same time. To see competitive brands at the same time, select either of the following Internet booking sites:

http://www.travelocity.com/

or

http://www.hotels.com

Find the lowest rate available for the night of your next birthday at a hotel near your hometown or school.

In addition to Internet booking sites operated by hotel franchise companies and independent site operators, many independent hotels, as well as hotels affiliated with chains, have developed their own Web sites. These technologically savvy hotels often link their sites with those of local area attractions, businesses, non-profit organizations, and other enterprises that are likely to need guest rooms on a regular basis.

LODGING ON-LINE

Some hotels are very creative in developing their own special Web sites. To view one such site, go to:

www.orleanscasino.com

Note how the hotel uses the site to advertise package specials by choosing "Hotel," then "Packages" on the drop-down menu.

RECEPTION AND GUEST SERVICE

While the front office is not, by itself, responsible for the entire experience of hotel guests, it is an area that is especially visible to guests. Because of its responsibility for providing so many guest services, it is important that the front office be properly staffed and managed. When a guest arrives at a hotel, it the responsibility of the front office staff to greet them and take care of them. Actually, the role of the front office begins even before guests arrive. The front office staff will interact with guests prior to their arrival, during their stay, and at the time of their departure.

ALL IN A DAY'S WORK

The Situation

"Listen here," said Mr. Zollars, "I booked a room at this hotel, and I'm staying here tonight!"

"Sir," replied Chuck Lee as politely as he could, "I'm sorry, but we don't have your reservation, or any available rooms!"

Mr. Zollars had arrived at the hotel where Chuck worked with a confirmation number for a reservation he had booked on-line at www.buyaroom.com.

The problem, Chuck realized, was that buyaroom.com communicated to the hotels listed on its site via fax: when a reservation was made through buyaroom.com's Web site, buyaroom would manually fax the reservation information directly to the hotel. This was necessary because buyaroom was not directly connected to the hotel's PMS. In Mr. Zollars's case, unfortunately, the fax from buyaroom.com had never come, and thus the reservation had never been made. Since the hotel had no available rooms, it was impossible to accommodate Mr. Zollars.

A Response

Hoteliers participating with Internet booking sites not operated directly by their franchisor must be very careful. Unless a reservation is immediately entered into a hotel's PMS at the time it is made, errors such as this one with Mr. Zollars can occur. An added problem is that it will be difficult to explain to Mr. Zollars that any complaints about his "reservation" must be directed to buyaroom.com. because the purchase was made from that company, and not directly from the hotel.

In this case, Chuck, the front office staff member, should be courteous, help Mr. Zollars find the nearest hotel that can accommodate him for the night, and then report the guest's difficulty to the hotel's front office manager. The manager, as promptly as possible, should contact buyaroom.com to devise a plan to eliminate future reservation transmittal issues. If these issues cannot be resolved, the hotel should seriously consider not participating with (that is, accepting reservations from) that specific Internet booking site. Otherwise it risks many more Zollars-type incidents.

Pre-arrival

Guest services at the front desk actually begin at the time the guest makes an advance registration. On the night before a guest's arrival date, the front office staff, as part of their nightly duties, request the PMS to print (or hold in memory) a **registration (reg) card** for all guests scheduled to arrive the next day.

LODGING LANGUAGE

Registration (Reg) Card: A document that provides details such as guest's name, arrival date, rate to be paid, departure date, and other information related to the guest's stay. In conversation, most often shortened to "Reg" card, as in: "Who filed the Reg card for room 417?"

The registration card is important because it forms the basis for the legal contract between the hotel and the guest. In this contract, the hotel agrees to supply a room, and the guest agrees to pay for it. While the procedures of the hotel and the features of the hotel's PMS dictate some of the information contained on a registration card, all such cards should accurately contain:

- Guest name
- Guest address/ contact information
- Guest telephone number
- Arrival date
- Departure date
- Number of adults/ children in the room

- Room rate to be paid
- Room type requested
- Form of payment used to reserve the room

When a guest arrives at the hotel, an accurate registration card should be ready and waiting. If not, the hotel's front office staff is not obtaining complete information at the time of reservation or, if the reservation was made by an Internet booking site or central reservation system, at the time the reservation was entered in the PMS. It is the job of the front office staff to create an appropriate registration card for every known arriving guest. In older PMS systems, the registration cards are pre-printed and held for the guest's arrival. Any changes to the registration card are initialed by the guest at check-in. In most modern systems, the PMS simply holds the registration card information in computer memory. It is revised, as needed, upon guest check-in, with a corrected copy printed (if requested) for the guest.

Creating accurate registration cards is more than simply a matter of good record-keeping. When guests arrive at the hotel, announce that they have a reservation, and state that they are ready to check in, a front office staff member should be able to quickly retrieve a copy of the registration card. Travelers arriving at a hotel to find that their reservation has been lost are likely to be very upset, especially if the hotel is sold out and has no acceptable hotel alternative available. Similarly, a registration card that contains a misspelled name, erroneous room rates, or incorrect room types will create negative first impressions for the guest and extra work for the front office.

Arrival and Stay

When guests arrive at the hotel, the role of the front office is to take care of their needs during the stay. During pre-arrival, registration cards will have been properly prepared for them. The next most important function that can be provided by the front office staff is that of correctly registering guests. This five-step process consists of:

1. *Greeting the guest.* When guests arrive at the front desk, a professionally dressed, well-trained staff member should greet them in a friendly way. Because most hotel guests arrive in the evening and check-in time can be very busy, it may not always be possible to avoid the need for guests to wait in line for registration. Proper staffing, however, should minimize the wait. When it is their turn to be registered, guests should, above all else, be made to feel welcome!

2. *Confirming the information on the registration card.* It is critical that all of the information on a registration card be accurate. This includes the spelling of the guest's name, the arrival and departure dates, room rate, and any other information related to the specific guest. Accuracy in departure date and room rate information is so important that both should be initialed by the guests. Since the registration card will serve as the record of the guest's stay, it must be complete and precise. In addition, misunderstandings regarding room rate (one of the most frequent causes of guest dissatisfaction) can be minimized if the room rate is clearly communicated and understood by both the hotel and the guest prior to room assignment.

3. *Securing a form of payment.* In most hotels, guests must either pay for their room in advance or provide a valid source of credit at registration. While many hotels accept checks, the most prevalent source of credit provided by guests a credit or debit card. These cards must be legitimate, however, before they represent an acceptable form of payment. To establish the card's legitimacy, the desk agent should **authorize** the card at the time of guest registration.

LODGING LANGUAGE

Authorize: To validate. When used in reference to a credit card offered by a guest at the time of check-in, this term refers to the desk agent's validation of the card. Validation means:

- The card is being used legally
- The card has sufficient credit remaining to pay for the guest's estimated charges.
- A hold for a dollar amount determined by front office policy has been placed on the card to ensure the hotel's payment.

Used as in "Lisa, Please authorize Mr. Patel's MasterCard for $1,000."

■

Hotels use a verification service to authorize credit cards. The front office staff member who is registering the guest enters the information from the card (account number and expiration date) as well as the dollar amount to be authorized by telephone modem and keypad or magnetic swipe. If the card is not stolen and is valid, the verification service issues an authorization code number that lets the hotel know it can accept the card for payment.

Effective front desk personnel always authorize the credit cards they accept as a promise of guest payment. In fact, one objective measure of how well a front office is managed is its consistency in securing and authorizing valid cards.

4. *Room assignment.* After a guest's registration information has been confirmed and an acceptable form of payment has been offered, the guest should be assigned to a specific guest room. In some hotels, all guest rooms are identical, and room assignment is of little consequence. In other hotels, the room types may vary greatly in perceived quality and/or rate based primarily on the room's
   - Location
   - View
   - Bed type
   - Amenities or room features

Whenever possible a guest's room preferences should be accommodated. There will be times, unfortunately, when a guest cannot be accommodated. This is most often the case when the hotel is overbooked and must walk the guest. Walking a guest is one of the most difficult situations that can be confronted by the front office staff. Recall that a guest who must be walked is one who has a confirmed reservation but cannot be accommodated by the hotel. When this occurs, it is imperative that the front office staff carefully follows the hotel's established policies for walking a guest. In all cases, when confronted with the task of walking a guest, the front office staff should:

- Apologize for the inconvenience.
- Clearly explain the hotel's walk policy.
- Offer any reasonable assistance possible to minimize the difficulties of the situation.

5. *Issuance of keys.* The final step in the registration process is the issuance of room keys. The actual number of keys to be issued is a matter of hotel policy and guest preference. It is important, however, that guest room keys be tightly controlled, because the theft, loss, or unauthorized duplication of keys could seriously threaten guest safety. Upon receiving room keys, the guests are either taken or directed to their rooms.

According to various court rulings, a guest who has been assigned to and enters a hotel room, enjoys many of the same constitutional rights in that room as in his or her own home. Protecting the privacy rights of guests is not simply the legal thing to do, it is also a courteous and considerate policy.

A professionally managed front office is one where guests are confident that their privacy is protected by all hotel staff members. This includes maintaining a guest's anonymity. To that end, front office staff should:

- Never confirm or deny that a guest is registered in the hotel without the guest's express permission to do so.
- Never provide information related to a guest's stay (arrival, departure, or room number, for example) to anyone without the guest's express permission to do so.
- Never perform registration tasks in such a way as to allow guest room information to be overheard by others in the front office area. For example, for a front office staff member to say aloud, *"Here is your key to room number 416, Mr. Franken,"* would be inappropriate because the guest's privacy would be violated by such a comment.
- Never mark room numbers directly onto keys.
- Never issue a duplicate room key to anyone without confirming by positive identification that the person is the room's properly registered guest.

At check-in, all guests should be confident that personal details of their stay will remain confidential, that information the hotel may have about them, including their address, telephone number, e-mail address, and credit card, is secure, and that no unauthorized person can gain access to their room.

One of the most challenging aspects of providing excellent guest service at the front desk relates to ensuring that guests are satisfied during their stay. When guests experience difficulties in the hotel, they will most likely turn to the front desk and its staff for assistance. During their stay and during check-out, guests are likely to bring up any issues that detracted from their experience. It is the responsibility of the front office staff to address these guest issues and to correct them if it is possible to do so.

Departure

Some hotels provide guests the option of using variations of a self-check-out system when they conclude their stay. In all of these systems, a copy of the guest's folio is made available prior to check-out, and if the guest has no objection to the items on the bill, the guest is charged the amount listed on the folio. These systems are designed to save the guest time during the check-out process. In the normal case, however, when guests come to the front desk to check out, the hotel staff must perform two important tasks. The first is the actual settlement of the guest's bill, which is a several-step process:

- Confirmation of the guest's identity
- Producing a copy of the bill for the guest's inspection
- Processing the guest's payment
- Revising the room's status in the PMS to designate the room as vacant and ready to clean

In most cases, guest check-out is a relatively straightforward process. This is especially true if the guest's form of payment was confirmed at check-in. In some cases, however, guests will have experienced a difficulty with their stay and an adjustment of their bill may be in order. It is important, however, that front office staff know the limits to their authority to do so. That is, an employee may be authorized to make adjustments up to a predetermined dollar amount, with a supervisor or manager required to authorize adjustments exceeding that amount.

The second essential task to be accomplished by the desk agent when a guest checks out is the rebooking of the guest for a future stay. If the guest's stay has been a positive one, it is appropriate, (and good front office management) to ask the guest if a future reservation can be made for them at the hotel or at another hotel in the chain. This is an often-overlooked selling opportunity.

GUEST ACCOUNTING

Accounting for guests, while less visible than providing guest services, is another critical responsibility of the front office. During their stay, guests are likely to have purchased a variety of hotel goods and services in addition to having rented their rooms. Accounting for guests simply means that all data related to a guest's use of the hotel is accurately collected, and that guests are properly charged for their purchases. Depending on the services and amenities offered by the hotel, there can be many sources of guest charges. The following list of products and services is not all-inclusive, but represents some of the many possible charges that hotel staff must accurately identify and **post** to the guest's folio:

- Guest room charges, including appropriate taxes
- In-room safe charges
- Pay-per-view movies/games
- Internet access charges
- Restaurant or bar charges
- Telephone tolls
- Gift shop purchases
- Laundry charges
- Parking charges
- Meeting room charges
- Audiovisual equipment rental

- Banquet food or beverage charges
- Business center charges

LODGING LANGUAGE

Post: Enter a guest's charges into the PMS in order to create a permanent record of the sale. Used as in "Please post this meeting room charge to Mr. Walker's folio."

■

Effective guest accounting in a hotel, as it relates to the front office, consists of two different but important tasks. The first is that of information (data) management and the second is the completion of the night audit.

Data Management

The front office is the center for the hotel's data-management systems that identify charges to be posted to guest folios. At the front office, the PMS and other accounting systems maintain the hotel's financial and operational records. In most cases, these systems are extensive and complex. Their management requires a talented and technologically well informed staff because an increasing number of important data-generating systems are, or should be, **interfaced** with the hotel's PMS.

LODGING LANGUAGE

Interfaced: The process in which one data-generating system shares its data electronically with another system.

■

The process of interfacing two data-management systems can be challenging because in most cases the systems have been manufactured by different companies. For example, the company that produces the hotel's PMS will not be the same as the company providing the hotel with its electronic guestroom door lock system. Clearly, however, the guest who is checked in to room 101 by the PMS should automatically be issued a key for room 101 (not for room 102!) by the electronic locking system. When the PMS and lock system are interfaced, this happens immediately. When they are not, a hotel staff member must produce the key separately, and this introduces the possibility of an error.

To complicate matters further, in many cases multiple system interfaces are required, but not all are completely under the control of the hotel. For example, a hotel that wishes to improve its **call accounting** system will find that a new system must be interfaced with the existing telephone system, the local telephone call provider's system, the long-distance call provider's system, and the hotel's PMS. The many challenges of implementing such an integrated system fall primarily to the front office.

LODGING LANGUAGE

Call Accounting: The system within the hotel used to document and charge guests for their use of the telephone.

■

Cell phones have had a negative impact on in-room telephone usage. Hotels face rising costs but declining revenues in this guest service area.

Telephones are one of the most complex data- and equipment-management areas in a hotel. Even the smallest of hotels is large enough to have its own private branch exchange, or **PBX.**

LODGING ON-LINE

Mitel is one of the best and most popular makers of hotel telephone systems. To view its site, go to:

www.mitel.com

When you arrive, click on "Solutions," then "Hospitality."

LODGING LANGUAGE

PBX: Short for "Private Branch Exchange." The system within the hotel used to process incoming, internal, and outgoing telephone calls.

Today's hotel PBX is highly automated, as it must be because of the significant use of telephones in the typical hotel. The PBX is the hotel's telephone system, and it is maintained by the front office. It includes the call-accounting system used to charge guests for telephone calls. For example, if a registered guest directly dials a person in another state from a hotel room, the hotel will actually be billed for the call. Of course, the hotel would want its cost for the call to be as low as possible while still providing that guests with quality long-distance service. The hotel will, depending on the distance and length of the long-distance call, post a charge to the guest's folio to offset the cost of the call. For hotels providing in-room fax machines, these calls, like all others, can be charged to the guest's folio when the call-accounting data system is interfaced with the PMS. The call-accounting system records the time, length, and number called of very telephone call made in each guest room (as well as those made from administrative phones). These call records must be accurate if guests are expected to pay for the calls they have initiated.

It is important to know that even local calls are not free for the hotel. Proper operation of the call-accounting system is critical because telephone calls are a significant source of revenue for many hotels. Telephone revenue, as a percentage of total hotel revenue, has been declining in recent years due to the increased use of cell phones and pagers; however, a properly managed call-accounting system is still important because telephone revenue that goes uncollected due to an improperly managed system negatively affects the hotel's bottom line.

In addition to telephone-related information, the front office must manage the guest data and charges that result from in-room services. Increasingly, guests can use the televisions, telephones, and/or hotel-provided keyboards in their rooms to access products and services sold by the hotel. As the traveling public becomes even more computer sophisticated, look for this trend to continue and expand. Currently, some of the most popular products and services guests can purchase from their rooms include movies, games, safes, and Internet connections.

Movies

Pay-per-view movie systems have long been a popular feature offered to hotel guests. Essentially, these systems offer guests the opportunity to view movies that are currently, or have just recently finished, showing in theaters. In addition, most pay-per-view providers offer a variety of adult-oriented movies. Guests pay the hotel for viewing the movies. Then, at month's end, the movie provider charges the hotel based on the number of movies viewed as well as for any equipment charges included in the hotel's pay-per-view contract.

LODGING ON-LINE

For a sample of the type of movies shown to guests on a pay-per–view system, review the offerings of Lodgenet, one of the largest pay-per-view movie and services providers. You can do so at:

www.lodgenet.com/guests/index.html

Today's in-room movie services include enhanced features that allow guests to review their folios on their television screens and even to check out of the hotel using a PMS-interfaced pay-per-view system.

Games

Many hotels offer guests the chance to play video games on the television screens in their rooms. The games are typically accessed in the same manner as pay-per-view movies. While these game services are very similar to pay-per-view movies (they are pay-per-play), the significant difference is the requirement for an in-room joystick, mouse, or keyboard to play the game. This means that the hotel must provide these electronic devices and keep them secure in the rooms. The front office is not responsible for the security of the in-room devices, but it is responsible for maintaining an effective PMS data interface so that all games played are, in fact, charged to the proper guest folio.

Safes

Recently, more hotels have begun offering in-room safes for guests' use. These safes are electronic and can be opened only by the guest and the hotel's own staff. Charges for the use of the safe are typically posted to the guest's folio through a PMS interface.

Internet Connections

In the late 1990s, some hotels began to aggressively market in-room Internet services. The intent was to capitalize on the increasing use of the Internet by travelers of all types. Some of these efforts met with success. Others, the victim of the infamous dot.com bust of 2001, were cancelled or delayed when companies offering the services failed to deliver because of defective business models. At many hotels, Internet usage is now offered as a free service. At hotels that do charge for it, however, access and usage fees must be properly identified and posted to the appropriate folio.

The management of data related to guest charges is important to a hotel's profitability. Each hotel will offer some free services and establish charges for other products and services. Purchases by guests must be identified and posted to the proper folio. The night auditor who performs the night audit has the final responsibility for completing this task.

Night Audit

Hotels must account for guest charges every day. An interesting accounting issue arises, however, because hotels are open seven days a week, 24 hours a day. It is this: When do one day's hotel sales end and another day's sales begin?

To illustrate the issue, assume that a hotel on an interstate highway checks in guests at the following times: 11:00 p.m., midnight, 1:00 a.m., 2:00 a.m., 3:00 a.m., 4:00 a.m., and 5:00 a.m.

At what point are these guests considered one night's guests, and at what point should they be considered the next day's?

Traditionally, the end of the day (and therefore the beginning of the next day) is not a fixed time at all. Rather, it is designated as the time at which the night auditor concludes (closes) the night audit. The night audit could, theoretically, be performed at any time during the day or night. Traditionally, however, it is performed in the very late evening/ early morning hours when the hotel's overall activity is at its slowest because most guests have, at that point, gone to sleep for the night and therefore will not be purchasing additional hotel products or services.

The night audit function is important for many departments in the hotel. Completing it consists of the following eight key items:

1. Posting the appropriate room and tax rates to the folios of the guests currently in the hotel.
2. Verifying the accurate status of all rooms in the PMS.
3. Posting any necessary adjustments to guest folios.
4. Verifying that all legitimate non-room charges have been posted throughout the day to the proper guest folio.

5. Monitoring guest account balances to determine whether any are over the guest's credit limit.

6. Balancing and reconciling the front desk's cash bank.

7. Updating and backing up the electronic data maintained by the front office.

8. Producing, duplicating, and distributing all management-mandated reports, such as those related to ADR, occupancy percentage, source of business, and in-house guest lists.

With a computerized PMS, some of these tasks may be completed automatically. In most hotels, the night auditor completes the audit between 1:00 a.m. and 4:00 a.m. It is important for this task to be completed correctly and on time because some guests will begin to check out of the hotel very early in the morning, and their folios must be as up to date as possible at that time. In a well-run front office, properly prepared folios will await these guests.

LODGING ON-LINE

Front Office management is a specialized and rapidly changing area of hotel operation. To purchase a complete and up-to-date text about professional procedures and methods used in front office management, go to

www.amazon.com

When you arrive, enter: "Professional Front Office Management" to view a selection of current texts.

ALL IN A DAY'S WORK

The Situation

"I just want to go to sleep," said Mr. Rosenbloom, the guest in room 205. "Tell those people next door to quiet down. It's 2:30 in the morning!"

Those people, as Shingi, the hotel night auditor, knew well, were in room 207.

Mr. Rosenbloom had first called the front desk at 1:00 a.m. that night, asking Shingi if she could do something about the noise and loud music coming from room 207. Shingi had promptly called room 207 to say, politely, that there had been a guest complaint and to request that the room hold down the noise level. The occupants of 207 quickly assured Shingi that they would keep it down; however, Mr. Rosenbloom called the front desk again at 1:45 a.m. saying that the noise and loud music coming from 207 had resumed.

After that call, Shingi had visited room 207, personally heard the loud noise and music, knocked on the door, and when the occupants answered it, again asked them politely to hold down the noise level, but also informed them if they did not, the police would be called to assist in evicting them from the room. The guests in 207 then assured Shingi that they would quiet down.

Now it was 2:30 a.m. and it appeared that the "party" in 207 was starting up again.

A Response

Hotels should, of course, respect the privacy of guests in their rooms, but guests must also respect the rights of other guests. In this case, the rights of room 207 are unreasonably infringing on the rights of room 205. In most hotels, front office policy stipulates that after two warnings the hotel's own security staff or the local police are to be summoned to warn and/or remove unruly guests. Front office staff should never physically confront unruly guests, but they must maintain control over inappropriate behavior occurring in the hotel. The hotel's management must implement policies designed to guide front office staff when faced with such situations.

CHAPTER OBJECTIVES REVIEW

If you have successfully studied the material in this chapter, you should be prepared to:

1. Explain the major activities that occur in a hotel's front office. (Objective 1)
2. Describe the process of forecasting hotel demand and establishing room rates. (Objective 2)
3. Review the major sources of hotel reservations. (Objective 3)
4. Explain the role of the front desk before, during, and after a guest checks into the hotel. (Objective 4)
5. Describe how the front office manages guest and hotel data, including the night audit process. (Objective 5)

LODGING LANGUAGE

Front Office	Guest History	Walk-in
Front Desk	Revenue Management (RM)	Curb Appeal
FOM	Revenue Manager	Confirmation Number
PMS	Rack Rate	Cancellation Number
Back-up System	Overbooking	Room Nights
Night Audit	Walked	Black-out Date
Night Auditor	No-show	Registration (Reg) Card
Folio	Corporate Rate	Authorize
Room Type	Transient	Post
RevPar	Non-yieldable	Interfaced
Sell-out	Group	Call Accounting
Historical Data	Upselling	PBX

FOR DISCUSSION

1. Hotels are not the only businesses that must employ talented employees who are oriented to guest service. Identify three other businesses that employ individuals in a significant guest service role. Could these businesses be a source of employees for a hotel's front office?
2. Some individuals are better than others are at providing quality guest service. Name five personal characteristics you would seek in a person who wanted to be employed at a front office you managed.
3. Some guests do not understand the need for hotel managers to adjust room rates to meet forecasted demand. How would you respond to a guest who complained about paying more than the average room rate on a night all the hotels in your area forecasted to be a sell-out situation?
4. Many factors can influence demand for hotel rooms. Identify three events or times of the year in your area that you believe would heavily increase room demand. Why would these events increase room demand?
5. Some hotels have greatly expanded the number of items they seek to maintain in guest histories. Identify five pieces of information about a guest that you believe hotels have a legitimate purpose in securing. Are there items that you, as a guest, would not share with a hotel? What? Why?

6. Interestingly, the restaurant business does not typically offer discounts for large groups. That is, a restaurant generally charges the same prices to a table of two as it would to a table of 22. In the hotel business, discounts are typically given for a group sale. Why do you think these two related industries approach pricing so differently?

7. Some Internet booking sites operate by letting guests bid for hotel rooms at whatever price the guest is willing to pay. If the bid is successful (that is, if a hotel is willing to sell a room for the suggested bid price), a non-refundable reservation is made. If you were managing a front office, would you want your hotel to participate in such an arrangement? Explain your reasoning.

8. Some hotels believe that self-check-in and check-out by guests will be appealing because it will save the guest time. Other hoteliers believe that guests desire contact with hotel staff during registration and check-out. Which position do you take? Does the type of hotel involved help determine your view?

9. When guests register at a hotel, they must supply such information as their name, address, and telephone number. Do you believe that hotels have the right to share this data with others, such as direct mail or advertising companies, without the express approval of the guest? Should such data be shared with the franchise company?

10. The night audit position in a hotel is an important one. What personal characteristics do you believe are necessary for an employee to enjoy the late night/early a.m. work shifts required of such a position?

TEAM ACTIVITIES

Team Activity 1

There are a variety of PMS systems on the market. Search the Internet with your team to identify three such systems. Each of them will promote its own features and advantages. Select two features or advantages for each PMS system you identified. Why would it be important for a hotelier to have the advertised feature or benefit?

Team Activity 2

One of the most important tasks facing front office managers and employees is that of monitoring demand for guest rooms and then yield managing rates to maximize the hotel's RevPar. Identify an event in your area that greatly affects hotel demand (or use a national event, such as the Indianapolis 500 or Mardi Gras). Use the Internet to check the price of five different hotels affected by the event one week before, during, and one week after the event. What can you determine about the forecasting strategy of each hotel you examined?

The Sales and Marketing Department

Chapter Objectives

1. To define the terms "sales" and "marketing" and to explain the relationship between a hotel's sales and marketing effort and its financial success.
2. To examine the sales and marketing activities that occur within a hotel as well as those that take place outside of it.
3. To identify the two major hotel markets and describe how each can be solicited to help maximize hotel revenues.
4. To teach you about the major sales and marketing tools used by those responsible for hotel sales and marketing.
5. To explain how hotel owners and managers evaluate a hotel's sales and marketing efforts.

Chapter Outline

THE IMPORTANCE OF SALES AND MARKETING

SALES AND MARKETING ACTIVITIES
 On-Property Activities
  Sales and Marketing Team
  Sales and Marketing Budgets
  The Sales and Marketing Plan
 Off-Property Activities
  Franchisor's Efforts
  CVB Efforts
  Other Efforts

HOTEL MARKETS
 Transient Travelers
 Group Travelers

SALES AND MARKETING TOOLS
 In-Person Sales Calls
 Print and Direct Mail
 Telephone
 E-mail
 Web Sites
 Client Appreciation Activities

EVALUATION OF SALES AND MARKETING EFFORTS
 Performance to Sales and Marketing Plan
 STAR Report

Overview: The Sales and Marketing Department

The economic health of a hotel is dependent upon its securing its fair share of the hotel rooms sold in its market. If a hotel does not do a good job of selling rooms, it will not get its fair share of business in the area, and as a result will not be as profitable as it should be. Ultimately, a well-run hotel must attract, maintain, and expand a strong guest base. This is the goal of all sales and marketing efforts.

The hotel sales and marketing effort takes place both inside and outside the hotel. Within the hotel, those responsible will establish a budget, create a marketing plan, and implement it. The marketing plan will detail what is to be done internally and externally to maximize hotel sales. In addition to efforts that take place within the hotel, hotel properties will also rely on the area's convention and visitors bureau to assist in hotel marketing. In a franchised hotel, the franchisor too will assist in property sales and marketing, and in this chapter you will learn about the resources they contribute to the sales effort.

While every hotel guest is a unique individual, hotels have traditionally viewed guests as falling into one or another of two broad categories: individual travelers and members of a group. In this chapter, we will closely examine these two segments to understand better how to effectively market and sell to each of them.

In very small hotels, the general manager may be responsible for sales and marketing. In larger hotels, the effort may be divided among many people. In both types of establishments, cases, however, there are common sales and marketing tools that are used to increase a hotel's sales effectiveness. In this chapter, we will examine the most popular of these and see how hoteliers utilize them to increase hotel revenues.

The owners and/or managers of a hotel continually evaluate the efforts of employees in all areas of the property. Naturally this holds for sales and marketing as well. There is a clear relationship between effort and success in sales and marketing but evaluating that relationship can be complex because a strong effort in a weak hotel market may actually yield less business than a weak sales effort in a strong market. Because this is true, evaluations of a hotel's sales effort must be carefully done. In this chapter, you will learn about the methods used in the hotel industry to evaluate fairly the staff members responsible for a hotel's sales and marketing effectiveness.

THE IMPORTANCE OF SALES AND MARKETING

Very few hotels operate in a non-competitive environment. In most cases, a guest chooses a hotel after considering several alternative properties. Not all hotels appeal equally to all guests. For example, a couple with children looking for a nearby weekend getaway may want to stay only at a hotel with a swimming pool their children can use. A business traveler may consider a free in-room high-speed Internet connection to be a very important feature. In both cases, the guest has needs and the hotel has facilities that may, or may not, meet them. In its simplest form, the goal of a hotel's sales and marketing effort is to find and attract guests whose needs match the services and facilities offered by the hotel. When this is done well, the hotel will sell its fair share of rooms to these guests and its profitability will be enhanced.

While every employee in a hotel may have an impact on a guest's experience, it is the job of sales and marketing personnel to attract guests. In smaller hotels, the general manager may be the person most responsible for selling the hotel's rooms. In larger hotels, a **DOSM** will be in charge of the sales and marketing effort.

LODGING LANGUAGE

DOSM: Short for "director of sales and marketing." Variations include DOS (director of sales) and DOM (director of marketing).

■

LODGING ON-LINE

Hoteliers who work full-time or part-time in the area of sales and marketing often decide to become members of the Hospitality Sales and Marketing Association International (HSMAI). To view its Web site, go to:

www.hsmai.org

The employee who is responsible for sales and marketing must identify and cultivate clients, plan the hotel's marketing efforts, determine appropriate room rates, negotiate sales contracts, and serve as a leader to the hotel's entire sales and marketing team.

Entire books and magazines are devoted to the topic of hotel sales and marketing. There are many different opinions about how it is best done. There are nearly as many approaches to the sales and marketing of hotels as there are people working in the area. On reason is that each hotel is unique, and as a result, how each hotel should best be sold and marketed may be unique.

Even definitions of the terms **sales** and **marketing** are often debated in the hotel industry. In fact, there is no universally accepted definition for these terms as they relate to the hotel business. For purposes of this text, we will consider "marketing" to be all activities designed to increase consumer awareness and demand by promoting and advertising the hotel, and sales to comprise activities related directly to **booking** guests.

LODGING LANGUAGE

Sales: Activities directly related to a client's purchase of hotel rooms or services.

Marketing: Activities directly related to increasing a potential guest's awareness of a hotel.

Booking: Hotel jargon for making a confirmed sale. Used as in: "What is the current level of bookings for the month?" or "How many out-of-state tour buses were booked into the hotel last month?"

■

A sale, or booking, is typically the result of effective marketing. That is, a potential guest sees or hears information about a particular hotel and then decides to utilize (book) the hotel's guest rooms or other services. As Figure 8.1 illustrates, when executed properly, increased marketing activities will lead to greater hotel profitability.

When not done, or when done poorly, hotel marketing activities may not lead to greater consumer awareness. When that happens, the hoped-for increases in sales levels may not occur. Sometimes a marketing activity increases consumer awareness at so a high cost to the hotel that total profits actually decrease. For example, paying excessively high rates to advertise in a magazine or newspaper and not receiving sales increases sufficient to pay for the ads.

The distinction between sales and marketing activities is sometimes clear-cut but more often is somewhat uncertain. For example, designing a hotel advertisement

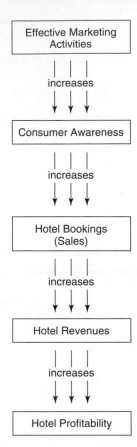

FIGURE 8.1   The Goal of Marketing Is Increased Profitability

and placing it in the local Yellow Pages telephone directory is a marketing activity designed to inform potential guests about the hotel. Typing the final contract document for a group reserving 100 sleeping rooms is clearly a sales activity. Representing the hotel at a trade show whose attendees are professional meeting planners, however, can be considered either marketing (an activity related to increasing awareness), or sales (activities directly related to booking business), or both. The way sales or marketing is defined is less important than knowing that both activities must be planned and executed well if the hotel is to achieve its desired ADR, occupancy rate, and profitability.

LODGING ON-LINE

Hotel brand Web sites are increasingly utilized by consumers who seek information about a specific hotel brand. The Cendant Corporation is one of the world's largest managers of hotel brands. To view its Web site, go to:

www.cendant.com

When you arrive, click on "Brands and Business Units" and then select a hotel brand Web site to visit.

SALES AND MARKETING ACTIVITIES

The goal of all hotel sales and marketing activities should be to increase sales and, therefore, revenues. One way to examine the sales and marketing efforts of hotels is to consider the activities involved before, during, and after, a sale, as illustrated in Figure 8.2.

Not all sales involve each of the activities we will examine, but each is part of the sales cycle. At every phase in the sales cycle, hotel employees must perform well or risk losing the sale to another hotel. The following events are typical of the actual hotel sales process:

- *Pre-sales Phase.* Allisha Miller, a manager at the Best Sleep Hotel, meets Mr. Jodi at a community golf outing held to raise funds for the American Cancer Society. Mr. Jodi mentions that he is this year's state chapter president of the Society of Antique Furniture Appraisers.

- At dinner following the golf outing, Allisha inquires about any meetings held in the city by the society. Mr. Jodi replies that the group meets annually in the area for three days, and that its board of directors votes each year on which hotel to select. In the past, he says, the group has always stayed at the Altoona Hotel (a competitor of the Best Sleep Hotel), and that members are relatively happy with that hotel.

- After dinner, Allisha invites Mr. Jodi to the Best Sleep Hotel for a **site tour**. Based primarily on the friendship established on the golf course, Mr. Jodi agrees to the meeting.

LODGING LANGUAGE

Site Tour: A physical tour of a hotel, hosted by a member of the hotel's staff.

■

- During the site tour, Allisha points out the Best Sleep's most significant features and subtly contrasts them to the Altoona Hotel, (but without criticizing the competitor). At the conclusion of the tour, Allisha asks Mr. Jodi if he could arrange to include the Best Sleep Hotel on the list of hotels allowed to submit a **bid** on the society's next meeting. Mr. Jodi agrees to do so.

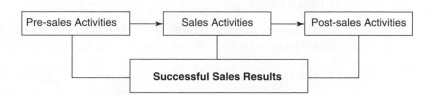

FIGURE 8.2 Three Types of Activities in the Sales Cycle

LODGING LANGUAGE

Bid: An offer by a hotel to supply sleeping rooms, meeting space, food and beverages, or other services to a potential client at a stated price. If the bid is accepted, the hotel will issue the client a contract detailing the agreement made between the hotel and the client.

- *Sales Phase.*
  - The Best Sleep's bid is prepared and submitted before the deadline established by the society. Room rates to be charged are based upon the hotel's estimate of the society's actual sleeping room **pickup**.

LODGING LANGUAGE

Pickup: The actual number of rooms purchased by a client in a specific time period. Used as in: "What was the Florida Furniture Society's pick-up last week?

- Based on the bids received, the society's board narrows its choice of hotels to two, one of which is the Best Sleep Hotel. The board, following a site tour, and with the personal support of Mr. Jodi, selects the Best Sleep Hotel for its next meeting.
- Allisha prepares a **group contract** for the society detailing the agreement with the hotel and specifically mentioning any **attrition** and cancellation penalties.

LODGING LANGUAGE

Group Contract: A legal document used to summarize the agreement between a hotel and its group client.

Attrition: The difference between the original request and the actual pickup of a group. For example, a group might reserve 100 rooms but actually use only 50. Because the room rate quoted to the group was based upon the use of 100 rooms, the hotel's standard group contract may require, in such a case, that the group pay a penalty for its failure to purchase the number of rooms it originally agreed to purchase.

- Allisha next establishes a group **block** for the society to ensure that sleeping rooms are reserved for its meeting.

LODGING LANGUAGE

Block: Rooms reserved exclusively for members of a specific group. Used as in, "We need to create a block of 50 rooms for May 10th and 11th for the Society of Antique Furniture Appraisers."

- Allisha monitors the society's block to ensure that the hotel meets its contractual terms. That is, it holds (reserves), for the group's purchase only, the required number of rooms for the length of time stipulated in the contract.

- Allisha attends a pre-event sales meeting of her hotel's staff. The staff reviews the needs and special requests of all the groups that will be coming to the hotel in the next week. One of these groups is the society, and Allisha reviews its contract terms with the staff.

- Allisha is present on the first day of the society's meeting to welcome the board members, Mr. Jodi, and others. Periodically, during the society's stay, Allisha meets with the group's main contact person(s) to make sure that all is going well.

- *Post-sales Phase.*

  - Allisha writes to each member of the society's board thanking them for choosing the Best Sleep Hotel. The letter is co-signed by the general manager Allisha hand-delivers a special token of appreciation to Mr. Jodi and thanks him for his assistance in securing the society's business.

  - The society is added to a preferred client list. This means that it will be contacted and recognized in some manner by the hotel on a regular basis.

  - Entries made in the sales activity calendar ensure that the hotel sales team will begin the bid process with the society next year in ample time to retain the business.

  - All written records related to the society's event are properly filed.

There are many activities that must be performed flawlessly in the competitive hotel sales process. People skills, organizational skills, and conflict-management abilities are essential characteristics of sales and marketing professionals. Many of the sales activities identified above are complex, and all are vitally important. Errors made in any of the processes required for a successful sale could cause as much client dissatisfaction as would errors in any of the hotel's operating departments.

The marketing activities of a hotel typically draw a great deal of attention. However, it is important to recognize that sales execution is just as important as the marketing activities. At the risk of oversimplification, sales can be defined as the process of servicing business currently identified, and marketing as the effort to generate new business. It makes little sense to expend significant resource attracting new clients (marketing) if the sales processes involving the hotel's current clients are not properly managed. In fact, until a hotel's sales efforts are smooth and efficient, it is probably best not to risk permanently alienating new clients by serving them poorly also.

The number of marketing and sales activities that *could* be undertaken by a specific hotel is immense. Before any such activities are contemplated, however, it is important to establish who on the hotel staff will be responsible for the property's sales and marketing efforts and how much money can be spent to support the efforts.

The process of assembling a sales and marketing team, establishing a budget, and identifying the sales and marketing activities to be carried out by the team are all measures undertaken inside (on) the hotel property. There are also significant efforts undertaken outside (off) the hotel property. These sales and marketing activities are performed on the hotel's behalf by its franchisor, the area **convention and visitor's bureau (CVB)**, and others.

LODGING LANGUAGE

Convention and Visitor's Bureau (CVB): An organization, generally funded by taxes levied on overnight hotel guests, which seeks to increase the number of visitors to the area it represents. Also called the "CVB" for short.

■

On-Property Activities

On property sales and marketing activities will be varied but are best begun by establishing a sales and marketing team, developing a budget to support the sales and marketing effort, and then creating and following a **marketing plan**. These are the topics of this section.

LODGING LANGUAGE

Marketing Plan: A calendar of specific activities designed to the meet the hotel's sales goals.

■

Sales and Marketing Team

Perhaps the most important task related to sales and marketing is determining who on the hotel staff will be responsible for sales. The answer should be "Everyone!" Every hotel employee who comes into contact with guests, or whose work in some way affects a guest's experience, is involved with sales and marketing. Therefore, in one sense, all on-property employee activities, from cleaning guest rooms to trimming the grass to picking up discarded bottles and cans in the parking lot, are sales and marketing activities, because all of these activities affect a guests' perceptions of a hotel and thus their willingness to stay there.

In larger hotels, the director of sales and marketing heads a sizable staff of professional salespeople. In a smaller, limited-service hotel, sales duties may be shared by the general manager and the front-office manager, or may be performed only by the general manager. Even the smallest hotels, however, can benefit from the development of a **sales and marketing committee**, chaired by the hotel's general manager or director of sales and marketing.

LODGING LANGUAGE

Sales and Marketing Committee: The team of employees responsible for coordinating the hotel's sales and marketing effort.

■

A sales and marketing committee is important because many areas of a hotel are affected by the sales effort. For example, assume that the general manager or director of sales and marketing wishes to create and promote a couples **inclusive**-priced weekend getaway package that includes a room at the hotel, chocolates placed in the room upon arrival, a complimentary pay-per-view movie, and a late check-out the next morning. The impact on the hotel's entire operation can be significant.

LODGING LANGUAGE

Inclusive: A single price that includes all charges.

■

In this example, an employee has to place the chocolates in the proper room before the guests arrive. In addition, the night auditor must be aware that the guest's first pay-per-view movie is included in the price of the package and thus the guests should not be charged for it (but should be charged for additional movies). The housekeeping staff must be informed that rooms reserved for this package will have to be cleaned later than usual because of the late check-out. In this example, a coordinated effort is clearly required. It is the role of the sales and marketing committee to provide the coordination, and to do so it should include representatives from all areas of the hotel.

Sales and Marketing Budgets

As is true in all areas of a hotel, the costs of sales and marketing efforts must be known and/or estimated if they are to be properly managed. When developing a sales and marketing budget, hoteliers must first establish their hotel's estimated or budgeted expected revenue levels. They then calculate the projected sales and marketing costs necessary to generate these revenues.

Annual sales and marketing budgets are typically prepared in advance of the coming year (see Chapter 9). Therefore, a sales and marketing budget for the period January through December might be prepared the preceding September or October.

Developing a realistic budget is an important part of creating an effective sales and marketing plan.

The budget is developed by projecting expenses on a monthly basis and then combining this information for a year. As the budget year evolves, adjustments can be made to the sales and marketing budget to account for changes in actual hotel revenue or in the sales and marketing expenditures. Typical expenses in the sales and marketing area include staff salaries and wages as well as the funds required to support the activities in the hotel's marketing plan.

LODGING ON-LINE

Budgeting is a skill that can be learned, and there are tools to help managers do just that. To review the features of one such tool, go to:

www.centage.com

When you arrive, try the free budgeting demo.

The Sales and Marketing Plan

Effective hotel marketing begins with the development of a marketing plan, which is simply a list of activities designed to meet the sales goals of the hotel. Activities often included in a marketing plan involve analysis of the hotel's competitors, the establishment of prices, and a calendar of specific tasks and expenditures to be made by the hotel's staff throughout the year.

The physical format of marketing plans can vary greatly, but most include the following:

- An overview of the area in which the hotel competes, including
  - Occupancy trends
  - ADR trends
  - Performance of the hotel in the market
- Competitive analysis, including a review of each competitor's
  - Strengths
  - Weaknesses
  - Price structure
- Competitive analysis of the hotel, including a review of its
  - Strengths
  - Weaknesses
  - Price structure
- Forecast of future market conditions, including:
  - Estimates of market growth or contraction
  - Performance goals and objectives for the hotel
  - Timeline for achieving these goals and objectives
- Plans relating to specific marketing strategies and activities designed to meet the hotel's goals and objectives, including those related to
  - **Advertising**
  - Promotions

- **Publicity**
- Development of a marketing budget to support the identified strategies and activities
- Selection of measurement and evaluation tools to help assess the marketing plan's effectiveness and to allow for needed modifications

---

LODGING LANGUAGE

Advertising: Information about a hotel that the hotel pays a fee to distribute.

Publicity: Information about a hotel that is distributed for free by the media.

■

In addition to advertising activities, an effective sales and marketing plan includes promotion and publicity-generating activities. These three terms are closely related, sometimes overlap, and are often confused; however, each plays a part in the successful sales and marketing of a hotel.

- *Advertising.* Hotels have numerous opportunities to advertise their products and services. The best advertising is clearly directed at the hotel's identified target markets, and it should be cost-effective, because advertising, by definition, must be paid for by the hotel.

- *Promotions.* In the hotel industry, the term "promotion" most often refers to a special packaging of products or services. For example, a hotel in a cold climate may create a "Summer Getaway" promotion to be marketed in the winter. The inclusive package might include a sleeping room, the use of the hotel's pool, a special "beach theme" dinner party, and complimentary rum-based drinks to remind guests of those consumed at the beach. Specially priced, this package would be promoted through advertising and publicity. Similarly, a franchise company may offer, as a special promotion, triple airline (frequent flier) miles for all stays completed between two fixed dates. Again, information about this promotion would be disseminated through advertising and, possibly, publicity.

- *Publicity.* Publicity refers to information about the hotel that is distributed free of charge, by the media. The good news is that publicity costs the hotel nothing. The bad news is that the publicity may be either good or bad. The news media is, of necessity, an independent force in the shaping of public opinion. Cultivating good relationships with the media is an important part of a hotel manager's job. When a good relationship exists, it may be easier for the hotel to achieve positive publicity. If, for example, the governor of the state is visiting your hotel, and this fact is mentioned in the newspaper, the publicity value is good. However, even with good media relationships, a highly publicized fire in a nearby hotel carrying the same brand affiliation as your hotel would be widely reported and might reflect poorly on your own property.

An annual marketing plan is essentially a blueprint or recipe for the sales and marketing effort. The sales and marketing committee should be carefully monitored to make sure that it undertakes and implements the activities and expenditures proposed are in the plan. The plan should be evaluated regularly to ensure that the activities yield the results anticipated by the hotel.

─────────────── **ALL IN A DAY'S WORK** ───────────────

The Situation

Darnell Claxton, the manager at the Best Sleep hotel, was listening carefully as Wanda McInty, the advertising sales representative, finished her presentation. She had arrived unannounced at the hotel 15 minutes earlier, and because she was associated with the local university, Darnell had agreed to see her without an appointment.

"So you see," said Wanda, "It's the actual football program that will be sold during the big State University home-coming football game next month. We're going to print thousands of copies. Advertising in it will give great exposure to your hotel. And best of all, the cost is only $2,000 for a full-page ad. All the local hotels are participating. Can we count on the Best Sleep to buy an ad? I have to turn in all the ad requests by Friday, so I really need your answer today".

A Response

Hotel sales and marketing plans should always allow some room for unanticipated activities and expenditures. Hoteliers responsible for managing sales and marketing efforts know, however, that literally hundreds of advertising and promotional opportunities are presented to them annually. In the great majority of cases, the hotel should pursue only planned (and budgeted-for) activities, and not those that are undertaken as an impulsive reaction to a persuasive sales pitch.

If advertising in the local university football program is indeed a part of Best Sleep's total marketing plan this year, then the advertising opportunity should be explored. If not, Darnell can politely reply that while such an expenditure is not in the budget this year, the sales and marketing team of the hotel will seriously consider it for next year, and he should see that they do so. True professionals who are selling advertising understand the hotel budgeting process, and they will appreciate Darnell's time and polite consideration of their proposal regardless of his final decision about the ad.

Off-Property Activities

In addition to the sales and marketing activities implemented by a hotel, there will also be off-property sales efforts undertaken by others. Several groups may benefit from increased room sales activity at a hotel and, therefore have an interest in assisting with a its sales and marketing efforts. Chief among these in a franchised hotel is the hotel's franchisor. In addition, the local CVB and others can benefit when hotels do a good job selling their products. Understanding the role each of these groups plays is essential to effective hotel marketing.

Franchisor's Efforts

Franchisors charge their franchisees monthly fees based upon the sales levels achieved by the franchisee's hotel(s). When the revenue achieved by a hotel increases, so do the fees collected by the franchisor. As a result, franchisors work hard to promote their brands. Some significant efforts include:

- *National call centers.* Many travelers prefer a certain hotel brand but may not know whether it is represented in specific geographic areas. For example, a traveler in Florida may enjoy staying at Best Sleep brand hotels but does not know if there is a Best Sleep in Denver. If Best Sleep advertises that travelers can call a toll-free number to learn about its locations and to make reservations, the Florida traveler might make the telephone call and, utilizing the information given by the national call center, reserve a Best Sleep room in Denver. All national hotel brands maintain a call center. Hotel managers should periodically call the national call center to carefully monitor the information about their hotel that the agents answering calls give to potential guests. Information about the hotel should be kept up to date and accurate to maximize the chances for the call center to sell its rooms.

A nationally recognized logo, the responsibility of a hotel brand's managers, helps the marketing efforts of all the hotels operating as part of that brand.

- *Brand-specific Web sites.* Hotel brands understand that using the Internet is a favorite way for travelers to get information about hotels. The best of the brands have created easily usable, highly informative Web sites that allow travelers using their own computers to make reservations and receive confirmation numbers.

- *National advertising.* Most hotels are too small to advertise on national television or take out an ad in a national newspaper such as *USA Today.* Collectively, however, the advertising fees collected by a franchisor can make such ad placement possible. When a brand develops a nationally recognized name and logo, it can be used in advertisements directed toward the brand's target customers. The result is national exposure and effective advertising for even the smallest of hotels affiliated with the brand.

- *Brand-specific promotions.* Earlier in this chapter you learned that hotels can create promotions to offer special services or packages of services designed to attract travelers. Brand managers also create and market special promotions. These can include special rates, room amenities, or upgrades given to members of the brand's **frequent guest program**.

LODGING LANGUAGE

Frequent Guest Program: A promotional effort administered by a hotel brand which rewards travelers every time they choose to stay at the brand's affiliated hotels. Typical rewards include free-night stays, room upgrades, and complimentary hotel services.

■

- *PMS training and support programs.* Because the PMS is so important to a hotel's ability to sell rooms effectively, most franchisors offer training programs related to its operation as well as technical support in times of hardware or software glitches or failure. These programs are typically free to franchisees or are supplied to them at a nominal fee.
- *Sales training programs.* The effective selling of hotel rooms is a skill that can be taught and learned. Well-managed hotel brands offer their franchisees frequent and inexpensive or free-to-attend classes and seminars and may distribute training materials to help managers teach rooms-selling skills to employees who need training of this type.

CVB Efforts

In addition to the sales and marketing efforts of a hotel and its franchisor, the local convention and visitors bureau may help to market the hotel. Professional hoteliers, whether their properties are large or small, are active members of their CVBs. By participating, they can influence the CVB in ways that increase business opportunities for their hotels. Not every effort by a CVB will result in additional room nights sold in an area, but the mission of any CVB is to increase the number of visitors to the area it represents, and of course, some of these visitors will require overnight accommodations. CVBs (also known as conference and/or tourism boards in many countries) are primarily not-for-profit organizations that represent a specific destination, such as a city or region. They serve as the major point of contact for their destination for meeting professionals and tour operators as well as individual visitors.

CVBs offer unbiased information about an area's lodging and entertainment facilities. They save visitors time and energy because they are a one-stop "shop" for local tourism information. They provide a full range of information about a destination and do not charge for their services because they are funded by a combination of taxes and membership dues. The advantages of a hotel enjoying a positive working relationship with its local CVB are clear.

LODGING ON-LINE

Professionally managed convention and visitors bureaus work hard to promote the areas they represent. One of the very best is the CVB of New York City. To view its Web site and explore the ways a CVB can help promote tourism-related and other visitors to a business community, go to:

http://www.nycvisit.com

A CVB may be operated as an independent entity or may be affiliated with a local area **chamber of commerce**.

LODGING LANGUAGE

Chamber of Commerce: An organization whose goal is the advancement of all business interests within a community or larger business region. Sometimes called "the chamber" for short.

■

LODGING ON-LINE

Chambers of commerce exist in nearly every community. There are also regional, state, and national chambers. Go to:

www.chamberofcommerce.com

Utilize the site's search engine to find and explore the chamber nearest you.

Other Efforts

Many individuals, businesses, and other entities profit when hotels sell more hotel rooms. Some of the most important of these are the travel agent and travel advisory groups. As we discovered in Chapter 1, travel agents assist transient and group travelers who come to a hotel for a variety of reasons, such as vacations, weddings, visiting friends and family in the area, or any number of other work-related and non-work-related reasons. Unlike the corporate traveler who may return to the same geographic area frequently, leisure travelers tend to visit a specific area or hotel less often. As a result, leisure travelers have traditionally relied very heavily on the advice of travel agents and other travel advisory groups to recommend hotels. A travel agent who books a client into a hotel is usually paid a commission for the booking. A large travel agency can influence a great many travelers to use a specific hotel. That is why contact with travel agents can be an important tactic in a hotel's sales and marketing efforts.

In addition to travel agents, many travelers are members of one or more travel advisory groups. These groups consist of individuals who share useful travel information, including information about hotels, with other members. One of the largest and most popular travel advisory groups is the American Automobile Association (AAA). AAA is a not-for-profit membership organization of over 80 motor clubs, with more than 1,000 agency offices serving over 44 million people in the United States and Canada.

AAA publishes a tour book that rates hotels for travelers. AAA evaluators visit hotels without announcing that they are coming (but at the hotel's specific request). They rate hotels on the following six characteristics:

- Exterior, grounds, and public areas
- Guestrooms and bathrooms
- Housekeeping and maintenance
- Room décor, ambiance, and amenities
- Management
- Guest services

Based on the evaluator's assessment, the hotel is assigned an overall property rating consisting of one to five diamonds (five diamonds is the highest possible score). The AAA rating book for 2003 listed the following approximate results:

- 0.2% were 5-diamond properties
- 2.8% were 4-diamond properties
- 53.2% were 3-diamond properties
- 34.5% were 2-diamond properties

> **One Diamond:** Essential, no-frills accommodations. These hotels meet basic requirements related to comfort, cleanliness, and hospitality.
> **Two Diamonds:** Modest enhancements to the one-diamond type property are required. Moderate prices prevail, and amenities and design elements are modest as well.
> **Three Diamonds:** These properties appeal to travelers with greater needs than those provided by two-diamond hotels. Marked improvements in physical attributes, amenities, and level of service above the two-diamond properties are evident in these hotels.
> **Four Diamonds:** These hotels are upscale in all areas. Accommodations are refined and stylish. The hallmark of a four-diamond hotel is its extensive array of amenities and a high degree of hospitality, service, and attention to detail.
> **Five Diamonds:** This highest level reflects a hotel of the first class. The physical facilities are extraordinary in every manner. The fundamental hallmarks at this level are meticulous service and the ability to exceed all guest expectations while maintaining an impeccable standard of excellence and personalized service.

FIGURE 8.3   What the AAA Diamond Ratings Represent

- 6.8% were 1-diamond properties
- 2.5% Failed 1-diamond rating

Figure 8.3 describes the rating system used by AAA. While it is similar to the rating/advising systems of other travel advisory groups that assign hotels stars or points to indicate relative quality, it is currently the U.S. rating system of greatest importance.

LODGING ON-LINE

AAA ratings are important to travelers as well as to hoteliers. To learn more about how to promote a hotel by working with this membership travel organization, go to its Web site at:

http://www.aaa.com

HOTEL MARKETS

The types of travelers who visit hotels are as varied as the hotels serving them. While travelers can be segmented in a variety of ways (as we saw in Chapter 7), most hoteliers consider travelers to be either transient or part of a group. Therefore "transient" and "group" are the two major hotel markets. Recall that transient travelers are individual hotel guests who are not part of a group or tour booking. Transient guests can be further subdivided by traveler demographics to gain more detailed information about them. For example, they can be considered corporate, leisure, or government travelers. The group market, on the other hand, refers to guests who are a part of a larger, multiple-traveler booking, such as those in a tour bus, wedding party, visiting sports team, or corporate training session. To understand how sales and marketing efforts can effectively target these two traveler markets, they will be examined in detail.

Transient Travelers

Individual transient travelers are important to nearly all hotels, but they are especially important to limited-service properties. This is so because limited-service properties are not typically built with as much meeting space as is often requested by groups and do not generally offer extensive food services. Transient travelers generally do not require meeting space or food services, and therefore they can freely choose between limited-service and full-service properties.

Transient travelers can be segmented (categorized) in a variety of ways. The best segmentations for a specific hotel to use depend upon the make-up of its own unique transient market. In most hotels the following transient categories are considered to be significant enough to **track**.

LODGING LANGUAGE

Track: Maintain extensive information on a specific type of traveler. For example, a hotel may wish to track the ADR, rooms used, and arrival patterns of transient military travelers to learn more about this traveler type.

■

- *Corporate.* This segment consists of business travelers. It is a very important segment because the room rates paid by business travelers are among the highest the hotel will receive. Business travelers have special needs, and the members of the sales and marketing team that sell to them must be keenly aware of both the source of these travelers and the hotel services they desire. Business travelers make up a large portion of the traveling public. This segment is increasingly changing from one dominated by male travelers to one divided almost evenly between male and female travelers. Business travelers are a demanding group, but one that pays well for what it wants.

  Groups of corporate travelers sometimes come together to form buying **consortia**. Consortia are simply multiple large buyers of hotel (or other hospitality) services that affiliate in order to obtain lower prices for their members.

LODGING LANGUAGE

Consortia: Groups of hotel service buyers organized for the purpose of reducing their clients' travel-related costs. A single such group is a consortium.

■

For example, a consortium representing dozens of large corporate travel departments may request that a hotel offer significant discounts if any of the corporate travelers represented by the consortium stay at the hotel. A hotel that agrees to work with the consortium will evaluate the potential volume level of this client, establish a **negotiated rate**, identify any blackout dates that apply, and then track the consortium's pick-up.

LODGING LANGUAGE

Negotiated Rate: A special room rate offered for a fixed period of time to a specific client of the hotel. As in "What is the negotiated rate we should offer the Travelsavers consortium next year?"

■

The corporate market is large, and as a result, many hotels assign their very best salespersons to this transient segment.

- *Leisure.* Leisure travelers are also an important market segment for many hotels. In some resort areas, they may constitute nearly 100 percent of all hotel guests. As mentioned earlier in this chapter, leisure travelers visit an area for a variety of personal and recreational reasons, and this group must be directly addressed in any successful sales and marketing plan.

- *Government.* Local, state and federal government workers (including military personnel) are a large part of the clientele of many mid-priced full- and limited-service hotels. Government travelers typically are allowed a **per diem** for their hotel stays, and this amount, for some hotels, represents an ADR attractive enough to aggressively seek these their business.

LODGING LANGUAGE

Per Diem: A daily, fixed amount paid for a traveler's food and lodging expenses. Established by companies, government agencies, or other entities, the per diem amount for a traveler will be based upon the costs associated with the area to which the individual travels. For example, the per diem for a traveler spending the night in New York City will be higher than for a traveler spending the night in a less expensive area of the country.

LODGING ON-LINE

The federal government establishes per diem rates to help control its travel costs. To view the rates established for military travelers by the Department of Defense, go to:

http://www.dtic.mil/perdiem/pdrates.htmlm

- *Long-term stay.* In some cases, when guests check in to a hotel they plan to stay for a very long time. These long-term or extended-stay guests are an emerging market segment. In fact, some entire hotel brands have been designed to appeal specifically to them. Not all hotels appeal to long-term stay guests, but most hotels have some clients who fit this category. At the less expensive end of the room rate scale, some properties that attract extended stay guests do so by providing larger rooms (or suites), cooking facilities, and refrigerators. At the higher end of the room charge scale, hotels have always appealed to some wealthy clients who prefer to live in an environment that provides food, security, and cleaning services rather than in an apartment. Long-term-stay guests come to hotels for a wide variety of reasons and include individuals working on construction projects, those seeking permanent housing in the area, and those whose homes are temporarily uninhabitable. This is a highly desirable market segment for several reasons, including the guaranteed occupancy the guests bring to the hotel, the ease of cleaning their rooms, and their relatively uncomplicated billing. A disadvantage is that these rooms are often sold at very low daily rates. Despite that fact, some hotels assign specific sales and marketing team members specifically to this segment and have great success with it.

LODGING ON-LINE

To view the features offered by one of the very best managed extended-stay brands, visit Hyatt Hotel's "Hawthorn Suites" Web site at:

http://www.hawthorn.com/

Group Travelers

For many hotels, 50 percent or more of their business is the result of providing lodging for group travelers. In fact, in some large hotels built primarily to house groups holding conventions, nearly 100 percent of their entire business may be group-related.

The actual definition of what constitutes a group varies by hotel. For example, two people traveling together are not likely to be considered a group by any hotel, whereas nearly all hotels would consider 100 people traveling together a group. For many hotels, the purchase of 10 or more rooms constitutes a minimum-sized group sale, but this can vary somewhat depending upon the hotel manager and the size of the hotel. Since there is no universally accepted definition of group, it is the hotel's manager who determines when a proposed sale requires the creation of a group contract.

A group contract details the responsibilities of each party in the purchase of a large number of hotel rooms. The group contract lets the hotel know how many rooms the group wishes to purchase and identifies a deadline date by which the purchase must be made. Typically, a group contract will include information related to the group's:

The ability to make effective presentations is an important skill utilized by managers on a hotel's sales and marketing team.

- Name
- Billing address
- Arrival date
- Departure date
- Requested room types
- Room rate(s) to be paid
- Date by which the requested rooms must be reserved
- Request for additional hotel services
- Form of payment
- Authorized representative

Group contracts can be lengthy and detailed because groups often make extensive use of hotel services in addition to sleeping rooms. These services can include:

- Catered meals
- Meeting space
- Audiovisual equipment
- Registration services
- Transportation
- Baggage handling
- Welcome receptions
- On-site activities

The needs of a specific group depend upon the reasons for their travel. Thus, the needs of a seniors group touring for leisure and stopping for one night on their way to a final destination will be different from the needs of a future bride wishing to secure weekend sleeping rooms for her wedding guests as well as the food and beverage services needed for her wedding banquet.

An effective sales and marketing plan will include significant efforts to attract **SMERF** and other groups that are potential clients of the hotel.

LODGING LANGUAGE

SMERF: Short for "Social, Military, Educational, Religious, or Fraternal groups" and organizations.

■

This is so because the group market segment is of significant size. Group members hold organizational meetings, may travel as a group, and frequently hold conferences and conventions. Additional market groups that may, depending on the hotel, deserve special marketing plan attention include sports teams, government workers, tour bus, or any other defined group large enough, in the opinion of the hotel's managers, to be worth soliciting. This can be more effectively done if the hotel begins by identifying the **meeting planner** used by the groups the hotel has targeted for solicitation.

LODGING LANGUAGE

Meeting Planner: A professional employed by a group to negotiate its contract with a hotel.

■

Professional meeting planners annually buy large numbers of sleeping rooms and reserve significant amounts of meeting and catering space. They may do so on behalf of many different groups and organizations as well as some corporations. Sophisticated buyers of hotel products, they often use comparison-shopping techniques, and can heavily influence a hotel's reputation based on their experience with it.

LODGING ON-LINE

Meeting Professionals International (MPI) is the world's largest association of meeting planning professionals with more than 19,000 members in 64 countries. To visit its Web site, go to:

http://www.mpiweb.org

Note the large number of member educational services it offers.

SALES AND MARKETING TOOLS

Regardless of whether they seek to attract transient business, group business, or both, the sales and marketing team will be able to utilize a variety of sales tools. The type of tool selected and its effectiveness depends, in many cases, upon the skill of the person developing and using the tool as well as the appropriateness of the tool for the market segment sought by the hotel. Among the many available selling tools, the five listed below are used by most hotels:

- In-person sales calls
- Print and direct mail
- Telephone
- E-mail
- Web sites

In-Person Sales Calls

The majority of guests who visit a hotel are not return guests. While some guests do return week after week or year after year, most guests do not. Because that is true, a hotel must continually seek new clients. Identifying and soliciting new clients is, arguably, the single most important task of a sales team. A sales **lead** can come from many sources.

LODGING LANGUAGE

Lead: Information about a prospect who is likely to buy products and services from the hotel.

■

When the sales and marketing team believes a lead represents the potential for a sale, the lead will be followed, if possible, by an in-person **sales call**.

LODGING LANGUAGE

Sales Call: A meeting arranged for the purpose of selling the hotel's products and services.

■

Networking can create leads. Leads can come from a convention and visitors bureau, from a referral by a current guest, from employees, or simply from a prospect's telephone call to the hotel.

LODGING LANGUAGE

Networking: The development of personal relationships for a business-related purpose. For example, a chamber of commerce–sponsored breakfast open to all community business leaders interested in improving local traffic conditions would be an excellent example of a networking opportunity for a member of a hotel's sales team.

■

A sales team's ability to seek out and cultivate quality leads is critical to its success. An effective sales and marketing team structures its work in a way that provides adequate time to follow up leads with a sales call, and even more important, reserves adequate time for **cold calling**.

LODGING LANGUAGE

Cold Calling: Making a sales visit/ presentation to a potential client without having previously set an appointment to do so.

■

Good salespeople seek opportunities to cold call whenever they can. The objective of these sales calls is to qualify prospective clients by identifying those with a high likelihood of using the hotel's rooms or services. Of course, the most likely prospects are further cultivated until a sale is made. Outstanding sales teams actively seek out and create sales opportunities by following up on sales leads and by making a predetermined number of in-person sales calls and cold calls each week. Such calls should be followed with a thank-you note or letter thanking the prospect for the meeting and inviting the prospect to the hotel for a site tour.

In addition to arranging meetings with potential clients outside of the hotel, sales and marketing teams should always be prepared to host a **drop in**.

LODGING LANGUAGE

Drop In: A potential group buyer of rooms or hotel services who arrives at the hotel without an appointment.

■

A drop in is potential buyer who arrives on the property and requests a site tour of sleeping rooms, meeting rooms, or banquet facilities. If a member of the hotel's staff is not available to meet with prospects when they arrive, a sales opportunity may be lost. Drop ins are a reminder to management that some member of the hotel's sales team should be available at the hotel for the maximum number of reasonable hours per day to conduct site tours if needed.

LODGING ON-LINE

One of the best sales and marketing resources available to hoteliers is a book written by Howard Feiertag and John Hogan. Feiertag, a faculty member in the hospitality management program at Virginia Tech University, is recognized as one of the country's foremost experts on hotel sales. The book is titled *Lessons from the Field; A Common Sense Approach to Effective Hotel Sales.* It is available from JM Press, Brentwood, Tennessee. To view its Web site, go to:

www.jmpress.com

The book may also be available from other specialized on-line booksellers

Print and Direct Mail

Not every potential client can be contacted by a personal sales call. Print material delivered by direct mail can be an effective sales tool for potential clients located far away from the hotel or for times when a hotel sales team is attempting to determine the quality of a potential sales lead prior to arranging a sales call. For example, assume that a hotel's sales team first identified and then sought to advertise its rooms and services to the 100 largest group tour bus companies in the country. While it is unlikely that a member of the hotel's sales team could visit 100 tour bus locations, the team could develop a **direct mail** advertisement to all of them.

LODGING LANGUAGE

Direct Mail: The process of sending an advertisement to clients by U.S. mail service. The total cost of a direct mail piece includes the expenditures for the advertisement's design, printing, and mailing.

■

Direct mail can be viewed as indirect sales call. A sales and marketing team can set a goal for the number of direct mail pieces to be mailed each month. If the number of direct mail pieces drops below established goals, the hotel's sales and marketing team leader should discuss the need to maintain appropriate direct mailing levels. This can be done simply by explaining that direct mail pieces can "visit" prospects when a direct sales call is not possible. Just as increasing personal cold calls will most often increase hotel sales, the greater the number of direct mail pieces sent out, the more likely is the hotel to meet its revenue goals.

Of course, like direct sales calls, these indirect sales calls must be effective in the selling mission. The rules for effectiveness in direct mail are similar to those for in-person sales.

The best direct mail pieces:

- Are eye-catching
- Reflect positively on the hotel's image
- Don't say too much

- Introduce relevant hotel features and benefits
- Support the benefits with proof statements
- Are cost-effective
- Ask for the sale (order) or a site visit

If possible, the direct mail piece should also include an incentive designed to encourage the person receiving it to book the hotel now rather than postpone the decision. An effective direct mail piece could be a skillfully created postcard, a well-written first-class letter, or even a cleverly fashioned package. In all cases, it should be designed to expand the sales reach of a hotel. It must do so in a cost-effective way, and it should result in measurable increases in the hotel's visibility and revenue.

Telephone

Even in this day of advanced technology, the ordinary telephone call still presents an excellent selling opportunity for most hotels. Many incoming calls to a hotel will be from potential guests and, therefore, should be answered and responded to in a professional manner. In addition, outgoing telephone calls should be used extensively by the sales and marketing team to identify prospects, set appointments, and solicit room sales.

When trained properly, the sales and marketing team can use the telephone to:

- Make transient reservations
- Answer questions about group reservations and bids
- Find prospects who may be interested in a site tour
- Identify prospects and arrange dates and times for in-person sales calls

All employees who use the telephone as part of their regular duties should be trained in telephone selling skills.

- Increase the speed and accuracy of information transmitted to the caller
- Overcome resistance to sales barriers (for example, room rate too high or the hotel's lack of specific amenities)
- Improve total hotel revenue generated by telephone

When potential guests call a hotel, the employees answering the telephone must be knowledgeable and confident from the first moment they pick up the phone. The caller will form an instantaneous impression not only of the hotel representative but of the hotel itself from the representative's demeanor on the phone. To make a sale or provide information professionally, it is important that inside sales representatives have effective telephone skills. They must use their voices to increase trust and project a favorable personal impression. They must use positive and proactive language to handle a variety of situations effectively. Because answering machines are so prevalent in today's business world, the hotel sales staff must also have the ability, when necessary, to leave clear, concise voice mail messages.

LODGING ON-LINE

The Educational Institute of the American Hotel and Lodging Association (AH&LA) produces up-to-date training material about how to effectively utilize the telephone as a sales tool. To view its most recent video, go to:

http://www.ei-ah&la.org

When you arrive, search for the video titled "Courtesy Rules, Better Telephone Skills Now."

E-mail

Today's active business person answers telephone calls, reviews the daily mail, and increasingly checks the e-mail in-box on a computer several times per day. The most effective hotel sales efforts recognize this fact and use it, as well as other more traditional forms of client communication, to improve hotel revenues.

Hotels have long communicated with guests by means of direct mailings, the telephone, and more recently by fax. Today, e-mail systems are a newer method of mass communication that is increasingly used. Hotel salespersons should include their e-mail addresses on their business cards. Since most hotel guests do so as well, an effective, up-to-date e-mail list is today's equivalent of traditional systems of manually filing business cards. Unlike direct mail, e-mails can be inexpensively sent to virtually hundreds of clients and potential clients in a matter of seconds. While each hotel must decide how best to use e-mail in its selling effort, there are some general principles related to the effective use of e-mail. These include:

- Maintain an up-to-date list of e-mail addresses
- Create e-mail sales messages that are short, but effective
- Send e-mails at the proper frequency (too many will be perceived as spam, yet too few will not be as effective)
- Provide a convenient way for recipients to be removed from your e-mail list

In addition to its usefulness in communicating a sales message directly to clients, e-mail is increasingly the preferred method of attaching and exchanging documents, such as sales proposals, menus, and contracts. Most e-mail systems automatically update the user's database whenever an e-mail is received, thus helping to keep e-mail addresses current.

Properly used, an e-mail database can be accessed whenever the hotel wishes to innovatively communicate a special rate, promotion, or new hotel feature to its client list. Improperly used, e-mails can irritate potential guests. They may become so annoying that the recipients simply delete them almost as quickly as they are sent! Well-designed e-mail communication systems will continue to play an important communications role in the hotel sales and marketing effort and should be utilized to their fullest potential.

Web Sites

Recognizing the growing popularity of the Internet, most large hotels have created their own Web sites to help increase revenues. In addition, large and small hotels affiliated with a brand often share Web sites with other brand franchisees. In this way, even small hotels can achieve some level of visibility on their own Web page. While the Internet is, in many respects, simply another marketing tool used by a hotel, its significance, growth, and potential require special attention. When properly utilized and managed, the Internet is an excellent vehicle for communicating with current and potential clients. In 2004, Internet hotel sales accounted for 18 percent of all reservations made, and that number is increasing yearly.

An important point for hoteliers to remember is that the Internet allows smaller hotels to compete on an equal footing with larger ones. The Internet, at this point in its development, delivers just three media components: audio, text, and images. Each can be just as good on a small hotel's Web site as on a larger competitor's site (or even better). An effectively designed Web site allows a hotel to take advantage of an inexpensive direct line to consumers. Some hotel sales and marketing teams have never used Web site advertising and may not know how to manage it properly.

Before the Internet came into wide use and hotels began to create Web sites, a sales team that wanted an individual consumer or travel agent to "see" and experience the hotel had to do a direct mail piece or arrange for site visits. Both of these strategies can be expensive. With a Web site, potential clients can "see" the hotel immediately and at a typical cost to the hotel of only a few hundred dollars per month.

Web sites can easily generate in-person and telephone sales opportunities. Consider, for example, that drop ins, callers, meeting planners, travel agents, and consortium members may all learn about a specific hotel by surfing hotel Web sites on the Internet. Individual transient guests can reserve rooms via the net, and meeting planners can view a hotel's rooms and meeting space through the hotel's on-line brochure or, more recently, on streaming video tours. In addition, many travel wholesalers sell on the Internet, and technology-savvy hotels can connect their own Web sites to wholesale sites likely to draw potential guests.

The appearance of a hotel's Web site has become increasingly important and will continue to be even more so. The placement of text, images, and other media, and white space, on a Web page makes a strong statement about the quality of a hotel's products and services. Despite this fact, most hoteliers simply do not have the ability to create an effective Web page, nor do they have the technical skill required to evaluate the site's effectiveness.

LODGING ON-LINE

Some companies specialize in providing Web site design and other technology application solutions to hotels. To view one such company's product offerings, go to:

www.acromarketing.com

Evaluating the quality of a Web site can be complex; however, there are some characteristics that all effective hotel Web sites have in common. These are identified in Figure 8.4 below.

LODGING LANGUAGE

Link: A relationship between two Web sites. When Web site users select a link at one site, they are taken to another Web site address. An external link leads to a Web page other than the current one; an internal link leads elsewhere on the current Web site.

■

Some hotels do not obtain the results they seek from their Web sites because they do not link their sites properly and do not take full advantage of Internet search engines to identify the sites to which they should link. Effective Web sites should be linked in a manner that maximizes their sales potential. For example, assume a hotel located near the stadium of a professional sports team. Internet users who enter the name of the team in a search engine (for example, Excite or Yahoo) are probably looking for information about the team, such as its roster, won/lost record, and schedule. They are not necessarily seeking hotel rooms. Therefore, linking with sites that appear on a search for the team's name may not be effective for the hotel despite the high number of hits to these sites. Alternatively, however, consumers who search for driving directions to the stadium are likely to be:

- Attending one or more of the games
- Unfamiliar with the area
- Potentially seeking a place to dine or stay overnight

- The site is easy to navigate.
- The site has some level of interactivity.
- The site is connected (has a **link**) to appropriate companion sites.
- The site allows for the on-line booking of a reservation.
- The site balances guest privacy needs with the hotel's desire to build a customer database.
- Updating and revising room rates on the site is easy.
- The site includes a virtual tour of the property (with at least enough pictures or streaming video to provide an accurate image of the hotel).
- The site complements the hotel's other marketing efforts.
- The site is in the language(s) of the hotel's major clients.
- The site address is easy to remember.

FIGURE 8.4 Characteristics of Effective Hotel Web Sites

In this example, Web sites that appear when "Stadium," "Stadium Driving Directions," and similar entries are entered into search engines are likely to produce guests for the hotel, even though the number of hits from these sites may be smaller. With which sites should a hotel link? The answer is: all of the sites affiliated with the hotel's major **demand generators**.

LODGING LANGUAGE

Demand Generator: An organization, entity, or location that creates a significant need for hotel services. Examples in a community include large businesses, tourist sites, sports teams, educational facilities, and manufacturing plants.

■

Once guests arrive at hotel Web site through effective link development, the site can be used to promote the hotel's packages, guest rooms, and other services. There are significant marketing cost savings when discounts on hotel products and services are offered on a Web site. Spending money on regular advertising means that a hotel must pay for everyone who sees (and doesn't see) the advertisement, regardless of whether a purchase is made. By contrast, when marketing dollars are spent by charging less for products purchased on-line, the hotel must only pay for the people who actually place orders. As a result the hotel is charged for this form of advertising only when it is effective!

Many Web shoppers are looking for the best quality of hotel they can select at the lowest price available, and Web advertising makes it easy for them to identify which hotel offers a low price. For many hotels, selling rooms on the Web for a reduced price makes good economic sense because it is often a much less expensive sales method than in-person sales calls or a direct mail campaign. Because of the increasing importance of the Web to total sales and marketing effort, a hotel should always promote its Web site to current clients and contacts by including the hotel's site address on staff business cards as well as on all advertising and promotional materials.

LODGING ON-LINE

For an example of how a hotel can effectively link its own Internet site to a site that may bring it additional business, visit the site of the Chicago Convention and Visitor's Bureau, at:

http://www.chicago.il.org/hotels_location

When you arrive at the site, click on "North Michigan Avenue"; then choose, "Ritz Carlton Chicago", and see how the hotel many call the best in North America has used its Web site to link to the city's.

Client-Appreciation Activities

Experienced hoteliers know that making a sale is only the beginning (and not the end) of the client/hotel relationship. Too many hotels lose clients simply because they did not let the client know how much their business was appreciated. Client-appreciation activities allow the hotel to express its gratitude to clients for their current business. These activities can include anything from inviting a client or group of clients to join the hotel manager for dinner or drinks, to organizing an elaborate, once or twice a year gala client-appreciation event. Golfing and sporting events, con-

Hoteliers can use a variety of social settings to demonstrate their appreciation of a client's business.

certs and theater tickets are all ways to express a genuine appreciation for business received. Gift giving is another traditional way to express appreciation to a hotel's best clients. Gifts given to clients as tokens of appreciation can range from the simple to the elaborate. It is, of course, important to first determine whether the client's employer permits the acceptance of gifts. In all cases, the goal of a successful client-appreciation event or activity is to solidify the business relationship with current clients and to communicate to potential clients the seriousness with which the hotel views the hotel/ client relationship. On a regular basis, hotels must objectively review and evaluate the quantity and quality of their client-appreciation activities.

EVALUATION OF SALES AND MARKETING EFFORTS

Evaluating sales and marketing efforts is one of the most difficult tasks faced by hoteliers. Reduced sales and guest counts, for example, are not always the result of ineffective sales and marketing. Hotel revenues may decline for reasons totally unrelated to sales and marketing.

Consider, for example, that a hotel with stagnant or declining revenues may not provide good service, and if so, it may well be the poor service, not poor selling efforts, that keeps sales from increasing. This could certainly be true when housekeeping, maintenance, or other staff members do not perform well. In other cases, the hotel may face lowered sales levels if the property is older or if newer competitors are capturing more of the market. Also, if the total market size declines, it is reasonable to expect that revenue levels, at least in the short run, will decline also.

Despite the difficulty of measuring and evaluating the efforts of the sales and marketing team, it must be done. Fortunately, there are a variety of tools available to help make this job easier. Certainly a hotel owner or general manager can subjectively evaluate the professionalism and appearance of the sales and marketing staff, their diligence at work, and their creativity in presenting the hotel's best features. Also, in some cases, the presence of increasing occupancies may indicate good efforts by the sales and marketing team, as may increases in ADR. It is important to remember, however, that both types of increases could result from an increase in guest demand and thus could mask a decline in the quality of sales and marketing efforts.

Fortunately, there are also quantitative reports designed to measure the actual end results of the sales and marketing effort. These include an evaluation of the hotel's Performance to Sales and Marketing Plan and the **Smith Travel Accommodations Report (STAR report).**

LODGING LANGUAGE

STAR Report: Short for the "Smith Travel Accommodations Report." Produced by Smith Travel Research, this report is used to compare a hotel's sales results to those of its selected competitors.

■

Performance to Sales and Marketing Plan

One valuable way to evaluate a hotel's sales and marketing effort is to compare the property's accomplishments to those originally identified in its Sales and Marketing Plan. Recall that the Sales and Marketing Plan identifies specific marketing strategies and activities designed to meet the hotel's revenue goals. Therefore, hotel owners and managers can compare the specific advertising, promotion, and publicity efforts originally planned by the sales and marketing team with the work this group actually completed.

In addition to evaluating what was done, the timeliness of efforts and conformity to established budgets can also be reviewed. To illustrate, assume that a hotel had intended, as part of its sales and marketing plan, to create a New Year's Eve package designed to attract local transient guests on the night of December 31st. The package was designed to include, for one special price, a guest room, champagne, party favors, and a complimentary in-room movie. Advertisement of the package was to begin in mid-November, with a total established advertising budget of $5,000.

If, as planned, advertising for the package really did begin in mid-November, and if the total amount spent on advertising was approximately $5,000, then the sales team has likely performed well. If, alternatively, the advertisement for the package was initiated four weeks late (mid-December), and if, as a result, the hotel could only sell out its rooms by spending substantially more on advertising than was originally planned, the team has not performed as well in terms of timing or adherence to budget. In this case, the team's efforts should be closely examined to identify the reason(s) for the advertising delay and its resulting negative impact on the budget.

In evaluating over-all performance of the sales and marketing plan, there are four important areas to consider:

- *What.* This simply means comparing what was planned to be done with what was actually done. "Plan your work, then work your plan" is an often-repeated phrase in the hotel business. Even the best sales and marketing plans will be ineffective if they are not implemented.
- *Who.* Even if a sales or marketing activity has been fully completed, the quality of accomplishment is typically dependent upon the expertise of the em-

ployees doing the work. It is important that the hotel assign employees skilled at sales and marketing to its essential sales and marketing activities. These activities are too important to be delegated to unskilled employees.

- *How Much.* Given a large enough marketing budget, virtually any hotel sales and marketing team could achieve improvements in hotel revenues. Realistically, however, marketing resources, like all resources in a hotel, are limited. It is important to undertake activities designed to improve revenues, but it is just as important to complete these activities in a cost-effective manner. By comparing actual marketing expenditures to the expenditures in the budget section of the sales and marketing plan, the cost-management abilities of the sales and marketing team can be properly assessed.

- *How Effective.* The most important evaluation of a sales and marketing plan is based on its ultimate effectiveness. Following implementation of the sales and marketing plan, did revenues go up, go down, or stay the same? Even the best plans are sometimes affected by unanticipated events and these must be considered. Nonetheless, if specific target goals of occupancy level and ADR have been established in a sales and marketing plan, it is reasonable to compare them with the actual results evaluate the over-all effectiveness of the sales and marketing effort.

STAR Report

While an assessment of the Performance to Sales and Marketing Plan tells the hotel's owner and management what has been done by the sales team, it does not, by itself, assess the relative quality of the results achieved. If a hotel has followed its sales and marketing plan, and is experiencing a 60 percent occupancy rate, it is difficult to know whether that level of occupancy is good or bad unless the occupancy level of competing hotels is also known. If, for example, your hotel is averaging a 60 percent occupancy and your competitors are averaging 50 percent, you may be pleased with the performance of the sales and marketing team. If, on the other hand, your direct competitors are averaging a 70 percent occupancy, it is clear that you are not achieving your fair share of the business available in your market. Similarly, if your ADR is $100, and your competitor's ADR is $80, your sales team is showing success in selling at a good rate. If your competitor's ADR is $120, you are comparatively less successful.

The hotel industry's most widely accepted means of assessing the comparative strength of a property's sales and marketing staff is the Smith Travel Accommodations Report (STAR report). It is by far the most credible independent measure of a hotel's comparative revenue generation. A STAR report details, among other information, a hotel's monthly ADR, occupancy percentage, RevPar, and relative share of the market. It also reports this same data on a hotel's **competitive set**.

LODGING LANGUAGE

Competitive Set: The group of competing hotels to which an individual hotel's operating performance is compared. Sometimes shortened to "Comp Set."

The STAR report is important because unbiased occupancy rate, ADR, RevPar, and resulting market share comparisons are important to a wide range of interest groups. These include:

- *Hotel Owners.* Hotel owners and investors want to know if the management team they have put in place is competing effectively in the marketplace. Managing the asset (hotel) to maximize its financial potential is an important goal, and the STAR report indicates, in many ways, how well this goal is being achieved.

- *Management Companies.* These companies know that their effectiveness as managing consultants will be based, to some degree, on how well they perform on the STAR report. Good results are used to demonstrate the value of these companies to owners.

- *Property Managers.* General managers and directors of sales and marketing want to know the effectiveness of their marketing plans and sales efforts as well as those of their competitors.

- *Franchisors.* Brand managers want a measure of how well their brands compete in the marketplace. Strong brand performance helps sell additional franchises. Weak performance helps indicate where brand managers can better assist current franchisees.

- *Appraisers.* These professionals interpret STAR report results to assist in establishing the financial value (worth) of a hotel.

- *The Financial Community.* Prospects asked to invest or lend money to buy or renovate hotels want to know about the sales strength of the hotel seeking funding. Good relative performance (a strong STAR report) helps persuade lenders to lend, while a weak STAR report indicates potential problems and will make it more difficult to secure funding.

A variety of groups are interested in the STAR Report for specific hotels or specific geographic areas. Many general managers and sales and marketing directors see the STAR report as the primary measure used to judge their own performance. STAR reports can provide a wealth of information to those sophisticated enough to read and analyze the data they contain. Fortunately, Smith Travel Research produces excellent materials that teach managers how to fully interpret their STAR reports.

LODGING ON-LINE

STAR Report interpretation and analysis is an important and often complex activity. To request instructional information on interpreting STAR reports, and to see the wide variety of benchmarking products produced by Smith Travel Research, go to:

www.str-online.com

Smith Travel Research (Smith) produces comparative reports on a daily, weekly, monthly, and annual basis. Hotels voluntarily submit financial data to Smith. In return, Smith maintains the confidentiality of the individual hotel data it receives. By combining the operating data submitted by selected competitors, an individual hotel's operating performance can be compared to that of its competitive set.

Understanding the competitive set is a key component of understanding the STAR report. Essentially, a competitive set consists of a group of hotels used to establish a performance benchmark. To illustrate, assume that you manage a 100-room limited-service property in a large city. You compete for most of your customers with five other hotels in your area, each of which has approximately the same number of rooms, services, approximate ADR, and quality as your own property. Assume also that you have identified these five properties to Smith Travel as the group you wish to consider as your competitive set. In nearly all cases, each of these hotels will, as you did, voluntarily submit monthly (or more frequent) actual sales data to Smith. This data is then tabulated and returned to your hotel in the form of a STAR report. Smith will only report the aggregate results of the competitive set. The company never releases or divulges information on an individual property or brand.

Operating comparisons produced by Smith can be customized, but popular comparisons include those related to:

- Occupancy
- ADR
- RevPar
- Market share
- Historical trends
- Monthly and year-to-date performance
- City, region or state performance

The STAR report assesses hotel performance, then assigns a score (index) that directly reflects a specific hotel's performance relative to its competitive set. A score (index) of 100 means that, on a selected operating characteristic such as ADR or occupancy percentage, a hotel has performed equal to its competitive set. A score above 100 means the hotel has outperformed its competitive set, and scores below 100 mean the competitive set has outperformed, on that characteristic, the specific hotel being scored.

To accurately gauge the overall effectiveness of a hotel's management, a property's STAR report must be examined in its entirety. When it is, a hotel's sales and marketing performance can be directly compared to the sales and marketing efforts of its competitors. As a result, STAR performance goals can be established for any operating factor, including occupancy rate, ADR, RevPar, market penetration, or growth. When STAR performance does not reach the goals set by the hotel's owners or managers, there can be a variety of problems, not all of which can be solved by the general manager or the sales and marketing team. Some of these include:

- Poor franchise (brand) name
- Poor signage
- Poor **room mix** for the market
- Substandard furnishings or décor
- Marketing/ advertising budget too small
- Marketing staff too small
- Marketing staff ineffective

LODGING LANGUAGE

Room Mix: The ratio of room types in a hotel. For example, the number of double-bedded rooms compared to king-bedded rooms, the number of smoking-permitted rooms to no-smoking rooms, and the number of suites compared to standard rooms.

--- **ALL IN A DAY'S WORK** ---

The Situation

"But I thought you said we did great," said Lance to Sabrina Davis, the general manager of the Crawford Hotel. "We must have done well, because we were packed during the Classic Car Convention! What did we do wrong?"

The Crawford was a limited-service property not affiliated with a brand. Lance, the property's front office manager, and Sabrina were reviewing the hotel's latest monthly STAR report. It showed that occupancy at the Crawford had increased 12 percent (from 60 percent to 67.2 percent) when compared to the previous year, and ADR had

increased 3 percent. That brought the RevPar increase for the property to approximately 15 percent when compared to the previous year.

"We did do well," replied Sabrina, "but our competitive set increased their occupancy by 12 percent, and they also increased their rate by 15 percent. They must have increased their rates during the convention more than we did!"

A Response

Managing room rates during high-volume demand periods can be difficult. In this case, a high-demand period (the Classic Car Convention) was evidently used by

the competitive set to drive rates higher than those achieved by the Crawford. The resulting "underselling" by the Crawford shows up in the STAR report as poor performance, despite RevPar increases for the hotel. Careful examination of the monthly STAR report, as is the case here, can provide valuable guidance to hotel managers. It is as important to independent hotels as it is to those that are franchised. In future high-demand periods, both Lance and Sabrina should closely monitor the rates charged by their competitors to ensure that the Crawford's rates stay in line with those of their competitive set.

Some hotel managers dislike STAR reports because they view them as an objective measure (score or index) of a subjective activity (management). Despite their limitations, however, STAR reports are perceived by many in the hotel industry as the best indicator of sales and marketing effectiveness. STAR reports, properly interpreted, are indeed a valuable tool for assessing the performance of a sales and marketing team as well as the entire property. Serious hoteliers should learn to analyze them and to then review them every month.

CHAPTER OBJECTIVES REVIEW

If you have successfully studied the material in this chapter, you should be prepared to:

1. Define the terms "sales" and "marketing," and to explain the relationship between a hotel's sales and marketing effort and its financial success. (Objective 1)
2. Describe those sales and marketing activities which occur within a hotel as well as those that take place outside of it. (Objective 2)
3. Categorize guests as belonging to one of the two major hotel markets and describe how each market can be solicited to help maximize hotel revenues. (Objective 3)
4. Name and describe the major sales and marketing tools used by those responsible for hotel sales and marketing. (Objective 4)
5. Describe two methods hotel owners and managers use to evaluate a hotel's sales and marketing efforts. (Objective 5)

LODGING LANGUAGE

DOSM	Booking	Pickup
Sales	Site Tour	Group Contract
Marketing	Bid	Attrition

Block
Convention and Visitor's
    Bureau (CVB)
Marketing Plan
Sales and Marketing Committee
Inclusive
Advertising
Publicity
Frequent Guest Program

Chamber of Commerce
Track
Consortia
Negotiated Rate
Per Diem
SMERF
Meeting Planner
Lead
Sales Call

Networking
Cold Calling
Drop In
Direct Mail
Link
Demand Generator
STAR Report
Competitive Set
Room Mix

FOR DISCUSSION

1. Effective marketing increases consumer awareness of a hotel. Sales is the personal aspect of client relations. Which do you believe is more important in the long-term success of a hotel? How would the specific characteristics of a particular hotel or hotel brand affect your answer?

2. You have learned that every employee in a hotel is responsible for sales and marketing. Identify three specific activities that each hourly hotel employee can be instructed to undertake to assist in the hotel's sales and marketing effort.

3. Convention and visitors bureaus receive most of their funding from special taxes levied on hotel guests. What other businesses benefit from the efforts of a CVB? Why do you think most communities refrain from assessing a CVB tax on those businesses?

4. Some hoteliers believe that the Internet will do away with the need for travel agents. Do you agree? Explain your reason.

5. Most hoteliers can easily identify potential transient business that originates from out of town. There is, however, a significant amount of transient business that is locally generated. Identify at least three such sources of transient business. What are some methods a hotel sales team could use to secure this business?

6. Those who purchase group rooms from a hotel often want to do so at a discount price. Identify three factors that a hotelier might consider before agreeing to give a significant discount for a group room purchase.

7. In large hotels with a full-time sales staff, hotel salespersons are typically paid a salary and (if their work is superior) a bonus for their work. In many other industries, salespersons are only paid the commissions they earn. Why do you think hotel salespersons are rarely, if ever, paid "commission-only" for their efforts?

8. The Internet has had a significant impact on how hotel rooms are sold. Identify three ways sales managers can utilize the Internet to help their hotel achieve greater sales revenues.

9. The properties selected to be a part of a specific hotel's competitive set will strongly affect how the hotel's sales performance is assessed. Identify at least three characteristics of a hotel that should be considered when selecting the specific hotels to be included in a competitive set.

10. Some in the hotel industry believe that too heavy an emphasis on the STAR report to evaluate a hotel's sales effort has a negative effect. Others defend the STAR as the only independent way to evaluate a sales team's effectiveness. Identify two positive and two negative aspects of STAR report utilization in an assessment of a hotel's sales effort.

TEAM ACTIVITIES

Team Activity 1

The distinctions between the terms "sales" and "marketing" are as many as there are authors writing about the topics. Identify at least three books, or book chapters, devoted to the sales and marketing area and compare the definitions of these two terms in each reference.

What were the similarities among the definitions? What were the differences? Why do you think HSMAI is titled as it is, rather than as "HMSAI"?

Team Activity 2

The rapid expansion of brands has made it more difficult for consumers to differentiate among them. Choose from the following segments of the lodging industry:

- Full-service
- Limited-service
- All-suite

Then select the largest three franchise brands in the chosen market and consider the brand's marketing efforts. What feature(s) have the brand managers chosen to emphasize? Do you think most consumers are aware of the distinctions advertised by the brand manager? What would you suggest the brand managers do differently?

9 The Accounting Department

Chapter Objectives

1. To explain the difference between centralized and decentralized on-property hotel accounting systems.
2. To teach you how hotels utilize long-range, annual, and monthly budgets to manage their income and expenses.
3. To describe the controls used to manage hotel revenues.
4. To describe the controls used to manage hotel expenses.
5. To explain how income statements, balance sheets, and statements of cash flows are used to report on the financial status of a hotel.

Chapter Outline

ON-PROPERTY HOTEL ACCOUNTING
    Centralized Accounting Systems
    Decentralized Accounting Systems
BUDGETING
    Long-Range Budgets
    Annual Budgets
    Monthly Budgets
INCOME CONTROL
    Operational Controls
    Cash Control

Allowances and Adjustments
Accounts Receivable Control
EXPENSE CONTROL
    Purchasing and Receiving
    Accounts Payable
FINANCIAL REPORTING
    The Income Statement
    The Balance Sheet
    The Statement of Cash Flows

Overview: The Accounting Department

An operating hotel generates a tremendous amount of financial data. Every sale of rooms, food, beverages, and other hotel products and services must be recorded, the money paid for these must be collected and safeguarded, and, as well, the hotel's operating expenses must be carefully recorded, monitored, and managed. Accounting involves the maintenance of accurate records about a hotel's financial activities.

In a large hotel, an employee known as the controller is responsible for the accounting function. The controller may work with a very large staff. In a smaller property, the hotel's general manager may perform the duties of the controller. In either case, the hotel will have either a centralized or a decentralized accounting system in place. In this chapter you will learn about both of these systems, and we will use the term "controller" to refer to the individual responsible for the hotel's accounting function.

The accounting function actually begins with budgeting. A hotel must be able to estimate the amount of money it will bring in (income) as well as the amount it must spend (expenses) to operate. Budgets are of three basic types. These are long-range budgets, annual budgets, and monthly budgets. Each budget type will be examined in this chapter.

In a hotel, the money to be collected from guests for purchases of rooms and other services must be carefully accounted for. This work must be done on a daily basis because many guests will only stay at the hotel one night. Thus, every morning at check-out time, each guest's properly tabulated bill (folio) must be ready for presentation to that guest. In addition, hotels that operate retail outlets, such as restaurants, lounges, and gift shops, must account for their daily sales. All areas of the hotel that collect money must protect these funds from possible theft. In this chapter you will see how hotels collect and protect their revenues.

In Chapter 4, we identified control as one of the four major functions of management. It is not surprising, then, that a primary job of the controller is to help control expenses. This is done through careful management of the hotel's purchasing, receiving, and bill-payment processes.

Finally, the financial performance of a hotel is important to those managing the hotel, but it is also important to many individuals and groups outside the hotel. These may include the hotel's owners, investors, stockholders, lenders, or governmental taxing authorities. These audiences all rely on accurate and timely accounting information to make informed financial decisions about the hotel. In this chapter you will learn about three of the most important financial documents prepared for use by those outside (as well as inside) a property. These are the income statement, the balance sheet and the statement of cash flows.

ON-PROPERTY HOTEL ACCOUNTING

Professional hotel managers know they will be held accountable for the financial success of their properties. Accounting is simply the method by which a hotel or any organization's financial performance is measured. To be useful, an effective accounting system must allow for the careful recording, summarizing, and analysis of every financial transaction that occurs. When an accounting system works well, hoteliers can use the financial information it generates to make good managerial decisions. When a system works poorly, decision-making is impaired because it is based on inaccurate or incomplete information.

In a hotel, the **controller** is the individual responsible for overseeing the accounting and bookkeeping functions.

LODGING LANGUAGE

Controller: The individual responsible for recording, classifying, and summarizing a hotel's business transactions. In some hotels, this position is referred to as the comptroller.

■

While accounting and bookkeeping are similar, the purpose of bookkeeping is primarily to record and summarize financial data. Accounting includes the development of the systems to collect and report financial information, analyzing this same information, and making finance-related recommendations to assist in managerial decision-making. In many ways, the controller can be considered the hotel's on-property accountant even if the person who performs this function is not a **C.P.A.**

LODGING LANGUAGE

C.P.A.: Certified public accountant. An individual designated by the American Institute of Certified Public Accountants as competent in the field of accounting.

■

In some cases, the financial records of the hotel must be examined by a C.P.A. before owners, investors, creditors, governmental agencies, and other interested parties will accept them as accurate. In larger hotels, the controller is likely to be a C.P.A., but in smaller properties it is more likely that an individual who is not a C.P.A. will be responsible for the bookkeeping and accounting functions. It would be a mistake to discount the importance of a C.P.A. to some hotels; however, it would be just as big a mistake to assume that only a person who has earned the C.P.A. designation can be an effective controller. This is true because today's accounting systems can be classified as either centralized or decentralized.

Centralized Accounting Systems

In a **centralized accounting** system, the financial data from your property is transmitted via computer (for example by fax, e-mail, network, Web page posting, etc.) to a central location where it can be recorded and then analyzed by management, or combined with data from other hotel properties for analysis.

LODGING LANGUAGE

Centralized Accounting: A financial management system that collects accounting data from individual hotels, and then combines and analyzes the data at a different (central) site.

■

To illustrate why some hotels operate under a centralized system, assume that you own five hotels in the southeastern United States. Assume also that your office is in the Midwest. If you wanted to know, on a daily basis, what the combined sales revenue for your five hotels was on the day before, you would want those hotels to have reported their previous day's sales to your office. For convenience, you would then have the sales revenues of the five hotels added together to yield one number that represented all your hotels' total sales for that day. Centralized accounting is most prevalent in companies that operate several hotels and wish to combine financial data or spread the costs of the company's accounting system over multiple properties.

If a hotel is one of a number of smaller hotels owned or managed by the same company, it is likely to operate under a centralized accounting system. If so, it is also likely that the company, rather than any individual hotel, will employ a C.P.A. for data analysis. Employing one highly trained C.P.A. in a central location is generally more cost-effective than having multiple C.P.A.s in multiple locations.

Decentralized Accounting Systems

In a **decentralized accounting** system, the general manager (small property) or the controller (larger property) must take a greater role in the preparation of financial documents.

LODGING LANGUAGE

Decentralized Accounting: A financial management system that collects accounting data from an individual hotel site and combines and analyzes it at the same site.

■

If neither the general manager nor the controller is a C.P.A., it is likely that the hotel's owners will, at least annually, employ the services of a C.P.A. to review the work of the on-property controller and give a professional opinion about the reliability of the financial statements he or she has prepared. This review process is called an **audit.**

LODGING LANGUAGE

Audit: An independent verification of financial records.

■

In some cases, audits of hotel accounting practices are viewed with the same dread as an individual's Internal Revenue income tax audit! That should not be the case. A hotel audit is routinely performed because hotel room nights, the principle saleable product of a hotel, are an extremely perishable commodity that cannot be held and controlled in a normal manner. This is true because unsold room nights disappear at midnight on each sale day. In addition, normal service to hotel guests includes a wide variety of transactions in which fairly large amounts of cash are handled. Finally, in smaller hotel properties, there are frequently a limited number of employees among whom duties can be divided and rotated.

In nearly very case; an audit will uncover areas of financial reporting and control that can be improved. This is to be expected and should not be cause for concern. If the individuals performing the hotel's accounting functions are professionals committed to excellence, the audit is a tremendous opportunity for growth and improvement. Frequent and detailed auditing of hotel records is vital because of the need to establish and maintain sound accounting systems.

LODGING ON-LINE

C.P.A. is a prestigious designation that carries with it significant responsibilities. The American Institute of Certified Public Accountants (AICPA) is the professional association of those who have earned the C.P.A. designation. To view its Web site and read about the C.P.A. code of conduct, go to:

www.AICPA.com

When you arrive, click on "Code of Conduct."

In this text, we will examine a decentralized accounting system to illustrate all of the many bookkeeping and accounting functions taking place in a modern hotel. In some hotels, all, some, or none of these functions may be centralized. It is essential, however, for hoteliers to understand the budgeting, income and expense control, and financial reporting procedures that are required in a professionally managed hotel.

BUDGETING

Just as individuals make purchasing and spending decisions based upon how much money they will earn, hotels too must estimate the amount of revenue they will generate, how much it will cost to generate that revenue, and how extra funds (if any) will be spent or invested. As a result, professionally managed hotels budget for their income (revenues), expenses, and profits.

Long-range hotel budgets are affected by the financial strength of both the local and national economies.

Some hoteliers may see the budgeting process as difficult and time-consuming. In fact, it need not be either of these. Properly prepared, a budget provides guidance to hotel managers and vital information to others interested in estimates of the hotel's future financial performance. It is crucial tool for effective hotel management.

In a business context, a budget is much more than a plan for spending cash resources. In fact, it is a plan for utilizing resources of all kinds, including cash, tools and materials, and labor, to operate the hotel in the most effective manner. Budgeting is sometimes described as a financial expression of a hotel's overall business strategy. This makes sense when you consider that a business strategy seeks to project where the hotel is going, how it will get there, what it will cost, and what the profit outcome will be if the strategy is implemented successfully. A well-developed budget, however, can do even more than project revenues and expense. If used properly, the budget is an important means of developing internal controls, another function that is critical to the controller's role.

Hotel managers create their budgets, monitor them closely, modify them when necessary, and (hopefully) achieve their desired results. Yet, some controller/general manager teams do a poor job developing budgets because they feel the process is too time-consuming. Developing a dynamic budget does take time, but good budgets assist the hotel in many ways, including:

1. Allowing management to anticipate and prepare for future business conditions.
2. Providing a communication channel that allows the hotel's objectives to be passed along to all of its operating units.
3. Encouraging department managers who have participated in the preparation of the budget to establish their own operating objectives and evaluation techniques and tools.
4. Providing the hotel's managers with reasonable estimates of future expense levels and serving as a tool for determining future room rates and other pricing structures.
5. Helping the controller and the general manager to periodically carry out a self-evaluation of the hotel and its progress toward its financial objectives.
6. Estimating the probable financial returns on their investments for the hotel's owners.

In the hotel industry, operating budgets generally are one of three types:

• Long-range
• Annual
• Monthly

And we will examine each of these.

Long-Range Budgets

A long-range budget is one that encompasses a relatively lengthy period of time, generally from two to five years, or in some cases, even longer. The general manager, with the help of the controller in large properties, prepares the budget, with input from each of the hotel's operating units. The general manager's role in the process would be, in conjunction with the sales and marketing team, to forecast the number of guest rooms available to sell, and predict occupancy percentages and ADRs given future market conditions, while the role of the controller (as well as the general manager) would be to estimate operating expenses.

Obviously, with such a long-term outlook, budgets are subject to changes due to unforeseen circumstances and market forces, but they are useful for long-term planning as well as for considering the wisdom of debt financing and refinancing, and for scheduling **capital expenditures.**

LODGING LANGUAGE

Capital Expenditure: The purchase of equipment, land, buildings, or other assets necessary for the operation of a hotel.

■

Annual Budgets

In many cases, preparation of the annual budget consumes a significant amount of time. This is so because in large, multi-unit hotel companies, annual budgets must be produced by the individual hotels, submitted to a central office for review, and then in some cases revised to ensure they are in keeping with the overall financial objectives and goals of the hotel company. This budget development process can begin as early as June or July for the following year.

As the name implies, annual budgets are developed to coincide, in most cases, with the calendar year. As such, they provide more detail than a long-term budget and are subject to less fluctuation based on unforeseen events. To be effective, annual budgets must be based upon management's best estimate of market conditions, the effectiveness of the sales and marketing team and its annual marketing plan, new hotels that may open in the area, existing hotels that may close, and any other economic factors that could reasonably affect the total revenues generated by the hotel.

ALL IN A DAY'S WORK

The Situation

"I don't know. It's a good brand, but their location isn't nearly as convenient as ours," said Peggy Richards, the manager of the Homestead Suites Hotel.

"But what will its opening do to our occupancy next year" asked Kevin Gustafson, the hotel's owner, "And how will it affect our ADR?"

Peggy and Kevin were preparing the Homestead's annual operating budget for the coming year. They were attempting to estimate revenues. This year had been a good one; their 100-room hotel had achieved a 70 percent occupancy rate with slightly better than a $78 per room ADR. The result was nearly $2 million in hotel rooms revenue. The problem and challenge, they both knew, was that a new competitor was scheduled to open an 80-room franchised property just a quarter of a mile from them on February 1st. While not an all-suite hotel, the new competitor would be offering newly built, large rooms, with high-speed Internet access in each room and a well-marketed frequent-guest program. Peggy and Kevin had already received invitations to the hotel's "Grand Opening" party.

A Response

Peggy and Kevin are wise to consider the impact of events outside their control when preparing their annual operating budget. New hotel openings, hotel closings, the state of the economy, and the effectiveness of a hotel's sales and marketing plan are all factors that must be considered when preparing a hotel's long-term, annual, and monthly budgets. Additional factors to be considered include planned property upgrades, the franchisor's marketing efforts, and the efforts of the local convention and visitors bureau.

Membership in the local chamber of commerce can lead to individual recognition as well as help keep hoteliers informed about community developments that may affect their hotels' annual budgets.

Monthly Budgets

The monthly budget is a natural component of the annual budget. In fact, many hotel managers produce their annual budgets by first producing 12 monthly budgets. You might wonder why a hotel with a well-developed annual budget should concern itself with accurate monthly budgets. The importance of the monthly budget, however, can be seen quite clearly in the example of the annual revenue and expenses of a hotel near a ski resort. In each of the winter months, revenues and expenses will probably be much more than one-twelfth of the annual revenue and expense budget. In a like manner, the revenues and expenditures for the summer months will fall far short of one-twelfth the annual budget. If this **seasonal hotel** is to effectively reach the annual targets, great care will need to be taken with each individual month's budget. Most hotels will see some variation in annual sales based on the time of year. As a result, monthly budgets are an excellent managerial tool for helping to determine whether or not the hotel is making progress toward the overall goals developed in the annual budget.

LODGING LANGUAGE

Seasonal Hotel: A hotel whose revenue and expenditures vary greatly depending on the time (season) of the year. Examples include hotels near ski resorts, beaches, theme parks, certain tourist areas, sporting venues, and the like.

■

While the complete development of a hotel's operating budget is beyond the scope of this chapter, it is important to understand that a significant part of a hotel's accounting function consists of preparing and monitoring long-range, annual, and monthly budgets that detail revenues, expenses, and profits.

LODGING ON-LINE

Hospitality Financial and Technology Professionals (HFTP) is the professional association for individuals working in the areas of hotel accounting and technology. To see its Web site and mission statement, go to:

http://www.hftp.org

INCOME CONTROL

One of the most important reasons for a hotel to have an effective accounting system in place is to safeguard the income (revenues) it earns. When a guest makes a purchase, the money paid to the hotel by the guest must be documented, collected, and safely held until it can be deposited into the hotel's bank account. Prior to that, however, it is necessary to confirm that the amount charged to the guest for the purchase was, in fact, the correct amount. An effective hotel accounting system includes the operational controls necessary to ensure that guests (and the hotel) are not defrauded by hotel employees. These same controls also help ensure that guests do not defraud the hotel. In addition, an effective system will include procedures for handling the cash collected on-property, billing guests to whom the hotel has extended credit, and collecting payments from them.

Operational Controls

On a daily basis, the hotel controller must confirm that the previous day's sales were recorded accurately. Recall from Chapter 7 that the previous day's hotel sales are tabulated by the night auditor and that the "end" of the day, (and therefore the beginning of the next day) is not a fixed time. Rather, it is the time at which the night auditor concludes (closes) the night audit. The controller checks the accuracy of the night audit and also makes sure that the night auditor is not defrauding the hotel. These two operational goals are accomplished by the accurate production of the **manager's daily** sales report.

LODGING LANGUAGE

Manager's Daily: A re-cap of the previous day's rooms, food and beverage, and other sales. The manager's daily may include additional hotel operating statistics as requested by the hotel's general manager. Sometimes referred to simply as the "daily."

■

The daily is prepared from data supplied every night by the PMS (see Chapter 7). In some cases, the PMS may actually produce the first draft of the daily. The controller uses the nightly data produced by the PMS for a variety of tasks, one of which is the preparation of the Daily.

Information that should be contained on the daily includes the following:

- For rooms:
  - Number of rooms available for sale
  - Number of rooms sold
  - Occupancy rate
  - ADR
  - RevPar
  - Other rooms revenue information desired by the general manager

- For foods and beverages:
  - Restaurant sales
  - Bar/lounge sales
  - Meeting room rentals
  - Banquet sales
  - Other F&B revenue information desired by the general manager

- For other income:
  - Telephone revenue
    - In-room movie revenue
    - No-show billings
  - Other income categories unique to the property

While the report is called the daily, which implies that it contains only one day's information, most controllers increase the value of the daily by including cumulative monthly data totals, as well as individual and cumulative data from the same day in the preceding year. A sample one-page daily for a mid-sized hotel, produced via Excel spreadsheet, could be designed in a manner similar to what is shown in Figure 9.1

The more detail desired by the manager, the more in-depth will be the manager's daily. Some managers prefer great detail, including in their daily information about room types sold, number of guaranteed reservations made, cash overage and shortages, or any number of other types of information that may be helpful in keeping abreast of the hotel's business on a daily basis. When the controller produces the daily, the job is made substantially easier because the PMS system is used to generate some parts or even all of the report.

An additional part of the controller's operational controls role is the documentation and verification of the night auditor's report. This report (see Chapter 7), generated by the night auditor and the PMS, will provide management a complete and detailed breakdown of the previous day's business. Often running 10 or more pages in length, the night audit report is used to verify credit card charges, cash on hand, revenue sales totals, detailed room revenue statistics, and **allowances and adjustments.**

LODGING LANGUAGE

Allowances and Adjustments: Reductions in sales revenue credited to guests because of errors in properly recording sales or to satisfy a guest who has experienced property shortcomings.

■

Manager's Daily Report				
THE BEST SLEEP HOTEL				January 15, 20xx
	Today	To Date	Last Year Today	Last Year to Date
Rooms Available	285	4275	285	4275
Rooms Occupied	**191**	**3035**	**180**	
Occ. %	67%	71%	63%	70%
ADR	$ 105.20	$ 103.98	$ 98.99	$ 100.20
RevPar	$ 70.50	$ 73.82	$ 62.52	$ 70.57
Rooms Revenue	**$ 20,093.20**	**$ 315,579.30**	**$ 17,818.20**	**$ 301,702.20**
Food and Beverage				
Banquets	$ 4,550.00	$ 68,250.00	$ –0	$ 71,250.00
Meeting Room Revenue	$ 1,250.00	$ 18,750.00	$ 150.00	$ 19,850.00
A/V Rental	$ 140.00	$ 2,240.00	$ 75.00	$ 2,500.00
Restaurant	$ 650.00	$ 8,450.00	$ 710.00	$ 10,650.00
Total F&B Income	**$ 6,590.00**	**$ 97,690.00**	**‡$ 935.00**	**$ 104,250.00**
Telephone Revenue				
Local Calls	$ 85.00	$ 1,105.00	$ 79.50	$ 1,033.50
Long Distance Calls	$ 210.00	$ 2,730.00	$ 185.00	$ 2,220.00
Other Income				
Gift shop	$ 231.25	$ 2,312.50	$ 221.00	$ 2,210.00
In-room movie sales	$ 185.00	$ 2,035.00	$ 78.00	$ 1,850.00
Guest Laundry	$ 71.50	$ 858.00	$ 61.50	$ 738.00
No Show revenue	$ 198.50	$ 2,580.50	$ 520.00	$ 3,200.00
Total Daily Revenue	**$ 27,664.45**	**$ 424,890.30**	**$ 19,898.20**	**$ 417,203.70**

FIGURE 9.1 Manager's Daily Report

The night audit report provides a wealth of information on room sales if the controller uses it properly. For example, the information (provided by the PMS) required to fully understand the daily sales revenue and RevPar on a given day includes information related to ADR, rooms sold, and market segment. figure 9.2 details the comprehensive information that can be provided on the guests staying in the hotel. This information is of importance to several of the hotel's operational areas.

As can be seen, the make-up of the guests in the hotel would be very different under these situations. In situation 1, the hotel is filled primarily with people on a tour (91 rooms) and leisure travelers (40 rooms). In the second situation, transient corporate travelers make up the largest portion of guests (75 rooms), followed by corporate travelers staying in a group (60 rooms). There are several reasons for the controller to analyze the night audit report. Two of the most important are information and accuracy. To understand the importance of information, consider again the data in Figure 9.2

Assume that the management of the Best Sleep Hotel knows, from past records, that the average leisure or tour room sold by the hotel houses 2.2 individuals, while

Manager's Room Revenue Detail Report

THE BEST SLEEP HOTEL   **January 15, 20XX**

Rooms Available   285
Rooms Sold   191
Occupancy %   67.0%

Market Mix	Situation 1 (285 Rooms Available)			Situation 2 (285 Rooms Available)		
	Rooms Sold	ADR	Total Revenue	Rooms Sold	ADR	Total Revenue
Transient Guests						
Corporate	25	119	$ 2,975.00	75	119	$ 8,925.00
Leisure	25	139	$ 3,475.00	5	139	$ 695.00
Government	0	0	$ 0.00	15	75	$ 1,125.00
Total Transient Guests	**50**		**$ 6,450.00**	**95**		**$ 10,745.00**
Group Guests						
Corporate	5	105	$ 525.00	60	105	$ 6,300.00
Leisure	40	118	$ 4,720.00	6	118	$ 708.00
Government	5	78	$ 390.00	30	78	$ 2,340.00
Total Group Guests	**50**		**$ 5,635.00**	**96**		**$ 9,348.00**
Tour Guests	91	88	**$ 8,008.00**	0		0
TOTAL GUESTS	**191**		**$ 20,093.00**	**191**		**$ 20,093.00**
ADR			$ 105.20			$ 105.20
RevPar			**$ 70.50**			**$ 70.50**

FIGURE 9.2   Two Alternative Guest Profiles/ Same RevPar

each corporate room sold is occupied, on average, by 1.1 persons. Obviously, the demands placed on the hotel's restaurants and recreational facilities will be very different, as will the housekeeping services required by these two groups. Taking all occupied rooms into consideration, the **house count** in the first situation is likely to be nearly twice that of the second situation. Because this is true, it is important for management to know not only how many rooms have been sold in the hotel, and the day's RevPar, but to what client type the rooms have been sold. It is the role of the controller to provide this information on a daily basis.

LODGING LANGUAGE

House Count: An estimate of the number of guests staying in a hotel on a given day.

■

The controller in a hotel should, on a daily basis, provide the property's management with the following information from the previous day (night audit);

- Rooms available
- Total rooms occupied

- Rooms occupied by guest type
- Occupancy percentage
- Total ADR
- ADR by guest type
- Total RevPar

To the above data may be added any additional decision-making rooms statistics or information required by management. The controller should have the accounting systems in place to verify the accuracy of all the operational information provided and should be prepared to **sign-off** on the accuracy of the night audit.

LODGING LANGUAGE

Sign-off: To verify or approve for accuracy or payment. Used as in: "Ms. Larson, will you sign-off on last night's audit?"

■

Cash Control

Because the position title of the controller is derived from the word "control," it is not surprising that one of the very most important functions of the controller is the development and maintenance of internal control systems. Hotels and the restaurants often routinely contain large amounts of cash, products, and equipment that can, if not carefully controlled, be the subject of fraudulent activities by guests or employees. A good controller carefully develops policies and procedures designed to protect the the hotel's assets, including cash.

Any business that routinely collects cash payments from guests must develop a system of safeguarding this important asset. Hotels are no exception. People unfamiliar with the hotel industry often think of "cash" as currency (coins and bills). In today's hotel environment, cash assets in addition to currency include credit and debit card charges, and personal and business checks. The potential to lose these assets to theft, fraud, or outright carelessness always exists, and it is the role of the controller as well as the general manager and the department head of each cash-handling area to develop and enforce a system of checks and balances and controls that will keep these important assets secure.

In many hotels, cash is collected in many other locations in addition to the front desk. Restaurants, bars, lounges, parking and vending areas, and gift shops are just a few examples of locations in a typical hotel that routinely process cash sales. In all of these situations, at least one person serves as a cashier/money handler. Bartenders may serve as their own cashiers during an evening shift. Likewise, the individual responsible for replenishing soft drink vending machines serves as a cashier of sorts when cash is removed from the machines. Even if the vending machines are serviced by an outside entity, theft from them can impact the hotel because commissions paid to the property are typically based upon a percentage of the revenue generated by the machines.

In hotels, cash assets are at greater risk from internal threats than from external ones. While there is always the potential for robbery by a non-employees, the greater threat to the security of the hotel's cash assets is the possibility of employee theft or fraud.

Any time a cashier is responsible for the collection of money, there are several areas of potential employee theft or fraud. The cashier may, for example, record a sale, collect payment from a guest, but keep the cash. Or the cashier may not record the sale at all and, again, keep the cash.

The methods used by cashiers to defraud guests and/or the hotel are varied and depend to a great degree upon the type of sale that is made. The methods used by a dishonest bartender to steal from the hotel's food and beverage department will be different from those used by a dishonest front desk agent. In either case, management must have systems in place to verify the amount of sales made and the cash receipts they produce. An effective, experienced controller is invaluable in designing and establishing these systems.

While thefts of cash (currency) by a cashier are fairly straightforward, some cashiers also have the opportunity to defraud guests who pay by credit card. These too must be guarded against. Some common credit-card-related techniques used to defraud guests include:

- Charging a guest's credit card for items not purchased, then removing an amount of money from the cash register equal to the erroneous charge.
- Changing the totals on credit card charges after the guest has left or imprinting additional credit card charges and pocketing the cash difference.
- Misadding legitimate charges to create a higher-than-appropriate total, with the intent of keeping the overcharge. This, of course, can also be done on a cash sale.
- Charging higher-than-authorized prices for products or services, recording the proper price, and keeping the overcharge.
- Giving, or selling, the credit card numbers of guests to unauthorized individuals outside the hotel.

The controller's revenue-control programs must be evident in every cash-handling area and on every shift. For example, a bartender working from 5:00 p.m. to 2:00 A.M. and serving as his or her own cashier might record $1,000 in beverage sales during that time period. If that figure is accurate, and there were no errors in handling change, the cash register should contain currency, checks, and bank charges equal to $1,000 plus, of course, the amount of cash in the register at the beginning of the shift (the **shift bank**).

LODGING LANGUAGE

Shift Bank: The total amount of currency and coins in a cashier's drawer at the beginning of that cashier's work shift. Used as in: "Let's start the 3:00 P.M. front desk shift with a $750. shift bank."

■

If, in our example, the bartender's drawer contains less than $1,000, it is said to be **short**; if it contains more than $1,000, it is said to be **over**.

LODGING LANGUAGE

Short: A situation in which a cashier has less money in the cash drawer than the official sales records indicate. Thus, a cashier with $10 less in the cash drawer than the sales record indicates is said to be $10 short.

Over: A situation in which a cashier has more money in the cash drawer than the official sales records indicate. Thus, a cashier with $10 more in the cash drawer than the sales record indicates is said to be $10 over.

■

Overages and shortages should be monitored by the controller, and when excessive, should be brought to the immediate attention of the appropriate manager for corrective action. Cashiers rarely steal large sums of money directly from the cash drawer because such theft is easily detected, but management should make it a policy to monitor cash overages and shortages on a daily basis. Some inexperienced managers believe that only cash shortages, but not overages, need to be investigated. This is not the case. Consistent cash overages as well as shortages may be an indication of employee theft or carelessness and must be investigated.

A dishonest cashier is sometimes able to avoid being short and still defraud the hotel. If, for example, the cash register has a void (erase) key, a dishonest cashier could enter a sales amount, collect for it, and then void the sale after the guest has departed. In this way, total sales would equal the amount in the cash drawer at the end of the shift. If the cashier then destroys the records involved with this sale, the cash register's total sales figure, and the cash drawer will balance. To prevent this, management should insist that all cash register voids be performed by a supervisor or at least be individually authorized by management. In addition, because today's computerized cash register equipment records the number, individual, and time at which cashier voids are performed, these, too, should be monitored.

Another method of hotel cashier theft involves the manipulation of reduced-price or complimentary rooms or products. Assume, for example, that at the Best Sleep Hotel, the sales and marketing team has produced and distributed a large number of guest coupons good for 50 percent off a guest's night stay. If the front desk cashier has access to these coupons, it is possible to collect the full charge from a guest without a coupon and then add the coupon to the cash drawer while simultaneously removing sales revenue equal to the value of the coupon. A variation is for the cashier to declare a room to be complimentary *after* the guest has paid the bill. In cases like this, the front desk agent would revise the PMS to indicate that the room was a comp, then remove revenue from the cash drawer in an amount equal to the comped room.

These kinds of fraud can be prevented by denying cashiers access to unredeemed cash-value coupons issued by the hotel, and by requiring special authorization from management to comp rooms. While the scenarios presented above do not list all the possible methods of revenue theft and fraud, it should be clear from this discussion that managers must have a complete revenue security system in order to be certain that all the sales revenue generated by the services and products sold by the hotel finds its way into the hotel's bank account.

It is important to regularly evaluate the cash-control systems in place on the property. This includes a through evaluation of:

- Cashier training programs
- Revenue recording systems and procedures
- Cash overage and shortage monitoring tactics
- Enforcement of employee disciplinary procedures for non-compliance with required procedures

Some cashiers find the theft of cash is very tempting. Today's sophisticated cash-management systems make it easier than ever to detect cashier theft, but an effective control system is still critical to the process.

Allowances and Adjustments

In a hotel, the issue of controlling allowances and adjustments is related to that of cash control. Recall that an allowance or adjustment is a reduction in a guest's bill resulting from a billing error or from a significant shortcoming in the product or services sold by the hotel. For example a guest who complains upon check-out that the room air-conditioner was so loud it was impossible to sleep, might, depending upon hotel policy, receive an allowance (reduction) on the bill of a specific dollar amount. The guest would pay the reduced amount and the cashier's drawer would balance because a record of the allowance would be made to explain the reduction in revenues. Similarly, a guest who checked in and was billed (during the night audit) at a nightly room rate of $99, but whose company had, in fact, previously negotiated a rate of $79 per night would have $20 adjusted off his or her folio when the error was discovered. The importance of a controller maintaining a detailed daily listing of any allowances or adjustments vouchers created by the managers or employees of the hotel is clear.

Vouchers are important because they help to balance actual revenue collected with monies previously billed to guests. From the perspective of the hotel's operating managers, however, vouchers are also important because they can identify shortcomings in hotel services, processes, and procedures that must be addressed, corrected and/ or improved.

Even in the best-managed hotel, some guests will have experiences that warrant adjustments of their bills.

Figure 9.3 shows an allowance and adjustment form used by a typical hotel. Note that the form has:

1. A sequence number for control purposes.
2. A space for the date the voucher is used.
3. A space for the name of the guest(s) for whom the adjustment was made.
4. A space for the guest's identifying room number or account.
5. A space for an explanation of the event or circumstances which justified the issuing of an adjustment.
6. A space for the initials or signature of the employee issuing the adjustment.
7. An identification number for reordering purposes.

In a small property, each of these vouchers would be tabulated and reviewed for accuracy by the controller or the general manager. In a larger property, the information on the vouchers might be combined and a summary of the information they contain would be passed on to the front office manager or whoever else is charged with monitoring this aspect of the accounting system.

The importance of reviewing these vouchers regularly becomes evident when you understand that there are three fundamental situations that could result in the completion of an allowance and adjustment voucher. These are:

- *Employee error in charges.* Despite appropriate training, employees can sometimes make errors in the amount they charge guests. This problem can range from charging guests the wrong room rate for their stay, to charging guest A for services actually used by guest B. When the error is discovered, the guest's folio (bill), must be adjusted to reflect the correct charge. Assume, for example, that Mr. and Mrs. York, staying in room 417 on a Saturday night, each have a

(1) ALLOWANCE/ADJUSTMENT

NO 348685

DATE (2) 19

NAME (3) *ROOM OR ACCT. NO. (4)*

EXPLANATION (5)

X (6)
SIGNATURE

11-09-0199 (7)

FIGURE 9.3 Allowance and Adjustment Voucher

drink in the hotel lounge. They sign the guest check charging the drinks to their room, but the bartender mistakenly charges the drinks to the guest in room 471. The Yorks check out on Sunday morning. On the following Monday, the guest staying in 471 approaches the front desk to check out. Upon reviewing the bill, the guest in room 471 will refuse to pay the incorrect charge. At that point, an allowance and adjustment voucher, removing the drink charges, must be prepared. In such a case, it may not be possible to collect on the charges originally incurred by the Yorks (remember that they left the hotel on the previous morning). Shortcomings in employee training programs, cash sales systems, or guest services techniques may become clear to the hotel's managers if a pattern of employee error is made apparent through the review of allowance and adjustment vouchers.

- *Hotel-related problems.* Despite the best efforts of the hotel's management and staff, some guests will still experience problems with the hotel's facilities or guest services. For example, an ice machine on a particular floor may, on a given day, have stopped working and, before it could be repaired by the hotel, inconvenienced a guest who had to walk to another section of the hotel for ice. Or, unfortunately, a hotel employee may not have been as courteous to a guest as desired, thus offending the guest. In both of these cases, and more, a guest may, upon check-out request (or demand!) a reduction in the bill. In these situations, an allowance or adjustment in the bill may need to be made, and the voucher would be filled out. The importance of such vouchers being seen by the hotel's managers on a daily basis is self-evident. Changes may be required in equipment inspection programs, guest service training, or a variety of other areas where management intervention is critical to correct recurring problems.

- *Guest-related problems.* In some cases it is the presence of other guests, rather than the hotel, that causes a particular guest to have an unpleasant experience at the hotel. Complaints ranging from excessive noise in adjacent rooms to rowdy guest behavior in public spaces can make some guests feel they should be compensated for the unpleasantness of their experience. If, in the opinion of the appropriate hotel staff member (front desk agent, front office manage, or **MOD**), an adjustment to the guest's bill is warranted, the allowance and adjustment voucher will be completed.

LODGING LANGUAGE

MOD: Manager on Duty. The individual on the hotel property responsible for making any managerial decisions required during the period he or she is MOD.

■

- The hotel's general manager would, of course, want to be made aware of all such incidents on a daily basis. Certainly the general manager would want to take corrective action to
  1. Eliminate the source of the guest disturbance
  2. Compensate affected guests appropriately

  The affected guests are likely to contact the general manager or the hotel's owners or the franchise brand organization with the same complaint. If management is unaware of problems on the property, corrective action cannot be taken. For that reason, the controller should share allowance and adjustment vouchers information with the appropriate managers every day.

The total dollar amount of allowances and adjustments compared to total overall rooms revenue can be tracked on a monthly basis using the following formula:

$$\frac{\text{Total Monthly Allowances and Adjustments}}{\text{Total Room Revenue}}$$

$$= \text{Room Allowance and Adjustment } \%$$

This percentage will vary based on the age of the hotel, the quality of staff and training programs, and even the type of guest typically served. Percentages ranging from 0.0 percent to 3.0 percent of total room revenue are most common.

Accounts Receivable Control

In some cases, a hotel's actual client will be a company or organization rather than an individual guest. For example, if a large insurance company employed 50 staff members and arranged to hold its annual staff training session at a hotel, the company itself would make the 50 required guest room reservations and would agree to pay for the charges. In a situation of this kind, the insurance company is likely to request that the hotel send it a bill for all the room charges incurred during the training session. If the hotel agrees to do so, it will have agreed to sell the rooms to the insurance company on credit.

When a hotel elects to extend credit to a guest, it creates a direct bill account and then, as the guest incurs charges; periodically prepares an invoice and sends it to the guest. This direct guest billing may occur on the same day the guest incurs the charge, at the end of each month, quarterly, or at any mutually agreed upon time. When a hotel extends credit to guests, the total dollar amount of the outstanding charges owed to the hotel by these guests is called the hotel's **accounts receivable (AR).**

LODGING LANGUAGE

Accounts Receivable (AR): Money owed to the hotel because of sales made on credit. Sometimes referred to as "AR."

■

There are many reasons, including guest preference, why a hotel might decide to extend credit to some guests. In all cases, however, it is the controller's job to establish:

1. Which guests will be allowed to purchase good and services on credit?
2. Is there a maximum amount the guest is allowed to charge?
3. How promptly will the guests receive their bills?
4. What is the total amount owed to the hotel and what is the length of time the monies have been owed?

The creditworthiness of guests is frequently debated between the sales and marketing team and the controller. In most cases, the sales and marketing staff will encourage the controller to extend credit (to complete the sale), while the controller often takes a more conservative view and may suggest that the hotel deny credit to the same potential guests. A good controller (working with the general manager) will establish a credit policy that maximizes the number of guests electing to do business with the hotel while minimizing the hotel's risk of creating uncollectable accounts receivable.

To assist in determining which guests should be able to buy on credit, a direct bill application (for credit) will be completed by the guest, reviewed by the controller or appropriate staff member, and then approved or passed on to the general manager for final approval or denial. Figure 9.4 is an example of a direct bill application.

To learn the reasons why a hotel would extend credit to a guest organization, consider the case of Rae Dopson, president of Dopson Construction, a mid-sized road construction firm. Rae's company has been awarded a state contract to construct two miles of new highway near the Best Sleep Hotel. The job is a big one and will last many months. It will involve the use of dozens of workers, each of whom will require Monday through Thursday night lodging near the worksite. Since the lodging of its workers will be an expense of Dopson Construction, it faces the alternatives of either (1) allowing the workers to stay at hotels of their own choosing and then reimbursing them for their lodging expenses, or (2) negotiate with a single hotel to place all of the business at that property, and then request that the hotel bill the company directly for all lodging expenses. Clearly, it is in the best interest of both the hotel and this company to select the second alternative. The bookkeeping of the construction company will be simplified if it is awarded direct bill status, and the construction company will also be able to negotiate a better nightly rate from the hotel because it can guarantee a predetermined number of room nights. The hotel also benefits from simplified billing. Other hotels that desire the business from Dopson Construction will compete for it, in part, by granting Rae's company direct bill status.

After a determination has been made that credit terms will be extended, it is the responsibility of the controller's office to bill guests promptly. It is also the controller's job to monitor accounts receivable and keep the hotel's managers informed as to their status. This is done by the preparation of an **accounts receivable aging** report.

LODGING LANGUAGE

Accounts Receivable Aging: A process for determining the average length of time money is owed to a hotel because of a credit sale.

■

Figure 9.5 shows an example of an accounts receivable aging report for a hotel with $100,000 in outstanding accounts receivable.

Figure 9.5 shows that the total amount owed to the hotel is $100,000. This amount can be broken down into four distinct time periods. One half of the total accounts receivable ($50,000) is owed to the hotel by guests who received their bills 30 or fewer days ago, while 5 percent ($5,000) is due from guests who have had more than 90 days to pay their bills. As a general rule, as the age of an account receivable increases, the likelihood of its being collected decreases. Also, as the total percentage of accounts receivable 90 days or older increases, the likelihood of collecting on these receivables decreases.

As a receivable account ages, an effective controller will contact the guest to find out whether a problem in billing, documentation, or some other issue is delaying payment to the hotel. In severe cases of non-payment, the guest's direct billing status could be revoked and the hotel would undertake collection efforts. The extension of credit and the collection of accounts receivable is an important component of the

Best Sleep Hotel

Application for Direct Billing

Date: _____   **Federal ID #** _____

Company/ Organization: _____

Division /Department: _____

Mailing Address: _____

Street Address	*Suite #*

City	*State*	*ZipCode*

(Area Code) Phone Number	*(Area Code) Fax Number*

BILLING ADDRESS: _____
(If different from above)   **(Name of Invoice Recipient–Attention to)**

_____

Street (PO Box #)	Suite #

City	State	Zip Code

List of those persons entitled to authorize (call in reservation):

1. _____   _____
   Full Name   **Title**

2. _____   _____
   Full Name   **Title**

3. _____   _____
   Full Name   **Title**

Please circle the charges employees are authorized to bill. Circle all that apply:

Room & Tax only	Phone	Restaurant Bills
All Charges	Movies	Banquet/Meeting Charges

Credit References:

1. _____
   Hotel Name

   _____
   Phone Number

2. _____
   Hotel Name

   _____
   Phone Number

3. _____
   Other

   _____
   Phone Number

FIGURE 9.4   Direct Bill Application

Company Bank:

Bank Name: _____   Account Type: _____

Account Number: _____

At least three credit references and at least one company bank are **required** to complete this application. At least two of the references must be hotel references, while the third may be a company with whom you have a billing history.

If for some reason the application cannot be completed with the requested information, please contact the Accounts Receivable Department of the Best Sleep Hotel.

Please allow at least 15 days for proper processing and approvals.
Applications must be approved **before** any direct billing may take place. You will be contacted by mail about your approval status.

By signing this document, I allow the creditors and bank listed above to release to the Best Sleep Hotel all necessary information for the proper processing and approval of this application. I understand that all accumulated charges are submitted to the accounting department upon the completion of each authorized function/stay. I also understand that payment is due within 30 days from the date of the invoice. I further understand that it is my company's responsibility to keep the list of authorized personnel updated and current to avoid improper or unauthorized usage of this direct bill account, and may do so by requesting an authorization/status change form from the Accounts Receivable Department of the Best Sleep Hotel.

Signature of Applicant: _____   _Date:_ _____

For Company Use Only:

Recommendation of Controller _____
_____
_____
_____
_____

Approved By

Signature: _____   _Date:_ _____

FIGURE 9.4   (continued)

Best Sleep Hotel: Accounts Receivable Aging Report For January, 200X
Total Amount Receivable $100,000.00

| | Number of Days Past Due | | | |
	Less than 30	30–60	60–90	90+
	$ 50,000			
		$ 30,000		
			$ 15,000	
				$ 5,000
Total	$ 50,000	$ 30,000	$ 15,000	$ 5,000
% of Total	50%	30%	15%	5%

FIGURE 9.5   Accounts Receivable Aging Report

1. All clients allowed direct bill privileges have a properly completed and approved direct bill application on file.
2. All direct bills are processed and mailed within three days of the guest's departure.
3. All direct bill clients have two files (paper or electronic). One file contains outstanding invoices; the other contains paid invoices.
4. Payments made by guests on their folio balances are recorded with copies of checks stapled to the front of the folio.
5. An accounts receivable aging report is prepared monthly.
6. The balance due to the hotel on the aging report matches the total uncollected amount charged to guests.
7. Monthly credit meetings are held with the sales and marketing team to communicate current credit policies.
8. Additional credit is denied to direct bill guests who exceed established payment deadlines.
9. Critically overdue accounts are given to a collections attorney.
10. **Write-offs,** if any, are approved by management and recorded.

FIGURE 9.6   Ten Key Elements for Accounts Receivable Management

hotel's income control system. Figure 9.6 lists 10 key elements that should be present in any controller's accounts receivable management system.

LODGING LANGUAGE

Write-off: A guest's direct bill that is considered uncollectible by management and as a result is subtracted from the hotel's accounts receivable total.

■

EXPENSE CONTROL

It is important to exercise complete control over a hotel's income, and it is just as important to maintain strict control over expenses. To operate properly, a hotel will spend money on staff, supplies, advertising, insurance, taxes, and a variety of other items. It is the job of the controller to see that the hotel pays its bills and maintains accurate records of doing so. Typically, the individual in charge of a specific area within the hotel will make the purchasing decisions for that area. For example, the front office manager may decide where to buy the electronic key cards used at the front desk and place an order for them. The key card vendor will ship the cards along with an invoice for their payment to the hotel. The payment made for the key cards and the recording of that payment will be the responsibility of the controller. Thus, the controller plays a role in the purchasing and receiving of hotel supplies as well as in the overall management of the hotel's **accounts payable (AP).**

LODGING LANGUAGE

Accounts payable (AP): The sum total of all invoices owed by the hotel to its vendors for credit purchases made by the hotel. Also called "AP."

■

Purchasing and Receiving

Perhaps the most important role the controller can play in the purchasing and receiving process is that of making sure that vendors are only paid for goods and services actually received. In some cases, the process is relatively easy. When a delivery of coffee is made by a coffee vendor, for example, it is a straightforward process to count the number of cases delivered and verify that the product delivered is the product ordered and that the price matches that which was agreed upon.

In other instances, the process of verification is more difficult. For example, a lawn service invoice may include charges for lawn mowing, edging, and chemical weed treatment. Both the quality of the work done (mowing and edging) and confirmation that it was, in fact, done (chemical weed treatment) must be verified by the person at the hotel who authorized the work. Obviously, the invoice should be paid if the services have been performed. However, payment should be withheld if all services have not been performed, or were not completed at the agreed-upon quality level. Thus, the controller should pay only those vendors who have delivered the hotel's authorized goods and services at the pre-authorized price, and in the manner agreed upon by both the hotel and the vendor.

Before an accounts payable invoice is paid, the controller should have a system in place that verifies the terms of the sale, the product prices quoted by the vendor, and a list of the products received by the hotel so that these can be checked against actual vendor's invoices. When a hotel purchases services, it must have a payment system in place to confirm that a member(s) of the property management team has:

Accurate verification of the products received by a hotel is an important part of the accounts payable process.

- Pre-authorized the work to be done
- Confirmed the cost of the work to be done
- Verified that the work has been satisfactorily completed before payment is made.

Accounts Payable

Just as a hotel will sell to some of its guests on a credit basis, many suppliers and service companies provide goods and services to the hotel on a credit basis. The hotel is billed by these vendors according to whatever credit terms have been established. For example, a dairy products vendor may deliver fresh milk daily to the hotel. Obviously, it makes little sense to pay that vendor 30 times per month for the milk products delivered. Typically, a vendor such as this would establish the creditworthiness of the hotel and then send the hotel an invoice on a weekly, bi-weekly, or monthly basis. The charges for goods and services used by the hotel, and invoiced by the vendor, but not yet paid make up the hotel's accounts payable.

There are four major areas of concern to controllers establishing an effective accounts payable management system. These are:

- *Payment of Proper Amounts.* Whatever their level of skill and experience, employees sometimes make mistakes in paying invoices. Data entry errors may be commonplace unless the controller has established solid procedures to ensure that legitimate invoices are paid only for the amount actually due. In a well-managed hotel, invoices and payments for invoices are checked for errors by at least two individuals. Software developed to match invoice numbers against hotel check numbers is invaluable in this process. Such software is used to help ensure that accounts payable are processed only for the actual amount of the invoices due.

LODGING ON-LINE

To view the features of a Windows-based software program that includes modules on accounts payable, go to:

http://www.hallogram.com/ias/

Scroll down and select "Accounts Payable" module to review this program's features.

- *Payments Made in a Timely Manner.* In addition to paying the right amount, an effective controller understands that there is a right time to pay each invoice. Some hotels gain a reputation with their suppliers for paying invoices very promptly. This can be good, but it is important to know that maintaining cash in the hotel's cash accounts is also valuable. An effective controller maintains good relations with vendors, many of whom are likely to be local businesses such as plumbers, electricians, and food vendors who are important for the hotel's continued success.

Customers, that pay their bills slowly are likely to be serviced slowly by their vendors. In fact, prompt payment of invoices is so important to many smaller businesses providing goods and services to a hotel that better purchase prices and delivery terms can often be negotiated if the hotel has a reputation for paying its bills on time. Some vendors will offer the hotel the choice of paying less than the

	Actual	Budgeted
Payroll and Related		
Chief Engineer	$ 4,444	$ 4,444
Engineer Assistants	8,450	9,000
Benefit Allocation	3,520	3,700
Total Payroll	16,414	17,144
Expenses		
Computer Equipment	425	500
Equipment Rental	1,000	0
Electrical & Mechanical Equipment	2,520	2,000
Elevators	600	580
Elevator Repairs	200	0
Engineering Supplies	250	300
Floor Covering	0	250
Furniture	0	1,000
Grounds	850	250
HVAC (heating/ventilation and air conditioning)	2,800	3,000
Kitchen Equipment	150	500
Laundry Equipment	0	400
Light Bulbs	250	200
Maintenance Contracts	2,500	2,500
Operating Supplies	185	300
Painting & Decorating	270	500
Parking Lot	1,000	200
Pest Control	350	500
Plants & Interior	280	300
Plumbing & Heating	1,585	500
Refrigeration & A/C	1,500	1,600
Signage Repair	0	0
Snow Removal	1,000	1,000
Swimming Pool	3,500	3,000
Travel & Entertainment	1,600	1,000
Telephone	150	200
Trash Removal	450	425
Uniforms	280	300
Total Expenses	$ 23,695	$ 21,275
Total Prop. Ops. & Maintenance	**$ 40,109**	**$ 38,419**

FIGURE 9.7   Best Sleep Hotel: Property Operations and Maintenance Expenditures for January

full invoice (discounts for on-time payments) if it pays promptly. In general, an effective controller should take advantage, whenever possible, of discounts offered by vendors for prompt payment. Some vendors will give a discount of 1–5 percent of the invoice price if a bill is paid within a specific time period. The controller should seize every opportunity to build positive vendor relations and lowest costs by managing the accounts payable process professionally.

• *Payment Records Properly Maintained.* While it may seem fairly simple to ensure that each accounts payable invoice is paid only once, that is not, in fact, the case. Careful attention to detail is needed to make sure that invoices are paid and recorded properly. An effective controller creates a system whereby total payments to vendors match vendor-submitted invoice totals, with no overpayments or underpayments.

- *Payment Totals Assigned to Proper Department or Area.* It is important for the controller to pay the hotel's bills, but it is equally important to know which area within the hotel has incurred a given expense. For example, a general manager may want to know how much money is being spent on plumbing repairs for a given month or year. Obviously then, the controller must keep a record of how much money is being spent by the maintenance department for plumbing parts and labor for that time period. To do so, controllers use a system of **coding** to assign actual costs to predetermined areas within the hotel.

LODGING LANGUAGE

Coding: The process of assigning incurred costs to predetermined cost centers or categories.

■

For example, the maintenance department will certainly be interested in its total expenditures for a month. The expenditure breakdown in Figure 9.7 shows where the money in the maintenance department is being spent and where it was over budget in the month of January. Note that each expense subcategory has been developed to help managers understand total property operations and maintenance expenditures.

ALL IN A DAY'S WORK

The Situation

"I know you signed off on it, but I'm just not comfortable processing payment on this one," said Kathy Waldo, "I need better back-up." Kathy, the general manager of the 65-room Best Rest Hotel handed the invoice from Pittsburg Plow, the hotel's snow removal and parking lot salting company, back to Ron. Ron was the head of maintenance and the person responsible for ensuring that the hotel's parking areas remained free of ice and snow in the winter. The invoice from Pittsburg Plow was for five parking lot saltings during December. It was now January, and Ron had submitted the Pittsburg Plow invoice he had received for December services.

The single-page invoice simply stated:

"Best Rest Hotel: December Saltings: 5 @ at $180.00 = Total due $900.00"

"How do you know there were five?" Kathy asked Ron. "And when were they? How do we know there weren't three or four, or just one!"

"I'm just not sure," replied Ron, "I'm not here 24/7. And sometimes they come in the middle of the night. But I do remember seeing the salt truck here at least once or twice last month."

A Response

Kathy is correct not to want to process payment. The hotel does not seem to have the kind of accounting systems in place that can verify whether it has received and can document the services for which it is billed. A solid system of services verification must be implemented to protect the hotel from fraudulent vendor billings for services such as salting, snow plowing, lawn care, fertilization of plants, and window washing in which the work may be done

in a manner, or at times, not easily confirmed. These systems can be as simple as having the vendor sign in at the front desk when working during off-hours, or as direct as requiring the vendor to make telephone contact with the appropriate hotel staff member when the work is started and/or has been completed. In all cases, however, it is unacceptable to pay a vendor for services when it is not clear whether the services were actually performed.

Working together, the general manager, the head of maintenance, and the hotel's salt/ plow vendor should work out a systems to verify the quality and quantity of work performed. Then the appropriate hotel staff member can sign off on the payment (invoice) for that work. If this cannot be achieved with Pittsburg Plow, a new vendor should be selected.

An effective controller will work with the employees involved in the purchasing process to code the hotel's expenses to the correct expense categories so that they can be accurately analyzed. Departmental expense categories can be developed by an individual hotel or a hotel company operating multiple hotels. In all cases, however, it is the role of the controller to implement a properly functioning expense coding system.

FINANCIAL REPORTING

In addition to producing budgets, safeguarding income, and managing expenses, the controller in a hotel is also responsible for preparing, or, in a centralized accounting system, supplying the information to prepare, the accounting documents known as **financial statements** that provide an overview of the hotel's fiscal standing.

LODGING LANGUAGE

Financial Statements: Financial summaries of a hotel's accounting information. Also called the hotel's "financials."

■

It is important that these financials accurately reflect the true fiscal health of the business. If a hotel's financial statements overstate its economic condition, potential buyers may be misled into thinking the hotel is worth more than it is, and thus might overpay to acquire it. Potential lenders to the hotel, in the same situation, may feel that the hotel could repay money loaned to it when, in fact, the hotel may not be able to do so.

Alternatively, if a hotel's financials inaccurately understate the value or economic strength of the property, its owners may not be able to achieve the sales price they want when they are ready to sell. Moreover, a lender may not loan money to the hotel, even though the hotel's true financial condition would indicate that it could easily repay any loans it obtained.

Business accounting is a dynamic professional field that is constantly being revised and improved by those who work in it. As in nearly all professional fields, there can be real differences of opinion as to how accounting is best done. To ensure that all accountants prepare accurate financial statements, as and that others in business can easily read and understand the financial statements, accountants follow a set of generally accepted accounting principles known as the **GAAP.**

LODGING LANGUAGE

GAAP: Short for "generally accepted accounting principles." Techniques, methods, and procedures utilized by all accountants in the preparation of financial statements.

■

As the hotel's accountant, the controller must also follow the GAAP. Even when the role of the on-property controller is simply to provide financial information to a centralized accounting system or to a C.P.A. retained by the hotel, the financial information reported must present a fair and accurate picture of the hotel's true financial position. While the hotel industry has not experienced blatant financial fraud on the magnitude of the Enron, WorldCom, and other highly publicized debacles, the experiences of these companies, and the consequences for their financial officers, point to the importance of honesty in reporting financial information.

LODGING ON-LINE

The 2002 Sarbanes-Oxley Act became law to help rebuild public confidence in the way corporate America governs its business activities. The Act has far-reaching implications for the tourism, hospitality and leisure industry. To examine an overview of its provisions, go to:

www.vigilar.com/sol_compliance_sarbanes_oxley.html

Accuracy and honesty are important, as we have seen, when the controller assists in preparing a budget that attempts to forecast a hotel's future financial performance. There are three additional key financial documents that look to the hotel's past accomplishments and present financial condition. These statements, each of which should be prepared monthly, are the:

- Income statement
- Balance sheet
- Statement of cash flows (SCF)

The Income Statement

The income statement is known by a variety of names. Technically, it is known as the income and expense statement. It is sometimes better known as the profit and loss statement, or, even more simply, as the **P&L.**

LODGING LANGUAGE

P&L: Short for "Profit and Loss" statement. The P&L records total hotel revenues and expenses for a specific time period. Same as income and expense statement.

■

The P&L, when properly prepared, lists the hotel's income (sales revenue) from all its income-producing areas (such as food and beverage, meeting space, telephone charges, movie rentals, and the like), all the expenses required to operate the hotel, **GOP,** and **fixed charges** for a specific time period. This specific time period is typically a month, **fiscal quarter,** or year.

LODGING LANGUAGE

GOP: Short for "Gross Operating Profit." This popular term is taken from a pre-1990 version of the Uniform System of Accounts for Hotels (USAH) published by the New York Hotel Association. It refers to hotel revenue less those expenses typically controlled at the property level. It is generally expressed on the income statement and in the industry as both a dollar figure and a percentage of total revenue.

Fixed Charges: The expenses incurred in the purchase and occupation of the hotel. These include rent, property taxes, insurance, interest, and depreciation and amortization.

Fiscal Quarter: Any three-month period within the 12-month period that makes up a company's operating year. For example, January, February, and March would make up the first fiscal quarter of an operating year that began on January 1st and ended on December 31st.

■

It is beyond the scope of this text to fully discuss the preparation and analysis of the income statement. It is important to know, however, that a competent controller will produce an accurate income statement in a timeframe that the hotel's owners and the property general manager find helpful for the proper management of the hotel. In no case should this time period extend beyond the middle of the next reporting period. For example, if the income statement is to be produced monthly, the completed January statement should be available to management no later than February 15th.

LODGING ON-LINE

To be of most value, a hotel's income statements must conform to industry standards. These standards are regularly reviewed and improved. To view a copy of the most current version of the Uniform System of Accounts for Hotels, go to:

www.amazon.com

When you arrive, enter "Uniform System of Accounts for Lodging" and you will be directed to the appropriate site.

An income statement that details monthly, quarterly, and /or annual revenue and expense can be prepared from the information identified in Figure 9.8.

With the information in Figure 9.8, the hotel's owners and managers can answer the question: How did the hotel perform during this time period?

A helpful format for the income statement is the **tri-columned statement** shown in Figure 9.9.

LODGING LANGUAGE

Tri-columned Statement: An income statement that lists (1) actual hotel operating results for a specific time period, a (2) budgeted operating estimates for the same time period, and (3) the actual operating results from the same time period in the previous year.

■

This Period's Actual		
		Revenues
	Less	Direct operating expense
	Equals	Departmental Operating income
	Less	Overhead expense
	Equals	Net Income (GOP)
	Less	Fixed expense
	Equals	Income before taxes

FIGURE 9.8   Income Statement Information

		This Period's Actual	This Period's Budgeted	Last Year Same Period Actual
	Revenues	$274,891	$268,500	$256,431
Less	Direct operating expense	99,851	93,975	96,253
Equals	Departmental operating income	175,040	174,525	160,178
Less	Overhead expense	59,853	57,500	53,193
Equals	Net income (GOP)	115,187	117,025	106,985
Less	Fixed expense	64,231	65,000	63,980
Equals	Income before taxes	50,956	52,025	43,005

FIGURE 9.9   Tri-columned Income Statement

With the income statement information shown in Figure 9.9, the hotel's owners and managers can evaluate and determine answers to the following types of questions:

1. How well did the hotel perform during this time period?
2. How well did the hotel perform compared to its performance estimate (budget)?
3. Where did the estimates vary significantly?
4. How well did the hotel perform compared to the same period last year?
5. Where were any significant financial changes from last year evident?

The Controller who supplies the information found on the hotel income statement provides an important benefit to those operating the hotel.

Balance Sheet

An income statement tells the general manager whether the month or other accounting period summarized has been a profitable one, but it is the balance sheet that provides a point-in-time statement about the overall financial position of the hotel. The balance sheet has often been described as a "snapshot" of the financial health of a hotel. This analogy is a good one, because the balance sheet captures the financial condition of the hotel on the day the document is produced. It does not tell how profitable the hotel was in a given accounting period, but it can be compared to previous or later snapshots to determine the hotel's financial condition.

LODGING ON-LINE

Learning to read a balance sheet is an important managerial skill. To find articles that may help you learn this skill, go to:

www.hotelbusiness.com

When you Arrive, enter "Hospitality Accounting" in the "Search Articles" field to find accounting-related articles.

The format of the balance sheet is really rather simple. First it lists the hotel's assets (what the hotel owns), then its liabilities, (what it owes), and finally, the difference between what is owned and what is owed (the owner's equity).

The assets owned by a hotel typically include such items as cash, monies owed to it by others (accounts receivable), the value of items in inventory (food, beverages, cleaning supplies, linens and the like), and **pre-paid expenses.**

Financial institutions are more likely to make construction loans to hoteliers whose financial statements demonstrate the owner's proven ability to operate profitable hotels.

LODGING LANGUAGE

Pre-paid Expenses: Expenditures made for items prior to the accounting period in which the item's actual expense is incurred.

■

The asset portion of the balance sheet also lists the value of the hotel's property and equipment (fixed assets), less any accumulated depreciation. Recall from Chapter 2 that depreciation reflects the reduction in the value of an asset as it wears out.

The liabilities section of the balance sheet includes current liabilities, generally defined as debts that will be paid within one year, and long-term liabilities, which are debts that will be paid in a time period longer than the next twelve months. Thus, for example, an invoice for dairy products that is due and payable on the day the balance sheet is produced would be considered a current liability. By contrast, the amount remaining to be paid on the hotel's twenty-year mortgage would, on the same date, be classified as a long-term liability.

The difference between what a hotel owns (assets) and what it owes (liabilities) represents the property owner's equity (if any) in the hotel. Figure 9.10 represents a sample balance sheet for the Best Sleep Hotel.

The information presented by the balance sheet is important, and it should be prepared as often, and in as timely a manner, as is the income statement. The balance sheet is especially useful when a specific time period (for example, the end of the

Assets		
Cash	$ 75,000	
Accounts receivable	50,000	
Inventories on-hand	25,000	
Pre-paid expenses	10,000	
Total Assets		$ 160,000
Property and equipment	$ 7,000,000	
(Less accumulated depreciation)	500,000	
Net property and equipment		6,500,000
Total Assets		**$ 6,660,000**
Liabilities and Owners' Equity		
Current liabilities		
Accounts payable	$ 75,000	
Wages payable	25,000	
Total current liabilities	$ 100,000	
Long-term liabilities		
Mortgage payable	$ 6,300,000	
Total Liabilities		$ 6,400,000
Owners' equity		260,000
Total Liabilities and Owner's Equity		**$ 6,660,000**

FIGURE 9.10   Simplified Balance Sheet for the Best Sleep Hotel as of January 1, 200X

current year) is compared to an earlier time period (for example, the end of the preceding year). The balance sheet's "point-in-time" perspective makes it a useful tool for management in the analysis of the overall financial health of the hotel.

Although little seems to have been written on this issue, it is important to realize that balance sheets may have significant limitations, especially in the hotel industry. A complete discussion of the balance sheet's limitations will be found in any fundamental accounting text. What is of most significance here is the fact that the assets listed on the balance sheet do not, into account the relative value, or worth, of the staff (see Chapters 4 and 5) actually operating the hotel.

Hotel companies are fond of saying that people (staff) are their most important assets, but the value of experienced, well-trained staff members is not quantified on the balance sheet. To clarify this very important concept, assume you are the general manager of a hotel and are considering a $1,000 expenditure for your sales and marketing team. You can spend the $1,000 either to replace an aging computer used by the sales staff or to send the sales and marketing team to a one-day training class to learn more about Microsoft Word and Excel, the software programs used at your property for producing sales contracts and guest invoices.

If you purchase the computer, the value of the assets (property and equipment) on the balance sheet will increase, but if you elect to "invest" in your staff by choosing the training program, no such increase will occur even though it is likely that the training class, rather than a single computer, will make a much greater difference in the effectiveness, efficiency, accuracy, and "worth" of the hotel's sales and marketing team. Experienced hoteliers recognize both the value and the limitations of the balance sheet when reviewing it.

The Statement of Cash Flows

Controllers produce or help to produce a hotel's income statement and balance sheet. As you have seen, the income statement details the financial performance of the hotel during a specified time period, whereas the balance sheet shows the hotel's financial position at the end of an accounting period. These two documents are extremely useful to management, but there is a third and equally important financial summary that should be produced by the hotel's accountant. That summary is the statement of cash flows.

The statement of cash flows provides answers to the following types of questions that cannot be answered by either the income statement or the balance sheet:

- How much cash was provided by the hotel's operation during the accounting period?
- What was the hotel's level of spending for building improvements for the period?
- How much long-term debt did the hotel add (or reduce) during the period?
- Will cash be sufficient for the next few weeks, or will short-term borrowing be required?

In the hotel business, "Cash is King." Savvy hoteliers who make this statement know it is critical not only for a hotel to be profitable, but also for it to maintain its **solvency.**

LODGING LANGUAGE

Solvency: The ability of a hotel to pay its debts as they come due.

■

The statement of cash flows shows the effects on cash of the hotel's operating, investing, and financing activities. A simplified illustration will clarify the importance of the statement of cash flows. Assume that a hotel's income statement shows sales revenue of $200,000 for the month. Assume also that the hotel shows a profit (income before taxes) of $50,000 for that month. All may seem well until it is realized that $100,000 of the monthly sales were made to a guest to whom the hotel has extended credit. Thus, the income statement may show the hotel has made $50,000 for the month, but that money is not yet on deposit in the hotel's bank accounts and is not available to help pay the hotel's debts (and in fact, the hotel has been required to use $50,000 of its own cash or credit to finance the operation of the property until the $100,000 is collected from the guest). As you can see, it is important to know how many dollars are in the hotel's bank account and in its accounts receivable.

In addition to credit sales, the general manager must be aware of the hotel's own short- and long-term cash needs if the hotel is to remain solvent. Since the cash standing of a hotel is vital, a statement of cash flows detailing that standing should be produced just as frequently as is the income statement and the balance sheet. In fact, the Financial Accounting Standards Board (FASB), the organization responsible for making accounting rules, has since 1988, required that the statement of cash flows be included with other financial statements when issued to external users.

LODGING ON-LINE

To stay abreast of issues and changes in procedures in the area of accounting, periodically visit the Web site of the Financial Accounting Standards Board (FASB). You can access it by going to:

www.accounting.rutgers.edu/raw/fasb/index.html

CHAPTER OBJECTIVES REVIEW

If you have successfully studied the material in this chapter, you should be prepared to:

1. Explain the difference between centralized and decentralized on-property hotel accounting systems. (Objective 1)
2. Discuss how hotels utilize long-range, annual, and monthly budgets to manage their income and expenses. (Objective 2)
3. Identify ways to ensure the security of hotel revenues. (Objective 3)
4. Identify ways to manage a hotel's expenses and accounts payable. (Objective 4)
5. Explain the importance of the income statement, balance sheet, and statement of cash flows to report the financial status of a hotel. (Objective 5)

LODGING LANAGUAGE

Controller	Sign-off	Financial Statements
C.P.A.	Shift Bank	GAAP
Centralized Accounting	Short	P&L
Decentralized Accounting	Over	GOP
Audit	MOD	Fixed Charges
Capital Expenditure	Accounts Receivable (AR)	Fiscal Quarter
Seasonal Hotel	Accounts Receivable Aging	Tri-columned Statement
Manager's Daily	Write-off	Pre-paid Expense
Allowances and Adjustments	Accounts Payable (AP)	Solvency
House Count	Coding	

FOR DISCUSSION

1. Identify two advantages of using a centralized accounting system in a hotel, as well as two disadvantages of such a system.
2. Identify two advantages of using a decentralized accounting system in a hotel, as well as two disadvantages of such a system.
3. Budgets may be affected by a variety of external events that are unforeseen by management. Identify three such events that could affect a hotel's long-term budget. Identify three events that could affect its annual budget.
4. While many hotels employ progressive disciplinary programs, theft is usually grounds for immediate termination. Would you implement an immediate termination policy at your hotel, or would you give a second chance to a cashier caught stealing? Why? What factor(s) would influence your decision?

5. One important decision that must sometimes be made by a hotel pertains to when to deny credit to a client or guest formerly allowed to charge purchases. What factors would influence your decision to deny future credit to a current client whose direct bill account was past due?

6. In some hotels, management has determined that any purchase made by a hotel staff member, above an established dollar amount must be pre-approved by the hotel's general manager or controller. Identify five factors that could influence your decision to implement a similar policy. How would this policy affect accounting procedures in the hotel?

7. Hotel controllers generally rely upon other managers in a hotel to verify many of the invoices submitted for payment. Assume that you are serving in the role of hotel controller and suspect a manager of submitting falsified invoices for the purpose of defrauding the hotel. Outline a procedure you would implement to prevent such abuse.

8. Some hoteliers believe that a hotel's balance sheet is the best indicator of its economic health, while others point to the income statement as the better measure of financial strength. Which document do you believe is most important? Give two reasons to support your answer.

9. The independent verification of financial information in a hotel is an important way to help prevent employee fraud. How often do you believe a controller's work should be audited? What factors would influence your decision?

10. Assume you are a banker asked to lend money to an operating hotel. Identify three pieces of financial information you would want to see before making the loan. How important would it be to you that the data submitted was accurate?

TEAM ACTIVITIES

Team Activity 1

Identify the person responsible for the duties of controller at a nearby hotel. Ask that person to answer the following questions. Have the team report the answers to the class.
In your hotel:

1. What is your greatest budgeting challenge?
2. What is your greatest income control challenge?
3. What is your greatest expense control challenge?
4. What is your greatest overall accounting challenge?

Team Activity 2

Assume that a potential client's meeting planners have applied for direct bill status at your hotel. They will agree to do business with your property only if they can purchase on credit. Your team must decide whether they will be granted credit. Identify the specific terms under which you would be willing to allow the potential client to buy on credit. Also identify the factors you considered prior to establishing this client's credit terms.

10 The Housekeeping Department

Chapter Objectives

1. To identify the areas of responsibility assigned to the housekeeping department of a lodging facility.
2. To explain how hoteliers should manage guest property that has been left behind (lost and found).
3. To show the importance of safety training for employees working in housekeeping.
4. To describe, in detail, how housekeepers should clean guest rooms and public space areas in a lodging facility.
5. To explain the processes required to clean the laundry generated by a lodging facility.

Chapter Outline

THE ROLE OF HOUSEKEEPING
  Areas of Responsibility
  Interactions
    Front Desk
    Maintenance
    Food and Beverage
MANAGING HOUSEKEEPING
  Staffing
    Executive Housekeepers
    Inspectors
    Room Attendants
    Other Housekeeping Staff
  Inventory Management
  Managing Lost and Found
SAFETY TRAINING
CLEANING RESPONSIBILITIES

  Employee Scheduling
  Guest Room Cleaning
    Sleeping Area
    Bathroom Area
    Kitchen Areas and Suites
    Public Space Cleaning
LAUNDRY OPERATIONS
  Laundry Processing
    Collecting
    Sorting/Repairing
    Washing
    Drying
    Finishing and Folding
    Storing
    Delivering
  Guest-Operated Laundry
  "Green" Hotels

Overview: The Housekeeping Department

For hoteliers working in a lodging facility, no one area within the hotel is more important than the others. For example, the sales and marketing or front office areas already reviewed in this text are no more important than housekeeping, the subject of this chapter. In virtually every industry survey of hotel guests, however, hotel (guest room) cleanliness is rated the single most important feature affecting their decision to choose (or not choose) a specific hotel. Guests want, first and foremost, a clean room. It is the role of the housekeeping department to provide that clean room as well as to clean most other areas of the hotel. For this reason, it is difficult to overestimate the importance of a well-managed and properly staffed housekeeping department.

In this chapter we will examine the areas of responsibilities of a hotel's housekeeping department as well as how the work of the department's employees affects the front office, maintenance, and, in full-service hotels, the food and beverage department.

You will learn that hoteliers who manage housekeeping must select and properly train their staff, manage product inventories, and also protect guest property that is accidentally left behind when guests check out. All of these functions will be examined in this chapter, as will the importance of safety training for everyone working in housekeeping. This can be especially challenging if, as is often the case, the staff of the department is multinational and therefore multilingual.

The job of the housekeeping department is complex and becomes more so every day. Properly cleaning a hotel requires knowledge of the many available tools and chemicals that make cleaning jobs easier. In this chapter we will closely examine how to use a checklist to evaluate the results of the housekeeping department's cleaning efforts.

In addition to cleaning rooms, the housekeeping department in most hotels is responsible for cleaning the sheets, towels, and other items processed in the hotel's laundry area. While some hotels do not do their own laundry on-site (on-premise), in most hotels the on-premise laundry (OPL) is a significant part of the housekeeping department's daily activities. In this chapter we will examine the steps utilized to process laundry in an OPL, as well as the unique features of on-premise guest-operated laundry facilities.

THE ROLE OF HOUSEKEEPING

The housekeeping department in a hotel is responsible for the hotel's cleanliness. Because that is true, every guest or visitor to the hotel will be able to readily see the results of the housekeepers' work. When a hotel's housekeeping staff is effective, guest satisfaction is high, employee morale is good, and ultimately the hotel is profitable. When the quality of the housekeeping staff's work is below industry standards, guest complaints soar, employees at the front desk and in other departments of the hotel become disillusioned about management's commitment to quality service, and profits suffer due to increased allowances and adjustments made at the front desk to compensate guests for poor experiences. In addition, guests who feel the hotel was not clean simply do not return.

Areas of Responsibility

The number of areas in a hotel that must be kept clean are so numerous that the housekeeping department will nearly always be the hotel's largest department in terms of number of employees. Depending on the type and size of the hotel, the housekeeping department will generally be responsible for cleaning and maintaining all of the following:

- Public Spaces
  - Lobby areas
  - Public restrooms
  - Front desk areas
  - Management offices
  - Game rooms
  - Exercise areas
  - Pool and spa areas
  - Employee break rooms and locker rooms
  - Selected meeting and food service areas
- Guest Areas
  - Elevators
  - Corridors
  - Stairwells
  - Guest rooms:
    - Sleeping areas
    - Bath areas
    - Kitchen areas
- Laundry Areas
  - Laundry preparation areas
  - Laundry supply closets
  - Guest linen and supplies storage areas

Decisions about the number of employees required to clean these areas and frequency of cleaning are the responsibility of the **executive housekeeper.**

LODGING LANGUAGE

Executive Housekeeper: The individual responsible for the management and operation of a hotel's housekeeping department.

■

It is sometimes unclear whether a space in a hotel is the responsibility of the housekeeping department or of another department. A good example is the dining area in a full-service hotel. In some hotels, it the general manager may decide that housekeeping staff clean the dining room, while in other hotels this would be the responsibility of the food and beverage department. The important rule is that every department must know and carry out its cleaning responsibilities.

There will always be areas in a hotel that call for management judgment about who should clean them. The general manager in conjunction with the executive housekeeper, must make these decisions so that the cleaning of every area of the hotel is the responsibility of a specific department. To facilitate this process, many hotels use a color-coded map of the entire property. Areas of cleaning responsibility are assigned to departments by color code. Each department is responsible for cleaning and maintaining the areas that match its assigned color. With this system, the responsibility for the cleaning of every area in the hotel is known by the department head assigned to the area, and accountability can be ensured.

Interactions

Providing perfectly cleaned guest rooms is a top priority for any well-run hotel. The cleaning of guest rooms is always the responsibility of the housekeeping department and must be executed flawlessly. The specifics of guest room cleaning will be examined later in this chapter. What is less well known, but of utmost importance, is the communication role the housekeeping department must play in relaying **room status** information to the front desk staff and room maintenance issues to those responsible for room repairs. In a hotel with a food and beverage department, housekeeping must also interact with that important area.

LODGING LANGUAGE

Room Status: The up-to-date (actual) condition of each of the hotel's guest rooms (for example; occupied, vacant, dirty etc.).

■

Front Desk

No front office manager wants to assign arriving guests to a dirty room. In fact, in a well-managed hotel, there is a strict policy not to assign a guest to a room unless it has been:

- Properly cleaned by the housekeeping department
- Verified as clean by a second member of housekeeping
- Its status has been correctly reported to the front desk

While this might, at first glance, appear to be a simple process, it is quite complex and contains the potential for a variety of miscommunications if not managed properly.

To examine the importance of maintaining accurate guest room status, let's examine the hypothetical stay of Mr. and Mrs. Flood. This couple checks into a room at the Best Sleep Hotel at 4:00 P.M. on Monday afternoon and are assigned to a room that the housekeeping staff has reported to the front desk is "clean and vacant." That is, housekeeping personnel have communicated that the room has been cleaned and inspected for cleanliness and that no other guest is occupying it. If, in fact, the room was properly cleaned and no other guest is assigned to it, the Floods, upon arriving at the room, should have no housekeeping-related complaints.

Consider, however, the problems that could occur if the room, instead of being clean, was scheduled for a cleaning that had not yet occurred. In this case, the couple would have been checked into a dirty room and, of course, will return to the front desk area unhappy and concerned about the overall quality of their stay. Similarly, if the room is cleaned but the Floods, upon their arrival, discover someone's possessions, (or someone!) in the room, they will again be upset and return to the front desk area unhappy and concerned about the quality of the hotel's management staff.

It is critical that a housekeeping staff continuously and accurately maintain the room status of all guest rooms in the hotel that are rentable. Figure 10.1 lists the room status definitions commonly used in U.S. hotels. Specific companies or areas of the country may vary the terms (and/or the abbreviations used to designate them); however, these terms or their equivalents must be used in the hotel if housekeeping is to accurately represent room status to the front desk.

It is easy to see that the housekeeping department must carefully report the status of rooms. The process of communicating room status between housekeeping and the front desk begins each morning when the housekeeping department receives, from the front desk, an occupancy report that was produced as part of the night audit.

This occupancy report will detail, for each room, the room status the PMS is displaying for front desk agents. If there are no discrepancies, the report will accurately show which rooms that are **stay-overs,** occupied, vacant, on-change, out of order, and so on. It is up to the housekeeping department to take this report and to, report room status changes to the front desk as they are made, just as the front desk should communicate its known room status changes to housekeeping.

LODGING LANGUAGE

Stay-over: A guest who is *not* scheduled to check out of the hotel on the day his or her room status is assessed. That is, the guest will be staying at least one more day.

■

If both the front office and housekeeping perform their jobs well, an accurate, up-to-date room status is maintained in the PMS throughout the day. Generally, the front desk notifies the housekeeping department of check-outs and other room status changes throughout the day by:

- calling the executive housekeeper or a housekeeping supervisor
- updating the PMS (when the housekeeping department has easy access to viewing it)
- using another communication device, such as a two-way radio

Term	Meaning
Clean and Vacant	The room is vacant, has been cleaned, and can be assigned to a guest
Occupied	The room is registered to a current guest
On-Change	The room is vacant but not yet cleaned
Do Not Disturb	The room is occupied but has not been cleaned due to the guest's request not to be disturbed
Sleep-out (sleeper)	The room is reported as occupied but was not used (bed not used; no personal belongings in room), and the guest is not present
Stay-over	The guest will stay in the room at least one more night
Due-out	The guest(s) have indicated this is the last day they will use the room
Check-out	The guest(s) have departed
Out of Order	The room is unrentable and thus unassignable at this time
Lock out	The guest has items in the room, but will be denied access until approved to re-enter by management
Late Check-out	The guests have requested and been given an extension of the regular check-out time

FIGURE 10.1 Room Status Terminology

Changes in room status made by housekeeping can be communicated to the front desk in a variety of ways, including

- having a housekeeping supervisor contact the front desk by telephone (from each room as its status changes)
- via radio or hand-held computer
- by using the telephone's interface with the PMS to make the changes via codes entered into the telephone in the affected room

At the end of the housekeeping shift, the housekeeping department will prepare a final room-status report based on a physical check of each room. This report is then compared to the updated PMS occupancy report to identify any discrepancies. If there are any, the front office manager must then investigate them. A discrepancy could occur if, for example, a front desk agent is fraudulently selling rooms to guests (assigning the guests to a room but not recording the income in the hotel's PMS). In this case, the discrepancy report would uncover the activity because the guest room, reported as "vacant" in the PMS, would show as "occupied" on the housekeeping room status report.

Maintenance

An additional and absolutely critical communication line must exist between the housekeeping and **maintenance** departments of the hotel. Repairs and replacements will inevitably be needed due to the wear and tear caused by guests using guest rooms.

LODGING LANGUAGE

Maintenance: The activities required to keep a building and its contents in good repair. Also, the department or area of a hotel responsible for these activities.

∎

For example, when light bulbs burn out in a guest room they must be replaced. This simple task may be assigned to housekeeping. If, however, a guest accidentally breaks the leg off of a chair in the room, or if a toilet is running constantly, housekeeping must request a repair. The ability of the housekeeping department to aggressively identify and then quickly report needed room repairs will make a significant difference in the satisfaction level of guests subsequently using the rooms. The actual method used by housekeeping to report room issues to the Maintenance department is detailed in Chapter 11.

A critical point to remember is that the housekeeping department, because its staff members are in the rooms most frequently, plays a crucial role in maintaining room quality by reporting room defects quickly and accurately to the employees responsible for eliminating them. Maintenance department employees then make the repairs and clean up their work or, if appropriate, contact housekeeping to retidy the room prior to renting it to a guest. When communications between housekeeping and maintenance are good, the rooms, guests, and hotel all benefit.

Food and Beverage

Some hotels have extensive food and beverage departments. When they do, linens, tablecloths, and napkins may be cleaned and pressed in the hotel's **OPL.**

When the housekeeping and maintenance departments communicate well, room quality is at its best. (*Source:* Clarion Hotel and Conference Center, Lansing, MI.)

LODGING LANGUAGE

OPL: Short for "On Premise Laundry".

■

When a hotel offers guests the choice of in-room dining, the housekeeping department may be responsible for returning used dishes and glassware to the food and beverage dish-washing area. Alternatively, housekeeping staff may simply remove these items by from the guest room to the hotel's hallways for pick-up by a food and beverage staff member.

In addition to providing laundry service and providing for in-room dining dish return, the housekeeping department in a larger property may be responsible for maintaining employee uniforms for food and beverage (and other departments).

MANAGING HOUSEKEEPING

The executive housekeeper in a hotel has responsibility for the cleanliness of the entire facility. He or she must know about personnel administration, budgeting, laundry sanitation, fabrics and uniforms, room-cleaning chemicals and routines, and of course, be guest-service-oriented.

ALL IN A DAY'S WORK

The Situation

"It isn't fair," Jenna Walbert, the executive housekeeper, said to Basil Josiah, the hotel's general manager. "My staff clean the men's employee locker room every day, but just look at this!"

Basil carefully inspected the area. Ashtrays overflowed, food was left on benches, dirty uniforms littered the floor, and newspapers were strewn about. It was a mess.

"The guys in food and beverage and maintenance do this every day," continued Jenna angrily. "Our

houseperson is too busy trying to keep the lobby carpets sharp to spend an hour a day down here cleaning up after our own staff. I think you should make the food and beverage and maintenance departments keep this place clean. *They* are the ones who are messing it up."

A Response

Accepting Jenna's suggestion may be tempting to Basil, but the solution to this problem is *not* the reassignment of cleaning responsibilities. The housekeeping department is typically

responsible for cleaning the entire hotel (including employee locker rooms). In this case, however, the male employees are abusing the system. Fairness in this case requires that the departmental managers responsible for the employees involved correct the situation immediately. Basil ends Jenna's difficulty by using his authority as general manager to enforce their compliance.

Managers in the housekeeping department must be among a hotel's most talented. The challenges of keeping a hotel clean are many, as are the special issues faced by the executive housekeeper and the housekeeping staff. The unique issues faced by the department may pertain to staffing, inventory management, and the management of guest property accidentally (or purposely) left behind.

Staffing

It is usually very difficult to staff a hotel housekeeping department. This is because of the large number of housekeeping staff needed, the difficulty of the work, and unfortunately, in some cases, a wage structure that does not induce the best potential employees to seek hotel housekeeping careers.

Properly approached and fairly treated, however, this department can be well staffed with stabile, highly professional employees who add tremendously to the success of the hotel. In most hotels, the key staff positions are executive housekeeper, inspector, room attendants, and, in some cases, housepersons.

Executive Housekeepers

A hotel with a highly trained, motivated, and professional executive housekeeper has a tremendous advantage over those establishments that do not employ such a person. An effective executive housekeeper is not only a valuable member of the hotel's management team, he or she is also an effective administrator, department motivator, and team player.

At many hotels, the executive housekeeper has worked up from an entry-level housekeeping position. In other hotels, the executive housekeeper may not have held any entry-level housekeeping positions. In either case, the skills required to be an effective executive housekeeper, like the skills needed by all managers, are related to planning, organizing, directing, and controlling the activities of the department. Executive housekeepers must have an unquestioned commitment to cleanliness, impeccable standards, unflinching dedication to their area, and human resource-related skills well above the average for managers. It is only with these characteristics that a hotel's executive housekeeper will provide the departmental leadership required in today's competitive hotel environment.

LODGING ON-LINE

The International Executive Housekeepers Association (IEHA) is the professional association for managers working in housekeeping. With over 6,000 members, the IEHA offers educational programs and certification and publishes a monthly magazine. To view its Web site, go to:

http://www.ieha.org/

Inspectors

The housekeeping departments of many hotels include one or two people in the position of **inspector (inspectress).** These employees report directly to the executive housekeeper.

LODGING LANGUAGE

Inspector (Inspectress): Employee responsible for physically checking the room status of guest rooms and performing other tasks as assigned by the executive housekeeper.

■

Regardless of a hotel's size, it is important that someone verify the actual readiness of guest rooms before they are listed in the PMS as clean, vacant, and available to sell. This job falls to the inspectors. An inspector physically enters and checks a guest room after it has been cleaned to determine whether any areas that should have been cleaned have been missed or if there are other defects in the room that require further attention.

In a very large hotel there may be several inspectors working at the same time. The primary responsibility of the inspector is to assess the quality of room cleanliness, but it is equally important to point out deficiencies to **room attendants,** get those deficiencies corrected, and report revisions in room status to the executive housekeeper or the front desk.

LODGING LANGUAGE

Room Attendant: Employee responsible for cleaning guest rooms. Also referred to as "housekeeper." Sometimes called "maids" by guests, but this term is *never* used by professional hoteliers.

■

An effective inspector has high standards of cleanliness and the ability to point out deficiencies in rooms reportedly cleaned by room attendants in a way that motivates the attendants to do their very best work—in other words, without appearing overly critical of sincere efforts to do a good job. Inspectors are truly a hotel guest's best friend, because their sharp eyes enforce the standards of cleanliness established by the executive housekeeper.

Room Attendants

Highly skilled and motivated room attendants are incredibly vital to a hotel's success. Yet many hotels find it difficult to recruit, select, and retain a sufficient number of room attendants to adequately clean the number of rooms sold. As a result, the hotel operates shorthanded in the room attendant area, and room cleanliness suffers. In addition, managers (and other non-housekeeping staff) end up cleaning rooms, and inspectors sometimes are not able to inspect because they are too busy helping to clean rooms.

When executive housekeepers are asked why these problems occur, their answers include:

- We don't pay enough to attract the right people.
- The work is too hard.
- There is a labor shortage.
- Today's workers simply won't work.
- Not enough people like to do the work a housekeeper is required to do.
- Workers don't care about doing a good job anymore.

It is sometimes tempting to accept such statements as the truth. You should not, however, because in nearly all cases they are simply not true. Interestingly, the best executive housekeepers not only have adequate numbers of room attendants on staff, they have a waiting list of room attendants from other hotels in the area hoping to join their staff. Remember that strategies designed to properly recruit and retain room attendants must be put in place if a hotel is to be perceived as the employer of choice for the area's best room attendants.

Properly cleaning guest rooms can be hard, physically demanding work. Some larger hotels used to employ **housepersons** (typically male) to perform the very labor-intensive tasks, such as carrying heavy loads of laundry and moving furniture within rooms. Today, such employees are just as likely to be female as male, and, as is true with laundry workers and public space cleaners, they comprise an integral part of the overall housekeeping department.

LODGING LANGUAGE

Housepersons: Employee responsible for assisting room attendants with their work.

■

Entry-level housekeeping wages are often among the lowest in the hotel. Nonetheless, it is possible and critical to build a highly motivated, dedicated staff of room attendants. The approaches to doing so are many but at minimum include:

- Treat room attendants with the respect they deserve at all times
- See that room attendants are supervised by excellent supervisors
- Maintain room-cleaning assignment policies that are perceived as fair by the room attendants
- Provide excellent, ongoing training
- Provide a realistic career ladder for room attendants
- Enforce housekeeping department policies that affect room attendants consistently and without favoritism
- Provide for room attendant safety through training and appropriate hotel policies
- Provide benefit packages that are competitive for the area
- Pay fair wages to part-time and full-time housekeeping staff

Many hotel general managers disagree about what constitutes fair wages for room attendants. Some simply pay room attendants an hourly wage. Others add incentives for extra effort, such as meeting established quality levels. Still others pay a designated dollar amount for each room cleaned. Regardless of the payment approach, it is important to treat room attendants fairly. Some hoteliers treat room attendants as if they are not important. Hotels that do this will, inevitably, lose their best room attendants to hotels that demonstrate real concern for these crucial staff members.

Other Housekeeping Staff

In addition to the executive housekeeper, inspectors, and room attendants, the housekeeping department will, depending upon its size, employ one or more housepersons to clean **public spaces,** records or payroll clerks who serve as administrative assistants to the executive housekeeper, and OPL workers.

LODGING LANGUAGE

Public Space: Areas within the hotel that can be freely accessed by guests and visitors. Examples include lobby areas, public restrooms, corridors, and stairwells.

■

The on-premise laundry in a hotel is often a hot and physically demanding place to work. Employees needed in this area include those actually moving items to be washed from the guest rooms to the laundry area, those loading and unloading washers and dryers, and those responsible for folding and storing the cleaned items as well as transporting them to carts or storage areas located near guest rooms. In some special cases, seamstresses may be employed to care for uniforms and guest clothes.

Inventory Management

The housekeeping department maintains a large number of products used in the cleaning and servicing of rooms. In addition, a large number of inventory items are required each time a room is cleaned. The following partial list gives some indication of the number of guest-room-related inventory items that must be maintained by the executive housekeeper:

Sheets (all sizes)	Acid-based cleaners
Pillowcases	Glassware
Bedspreads	Cups
Bath towels	Coffee/coffee filters
Hand towels	Laundry bags
Washcloths	Laundry tags
Soaps	Clothes hangers
Shampoos	In-room literature and signage
Conditioners	Television viewing guides
Sewing kits	Telephone books
Glass cleaners	Pens
Furniture polish	Paper/pads/stationery

If too many units of any item are kept in storage, the hotel may have committed money to housekeeping inventory that could be put to better use elsewhere in the hotel. Alternatively, if too few items are kept on hand, housekeepers may not have what they need to properly clean and service rooms. Therefore, the executive housekeeper must know how much of each item is in use, in storage, and/or on order. Purchasing and receiving replacements for some items, such as custom bedspreads, drapes, or logo items, may take weeks or even months. In light of this, an actual monthly count of all significant housekeeping supplies is strongly recommended.

A second value of monthly inventories is that they allow the executive housekeeper to compute monthly **product usage reports.**

LODGING LANGUAGE

Product Usage Report: A report detailing the amount of an inventoried item used by a hotel in a specified time period (week, month, quarter, or year).

■

Figure 10.2 shows a monthly product-usage report for king-sized bed sheets. It is completed using actual product counts taken at the beginning of each month by the housekeeping staff (*note:* the same format can be used to compute product usage in any department and for any product in the hotel).

When determining the count of products in housekeeping, it is important to remember to count the total number of products on hand, whether they are in use, in storage, or in reserve. To accurately determine the total number of king-sized bed sheets actually on hand, for example, physical counts would need to be taken in:

- Guest rooms
- Room attendant carts
- Soiled linen areas (including inside washers and dryers)
- Clean linen storage areas
- New product (unopened) storage areas

Department:	Housekeeping		Item:	King-size Sheets
Prepared By:			Date:	
For Period:			to	

Count on:	January 1			850 units
		Plus		
Purchased in month				144 units
Total in service				994 units
		Less		
Count on:	February 1			877 units
Total Monthly usage				**117**

FIGURE 10.2   Best Sleep Hotel Product Usage Report

Note in Figure 10.2 that 117 bed sheets were used in the month. This may mean that the sheets were taken out of service because they were too badly stained to continue using, that they had become torn or frayed beyond use, and/or that they were stolen. Regardless of the reason, if the physical count of the king-sized bed sheets is accurate, management knows the number and can easily compute the cost of king-sized sheets taken out of service in January. The executive housekeeper, assisted, if necessary, by others on the housekeeping staff, should compute monthly usage rates on all significant housekeeping items.

Managing Lost and Found

Guests often either intentionally or accidentally leave valuable items in their rooms when they check out. As a result, the housekeeping department must have specific, written lost and found procedures in place.

Sometimes it is hard to know what to do with property whose ownership is unknown. In most states, the law makes a distinction between three types of property whose ownership is in doubt. Each of the three types of unclaimed property requires a different response by the housekeeping staff. The three property types are:

- **Mislaid property.** The owner has unintentionally left the item(s) behind.
- **Lost property.** The owner has unintentionally left the item(s) behind and then forgotten them.
- **Abandoned property.** The owner has intentionally left the item(s) behind.

LODGING LANGUAGE

Mislaid Property: Items the owner has unintentionally left behind.

Lost Property: Items the owner has unintentionally left behind and then forgotten.

Abandoned Property: Items the owner has intentionally left behind.

■

The law requires that hotels safeguard mislaid property until the rightful owner returns. For example, a laptop computer left in a guest room is to be protected by the hotel until its owner returns. To throw or give the computer away on the same day it was discovered in the room would be illegal. In fact, if the hotel were to give it away to someone other than its rightful owner, the hotel would be responsible to the owner for the value of the computer. Executive housekeepers must make sure that a policy is in place requiring that employees discovering mislaid property identify it as such to their supervisor.

In the case of a laptop computer, it is very likely that the guest who mislaid it will contact the hotel to arrange for its return. If that does not happen in a reasonable time (in most states 60–90 days), the mislaid property would now legally be considered lost property (property that the owner has forgotten).

A hotel must hold lost property until the rightful owner claims it. In many states, the item's finder must make a good faith effort to return the lost item to its owner. For example, if a leather jacket is left in a guest room, and the hotel staff discovers the owner's name and telephone number sewn into the lining, they must attempt to reach the jacket's owner. As with mislaid property, employees who find lost property in the course of their work should be required to give the property to their employer.

How long a hotel must hold lost property depends upon the value of the property. In general, the greater value, the more reasonable it is to hold the item for an extended period. The executive housekeeper, in consultation with the general manager, should establish the length of time mislaid and lost property will be held before the hotel disposes it of. In most cases, 90 days is a reasonable time to hold items found in a hotel.

In the case of abandoned property, the owner has no intention of returning to retrieve the item(s). Interestingly, the law does not require a hotel to attempt to find the owner of abandoned property. Most of the guest items left in hotel rooms fall into this category. Magazines, worn-out clothing, personal toiletry items such as combs and razors, and a variety of grocery items are often abandoned.

It can be difficult for a hotel manager to know when an item has been abandoned rather than misplaced or lost. When in doubt, property left behind in a room or found in a lobby area should be treated as either mislaid or lost. After it is held for a reasonable period, the hotel should dispose of it. Some hotels give such items to local charities; others give them to the hotel employee who found them.

Regardless of the hotel's abandoned property policy, it is the job of the executive housekeeper to have a written lost and found procedure in place that protects guest property until it is claimed or declared abandoned. In large hotels with designated safety and security departments, the head of that department may develop this policy and may even be responsible for safekeeping misplaced or lost items.

Pre-printed forms on which to record information about lost and found items are readily available from many business stationery sources and can be useful. Regardless of the form(s) used, the executive housekeeper should protect the hotel with a written record of:

- The date the item was found
- A description of the item
- Location where the item was found (room number; if applicable)
- Name of the finder
- Supervisor who received the item

When the item is returned to the rightful owner or disposed of, the written record should include:

- The date the item was returned to the owner
- Owner's name/address/telephone number
- The name of the housekeeping manager returning the item
- Method of return (for example, by mail, in person, etc.)
- Date the property was declared to be abandoned
- Name of hotel employee (or charity) receiving the abandoned property

LODGING ON-LINE

A number of companies sell complete "lost and found" documentation packages that include forms and log books. The American Hotel Registry is a full-service hotel products supplier. To view this innovative company's lost and found (and other) product offerings, go to:

http://www.americanhotel.com/

SAFETY TRAINING

Employee accident rates in the housekeeping department are often among the highest in the hotel. There are two reasons for this. The first is the simple fact that the housekeeping department is usually one of the hotel's largest in terms of the number of workers employed. The second reason, however, relates to the physical nature of the job. Housekeepers often work with equipment and supplies that must be very carefully handled if accidents are to be avoided. Proper housekeeping equipment and supplies help improve productivity and safety as well as reduce accidents and therefore should be provided to each housekeeper and placed, where appropriate, on every **room attendant cart.** If they are not, unnecessary on-the-job injuries will result, and medical costs related to accidents will increase.

LODGING LANGUAGE

Room Attendant Cart: A wheeled cart that contains all of the items needed to properly and safely clean and restock a guest room.

■

Training the housekeeping staff properly is just as important as providing them with the necessary tools and supplies to do their jobs. Employee training is always a crucial aspect of the executive housekeeper's job, and safety training is the most essential element of training. The executive housekeeper must make sure that the department has the necessary equipment, supplies, and training programs in place to minimize threats to worker safety.

Housekeeper's jobs often require the use of machines, such as vacuum cleaners, washers, dryers, high-capacity linen ironing and folding apparatus, and other equipment. Workers should never be allowed to operate these until they are fully trained. Supplies used by housekeepers in the completion of their daily tasks include powerful cleaners and chemicals. Properly used, they make the workers' jobs easier. Improperly used, the same chemicals and cleaners can cause nausea, skin rashes, vomiting, blindness, and even death. A good rule to follow is that all housekeeping employees handle only machinery and supplies that they have been properly and thoroughly trained to handle.

All hotel employees require both general and department-specific training, and the housekeeping department is no exception. In housekeeping, specific areas of training concern most often include:

- Handling chemicals
- Cleaning procedures
- Correct lifting techniques
- Properly entering guest rooms
- Contending with guest rooms containing:
  - Firearms
  - Uncaged pets/animals
  - Individuals perceived to be threatening
  - Guests who are ill/unconscious
  - Drugs and drug paraphernalia

- Blood and potential **blood-borne pathogens**
  - Unsafe (damaged) furniture or fixtures
- Guest service
- Guest room security
- Lost and found procedures

LODGING LANGUAGE

Blood-borne Pathogen: Any microorganism or virus carried by blood that can cause a disease.

The special training required by housekeeping staff in regard to blood-borne pathogens and lost and found items deserves special attention.

Blood-borne pathogen training is especially important for room attendants because they may come into contact with body fluids and/or bloody sheets, towels, or tissues while cleaning guest rooms. Employees who are not trained in the proper procedures for such situations could be infected. Needles left by intravenous drug users or guests with medical conditions requiring the use of hypodermic needles may also threatens the safety of room attendants. Human immunodeficiency virus (HIV) and Hepatitis B are serious diseases spread by blood-borne pathogens. Health threats must be addressed through proper training, and it is the responsibility of the hotel's managers to ensure that such training takes place.

Potential exposure to blood-borne pathogens is one reason that all room attendants must have access to proper safety equipment. (*Source:* Joshua D. Hayes)

LODGING ON-LINE

The federal government is very involved in the development of standards, education, and training materials for workers who could be exposed to blood-borne pathogens. To view a Web site devoted exclusively to this topic, go to:

www.osha-slc.gov/SLTC/bloodbornepathogens/index.html

LODGING ON-LINE

Because housekeepers often come from a variety of backgrounds, language barriers in the housekeeping department can make training difficult. To view an innovative, dialogue-free video training program for room attendants developed for the Educational Institute of the American Hotel and Lodging Association (E.I.), with the vision and support of then executive director, E. Ray Swan, and now marketed extensively by E.I., go to:

http://www.ei-ahla.org/ei1/product_display2.asp

CLEANING RESPONSIBILITIES

Because it is responsible for cleaning so many different areas, an effective housekeeping department must have a flexible, talented staff and must implement detailed procedures for cleaning and inspecting guest rooms and the hotel's public spaces. While it is beyond the scope of this book to detail the specific how-tos of guest room and public space cleaning, it is important to know that employees must be carefully scheduled to clean these areas, and that standards of cleanliness for all areas must be established and strictly enforced.

Enforcement of cleaning standards generally takes the form of the systematic inspection of guest rooms and public space by the department's inspectors, the executive housekeeper, and even the hotel's general manager. As mentioned earlier in this text, however, in some hotels effective inspection programs utilize the hotel's room attendants and other non-supervisory housekeeping staff in the role of inspector. The front office manager can also be a valuable resource in the inspection/quality control programs initiated by the executive housekeeper. This is so because it is often the front desk area of the hotel that receives, directly from guests, any negative comments about guest room or facility cleanliness.

Employee Scheduling

Properly scheduling employees in the housekeeping department requires skill on the part of the manager making the schedule and flexibility on the part of the staff. Depending upon the size and occupancy rate of the hotel, it is not unusual to find housekeeping staff working at any time of the day or night. Public space cleaners may find that late night or early morning hours are best for completing their work. To complete the number of laundry loads needed to support the hotel's occupancy levels, laundry staff may find that they too may have to work very late at night or very early in the morning.

Room attendants' work schedules are generally less flexible with regard to when they can work. This is because guests in stay-over rooms will expect their rooms to be cleaned between the time they leave them in the morning and the time they are reasonably likely to return after their day's activities. Therefore, unless the guest requests alternative times, stay-over rooms in the typical hotel should be cleaned between 8:00 A.M. and 3:00 P.M. In addition, the housekeeping staff must have cleaned enough rooms to allow front desk staff to assign guests to cleaned and vacant rooms at the check-in time established by the hotel. Thus, if check-in is at 3:00 P.M., enough rooms must be ready to allow guests to be assigned one promptly upon their 3:00 P.M. arrival. If this is not done, and a front desk agent greets a guest with the words, *"Your room is not ready yet; housekeeping is still working on cleaning rooms,"* the guest is likely to be dissatisfied.

The number of room attendants to be scheduled on any given day depends upon several factors, including the size of the guest rooms, the amenities in the rooms, the number of rooms to be cleaned, and the amount, if any, of **deep cleaning,** taking place.

LODGING LANGUAGE

Deep Cleaning: Intensive cleaning of a guest room. Typically includes thorough cleaning of such items as drapes, lamp shades, carpets, furniture, and walls. Regularly scheduled deep cleaning of guest rooms is one mark of an effective housekeeping department.

■

Larger guest rooms generally take more time to properly clean than smaller ones, and rooms with special amenities, such as refrigerators, microwaves, stoves, and dining areas, require more of an attendant's time than those without these features.

The actual number of rooms to be cleaned is the variable that is most critical to effective scheduling, and it is important to realize that this number is subject to normal, but rapid, fluctuation. Assume, for example, that an executive housekeeper wishes to inform employees one week ahead of time about next week's work schedule. For example, if Monday is the first day of the month, the executive housekeeper would like to post, on Monday, the room attendants' work schedule for the week of January 8th through the 15th. Based upon the room sales forecast provided by the general manager or front office manager, the executive housekeeper determines how many room attendants are needed and then posts the schedule. If, however, on the fifth day of the month the sales and marketing team makes a large (75 rooms per night), but last-minute sale to guests arriving on the seventh and staying through the tenth, more room attendants will be needed than on the schedule. Alternatively, if significant numbers of guest reservation cancellations occur, fewer room attendants will be needed. This can be the case when inclement weather, airport closings, or other unusual events cause major disruptions in typical travel patterns.

Some inexperienced executive housekeepers, in an attempt to firmly quantify the number of workers needed on a given day, rely exclusively on a **minutes per room** target to establish the room attendants' schedule.

LODGING LANGUAGE

Minutes Per Room: The average number of minutes required to clean a guest room. It is determined by the following computation:

$$\frac{\text{Total number of minutes worked by room attendants}}{\text{Total number of guest rooms cleaned}} = \text{Minutes per room}$$

■

For example, if a thorough cleaning typically takes 30 minutes, and an estimated 100 rooms will be sold, the two-step formula used to compute the number of room attendant work hours to be scheduled is:

$$30 \text{ minutes per room} \times 100 \text{ rooms} = 3000 \text{ minutes}$$

$$\frac{3000 \text{ minutes}}{60 \text{ minutes per hour}} = 50 \text{ hours of room attendant time}$$

The actual number of room attendants scheduled would then depend upon how many of them work full-time and how many part-time.

Experienced housekeepers rely on both rooms per minute computations *and* information about the guests to determine the actual number of room attendant hours that should be scheduled on a specific day. For example, executive housekeepers know that it takes more minutes to clean a room in which the guest has checked out than one in which the guest is a stay-over. As a result, when the percentage of guest rooms that are stay-overs increases, the number of room attendant minutes (and therefore the total number of hours) required to clean those rooms declines. Likewise, when a room has multiple occupants, it is more likely to take longer to clean it than a room housing only a single guest. With experience, executive housekeepers can develop a hotel-specific formula that uses both minutes per room and the unique characteristics of the hotel's guests and sales patterns to determine achievable productivity levels and thus scheduling requirements for room attendants.

Guest Room Cleaning

Effective guest room cleaning is the heart of the housekeeping department and also of the entire hotel operation. In most hotels, this activity, more than any other, will determine the long-term success or failure of the property. It must be done extremely well. A motivated executive housekeeper and well-trained staff are required, but so too are regular inspections that identify areas for improvement and reinforce good practices.

Some hoteliers evaluate the effectiveness of a hotel's housekeeping departments only by computing the labor, cleaning, or guest supplies **cost per occupied room.**

LODGING LANGUAGE

Cost Per Occupied Room: Total costs incurred for an item or area, divided by the number of rooms occupied in the hotel for the time period examined. For example, in a hotel that spent $7,000 on room attendant wages in a week that it sold 1,000 rooms, the cost per occupied room for room attendants would be computed as

$$\frac{\$7,000 \text{ room attendant cost}}{1,000 \text{ rooms sold}} = \$7 \text{ room attendant cost per occupied room}$$

■

It is wrong to think that achieving lower costs per occupied room or spending fewer minutes cleaning each room is always better. In fact, spending too little money or time cleaning each guest room is as bad, or worse, than spending too much. The proper approach is to inspect the guest rooms and then determine whether the hotel is maximizing the effectiveness of the housekeeping department. If it is not, more staff training or additions to staff may be required to maintain established standards, and management must address these issues.

It is a good idea to develop inspection sheets that identify areas to be evaluated during routine inspections of public spaces, guest bathroom and sleeping room areas, and the laundry. They can focus attention on every area affecting guest satisfaction. Of course, the property inspection sheets a hotel develops should consider the hotel's specific needs and characteristics. Inspection checklists, however, can provide an excellent starting point for examining the cleaning process.

GUEST ROOM SLEEPING AREA INSPECTION

Date: _____ Inspected by: _____

Room Number: _____

ITEM/AREA	OUTSTANDING	ACCEPTABLE	UNACCEPTABLE	COMMENTS
All light bulbs functioning	❑	❑	❑	
Lamps clean/functioning	❑	❑	❑	
Carpet unspotted	❑	❑	❑	
Drapes/cords/hooks in place	❑	❑	❑	
Outside windows/ ledges clean	❑	❑	❑	
Bedspread clean	❑	❑	❑	
Pillows in good condition	❑	❑	❑	
Pictures straight/ dusted	❑	❑	❑	
Air vents dusted	❑	❑	❑	
Mirrors clean	❑	❑	❑	
TV clean/ dusted	❑	❑	❑	
Counters/ furniture dusted	❑	❑	❑	
Guest amenities (iron/boards, etc.) in place	❑	❑	❑	
Guest literature in place	❑	❑	❑	
Telephone clean	❑	❑	❑	
Telephone handset clean	❑	❑	❑	
Night stand clean	❑	❑	❑	
Furniture dusted	❑	❑	❑	
Closet doors clean	❑	❑	❑	
Closet shelf clean	❑	❑	❑	
Proper number/ type hangers	❑	❑	❑	
Laundry bags in place	❑	❑	❑	
Extra pillows/ blankets in place	❑	❑	❑	
Refrigerators/ microwaves clean	❑	❑	❑	
Dresser top clean	❑	❑	❑	
Dresser drawers clean	❑	❑	❑	
Area under bed or bed box clean	❑	❑	❑	
Coffee pot clean	❑	❑	❑	
Coffee items stocked	❑	❑	❑	
Waste basket in place	❑	❑	❑	
Logo items in place	❑	❑	❑	
Inside of corridor door clean	❑	❑	❑	
Print material posted on door	❑	❑	❑	
Evacuation sign in place	❑	❑	❑	
Do Not Disturb sign in place	❑	❑	❑	
Other _____	❑	❑	❑	
Other _____	❑	❑	❑	
Other _____	❑	❑	❑	
Other _____	❑	❑	❑	
Other _____	❑	❑	❑	

FIGURE 10.3 Sample Guest Room Sleeping Area Inspection Sheet

Sleeping Area

The sleeping area of a guest room is typically the first part seen by the guest when entering the room. It must be absolutely clean. Figure 10.3 is an example of an inspection sheet that could be used to inspect the sleeping area of a guest room. Recall that the actual inspection sheet used would, of course, be developed specifically for the hotel inspected.

Bathroom Area

The bathroom area of a guest room is very closely inspected by guests for cleanliness. Inadequate cleaning of this area by the housekeeping staff will inevitably result in guest dissatisfaction and complaints. Like the sleeping area of the guest room, the bathroom area must be absolutely clean. Figure 10.4 is an example of an inspection

---

GUEST ROOM BATH AREA INSPECTION

Date: _____   Inspected by: _____

Room Number: _____

ITEM/AREA	OUTSTANDING	ACCEPTABLE	UNACCEPTABLE	COMMENTS
Lights working	❑	❑	❑	
Light fixtures clean	❑	❑	❑	
Fans working	❑	❑	❑	
Air vents clean	❑	❑	❑	
Telephone clean/functioning	❑	❑	❑	
Shower head clean	❑	❑	❑	
Bathtub fixtures clean	❑	❑	❑	
Tile and tub clean	❑	❑	❑	
Safety handles clean	❑	❑	❑	
Shower rod clean/all hooks in place	❑	❑	❑	
Shower curtain clean	❑	❑	❑	
Toilet free of water stains inside	❑	❑	❑	
Toilet exterior and back clean	❑	❑	❑	
Sink fixtures clean	❑	❑	❑	
Sink and stopper clean	❑	❑	❑	
Mirror(s) clean	❑	❑	❑	
Counter tops clean	❑	❑	❑	
Hair dryers/other amenities clean	❑	❑	❑	
Floor tiles clean	❑	❑	❑	
Soaps/amenities in place	❑	❑	❑	
Electrical switches/outlets clean	❑	❑	❑	
Towel bars clean	❑	❑	❑	
Proper terry in place	❑	❑	❑	
Tissues in place	❑	❑	❑	
Toilet paper holder clean	❑	❑	❑	
Toilet paper and replacement roll in place	❑	❑	❑	
Wall coverings clean	❑	❑	❑	
Inside door clean	❑	❑	❑	
Locks polished/ working	❑	❑	❑	
Exterior of bath door clean	❑	❑	❑	
Other _____	❑	❑	❑	
Other _____	❑	❑	❑	
Other _____	❑	❑	❑	
Other _____	❑	❑	❑	
Other _____	❑	❑	❑	

FIGURE 10.4   Sample Guest Room Bath Area Inspection Sheet

sheet an executive housekeeper or a general manager would use to inspect the bathroom area of a guest room. The actual inspection sheet used would be tailored specifically for the bathroom area inspected.

Kitchen Areas and Suites

Many hotels have guest rooms that include in-room kitchen facilities for guests. In addition, all-suite hotels may include kitchens, living room areas, and equipment and features that require separate inspection. Figure 10.5 is an example of an inspection sheet that could be modified for use in guest rooms that include kitchen facilities or in suites.

Public Space Cleaning

The public space in a hotel is one of the first areas seen by the guests. In a larger hotel, the efforts of one or more full-time **housepersons** will be required to maintain proper cleanliness levels.

LODGING LANGUAGE

Houseperson: The employee responsible for the cleaning of public spaces (the house). Also sometimes referred to as a PA (public area cleaner) or porter.

KITCHEN AND SUITE INSPECTION

Date: _____   Inspected by: _____

Room Number: _____

ITEM/AREA	OUTSTANDING	ACCEPTABLE	UNACCEPTABLE	COMMENTS
Range top clean	❏	❏	❏	
Oven clean	❏	❏	❏	
Refrigerator clean	❏	❏	❏	
Freezer empty	❏	❏	❏	
Ice trays available	❏	❏	❏	
Microwave clean	❏	❏	❏	
Dishwasher empty/ clean	❏	❏	❏	
Appropriate glassware in place	❏	❏	❏	
Appropriate flatware in place	❏	❏	❏	
Appropriate dishware in place	❏	❏	❏	
Appropriate pots/ pans/ cooking utensils in place	❏	❏	❏	
VCR/ DVD in working order	❏	❏	❏	
High-speed Internet in working order	❏	❏	❏	
Sofa-bed clean/ easily pulled out	❏	❏	❏	
Other _____	❏	❏	❏	
Other _____	❏	❏	❏	
Other _____	❏	❏	❏	
Other _____	❏	❏	❏	
Other _____	❏	❏	❏	
Other _____	❏	❏	❏	
Other _____	❏	❏	❏	
Other _____	❏	❏	❏	

FIGURE 10.5 Sample Kitchen and Suite Inspection Sheet

Perfectly clean and well-kept public spaces make a positive impression on a hotel's guests.

Guest room suites require special housekeeping attention.

The importance of guest room cleanliness is a consistent theme in this chapter because it is very critical to the long-term success of the hotel. Public spaces, however, are equally important because they form the basis for a guest's initial impression of the property. It is essential, therefore, that the goals for all public space areas include excellent appearance and impeccable cleanliness. Every hotel will have its own requirements for public space cleaning based on its size and product offerings. For example, in a smaller limited-service hotel that offers a complimentary breakfast, the breakfast area may become part of the houseperson's daily cleaning assignment. In a larger full-service hotel, the food and beverage department would assume the responsibility for cleaning dining areas. Figure 10.6 is an inspection checklist designed to help examine some public spaces common to many hotels. It should be modified to reflect the needs of the hotel using it.

PUBLIC SPACE INSPECTION

Date: _____   Inspection assisted by: _____

ITEM/AREA	OUTSTANDING	ACCEPTABLE	UNACCEPTABLE	COMMENTS
Lobby/Front Desk				
Entrance door/ glass clean	❑	❑	❑	
Ashtrays clean	❑	❑	❑	
Front Desk counter area clean	❑	❑	❑	
Drapes/ window treatments clean	❑	❑	❑	
Decorative pieces dust-free	❑	❑	❑	
Carpets, floors clean	❑	❑	❑	
Furniture straight/clean	❑	❑	❑	
Pictures straight/dusted	❑	❑	❑	
Lobby telephones clean	❑	❑	❑	
Ceiling/wall vents clean	❑	❑	❑	
Pool/ Spa/ Exercise Areas				
Wet terry collected	❑	❑	❑	
Terry supplies adequate/properly placed	❑	❑	❑	
Carpet unspotted/clean	❑	❑	❑	
Floors clean	❑	❑	❑	
Windows/ledges clean	❑	❑	❑	
Exercise equipment clean	❑	❑	❑	
Wall coverings clean	❑	❑	❑	
Public restrooms clean	❑	❑	❑	
Air vents dusted	❑	❑	❑	
Safety equipment clean/in place	❑	❑	❑	
Administrative Areas				
Light bulbs/lamps clean and functioning	❑	❑	❑	
Telephones clean	❑	❑	❑	
Carpet unspotted	❑	❑	❑	
Windows clean	❑	❑	❑	
Upholstered furniture clean	❑	❑	❑	
Furniture/desks dusted	❑	❑	❑	
Waste containers clean/in place	❑	❑	❑	
Pictures, wall hangings straight/ dusted	❑	❑	❑	
Vents dusted	❑	❑	❑	
Wall coverings clean	❑	❑	❑	

FIGURE 10.6   Sample Public Space Inspection Sheet

--- **ALL IN A DAY'S WORK** ---

The Situation

"Your maids are thieves," said the middle-aged lady standing at the front desk to Levine Parsons, the hotel's front office manager.

"I'm in room 253," the woman continued, "and when I left my room this morning I put my diamond earrings on the night stand. When I got back to my room, they were gone! I want you to call the person who cleaned my room and tell them to give me back my property. If you don't I'm going to sue you and your hotel! My husband is a lawyer!"

A Response

Unfortunately, hotel guests often accuse room attendants of theft. For this reason,

it is very important for hoteliers to be familiar with their state's innkeeper liability laws. A hotel is not a bank. In most states, the guest in this situation would not be able to recover the cost of the earrings from the hotel, nor would she have grounds for a lawsuit if the hotel routinely informed all its guests that they had access to no-cost safety deposit boxes for the safekeeping of their valuables.

To assist Levine in this situation, however, the hotel must have written procedures in place so that she can investigate accusations of theft and, in the proper manner, talk with involved

employees about their alleged actions. In most cases, accusations against room attendants will be spread somewhat equally among all room attendants. When they are not (for example, when one specific room attendant is accused more frequently than others), managers must take the appropriate actions to protect guests' property. While an accusation of theft is certainly not proof of wrongdoing, a reasonable manager would not continue to allow one employee with multiple accusations to be in a position to continue to cause harm to the hotel's reputation.

LAUNDRY OPERATIONS

Hotels sell overnight rooms, and as a result, the sheets, towels, pillows, blankets, and other fabric items used by guests must be professionally cleaned and disinfected. Some fabric items are cleaned daily; others are cleaned on a systematic schedule determined by the executive housekeeper. Still other items, such as shower curtains, may be made of vinyl or plastic, yet these too must be cleaned regularly. Processing these items and others is the job of the hotel's laundry staff, which is an important division of the housekeeping department.

Hotels have traditionally been designed with space for processing their own laundry, but more recently, as extended-stay hotels have gained popularity, some are also providing laundry areas inside the hotel so that guests can do their own personal laundry. In this section, we will examine both the processing of a hotel's laundry and the unique features of a guest-operated laundry.

Laundry Processing

Hotels generate a tremendous amount of laundry. Some hotels, especially very small ones, may not actually do their laundry on-site. Most hotels, however, will do their own laundry. Significant time, space, equipment, and expertise are required to properly wash, dry, and fold the large amount of **linen** and **terry** generated by a hotel. Table linens, including the tablecloths and napkins used in the food and beverage department, employee uniforms, and other laundry items must also be processed. Not surprisingly, laundry represents one of the hotel's major expenses, and an on-premise Laundry (OPL) must be managed properly if the hotel is to control this important cost.

LODGING LANGUAGE

Linen: Generic term for the guest room sheets and pillowcases (and food and beverage department tablecloths and napkins) washed and dried in the laundry area.

Terry: Generic term for the bath towels, fabric bath mats, hand towels, and wash cloths washed and dried in the laundry area.

■

A hotel's laundry needs vary with its size and product offerings. A smaller extended-stay or limited-service property (100 rooms or less) may do less than 500,000 pounds of laundry per year. At this volume level, the hotel may use linens that are wrinkle-free, and the OPL may consist simply of washers and dryers. Larger, full-service hotels with extensive food and beverage volume have expanded laundry needs because of the tablecloths and napkins to be processed and the increased linen and terry needs that occur when there are more guest rooms. These properties may require additional equipment to press and fold laundered items. In very large hotels, the OPL may process well over 1 million pounds of laundry per year and employ dozens of workers. It will also maintain a substantial number of pieces of high-volume laundry-related equipment. Regardless of its size, the OPL is a major responsibility of the housekeeping department and the executive housekeeper.

LODGING ON-LINE

Large-volume OPLs require large-volume equipment. One of the hotel industry's leading suppliers of large-volume laundry equipment is the Pellerin Milnor Corporation. To review some features of its "tunnel washer" designed specifically for OPLs processing laundry for hotels of 500 rooms or more, go to:

http://www.milnor.com/CBWwhatis.asp?model=36

When most people think of a laundry they think of clothes washers and dryers. In an OPL, the process is more complex, involves more equipment, and actually begins not in the laundry area but in the guest rooms, pool area, dining rooms, and meeting spaces. It is in these areas that room attendants collect the soiled linen and terry that is to be cleaned by the OPL. Operating an effective OPL is a multistep process that includes:

- Collecting
- Sorting/Repairing
- Washing
- Drying
- Finishing/Folding
- Storing
- Delivering

Collecting

Room attendants collect soiled linen from guest room sleeping areas and used terry products from guest room bath areas, spa areas, and pools. In the guest rooms, room attendants strip beds and put dirty linens directly into laundry bags attached to their cleaning carts. When full, these laundry bags are either hand carried or carted to the

OPL. Dirty linen and terry should never be used as rags to actually clean a guest room because doing so could damage them. Sometimes laundry is pre-sorted in the guest room before it reaches the OPL. This is the case when linen or terry is blood-stained and must be placed separately into a **biohazard waste bag** to help OPL workers avoid exposure to blood-borne pathogens. Bags of this type should be placed on every housekeeping cart, and room attendants should be required to use them.

LODGING LANGUAGE

Biohazard Waste Bag: A specially marked plastic bag used in hotels. Laundry items that are stained with blood or bodily fluids and thus need special handling are put into these bags for transport to the OPL.

■

The food service department generates tablecloths and napkins to be cleaned, and in larger hotels, employee uniforms may be processed in the OPL. As a result, the executive housekeeper must also have efficient methods in place to collect these items from their various locations and deliver them to the OPL.

Sorting/Repairing

Once in the OPL, laundry is sorted both by fabric type and degree of staining. Different fibers and colors require different cleaning chemicals in the wash and, in many cases, different water temperatures or length of washing. Linens made of 100 percent cotton, for example, are washed in a different manner than an employee uniforms with a high polyester content. Similarly, a white terry wash cloth used by a guest to polish black shoes would not be washed in the same load as the regular terry collected in the hotel because the heavily soiled cloth would need special pre-wash stain removal treatment to come completely clean. In some hotels, an item like this may be laundered in a special washer designated only for heavily stained laundry. In some cases, a tear or rip in a cloth item can be repaired. These repairs are typically made prior to washing.

Washing

Washing is the most complex part of the laundering process. Today's laundry items are made from very durable fabrics, and washers can be pre-set to dispense cleaning products into the water at the right time and in the right amounts. Even so, executive housekeepers must still teach laundry workers to monitor washing times, wash temperatures, chemicals, and **agitation** when washing laundry.

LODGING LANGUAGE

Agitation: Movement of the washing machine resulting in friction as fabrics rub against each other.

■

Length of washing time is a key factor because heavily stained items need to be washed longer than lightly soiled items. Too long a washing cycle may waste time, water, energy, and chemicals. If the washing cycle selected is too short, the laundry may not be cleaned. Wash water temperature is important because some fabrics can handle exposure to very hot water whereas others cannot. Generally, hot water cleans better than cold, but fabrics washed in water too hot for their fiber type can be damaged.

The chemicals used to wash items are determined by the type of fabric. Chemicals used in the laundry area include detergents, bleaches, heavy stain removers, and fabric softeners. The amount of each to be used should maximize the cleanliness of the fabric washed and control the cost of chemical usage.

Lastly, agitation length and strength must be determined for each fabric type. Agitation is the friction of the laundry against itself during the wash cycle. With too little agitation (caused when the washer is packed too full), items washed will not be cleaned properly. With excessive agitation, the fabrics washed will wear out too rapidly because of the damage done to their fibers.

Some large and small hotels have begun using an **ozone system** for washing laundry items.

LODGING LANGUAGE

Ozone System: A method of processing laundry that utilizes ozonated cold water rather than hot water to clean and sanitize laundry items.

■

Ozone is an extremely powerful oxidant that is 150 percent more effective than chlorine bleach. It destroys bacteria, deactivates viruses, and controls odors. An ozone system replaces the hot water normally used for washing with highly ozonated cold water. The result is better cleaning, reduced energy costs, and longer fabric life.

LODGING ON-LINE

Ozone laundry systems have become increasingly popular in hotels. To learn about these low-temperature washing systems, go to:

www.PuroTek.net

When you arrive, click on "Laundry" and then click on "Hospitality."

The next step in the wash cycle is water extraction. Removing as much water as possible makes the washed laundry lighter and easier for laundry workers to handle. In addition, items that require drying will do so more quickly. When the water has been extracted from the cleaned fabrics, the wash cycle is complete.

In today's modern washing machines, the time, temperature, chemical input, and agitation levels can be pre-set. These must first be determined, however, in consultation with the washing equipment manufacturer and the chemical supplier if wash results are to be maximized and OPL costs are to be controlled to the greatest degree possible.

LODGING ON-LINE

The number of possible setting combinations on a commercial washer/water extractor is large. To review one manufacturer's options utilizing microchip technology to pre-select settings, go to:

http://www. speedqueen.com/opl/products/prod_micromaster_features.htm

---

Drying

Some fabrics do not need to be dried after they are washed. This is the case with some linens that are removed from the washer and then immediately ironed. Terry, however, as well as most other fabrics, must be properly dried before folding or ironing. Drying is the process of moving hot air (140–145 degrees F.) through the fabrics to vaporize and remove moisture. Fabrics that have been dried must go through a cool-down period in the dryer before they are removed from it. This minimizes any damage to the fabric and helps prevent wrinkling. Once removed from the dryer, however, these items should be immediately finished.

Finishing and Folding

The finishing of fabrics is important because washers and dryers should not produce more clean laundry than workers can readily process by ironing and/or folding. Since hotels increasingly use wrinkle-free fabrics, finishing work today involves more folding than ironing. Regardless of how much ironing is done, the space required for finishing laundry must be adequate. In larger hotels, the folding of linens and terry may be done by machine, while in smaller properties it is generally done by hand. The finishing area must be very clean so that the finishing process itself does not soil the laundry. Once the laundry has been finished, it moves to the storage area(s) of the housekeeping department.

Storing

The storage of linens is important because many fabrics must "rest" after washing and drying if the damage to them is to be minimized. Most laundry experts suggest a rest time of 24 hours for cleaned laundry. Therefore, the housekeeping department

Properly processing laundry items prolongs their lives.

should strive to maintain **laundry par levels** of three times normal usage. For example, in a 150-room hotel, there should be enough linen and terry to have:

- One set in the rooms
- One set in the laundry (being washed and dried)
- One set in storage

In this manner, the hotel will have adequate products for guests and enough reserve to permit the laundry to rest before being put back into rooms.

LODGING LANGUAGE

Laundry Par Levels: The amount of laundry in use, in process, and in storage.
∎

If laundry par levels are too high, storage may be difficult and too much money will have been committed to laundry inventories. If laundry par levels are too low, guests may not receive the items they need. As well, room attendants may not be able to complete their work in a timely manner because they must wait for laundry products before they can finish cleaning the rooms. In addition, fabrics may not be allowed to rest properly if they are needed immediately to make up rooms that must be sold.

Delivering

In smaller hotels, room attendants may go to laundry storage areas in the OPL to pick up linen and terry items. In larger properties, these items may be delivered to housekeeping storage areas located in various parts of the hotel. Because linens and terry are frequent targets of theft by hotel guests and staff, the storage areas containing them should be kept locked, and the housekeeping staff should inventory them on a regular basis.

As with guest rooms, management should inspect OPL areas on a regular basis. Figure 10.7 is a sample inspection sheet that can be modified and used. Note the specific reference to **material safety data sheets.**

LODGING LANGUAGE

Material Safety Data Sheets (MSDS): Written statements describing the potential hazards of, and best ways to handle, chemicals or toxic substances. An MSDS is provided to the buyer by the manufacturer of the chemical or toxic substance and must be posted and made available in a place where it is easily accessible to those who will actually use the product.
∎

Guest-Operated Laundry

Guest-operated laundry equipment is very common in apartments, condominiums, and college residence halls. In hotels, guest-operated laundries are popular with families traveling on vacation, long-term-stay guests, and even business travelers who like to travel with as few clothing items as possible. The ability to do one or more loads of laundry at their own convenience and within the hotel is increasingly appealing to many travelers. Some all-suite hotel chains (for example, Hawthorn Suites) have mandated that all of their hotels have an on-premise guest-operated laundry facility.

Most guest-operated laundry facilities consist of a room with one or more coin-operated home-style washers and dryers. Ample space is typically provided for the

LAUNDRY AREA INSPECTION

Date: _____   Inspection by: _____

ITEM/AREA	OUTSTANDING	ACCEPTABLE	UNACCEPTABLE	COMMENTS
Bags and carts used to collect laundry are clean and in good condition	❑	❑	❑	
Area used to sort laundry is clean/ uncluttered	❑	❑	❑	
Washers clean inside and out	❑	❑	❑	
Washing instruction signs easily read	❑	❑	❑	
Area around washers clean/ free of clutter	❑	❑	❑	
Chemicals properly labeled and stored	❑	❑	❑	
Material Safety Data Sheets (MSDS) readily available	❑	❑	❑	
Dryer temperatures controlled, posted	❑	❑	❑	
Folding area adequate, clean of all debris	❑	❑	❑	
Storage areas clean, labeled	❑	❑	❑	
Other _____	❑	❑	❑	
Other _____	❑	❑	❑	
Other _____	❑	❑	❑	
Other _____	❑	❑	❑	
Other _____	❑	❑	❑	

FIGURE 10.7   Sample Laundry Area Inspection Sheet

sorting, folding, and ironing of laundry. Most guest-operated laundries also contain vending machines where detergents, bleach, and fabric softeners may be purchased. Large-screen televisions and/or background music can help to make these areas a pleasant hotel amenity.

Hotels may develop and maintain their own guest-operated laundry areas, but in many cases the hotel will enter a partnership with a company whose business is the management of coin-operated laundry facilities. These companies typically provide and maintain the laundry equipment, fill vending machines with needed cleaning products, and share with the hotel, on a predetermined basis, the revenue generated by the laundry's operation. The hotel, in return, maintains the cleanliness and security of the laundry area. The many advantages of this partnership to a hotel include monthly commission checks and the elimination of the costs associated with buying, installing, and maintaining guest laundry equipment, and the cost of providing and servicing laundry-product-related vending machines.

LODGING ON-LINE

Limited-service hotels are not the only lodging properties offering guest-operated laundry facilities. Even large hotels find that many guests desire this feature. To see one large hotel's use of guest-operated laundry facilities in its marketing effort, go to:

www.adamsmark.com/denver/guest.asp

Note the placement of the "Coin-operated laundry" on the hotel's list of guest amenities.

"Green" Hotels

Many hoteliers participate in efforts that are viewed as worthwhile by society as a whole and by their local communities more specifically. Environmentally friendly activities are increasingly supported by the hotel industry. The term **green hotel** has evolved to describe a hotel that utilizes environmentally friendly practices that may enhance but do not detract from guest experiences at the property.

LODGING LANGUAGE

Green Hotel: A lodging property that utilizes environmentally friendly practices in ways that enhance or, at least, do not detract from its guests' experiences.

■

There is a relatively long history of hospitality industry concerns about the environment. Early efforts continue today with a focus on the conservation of water in restaurants and hotel food and beverage operations. Table tents or menu language emphasize the property's interest in this environmental concern. One tactic: glasses of drinking water are served on request rather than routinely as part of beginning meal service. These efforts are not intended to limit the amount of water actually consumed by guests. Rather, they address concerns about the significant amount of water used to wash the glasses, the energy required to heat the water during the sanitizing cycle, and the detergent waste water that must be recycled in the community.

Many hotels utilize environmentally friendly conservation efforts in their guest rooms. Figure 10.8 illustrates the type of information that can be used to convey the program's intentions to hotel guests and to solicit their participation. As you'll note, guests are invited to help reduce detergent, water, and environmental pollution by allowing housekeeping staff to reuse their bed and bath linens.

Green hotels can do much more than invite guests to participate in within-guest-room conservation efforts. For example, non-synthetic (botanical) cleaning chemicals including cleansers and disinfectants can be used. Newly developed products work very well. They leave a pleasant aroma and help to eliminate the microorganisms with which they come in contact. Some housekeepers report, as well, that they do not suffer from the allergies and headaches that can arise when more harsh synthetic products are used.

Help Us To Conserve Our Natural Resources

We at the _____ Hotel want to do our fair share to help conserve our country's limited natural resources. Want to help?

If your bed and bath linens are reused during your stay, water and energy consumption can be reduced, as will the amount of detergent waste water that must be recycled.

If you would like your sheets and pillowcases replaced, just leave this card on the pillowcase. If you would like your bath linens replaced, simply leave them on the floor.

Thanks! for helping to conserve our environment.

FIGURE 10.8 Linen Change Request Form

Hoteliers continue their environmentally friendly concerns by purchasing and using organic (non-synthetic) fertilizers, herbicides, and pesticides to maintain exterior landscapes without harming the environment. These products can be just as effective as their more traditional counterparts, but they do not contribute to pollution-related problems that can otherwise affect the environment.

Waste management programs, including the minimization of garbage, recycling, and the use of environmentally friendly packaging materials, are additional tactics used by many hotels. In some states, bottle deposit fees must be paid and are refunded when applicable containers are returned. In other areas, paper, glass, garbage, and other materials must be sorted prior to refuse pick-up. All of these tactics help the community in its recycling efforts.

Some hotels, especially in locations with access to beaches, reefs, and other native and prestige areas, are very concerned about protecting the habitat. Ongoing employee and guest education about environmental concerns and community outreach efforts are part of campaigns to demonstrate what can be done and to encourage community-wide participation. Other hotels offer property tours that enable visitors to view natural areas and to learn about the flora and fauna native to the location.

The phrase "think globally and act locally" maybe overused. It does, however, suggest the increasing role that many hoteliers play in working to conserve resources without sacrificing the quality of their guests' experiences as they do so.

CHAPTER OBJECTIVES REVIEW

If you have successfully studied the material in this chapter, you should be prepared to:

1. Identify the areas of cleaning responsibility assigned to the housekeeping department of a lodging facility. (Objective 1)
2. Explain how hoteliers should manage guest property that has been left behind (lost and found). (Objective 2)
3. Show the importance of safety training for employees working in housekeeping. (Objective 3)
4. Describe, in detail, how housekeepers should clean guest rooms and public space areas in a lodging facility. (Objective 4)
5. Explain the processes required to clean the laundry generated by a lodging facility (Objective 5)

LODGING LANGUAGE

Executive Housekeeper	Mislaid Property	Terry
Room Status	Lost Property	Biohazard Waste Bag
Stay-over	Abandoned Property	Agitation
Maintenance	Room Attendant Cart	Ozone System
OPL	Blood-borne Pathogen	Laundry Par Levels
Inspector (Inspectress)	Deep Cleaning	Material Safety Data Sheets
Room Attendant	Minutes Per Room	(MSDS)
Houseperson	Cost Per Occupied Room	Green Hotel
Public Space	Houseperson	
Product Usage Report	Linen	

FOR DISCUSSION

1. Many hotels find it difficult to hire and retain housekeeping staff. Identify three reasons you believe contribute to this difficulty. What could the general manager of a limited-service hotel do to help overcome these obstacles?

2. Some hoteliers feel that room attendants must be able to fluently speak the language of the majority of the hotel's guests to do their jobs effectively. They feel that guest contact is an important role of the room attendant's job, and to converse with guests they must have strong language skills. Other hoteliers feel that a command of the principal language used by guests is not required. If the hotel you managed was in the United State, would you require room attendants at the hotel to be fluent in English? What are some factors that would influence your decision?

3. Housekeeping is one of the departments in the hotel that must work every holiday because the hotel is open and often very busy. Assume you have a housekeeping department with 12 employees and your hotel recognizes New Year's Day, Memorial Day, Fourth of July, Labor Day, Thanksgiving, and Christmas as paid holidays. Also assume that at least one-half of your housekeeping employees need to work each holiday. What factors would influence you as you develop a scheduling system that fairly assigns holiday work days and off days to these employees?

4. Some executive housekeepers allow room attendants to work independently, with only one attendant assigned to each room to be cleaned. Others prefer a system that teams two or more attendants together for each room assigned to be cleaned. Identify two advantages and disadvantages of each approach. Which would you use in your hotel? Why?

5. In some hotels, abandoned property found by employees is given to the finder after an established period of time. In other hotels, such property is given to designated charities. Identify an advantage and a disadvantage of utilizing the charity approach.

6. Some hotels allow, and even encourage, the tipping of room attendants. This is typically done through the placement of a tip envelope with the employee's name on it in the guest room. Identify three factors that you believe would encourage a guest to tip a room attendant. Are these factors influenced most by the hotel's management or by the hotel's individual room attendant(s)?

7. Housekeepers (room attendants) have easy access to guests' personal belongings. As a result, some hotels require applicants for a room attendant position to undergo a criminal-background check. Would you implement such a policy at a hotel you managed? Would you require that all hotel employees (or just room attendants) undergo such a background check? Explain your decision.

8. Housekeeping is very physically demanding work. Identify five things a hotel's executive housekeeper or general manager could do to make the work of housekeeping employees as physically light (less strenuous) as possible.

9. Some hotels do an excellent job of maintaining public space cleanliness yet do not maintain back-of-the-house areas (which cannot be seen by guests) in a similar manner. How do you think such an operating standard would be viewed by employees of the hotel?

10. In an effort to conserve natural resources and reduce costs, some hotels change sheets and towels in stay-over rooms only when requested to do so by the guest. Identify a positive and negative aspect of this policy.

TEAM ACTIVITIES

Team Activity 1

Housekeeper safety and security should be the most important factor to consider when developing room-cleaning procedures. Identify a step-by-step procedure to be used when a hotel housekeeper encounters blood or body fluids on linens or terry found in a guest room.

Team Activity 2

In the normal course of their jobs, housekeeping employees often recover abandoned property. Assume that your team is the supervisory staff of a housekeeping department and you have been asked by your general manager to draft a hotel policy regarding the finding of cash. In your policy, detail what is to happen when cash is found, how long it will be held, and what will happen to it after the holding period has ended.

The Maintenance Department

Chapter Objectives

1. To identify the areas of responsibility assigned to the maintenance department of a lodging facility.
2. To explain the importance of routine maintenance in a professionally managed hotel.
3. To explain the importance of preventive maintenance in a professionally managed hotel.
4. To explain the importance of emergency maintenance in a professionally managed hotel.
5. To explain the processes required to properly manage and control utility consumption in a lodging facility.

Chapter Outline

THE ROLE OF MAINTENANCE
  Areas of Responsibility
    Engineering
    Maintenance
    Renovation
  Interactions
    Front Desk
    Housekeeping
    Food and Beverage
MANAGING MAINTENANCE
  Staffing
    Chief Engineer
    Maintenance Assistants
  Routine Maintenance
    Exterior
    Interior

  Preventive Maintenance
    Public Space
    Guest Rooms
    Food Service
    Laundry
    Other Areas and Equipment
  Emergency Maintenance
MANAGING UTILITIES
  Electricity
    Lighting
    HVAC
  Natural Gas
  Water
MANAGING WASTE

Overview: The Maintenance Department

Hotel guests have expectations about a hotel that simply must be met. These include such basic items as ample hot water for baths and showers, guest room lights that work, and comfortable temperatures in the hotel's public spaces and guest rooms. Employees working in a hotel expect that the tools and equipment they need to do their jobs will be safe and in good condition. In addition, the owners of a hotel have expectations. Among other things they expect that the building and its contents will be diligently repaired and maintained to protect the value of their investment in them. All of these expectations are met and fulfilled by a hotel's maintenance department.

In some hotels, the maintenance department is known as the maintenance and engineering department or as the engineering and maintenance department. For that reason, the head of the maintenance department is commonly referred to as the chief engineer. Regardless of the name used to identify the department, the chief engineer and the department's staff are responsible for properly maintaining the hotel's grounds and physical plant.

A well-run maintenance department assists the hotel's sales effort by providing guests with the very best experience possible as related to the appearance and functioning of the building's exterior and interior. This makes it easier for the sales and marketing team to sell the hotel. In this chapter you will learn about the major areas of responsibility of the maintenance department and how it interacts with the front desk, housekeeping, and food and beverage departments of the hotel.

The chief engineer and his or her staff are responsible for the routine maintenance of the hotel. This includes such tasks as lawn care and adding appropriate chemicals to the hotel's swimming pool. In addition to routine maintenance, every chief engineer or manager in charge of maintenance should develop an effective preventive maintenance program. Preventive maintenance programs are implemented to prolong the life of a hotel's facilities and equipment and to ensure their peak operating efficiency. It is also important that the department be ready for any emergency maintenance that may be required. In this chapter you will learn about routine, preventive, and emergency maintenance.

In most cases, a hotel's chief engineer will also have responsibility for helping the hotel's general manager monitor and manage utility usage. When utilities such as water, gas, and electricity are not well managed, and the equipment that utilizes these resources is not well maintained, the hotel's operating costs will be higher than they should be and, as a result, profits will be lower than they should be. In this chapter, you will learn how the maintenance department can effectively oversee this important concern.

THE ROLE OF MAINTENANCE

Every hotel has a variety of valuable assets. These include the hotel's staff, its cash in the bank, its customer base, and its reputation. The hotel's grounds, buildings, and equipment, comprise the hotel's most visible (and, usually, most expensive) asset and directly affect the value of the hotel's other assets. How guests perceive the hotel's facilities makes a tremendous impact on profitability. It is important, then, for the hotel's managers develop systems to protect its physical assets by performing essential maintenance on the hotel's facilities.

When a hotel's building, equipment, and grounds are properly maintained, guests will be more likely to perceive a positive experience during their stay, and the hotel's ability to increase sales is enhanced. This is the primary job of the maintenance department. When guests experience poor facilities, such as potholes in parking areas, leaking faucets, burned-out light bulbs, poor heating/cooling capacities, or insufficient hot water, their dissatisfaction increases, and the hotel's sales potential is diminished. In addition to guest satisfaction, however, an effective maintenance department will achieve many other important goals, including:

- Protecting and enhancing the financial value of the building and grounds
- Supporting the efforts of other hotel departments
- Controlling maintenance and repair costs
- Controlling energy usage
- Minimizing guests' facility-related complaints
- Increasing the pride and morale of the hotel's staff

These goals can be achieved if the maintenance department effectively performs **preventive maintenance, routine maintenance,** and **emergency maintenance,** and if it properly manages the hotel's utility usage.

LODGING LANGUAGE

Preventive Maintenance: Maintenance activities designed to minimize maintenance costs and prolong the life of equipment.

Routine Maintenance: Maintenance activities that must be performed on a continual (ongoing) basis.

Emergency Maintenance: Maintenance activities performed in response to an urgent situation.

■

Areas of Responsibility

The staff in the maintenance department of a hotel is fully responsible for the facility's upkeep (maintenance), but it is also responsible for selected **engineering** tasks and (when required) specific renovation tasks.

LODGING LANGUAGE

Engineering: Designing and operating a building to ensure a safe and comfortable atmosphere.

■

These three distinct areas of responsibility sometimes overlap. To understand the complete role of the maintenance department, we will examine its engineering, maintenance, and renovation activities separately.

Engineering

Some hoteliers use the terms "engineering" and "maintenance" interchangeably. Thus, in some hotel companies, the department responsible for the care of the hotel is as likely to be called "engineering" as "maintenance," and in some cases, its name will be a combination of both terms (maintenance and engineering). Engineering, as a building specialty, however, is different from maintenance.

The engineering of a building refers to the application of physics, chemistry, and mathematics to design and operate a building that provides a comfortable atmosphere for guests and employees. For example, in a hotel lobby area that must be air-conditioned, the building's engineer calculates the amount of air-conditioned air required to properly cool it. Factors that must be taken into consideration in such a calculation include the temperature and humidity of the outside air, the desired lobby temperature, the temperature at which air-conditioned air enters the lobby, and the movement of the air once it is inside the lobby. Based on these calculations, the size of the air-conditioning unit required to cool the lobby is determined, as are the optimum number and location of air vents and fans delivering the cold air to the area. The knowledge required to balance these features and make the right decision about air-conditioner capacity is significant.

Improperly engineered facilities can result in underpowered (or overpowered) equipment, increased building deterioration, excessive energy usage, and higher-than-necessary operating costs. The head of the maintenance department in an operating hotel will not have actually designed the building's **HVAC** systems, but must be thoroughly familiar with them as well as with the engineering of the building's electrical, water, and waste systems.

LODGING LANGUAGE

HVAC: Shorthand term for "heating, ventilating, and air-conditioning."

■

In very small hotels, the entire maintenance department may consist of only one full-time (or even part-time) maintenance staff member. Whatever a hotel's size, however, there are engineering issues to be addressed, because providing a safe and comfortable environment is an ongoing process that must be continually administered.

LODGING ON-LINE

Engineering a building's heating, refrigeration, ventilation, and air-conditioning systems is quite complex, and special knowledge is required to manage it. To familiarize yourself with an organization whose members specialize in this field, review the Web site of the American Society of Heating, Refrigerating, and Air Conditioning Engineers, at:

www.ashrae.com

Maintenance

Maintenance, as the term implies, refers to "maintaining" the hotel's physical property. It has been said that maintenance costs are like taxes; if they are not paid one year, they will be paid the next year—and with a penalty!

The maintenance-related costs of a hotel are often related to the hotel's age. As a building ages, its maintenance costs generally increase. Even brand-new hotels, however, require **POM**-related expenditures. These costs include staff wages and benefits, replacement parts, contract services, and energy costs that are listed separately on the income statement (see Chapter 9).

LODGING LANGUAGE

POM: Short for "property operation and maintenance." The term is taken from the Uniform System of Accounts for Hotels and refers to the segment of the income statement that details the costs of operating the maintenance department.

■

The maintenance department should maintain the property in the most effective manner possible given the budget assigned it. To do so, hotel maintenance must be:

- *Planned.* From routinely changing air filters in heating and cooling units to awarding a contract for tree trimming, the maintenance department performs too many tasks to leave these activities to chance. An effective maintenance manager is a careful administrator who reviews every piece of equipment and required activity in the hotel and then plans what should be done, when it should be done, and who should do it.

- *Implemented.* Some maintenance managers know what should be done in their properties and have good intentions of completing all the required tasks, yet do not do them. Shortages of properly trained staff, insufficient budgetary allocations, lack of supervisory skills, inadequate tools, and/or underestimation of the time required to perform a given task can all adversely impact the ability of the department to achieve its goals.

   Many excellent checklists and suggested activities have been developed for maintenance departments. Virtually every franchisor offers such checklists free of charge to its franchisees because it is in the best interests of the franchisor for every hotel in the system to represent the brand well.

   Checklists and suggested activities that are not properly implemented, however, will not result in an acceptable maintenance program. Thus, when evaluating a maintenance department, the important factor is not whether it has planned an acceptable maintenance program for the hotel, but the degree to it has effectively implemented the planned program.

- *Recorded.* Record-keeping is an immensely important maintenance function. Routine, scheduled maintenance tasks cannot be properly planned unless maintenance personnel know when these tasks were last performed. For example, if the plan calls for lubricating hot water pumps every six months, a written record must be kept of the last time the pumps were lubricated. Similarly, if a faucet in a guest room is replaced, a record should be kept of when the replacement was made. This will enable the maintenance department to evaluate the quality (length-of-life) of the faucets used and to take advantage of any warranty programs that apply to the replacement parts and to new equipment purchased by the hotel.

   In many cases, such as fire-suppression systems, elevators, and other safety-related equipment, local ordinances or laws may require that records documenting the performance of system maintenance be kept on file or displayed publicly. Even when it is not mandated by local ordinance, however, excellent record-keeping in all areas of the maintenance department is a good indicator of overall departmental effectiveness.

The cost of maintaining a building is very closely related to its original design and size and to the facilities it includes. Hotels with food service and banquet facilities, swimming pools, and exercise rooms, for example, will experience greater maintenance costs than limited-service hotels that do not have these facilities. High-rise buildings will have elevator systems that must be maintained, while one-story hotels will not. Resort facilities spread over any acres will need more landscape care than those located on smaller plots of ground.

The materials and construction techniques used in building the hotel will also affect its POM costs. A hotel with an exterior that must be painted will experience exterior painting costs, while a hotel made of masonry will not. Energy costs will also be affected by construction. Hotels built with good insulation and well-made windows will generally experience lower energy costs than those that are not built this way.

The finishes and equipment specified for installation by the hotel's builders have a tremendous impact on long-term POM costs. Durable finishes and high-quality, long-life equipment may initially be more expensive, but will generally reduce operating and maintenance costs.

Renovation

Even with the very best of maintenance programs, hotel buildings wear out with use and must be renovated to compete against newer properties. Hotel buildings have a predictable life span that directly affects their maintenance and renovation needs. Figure 11.1 details the typical life span of a hotel. As can be seen, the challenges of maintaining a building increase as it ages.

Because every hotel will at some point need renovation and refurbishment, its owners must take steps to reserve funds for the time when renovation is undertaken. This is often done by establishing an **FF&E reserve.**

LODGING LANGUAGE

FF&E Reserve: Funds set aside by ownership today for the future "furniture, fixture, and equipment" replacement needs of a hotel.

■

Generally, FF&E reserves average 2–4 percent of a hotel's gross sales revenue. If designated funds are not reserved, the hotel will not be able to carry out needed minor renovations, major renovations, or **restoration** when needed.

LODGING LANGUAGE

Restoration: Returning a hotel to its original (or better than original) condition.

■

Figure 11.2 lists specific items that must be considered when planning a hotel's short- and long-term renovation program.

Building Age	Building Characteristics and Requirements
1–3 years	Low maintenance costs incurred
3–6 years	Maintenance costs increase
6–8 years	Refurbishment required; average maintenance costs incurred
8–15 years	Minor renovation and refurbishment required
15–22 years	Major renovation and refurbishment required
22+ years	Restoration required; high maintenance costs incurred

FIGURE 11.1   Hotel Life Span

	Minor Renovation	Major Renovation
Guest Rooms	Drapes, bedspreads	Bed frames, mattresses
	Lamps, shades	Wall lights
	Carpets	Wall vinyl
	Upholstered furniture	**Case goods**
	Faucets	Sinks, countertops
	Mattresses	Televisions
Food and Beverage	Carpets, chairs, reupholster booths	Decorative lighting
	Table top décor	Tables
	Dishes, flatware	Serving equipment
		Wall coverings
Public Space	Table lamps, lobby furniture	Overhead lighting
	Lobby carpet	Corridor carpet
	Lobby wall coverings	Corridor vinyl
	Meeting rooms	Restrooms

FIGURE 11.2   Selected Hotel Renovation and Replacement Considerations

---

LODGING LANGUAGE

Case Goods: Non-upholstered furniture, such as guest room dressers, tables, desks and the like.

∎

Refurbishment and minor renovation is actually an ongoing process in most hotels. Major renovation should take place every six to ten years. Costs are high whenever a hotel undergoes renovation. Extra cleaning costs are likely to be incurred during construction. Moreover, it is almost inevitable that guest services will be disrupted, resulting in unhappy guests who must be soothed, and in lost revenue from out-of-service areas that normally generate revenue.

Restoration takes place when a hotel undergoes a so complete renovation that walls are relocated, rooms and public space are totally reconfigured, and mechanical systems are replaced with more modern ones. The typical hotel undergoes a restoration every 25 to 50 years. Restorations are a challenging time for management, the maintenance department, and guests. If restoration is not undertaken when needed, however, the revenue-producing potential of the hotel will decline.

Interactions

The efforts of the maintenance department affect the guests, the hotel's managers, and even the hotel's line employees. On a departmental basis, maintenance has the most interaction with the front desk and housekeeping. In full-service hotels, the food and beverage department will also regularly interact with maintenance.

Front Desk

The maintenance department interacts with the front desk in many ways. Among the most important of these are:

- *Providing room-status updates.* When a room or its contents are damaged and cannot be rented to another guest, the maintenance department will take it out of order. The front desk must be informed about the room's status, including how long it will be unrentable and the date when it is likely to be back in service.

- *Responding to guest service requests.* Guests occupying hotel rooms generate a variety of requests for assistance from the maintenance department. Such requests can include, for example, adjustment of the reception on televisions, replacement of light bulbs, adjustment of in-room heating or cooling (HVAC) units, and the resolution of plumbing complaints. Guests with such needs or concerns will typically call the front desk, whose staff must then relay the request for service to a member of the maintenance staff.

- *Communicating information about specific hotel conditions.* The normal maintenance performed in a hotel can result in disruption to regular building functions and/or guest services. When, for example, a swimming pool must be closed for resurfacing, or when water must be temporarily shut off to make plumbing repairs, or when a power outage disrupts electrical service to the entire hotel, the maintenance department must keep the front desk well-informed of the status of the repairs or disruption and how these will affect the hotel's guests and employees.

Additional interactions between the maintenance department and the front desk can include assisting with guests' needs in meeting rooms, the servicing or repairing of front office equipment and furniture, and carefully coordinating the scheduled maintenance of rooms with the front office manager to minimize disruption to guests and any negative impact on hotel revenues.

Housekeeping

Making minor repairs in guest rooms is a major responsibility of all maintenance departments. Because the housekeeping department cleans the rooms, its staff members have a critical part in identifying major and minor repair issues and reporting them to maintenance. When these two departments work well together, minor issues such as loose handles on dressers and drawers, torn wall vinyl, and leaky faucets can all be quickly identified and repaired.

Food and Beverage

The food and beverage department of a hotel may be very small, as in many limited-service properties, or extremely large, as in a convention or resort hotel. In both cases, however, the normal repair and maintenance on items such as kitchen cooking equipment, refrigerators and freezers, dishwashing equipment, and ice makers is performed by the maintenance department. Repairs to dining or meeting room tables and chairs may also be done by the maintenance staff.

MANAGING MAINTENANCE

The job of maintaining a building begins immediately after it is designed, engineered, and built. With a properly trained staff, maintenance tasks can be planned and implemented to maximize the life of the property while minimizing the cost of operating the building. Managing maintenance in a hotel is a process that can be examined in a variety of ways. One helpful approach is to consider maintenance as either routine, preventive, or emergency.

Staffing

The talent employed in the maintenance staff crucially affects a hotel's profitable operation. This is true because so much of a guest's impression of the quality of a hotel is dependent on the work of the maintenance department. Thus, the quality of the maintenance staff and the quality of their work will, in the guest's eyes, represent the quality of the entire hotel. When maintenance work is performed poorly or not at all, it shows. The solution to this potential problem lies in the selection of an excellent manager to head the maintenance department. In most hotels, there will also be a need for appropriately trained maintenance assistants.

Chief Engineer

In the hotel industry, the head of maintenance may hold a variety of titles. The most widely used titles are **chief engineer** and **maintenance chief.** Whatever the title, the person who has this role is the head of one of the hotel's most important departments.

LODGING LANGUAGE

Chief Engineer: The employee responsible for the management of a hotel's maintenance department. Sometimes referred to as "maintenance chief."

Maintenance Chief: The employee responsible for the management of a hotel's maintenance department. Sometimes referred to as "chief engineer."

■

In smaller hotels the chief engineer may take a very hands-on role in the maintenance effort. This could involve actually performing maintenance and repair tasks. In larger hotels, with a larger staff, the chief engineer serves in an administrative role that consists of planning work, organizing staff, directing employee efforts, and controlling the POM budget. Regardless of a hotel's size, the chief engineer must be well-organized, attentive to detail, and a cooperative member of the management team.

Maintenance Assistants

In addition to the chief engineer, the maintenance department may employ one or more individuals with varying degrees of skill in the areas of:

- Engineering
- Mechanics
- Plumbing
- Electricity
- Carpentry
- Water treatment (for pools and spas)
- Landscaping
- Grounds maintenance

The needs of each a specific hotel dictate the actual skill, make-up, and number of maintenance staff required. It would be difficult to find one person skilled in all of the technical maintenance areas needed in a hotel. When the necessary skills or manpower needs exceed the capabilities of the in-house staff, the chief engineer (sometimes in consultation with the general manager) must decide to **outsource** work. The ability to effectively determine which tasks are best performed by in-house or outsourced staff is a characteristic of an excellent chief engineer.

LODGING LANGUAGE

Outsource: To obtain labor or parts from an outside provider. Typically done to reduce costs or obtain specialized expertise.

■

Routine Maintenance

When managing a hotel's routine maintenance, the chief engineer is simply directing the customary care of the facility. For example, in hotels with lawns and plant beds around entrances or parking areas, it is customary to periodically cut and edge the grass and to maintain the visual integrity of the plant bed by pulling weeds and replacing foliage as needed. If this work is not done, the curb appeal of the hotel suffers. Cleaning interior windows, picking up trash in the parking lot, and shoveling snow in climates that require it are additional examples of routine maintenance. Often, only limited employee training is required to adequately complete routine maintenance tasks.

The chief engineer generally is the one who decides whether to perform routine maintenance work in-house or to pay an outside vendor to perform it. Regardless of the decision, an effective chief engineer must be concerned with both the exterior and interior of the hotel.

ALL IN A DAY'S WORK

The Situation

"The telephone is ringing off the hook!" Dani Pelley, the front office manager, told Lindsey Noel, the hotel's general manager. "I called maintenance, and they said they were looking into it."

"It" was a complete outage of the satellite system used to deliver television reception to the hotel. The pay-per-view features of the hotel (which were VCR-based) still worked, but the free-to-guests channels were completely down, and guests were calling the front desk to complain or to request a repair on their television sets.

"What do we do now?" asked Dani.

Lindsey picked up the walkie-talkie, radioed the chief engineer, and got the bad news: Satellite reception was indeed down. The hotel's equipment was not at fault, but the satellite service provider was experiencing equipment difficulty. The chief had just gotten off the telephone with them to report the problem, and they estimated a repair time of between two and 24 hours. Until the problem was fixed, there would be no free-to-guests channels reception.

A Response

Sometimes hotels experience maintenance or facility problems that are simply beyond their control. In this situation, the most important thing for management to do is inform guests (and appropriate hotel employees) about the problem, keep them updated as to any changes in the estimated repair time, and be prepared to make room-rate adjustments or provide other compensation as approved by management. In smaller hotels, calling each room may be appropriate. In larger properties that are so equipped, activating the telephone message light in each room and recording a message explaining the problem may be a good solution.

Exterior

On the outside of the hotel, lawn care, landscaping, and leaf and snow removal are important issues. Just as important is attention to the details required for the care of the hotel building. This includes such items as routine roof inspection and repair, window cleaning and window seal inspection, and the care and painting, if required, of the building's exterior finishes. The location of the hotel will dictate, to a large degree, the items that must be considered for routine exterior maintenance. A resort hotel in Florida will have needs different from those of a downtown high-rise hotel in the upper Midwest. Regardless of the setting, however, maintaining the outside of the hotel improves curb appeal, operational costs, and ultimately the building's value. The maintenance department must ensure that routine exterior maintenance is performed well and in a timely manner.

Interior

The chief engineer must also supervise routine maintenance inside the hotel. Some areas include the care of indoor plants, the washing of interior windows (if not assigned to housekeeping), and, in some cases, the care and cleaning of floors and carpets.

One significant task nearly always assigned to the maintenance department is the changing of light bulbs. Regardless of their type, light bulbs will burn out and then must be replaced. In some instances, individual light bulbs are immediately replaced when they burn out. That is, the maintenance department implements a **replace as needed** program for bulbs.

LODGING LANGUAGE

Replace as Needed: A parts or equipment replacement plan that delays installing a new part until the original part fails or is near failure. For example, most chief engineers would use a replace as needed plan in the maintenance of refrigeration compressors or water pumps.

■

The cost to a hotel of replacing a light bulb consists of two components. These are the price of the bulb itself and the labor dollars required to change the bulb. Therefore, in special cases, such as the light bulbs in a hotel with high ceilings that require special lifts or ladders for access, the hotel may implement a **total replacement** program that involves changing all bulbs, including those that have not burned out, on a regularly predetermined schedule.

LODGING LANGUAGE

Total Replacement: A parts or equipment replacement plan that involves installing new or substitute parts based on a predetermined schedule. For example, most chief engineers would use a total replacement approach to the maintenance of light bulbs in high-rise exterior highway signs.

■

This approach, while it involves the discarding of some bulbs or lamps with life remaining, significantly reduces bulb-replacement labor costs and makes the hotel's total bulb-replacement costs lower.

Another form of routine maintenance involves items related to guest rooms and public spaces that must be attended to on a regular basis when they malfunction, wear out, or break and need fixing or replacement. For example, a room attendant in a guest room may notice that a chair leg is broken or that the tub drains slowly. A front desk agent may report that a guest has complained about poor television reception or reported a toilet that does not flush properly. When events such as these occur, the maintenance department is notified via a **work order,** or maintenance request. Figure 11.3 shows a sample work order.

LODGING LANGUAGE

Work Order: A form used to initiate and document a request for maintenance. Sometimes referred to as a "maintenance request."

■

In a well-managed hotel, any staff member who sees an area of concern can initiate a work order. Work orders are prenumbered, multicopy forms that, depending on the number of copies preferred by the general manager, are used to notify maintenance, the front desk, housekeeping, and others who may need to know when a maintenance request is initiated or completed. In some hotels, blank work order forms are placed in the guest room for guests to initiate.

Regardless of their original source, the work orders, once received by the maintenance department, are reviewed and prioritized. For example, a work order indicating an inoperable guest room lock would take priority over one addressing a crooked picture in another guest room. A maintenance employee completes the task(s) called for on the work order and informs the proper departments, and the information related to the work performed is carefully retained. In a well-run department, the chief engineer keeps a room-by-room record of replacements or repairs

---

Best Sleep Hotel Work Order

Work Order Number: _____(Preassigned)_____ Initiated By: _____

Date: _____ Time: _____ Room or Location: _____

Problem Observed: _____

_____

_____

Received On: _____ Assigned To: _____

Date Corrected: _____ Time Spent: _____

M&E Employee Comments: _____

_____

_____

_____

_____

Chief Engineer Comments: _____

_____

_____

_____

_____

FIGURE 11.3   Work Order

made. This is because keeping a history of the room and its contents facilitates making decisions about repairing or replacing in-room items.

Some general managers evaluate the effectiveness of their maintenance department based on the rapidity with which maintenance work orders are completed. While the timely completion of maintenance requests should not be the only criterion for judging a maintenance department, it is an important indicator of effectiveness and efficiency. When work orders are not completed promptly (or at all), the maintenance department loses credibility in the eyes of the hotel's staff and guests. An effective chief engineer monitors the speed at which work orders are prioritized and completed and then, if needed, takes corrective action.

Preventive Maintenance

When not performing routine maintenance or responding to work orders, the maintenance department has a good many other maintenance-related tasks to perform. In fact, many hoteliers believe that the most important maintenance performed in a hotel is its **PM (preventive maintenance) program.**

LODGING LANGUAGE

PM (Preventive Maintenance) Program: A specific inspection and activities schedule designed to minimize maintenance-related costs and to prolong the life of equipment by preventing small problems before they become larger ones.

■

An effective PM program saves a hotel money by reducing:

- Long-term repair costs (because equipment life is prolonged)
- Replacement parts costs (because purchases of parts can be planned)
- Labor costs (because PM can be performed in otherwise slow periods)
- The dollar amount of adjustments and allowances due to guest dissatisfaction
- The costs of emergency repairs (because they will occur less frequently)

In addition to saving money, a good PM program reduces guest complaints, eases the job of the sales staff, improves the eye appeal and functionality of the hotel, and improves employee morale.

Schedules for PM programs can come from a variety of sources. Equipment suppliers often suggest maintenance activities, franchisors may mandate PM schedules, and local ordinances may require specific PM activities (such as boiler equipment or water heater inspection). Most important of all, the chief engineer's skill and experience and knowledge of the hotel's needs will dictate the PM schedules.

Most PM activities involve basic inspection, replacement, cleaning, and lubrication. PM is not generally considered to be a repair program, nor should it be viewed as one. Repairs must be completed when they are needed, whereas PM activities should be performed as scheduled.

Some chief engineers design PM programs that are segmented into activities to be performed daily, weekly, monthly, semi-annually, and annually. Others segment the hotel into major areas (for example food service and laundry) and then develop area-specific PM schedules. In both cases, the PM program should identify what is to be done, when it is to be done, and how it is to be done. It should also provide an easy method to document the completion of the activity.

Figure 11.4 is a sample daily, monthly, and annual PM task list for a dryer in the laundry area.

The chief engineer should have a written and complete PM program in place. All of the hotel's equipment, including furnaces, air-conditioners, water-heating equipment, and elevators, must have individual PM programs. In addition, the maintenance department must create specific PM programs for the following areas:

- Public space
- Guest rooms
- Food service
- Laundry
- Other equipment

Public Space

Public space PM programs are vitally important but relatively simple to develop. In public spaces such as lobbies, corridors, and meeting areas, PM programs should include such items as windows, HVAC units, furniture, lights, elevators, and carpets. In fact, carpet care is one of the most challenging PM activities of all. Carpet care duties are often shared between housekeeping and maintenance, with housekeeping taking responsibility for minor (spot) cleaning issues, and the maintenance department responsible for long-term carpet PM.

LODGING ON-LINE

Carpet and area rug care can be complex, but a variety of resources are available to help determine how to best care for these items. To view one such free resource, go to the Web site of the Carpet and Rug Institute at:

www. carpet-rug.com

PM ACTIVITY: LAUNDRY AREA DRYER

DAILY
- ❑ Clean lint trap
- ❑ Wipe down inside chamber with mild detergent
- ❑ Clean and wipe dry the outside dryer shell

MONTHLY
- ❑ Vacuum the inside of dryer (upper and lower chambers)
- ❑ Check and tighten, if needed, the bolts holding dryer to floor
- ❑ Check all electrical connections
- ❑ Check fan belt for wear; replace if needed
- ❑ Lubricate moving parts

ANNUALLY
- ❑ Check pulley alignment
- ❑ Adjust rotating basket if needed
- ❑ Lubricate motor bearings
- ❑ Lubricate drum bearings if needed

FIGURE 11.4   Sample PM Task List for Laundry Area Dryer

It is important for public space appearances to be well maintained, because they significantly influence guest opinions about the entire hotel. Professional hoteliers know that a good first impression goes a long way toward ensuring a satisfactory guest stay.

Guest Rooms

The hotel's guest rooms are perhaps the most important and certainly the most extensive area for PM. Unfortunately, some chief engineers do not implement aggressive guest room PM programs. The guest room PM program is critical to the hotel's sales effort, to its ability to retain guests, and to the maintenance of the asset's monetary value. In fact, there are few things a chief engineer should pay more attention to than the PM program used for guestrooms.

An effective PM program requires a quarterly, or more frequent, inspection of guest rooms with a careful examination of each item on the guest room **PM Checklist.**

LODGING LANGUAGE

PM Checklist: A tool developed to identify all the critical areas that should be inspected during a PM review of a room, area, or piece of equipment.

■

The checklist for any PM area should be developed to help maintenance staff with their inspections. Figure 11.5 is a sample PM checklist used for guest rooms.

Note that the extensive checklist in Figure 11.5 can be tailored for each individual property. For example, hotels that have in-room microwaves and refrigerators must add these items to the guest room PM checklist. If some guest rooms contain whirlpool-type tubs, these should be included. It is the responsibility of the chief engineer to develop a custom PM checklist and inspection schedule for guest rooms and then to see that the inspections are performed when scheduled. When they are performed, guest room quality complaints will be minimized and long-term repair costs will be reduced because small problems will be uncovered and attended to before they become big ones.

Food Service

There are three major PM concerns in the food service area. The first is back-of-the-house equipment. The ovens, ranges, griddles, fryers, and other production equipment in the kitchen are heavily used and of course, must be properly maintained. Specialty equipment such as dishwashers, fryers, and convection ovens may require the PM expertise of specifically trained technicians. If so, these outsourced vendors should be selected and their work scheduled by the chief engineer or the food and beverage director. In all cases, every piece of kitchen as well as mechanical bar equipment should be included in the PM program.

A second area of PM concern in the food services area is the dining space used by guests. Included in this program are chairs, tabletops, and bases. An especially annoying PM issue for guests involves table leveling; there is simply no excuse for wobbly tables or for foreign objects placed under tables to make them level. In addition, PM must include fixed seating, booths, self-serve salad or buffet areas, lighting fixtures, and guest-check processing equipment.

	The Best Sleep Hotel Guest Room PM Checklist											
	Place an "x" by any item not meeting hotel standards											
Year _____		Room Number _____										
Area Inspected	Item Inspected		Quarter				Area Inspected	Item Inspected		Quarter		
		1	2	3	4				1	2	3	4
Entrance	Number sign						Bathroom	Floor tile/grouting				
Door	Exterior Finish						continued	Telephone				
	Interior Finish							Blow Dryer				
	Peep hole							GFI plug operational				
	Door closer						Drapes	Drape Hooks				
	Deadbolt							Drape wand				
	Lock/lock plate							Valance				
	Evacuation/fire safety plan							Drape rods and brackets				
	Innkeeper's laws frame						Bedroom	Entrance ceiling				
	Hinges							Room ceiling				
Closet	Shelf Stable							Night Stand				
	Clothes Hooks							Night stand drawers				
	Clothes Rod							Dresser				
	Carpet/Covebase							Dresser drawers				
	Luggage Rack							Headboard				
	Vinyl/Walls							Desk				
	Closet door finish							Desk chair				
	Closet door operation							Upholstered chairs				
	Closet door mirror							Bed frames				
Fixtures,	Entry light							Mattress (condition)				
lights and	Closet light							Mattress (turned)				
bulbs	Swing lamps							Mirrors				
	Dresser lamps							Art work				
	Desk lamp							Wall vinyl				
	Pole lamp							Electrical switches				
	Bathroom						HVAC	Filters changed				
	Smoke Detector							Fan				
	Sprinkler head							Motor				
Bathroom	Door Finish							Controls				
	Door lock							Condensate pan				
	Ceiling condition							Wiring				
	Overhead Fan						TV/Radio	Picture quality				
	Toilet operation							Swivel				
	Toilet caulking							Lock down				
	Tub diverter spout							Volume				
	Tub tile/grouting							Remote control				
	Tub stopper							Cabinet condition				
	Shower head							Connections				
	Curtain rod secure							Video game controls				
	Safety bar secure						Telephone	Line 1				
	Non-skid surface							Line 2				
	Sink Faucet							Jacks secure				
	Sink stopper						Connecting	Interior Finish				
	Piping						Door	Exterior Finish				
	Aerator							Frame				
	Toilet Paper holder							Door Stop				
	Towel rack							Lock(s) operation				
	Mirrors							Door knob				
	Vinyl Walls							Hinges				
							Other					
Inspector initials												
The Best Sleep Hotel, 20XX												

FIGURE 11.5 Guest Room PM Checklist

A third area of PM concern in food and beverages (and one that is often overlooked) includes meeting and conference rooms and equipment. Included in this PM program are light fixtures, tables, chairs, and wall coverings within the hotel's meeting rooms and related food service equipment. In addition, the PM program must include transport carts and any audiovisual-related items owned by the hotel. These may include flip chart stands, TVs, overhead projectors, computer projection units, and speaker telephones.

Laundry

In the laundry, the washers, dryers, folding equipment, water supply lines, drains, lighting fixtures, and temperature-control units require PM programs. The clothes dryer is an especially important concern (because of the potential for fire). Dryer drum temperatures can be very high, and the lint build-up during the natural drying process requires vigilance on the part of the maintenance department as well as housekeeping personnel. Lint traps should be cleaned at least once per day (or more often) and should be thoroughly inspected monthly.

In many cases, the company supplying laundry chemicals to the hotel maintains the equipment used to dispense chemicals into the washers. This does not relieve the maintenance department of responsibility. If chemical usage is too high, this may be because the chemical supplier has adjusted equipment to overdispense chemicals in an effort to sell more products. For this reason and because improperly maintained chemical-dispensing units may result in substandard laundry quality and even cause damage to linen and terry, the maintenance department should make chemical dispenser maintenance an important part of the laundry PM program, even if it is performed in conjunction with the dispensing equipment supplier.

LODGING ON-LINE

Johnson Diversey is a company that supplies chemicals to hotel laundries. It does an excellent job of PM on its own dispensing equipment. To view the company's Web site, go to:

www. johnsondiversey.com

When you arrive, click on "Lodging" under the "Industries Served" tab.

Other Areas and Equipment

Additional areas of concern when developing a PM program include pools and spas, front desk equipment, electronic locks (if not included in the guest room maintenance program), exterior door locks, motor vehicles such as courtesy vans, and in-hotel transportation equipment (including housekeeper's carts and luggage carts), to name but a few. As can be seen, a quality PM maintenance program involves a vast number of pieces of equipment and areas of the hotel. An effective chief engineer develops, maintains, and documents an effective and comprehensive PM program that both reduces repair costs and enhances the image of the hotel.

Emergency Maintenance

The strongest rationale for implementing well-designed and aggressive routine and preventive maintenance programs is the ability to manage and minimize repair costs. Despite the very best routine and preventive maintenance efforts of the chief engineer

---

LODGING ON-LINE

A comprehensive PM program for hotels is sometimes easier to maintain than to begin because there are so many pieces of equipment to be included. Today, software exists to help a chief engineer decide what must be maintained and how frequently to schedule PM. To view one software company's hotel-oriented PM program, go to:

www.attr.com

---

and the maintenance staff, however, a hotel sometimes requires emergency maintenance. Emergency maintenance occurrences are generally defined as those that:

- Are unexpected
- Threaten to negatively impact hotel revenue
- Require immediate attention to minimize danger or damage
- Require labor and parts that may need to be purchased at a premium

For example, assume that a water pipe bursts in one of the hotel's unoccupied guest rooms in the middle of the night. A short time later, the guests in the room one floor below the room with the broken pipe call the front desk to complain about water coming into their room from the ceiling. Clearly, this situation requires emergency maintenance. If not attended to immediately, extensive repair work to the pipe as well as the ceilings and walls around the leak may be required.

Hotels managers can encounter a variety of situations that require immediate attention from the maintenance department. Some of these include:

- *No heat (air-conditioning) in room.* This is especially an emergency during extremely cold or hot weather, and when the HVAC unit controlling air temperature is not working due to mechanical malfunction.

- *No electricity in room.* Blown fuses in a hotel are fairly common. Even more common is a blown **GFI outlet.** While these are easy to reset, many guests will not know how to do so. The result can be frequent emergency power outage calls to the front desk, followed by the need for maintenance staff to reset the outlets.

LODGING LANGUAGE

GFI Outlet: Short for "Ground Fault Interrupter." This special electrical outlet is designed to interrupt power ("trip" or "blow") before significant damage can be done to a building's wiring system. These are most commonly installed in the bathroom or vanity areas of a hotel room, where high-voltage usage (hairdryers) or high moisture levels can cause electrical power interruptions.

- *Gas leaks or smell of gas.* This is a very serious situation because sparks from phones (even cell phones) can ignite gas. Immediate shut-off is required in a situation of known gas leakage. If appropriate, the hotel's natural gas provider should also be contacted in such emergencies.

- *Interior flooding.* In most cases, the action required in these emergencies involves shutting off the water at the source of the leak and then making the appropriate plumbing repair. In most cases, repairs of this type must be made quickly to avoid damaging furniture, flooring materials, and other guest rooms or public areas of the hotel.

- *Toilet stoppage.* This extremely common situation always requires prompt maintenance attention. A guest may tolerate a slow drain in a sink or tub, but a toilet stoppage emergency is quite a different matter. To avoid further problems including flooding, these emergencies must be addressed immediately.

While minor emergencies are not typically brought to the attention of the hotel's general manager, the chief engineer should notify the general manager or other appropriate hotel management and/or staff when doing so is necessary to protect the well-being of guests and the hotel.

Emergency repairs are expensive. They sometimes require the authorization of overtime for maintenance staff or outside repair personnel. In addition, needed repair parts that might normally be purchased through customary sources may need to be secured quickly (and at a premium price) from non-customary sources. While it is not possible to avoid all emergency maintenance, effective routine and preventive maintenance programs reduce the number of times emergency maintenance is required and the total cost of property maintenance.

MANAGING UTILITIES

Utility management is an important part of a hotel's overall operation. Utility costs in hotels include expenses for water and sewage, gas, electricity, or other fossil fuel for heating and cooling the building, fuel for heating water, and, in some cases, the purchase of steam or chilled water. Hotels with active programs to conserve energy find that the procedures they use are not only environmentally friendly but save money.

Energy-related expenses, that were once taken for granted by the public and most hoteliers became very important and costly during the energy crisis of 1973. Since then, these costs have moderated somewhat. When the cost of utilities is relatively low, few Americans, including hoteliers, take strong measures to conserve resources and implement **energy management** programs. Alternatively, when energy costs are high, managers have a heightened sense of awareness about these costs. Every hotel manager, and every hotel staff member, should always practice energy-effective management.

LODGING LANGUAGE

Energy Management: Specific policies and engineering, maintenance, and facility-design activities intended to control and reduce energy usage.

■

It is important to remember that, in most cases, the utilities cost for lighting, heating, and operating hotel equipment will be incurred regardless of occupancy levels. While it is true that higher hotel occupancy will result in some incremental increase in utility costs, (for example, more rooms sold will result in increased water consumption for bathing), as much as 80 percent of total utility costs for a hotel are actually fixed. A hotel's original design and construction and the age of its buildings significantly affect its energy usage. Its usage is most affected, however, by the regular maintenance and **calibration** of the equipment consuming energy.

LODGING LANGUAGE

Calibration: The adjustment of equipment to maximize its effectiveness and operational efficiency.

■

Depending on the location of the hotel, energy costs can represent as much as 3–15 percent of total operating costs. In addition, energy is a valuable resource, and as responsible members of the hotel industry, we should all try to conserve it. It is easy to see why an effective maintenance department should be very concerned with conserving energy and controlling utility costs.

Electricity

Electricity is the most common and usually the most expensive form of energy used in hotels. To be effective, the hotel's electrical source must be dependable, and it will be if the maintenance department maintains the hotel's electrical systems in a safe manner. While some hotels have a **back-up generator** for use in an emergency outage situation, most will rely on one or more local power providers to deliver electricity.

LODGING LANGUAGE

Back-up Generator: Equipment used to make limited amounts of electricity on-site. Utilized in times of power failure or when the hotel experiences low supply from the usual provider of electricity.

■

In some locations, electric bills account for more than 50 percent (and sometimes as much as 80 percent) of a hotel's total utility costs. Controlling electrical consumption can really pay off for a hoteliers interested in lowering utility bills.

Electricity is used everywhere in a hotel. It powers the administrative computers, operates fire safety systems, keeps food cold in freezers and refrigerators, and provides power for security systems, to name but a few uses. When considering the total electrical consumption of hotels, however, the two most important uses of electricity, and therefore those the chief engineer must manage most carefully, are related to lighting and HVAC systems.

Lighting

The lighting in a hotel is tremendously important for curb appeal, guest comfort, worker efficiency, and property security. Lighting is sometimes referred to as illumination, and light levels are measured in **foot-candles.** Generally, the greater the number of foot-candles, the greater the illumination. Hotels require varying degrees of illumination in different locations, and the types of light fixtures and bulbs used play a large role in producing the most appropriate light for each hotel setting.

LODGING LANGUAGE

Foot-Candle: A measure of illumination. One foot-candle equals one lumen per square foot.

■

Artificial light is produced to supplement natural (sun) light. Natural light is cost-effective and, when used properly, can reduce utility costs by limiting the amount of artificial light that is needed. When lighting must be supplemented, the hotel can choose from two basic lighting options. The first of these is **incandescent lamps.**

LODGING LANGUAGE

Incandescent Lamp: A lamp in which a filament inside the lamp's bulb is heated by electrical current to produce light.

■

Incandescent lamps are what most people think of when they think of the light bulbs used in their homes. Incandescent bulbs have relatively short life spans (2,000 hours or less) and thus must be frequently changed. They are fairly inefficient, since they produce only 15–20 lumens per watt. For example, a 100-watt bulb produces 1,500–2,000 lumens. Incandescent lights are popular, however, because they are easy to install, easy to move, inexpensive to purchase, and have the characteristic of starting and restarting instantly. Incandescent lamp bulbs can be made in such a way as to concentrate light in one area (these are known as spotlights or floodlights).

In cases where a conventional incandescent light is not best suited for a specific lighting need, hotels can select an **electric discharge lamp** as a second lighting option.

LODGING LANGUAGE

Electric Discharge Lamp: A lamp in which light is generated by passing electrical current through a space filled with a special combination of gases. Examples include fluorescent, mercury vapor, metal halide, and sodium.

■

Electric discharge lamps do not operate directly from electricity. They must use a **ballast.**

LODGING LANGUAGE

Ballast: The device in an electric discharge lamp that starts, stops, and controls the current to the light.

■

Electric discharge lamps have longer lives (5,000–25,000 hours), and higher efficiency (40–80 lumens per watt) than incandescent lamps. The most common lamp of this type is the fluorescent, and it is frequently used where high light levels and low operating costs are important. If an electric discharge lamp stops working, either the bulb or the ballast may need replacing.

Other types of electric discharge lamps include those for parking areas or security lighting. In cases such as these, sodium lamps are a good choice because they can generate 200 lumens per watt used and have extremely long lives, but the cost of purchasing and installing these lights is also greater than for fluorescent lamps.

In the late 1980s, the compact version of the fluorescent light known as the **CFL** became popular in many hotels. These lights were designed to combine the energy efficiency and long life of a traditional fluorescent light with the convenience and ballast-free operation of an incandescent light. For many applications, they provide an excellent blend of operational savings and convenience.

LODGING LANGUAGE

CFL: Short for "Compact Fluorescent Light."

■

LODGING ON-LINE

The proper use of indoor and outdoor lighting in a hotel is important in many ways. To obtain a better understanding of how lighting works, visit the General Electric Company's lighting Web site. Go to:

www.gelighting.com

When you arrive, select "Lighting Institute," then select "Understanding Light," then select "Introduction to Lighting."

CFLs are increasing in popularity because they are:

- *Energy-efficient.* CFLs use about one-fourth the energy of traditional incandescent light bulbs. For example, a 26-watt CFL produces the same amount of light as a typical 100-watt incandescent bulb.
- *Cost-effective.* Because CFLs use about one-fourth the energy of incandescent bulbs, hotels using them save money on their electric bills. While the initial purchase price of a CFL is higher than an incandescent, it lasts about 10 times longer.
- *Environmentally friendly.* Power plants that generate electricity also produce pollution. Since CFLs use less electricity to produce the same amount of light as incandescent light bulbs, reducing the amount of electricity used also reduces the amount of pollution produced.

When selecting lighting, hotels can choose from a wide choice of lamps, bulbs, and light fixtures. The proper type, the color of the light, and the operational costs must all be taken into consideration when selecting lighting fixtures and lamps. In all cases, however, lighting maintenance, including lamp repair, bulb changing, and fixture cleaning, must be an integral part of the hotel's PM program.

HVAC

Another significant consumer of electrical power is the hotel's HVAC system. Heating, ventilation, and air-conditioning are considered together in the hotel's maintenance program because they all utilize the hotel's air-treatment, thermostats, and **duct** and **air handler** systems.

LODGING LANGUAGE

Duct: A passageway, usually built of sheet metal, that allows fresh, cold, or warm air to be directed to various parts of a building.

Air Handler: The fans and mechanical systems required to move air through ducts and to vents.

■

A properly operating HVAC system delivers air at a desired temperature to rooms in the hotel. The efficiency with which a hotel's HVAC system operates, and thus the comfort of the building, is affected by a variety of factors, including:

• The original temperature of the room
• The temperature of the air delivered
• The relative humidity of the air delivered
• The air movement in the room
• The temperature-absorbing surfaces in the room

HVAC systems can be fairly straightforward or very complex, but all consist of components responsible for heating and cooling the hotel.

Heating Components   While it is possible for all of a hotel's heating components to be run by electricity, this is not normally the case. Heating by electricity, especially in cold climates, is generally not cost-effective. Because of this, hotels heat at least some parts of their buildings using natural gas, liquefied petroleum gas (LPG), steam, or fuel oil, although electricity can be used to heat small areas.

In most hotels, the heating of hot water is second in cost only to the heating of air. A hotel requires an effective furnace (or heat pump system) for heating air, and a boiler of the right size for heating water. Regardless of the heat source, fans powered by electricity move warm air produced by the furnace to the appropriate parts of the building. Similarly, electricity powers pumps to move hot water produced by the hot water heater. The maintenance of these two heating components can be complex, but an effective chief engineer maintains them in a manner that is safe and cost-effective, performing calibration and maintenance tasks in accordance with manufacturer's recommendations and local building code requirements.

Cooling Components   Just as a hotel must heat air and water, so too it must frequently cool them. The major cost of operating air-cooling or air-conditioning systems is related to electricity usage. Essentially, in an air-conditioning system, electrically operated equipment extracts heat from either air or water and then utilizes the remaining cooled air or water to absorb and remove more heat from the building. The effectiveness of a cooling system is dependent on several factors, including:

• The original air temperature and humidity of the space to be cooled
• The temperature and humidity of the chilled air entering the room from the HVAC system
• The quantity of chilled air entering the room
• The operational efficiency of the air-conditioning equipment

Some cooling systems are designed to produce small quantities of very cold air that is then pumped or blown into a room to reduce its temperature, while other systems supply larger quantities of air that is not as cold but has the same room-cooling affect because the quantity of air supplied is greater.

The ability of a cooling system to deliver cold air or water of a specified temperature and in the quantity required determines the overall effectiveness of a cooling system. Very often, especially in hot humid weather, the demands placed upon a hotel's cooling system are intense. The ability of the maintenance department to maintain cooling equipment in a manner that minimizes guest discomfort (and the resulting complaints) is critical to the success of the hotel. Effective routine and PM maintenance on cooling equipment is a crucial part of the chief engineer's job in climates where air-conditioning is a frequent need.

Natural Gas

In some geographic areas where natural gas is plentiful and cost-effective, hotels use it to heat water for guest rooms and to power laundry area clothes dryers. Natural gas is also used in many hotel HVAC systems to directly or indirectly provide heat to guest rooms and public spaces.

Interestingly, the overwhelming majority of chefs and cooks prefer natural gas when cooking because of its rapid heat production and the amount of immediate temperature control it allows. Cooking with natural gas is also economical. It costs about half as much to cook with a natural gas range as with a similar electric range. Although a natural gas range may cost somewhat more than an electric model, these durable pieces of cooking equipment will pay the hotel back with energy savings and years of reliable service. Many of the new models of natural gas cooking equipment use an electronic spark ignition rather than a continuously burning **pilot light,** thereby saving as much as 30 percent on energy costs when compared to a unit using a pilot light.

LODGING LANGUAGE

Pilot Light: A small permanent flame used to ignite gas at a burner.

■

Managed properly, natural gas is an extremely safe source of energy. If a hotel is using natural gas equipment of any type, each gas hot water heater, furnace, or other piece of equipment should have a PM program designed specifically to minimize operating costs, ensure safety, and maximize the efficiency of the unit. This is especially important because the combustible nature of natural gas requires that gas leaks be avoided at all times. In addition, the calibration of the oxygen and fuel mixture required to maximize the efficiency of the combustion process must be continually and carefully monitored.

LODGING ON-LINE

Gas equipment manufacturers are understandably proud of their products. For more information on gas-operated food service equipment as well as managerial tips and restaurant operations information, go to:

www.cookingforprofit.com

Water

Aggressively managing a hotel's water consumption is very cost-effective because it pays three ways. Conserving water:

1. Reduces the number of gallons of water purchased
2. Reduces the amount the hotel will pay in sewage (water removal) costs
3. Reduces water-heating costs because less hot water must be produced

Water costs can be dramatically reduced if the maintenance department carefully monitors water usage in all areas of the hotel. Figure 11.6 lists just a few of the activities a hotel can undertake to help reduce water-related costs. Working together, the hotel staff led by the chief engineer, should implement every water-saving activity that improves the hotel's bottom line and does not negatively affect guest satisfaction.

MANAGING WASTE

Hotels generate a tremendous amount of solid waste (trash). Sources of waste include packaging materials, such as cardboard boxes, crates, and bags used in shipping hotel supplies, kitchen garbage, guest room trash, and even yard waste generated from the hotel's landscaping efforts. Increasingly, the hotel industry has come to realize that excessive waste and poorly conceived waste-disposal methods are detrimental to the environment and represent a poor use of natural resources. In addition, as landfills become scarce, the cost of solid waste disposal has risen. Because of this, hotels have encouraged manufacturers that ship products to them to practice **source reduction** and have aggressively implemented creative programs to reduce the generation of their own solid waste.

Guest Rooms
- Include inspection of all guest room faucets on the PM checklist
- Inspect toilet flush valves monthly; replace as needed
- Consider installing water-saver showerheads
- Investigate earth–friendly procedures designed to enlist the aid of guests in the water conservation process

Public Space
- Include inspection of all public restroom faucets on the PM checklist
- Install automatic flush valves in men's room urinals
- Where practical, reduce hot water temperatures in public restrooms
- Check pool and spa fill levels and water pump operation daily

Laundry
- Include, as part of the PM program, the monthly inspection of water fittings on all washers
- Pre-soak stained terry and linen rather than double washing
- Use the lowest hot water wash setting possible while still ensuring clean terry and linen

Food Service
- Serve water to diners only on request
- Operate dishwashers only as needed
- Use sprayers, not faucets, to prerinse dishes and flatware intended to be machine-washed
- Use chemical sanitizers rather than excessively hot water to sanitize pots and pans
- Use sprayers (not faucets) to rinse/wash produce prior to cooking or storage

Outdoors
- Inspect sprinkler systems for leaking and misdirected spraying daily
- Utilize the sprinkler system only when critically needed. Do not overwater
- Minimize the use of sprayed water for cleaning (driveway and parking areas, for example); sweep and spot clean these areas as needed

---

FIGURE 11.6   Sample Water Conservation Techniques

ALL IN A DAY'S WORK

The Situation

"This doesn't make any sense," said Tamara, the hotel's controller. "Occupancy was about the same this month as it was for the same month last year. But our water bill is 40 percent higher than the same time last year!"

Terrell, the maintenance chief, looked at the bill from the hotel's local water company. "I don't know what's happening either," he said. "For the bill to go up that much, something must really be wrong!

"I'll say it's wrong," said Jack, the general manager of the hotel. "Terrell," continued Jack, "you've got to find out what's going on here. This leak is really affecting our profits!"

A Response

Unexpected increases in utility costs are always unwelcome. In this situation, a large increase in water costs indicates either a broken water line on the property, defective equipment that can result in excessive water usage (for

example, malfunctioning ice machines or equipment with water-cooled motors), or a large number of small waste areas (such as multiple toilets that are leaking water into their overflow valves).

Of course, it is also possible that the meter measuring the amount of water used by the hotel is defective. In all cases, however, it is the responsibility of the maintenance chief to systematically identify and eliminate these potential sources of wasted water and their effect of "draining" the hotel's profits!

LODGING LANGUAGE

Source Reduction: Effort by product manufacturers to design and ship products in a way that minimizes packaging waste resulting from the product's shipment to a hotel.

■

Source reduction involves decreasing the amount of materials and/or energy used during the manufacture or distribution of products and packages. Since it stops waste before it starts, source reduction is the top solid waste priority of the U.S. Environmental Protection Agency.

Source reduction is not the same as recycling. Recycling is collecting already used materials and making them into another product. Recycling begins at the end of a product's life, while source reduction takes place when the product and its packaging are being designed.

One way to think about source reduction and recycling is that they are complementary activities: combined, source reduction and recycling have a significant impact on preventing solid waste and saving resources. Source reduction conserves raw material and energy resources. Smaller packages and concentrated products, such as detergents and other cleaners, typically use fewer materials and require less energy to transport. In addition, source-reduced cleaning products take up less storage space and are easier to use. Recycling, minimizing waste generation, and wise purchasing can all help reduce waste disposal costs and should be implemented wherever possible.

LODGING ON-LINE

A growing proportion of the population, including many hoteliers, aggressively embraces earth-friendly hotel operating procedures. The Green Hotels Association is one such group. For an overview of the group's philosophy, go to:

http://www.greenhotels.com

Once there, review the "Meeting Planner's Questionnaire" found at the site to see the types of activities this group encourages hotels to undertake.

In addition to improving conservation efforts and controlling costs, effective waste management means keeping inside and outside trash-removal areas clean and, to the greatest degree possible, attractive. This can be achieved by proper sanitation procedures and by enclosing the trash-removal areas with fencing or other eye-appealing materials.

Poorly maintained trash-removal areas are unsightly and can attract insects, rodents, and other scavenging animals. The chief engineer should regularly inspect these areas for preventive maintenance of fencing or other surrounds and for the quality of sanitation in the trash-removal areas.

CHAPTER OBJECTIVES REVIEW

If you have successfully studied the material in this chapter, you should be prepared to:

1. Identify the areas of responsibility assigned to the maintenance department of a lodging facility. (Objective 1)
2. Explain the importance of routine maintenance in a professionally managed hotel. (Objective 2)
3. Explain the importance of preventive maintenance in a professionally managed hotel. (Objective 3)
4. Explain the importance of emergency maintenance in a professionally managed hotel. (Objective 4)
5. Explain the processes required to properly manage and control utility consumption in a lodging facility. (Objective 5)

LODGING LANGUAGE

Preventive Maintenance	Outsource	Foot-candle
Routine Maintenance	Replace as Needed	Incandescent Lamp
Emergency Maintenance	Total Replacement	Electric Discharge Lamp
Engineering	Work Order	Ballast
HVAC	PM (Preventive Maintenance)	CFL
POM	Program	Duct
FF&E Reserve	PM Checklist	Air Handler
Restoration	GFI Outlet	Pilot Light
Case Goods	Energy Management	Source Reduction
Chief Engineer	Calibration	
Maintenance Chief	Back-up Generator	

FOR DISCUSSION

1. Many chief engineers find that maintaining an older hotel is more challenging than maintaining a newer property. Name five areas in a hotel you believe would become more difficult to manage as the hotel ages.
2. Many hotel general managers require the entire maintenance staff to go through extensive guest-service training programs. Why do you think they feel this training is important?
3. For many routine maintenance replacement items, a hotel manager has a choice between doing all of the maintenance at once (such as changing air filters in all guest rooms quarterly) and doing it as needed (such as replacing hot water heater

pumps when they stop working). In other cases, such as replacing parking lot light bulbs or fan belts on motors, the manager has a choice between systematic total replacement and a "replace as needed" approach. Assume you were required to decide on a replacement program for exterior parking lot lights in a hotel with parking for 150 cars. What factors would influence your decision?

4. In some hotels the cleaning of exterior sidewalks and parking areas is the responsibility of housekeeping. In others it is the responsibility of maintenance. Name three factors that would likely influence which department would be assigned this important cleaning task.

5. In most hotels, a representative from the maintenance department must be available 24/7 in case of a hotel emergency. How do you think such employees could be fairly compensated for this responsibility?

6. Lawn care is an example of a maintenance task that can be done in-house or outsourced. Assume you operate a 135-room hotel with three acres of total lawn and landscape area. Identify three factors that might influence your decision to select an outside lawn care service for your hotel's lawn and landscape work.

7. Maintaining food service equipment often requires specialized skill and replacement parts. Name three factors that you would consider before deciding to outsource the preventive maintenance of such equipment.

8. Water conservation is important in a hotel. List four things you could do as a hotel guest to help conserve water. Do you think hoteliers should inform guests about activities like the ones you listed? If so, how?

9. Maintenance staff are often highly skilled at specific building-related trades (for example plumbing, electricity, carpentry, and HVAC repair). What are some steps a maintenance chief could undertake to ensure that the skills of the maintenance staff were kept up-to-date?

10. Many hotels have implemented aggressive recycling programs. What factors would be likely to influence a hotel manager's decision to begin such a program?

TEAM ACTIVITIES

Team Activity 1

For major hotel repairs that cannot be done in-house, some hoteliers prefer to establish a relationship with one prime contractor in each field or trade (for example, plumbing, heating, and electrical) and then employ that contractor as needed. Other managers prefer to solicit competitive bids for each major project and then select the best bidder. Identify three advantages and three disadvantages to each approach. Which approach would you suggest at a hotel managed by your team?

Team Activity 2

Maintenance staff members must often enter occupied guest rooms to address rooms-related emergency repairs. The result is often interaction with unhappy guests. Write a script two team members can present in a role-play format. In the role-play, assume it is a hot summer day, and a maintenance staff member is explaining to an unhappy guest that the air-conditioning unit in the room is actually working properly. However, the guest continues to complain that the room is too hot and implores the staff member to fix it.

Food Service and Meeting Management in Limited-Service Hotels

Chapter Objectives

1. To explore the range of food services offered by limited-service hotels.
2. To discuss management concerns important when implementing a high-quality and cost-effective lobby food service, including pre-service activities of menu planning, purchasing, receiving, storing, and setting-up, during service maintenance activities and after service clean-up duties.
3. To explain the importance of informing guests about the availability of lobby food services, assisting them with food services, and providing attractive serving and dining areas for their enjoyment.
4. To review alternatives to manage small group meetings, including the provision of food services for session attendees.

Chapter Outline

RANGE OF FOOD SERVICES
  Breakfast Alternatives
  Other Food Services
MANAGEMENT OF LOBBY
FOOD SERVICES
  Menu Planning
  Purchasing
  Receiving and Storing

Setting Up Breakfast Service
Maintaining Breakfast Service
Cleaning Up
GUESTS AND LOBBY FOOD SERVICES
MANAGING MEETINGS
  Small Meetings Business
  Meeting Procedures
  Meeting Food Services

Overview: Food Service and Meeting Management in Limited-Service Hotels

This chapter addresses the food services and meeting space alternatives offered by limited-service hotels. The subject is important because it represents a significant difference between limited-service properties and their full-service counterparts. As you have learned, the term "limited service" indicates minimal, if any, availability of food services and meeting spaces. By contrast, the term "full-service" refers to the availability of more extensive food services and, often, a much greater square footage of meeting space.

The range of food services available in this segment varies from properties offering deluxe hot breakfast buffets made to order for guests and with the ability to prepare a wide range of menus for those attending meetings to hotels that offer the most simple continental breakfast: coffee, juice and bread, a muffin or bagel. The space allocated for food services likewise varies from hundreds of square feet (or more) to just several square feet. Some, but relatively few, limited-service properties market their public spaces and food services for holiday parties, family occasions, and other events in direct competition with full-service hotels in the area.

Managers of limited-service hotels utilize the same basic principles to manage their food service operations as do managers in full-service hotels or any other quantity food-production operation. They must begin by planning the menu, and this, in turn, indicates what menu items will be needed. These products must be purchased, received, and stored. Serving areas must be set up and maintained during times of guest service, and they must be cleaned at the end of the meal period.

Many guests make their hotel selection decision based upon the availability, variety, and quality of the lobby food services that are available. Marketing concerns that focus on the wants and needs of present and potential guests are very im-

portant factors to be considered in the planning and delivery of food services. Hopefully, many guests will be repeat visitors and will know about the food services that are offered. Others may have visited properties of the same brand and will know something about how food service works at the hotel. Others, however, will have no experience with the brand, and it is important to inform them properly about details of the lobby food services, including hours of operation and the types of products available. This can be done when they check in and by means of information provided in guest rooms and in public areas.

Limited-service hotels are often excellent choices for small group meetings. Some properties are planned with this market in mind; the general managers of others must be creative in finding ways to make the limited available space useful for accommodating the needs of small groups. Some properties actively seek out small meetings; others have an ongoing meetings business without the need to do so, and still others are less proactive and just accept the business if it comes to them. Likewise, some properties provide no food services for groups, others help meeting planners to obtain food services from outside sources, and still others offer menus with prepared/purchased items to accommodate the group's needs.

Food services and meetings business are relatively new features of the limited-service segment, and the best managerial efforts to market and operate these programs are still evolving. One thing appears certain: many members of the traveling public enjoy the food services and meeting alternatives offered by limited-service properties. Independent owners and operators and their multi-organization counterparts will continue to plan and implement ways to stay competitive by offering consistently high-quality food services and meeting alternatives.

RANGE OF FOOD SERVICES

Throughout this book we have referred to limited-service hotels as being lodging properties that do not provide extensive food service options for guests. For example, unlike their full-service hotel counterparts, hotel guests in limited-service properties do not have access to à la carte dining or room service delivered by property employees. As will be seen later in this chapter, the banquet and meeting facilities, if any, offered in limited-service hotels are typically modest in terms of the number of guests that can be accommodated and in the type of food services available to meeting attendees. Another difference is that limited-service managers do not market food services to the general public, whereas managers in full-service properties frequently rely on local residents to visit their dining rooms. Some full-service properties also offer off-site food services (limited-service properties do not), and full-service managers aggressively sell meetings with or without assorted food services and banquets. By contrast, limited-service properties with meeting space may market meetings-only business to small groups and typically offer only minimal, if any, food services as part of the hotel meetings package that is sold.

Historically, full-service hotels have offered food services in dining rooms (areas) adjacent to or near their lobby areas. Some, especially very large hotels with **atriums** or other large, open lobby areas, may offer à la carte dining in public spaces that are not in separate rooms. Large full-service hotels may also have small retail areas selling coffee, pastries, and sandwiches and even bars dispensing alcoholic beverages in lobby areas.

LODGING LANGUAGE

Atrium: A large, open central space used by some hotels for registration, lobby, retail sales, and food services, among other purposes.

■

Limited-service hotels typically offer breakfast and do so in their relatively small lobby areas. Ironically, then, they became similar to large, atrium-type hotels in the multi-purpose use of lobby areas. Many limited-service properties offer creatively designed multi-purpose spaces with attractive tables and chairs that can be used for food consumption during the designated breakfast hours and for guest waiting and other purposes during the rest of the day. A very small service kitchen may be located adjacent to the public area, and service counters, storage cabinets, and other space and equipment used for food services are attractively designed into the lobby environment.

Since food services in these properties are most typically offered in the lobby, a new term, **lobby food services,** has come into use.

LODGING LANGUAGE

Lobby Food Services: Food services offered by limited-service hotels.

■

Figure 12.1 reviews the types of food services offered by limited- and full-services hotels. Over time, and with the evolution of lobby food services, the distinc-

Factor	Type of Hotel	
	Limited-Service	Full-Service
À la carte dining available	No	Yes
Room service available	No	Sometimes
Banquet capabilities	Modest, if any	Yes
Alcoholic beverages available	Sometimes	Usually
Off-site food services available	No	Sometimes
Offer meetings with limited food services	Sometimes	Yes
Offer meetings with extensive food services	No	Yes
Markets food services to general public	No	Yes
Locations of food services (Dining)	Usually in lobby	Dedicated area(s) in property
Food preparation/storage areas	Minimal	Extensive
Payment for consumed food	Included in room rate	Charges in addition to room rate

FIGURE 12.1   Food Services in Limited- and Full-Service Hotels

tion between very minimal food service (in limited-service properties) and very extensive food services (in full-service hotels) is becoming blurred. The reason for this is that both types of hotels are attempting to determine exactly what their guests want and to find ways to cost-effectively meet their guests' expectations.

Breakfast Alternatives

When most people think about food services in limited-service hotels, they think about breakfast, because food and beverages items available during the early morning (breakfast) hours are most commonly offered by these properties. Actually, some limited-service hotels offer other types of food and beverage services, and these will be examined in the next section of the chapter.

What types of breakfasts are offered by limited-service hotels? Figure 12.2 answers this question.

Figure 12.2, reviews a range of breakfast food services from modest to extensive. Some properties offer a limited **continental breakfast.** The simplest continental breakfast requires no cooking equipment and very little preparation or service space. A simple coffee maker and supplies (disposable cups, napkins, stir sticks, sugar/cream), a pitcher (or individual portions) of juice, a simple bread item with butter and, perhaps, jelly or a pastry (doughnut or sweet roll) illustrate the requirements for a limited continental breakfast with few guest choices.

WHAT'S IN A NAME?

While the term "limited-service" is widely used to represent the segment of the lodging industry without extensive food service capabilities, many owners and managers of properties in this segment do not like the name. They point out that their service to guests is not limited in regard to guest registration, room accommodations, cleanliness, safety, or other non-food-service amenities and is, in reality, equal to that of their full-service peers. The need for hotels of any size or category to consistently deliver service meeting the expectations of their guests is standard throughout the industry. In this context, then, limited-service properties actually provide selected "full-service" service to guests who do not require or desire extensive on-site food service or meeting alternatives.

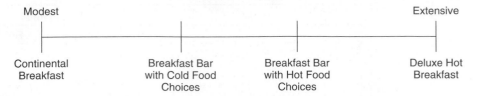

FIGURE 12.2   Range of Breakfast Food Services in Limited-Service Hotels

---

LODGING LANGUAGE

Continental Breakfast: A simple breakfast consisting of fruit juice or fruit, coffee, and toast or a pastry.
■

A breakfast bar with cold food choices offers guests additional variety. This might, for example, include a selection of juices and several types of breads, rolls, and pastries along with coffee and milk. Other items (yogurts, fresh fruits, and assorted breakfast cereals) may also be available.

A breakfast bar with hot food choices expands the variety of menu items available to guests even further. Perhaps, for example, a toaster is available for bread, bagels, and prepared waffles and/or a waffle maker with pre-portioned batter available in individual portion cups.

At the extreme range of Figure 12.2, some limited-service properties offer a **deluxe hot breakfast** with numerous food offerings. For example, there may be a buffet to allow guests to self-serve eggs (perhaps several styles), bacon, sausage,

The availability of complimentary food services may increase the market share of a hotel in competition with others.

ham, potatoes, and other items that are prepared on-site in a small kitchen. In other properties, guests order desired items that have been prepared in advance or, alternatively, are prepared to order. In relatively few properties, a limited table service breakfast is available.

LODGING LANGUAGE

Deluxe Hot Breakfast: A breakfast with hot food choices offered by a limited-service hotel.

■

As the complexity of the breakfast food services increases, so does the amount of storage, equipment, preparation and service space, number of labor hours required, and skill levels of food service employees. In addition, associated operating expenses can rise dramatically. The decision about the type of food services to offer is critical and is an important part of the package marketed to prospective guests. Consider, for example, a new property being built or an existing facility being renovated. The space and equipment needs to offer a modest continental or a deluxe hot breakfast are vastly different. Including this space if it will not be used or excluding space that will later be required has significant financial consequences. As well, guests looking for value in their room rate will make personal decisions about the worth of the breakfast option they are paying for. It is important to design food service needs into the property at the time it is constructed or when major renovation is done.

Other Food Services

In addition to the breakfast offered by many limited-service hotels, some properties in this segment also offer their guests other food services alternatives. These include:

- *All-day hot beverage service.* Brewed coffee and hot water for tea along with required supplies may be available at a "help-yourself" beverage station in the lobby 24 hours per day.
- *Food and beverage items for a* **manager's reception.** Some limited-service hotels offer complimentary foods, including appetizers, snacks, **finger foods,** and even alcoholic beverages, during a specified time period (for example, from 5:00 p.m. to 6:30 p.m.). This practice originated to provide opportunities for management staff to greet guests, but in many properties there are no management staff available, and instead it has evolved into a "manager-hosted" event.

LODGING LANGUAGE

Manager's Reception: A time, usually during the late afternoon/early evening, when complimentary foods and beverages are offered to guests of limited-service properties.

■

LODGING LANGUAGE

Finger Foods: Small sandwiches, salty snacks, sliced vegetables, and other foods that do not require flatware or other service items for guest consumption.

■

- *Meetings-related food services.* As you will learn later in this chapter, some limited-service properties have meeting spaces available for small groups. These properties may offer food and beverage services ranging from simple coffee breaks to relatively simple buffets for entire meals.
- *Special-event food services.* A few limited-service properties with food preparation space and equipment that enables them to offer deluxe hot breakfasts may market their facilities for small private parties, such as wedding receptions and anniversaries, and for public events, such as New Year's Eve or Mardis Gras parties. Just as at their full-service hotel counterparts, these public events are often packaged with a guest room rental.

MANAGEMENT OF LOBBY FOOD SERVICES

Let's go behind the scenes to learn more about how breakfast food service is planned and operated in a limited-service hotel. Figure 12.3 outlines the process.

Let's review Figure 12.3, beginning with Step 1 (Menu Planning).

Menu Planning

What items should be offered on the breakfast menu? Many factors must be addressed, and Figure 12.4 reviews some of them.

Owners and managers of independent hotels can make their own decisions about what to offer guests. Corporate hotels (those owned by a multi-unit hotel organization) and franchised properties typically impose limitations on planners. Menus are planned or, at least, breakfast components are specified to standardize the breakfast within the brand so as to meet the expectations of guests who visit different properties. Standards may also be established to specify items (hot coffee, orange

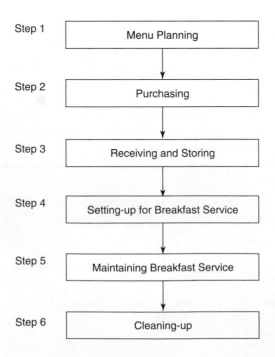

FIGURE 12.3 Managing Breakfast Operations in a Limited-Service Hotel

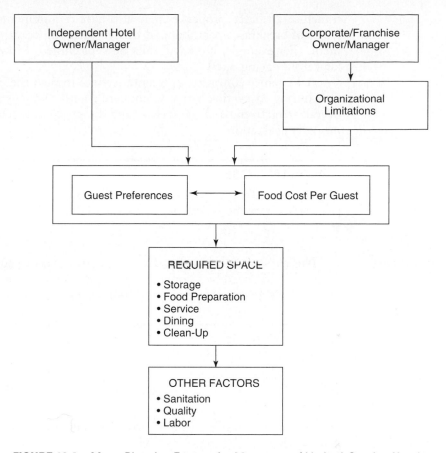

FIGURE 12.4   Menu Planning Factors for Managers of Limited-Service Hotels

juice, and sweetened and unsweetened cereal). As well, properties may be required to offer specific brands of items (for example, Kellogg breakfast cereals and Smuckers assorted jellies). The reason: many consumers, including hotel guests, recognize popular brands and equate them with high quality and good value. Corporate- and

---

BREAKFAST ITEMS ARE REQUIRED

Many lodging brands now require their hotels to offer breakfast items. Coffee, tea, milk, fruit juices, dry cereals, fresh fruits, and sweet and non-sweet breads are all common breakfast items that may be required. Properties can offer additional and/or upgraded items if their owners and managers believe they will be beneficial in a specific market.

Holiday Inn Express introduced its Express Start Breakfast Bar with two signature items. All Holiday Inn Express hotels were required to have breakfast bar areas designed to provide the atmosphere of a small café. Guests enjoy two **signature items**: a cinnamon roll made from an exclusive recipe and a special gourmet coffee with four different blends.

Many hotels that do not offer signature items do offer brand-name products. For example, Starbucks coffee is provided in many properties (with signage to announce its availability), and branded products of many types allow guests to identify the hotel's food services with the quality represented by the brands that are served.

---

franchise-affiliated properties may also have requirements regarding the number of hours of breakfast operation, and this, in turn, impacts the necessary serving equipment. (For example: How will milk be kept chilled? How can bread and pastries be kept from drying out?)

A franchise company representative will inspect the hotel's food services operation during inspection visits. Compliance with required standards, cleanliness, and overall attractiveness of the serving and dining areas will be important aspects of the property evaluation.

LODGING LANGUAGE

Signature Items: Food or beverage products produced by a hospitality operation that are unique to the property and/or that the general public associates with it.

■

Numerous menu planning factors are important to any planner regardless of the limitations imposed by a company or brand. These too are suggested in Figure 12.4. For example, guest preferences and **food cost per guest** served are important.

LODGING LANGUAGE

Food Cost Per Guest: The amount expended for breakfast for each guest. Calculated as: Total Breakfast Food Cost ÷ Number of Guests Served.

■

Guest preferences and food cost per guest must be discussed at the same time because they are so interrelated. Menu planners often use an elimination process that involves a consideration of items guests prefer and the property's ability to provide them within financial limitations.

Assume, for example, that a limited-service manager has a budgeted food cost per guest of $1.75 (in other words, it is estimated that the average guest will consume breakfast items costing approximately $1.75). At this cost, it may be possible to offer something in addition to a modest continental breakfast, but it is not possible to offer a wide variety of breakfast items. By contrast, a property with a budget of $3.50 per guest is able to offer additional (more expensive) items without exceeding the food cost per guest goal. In both cases, the food cost per guest must be factored into the room rate. While breakfast may be free to guests, it is not free to the hotel.

BREAKFAST COST PER WHAT?

Food cost per guest is one popular way to compute the cost of providing a complimentary breakfast, but there are other ways. Some hoteliers prefer to compute their food cost per occupied room. The formula for food cost per occupied room is similar to the one for food cost per guest. It is calculated as:

Total Breakfast Food Cost ÷ Number of Occupied Rooms

The advantage of this method is that keeping count of the number of guests actually using the breakfast area is not required because it is the number of rooms occupied, not guests served, that is critical to the computation.

Limited-service properties utilizing an **accrual accounting system** calculate breakfast food costs for a fiscal period (typically one month) as follows:

Beginning Inventory of food items
+ Purchases of food items
− Ending Inventory of food items
Food Cost

LODGING LANGUAGE

Accrual Accounting System: An accounting system that matches expenses incurred with revenues generated. Revenue is considered to be earned when products/services are provided (not when money is received); expenses are incurred when products, labor, and other costs are expended to generate revenue (not when the expenses are paid for).

■

Properties using a **cash accounting system** to determine the cost of food consider the amount of money paid during the fiscal period (month) for food, supplies, and related breakfast items.

LODGING LANGUAGE

Cash Accounting System: An accounting system that considers revenue to be earned when it is received and expenses to be incurred when they are paid for.

■

Figure 12.4 indicates that the space needed for storage, food preparation if applicable, service, and dining is another important consideration when menus are planned. New construction that incorporates the space needed for a limited food service operation allows for an ideal design in terms of location within the hotel and the required square footage. By contrast, existing properties that were not designed for breakfast service can face significant challenges. Depending upon the type of breakfast offered (and this will likely evolve over the life of a property and the competitive challenges it faces), the amount of space required for food storage, preparation, and clean-up can be equal to, if not greater than, the amount of space required for the guest serving area. Additional space is also needed for guest seating and can range from "anywhere there is room for a table and chairs" to well-thought-out, functional, and attractive lobby spaces.

Limited-service properties designed for small business meetings may have a separate room that is used for breakfast service and that then becomes available for meeting space after breakfast clean-up is completed. Still other properties use lobby space for service and dining, with an adjacent room that can be used for overflow breakfast service (if the space is not reserved for an all-day meeting) and for meetings after breakfast service has ended.

Figure 12.4 indicates that still other factors must be considered in planning menus for limited-service hotel breakfasts. Sanitation concerns are critical. Equipment is required to keep perishable items such as dairy products at the proper temperature before use and during service. Reusable pitchers, trays, tongs, and other items must be properly washed, rinsed, and sanitized between uses, and, as noted

---

WHY SO MUCH STORAGE SPACE?

Much less storage space is required for limited-service hotel breakfast operations than for three-meal-a-day à la carte food preparation in a full-service restaurant. Nonetheless, there must be space for refrigerated storage (of milk, butter, and other dairy products), for frozen storage (if frozen juices, waffles, and/or other bread/pastry products are used), and dry storage. Cases of disposable plates, flatware, cups and glasses, napkins, and related items are very bulky. Space may be needed for a coffee maker, small ice bin, sink (many local health departments require a water source in any food preparation area, and this is a good idea even if it is not required!), and for storage of all items (such as pitchers, toasters, and serving trays) that cannot remain in the lobby. *Note:* properties designed to offer breakfast service frequently utilize very attractive serving counters with attractive built-in lockable storage for many items under the serving counters and elsewhere in the serving area.

---

earlier, a sink meeting local sanitation ordinances is often required. Refuse from food preparation and after guest use must be quickly removed from the lobby area and properly maintained until it can be disposed of.

Product quality is another important factor to consider when menus are planned. Earlier in the chapter we noted that many products are purchased on a brand-name basis to help ensure quality. Items such as fresh fruits, baked goods, and other non-branded items must be purchased from reputable suppliers. Hoteliers buying these products should be just as concerned about value (price relative to quality) as their guests, who are looking for value in the lodging dollars they spend.

Labor is another factor that cannot be forgotten even when little or no food preparation is required. It is typically easy to recruit and select applicants because no experience and/or culinary skills are required. Some applicants may desire a part-time job during the early morning hours so that the rest of their day is free for personal use. Many properties utilize a part-timer specifically for breakfast service duties. Others combine tasks so that a staff member can be used for food service and then complete a shift in housekeeping or some other department. In very small properties, the night auditor or front desk clerk may set up the food service. A food service attendant may then arrive to maintain the serving area and to clean up after service concludes. Regardless of the staffing plan, however, the food service attendant must be responsible, have a positive guest focus, be able to work quickly, and be able to perform many tasks at the same time.

Who plans the menu? In a limited-service property, this responsibility typically rests with the general manager, who must attempt to meet franchisor standards, please the guests, and stay within the budget. Remember that the availability of the complimentary breakfast is a significant factor in the decisions of many of the guests who select limited-service hotels. The menu planner must earnestly attempt to determine what the guests prefer (and do not prefer!) as part of the ongoing process of menu evaluation and improvement that helps to keep the property competitive. Despite the fact that franchise brands (and their breakfast requirements) are national (and international), the food preferences of many guests are regional, and these guest preferences must be addressed when deciding what to put on the breakfast menu.

Purchasing

After the menu is planned, the items required will be known and can be purchased. Limited-service properties that are part of a multi-unit organization may pool their purchase needs by using a **centralized purchasing** system. For example, assume that independent hotel owners or franchisees with several properties in the same area offer the same (or, at least, many of the same) menu items on their breakfast menus. These owners can combine the purchase needs for all the properties and than select a supplier to provide all the participating hotels with dairy or food products or disposable supplies for a specified time period, such as six months. Suppliers frequently quote a lower price per unit (for example, a case of napkins) as the number of cases ordered increases.

LODGING LANGUAGE

Centralized Purchasing: A purchasing system in which participating properties develop common purchase requirements and combine purchase quantities. Suppliers frequently lower the price per purchase unit (per pound or per gallon, for example) as the quantities of items to be purchased increases.

Other hotel managers do not purchase from wholesale suppliers. Instead, they purchase from large retail stores that sell products in large "commercial" sizes and/or from food wholesalers with retail outlets. For example, Gordon's Food Service (GFS) is a very large supplier of food and other products to hotels, restaurants, and institutional purchasers in several midwestern states. It also has retail outlets offering products sold in bulk to customers coming into the stores.

LODGING ON-LINE

Food, beverage, and supply products needed for food services in limited-service hotels can be purchased from large commercial warehouses. To learn how one food service distributor can help with the purchasing task, go to:

www.gfs.com

When you arrive at this site, click on "market place stores." Then click on "product categories" to see the types of products that are available. Also, click on "commercial savings program" to learn about the benefits to businesses such as limited-service hotels. If a property is planning a special event, check out "event planning" and preview a sample menu created on the company's "menu wizard."

What quantity of food and supplies should be purchased? Many limited-service properties utilize a **par inventory system** to help manage the purchase of many required items.

LODGING LANGUAGE

Par Inventory System: A system of managing purchasing and inventory levels based upon the requirement that a specified quantity of product be available in inventory. For example, if a par of five cases of disposable coffee cups is established, the quantity necessary to bring the inventory level back to five cases is ordered when coffee cups are purchased.

Extremely perishable products, such as fresh breads and pastries must typically be ordered daily. Other items (for example, dairy items and fresh fruits) may be ordered several times weekly. Still other items (for example, dry cereal and frozen products) can be ordered several times (or fewer) monthly depending upon the amount of available inventory space and the amount of money the manager is willing to tie up in inventory. This, in turn, relates to the per purchase unit savings to be realized from purchasing in a larger quantity than needed for immediate use.

Par inventory systems do not work well for perishable foods. Items such as fresh pastries and dairy products are typically purchased in quantities that relate more to forecasted occupancy levels than to par levels. This is so because more of these products are purchased as more rooms are sold, and fewer are purchased when occupancy levels are lower.

Managers are often confronted with two purchasing challenges regarding the correct amount of food to order. First, low sales forecasts may turn into a busy breakfast if many reservations with short booking times and/or walk-in guests arrive. At times like these, it may be necessary for hotel staff to purchase products from a local retail or wholesale outlet at a higher-than-planned price. Second, it can be difficult to know the guests' selection preferences, and these can change on an almost daily basis. For example, if numerous guest rooms have been reserved for the use of junior sports teams during a specific weekend, more sweet cereals and pastries will be consumed and must be available.

As food usage rates relative to occupancy levels are analyzed, managers can begin to accurately determine the quantities of items to be in par and to be purchased on a daily (or other) basis. Doing so is necessary to control food costs. Money that is wasted when products must be discarded does not benefit the guests or the property. By contrast, money saved through effective purchasing and food handling is available to purchase more products and/or better-quality products and, at the same time, provide guests a better breakfast value. This, in turn, yields a competitive marketing edge for the property.

Receiving and Storing

After products are purchased, the **receiving** and storing processes become important. If a manager purchases products at a retail or wholesale outlet, there are few, if any, concerns about receiving. What has been purchased can be transported to the hotel and put in storage. However, if suppliers deliver products to the hotel, special procedures are in order.

LODGING LANGUAGE

Receiving: The point at which ownership of products being purchased transfers from the seller (supplier) to the hospitality operation.

■

Often there will not be a food services employee available when orders are delivered. In such cases other arrangements for receiving must be made. Should receiving be done by the front desk clerk (who may be busy) or the general manager (who may be unavailable)? Each property must address this question with the approach that is best for it. In all instances, however, the employee who does the receiving should be properly trained to do at least four things:

- Confirm (typically by counting and reading labels) that the correct items and quantity of each item noted on the **delivery invoice** were ordered and have been delivered to the hotel.

- Sign the delivery invoice.
- Move products that have been received into the appropriate storage area.
- Retain the signed delivery invoice and route it to the individual with accounting/bookkeeping responsibilities.

LODGING LANGUAGE

Delivery Invoice: A statement from the supplier that accompanies product delivery and provides information to establish the amount of money due to the supplier. This information includes name of product, quantity, and price, and must be signed by a hotel representative to confirm that the products were delivered.

■

Many of the products that are received will be expensive and/or prone to theft. Many will also be susceptible to quality deterioration. Therefore, it is important that they be quickly moved to their proper locked storage areas. If an inventory par level is being maintained, it will be necessary for someone to update inventory records with the quantities of incoming products.

Setting Up Breakfast Service

A significant amount of effort is required to prepare for even a relatively simple breakfast for hotel guests. It is very unlikely that all (or even most) of the hotel's guests will want to have breakfast at the moment service begins. In fact, there may be only a very few or even no guests present at the beginning of service. (If this is consistently the case, the general manager may wish to reevaluate the breakfast's start time.) However, the first guest should be able to select from the full variety of

---

WHO ATE THE DOUGHNUTS?

Doughnuts and other fresh pastries are delivered daily to many limited-service hotel properties for breakfast use. They may arrive before the food service attendant begins the work shift. Hopefully, these items will be properly received by the front desk clerk, night auditor, or other responsible employee and will then be quickly moved into a secure storage area. If this does not happen, the opportunity for employees and other non-guests to consume a free breakfast is obvious.

Less-than-careful managers may have the philosophy that "Who cares about a few doughnuts?" In fact, the manager should care a great deal! Why? If each doughnut costs 25 cents and 10 doughnuts are consumed inappropriately each day, a property with a 10 percent bottom line (net income before taxes) must generate $25 each day to yield the $2.50 profit required to purchase the doughnuts.

(10 doughnuts @ $0.25 = $2.50 ÷ .10 profit = $25.00 ÷ in revenues)

If this consumption continued each day, the hotel would require revenues of $9,125 each year ($25/day × 365 days/year) just to pay for these unaccounted-for doughnuts. To continue with our example, if the property's ADR was $65, it would need to rent 140 rooms ($9,125 ÷ $65.00) just to compensate for the doughnut costs that would otherwise not need to be purchased.

No hotel (or any other business!) can afford to throw away more than $9,000 revenue annually on wasted expenses. In fact, doughnuts (and every other expense) add up quickly in the hotel business, where the details are very important.

foods that will be available to those having breakfast later in the morning. In other words, all the food items to be offered should be available when the service begins. It is not appropriate to get the coffee ready and then begin preparing breakfast service for later-arriving guests. Hotel managers must carefully work out how long it takes to prepare for breakfast service, determine the most reasonable start and end times for service based upon guest desires, and then schedule labor accordingly.

Hotels offering breakfast will require one or more attendants. The performance of a food service attendant is affected by at least three factors under the hotel manager's control:

- *Proper Training.* Training is just as important for a food service attendant as for any other hotel employee. Training should include such matters as where food and supply items are located, how to operate coffee machines and other equipment, and where refuse should be placed as waste receptacles become filled.

- *Development of a Work Task Checklist.* Just as cooks need recipes, food service attendants can use a "recipe" that indicates the tasks to be done as breakfast is readied for service, as guests are served, and as clean-up activities are undertaken. The sequence in which tasks are to be done should be specified.

- *Serving Diagram.* A graphic illustrating "what goes where" can be very helpful in the efficient set-up of a serving area. Figure 12.5 illustrates a sample lobby food services set-up that can be used to train new food service attendants and remind experienced ones about the location of menu items on serving lines.

Maintaining Breakfast Service

Ongoing work will be necessary to replenish the food services area and keep it clean and sanitary during service. An efficiently designed storage area and serving kitchen are an important first step in the process of speeding the flow of work in the area and reducing the attendant's travel time between the area and the serving line. The attendant must be able to anticipate when items must be replenished. (Is there time to wipe several tables before I refill the decaf coffee? Do I need to make more coffee since breakfast service ends in 10 minutes?) Some limited-service hotels offer hot

---

WHAT ABOUT FOOD SERVICE TRAYS?

Some guests prefer to pick up breakfast items from the food service area and take them to their rooms. The number of such guests may increase when there is no available dining space. It seems logical, therefore, for hotel managers to anticipate a need for food service trays to accommodate these guests.

On the other hand, some managers believe that the availability of trays encourages excess food consumption, waste, and removal from the property for later consumption. These properties may not make food service trays available.

A third group of hotel managers recognize the need to please the guests and also the problems just noted. Their solution: Have trays available out of sight in case a guest requests one during a slow time and make them readily available during busy serving periods.

There is no easy way to decide on tactics that will please the guests and at the same time be cost-effective. While it is likely that some guests will take advantage of the property, the vast majority of them will not. Unfortunately, excessive costs must be spread among all guests, and the manager has the responsibility to minimize these costs.

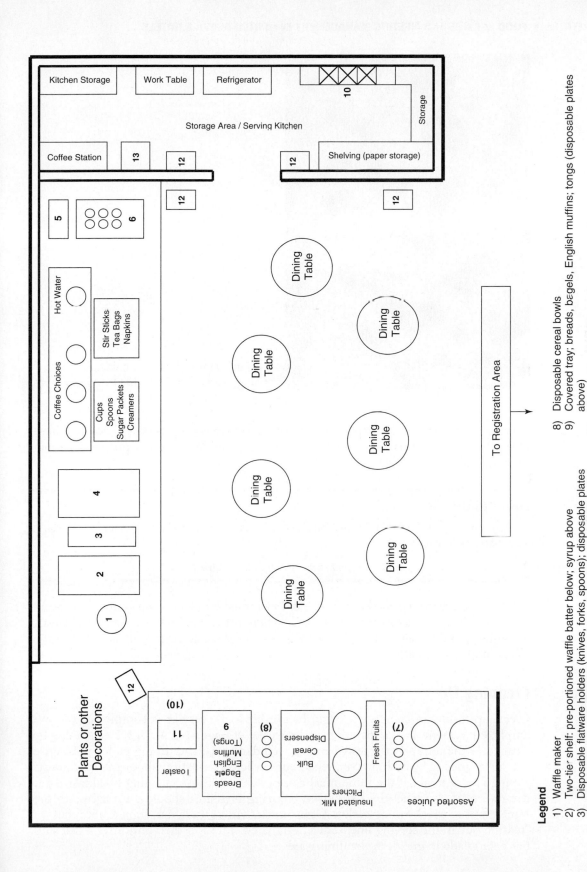

Legend

1) Waffle maker
2) Two-tier shelf: pre-portioned waffle batter below; syrup above
3) Disposable flatware holders (knives, forks, spoons); disposable plates
4) Covered tray: muffins and pastries; tongs; disposable plates above
5) Guest trays
6) Disposable cups/lids
7) Disposable juice cups

8) Disposable cereal bowls
9) Covered tray: breads, bagels, English muffins; tongs (disposable plates above)
10) Disposable plates
11) Pre-portioned butter, jelly, cream cheese
12) Waste basket
13) Ice machine

FIGURE 12.5   Sample Layout of Lobby Food Services Showing Placement of Menu Items

One good thing about a breakfast bar is that guests can select what they prefer.

beverages 24 hours daily; hopefully, the coffee service station is in a location convenient for breakfast service and for those using the lobby for other purposes during the remainder of the day.

LODGING ON-LINE

To learn about coffee-brewing, food-serving, and other equipment useful in serving breakfasts in limited-service hotels, go to:

www.aacommercialproducts.com

Serving areas must be kept tidy, and spills must be cleaned up immediately and correctly. These tasks can be very difficult when, for example, there are many guests, including families with young children (who are prone to have spills), enjoying the lobby food services at the same time.

Cleaning Up

Clean-up tasks can sometimes begin before breakfast service is completed. For example, equipment and preparation tables in the storage area/serving kitchen can be cleaned as the number of guests being served decreases, and dining tables not in use can be cleaned as well. However, recall our earlier observation about the first guests having access to all of the same meal components as those enjoying breakfast later; the reverse is also true: the last person enjoying breakfast should have access to the same items as those dining earlier. Clean-up activities, therefore, should not focus on "tearing down" the serving line until a designated time and then only after a **last-call** has been made to guests in the dining area.

This limited-service hotel offers a "signature" coffee bar and cinnamon roll.

LODGING LANGUAGE

Last Call: Notice given to guests that service will end at a specified time. For example, guests in a hotel bar may be notified 20 minutes before closing time that last drink orders must be placed, and guests in a lobby breakfast service may be informed that service will end in 10 minutes.

NEVER FORGET ABOUT SANITATION!

It is easy to think about the need to consistently use food-handling practices that incorporate sanitation concerns when one works with potentially hazardous foods, such as meats, seafood, and other items that we associate with food-borne illness. However, sanitation is just as important when handling any food products, including those typically available in a limited-service hotel's breakfast offering. It should be obvious that food service attendants should not cough or sneeze around food, handle food products with their bare hands, and touch any food (including foods in individual containers) after handling garbage.

Should the hotel manager assume that staff members employed for these positions know and consistently practice effective food-handling procedures? (No!) Does the manager have the responsibility to incorporate sanitation information into the training that is provided? (Yes!) Fortunately, there is excellent information on sanitation training available from the National Restaurant Association and the Educational Institute of the American Hotel & Motel Association. Local health departments may also have information if not training programs available. Sanitation training should be incorporated into activities designed to prepare food service attendants for their work. As well, hotel managers should observe the work of food service attendants to make sure that these important procedures are consistently incorporated into their work habits.

Removing all food items to their proper storage areas and disposing of items that cannot be reused, such as fresh pastries, frozen waffles (which will have thawed), and coffee cream in serving pitchers, if used, are important tasks. Serving equipment and food/beverage items and supplies should be placed under lock as part of clean-up and closing duties. Clean-up of the equipment, preparation and storage areas, food serving counters, and lobby tables/chairs are among the tasks that are the responsibility of food service attendants in many limited-service properties. Hopefully, the job descriptions for these employees will specify whatever other duties, if any, are among their responsibilities, such as cleaning floors and removing food service trash.

LODGING ON-LINE

Most limited-service hotels use disposable serviceware because they find this more cost-effective than utilizing reusable items. To learn about environmental issues relative to the use of disposable products, go to:

www.p2pays.org/ref/13/12198.pdf

What, if any, concerns should managers of limited-service hotel properties have about the environment as disposable serviceware is selected and used?

ALL IN A DAY'S WORK

The Situation

"I wish our manager was here every time guests complain about our complimentary breakfast," said Caesar, a front desk clerk at the Seaside Inn Lodge. He was talking to his friend, Romaro, a housekeeper at the 65-room limited-service hotel. "Lots of guests complain to me," he continued, "and I've seen guest comment cards with the same complaints. I know our manager is aware of the problems because I talked to him several times. I guess he is concerned about it, but all he talks about is cost, cost, cost. His idea is to provide large quantities of cheap food."

"Yes, I guess there is a problem," said Romaro, "But, after all, the food is free, and there is plenty of it. I think our prices are lower than some of the other hotels in the area, and if I were the boss, I would do the same thing: try to offer plenty of food as the way to keep guests coming back."

"I don't know," said Caesar, "If I were the boss, I think I would raise the room rate by one or two dollars and put all of that extra money into buying better-quality food."

A Response

Many guests select a limited-service property, in part, because of the complimentary food services it offers. Guests want to enjoy this amenity, and it is an essential factor in their assessment of value ("what they pay for what they get"). Serving lots of food that guests do not enjoy (the manager's tactic) and charging guests more as the first step in improving food services (Caesar's suggestion) are both likely to be ineffective tactics. The manager and his staff can determine what guests like and do not like about the food services program. They can do so by being there during the serving period and by talking with guests. They can carefully analyze guest comment cards (and perhaps develop one specifically applicable to food services). They can also look in the garbage cans and ask housekeepers about the amount of food products left in rooms. If they spend less to purchase what guests don't want and spend more to purchase what guests do desire, it may be possible to please their guests without the need to raise prices.

The general manager should also try to come up with ways to reduce costs that do not compromise quality. How much do other properties spend per guest? (This question can be asked and answered at local association meetings and by reviewing trade publications.) What suggestions do suppliers have based upon their experience with other limited-service properties? What about the hotel's employees? (You have learned about empowerment and employee input to decision-making and the benefits that a diverse range of staff members can bring to the problem-resolution process.) The general manager should give a high priority to improving the food services operation because it is a concern to guests, and guests who are not satisfied may make other lodging choices.

GUESTS AND LOBBY FOOD SERVICES

We have focused attention on the guests in our discussion of the importance of food services in their hotel selection decisions and of menu-planning activities that address guest preferences. Guest concerns were also noted when we discussed the schedule for breakfast service, and when we stated the importance of keeping the serving line replenished and clean during the hours of service. In this section, we will explore additional guest-related concerns applicable to food services.

Increasingly, guests make hotel selection decisions after studying the alternatives on the Internet. Food service amenities should be emphasized on the property's home page and in its other sales and marketing activities.

Front desk clerks should be trained to provide information about food services, including hours of operation, when guests check in. Since this can be time-consuming, some properties provide written information to guests as part of the registration process. Supplemental information can also be provided in a hotel directory packet in the guest rooms.

The number of guests to be served relates to the hotel's occupancy rate. As the number of guests increases, there is a greater likelihood that guest service will suffer unless specific management actions are taken. For example, on especially busy shifts, is there a need for another food service attendant or for an employee to begin work earlier and/or to stay later? Should space-consuming sofas be removed to accommodate additional dining-area tables and chairs? Must additional quantities of food, disposable supplies, and/or other items be purchased?

Independent hotels may offer complimentary food services to compete with multi-unit hotel chains.

LODGING ON-LINE

To what extent do limited-service hotel organizations advertise their available food services on-line? To find out, check out the following Web sites:

Fairfield Inns	www.marriott.com/fairfieldinn
Comfort Inns	www.comfortinns.com
Wingate Inns	www.wingateinns.com
Holiday Inn Express	www.ichotelsgroup.com

Which, if any, of these sites provide the information you would like to know about their food services before selecting them as a limited-service hotel franchisor? What, if any, additional information would you as a prospective guest like to know?

MANAGING MEETINGS

The opportunities and alternatives for limited-service hotels to offer meetings are about as broad as the options for them properties to offer food services. For example, some new properties are designed with a lobby or off-lobby dining area and a second area that can be used for meetings. Other limited-service properties are designed with a multi-purpose area that can be used for both of these functions (sometimes with a moveable wall to separate areas, if necessary). Owners of existing properties often find creative ways to utilize space already available for meeting and/or food services purposes.

Small Meetings Business

Some limited-service hotels actively solicit small meetings business from out-of-town groups that will involve the need for some or all of the attendees to rent sleeping rooms and, as well, from local groups that will require few, if any, guest room rentals. By contrast, other properties are less aggressive in marketing meeting spaces but typically provide them when available for guests and others who request space.

It seems strange, in these times of great competitive pressure in the hospitality industry, that hotels of all sizes do not aggressively and creatively seek small meetings business. Very often the idea of marketing to groups calls to mind conventions and conferences attracting hundreds or even thousands of attendees. In fact, how-

ATTRACTIVE DINING AREAS

The lobby areas in many limited-service hotels are multi-purpose. They are used for guest registration, guest waiting and pick-up areas, and frequently for food service. Many properties make their lobby areas attractive and inviting for guests using the space for these and/or other reasons. Attractive tables and chairs, inexpensive flowers or other decorations, waste cans of the appropriate size and placed out of the way with an adequate supply of liners nearby are among the features that guests expect. Cleanliness of the serving line and dining and lobby areas is an absolute must.

Location-specific decorations can provide a unifying theme. For example, a property near an airport and another near a beach have natural opportunities to create and follow-through on a theme that can be pleasant for the guests.

ever, the average business meeting involves fewer than 25 people.[1] Meetings of this size can be accommodated by many limited-service properties.

The small meetings market is vast. In addition to business groups, it includes numerous other community-based organizations that are looking for a place to meet for just a few hours, a day, or even longer. Families that reserve a large block of rooms sometimes use the meeting room as a during-the-day gathering place. The availability of this space may serve as an incentive for families to use the property. Limited-service hotels and other properties that reach out to these groups and do an excellent job of accommodating their meetings can build a repeat business that may eventually grow to a significant percentage of the hotel's revenue base.

The hotel's marketing team can identify potential meetings clients through the local chamber of commerce and other community groups and/or contacts. Within-hotel advertising messages can reach existing guests, and advertisements can be placed in community publications. Front desk clerks can be trained to route incoming calls requesting information about the hotel as a meeting site to the appropriate person(s) and should get a call-back telephone number from the caller if this person is not available.

Meeting Procedures

In some hotels, meeting space is reserved by contacting the front desk. The front desk agents at these properties must be trained in the procedures for selling and reserving meeting space or, at least, must know about the importance of group meeting business and follow through by contacting the person with group sales responsibilities. By contrast, in other hotels a sales office is available, and personnel with this function sell and reserve meeting space. In still other hotels, the general manage negotiates with meeting planners.

Hotels with separate meeting rooms can typically accommodate up to 50 (or more) people depending upon whether chairs or tables and chairs will be needed.

WHY NOT MARKET THE MEETING ROOM?

Why would some limited-service properties have a meeting room available and not aggressively market it to prospective groups needing space? For some properties, this is not necessary because their meeting space is regularly booked and a concerted selling effort is not required. Other properties regularly receive referrals from the local convention and visitors bureau, chamber of commerce, or other organizations. If a property does not have a full-time sales staff, its managers typically set their priorities on generating revenues in the area that is most profitable: rental of guest rooms.

Hotels actively seeking the small meetings business may have a great competitive edge over other properties for several reasons. First, planners of small meetings may be looking for space and may be more likely to think about small rather than large hotels. Second, many large hotels actively pursue the business of larger groups and do not market as aggressively to small groups. Third, limited-service properties can offer the promise of fewer logistical problems. Parking, an easy-to-find meeting room within the property, and the availability of hotel personnel (the front desk clerk) immediately outside the meeting room door (in many properties) are examples of amenities that could be attractive to the planners of small group meeting.

---

[1]John Hogan, "Hotel Common Sense: Recognizing the Value of the 'Small Meetings' Markets," Hotel On-line Special Report, April 2, 2004.

LODGING ON-LINE

To see how one limited-service hotel chain can help meeting planners, go to:

www.ichotelsgroup.com

When you reach the site, click on "meetings and events." You will find help for professional planners (how to find a facility) and for the occasional planner. For example, after the type of event (meeting, sleeping rooms only, weddings/special events, tour/travel groups and sports groups) is selected, the site allows planners to find and select a facility and to request a price proposal.

(Local fire codes will mandate maximum occupancy levels.) An adjacent storage space may also be needed to store tables, chairs, audiovisual equipment (if available), a podium, and food service-related equipment offered for meetings when these items are not in use.

Many limited-service hotels develop a meeting room charge policy that relates to the revenues being generated. If, for example, a specified number of guest rooms are rented, the meeting room fee may be reduced or eliminated. A second example: some hotels charge a specified amount for each attendee that includes the meeting room, audiovisual equipment rental, and refreshment break(s) and/or a light meal. Other properties charge a flat rate for the meeting space. As with guest room rental charges, rates are often negotiable based in large measure upon the demand for the meeting room at the time for which it is requested.

What about audiovisual (AV) equipment? Some properties provide a speaker's podium, a dry erase board, and, perhaps, an overhead projector at little or no cost. The meeting sponsors bring in or rent whatever additional equipment is needed. Sometimes this equipment is rented by the hotel with charges passed on at cost or

The meeting room in a limited-service hotel can be perfect for a small group-training session.

with a **mark-up.** In other properties, meeting planners are given a list of companies in the area that they can contact about the rental of AV equipment.

LODGING LANGUAGE

Mark-up: A fee added to a supplier's charges that the hotel bills a guest or group to compensate for value added by the hotel.

■

Meeting Food Services

The relatively few limited-service properties that offer hot deluxe breakfasts have the capacity to prepare the elaborate refreshment breaks and meals desired by meeting attendees, but most of their counterparts cannot offer these options. Figure 12.6 illustrates the role of limited-service hotels in providing food services for on property meetings.

As you review Figure 12.6, note that some limited-service hotels have no role in the provision of food services but permit groups to bring in and provide their own refreshment breaks and/or meals. The meeting planners may make their own contacts with potential caterers, or alternatively the hotel may provide the group with a list of caterers in the area: Sometimes three types of caterers are suggested for the meeting planners' consideration: economy, mid-scale, and up-scale.

It is important for hotel managers to contact their local health department to make sure that they meet all the equipment and facility requirements for the service of food to the public. As well, the property's attorney should be contacted to determine the extent, if any, of the property's liability if food-borne illness problems arise from foods brought in by meeting attendees and/or an outside caterer.

As Figure 12.6 shows, some hotels contact caterers to make food service arrangements for groups. Sometimes this service is provided as part of a package of meeting amenities. The hotel may pay the caterer for the food services and then bill the group for the food service charges, sometimes including a mark-up. Alternatively, the group may be direct-billed by the caterer.

Figure 12.6 also indicates that limited-service properties may provide food services for group meetings. Some property managers prepare menus to illustrate the range of food and beverage items that can be offered and present these to the meeting planners. The hotel's representatives can also assess whether other menu items are possible given the property's limited facilities. Some of the items on the property's breakfast menu (pastries, bagels, juice, and coffee, for example) may be acceptable for a mid-morning refreshment break. Other items that do not need on-site

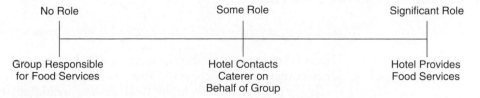

A hotel's role may vary on a by-group basis with some hotels offering all these options to meeting planners.

FIGURE 12.6   Role of Limited-Service Hotels in Meetings Food Services

—————————————————— ALL IN A DAY'S WORK ——————————————————

The Situation

The week of the Fourth of July is always slow in Carsonville, a small town known for its liberal arts college. This year, the Fourth of July is on a Tuesday, and Leilani, the general manager of a 65-room, franchised, limited-service hotel in the town, had resigned herself to almost no business for the entire week. She couldn't believe the phone call from a meeting planner who wanted to book about 75 percent of her rooms for Wednesday through Saturday of that week. The only problem: a large number of meeting attendees will be driving in, and the hotel's meeting room will not accommodate the group. There is one

option: use the larger room where the hotel's complimentary breakfast bar is available.

"It's amazing," thought Leilani, "We can book three-quarters of our rooms and, with our normal business, basically have a full house for most of what would normally be one of the slowest weeks in the year. However, what do I do about the guests who will be staying here in the 10 or 15 rooms that are not part of the meeting? Should I tell them we are full when they call for a reservation or stop by to ask about rates? Do I sell them rooms at a reduced price and indicate that there is no breakfast available that week? Is there something else I could do?

A Response

Leilani's franchisor will certainly require that she offer breakfast to all of her guests. Hoteliers, however, are noted for their creativity. In this case, the ability to provide a breakfast alternative for a few rooms (the non-meeting attendees) will allow Leilani to transform the week from unprofitable to profitable. In addition to her current ideas, converting a vacant guest room into a "private" breakfast area may be an option, and so is offering room-service trays to those guests not attending the meeting. As a last alternative, she may find that contacting a local restaurant and buying breakfast for her non-meeting guests is be the best solution of all!

preparation (for example, snacks, cookies, and fresh fruit) can be purchased and made available by the hotel.

Creative menu planners may be able to offer a lunch of tossed salad, a sandwich deli tray (sliced ham, turkey, roast beef, and cheeses with assorted breads and buns), and a baked dessert along with an assortment of hot and cold beverages. These and/or related items can be purchased locally and provided to meeting attendees (typically with a mark-up) without on-site preparation.

When a limited-service property is located adjacent to or very near a restaurant, the hotelier may make arrangements with the restaurant manager that enable meeting attendees to reserve tables at the restaurant for meals. Some restaurants have small private rooms where attendees can sit, eat, and continue their discussions. In some cases, the hotel receives a business referral fee for this added business.

In summary, managers must know their property's limitations. As seen above, almost any hotel could offer a continental breakfast to meeting attendees. Many could, as well, offer sandwich-type items. All properties could work with groups and local catering organizations to help meet the needs of (and to encourage) group meeting planners.

CHAPTER OBJECTIVES REVIEW

If you have successfully studied the material in this chapter, you should be prepared to:

1. Discuss the range of food services offered by limited-service hotels. (Objective 1)
2. Discuss management concerns that are important when implementing a high-quality and cost-effective lobby food service, including the pre-service activities of menu planning, purchasing, receiving, storing, and setting up, during-service maintenance activities, and after service clean-up duties. (Objective 2)

3. Explain the importance of informing guests about the availability of lobby food services, assisting them with the use of the food services, and providing attractive serving and dining areas for their enjoyment. (Objective 3)
4. Identify approaches to managing small group meetings, including the provision of food services for session attendees. (Objective 4)

LODGING LANGUAGE

Atrium	Signature Items	Par Inventory System
Lobby Food Services	Food Cost per Guest (Limited-	Receiving (Food Service)
Continental Breakfast	Service Hotels)	Delivery Invoice
Deluxe Hot Breakfast	Accrual Accounting System	Last Call
Manager's Reception	Cash Accounting System	Mark-up
Finger Foods	Centralized Purchasing	

FOR DISCUSSION

1. Name at least three daily sanitation-related concerns that you would have if you were the general manager of a limited-service hotel offering a complimentary breakfast bar.
2. How would you determine the food cost per guest to budget for the operation of your limited-service hotel's breakfast? What indirect costs, if any, such as for lobby cleaning, administrative expenses, and related costs other than food and direct serving labor, would you allocate to the food services operation? Why?
3. What, if any, kind of menu planning assistance for your limited-service hotel's breakfast program might you receive from food suppliers?
4. What types of control do you think could be useful to ensure that only hotel guests utilize the food services that are available at a limited-service hotel?
5. What are the advantages of providing within-guestroom information about the complimentary breakfast service in your limited-service hotel? Disadvantages?
6. Assume that you observe two children repeatedly coming down to the lobby area during the time that the breakfast bar is in operation, and that each time these two children take large amounts of food back to their room. Assume also that you know they are guests with their family at the property. What, if anything, would you say to the children and/or to the parents when they check out?
7. What are three alternatives you could give to a meeting planner hoping to provide lunch to meeting attendees in your limited-service hotel's small meeting room?
8. What factors would you consider in deciding whether your hotel should purchase and then rent audio visual equipment (for example, a digital projector and screen) to groups conducting business meetings at your property?
9. Assume that your property offers a fairly comprehensive complimentary breakfast program but does not feature hot foods. What are some kinds of menu items you could offer to meeting planners for their morning and afternoon refreshment breaks?
10. Identify at least three specific groups that all general managers of limited-service hotels could target for small group meetings sales.

TEAM ACTIVITIES

Team Activity 1

Select several limited-service properties in your area that offer complimentary food services. Contact these properties and ask about the most significant operating problems that arise in the operation of the food service program. What suggestions can your team make to resolve these concerns?

Team Activity 2

Review recent articles in full-service hotel and commercial food services trade magazines. Identify at least one production and one non-production issue that would be equally applicable to managers in limited-service properties offering a complimentary breakfast operation. How would these issues affect a limited-service hotel?

13

Food and Beverage Operations: Full-Service Hotels

Chapter Objectives

1. Describe the types of guests served by hotel food and beverage operations.
2. Review the organization of large and small hotel food and beverage operations.
3. Discuss basic guest- and operations-related concerns important when a hotel's menu is planned.
4. Review procedures for purchasing, receiving, storing, issuing, and producing food and beverage products and delivering them to guests.
5. Explain activities necessary to prepare dining areas for service and to serve à la carte meals.
6. Present management concerns applicable to room-service operations.
7. Provide basic information about important management concerns related to banquet operations.

Chapter Outline

FOOD AND BEVERAGE GUESTS
ORGANIZATION OF HOTEL FOOD AND BEVERAGE OPERATIONS
    Small Hotels
    Large Hotels
MENU PLANNING
    Guest Concerns
    Operating Concerns
FOOD SERVICE CONTROL POINTS
    Purchasing
    Receiving, Storing, and Issuing
    Production
    Serving and Service
À LA CARTE DINING
    Getting Ready for Service
    Service Procedures

ROOM SERVICE
    Profitability
    Menu Planning
    Operating Issues
    In-Room Service
BANQUET OPERATIONS
    Profitability
    Menu Planning
    Banquet Event Orders and Contracts
    Other Banquet Concerns
        Banquet Room Set-up
        Banquet Service Styles
        Control of Beverage Functions

Overview: Food and Beverage Operations: Full-Service Hotels

Full-service hotels offer food and beverage products and services to guests staying at the hotel and to others living in the community or visiting the property. People attending conventions and meetings and other groups desiring food and beverage service can also enjoy banquets at these hotels. Many properties must typically accommodate the diverse needs of a wide range of guests in planning and implementing food and beverage operations.

The organization of a hotel's food and beverage department depends upon the volume of revenue generated. Small properties may have a food and beverage manager who directs the work of the employees responsible for food production and food beverage service. As the operation grows in size, specialized positions (for example, specialized chefs for dining room and banquet food production and managers for separate dining rooms) become necessary.

The food management process begins with menu-planning efforts that focus on what the guests will want and what can be produced profitably. After menus are planned, ingredients must be purchased, received, stored, issued, and produced. As well, meals must be served to guests in the dining room, and several styles of food service can be used.

Full-service hotels have one or more dining areas (for example, a coffee shop and/or a dining room) along with other areas, such as a pool snack bar and lobby outlets, where food and beverage products may be available. The wide range of procedures needed to get ready for service and to actually deliver meals in à la carte dining outlets must all consistently meet the appropriate standards.

Some hotels have a unique type of food service not available in other industry segments: room service. A wide range of menu-planning factors, operating issues, and guest-related concerns must be addressed in managing this food service operation.

Few, if any, organizations in the hospitality industry can provide the type of banquet facilities found in many hotels. A hotel's banquet room can range from a small space accommodating 50 or fewer persons to large convention/conference facilities that may seat thousands. There is significant profit opportunity in banquet operations when they are effectively managed. As with any other type of food service operation, the first managerial consideration is menu planning driven by the identification of the guests to be served.

Much of a banquet's success relates to agreeing about (seemingly) numerous details. Two tools—banquet event orders and banquet contracts—help to minimize misunderstandings. Other banquet concerns, including issues relating to the provision of alcoholic beverages during events, are also very important.

As you read this chapter you will learn that the food and beverage operation in a full-service hotel is much more complicated than that in a limited-service property (see Chapter 12). Food and beverage managers with specialized knowledge, skills, and experience are required; the operation's acceptance by guests and its profitability are a direct result of their abilities.

FOOD AND BEVERAGE GUESTS

Full-service hotels offer **à la carte** and, perhaps, other food services for travelers who stay at the property and for others, including residents of the local community.[1] Is the hotel attempting to attract motorists on a nearby roadway traveling for pleasure

---

[1]This and the next three sections of this chapter are loosely based upon Chapters 10 and 11 in *Introduction to Hospitality: Careers in the World's Most Exciting Industry* by Jack D. Ninemeier and Joe Purdue. Published in 2005 by Prentice Hall.

and/or business? Is the property located in a city's business district? Does it do a large volume of convention business, and/or is it a resort (destination) property? The food services offered by the hotel must be planned to meet the dining needs of those to whom the property is marketed.

LODGING LANGUAGE

À la Carte: A food service offering items on an individually priced (by-item) basis, typically in a dining room.

■

Most full-service hotels also generate revenues from people living in the community who enjoy the same types of dining options as the hotel's guests. For example, residents of a rural community may enjoy the no-nonsense, value-priced meals offered by a lodging property on an interstate near the community which appeals to the motorists passing by. Residents of a large city may like to celebrate special occasions in the dining outlet of a hotel serving upscale business and pleasure travelers. It is a challenge for managers in hotel food services to identify their guests and to understand and consistently provide what they need. If they do not accomplish this, others (their **competitors**) will provide the products and services that are desired.

LODGING LANGUAGE

Competitors: Businesses that provide products and services to the same market of guests.

■

Figure 13.1 illustrates the types of food and beverage products/services that guests might desire in a specific property.

Let's look briefly at each of these alternatives:

* *À la Carte Dining.* Depending upon its size, a hotel might have one or more à la carte dining alternatives. For example, a small property might have a coffee shop

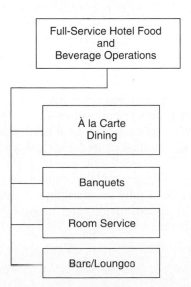

FIGURE 13.1 Food and Beverage Services Offered by Full-Service Hotels

or a dining room. A very large property may have several theme restaurants and a coffee shop. It may also offer one or more quick-service outlets in its lobbies and/or in a swimming pool area or other locations around the property.

- *Banquets.* Many hotels offer **banquet** functions for groups of guests meeting at the property and for others celebrating special occasions.

LODGING LANGUAGE

Banquet: A food and/or beverage event held in a hotel's function room.

■

- *Room Service.* Some hotels deliver food and beverage products to guest rooms. This type of food and beverage service is unique to lodging properties.
- *Bars and Lounges.* Some hotels have a bar/lounge located near the à la carte dining room. In some properties, bar/lounge guests may also order food items. Sometimes all à la carte menu items are served in the bar/lounge, whereas in other properties, a separate and more limited bar menu may be offered.

Many full-service hotels provide food services to their employees. Large hotels may employ hundreds or even thousands of staff members. Employee cafeterias are sometimes available for their exclusive use, and a subsidized (no- or low-cost) meal is offered.

ORGANIZATION OF HOTEL FOOD AND BEVERAGE OPERATIONS

The organization of a food and beverage operation in a full-service hotel depends upon its size (revenue volume). Small hotels tend to generate lower revenues from food services than their higher-revenue counterparts. The average full-service hotel generates approximately 28–40 percent of its total revenue from food and beverage sales.[2] Some properties, especially those with large-volume convention/meeting/banquet business, generate food and beverage revenues that are a much greater percentage of total hotel revenues.

Small Hotels

Figure 13.2 shows how a food and beverage operation might be organized in a small hotel. The hotel's general manager supervises a food and beverage manager who, in turn, manages the work of someone responsible for food production (the head cook), dining room service (the restaurant manager), god banquet and beverage production/service (the head bartender). In a small operation, managerial functions are combined into just a few positions. For example, the food and beverage manager may be responsible for food/beverage/supply purchasing, the applicable accounting and control activities, and banquet operations, among many other duties. By contrast, as will be seen later, larger operations have specialized positions for these tasks.

---

[2]*Hotel Operating Statistics: Report for the Year 2004* (Hendersonville, Tenn.: Smith Travel Research, 2005).

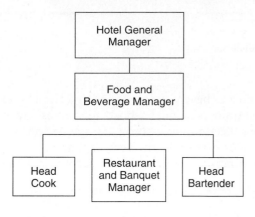

FIGURE 13.2   Organization of Food and Beverage Management Positions in Small Hotels

Large Hotels

As a hotel's food service operation becomes larger, additional managerial positions are needed, as illustrated in Figure 13.3.

The food and beverage manager in Figure 13.2 is now the director of food/beverage operations. He or she supervises the work of an executive chef who, in turn, supervises a sous chef (with responsibility for food production for à la carte dining and room service) and a banquet chef (with responsibility for food produced for group functions). The director of food/beverage operations may also direct the work of a catering manager (who interacts with clients and sells group functions) and a banquet manager (who is responsible for banquet set-ups/tear-downs and service at banquets). Other **direct reports** of the director of food and beverage operations are the restaurant manager (responsible for service in the à la carte dining room[s]), the room service manager, and the beverage manager (who is responsible for the head bartenders at each beverage outlet.)

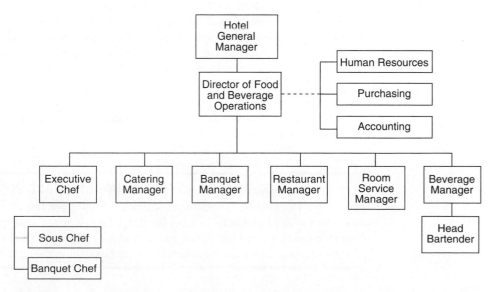

FIGURE 13.3   Organization of Food and Beverage Management Positions in Large Hotels

LODGING LANGUAGE

Direct Report: One's immediate supervisor.

■

The director of food and beverage operations in a large hotel also has the benefit of technical assistance from personnel whose specialties involve human resources (including recruitment, selection, orientation, compensation/benefits administration and interpretation/implementation of the ever-expanding body of legal issues relating to employment), centralized purchasing, and accounting/financial management.

LODGING ON-LINE

Hotel F&B Executive is a trade magazine addressing the managerial and operational concerns of those was manage food and beverage departments in lodging properties. Check out its home page at:

www.hfbexecutive.com

While reviewing this site, you can note the subjects treated in the current and past issues of the magazine. (What are the concerns of food and beverage executives as indicated by the article titles?)

Click on "E-Magazine—Reader Picks" for detailed information about suppliers and products used by the hotel food service industry.

MENU PLANNING

A food service manager in a hotel or any other type of organization must be consistently concerned about several important processes if the operation is to be successful. These are illustrated in Figure 13.4.

We will briefly discuss each of these processes later in this chapter. They are presented here to emphasize that they are sequential, and that the first on the list, menu planning, is, according to many industry experts, the most important. In their view, "it all starts with the menu!" Menus must offer items desired by the guests. Managers must use marketing principles to learn what guests will buy and at what price if they are to effectively differentiate their business from that of their competitors.

In other words, an effective menu focuses on the guests and addresses operating concerns. Entire books have been written on the topic of **menu planning.**[3] Two of the most important considerations relate to the guests (what they want and will pay for) and to the resources available to provide menu items that consistently meet required quality standards.

PROBLEMS AND PROFITS IN HOTEL FOOD SERVICES

Food service departments in hotels have some unique challenges. One of the most important is the inability of many to be profitable. At many (most) full-service hotels, food and beverage sales bring in fewer revenue dollars and bottom-line profits, than the rental of guest rooms. Financial management concerns create an umbrella under which hotel food services must constantly operate.

[3]See, for example, Jack Ninemeier and David Hayes, *Menu Planning, Design and Evaluation.* (Richmond, Calif.: McCutchan Publishing Corp., 2003).

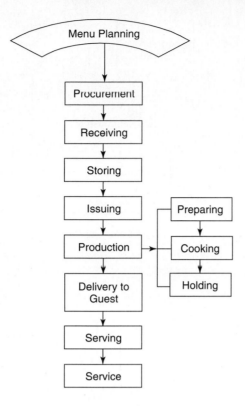

FIGURE 13.4   Overview of Food Service Processes

LODGING LANGUAGE

Menu Planning: The process of ascertaining which food/beverage items will most please the guests while generating acceptable revenue and/or cost objectives.

■

Guest Concerns

The guests are the most important consideration when planning the menu, and it is critical to know what items they will order. What guest-related factors should be considered in planning a menu? Figure 13.5 helps answer this question.

Figure 13.5 suggests that many guest-related factors should be considered:

- *Purpose of Visit.* Guests want (desire) an experience in line with the purpose of their visit. They may just be hungry (for example, when travelers on an interstate highway stop at a roadside hotel), they may be discussing business, or they may be a couple or a family visiting an upscale hotel restaurant to celebrate a special occasion.
- *Value.* The concept of **value** relates to a guest's perception of the selling price of an item relative to the quality of the menu item, service, and dining experience. Guests want to get what they pay for; they do not want to feel cheated, and, increasingly, many guests will pay more for a higher perceived quality of dining experience.

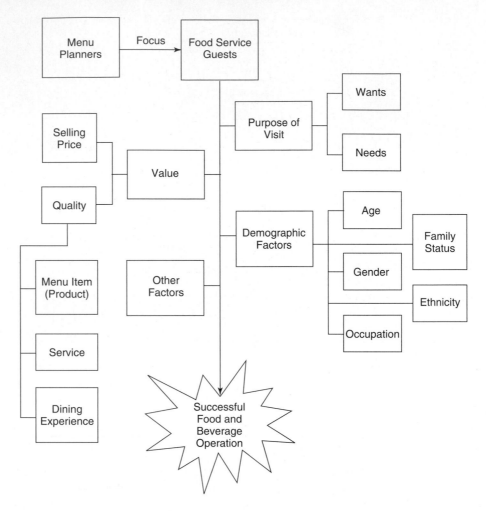

FIGURE 13.5   Menu Planning: Focus on Guests

LODGING LANGUAGE

Value: The guest's perception of the selling price of a menu item relative to the quality of the menu item, service, and dining experience received.

■

• **Demographic Factors.** Concerns such as the guests' age, marital status, gender, ethnicity, and occupation are likely to impact menu item preferences. Knowing the answer to the question "Who will be visiting our hotel's restaurant?" will help in the menu-planning task.

LODGING LANGUAGE

Demographic Factors: Factors such as age, marital status, gender, ethnicity, and occupation that help to describe a person.

■

The maitre d' is ready to greet guests in this full-service hotel restaurant.

- *Other Factors.* Social factors such as income, education, and wealth may influ-ence what a guest desires. Other factors, including guests' lifestyles and even their personalities (for example, the extent to which they like to try "new" foods) can be relevant to menu-planning decisions.

The goal of every menu planner is to offer items that please the guests. When guests are satisfied, they are more likely to provide **repeat business.** At the same time, they will tell their friends, and word-of-mouth advertising helps the food and beverage operation to remain successful.

LODGING LANGUAGE

Repeat Business: Revenues generated from guests returning to a commercial hospitality operation as a result of positive experiences on previous visits.

■

Operating Concerns

Figure 13.6 highlights some of the ways that the menu, once planned, impacts the food services operation.

Let's review these operating aspects:

- *Product Purchases.* All the ingredients required to produce all the menu items must be consistently available in the required quantity and quality and at the right cost. Otherwise, guests may be disappointed because desired items are not available. Moreover, there will likely be significant operational disruptions when alternative menu items need to be produced.

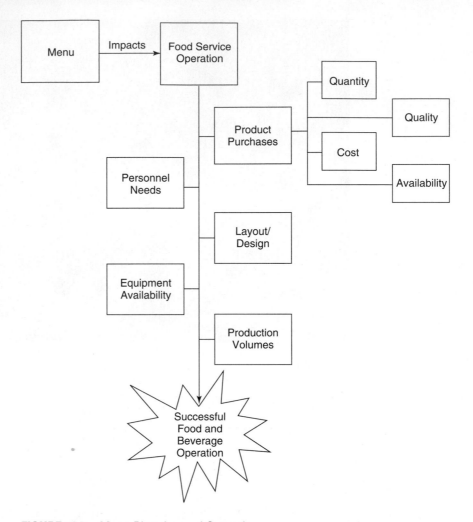

FIGURE 13.6   Menu Planning and Operations

- *Personnel Needs.* Staff members must be available to produce and serve the items required by the menu. Consider the differences in the experience and skill levels necessary, for example, for an effective server in a hotel's coffee shop and a server performing tableside flaming activities in an upscale hotel restaurant.
- *Layout/Design Concerns.* If a menu specifies a self-service salad bar, the space must be available for the serving counters and, as well, to accommodate the guest **traffic** in the salad bar area. A menu featuring fresh-baked breads requires the space (square feet) necessary for an on-site bake shop (or, at least, bake ovens).

LODGING LANGUAGE

Traffic: The number of people, such as guests and/or employees, occupying/moving about in a specified area.

◾

- *Equipment Availability.* If the menu requires fried foods and grilled items, deep-fat fryers and grills will be necessary based upon anticipated business volume. The space needed to locate the equipment and adequate ventilation as required by local/other fire safety codes must be considered.
- *Production Volumes.* It is difficult (impossible?) for a kitchen with one oven to produce baked appetizers, entrées, desserts, and breads in any significant volume. The menu planner in this operation must be careful about the potential to **overload** the oven.

LODGING LANGUAGE

Overload: Requiring equipment to produce more than it is reasonably capable of producing.
■

LODGING ON-LINE

After the menu is planned, it must be designed. A great resource to help you learn more about menu design is:

www.themenumaker.com

At this site you can review menu samples and designs and look at sample menu jackets. Also, click on "design your own" and learn "secrets" about menu design.

MENU DESIGN IS ALSO IMPORTANT

After the menu is planned, it must be designed. A menu may be a simple placecard at a banquet table or a name card identifying the item available next to each help-yourself serving dish on a buffet line.

Most hotel restaurants, whether upscale or casual, and most room service operations make a menu available to guests. Traditionally, the purpose of providing a menu was to simply inform guests about available items. Today, however, menus can be powerful in-house selling tools. They are designed to influence/encourage the guests to select items that are popular and profitable. Several different evaluation processes can be utilized with almost any type of menu to take advantage of the selling opportunities that an effectively designed menu can provide.

FOOD SERVICE CONTROL POINTS

After the menu is planned, other processes must be effectively managed to help the hotel's food and beverage operation successful. Figure 13.4 indicates the processes that must occur after the menu is planned. They will be reviewed in this section.

Purchasing

Once the menu is planned, the **food items** and **ingredients** needed to deliver it will be known. These are the items to be purchased. Figure 13.7 identifies five special concerns in **purchasing.**

LODGING LANGUAGE

Food Items: Food selections that will be available for the guests.
■

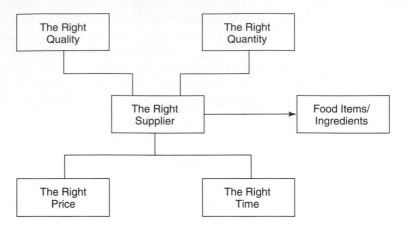

FIGURE 13.7 Five Special Purchasing Concerns

LODGING LANGUAGE

Ingredients: Individual components of a food item; for example, flour and sugar are ingredients in bread.

Purchasing: The process of determining the right quality and quantity of food products and ingredients to be purchased and of selecting a suppler that can provide these items at the right price and the right time.

■

Quality is perhaps the single most important concern when purchasing food and beverage items. The purchaser must consider the intended use of the items; the closer an item is to being suitable for its intended use, the more appropriate is its quality.

LODGING LANGUAGE

Quality: Suitability for intended use; the closer an item is to being suitable for its intended use, the more appropriate is its quality.

■

Maraschino cherries might be required at the bar for a drink garnish and in the kitchen as an ingredient in a fruit gelatin salad. A whole cherry with stem (at a relatively higher cost) may be needed at the bar because it is attractive; chopped cherry pieces (at a relatively lower cost) might be best in a gelatin salad. You cannot consider quality without first knowing how the product will be used.

Another purchasing factor relates to the quantity of items needed. If too much product is purchased, money that could be utilized for other purposes is tied up in inventory. The quality of some products can deteriorate in storage, space must be available to house excess inventory, and there is increased chance of **theft** and **pilferage.** By contrast, when an inadequate quantity of product is available, **stockouts** can occur. Guests may be disappointed because a desired item is not available, and operating concerns can arise if substitute items must be produced.

LODGING LANGUAGE

Theft: Stealing all of something at one time; for example, a thief might steal a case of liquor.

Pilferage: Stealing small quantities of something over a period of time; for example, a thief might steal one bottle from a case of liquor.

Stockout: The condition that arises when a food/beverage item needed for production is not available on-site.

■

The price is right when the cost of a food item or ingredient provides a good **value.** Wise purchasers realize that they are purchasing more than just products from a supplier. They also receive product information and service. The perceived value of these three factors (product quality, information, and service) should most influence purchase decisions.

LODGING LANGUAGE

Value: the relationship between the price paid and the quality of a product, supplier information, and service received.

■

The right time for product delivery must also be considered. Suppliers offering a good deal on an item for tomorrow's banquet delivered next week are not providing value. Purchasers who frequently **expedite** orders should look first at their operation to determine whether there is an internal problem. If not, they should select suppliers who consistently deliver required products on a timely basis.

LODGING LANGUAGE

Expedite: Facilitating delivery of food, beverage, or other products previously ordered from suppliers.

■

Finally, as noted in Figure 13.7, the right supplier consistently delivers the right quality and quantities of product at the right price and at the right time. Some food services managers try to have only a few suppliers so that they can eliminate paperwork and enhance their relationship with suppliers. Other managers believe that interactions with many suppliers are beneficial to the operation. Whichever of these (or intermediate) approaches is used, the importance of purchasing cannot be overlooked.

LODGING ON-LINE

Today, there are numerous ways that electronic systems can help with purchasing, receiving, storing, and issuing. To learn about some of these systems, go to:

www.calcmenu.com

www.foodtrak.com

www.tracrite.net

www.ibertech.com

As you review these Web sites, you will learn a great deal about how modern food and beverage managers can save time while implementing cost-effective control systems.

Receiving, Storing, and Issuing

After products are purchased, they must be received, stored, and issued to production areas. Receiving occurs when products are physically delivered. **Storing** is the process of holding products in a secure space with proper temperature, humidity, and product rotation until they are needed. **Issuing** involves moving products from the storage area to the place of production. Basic receiving, storing, and issuing procedures are similar for food and beverage products. They must be protected until used so that menu items can be produced at the lowest possible cost.

LODGING LANGUAGE

Storing: The process of holding products under optimal storage conditions until needed.

Issuing: The process of moving products to the place of production.

■

Production

Production is the process of readying products for consumption. It involves cooks working in the kitchen and bartenders working in bars.

LODGING LANGUAGE

Production: The process of readying products for consumption.

■

Effective food or beverage production requires the use of **standard recipes** to indicate the type and quantity of ingredients, preparation methods, and portion tools along with production instructions. Some items may be produced from **scratch;** others can be purchased in a **convenience food** form. A **make/buy analysis** is needed to determine which items should be made from scratch and which should be purchased as a convenience food.

LODGING LANGUAGE

Standard Recipe: A written explanation about how a food or beverage item should be prepared. It lists the quantity of each ingredient, preparation techniques, portion size/portion tools, and other information to ensure that the item is always prepared the same way.

Scratch: The use of basic ingredients to make items for sale. A stew may be made on-site with vegetables, meat, and other ingredients, and a Bloody Mary mix can be made on-site with tomato juice and seasonings.

Convenience Food: Food or beverage products that have some labor "built in" that otherwise would have to be added on-site. Alfredo sauce can be purchased in a ready-to-serve form (just heat it), and a Bloody Mary mix can be purchased ready-to-pour.

Make/Buy Analysis: The process of considering quality, costs, and other factors in scratch and convenience food alternatives to determine how products should be purchased for the operation.

■

The production of food items generally requires more elaborate and extensive preparation skills than are needed for beverages. A menu may offer a range of items requiring different levels of preparation skills. For example:

- hamburger patties that must only be grilled or oven-baked
- casserole-type dishes that involve the need to clean, pre-prepare (cut/chop), and cook numerous ingredients
- elaborate sauces that require experience in stock reduction and preparation to prepare a sauce that in itself is an ingredient (**chained recipe**) in another menu item

---

LODGING LANGUAGE

Chained Recipe: A recipe for an item (such as a sauce) that is itself an ingredient in another recipe (such as a steak).

■

Items that are produced can be made individually (**per portion**) or by **batch cooking.** Some ingredients require **preparing** as a first step in production to get them ready for **cooking.** (For example, fresh celery must be cleaned and chopped if used in a stew.) A final step, **holding,** may be necessary until menu items are served.

LODGING LANGUAGE

Per Portion: A single serving of food; for example, a portioned hamburger patty.

Batch Cooking: Preparing several portions of food at the same time.

Preparing: Steps involved in getting an ingredient ready for cooking or serving.

Cooking: Applying heat to a food item.

Holding: Maintaining food items at proper serving temperature after they are prepared. Holding involves keeping hot foods hot and cold foods cold.

■

Serving and Service

When a hotel has a dining room, food items prepared by cooks are transferred to employees who then serve them to guests. Bartenders preparing drinks in a **service bar** also produce items for transfer to employees who serve guests. The process of moving products from production to service personnel is called **serving.** Personnel then deliver food and beverage products to guests in a process called **service.**

LODGING LANGUAGE

Service Bar: A bar where drinks prepared by bartenders are given to personnel who serve them to guests.

Serving: The process of moving prepared food or beverage items from production staff to service personnel.

Service: The process of transferring food and beverage products from service staff to the guests.

■

Systems for food and beverage serving must be effectively designed to minimize service bottlenecks that can lower food quality (such as cold food) and lengthen

These guests are enjoying a business meal in the dining room of a full-service hotel.

guest waits (for example, when many slow-to-prepare ice cream drinks hinder the production of other drinks). The speed and manner in which products are delivered to guests is very important: the perceived quality of service is important when guests evaluate their food service experience.

LODGING ON-LINE

Hotel restaurant managers have lots of high-tech options available when they develop and implement guest reservation systems. Check out the following:

www.crossfirereservations.com/

This site has a demo that allows you to see features of the program.

À LA CARTE DINING

You have learned that à la carte food services allow guests in a hotel's restaurant to order and pay for the specific menu items they desire. These meals are typically served in a designated dining area, such as a dining room, pool snack bar, or coffee shop. There are many activities included in preparing for and providing service to guests in à la carte dining operations. Some of them are discussed in this section.

Getting Ready for Service

The work of the food and beverage server begins long before the first guests arrive. For example, **mise en place** activities are necessary.[4]

[4]*Restaurant Operations Management: Principles and Practices* by Jack D. Ninemeier and David K. Hayes. © 2006 Prentice Hall.

LODGING LANGUAGE: SERVICE STYLES

Prepared food can be presented to guests in several ways:

- *American (Plated) Service*. Food is pre-portioned onto serviceware (plates or bowls, for example) in the kitchen and is then served to guests seated at tables in the dining area.
- *Traditional French Service*. Food such as a classic Caesar Salad or a flaming Steak Diane is prepared and cooked at the guests' tables.
- *Russian (Platter) Service*. Food is placed on serviceware in the kitchen, brought to the guests' tables by servers, and individual portions are then served onto the guests' plates.
- *English (Family) Service*. Food is brought to the table by the server in serving dishes and placed on the guests' tables so that they can pass food items to one other.
- *Buffet (Self-Service)*. Guests help themselves to a variety of food placed on a serving counter.
- *Counter Service*. Guests place orders with service personnel behind a counter who retrieve food for the guests.

Service styles can be combined in the same meal. For example, a Caesar Salad may be prepared tableside (French Service), and the entrée may be pre-plated in the kitchen (American Service).

LODGING LANGUAGE

Mise en Place: French term meaning "everything in its place"; cooks and bartenders must get ready for production; servers must get ready for dining service.

Examples of mise en place activities for service staff include seeing that:

- tables, chairs, and booths are clean, safe, and steady

This dining room is ready for the first guest of the evening.

- tablecloths, if used, are correctly placed and are clean and free of burns, holes, and tears
- **place settings** are placed according to the hotel's standards (see an example in Figure 13.8) *Note:* There are many standards for setting tables (example: forks are placed to the guest's left, knives to the guest's right). However, consistency should be a priority concern of the dining room manager (that is, every place setting in the dining room should always be the same).
- there are no water spots or fingerprints on glassware, flatware, cover (base) plates, or other serviceware.

LODGING LANGUAGE

Place Setting: The arrangement of plates, glasses, knives, forks, and spoons (flatware), and other service items arranged on a dining table for one guest.

■

Note: Serving pieces are typically placed such that guests use the outside items first and then move toward the center of the place setting. When looking at Figure 13.8, note the arrangement of the forks. Guests will first enjoy a fish course, followed by the entrée. Since a formal European meal is being served, the salad course is served after (not before) the entrée, so the salad fork is placed closest to the center of the place setting.

Preparing for service extends beyond checking guest tables. All **condiments** must be filled, **service areas** must be stocked with necessary supplies (for example, coffee filters, napkins, and menus), and, hopefully, service staff will participate in a daily **line-up** pre-shift training session.

LODGING LANGUAGE

Condiments: Salt, pepper, ketchup, mustard, syrups, and related items that guests apply to food to adjust its taste to their personal preference.

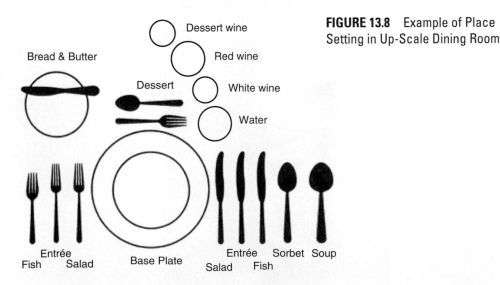

FIGURE 13.8   Example of Place Setting in Up-Scale Dining Room

Service Areas: Non-public areas close to the dining room used to house coffee machine, ice bins, serviceware, and related supplies needed by service staff.

Line-Up: A brief informational training session held before the work shift begins.

■

Topics for the daily food server line-up can include:

- **server station** assignments
- daily specials
- product knowledge information (including opportunities to sample new items)
- estimates of business volume during the shift based upon reservations and/or other information
- a mini-training session on a topic such as procedures to resolve a recurring service-related problem
- other issues as necessary

LODGING LANGUAGE

Server Station: An area of the dining room with tables/booths assigned to a specific food server.

■

LODGING ON-LINE

Technology can help servers place orders from the guest's table to the food/beverage production areas. One system uses a palm device that sends a wireless signal to the main system through an access antenna. To learn about the wireless waitress system, go to:

www.thewirelesswaitress.com/

This site allows you to take a virtual tour of a restaurant featuring the system.

Service Procedures

Many steps are typically involved in the interaction between servers and guests as the dining process evolves. These are identified in Figure 13.9.

The server's first step is clear; the next several steps may not be. It is important to approach the table as soon as possible after the guests are seated (Step 1). A hospitable and genuine greeting is important. ("Hello, welcome to Parker's Restaurant. We are pleased that you're here, and our goal is to make your visit a memorable one.") Eye contact, a feeling of self-confidence, and a genuine spirit of hospitality are helpful in this initial guest contact.

"WHO GETS THE SPAGHETTI?"

"Who gets the spaghetti?" is a question that will never need to be asked (and should never be asked!) in a well-managed dining area. Servers should use a numbering system so that they know who gets the spaghetti. Each table in the dining room is assigned a number (this helps with server station assignments), and each seat (space) at each table (booth) is also numbered. There is no question about who gets the spaghetti because the server will have written the table/seat number corresponding to the guest ordering the spaghetti on an order pad when the guest's order was placed.

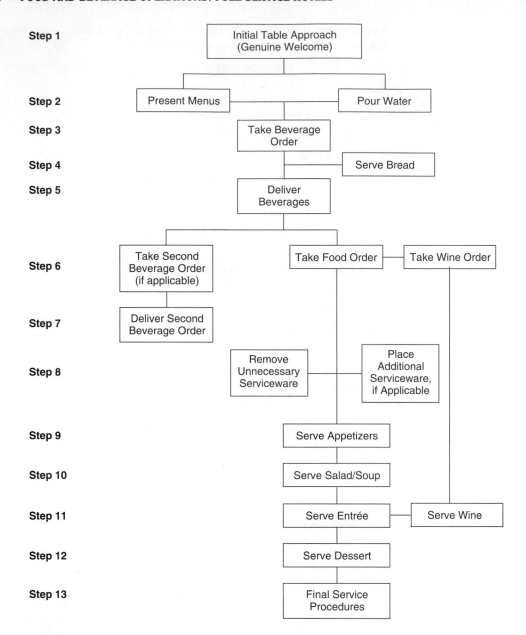

FIGURE 13.9   The Service Sequence

Step 2 in the service sequence depends upon the property. Guests may be provided with menus by the receptionist as they are seated, and a busperson may serve water to them before the server reaches the table. Menu presentation and providing water should be among the first steps in the service process regardless of which staff member does so.

When presenting the menu, the server can mention any specials available in addition to what is on the menu.

A beverage order can be taken (Step 3), and bread can be brought to the table after the beverage order is taken (Step 4). Trays should be used to carry beverage orders (and everything else!) to the table. Beverages should be served from the guest's right side with the server's right hand. (They are removed this way as well.) Service trays should not be placed on the guest's table when the server takes/delivers an order.

After beverages are delivered (Step 5), three activities then become important (in Step 6) when the server next returns to the table:

- Take a second beverage order (if applicable).
- Take the food order.
- If applicable, take a wine order.

As orders are taken, servers should:

- Be complete; ask questions. If a guest orders a steak, ask about the desired degree of doneness. If a guest orders a baked potato, ask about preferred condiments.
- Repeat orders to help ensure accuracy.
- Be alert to guests' needs. For example, if they appear rushed, suggest items that can be prepared/served quickly.
- Pick up the menus after each guest has placed an order and return them to their proper storage location.

After food/wine orders are taken, a second round of beverage orders can be delivered, if applicable (Step 7), and (Step 8) servers should remove items that will not be needed, such as pre-set wine glasses if no wine is ordered. Additional service items that will be needed after orders are known should be brought to the table (Step 8). These may include serrated knives (if steaks are ordered) and special condiments, such as tartar sauce for seafood.

Steps 9–12 review the sequence of serving appetizers, salads/soups, entrées (and wine, if applicable), and desserts. Attention to details is very important. Does a guest need more water or other beverage, was an item of flatware dropped on the floor (and need replacement), or does someone have second thoughts about a condiment not requested earlier? Another point: returning to a table and asking, "Is everything okay?" is doing the correct thing in the incorrect way. It is important to be available for additional service. It is not professional however, to imply that something may not be acceptable. A better tactic: approach the table, gain eye contact with the guests, and inquire, "Is there anything else I may do to assist you?"

Step 13 notes final service procedures:

- presenting the check
- assisting the guests with payment
- ending with a hospitable "Thank you; I enjoyed serving you; please visit us again real soon."

LODGING ON-LINE

Restaurant managers need many different types of dining room furniture and supplies. To review a Web site featuring a wide variety of these items, go to:

www.foodservicedirect.com

This site allows you to view products either by type (flatware, glassware) or by manufacturer.

ALL IN A DAY'S WORK

The Situation

"Whose job is it, anyway?" asked Francis, a frustrated food server at the Barkley Grill in the Mountain View Hotel, to Louis, the dining room manager.

"I'm glad we're very busy tonight, and I'm working as hard as I can to provide the quality of service that our guests want," he continued. "When I go to one table, however, the guests already have a menu. When I go to another, they do not. The same with water: sometimes guests have received water before I arrive and sometimes they have not. I'm glad when they have a menu and water; it helps speed service. But, I have to waste a lot of time picking up menus and preparing water glasses to bring to the table because I never know whether guests will have them when I arrive. If they do, I look silly, and I have to return them to the server station before I can take the order. I don't save time; I actually waste time which could be better spent on more productive tasks."

A Response

Francis is right about the problem. The policy may be that the receptionist should provide menus to the guests and the busperson should bring water. However, if staff are not properly trained, what actually happens may not be what policy dictates. Louis can confirm the problem ("Let's talk about this at the end of the shift when we are better able to do so. In the meantime, I'll try to help out wherever I can so that you and the rest of the staff will not have to waste time.")

Francis has a legitimate complaint and did the right thing by discussing the problem with his supervisor. Louis should give a priority to meeting with dining service staff and agreeing upon who does what. Once this is determined, effective training programs can help to implement the agreed-upon procedures.

ROOM SERVICE

Many full-service hotels offer room service; some do so 24/7 (24 hours per day; 7 days per week).[5] Guests of all types utilize room service, ranging from the business traveler wanting a quick breakfast to small groups desiring a lunch during their meetings in guest room suites to couples desiring a romantic meal alone.

Large hotels will employ a room service manager with total responsibility for this service. They may even have a separate food preparation area to produce room service orders taken and delivered by, respectively, order takers and room service attendants. In very small hotels, on the other hand, the food and beverage manager may plan the room service menu, which is prepared by the same cook who produces the restaurant meals. They are delivered to the guest room by a restaurant server according to the order written up by the front desk clerk or dining room receptionist who serves as the order taker.

Profitability

Guests noting the high prices on the menu often think that hotels make a lot of profit on room service. In fact, this is not so.

If room service is not profitable for the hotel, why is it offered? First, it is a service to guests; some may select properties on the basis of its availability. (Among these guests are those arriving on late airline flights and others wanting food/beverage services for small business meetings in guest rooms.) Also, hotel rating services such as the American Automobile Association (AAA) assign their highest ratings to properties that offer room service (among other amenities).

Why does room service frequently lose money? High labor costs are one reason. Much time is needed to transport food from the kitchen to guest room areas. The

---

[5]This and the following section are adapted from David Hayes and Jack Ninemeier, *Hotel Operations Management* (Upper Saddle River, N.J.: Pearson Education, 2004).

capital costs incurred to purchase equipment, such as delivery carts and warming devices, can be significant. If costs were allocated for elevators to transport items, for staging areas to store room service carts and to prepare them for deliveries, and for similar costs, the expenses would even be greater. Finally, items such as glasses, cups, flatware, and serviceware increase room service costs. The need to return soiled room service items to kitchen areas often creates problems. (The question of "whose job is it?" arises. Housekeeping personnel, maintenance and security staff, and even managers may notice but not pick up and return these items.)

In some hotels the room service department provides food and beverage service in **hospitality suites** and for other group functions in a guest room. In convention properties, vendors and exhibitors may invite customers to visit hotel rooms for **hosted events.** When these services are provided by room service rather than by banquet service (see below), the likelihood of room service profitability increases.

LODGING LANGUAGE

Hospitality Suite: A guest room rented by a supplier/vendor, usually during a convention/conference, to provide complimentary food and/or beverages to invited guests.

Hosted Events: Functions which are complimentary for invited guests; costs are borne by the event's sponsor. A hosted bar may offer free beverages to wedding party guests, and a corporate sponsor may pay for a hosted reception in a hospitality suite.

■

Menu Planning

Special concerns are important when planning room service menus. As with any other food service alternative, quality is important. Room service menus should only offer items that can be transported relatively long distances from food preparation areas without decreases in quality. As noted above, many guests perceive room service prices to be high, and they will demand that food quality requirements be maintained to help justify the prices. Unfortunately, some popular items (omelets and french fries, for example) are not ideal room service menu items because of quality problems that arise when they are held at serving temperatures for long periods of time during transport to guest rooms. (*Note:* A manager can easily check food quality in a hotel restaurant or a banquet setting by sampling various items. However, managers have less access to products served in room service. Efforts to solicit feedback from guests are a critical way of seeing whether quality requirements are consistently attained.)

Cross-selling on room service menus is also possible. A room service breakfast menu can indicate that the hotel's Sunday brunch in the dining room is very popular. An invitation on the room service breakfast menu to call about daily dinner specials in the dining room can interest guests in thinking ahead about evening plans.

LODGING LANGUAGE

Cross-selling: Messages designed to advertise the availability of other services. For example, a dinner menu may provide information about a hotel's Sunday brunch.

■

Hotels in airports and other locations housing international guests have another room service challenge: language barriers. A non-English-speaking guest alone in a guest room with a menu written in English will have great difficulty in ordering. Alternatives such as pictures and menu item descriptions written in the languages most used by the hotel's international guests may be solutions.

If there are minimum order charges, mandatory tipping policies, and/or other requirements for guest room orders, these should be clearly indicated on the menu and may also be stated by the order taker.

Operating Issues

Trained order takers are needed regardless of whether this is full-time position or only one part of many responsibilities. Communication problems occur all too frequently in room service. If the employee fails to take a complete order, guest dissatisfaction is likely. The same types of questions that are asked in an à la carte restaurant must be asked by the room service order taker:

- How would you like your steak prepared?
- Would you like sour cream with your baked potato?
- Would you like a glass of wine to complete your dinner? (Tonight's special wines would go well with your entrée, and they are a great value.)

It is difficult to correct errors in any food service operation. However, an inaccurate order in the dining room can sometimes be quickly corrected. For example, if catsup for french fries is omitted, it can be immediately provided. However, if catsup is omitted from the room service tray, a relatively long and time-consuming trip back to the kitchen will be necessary. Should the guest wait with cold food (lowerer quality) as a result? Alternatively, should the guest consume the meal without the desired condiments? Either way, guest dissatisfaction will result, and the negative impression may carry over to other hotel experiences. At the same time, servers who must spend additional time on this work task will be unavailable to serve other guests who, in turn, may become dissatisfied as the wait for their room service order increases. A minor problem, then, can create a ripple effect that impacts the perceptions of many guests about the entire lodging experience.

Opportunities for **suggestive selling** are very useful for room service. The room service **guest check average** can be increased if guests are informed about items they may not have initially ordered, such as appetizers or desserts, because they didn't know or think about them.

LODGING LANGUAGE

Suggestive Selling: Information suggested by an order taker (in a room service operation) or by a server (in an à la carte dining operation) to encourage guests to purchase items they might otherwise not have ordered.

Guest Check Average: The average amount spent by a guest in a room service or dining room order. The guest check average typically includes the food and alcoholic beverage sales.

Guest Check Average = Total Revenue ÷ Total Number of Guests Served.

■

Room service orders, like those in à la carte dining operations, may be handwritten or, increasingly, are entered into an **electronic cash register (ECR)** or **point-of-sale terminal (POS).** Orders can then be printed on hard-copy tickets given to the room service cook(s). (A copy is also given to the server when the order is transported to the guest room.) Alternatively, the order can be transmitted to the cook(s) with a **remote printer.** It is important for the room server to carefully note whether the items that have been plated (portioned) and placed on the cart for delivery are, in fact, the ones that were ordered.

LODGING LANGUAGE

Electronic Cash Register (ECR): A standalone computer system that includes an input device such as a keyboard, an output device such as a printer, a central processing unit, and some storage (memory) capacity.

Point-Of-Sale Terminal (POS): A computer system that contains its own input and output components and, perhaps, some memory capacity, but without a central processing unit.

Remote Printer: A unit in a food or beverage preparation area that relays orders entered through an electronic cash register and/or point-of-sale terminal.

■

Technology has improved room service order taking. Modern systems typically indicate the room number and the name of the guest registered in the room from which the order is placed. Using the guest's name is an effective selling tactic, and it has become easy for the order taker to do so. When orders are placed, information about whether the guest can charge the meal becomes available. (Guests who pay cash for a room when checking in are usually not permitted to charge room service or other purchases to their room. As guests using a credit card near their pre-established credit limit, this information is also readily available when automated systems are used.)

LODGING ON-LINE

Want to see a detailed job description for the position of room service manager? If so, go to:

www.workinfo.com/free/JobDescript/JD20.htm

In-Room Service

From the guests' perspective, room service does not end when the order reaches the guest room; it begins there. Room service attendants must be adequately trained in service procedures that include:

- asking guests where the room service meal should be placed
- explaining procedures for retrieval of room service items
- presenting the guest check and securing payment
- opening bottles of wine, if applicable
- providing an attitude of genuine hospitality (rather than being rushed to make another room service delivery)

This hotel guest is ready to enjoy a meal in his room.

Managers must know how, if at all, room service in their hotel can be improved. Sometimes, a section relating to room service is included in a general guest rating form used to evaluate the entire property. Alternatively, a specific evaluation form provided when room service is delivered can be used.

The results of guest feedback should be randomly requested from the room service manager and reviewed by the general manager. When results are favorable, affected personnel should be complimented. If challenges arise, the general manager should work with affected staff to resolve the issues. Follow-up is important so that the same problem or others related to it do not re-occur.

Surveys about the hotel and its products/services are increasingly offered through the guest room communication (television) system. This data can be available to the general manager immediately.

BANQUET OPERATIONS

Offering a wide variety of types and sizes of **banquet** events sold by **catering** staff is an important factor separating hotel food and beverage departments from many of their counterparts in other segments of the hospitality industry. The volume of banquet business helps determine whether banquet operations are the responsibility of food production and service staff or, alternatively, whether employees with specialized banquet duties are utilized. The hotel's marketing and sales staff will normally be responsible for generating banquet business and for negotiating contracts for specific banquet events. However, there is an old saying: "You are only as good as your last banquet." Repeat business generated from guests who have enjoyed previous

---

ALL IN A DAY'S WORK

The Situation

Mr. Vuki was chairing the weekly executive committee meeting. The current topic was guest feedback from a newly implemented comment card distributed in guest rooms, the dining room, and at the front desk. Some department heads expressed satisfaction (or at least relief!) because the guest comment ratings were 90 percent Positive, or more, on every factor assessed. "We must be doing a good job," said the food and beverage director. "There are no consistent complaints about anything."

Mr. Vuki, however, had a different thought. "Yes, at least nine guests out of ten think we are doing an excellent job. However, we should not be satisfied until every guest says we are doing a good job. The difference between where we are now and a perfect score represents improvements we can still make."

"Let's look at room service, for example," Mr. Vuki said. "Last week we had two complaints about cold food, and one guest remarked that the order was incomplete. Also, I am carrying more room service trays back to the kitchen that I find in the hallways as I walk around on the guest room floors."

"Yes," said the executive housekeeper. "My housekeepers tell me that they are also making more frequent calls to the kitchen to pick up room service trays left from the night before as well as from breakfast."

Suddenly, the food and beverage director was on the defensive. "We are short of employees in every service position. We have just hired and are now training several waiters and waitresses who, we hope, can work both in the dining room and, as necessary, in room service. In the meantime, I need your help in addressing these issues."

A Response

Mr. Vuki is correct to emphasize the need (opportunities) to improve the operation still further even in times when guest comment scores are relatively high. The executive committee meeting provides an excellent opportunity to discuss issues impacting more than one department. However, the food and beverage director should have explored service staffing issues with affected department heads as soon as he became aware of the problem. It was not necessary to wait until comments were made in the executive committee meeting.

Mr. Vuki should discuss issues of teamwork and cooperation among all department heads and their employees, and he should facilitate a discussion and agreement about what can be done to address the issues about cold food and unreturned room service trays.

---

banquets can be very helpful in selling future ones. By contrast, the negative word-of-mouth advertising created by dissatisfied banquet guests can significantly increase (and undo) the work of the sales and marketing staff.

LODGING LANGUAGE

Banquet: A special and often elaborate meal served (usually in a private dining area) to a select group of guests.
Catering: The process of selling a banquet event.

■

Hotels with extensive convention/meeting business have special banquet needs. Large properties will often have a separate convention services department whose personnel plan and coordinate all activities (including those that are food- and beverage-related) for the groups visiting the hotel. General managers of small hotels in which the food and beverage director administers the banquet function and their counterparts in larger properties with specialized banquet managers have something in common: they must all know and understand how banquet functions work, how

The hotel function room is often elaborately set for a buffet.

they can be evaluated, and how banquets can better meet the hotel's profitability and guest-related goals.

Profitability

Banquets are generally more profitable than restaurant (dining room) operations in hotels for several reasons:

- Banquets are frequently used to celebrate special events. This provides the opportunity to sell menu items that are more expensive and, therefore, higher in **contribution margin.**
- The number of meals to be served is known in advance; in fact, there is a formal **guarantee.** Also, the event will have known starting and ending times. This makes it easier to schedule production and service labor and to reduce the "peaks and valleys" in labor that often occur during, respectively, busy and slow periods in à la carte dining room operations. Also, there is less likelihood of overproduction of food with subsequent waste.
- Banquet planners are frequently able to sell a **hosted bar** or a **cash bar** that enables increased sales of alcoholic beverages to guests desiring them.
- There are opportunities to rent banquet rooms in addition to selling food and beverage products.
- Servers like banquet events because, typically, mandatory service charges increase their income.

LODGING LANGUAGE

Contribution Margin: The amount of revenue remaining from food revenue after the cost of the food used to generate the sale is paid for.

Guarantee: A contractual agreement about the number of meals to be provided at a banquet event. The event's sponsor agrees to pay for the number of guests served or the guarantee, whichever is greater.

Hosted Bar: A beverage service alternative in which the host of a function pays for beverages during all or part of the banquet event; also called an "open bar."

Cash Bar: A beverage service alternative where guests desiring beverages during a banquet function pay for them personally.

■

The banquet business is very desirable, and the general manager should do everything possible to gain a significant market share of the community's banquet business for the hotel.

Menu Planning

Most of the factors involved in planning a menu for the hotel's restaurant(s) are important when planning banquet menus. These include concerns about:

- guest preferences
- the ability to consistently produce items of the desired quality
- the availability of ingredients required to produce the menu items
- production/service staff with appropriate skills
- equipment/layout/facility design issues
- nutritional issues
- sanitation concerns
- peak volume production/operating concerns
- the ability to generate required profit levels at the selling prices that are charged

In addition, there are special concerns applicable to planning banquet menus. The menu planner must be confident that the items to be offered can be produced in the appropriate quantity at the appropriate level of quality and within the required time schedule. The old saying that "the guest (host) is always right" must be tempered when banquet menus are planned. The hotel, not the host, will be criticized if there is a failure to deliver according to anticipated standards. For example, consider a host desiring a flambéed entrée, table-side Caesar salad, and hand-made pastries for hundreds of guests. These items are very labor-intensive and a large amount of specialized service/equipment is needed. Personnel in the sales and marketing department of most hotels would be setting up a no-win situation if they booked this event. If the hotel accepts the business and cannot effectively deliver the promised banquet event, the guests will be upset. If the host cannot be sold on a more practical menu, business will be lost. However, it is in the hotel's best short- and long-term interests to refuse banquet business that cannot be delivered according to quality standards.

Many hotels have preestablished banquet menus that consider the hotel's production limitations and profitability goals. These menus are an excellent starting point for negotiations with prospective clients. Often these menus can be used without change; sometimes relatively minor changes, such as the substitution of a specific vegetable or dessert, can be made.

LODGING ON-LINE

Want to view the banquet menus used by many hotels around the world? If so, just type "hotel banquet menus" into your favorite search engine.

On other occasions a menu designed specifically for a special event is needed. A talented banquet planner working with the property's executive chef can develop a menu that meets the guests' expectations and the hotel's financial requirements. By contrast, when there is not close cooperation between the marketing and sales department and the food production personnel, concerns to generate short-term business may overshadow longer-term goals of consistently pleasing guests to generate repeat business.

Banquet Event Orders and Contracts

Banquet planning involves paying attention to numerous details. Most hotels utilize a **banquet event order (BEO).** A sample BEO is shown in Figure 13.10. It summarizes banquet details and helps to prevent communication problems between hotel staff and the event sponsor(s).

LODGING LANGUAGE

Banquet Event Order (BEO): Form used by sales and food production/service personnel to detail all the requirements for a banquet event. Information provided by the client is summarized on the form, and it becomes the basis for the formal contract between the client and the hotel.

■

The information in the BEO describes specific details about the event. However, a banquet contract will also be needed. It is wise to have the hotel's standard banquet contract reviewed by a licensed attorney to ensure that the best interests of the hotel are legally protected. Topics to be addressed by banquet contracts typically include:

- *Last date.* The last date that the banquet space will be held without a signed contract.
- *Time.* The date when an attendance guarantee must be received.
- *Cancellation policies.* This should include an explanation of fees to be assessed if the banquet contract is canceled. For example, assume the contract date is 180 or more days in advance of the event. There may be a cancellation fee of 50 percent of the anticipated billing if the contract is voided more than 60 days before the event, or a 100 percent fee may apply if a cancellation occurs 60 days or less from the date of the event.
- *Guarantee-reduction policy.* For example, if the final guarantee is less than a specified percentage of the initial guarantee, an additional charge (often equal to the meeting room charge) may be assessed.
- *Billing.* Information about the amount and schedule for guest payment is frequently included. Typically, the full remaining payment is due at the end of the event.

EVENT DATE:	BANQUET EVENT ORDER (BEO) #:
Organization:	
Billing Address:	**Business Phone #:**
	Business Fax #:
Contact Name:	**Business E-Mail**
Account Executive:	**Room Rental: $**
Guaranteed: ( ) persons	
BEVERAGES	**ROOM SET UP**
❑ Full ❑ Limited ❑ Hosted bar ❑ Non-hosted bar	❑ Classroom ❑ Theater ❑ Other: _____
❑ With bartender ( ) bars	❑ Diagram below
❑ Cash bar ( ) cashiers	
❑ Premium ❑ Call ❑ House	Need:
( ) per drink ( ) bar package	❑ Registration table / chairs:_____
( ) hours of operation	❑ Wastebasket
Time: **Room:**	❑ Easels
	❑ Podium: ❑ standing ❑ tabletop
	❑ Pads / pencils / pens / mints
Bar Opening/Closing Instructions:	❑ Water / glasses
Bar to close at: _____ AM / PM	
Bar to reopen at: _____ AM / PM	Diagram:
Wine with Lunch / Dinner	
_____ with entrée, _____ servers	
Time: Location:	
Additional Instructions:	**Linen:** ❑ White ❑ Other:_____
	Skirting:
FOOD MENU	**Napkin:** ❑ White ❑ Other:_____
_____ baseplates _____ waterglasses _____ butter rosettes on lemon leaves	**Music:**
❑ Introduction ❑ Invocation ❑ Nothing before meal	**AUDIO/VISUAL**
First Course Served at: _____ AM / PM Meal Served at: _____ AM / PM	❑ Microphone: _____ ❑ Slide Projector - package:_____ ❑ Overhead Projector - package:_____ ❑ VHS / monitor / package: _____ ❑ Mixer, _____ channel ❑ AV - cart ❑ White board / markers ❑ Screen ❑ Flipchart/pads/tape/pens ❑ LCD projector
	COAT CHECK
	❑ Hosted ❑ Cash: _____ ( ) Attendant(s) ( ) Coat Racks
BEVERAGE MENU	**PARKING**
	❑ Hosted ❑ Cash: $_____ Fee per car: $ _____
	BILLING (METHOD OF PAYMENT)
	Deposit received: $_____

FIGURE 13.10   Sample Banquet Event Order (BEO)

- *Beverage Control.* Information about the service of alcoholic beverages (if applicable).

Other Banquet Concerns

Banquet room set-up, service styles, and control of beverage functions are among the other special concerns of hotel banquet managers. These will be discussed in this section.

Banquet Room Set-Up

In large hotels, banquet rooms (also called **function rooms**) may be set up by house-keeping (public space) staff. In small properties, this activity may be the responsibility of staff members in the food and beverage department. Regardless of who is responsible, the activities are basically the same.

LODGING LANGUAGE

Function Room: Hotel public spaces, such as meeting rooms, conference areas, and ballrooms, that can be subdivided into smaller spaces available for banquet, meeting, or other group rental and/or use.

■

The space assigned for the banquet is normally determined when the banquet event is booked and will be specified on the banquet event order. Unfortunately, hoteliers are sometimes confronted with ethical, financial, and/or legal issues when, for example, space originally committed to one event is reallocated to attract another event. This often occurs when more profitable events are brought to the attention of the personnel in the marketing and sales department after commitments with groups hosting smaller events have been made.

Numerous details are involved in setting up a banquet room. Size is determined by the number of guests expected, although local fire safety codes/ordinances may also impact this decision. The type (round or rectangular, for example) and size of dining room tables, the number of seats per table, and the required space for aisles, dance floors, head tables, reception/buffet lines, or other purposes impact requirements. Timing also becomes critical when the same space must be used for different functions throughout the same day or when a very large evening event precedes a very large breakfast event in the same space the following day.

Banquet Service Styles

Banquet events can involve numerous ways to serve food and beverage products to guests. Most of these styles are applicable to dining room service, and several (American, French, Russian, English, and Buffet) were discussed earlier in this chapter. Another style sometimes used at banquets is called Butler Service: appetizers and pre-poured champagne, for example, can be passed by service personnel circulating among guests standing at a reception. Frequently more than one service style is used during a single banquet event.

Service styles can differentiate an elegant (and higher-cost) banquet from its less-elegant (and lower-priced) counterpart. For example, a Caesar salad might be prepared as a demonstration for those seated at a **head table;** pre-portioned servings of the Caesar salad could then be brought to guest tables for service. Alternatively, vegetables for a soup course could be brought to the guest table in a bowl (American service); service staff could pour broth from a sterling pitcher into each guest's bowl at table side (modified Russian service). These are examples of simple ways to make a banquet appear more elegant.

LODGING LANGUAGE

Head Table: Special seating at a banquet reserved for special guests.

■

Control of Beverage Functions

Many banquets offer alcoholic beverages. Examples include receptions before an event, wine service during a function, and continuing service of beverages during and after the meal service has concluded.

Banquets offer increased opportunities to sell **call brand** or **premium brand** *beverages* in addition to or in place of the property's **house brand beverages.**

LODGING LANGUAGE

Call Brand Beverages: High-priced and higher-quality alcoholic beverages sold by name (such as Johnny Walker Red Scotch) rather than by type of liquor (scotch) only.

Premium Brand Beverages: Highest-priced and highest-quality beverages generally available, such as Johnny Walker Black Scotch; also called "super call."

■

LODGING LANGUAGE

House Brand Beverages: Alcoholic beverages sold by type (scotch) rather than by brand that are served when a call or premium brand beverage is not requested; also called "speed-rail," "well," or "pour brand."

■

There are several common ways that beverages sold at banquet events can be charged for and priced. They can be sold at a cash bar where guests desiring beverages pay for them personally. Some events may offer an **open bar** in which beverages are paid for by the host. Still other events have a combination cash and open bar: guests are issued drink tickets for complimentary drinks and can then purchase additional beverages. Another variation occurs when drinks are complimentary for a specified time period (for example, before dinner) and are purchased (cash bar) by guests after that time.

LODGING LANGUAGE

Open Bar: A beverage service alternative where the host of a banquet function pays for beverages during all or part of the event; also called "hosted bar."

■

There are several ways that beverage charges can be assessed:

- *Individual drink price.* Cash (or a ticket sold for cash) is collected when each drink is sold. Alternatively, a manual or electronic tally can be made of the number of each type of drink sold, and the host is charged at an agreed-upon price-per-drink basis at the end of the event.
- *Bottle charge.* Often used with an open bar, beverages are charged on a by-bottle basis for each bottle consumed/opened. Normally, every bottle opened is charged for at a full, agreed-upon rate; guests are not allowed to take open bottles away from the hotel.
- *Per-person charge.* This method involves charging a specific price for beverages based upon event attendance. The same number of guests used for the guarantee

(discussed earlier) may become the basis for the per-person charge. A deduction from the guarantee is made for minors attending the event because they will not consume alcoholic beverages.

- *Hourly charge.* This method involves charging the host a specific price for each hour of beverage service. Properties using this method must determine the number of guests to be present (the guarantee can be used with adjustment for minors) and then estimate the number of drinks to be consumed per hour.

Some hotels charge a **corkage fee** for alcoholic beverages brought into the property for use during an event. Although this is often misunderstood by guests, hotels *do* incur fees when pre-purchased beverages are brought in. The beverages must be served (labor costs are involved) and the bar/dining areas must be cleaned; glasses subject to breakage are used and washed; stir sticks, cocktail napkins, appropriate garnishes, if applicable, and other supplies will also still be necessary.

LODGING LANGUAGE

Corkage Fee: A charge assessed when a guest brings a bottle (for example, of a special wine) to the hotel for consumption at a banquet function or in the hotel's dining room.

■

LABOR CHARGES

Costs for the labor required to produce and serve food is normally included in the banquet charge. Sometimes, especially when the number of guests is small and the variety of services requested is large, additional charges for the following types of labor are assessed:

- bartenders and barbacks (bartender assistants)
- beverage servers
- beverage cashiers
- security personnel
- valet (parking) staff
- coat room employees

CHAPTER OBJECTIVES REVIEW

1. Describe the types of guests served by hotel food and beverage operations. (Objective 1)
2. Review the organization of large and small hotel food and beverage operations. (Objective 2)
3. Discuss basic guest- and operations-related concerns important when a hotel's menu is planned. (Objective 3)
4. Review procedures for purchasing, receiving, storing, issuing, and producing food and beverage products and delivering them to guests. (Objective 4)
5. Explain the activities involved in preparing dining areas for service and in serving à la carte meals. (Objective 5)

6. Present management concerns applicable to room service operations. (Objective 6)
7. Provide basic information about important management concerns related to banquet operations. (Objective 7)

LODGING LANGUAGE

À la Carte (food service)	Production	Hosted Events
Competitors	Standard Recipes	Cross-selling
Banquet	Scratch	Suggestive Selling
Direct Report	Convenience Food	Guest Check Average
Menu Planning	Make/Buy Analysis	Electronic Cash Register (ECR)
Value	Chained Recipe	Point-of-Sale Terminal (POS)
Demographic Factors	Per Portion	Remote Printer
Repeat Business	Batch Cooking	Banquet
Traffic	Preparing	Catering
Overload (equipment)	Cooking	Contribution Margin
Food Items	Holding	Guarantee
Ingredients	Service Bar	Hosted Bars
Purchasing	Serving	Cash Bars
Quality (food/beverage products)	Service	Banquet Event Order (BEO)
Theft	Mise en Place	Function Room
Pilferage	Place Setting	Head Table
Stockout	Condiments	Call Brand Beverages
Value	Service Areas (dining room)	Premium Brand Beverages
Expedite	Line-up (training)	House Brand Beverages
Storing	Server Station	Open Bar
Issuing	Hospitality Suite	Corkage Fee

FOR DISCUSSION

1. Assume you are the food and beverage manager in a hotel in New York, San Francisco, New Orleans, or Honolulu that attracts guests from all over the world. What menu-planning tactics could you use that recognize the diverse food preferences of the international markets served by your property?

2. Assume you are interested in a career in a hotel food and beverage operations. What would be the pros and cons of starting work in a small hotel? In a large hotel?

3. Assume you are a food and beverage director working with the hotel's chef to plan a new menu. You want to add a deep-fried item to the new menu. What information would the chef want from you before implementing such a change?

4. It has been said that a hotelier will pay for food items of the quality purchased even though food items of the same quality are not received. What are some procedures that you as a food service manager would use to help ensure that proper receiving procedures are in use in your hotel?

5. You have learned about several service styles in common use in hotel à la carte dining and banquet operations. How would you determine which style(s) to would use for your operation?

6. There are numerous tasks that servers must perform in order to make their guests' dining experience a memorable one. What are some basics you would use

as a hotel restaurant manager to train new service staff in the proper way to perform these tasks?

7. Some hotels use dining room servers and room service attendants interchangeably. What special training would a room service attendant need to become an efficient dining server?

8. Communication problems often impact the effective planning and delivery of banquets. It is natural for marketing and sales department personnel to want to do whatever they can to fill the hotel's guest rooms and public function spaces. It is also natural for food production staff to be concerned about banquet events being sold to guests. What are some types of issues that can cause conflict between these two hotel departments?

9. The food and beverage department and its housekeeping counterpart employ the vast majority of the employees in a full-service hotel. These departments are very labor-intensive because it is not practical to use technology to replace human workers in these areas. To what extent do you think technology will replace employees in the food and beverage department in the future? Why?

10. Assume that you are a motorist stopping at a roadside hotel with a coffee shop. Assume also that you are a business person staying in a five-star hotel about to dine in the property's high-check dining room on the 60th floor of the property. What are some expectations you would have that would be the same for both dining areas?

TEAM ACTIVITIES

Team Activity 1

Today all large hotel organizations use the Internet to advertise products/services to prospective guests. Find the Web sites for several of your favorite hotel organizations. To what extent do they advertise their à la carte dining opportunities? Their room service and banquet operations? Do their advertising messages give any suggestion about the importance their guests place on food and beverage alternatives when making hotel-selection decisions? (While reviewing these sites, check out the "employment opportunities" or similar section and review the types of positions for which the organizations are currently recruiting. Are there position vacancies in food and beverage operations?)

Team Activity 2

Visit a hotel in your area and request permission to borrow a menu from the à la carte dining room. Pretend you are a consultant to the property who has been asked to make improvement suggestions. Carefully study the menu from the perspectives of both the guests and the property managers. What suggestions would you make to improve the effectiveness of the menu?

14 Safety and Security

Chapter Objectives

1. To stress the importance of keeping hotel guests and employees safe.
2. To identify a variety of internal and external resources available to help hoteliers meet their safety and security goals.
3. To describe safety threats that are unique to the hotel industry.
4. To stress the importance of property security.
5. To identify internal, external, and area-specific threats to hotel security.

Chapter Outline

THE IMPORTANCE OF SAFETY
   Legal Liability for Guest and Employee Safety
   Hotel Responsibility for Guest Safety
      Facility
      Staff Training
      Policies and Procedures
SAFETY RESOURCES
   Internal Resources
      Recodable Locks
      Alarm Systems
      Surveillance Systems
      Emergency Plans
   External Resources
      Local Law Enforcement
      Property Insurers
SPECIAL SAFETY-RELATED THREATS
   Swimming Pools
   Spas

   Exercise Facilities
   Parking Areas
PROTECTING PROPERTY FROM SECURITY THREATS
   Internal Threats
      To Cash
      To Other Assets
   External Threats
      To Cash
      To Other Assets
   Area-Specific Threats
      Front Office
      Housekeeping
      Food and Beverage
      Sales and Marketing
      Maintenance
HOTEL CRISIS-MANAGEMENT PLANS

Overview: Safety and Security

Hotel guests depend upon the hotel to maintain an environment in which they will be as safe as possible. Guests, however, are not the only people concerned about safety. Employees count upon the hotel to provide working conditions that allows them to do their jobs free from concerns about unnecessary risks. The owners of a hotel want its managers to develop practices and procedures that will safeguard the hotel's assets and minimize the owner's legal liability. In addition, there are governmental agencies at all levels which are charged with monitoring the safety related efforts of hotels.

The hotel industry is committed to safety. To achieve this goal, it relies upon a variety of internal security–oriented tools, including recodable locks, alarm systems, surveillance systems, and emergency plans that can be used to reduce safety and security risks. In this chapter, you will learn about all of these. You will also learn how external resources, such as local law enforcement personnel and the hotel's insurers, help properties to be safe and secure.

Depending upon their location and the services offered, some hotels have unique safety and security issues. These include protecting guests in swimming pool areas, spas, exercise areas, and in nearly all cases, parking lots. While hoteliers cannot guarantee their guests' safety, they have a responsibility to exercise reasonable care in protecting the welfare of guests. In this chapter, you will learn how hotels can meet the reasonable-care standard.

Threats to the security of hotel assets can come from both internal and external sources. To protect assets adequately, programs must be in place to guard against these threats. In this chapter you will learn about ways to reduce the chances of incurring losses due to dishonest guests and employees. In some cases, safety and security threats are unique to specific hotel departments. For example, in the front office, cash is routinely kept on hand and must be safeguarded, while the housekeeping department must control theft of room supplies and furnishings by employees or guests. This chapter examines in detail the important department-specific security concerns of the front office, housekeeping, food and beverage, sales and marketing, and maintenance and engineering.

THE IMPORTANCE OF SAFETY

Regardless of the size of the hotel, all of its employees must be concerned about **safety** and **security.** Concern for the safety of guests and the security of their possessions is not merely good business; it is also a legal responsibility of the hotel's ownership and becomes an important responsibility of each hotel staff member. Employees and other non-guests visiting the hotel also have a legal right to expect that management, will protect their health and well-being to the greatest degree possible.

LODGING LANGUAGE

Safety: Protection of an individual's physical well-being and health.

Security: Protection of an individual's or business's property or assets.

■

Legal Liability for Guest and Employee Safety

Since the earliest days of travel, guests have been rightfully concerned about their safety while they are sleeping. Innkeepers and hoteliers have responded to these concerns by striving to provide a safe haven for travelers. In addition to the good intentions of hotel managers, however, there are laws that require those who operate hotels to provide the traveling public with a safe and secure environment. These laws, however, do not hold hotels responsible for everything that could happen to guests during their stay.

For example, a guest may slip and fall in a bathtub. The hotel will not be held responsible for any resulting injuries if it is determined that it has exercised **reasonable care** in the manner in which it provides and maintains its bathtubs.

LODGING LANGUAGE

Reasonable Care: A legal concept identifying the amount of care a reasonably prudent person would exercise in a specific situation.

■

Assume, however, that the hotel had purchased bathtubs with surfaces that became extraordinarily slippery when wet. Assume also that many guests had slipped and fallen in the tubs and that management knew about these instances. In addition, assume that the hotel's franchisor, on several occasions when the hotel was inspected, had advised the hotel's owners to install slip-resistant materials on the floor of the tubs to reduce the chances of injury. If, in the face of this information, the hotel's owners refused to install the non-slip surfaces, they would, in all likelihood, be held liable for the guest's fall if a lawsuit was filed.

As a hotelier, it is important to remember that the legal standard of reasonable care means that you must operate your hotel with a degree of care equal to that of other reasonable persons (hoteliers). For example, if you know, or should have known, about a threat to the safety of your guests, it is reasonable to assume that you would either immediately eliminate the threat or clearly inform your guests of it. Not to do so would indicate that you exhibited an absence of reasonable care for the safety of your guests.

If a threat to guest safety results in loss or injury, and it is determined that the hotel did not exercise reasonable care in regard to that threat, the hotel may be held wholly or partially liable for the resulting loss or injury. If a hotel is found to be liable for injuries to a guest or employee, it will probably have to bear the cost of that liability. For example, assume that a hotel manager knew about a defective lock on a guest room door but did not authorize an immediate repair. Subsequently a guest rented the room with the defective lock and was robbed and assaulted by an assailant who obtained unlawful entry to the room via the door with the defective lock. In this case, it is highly likely that an attorney hired by the guest to seek **damages** against the hotel would be successful. In this hypothetical case, the damages would include **compensatory damages** and possibly even **punitive damages.** These damages could amount to extremely large amounts of money the hotel would be required to pay the injured guest—costs that could have been avoided had the guest room lock been repaired, as it should have been, in a timely manner.

LODGING LANGUAGE

Damages: The actual amount of losses or costs incurred due to the wrongful act of a liable party.

Compensatory Damages: A monetary amount intended to compensate injured parties for actual losses or damage they have incurred. This typically includes such items as medical bills and lost wages. Also known as "actual damages."

Punitive Damages: A monetary amount assessed to punish liable parties and to serve as an example to the liable party as well as others not to commit the wrongful act in the future.

■

It is important to note that hoteliers do not do their job of maintaining a safe property properly simply to avoid paying damages. A demonstrated concern for guest safety is not merely a good business practice; it is also the right thing to do. Guest safety is an important part of every hotel employee's job, and it is the job of the hotel's managers to make sure that employees, as well as guests, are safe while on the property.

Hotel Responsibility for Guest Safety

You have learned that a hotel can be held legally responsible for the results of injury to guests (and employees) if it does not exercise reasonable care. To demonstrate reasonable care, a hotel must address three main issues. These are:

1. The hotel's facility
2. The hotel's staff
3. Policies and procedures implemented by the hotel

Each of these plays an important part in the safety and security of overnight guests and those who work in or visit a hotel.

LODGING ON-LINE

Some hoteliers take the issues of guest safety and security so seriously that they have established separate trade associations designed to assist one another's safety efforts. Canadian hoteliers are leaders in this area. To view the Web site of the Alberta Hotel Safety Association (AHSA), go to:

http://www.albertahotelsafety.com

Facility

Every hotel offers different products and services to guests in a variety of different locations and settings. Each hotel, however, should be as safe as possible. This is not to imply that accidents cannot happen, but that the management and staff of the hotel should develop and maintain an active **threat analysis** program.

LODGING LANGUAGE

Threat Analysis: A systematic procedure designed to identify and eliminate identifiable safety risks.

■

A threat analysis program is an organized procedure by which a hotel facility is assessed for possible hazards. For example, in a hotel with a parking lot, the lights in the parking area should be periodically checked to see if they are functioning properly. If it is discovered that they are not working properly, they pose a potential safety hazard and that hazard must be eliminated by repairing the lights.

In some cases, it may not be possible to completely eliminate a safety risk. When this is the case, reasonable care demands that guests *must* be informed of the risk.

For example, most observers would agree that swimming in a hotel's swimming pool without a lifeguard present presents a risk to safety. However, most hotels with swimming pools do not employ a full-time lifeguard during the time the pool is open for use by guests.

In this case, the known risk (absence of a life guard) must be communicated to guests. Signage can be developed to communicate the risk. Possible wording alternatives, posted in the pool area in the language(s) of guests, and in a highly visible location, might include:

- Swim At Your Own Risk
- No Lifeguard On Duty
- Adult Swimmers Only
- Children Must Be Supervised By An Adult
- Children Under the Age of 16 Must Be Supervised by an Adult
- No Running or Diving

Note that each of these statements seeks to inform swimmers about risks related to swimming in an area without a lifeguard present. In most cases, if no lifeguard is present during most of the time a hotel's pool is open, the hotel's **insurer** would provide the actual language to be used to inform swimmers of their safety risk.

LODGING LANGUAGE

Insurer: The entity providing insurance coverage to a business.

■

Additional steps that can be taken in a threat analysis program are to prohibit behavior by guests and others that could pose a threat to safety. For example, a hotel might establish and enforce a policy prohibiting the use of glassware (glass bottles or drinking glasses) in a pool area. It would do so to eliminate the threat to safety that could come from broken (and thus nearly invisible) glass fragments in a pool area where people are likely to be bare-footed.

Each hotel facility will have its own safety issues; however, three steps are important parts of an effective threat analysis program and can help to demonstrate a hotel's commitment to using reasonable care to protect guests from harm. These three step include:

- Identifying and removing threats to safety
- Informing guests about existing safety threats
- Prohibiting behavior that creates safety threats

Staff Training

It takes the efforts of every employee in the hotel to eliminate, to the greatest degree possible, threats to the safety and security of guests and their property. In larger hotels, there may be a full-time director of safety and security and a staff of departmental employees who routinely patrol the hotel's grounds, make safety and security checks, and direct the hotel's safety programs. In other cases, the hotel may contract with a private security firm to provide security services. In still other cases, off-duty police may be hired to assist with the hotel's security efforts. However, even in the smallest of limited-service hotels, all employees need to be trained in security and safety methods.

Training employees to protect guests and themselves and to assist the hotel's security efforts is an ongoing process. One way to view the safety-training needs of employees is to think about the training required by all employees and the training essential only to members of a specific department. For example, teaching all employees to promptly report any unauthorized or suspicious person found loitering in the hotel's parking lot is appropriate, whereas training about the safe handling of food would be appropriate only for those employed in the food and beverage department.

Specific hotels or hotel companies develop and implement many fine safety-training programs. In addition, excellent training materials related to safety and security are developed and continually updated by the Educational Institute of the American Hotel and Lodging Association (E.I.). These materials are made available to hotels at a very reasonable cost.

LODGING ON-LINE

The Educational Institute (E.I.) offers a variety of safety and security related training products suitable for all of a hotel's employees and other programs that are departmental-specific. In addition, E.I. offers a self-paced training program leading to the Certified Lodging Security Officer designation (CLSO). To learn about that program and others, go to:

www.ei-ahla.org

and enter "Safety and Security" in the search field.

In most limited-service hotels, safety and security is not a completely separate department. Instead, safety and security programs are administered within each hotel department and are overseen by the general manager or a designated **safety and security committee.**

LODGING LANGUAGE

Safety and Security Committee: An interdepartmental task force consisting of hotel managers, supervisors, and hourly employees responsible for monitoring and refining a hotel's safety and security efforts.
■

Many hotels find that maintaining an effective safety and security committee is preferable to a separate safety and security department because the very operation of the committee reinforces the message that guest safety and hotel security is the responsibility of every one of its managers, supervisors, and employees.

Regardless of the size or organizational structure of the hotel's safety and security efforts, the training of employees is a key component of any effective program.

Managers are not the only persons interested in the safety of a hotel's employees. In 1970, the federal government passed the Occupational Safety and Health Act, which created, within the Department of Labor, the Occupational Safety and Health Administration (**OSHA**).

LODGING LANGUAGE

OSHA: The Occupational Safety and Health Administration. A federal agency, established in 1970, that is responsible for developing and enforcing regulations to help ensure safe and healthful working conditions.

■

The purpose of the Occupational Safety and Health Act is to bring about safe and healthful working conditions. OSHA has been very aggressive in enforcing the rights of workers. Together with its state-level partners, OSHA has approximately 2,100 inspectors, and additional complaint-discrimination investigators, engineers, physicians, educators, standards writers, and other technical and support personnel located in over 200 offices throughout the country. This staff establishes and enforces protective standards, and assists employers and employees through technical assistance and consultation programs.

All hotels are legally required to comply with the extensive safety practices, equipment specifications, and employee communication procedures mandated by OSHA. The OSHA requirements call upon employers to:

- Provide a safe workplace for employees by complying with OSHA safety and health standards
- Provide workers with tools and equipment to do their jobs that meet OSHA specifications for health and safety
- Establish training programs for employees who operate dangerous equipment
- Report to OSHA within 48 hours any worksite accident that results in a fatality or requires the hospitalization of five or more employees
- Maintain the "OSHA Log 200" (an on-site record of work-related injuries or illnesses) and submit it to OSHA once per year
- Display OSHA notices about employee rights and safety in prominent places within the hotel
- Provide all employees access to the Material Safety Data Sheets (MSDS) that provide information about the dangerous chemicals they may be handling during work (see Chapter 10)
- Offer no-cost hepatitis-B vaccinations for employees who may have come in contact with blood or body fluids

OSHA inspectors have the legal authority to inspect a hotel to see whether it is in compliance with their regulations. When OSHA was established, few businesses viewed it as a partner in their worker-safety efforts. Today, astute hoteliers recognize that compliance with OSHA standards results in fewer accidents, lower insurance costs, and a healthier workforce.

LODGING ON-LINE

OSHA maintains an active Web site with valuable information that can be easily accessed. To stay current on OSHA regulations and enforcement programs, visit and bookmark:

www.osha.gov/

In addition to OSHA, hotel operators may find that there are state and local laws regarding employee safety that also must be followed. In some cases, a state or local governmental agency may share responsibility for enforcing employee and guest safety-related issues. For example, in most cities, the local fire department will be responsible for ensuring that locally required fire-suppression systems are in place and operational.

Policies and Procedures

The specific safety and security policies and procedures that are best for an individual hotel will vary based upon its size, location, physical layout, and the guest amenities offered. In all cases, however, written policies and procedures help inform all hotel employees of what is expected when responding to safety and security threats. While a text or a legal manual can identify the importance of standardized policies and procedures, each hotel must consider its own property-specific threats, concerns, and solutions. These solutions, formalized in writing and consistently followed by every employee, will go a long way toward establishing that the hotel demonstrates reasonable care.

SAFETY RESOURCES

Fortunately, hoteliers have a number of resources at their disposal as they seek to create lodging environments that are safe and secure. In this section we will examine some of the most important of these.

ALL IN A DAY'S WORK

The Situation

J.D. Ojisima, the general manager of the hotel, walked quickly to the hotel's pool area.

"There are an awful lot of kids and only one adult down at the pool," was the statement made a few minutes earlier to the front office manager by the housekeeper, who had gone to the pool area to replenish the towel supply. All housekeepers in the hotel had been trained to report any activity that could possibly be considered dangerous, and this housekeeper had performed well.

Because she could not leave the front desk area unattended, the front office manager had called J.D. to ask for assistance.

"What's the problem?" stated the guest when J.D. arrived at the pool. " I rented a room at this hotel to hold my son's eleventh birthday party. These are his friends. Are you saying we are not allowed to invite friends to visit when we are registered guests in your hotel?"

J.D. quickly counted over 25 children attending the party and only one adult: the father who had rented the room for the party.

A Response

Here is a case where facilities, staff, policies, and procedures must all play a part in how the hotel responds to a safety threat. Children should be able to use a hotel's pool with adult supervision. In this case, however, most reasonable people would doubt whether one adult can effectively supervise 25 young children.

Generally, J.D.'s first responsibility would be to satisfy the guest. In this case, however, the greater responsibility is to safeguard the children and the hotel. As a result, J.D. must act decisively to remove the threat, even if it means upsetting the guest.

If no additional adults are present to help with supervision, J.D. should act to remove enough of the young swimmers from the water to ensure the safety of all. In the future, J.D. should address and formulate a written policy (if one does not currently exist) regarding the issue of the friends of registered guests and their permitted use (or non-use) of hotel swim facilities as well as a reasonable adult/child supervision ratio that can be enforced by all hotel employees.

Internal Resources

Internal safety and security systems have advanced rapidly in the lodging industry. Among the most important internal tools available to hoteliers are:

- Recodable locks
- Alarm systems
- Surveillance systems
- Emergency plans

The appropriate selection and use of these tools depends upon the safety and security needs of the individual hotel.

Recodable Locks

The purchase and use of a **recodable locking system** by a hotel was once such a significant event that the hotel could actually market its use of such locks to potential guests. Today, recodable locks are the industry standard and no hotel should operate without them.

Individual electronic keys add to guest safety and property security. (*Source:* Joshua D. Hayes)

It is critical that swimming pool areas be cleaned and monitored on a regular basis.

LODGING LANGUAGE

Recodable Locking System: A hotel guest room locking system designed so that when guests insert their "key" (typically an electromagnetic card) into the guest room lock for the first time, the lock is immediately recoded, canceling entry authorization for the previous guest's key.

■

The typical installed cost of a recodable locking system is approximately $300–$500 per guest room. Most such systems in use today are independent and standalone. That is, no wiring to a central computer or PMS is required. Except in life-threatening emergencies, only standard magnetic strip cards issued to guests or hotel staff will open the lock. This means that the hotel's entire room security system is controlled by software programmed into the individual locks, which are activated by **keycards** coded by a card-issuing computer.

LODGING LANGUAGE

Keycards: The electromagnetic card used in a recodable locking system.

■

Keycards are time-sensitive and can be issued up to 12 months in advance. Thus individuals or groups can be sent room keys when reservations are confirmed to speed registration.

In a recodable locking system, each lock contains a card reader and electronic lock control module connected to a motor-actuated lock mechanism. Standard AA alkaline batteries power the entire lock. A warning light visible only to staff warns when the batteries are within three months of needing replacing. When a guest inserts the keycard into the lock for the first time, it is immediately recoded, thereby canceling entry authorization for the previous guest. In a quality system, multiple keycards can be issued to the same guest. In addition to guest rooms and exterior doors, recodable locks can be used to limit guest access to designated areas, such as special elevator floors, swimming pools, spas, exercise rooms, and reserved breakfast or bar areas. They can also limit employee access to specified storage areas within the hotel.

The safety and security challenge for the individuals managing a recodable lock system is to ensure that front desk agents do not issue keys to individuals not properly registered in the guest room. For example, assume the (very common) situation where a guest approaches a front desk clerk and states, "I have misplaced my room key. Can you please give me another?"

The hotel staff member responding to the guest must:

- Be trained to issue duplicate keys only to confirmed registered guests.
- Maintain an accurate data system that identifies registered guests and their assigned room numbers.

The advantages of an interfaced recodable locking system and PMS are clear in this case.

Because guest rooms must be regularly cleaned and maintained, management issues master keycards to hotel employees who need them. With today's recodable lock systems, an electronic record is kept of all keycards used in the lock for a specific period of time. As a result, should the need arise, management can determine whose keycard was used to open a lock and at what day and time the key was used.

Unlike non-recodable locks, the use of recodable locks seriously reduces the possibility that guests can be victimized in their room by someone who had rented the same room on a previous night. In addition, recodable locks help reduce the incidence of employee theft from rooms.

LODGING ON-LINE

To view the operational features of one of the most popular recodable locking systems, go to:

www.tesalocks.com

and click on "Hotels and Resorts."

Alarm Systems

Alarms of many types are used in the hotel industry. They can be either audible or silent. Audible alarms typically consist of high-pitched buzzers, bells, or other noises. Alarm devices, whether audible or silent, normally consist of electrical connections, photoelectric light beams, seismic detectors, infrared beams, magnetic contacts, or radio frequency (RF) fields that, when activated, create the alarm.

Alarms many be classified as either an **internal alarm** or a **contact alarm.**

LODGING LANGUAGE

Internal Alarm: A warning system that notifies an area within the hotel if the alarm is activated.

Contact Alarm: A warning system that notifies (contacts) an external entity, such as the fire or police department, if the alarm is activated.

■

Internal alarms generally are designed to serve as a deterrent to criminal or mischief activity. For example, a warning buzzer on a hotel's fire exit door would typically be wired only to notify hotel personnel if the door was used. In a like manner, an alarm on a liquor storeroom door might serve to notify a manager or the food and beverage director. Conversely, an alarm activated by a front desk agent during or after an armed robbery would most likely be wired directly to the local police department for the purpose of contacting them immediately.

Some important areas that may be protected by internal alarms include:

- Storage areas
- Hotel facilities, such as pools, spa, and exercise areas
- Hotel grounds and perimeter

Some important areas that are more likely to be protected by contact alarms include:

- The front desk
- Food and beverage cashier stations
- The controller's office

Hotel fire alarms are so important that they are mandated by federal law and local building codes. Good hotels have these devices wired as both internal and contact alarms. Remember that in case of a fire, hotel employees, guests, and the fire department would all need to be made aware of the danger. Thus, heat or smoke detectors in a guest room may set off an internal alarm that would be heard by the guest in the room as well as staff at the front desk and should be checked immediately by the appropriate hotel employee. By contrast, a fire alarm activated in a public area may result in an automatic contact and summons of firefighters because the alarm was wired directly to the local fire department.

The hotel staff responsible for doing so should periodically and frequently check all alarms for proper operation. This is necessary because a hotel with a nonfunctioning alarm system will have great difficulty demonstrating that it exercised reasonable care toward employee and guest safety should the need ever arise. An effective and comprehensive alarm system is an invaluable tool in every hotel's complete safety and security efforts.

Surveillance Systems

Properly implemented, electronic surveillance can play a major role in a hotel's safety and security programs. Surveillance is generally done in one of two ways. The first involves simply recording, via a VCR (or DVD), the activity within an area of the hotel. Thus, for example, a hotel could set up a VCR that records the activity outside a liquor storeroom. Then, if the storeroom was broken into on a given night, a videotaped record of the break-in would exist that could be useful in identifying the thieves. VCR surveillance systems are most frequently used to record activity at the front desk, near entrances and exits, in parking areas, and near cashiers.

Some hotels use **closed-circuit television (CCTV)** as a tool in their safety and security programs.

LODGING LANGUAGE

Closed-Circuit Television (CCTV): A camera and monitor system that displays, in real time, the activity within the camera's field of vision. A CCTV consisting of several cameras and screens showing the camera's fields of vision may be monitored in a single location.

■

The potential uses of CCTV in a hotel are many. CCTV can be used, for example, in a multiple-entry property where management desires to monitor activity outside each entrance. To be most effective, a CCTV system must be monitored. Viewing monitors are typically placed in a central location and viewed by an assigned employee who is trained to respond appropriately to activities seen on the monitor. For example, if an outside entrance is being monitored, and the monitor shows that a break-in is being attempted, the employee may be trained to summon the local police. Some hotels that use CCTV also have an intercom in the area being monitored, thus extending the effectiveness of the employee monitoring the system by making it possible to talk with anyone observed in the monitored area. States generally mandate the use of CCTV to improve security in casino hotels.

Some hotel managers attempt to create the illusion of having a CCTV system in place, when, in fact, the cameras are not truly cameras or the monitors are not constantly monitored. This is typically done in an effort to save money on the cost of operating the CCTV system. The rationale is that the mere presence of the cameras will deter criminals, since they will not realize that they are not actually being observed. The courts and juries have found, however, that this approach does not establish reasonable security care by a hotel because victims may mistakenly think that help is on the way (because they believe their situation is being monitored) and base their behavior on that belief. No help is likely to arrive if the monitors are not being viewed. Hotel managers who wish to operate an unmonitored CCTV should consult with both their insurers and their legal counsel before implementing such an approach.

When considering the use of either a VCR or CCTV system, the issues for management involve balancing guest and employee privacy with safety, and assessing whether visible cameras increase or detract from a guest's sense of security.

Emergency Plans

Despite a hotel staff's best efforts, safety and security emergencies will occur. When they do, the hotel must be ready to respond appropriately. Pre-planning is the very best tool available to managers concerned with safety and security. In unforeseen emergencies, it may not be possible to determine the proper response until the actual event occurs. But in the case of crises that are foreseeable (such as severe weather storms or power outages), some of the actions a hotel must be prepared to take will be quite similar, if not the same, in each crisis.

To prepare the hotel for a crisis, a hotel's managers should develop and implement an **emergency plan.**

LODGING LANGUAGE

Emergency Plan: A document describing a hotel's predetermined, intended response to a safety/ security threat it may encounter.

■

An emergency plan is, quite simply, the identification of a threat to the safety and/or security of the hotel as well as the hotel's planned response to the threat. For example, an emergency plan for a hotel near a heavily wooded area might include an evacuation plan to be implemented in case of a forest fire. A hotel on a Florida coast might include in its emergency plan a method of evacuating the hotel in the event of an impending hurricane.

Responses to events such as the following are included in most hotels' emergency plans:

- Fire
- Power outages
- Severely inclement weather
- Robbery
- Death or injury to a guest or employee
- Bomb threat
- Intense negative publicity by the media

In all of the above cases, the hotel's management and employees may be called upon to react quickly. The emergency plan prepares them to do so. This can be accomplished because many crises share similar characteristics that can, to some degree, be controlled by pre-planning: These characteristics include:

- Extreme importance
- Disruption of normal business
- Potential for human suffering
- Financial loss
- Potential scrutiny by the media
- Threat to the reputation or health of the business

An emergency plan must be a written document. This is important because it must identify precisely what is expected of management and employees in times of crisis. In addition, if the hotel becomes subject to a lawsuit as a result of the crisis, a written emergency plan can help show that it exercised reasonable care in preparing for the crisis.

An emergency plan should be kept simple because it will likely be implemented only in a time of heightened stress. A clearly developed emergency plan should include, for each crisis identified:

- The type of crisis
- Who should be told when the crisis occurs (include telephone or pager numbers)
- What should be done (and who should do it) in the event the crisis occurs
- Who should be informed of the results or impact of the crisis when it is over

The actual plan should be reviewed frequently by management and should be shared with employees so that they know what to do during the emergency. Where practical, hotels should practice the implementation of their plan. By doing so, they demonstrate strongly their commitment to ensuring the safety and security of the hotel and everyone in it.

External Resources

Hoteliers are not alone in their efforts to provide for guest safety. Local law enforcement officials also are charged with maintaining individual safety and community security. They are natural allies of hoteliers. In addition, the hotel's insurers have a deep-seated interest in the safety and security efforts of the hotel's owner and staff. These two resources are readily available to hoteliers and should be utilized to the greatest extent possible.

Local Law Enforcement

Hotel employees can and should be well-trained, but their safety and security efforts will be helped tremendously when the hotel's managers establish and maintain an excellent relationship with local law enforcement professionals. Hotel general managers should personally know the individual(s) responsible for law enforcement in the area where their hotel is located. Local law enforcement officials can advise and assist managers and, in many cases, provide no-cost safety and security training for the hotel's employees. In addition, they can advise hoteliers on the best procedures and processes to be used in working together to remove unruly guests from the hotel (an event that, unfortunately, does occur in many properties).

In many communities, a general manager can request a property safety and security review from the local police. This will likely result in the identification of specific steps the hotel can take to reduce safety and security threats as well as actions it can take to make improvements. Good managers make it a point to meet frequently with local police, because they are an important source of information and assistance.

Property Insurers

Risk is inherent in running any business, and hotels are no exception. Hotels seek protection from risk by purchasing insurance. Doing so makes good financial sense. Some types of insurance coverage may be required by law (such as **workers' compensation**). Other insurance is required by the hotel's lenders (when the hotel has been purchased with borrowed money) to protect their interest in the property.

LODGING LANGUAGE

Worker's Compensation: An insurance program designed to assist individuals who are victims of a work-related injury or illness.

■

When assessing risk, and before selling insurance to a business, an insurance company predicts the average number of times the risk is likely to result in actual loss or damage. The average monetary value of the loss is then established. The **premiums** (fees) for the insurance to protect against the loss are then determined. These fees must be low enough to attract those who want to buy the insurance, but high enough to support the number of losses that likely to be incurred by the insurer.

LODGING LANGUAGE

Premiums: The fees paid for insurance.

■

The fewer the number of **claims** (potential losses), workers injured, and lawsuits that result from safety- and security-related incidents, the lower the risk that the insurance company will have to pay out money.

LODGING LANGUAGE

Claim (Insurance): A demand for compensation as the result of loss, injury, or damage.
■

When there are few claims, the premiums charged for insurance are lower. As a result, it is in the best interest both of hotels (because they want to minimize the insurance premiums they pay) and of their insurers (because they want to avoid paying claims) to minimize the number of losses incurred. Because this is so, insurers should be partners with hoteliers in finding ways to reduce accidents and other sources of potential loss or damage. Just as a hotel's managers should know and work cooperatively with local law enforcement officers, the hotel's insurance companies should be consulted on a regular basis to identify policies, procedures, and actions that can be taken to reduce potential claims by improving the property's safety and security.

SPECIAL SAFETY–RELATED THREATS

Every business has unique threats to safety and security, and hotels are no exception. These unique threats often require extra caution or effort on the part of the hotel's staff. For many hotels, four of the most important of these areas of special concern are swimming pools, spas, exercise facilities, and parking lots.

Swimming Pools

Hotel swimming pools are exceptionally popular despite the fact that they are typically used by only a small percentage of hotel guests. Consistently, in opinion polls regarding desirable services, travelers rank the presence of a swimming pool near the top of the list of hotel amenities that influence their hotel selection. The potential legal liability resulting from accidental slipping, diving, or even drowning, however, requires that the individual(s) responsible for taking care of the pool area be extraordinarily vigilant in enforcing pool safety procedures

It is not possible to avoid every possible accident in a pool area. It is possible, however, to minimize the chances for accidents. Figure 14.1 lists 10 key practices that affect swimming pool safety and legal liability. They should be reviewed on a monthly basis with affected employees to ensure consistent compliance.

Most hotels do not employ full-time lifeguards at their pools. If lifeguards are provided, they must know effective surveillance and rescue procedures and techniques specific to the facility they are protecting. When groups (especially children) are using a pool, it is the responsibility of the group leaders to provide supervision, regardless of whether lifeguards are provided. When lifeguard services are not provided, the group should be advised that there are no lifeguards on duty and that its leaders must provide stringent and effective surveillance and supervision while the participants are in, on, and around the water. The hotel should provide the group leaders with specific supervisory and safety guidelines to be followed while the pool is in use. This can be done verbally or by use of a written "Pool Rules" fact sheet. The hotel's staff should continuously assess the numbers of guests in, on, and

1. Post the pool's operating hours and open the pool only during those hours.
2. Clearly mark the depths of pools accurately the on sides and ends and in both metric measure and feet/ inches.
3. Ensure that the pool and pool area are properly illuminated and that any electrical components are regularly inspected and maintained to comply with local electrical codes.
4. Install self-closing and self-latching and/or locking gates to prevent unauthorized access to the pool area. If possible, lock the entrance to the pool with a recodable lock.
5. Have appropriate life-saving equipment on hand and easily accessible as well as at least one cardiopulmonary resuscitation (CPR) certified employee on duty at all times the pool is opened.
6. Allow pool use only by registered guests and specifically authorized others.
7. Contact the hotel's insurer to determine the number, placement, and content of necessary pool warning signs.
8. Post all pool policy and information signs in the language(s) of guests. Enforce the policies at all times.
9. Provide an emergency telephone in the pool area that rings directly either to the front desk or to 911 depending on the preference of the hotel's insurer.
10. Carefully document all activities related to pool maintenance, local ordinance compliance, and operating policy enforcement.

FIGURE 14.1   Swimming Pool Safety

around the water to determine how many adults are needed to ensure the safety of the group members.

Spas

Hotels that have common area spas, whirlpools, or hot tubs face special safety and liability concerns. While spas are popular, they can be dangerous to young children, the elderly, intoxicated individuals, and people on special medications. As with pools, it may be impossible to prevent all possible accidents, but the practices listed in Figure 14.2 can go a long way toward improving guest safety and minimizing the legal liability of the hotel. Management should review these practices with staff on a monthly basis to ensure compliance.

1. Inspect and document the inspection of spa drain covers on a daily basis.
2. Post all spa policies signs in the language(s) of guests.
3. Install a thermometer and check the spa temperature frequently; recording your readings. A range not to exceed 102–105 degrees Fahrenheit (38.9–40.6 degrees Celsius) is recommended.
4. Display spa temperatures in a manner that is easily readable by guests.
5. Clearly mark the depths of the spa in both metric measures and feet/inches.
6. Do not allow the consumption of alcohol while using the spa.
7. Install non-slip flooring surfaces around the spa and provide stairs/ladders for entry and exit.
8. Prohibit spa use by children and non-guests.
9. Provide an emergency telephone in the spa area that rings directly either to the front desk or to 911 depending on the preference of the hotel's insurer.
10. Carefully document all activities related to spa maintenance, local ordinance compliance, and operating policy enforcement.

FIGURE 14.2   Spa Safety

Exercise Facilities

Many hotels offer their guests the use of a fitness center or exercise room. These areas typically contain a variety of types and kinds of exercise equipment. In most cases, these rooms are not staffed by the hotel on a full-time (or even part-time) basis. The rooms do, however, require regular attention. Hotel staff should pick up hazardous items (towels and weights, for example) that might litter the floor and cause falls, and they should monitor exercise equipment for malfunctions or breakage and remove any machine that is broken or unsafe.

Statistics provided by insurers indicate that treadmills are, by far, the most dangerous apparatus in an exercise room. Even an experienced user can slip, trip, or lose balance on a treadmill. Falls from treadmills can cause serious physical harm, including broken limbs, concussions, and other serious injuries. Accidents are not the only safety risk. Equipment can easily transmit bacteria and other germs. Hoteliers operating exercise facilities must do their best to create a safe exercise environment. One way to do so is by the use of posted signs.

Signs act as a constant reminder of the dangers inherent to exercise facilities. In general, signs can be classified into four types:

• *Policy Signs.* Signs stating rules and regulations involving the use of the facility.
• *Warning Signs.* Signs stating specific risks in an area of the facility or with a particular piece of equipment.
• *Directional Signs.* Signs indicating entrances, exits, fire evacuation plans, and other safety information.
• *Emergency Signs.* Signs indicating where various emergency items are stationed, such as fire extinguishers, first aid kits, and telephones.

Signs in the exercise room (as well as in other areas where safety communications are important) should be made of durable material that will hold up well. They should be use letters of a size that is easy to read from at least five feet to ten feet away. Signs should be printed in bright colors that will attract the reader's attention (signs with a white background and colored letters are the best) and should be placed from four feet to six feet from the floor for easy viewing. Computer printouts and handwritten signs can act as temporary or emergency communication devices but should be avoided in most cases.

Parking Areas

Many hotels have parking areas for guest vehicles. While hotels do not insure the vehicles parked in their lots, they are responsible for providing reasonable care in the protection of vehicles and guests using the lots. Figure 14.3 lists ten key practices that affect the safety of parking areas. They should be reviewed on a monthly basis to ensure compliance.

The hotel's manager on duty (MOD) sho uld be assigned, as part of his or her daily responsibilities to conduct a walk-around of the parking area as part of the hotel's overall safety and security program. This walk-around should be documented. Figure 14.4 is an example of a manager on duty checklist related to parking areas in a hotel.

Despite a hotel's best safety-related efforts, accidents can and will happen. When they do, an **incident report** should be prepared to document the "who, what, where, how" and the hotel's response to the accident or injury.

1. Inspect parking lot lighting on a daily basis. Arrange for replacement of burned-out lights immediately.
2. Inspect parking lot surfaces daily and arrange for pavement patches immediately if they threaten guest safety. Keep surfaces free of ice and snow in inclement weather.
3. Ensure that parking lot stripes and directional signs are easily seen to avoid pedestrian/ vehicle accidents.
4. Post easily readable signs in the parking lot reminding guests not to leave valuables in their vehicles.
5. If valet parking is provided, document the training of all drivers employed.
6. Require guests to identify their vehicles by license number or make/color upon check-in.
7. Keep landscaping around parking lots well trimmed to avoid dangerous areas that may provide hiding places for individuals who could threaten guest safety or property security.
8. If possible, arrange for regular and frequent parking lot drive-through patrols by local law enforcement officials.
9. Arrange for daily daytime and nighttime walk-through patrols by hotel staff.
10. Use a manager's daily log to document parking lot maintenance procedures.

FIGURE 14.3   Parking Lot Safety

LODGING LANGUAGE

Incident Report: A document prepared to record the details of an accident, injury, or disturbance and the hotel's response to it.

■

An incident report should be filled out whenever a guest or employee suffers an accident or injury (a safety-related event) as well as when there has been a loss or damage to property (a security-related event).

LODGING ON-LINE

For an excellent (and free) example of a hotel incident report, go to:

www.hospitalitylawyer.com

Then use the Search field and enter the words "Incident Report."

This site charges no fee and is an exceptional source of up-to-date information related to safety and security.

Other examples of safety-related documentation that should be maintained by the hotel include minutes from safety and security committee meetings, general staff meeting notes relevant to safety issues, records of employee training related to safety and security, and safety seminars attended or certifications acquired by employees.

PROTECTING PROPERTY FROM SECURITY THREATS

As you learned earlier in this chapter, safety-related programs are designed to keep people safe from harm, and security-related efforts are directed toward the protection of property from the threat of theft or damage. The safety of people is always more important than the security of property. Good hoteliers know, however, that

Best Sleep Hotel

Performed by: _____

Date of Inspection: _____ Time of Inspection: _____

To ensure the integrity of your walk-through, this checklist should be completed in sequence as it appears.

As appropriate, a check must be placed in the "yes" or "no" column to the right of this paper. If "no" is required, please indicate the problem in the "comments" section. If a work order is submitted, note the work order number in the "comments" section.

ITEM	YES	NO	COMMENTS
Outdoor parking lot is well-lighted.	❏	❏	
Outdoor parking lot is free of trash and debris.	❏	❏	
Painted stripes are easily seen and in good condition.	❏	❏	
Directional signs are posted in conspicuous locations.	❏	❏	
Lot is patrolled at irregular intervals.	❏	❏	
All entrance gates are locked after 8:00 p.m. with the exception of the main entrance.	❏	❏	
Emergency call boxes are located throughout the parking lot and are functioning properly.	❏	❏	
Closed circuit cameras function properly and send clear images to security.	❏	❏	
Gangs or vagrants are noticed.	❏	❏	
Cars are checked for length of stay; (note cars that are covered with tarp or excessive dirt).	❏	❏	
Security is aware of long-term stay automobiles.	❏	❏	
Correct percentage of Americans with Disabilities Act (ADA) parking is available and well-marked.	❏	❏	
Grass areas and bushes are well-maintained.	❏	❏	
Bushes and plants are trimmed and away from entrance doors.	❏	❏	
Walkways are well-lighted.	❏	❏	
Walkways are free of trip hazards	❏	❏	
Outside entrances are free of trash and debris	❏	❏	
All external doors leading to the inside are closed, locked and card accessible.	❏	❏	
Key card readers work properly at each entrance.	❏	❏	
All entrances are well-lighted.	❏	❏	
All entrances are secured.	❏	❏	
Directional signage at each entrance is compatible with ADA requirements.	❏	❏	
Outdoor ADA requirements are met regarding wheelchair ramps.	❏	❏	
Other:	❏	❏	
Other:	❏	❏	
Other:	❏	❏	

FIGURE 14.4   MOD Checklist for Parking Areas

they must use sound judgment and establish effective programs to protect the personal assets of guests as well as the assets of the hotel itself. Not to do so would be a disservice to the traveler and the hotel's owners.

Threats to the security of assets can come from individuals inside the hotel (internal threats) or outside the hotel (external threats). In both cases, these individuals seek to steal or damage property that rightfully belongs to the hotel's guests, employees, or owners. Effective hoteliers design, implement, and monitor security programs that reduce, to the greatest extent possible, the internal and external threats to asset

The Situation

RING!!!!!!! RING!!!!!!! RING!!!!!!! RING!!!!!!!

The telephone woke Dale Parrot, the front office manager at the Better Inn and Suites hotel, from a deep sleep. It was 3:00 a.m. on Sunday morning.

"Mr. Parrot," said Shingi Rukuni, the night auditor and only employee on duty at the hotel, "Room 219 is having a really loud party. I'm getting lots of guest complaints from rooms located near theirs."

"Did you call the room and ask them to hold it down?" asked Dale.

"Yes, I did," replied Shingi. "I called them at 10:00 p.m., when the party started, then again at 1:30 a.m., 2:15, and 2:45, when the complaints really started coming in. They just stop for a couple minutes, then start right up again. I think they're drunk. I don't know what to do next!"

A Response

Surprisingly, the problem in this case is *not* the noise coming from room 219. Unruly guests are a fact of life in most hotels. The auditor's uncertainty about what to do about it indicates a lack of training by the front office management staff or a lack of direction from the hotel's general manager. Whatever the hotel's policy toward unruly guests (number of specific warnings before the guest is asked to leave or is escorted off the property by local law enforcement officials), it should be documented, clearly communicated, and then followed. The comfort (and safety) of all the hotel's guests must be considered (as should the latitude to be allowed for "partiers") before the hotel's forced-removal policy is established.

security. In addition, hoteliers must know about the unique and specific threats to asset security that exist in individual hotel departments. It is not possible to eliminate all potential for property loss or damage. However, knowledge of specific lodging-industry threats to security, as well as implementation of activities developed to minimize the impact of these threats, can help hoteliers show evidence of the reasonable care the law requires them to demonstrate.

Internal Threats

Sometimes employees steal assets owned by guests or the hotel. When it is clear that an employee is involved in such activity, the response of management should be appropriate and, above all else, consistent. Some hotels include a phrase in their employee handbook warning that theft will be grounds for dismissal. When the theft or loss of property involves significant amounts of money, the hotel may pursue the filing of criminal charges against the employee. Regardless of the approach used, it should be applied equally to all employees and at all levels.

Consider what happens, for example, when a supervisor or manager involved in criminal activity is caught but then allowed to resign, while in the same hotel, an hourly employee caught in the same activity is fired and/or prosecuted. This would leave the hotel open to charges of discrimination or unfair labor practices against which it may be difficult to defend. It also sends the hotel's employees a mixed message about management's view of theft.

If the hotel wishes to communicate to employees that theft of all types will be dealt with swiftly and consistently, it must treat internal threats to property security just as seriously as the threats posed by non-employees. A hotel faces two basic types of internal asset threats: those related to cash and those related to other assets.

To Cash

In many cases, when hoteliers consider employee theft, they think of employees stealing money. **Embezzlement** is a potential problem in hotels, but using procedures and policies designed to prevent it can minimize its likelihood.

LODGING LANGUAGE

Embezzlement: The theft of a company's financial assets by an employee.

■

Some hotels are so concerned about employee theft that they **bond** employees who are in a position to embezzle funds.

LODGING LANGUAGE

Bond(ing): Purchasing an insurance policy to protect against the possibility that an employee will steal.

■

There are many ways that employees can defraud their employers of cash, and managers (as well as hotel owners) must stay current in the areas of cost- and revenue-control systems. Good financial controls based on solid control principles go a long way toward reducing employee theft. Of particular importance are controls related to cashiering positions, because cashiers can steal from the hotel in a variety of ways. Typical methods of **fraud** related to cashiering include:

- Charging guests for items not purchased, then keeping the overcharge.
- Changing the totals on credit card charges after the guest has left or imprinting additional credit card charges and pocketing the cash difference.
- Misadding legitimate charges to create a higher-than-appropriate total with the intent of keeping the overcharge.
- Purposely short-changing guests when giving back change and then removing the extra change from the cash drawer.
- Voiding legitimate sales as mistakes and keeping the cash amount of the legitimate sale.
- Charging higher-than-appropriate prices for hotel goods or services, recording the proper price, and then keeping the overcharge.

LODGING LANGUAGE

Fraud: The intentional use of deceit, trickery, or other dishonest methods to take another's money or property.

■

In addition to cashier theft that can affect the hotel or hotel guests, employees can steal cash in the accounts-payable area (by paying the hotel's bills in such a way as to funnel money to the embezzling employee) or the accounts-receivable area (by fraudulently diverting funds intended for the hotel to the embezzling employee). The responsibility for preventing the theft of hotel funds falls to the controller (or general manager) and each hotel department head involved in the handling of cash.

To Other Assets

Cash is not the only hotel asset that can be stolen by employees. In fact, the number and type of assets that can be unlawfully taken by employees is large. Those responsible for a hotel's asset security often find it helpful to create programs designed to protect the three non-cash assets most subject to employee theft. These three loss areas involve the stealing of time, company property, and services.

It may seem strange to consider time a hotel asset, yet it is the asset most easily taken by employees. In nearly all cases, employees are paid for their work by the hour or, as in the case of salaried individuals, by the week or month. In effect, the hotel is exchanging one asset (cash), for another (employee time). When an employee takes a hotel's cash but does not reciprocate by giving the hotel back the time agreed upon, the hotel loses. The theft of time can consist of employees fraudulently filling out time sheets or punching time cards. In some large hotels, particularly those with weak supervision programs, theft of time may result from employees simply disappearing for hours at a time with the result that work they should have performed is not completed.

The best way to prevent theft of time by employees is to have strong controls in place with regard to time cards. To help in this area, more and more hotels are issuing individual employee swipe cards to reduce the chances of one employee fraudulently checking (punching) another employee in or out.

Managers must be vigilant when considering plans to reduce employee theft that involves lack of productivity. This can be challenging, especially in large properties. Good supervision, however, and a realistic work load for each employee on a work schedule that is reviewed daily will help improve the hotel's ability to detect such theft.

Company property can disappear through the actions of employees as easily as through those of guests. In fact, employees usually know best which assets management has neglected to protect as well as it could. From food in a food storage area to zippered laundry bags in housekeeping, employees often find that the physical assets of a hotel are of a type they could use personally. That makes these items very susceptible to employee theft. The best approach to preventing the theft of company property involves:

- Carefully screening employees prior to hiring
- Reducing the chances for theft through the use of effective recodable locks, inventory systems, and other security measures
- Informing managers and employees of the penalty for theft
- Treating all proven cases of similar theft in a similar manner

It is unlikely, even with the best controls, that all employee theft in a hotel can be eliminated. There are simply too many opportunities for dishonest employees to take advantage of their access to the hotel's physical resources. Effective employee screening, however, and the creation of an environment that discourages stealing and consistently disciplines, terminates, or prosecutes employees for known cases of theft will help reduce the problem.

Some employees steal company property, and others steal services provided by the hotel. In many ways, this type of theft is even harder to detect than the theft of company property. For example, assume that a front office supervisor, working late at night, spends an hour or more per day making a long-distance call to his girlfriend who lives several states away. This inappropriate use of hotel assets will result in the hotel's incurring a larger-than-necessary long-distance telephone bill for the month (as well as experiencing the theft of time discussed earlier). This theft of services may go undetected unless someone at the property is monitoring the long-distance telephone bills generated by each administrative telephone extension number. In-room movies and games, telephone tolls, copy and faxing services are among the services susceptible to employee theft. Proper managerial controls must be in place to minimize, to the greatest degree possible, the chances for loss of hotel services.

External Threats

Since hotels are open 24/7, they are susceptible to asset threats any time of the day or night. Guests or non-guests can pose these threats. As is the case when protecting assets from threats posed by employees, hoteliers protecting hotel assets from the illegal activities of non-employees must be aware of, and guard against, threats to cash and non-cash assets.

To Cash

Nearly all hotels keep some money on the property at all times. Because that is true, and because some hotels are laid out in a way that offers thieves the chance to make a rapid getaway by automobile, hotel staff members can sometimes be confronted by armed or unarmed robbers. Preventing such robberies is best achieved by management working with the hotel staff and local law enforcement officials to identify and eliminate the opportunities for thieves to rob the hotel.

It is important for hoteliers to understand that a robbery is *not* an occasion to protect cash assets. A robbery is a time to protect staff! In the event of a robbery, the hotel staff member(s) involved should obey the robber's demands and make no movements that might be perceived by the robber as an attempt to stop the crime. Employees should do *nothing* to risk or jeopardize their lives. Employees can, of course, be trained to observe the robber carefully for the purpose of later recalling physical characteristics, such as height, weight, color and length of hair, color of eyes, mustaches or beards, tattoos, accents, or other identifying characteristics. During a robbery, complying with the robber's demands and observation of the robber should be the employee's only concern.

To help apprehend robbers, many managers install a contact alarm system in their cashier's cash drawers. This alarm is activated when a predetermined bill or packet of bills is removed from the cash drawer. The alarm is wired to summon local law enforcement officers trained to deal with robbery-in-progress situations. If no such alarm is in place, an employee who is robbed should, at the earliest safe opportunity, contact local law enforcement officials as well as others indicated in the robbery section of the hotel's emergency plan.

To Other Assets

Robbers steal from hotels, but so do guests. In fact, guests are much greater threats than robbers to the non-cash assets of hotels. Most often, the targets of guests are not cash but the products and services the hotel sells. Every experienced hotel manager has a "you won't believe this one" story about a guest who removed (or tried to remove!) a significant asset from a hotel illegally. From furniture and artwork to minor items such as towels, robes, and ashtrays, guest theft costs hotels millions of dollars annually in lost assets.

The reality for most guest theft, however, is that it is simply recognized as a cost of doing business. It makes little sense, for example, to accuse a guest of stealing a wooden clothes hanger (even if the hanger was, in fact, stolen by the guest) and then attempt to charge the guest for the item.

Some hotel managers place small signs in guest rooms offering to sell guests those items that frequently disappear. Other managers, in an effort to deter theft, word guest room signs in such a way as to imply that a room attendant will be held financially responsible for any loss of guest room items. Whether managers use these in-room signs (neither of which is recommended by the authors) or other less obtrusive approaches, guests and visitors to a hotel represent a significant threat to asset security. Therefore it is good business practice to take precautions designed to reduce theft. To that end, security-conscious hoteliers:

- Hang all artwork in lobbies and guest rooms with lockdown-style hangers
- Avoid placing valuable decorations and décor pieces in areas where guests can easily take them
- Train room attendants to alert management if excessive amounts of terry cloth products or in-room items are missing from stay-over rooms
- Bolt televisions and in-room computers securely to guest room furniture
- Train all employees to be alert regarding the loss of hotel property and to report any suspicious activity they encounter

It is important to remember that theft of services by guests can happen just as easily as the theft of physical assets, and proper controls must be in place to prevent these occurrences. Just as retail stores endure losses from shoplifters, hotels lose items to guest pilferage. However, retail stores and their hotel counterparts must diligently seek to limit the losses caused by shoplifters through the implementation of policies and procedures designed to reduce such losses.

Area-Specific Threats

Threats to a hotel's assets can occur at any time and in any department. Some departments, however, by the nature of their operation, are subject to specific security threats of which hoteliers should be especially aware. These include the front office, housekeeping, food and beverage, sales and marketing, and maintenance departments.

Front Office

In addition to the threats to cash posed by employee theft or robbery, the largest area of concern at the front desk is the fraudulent selling of rooms. Consider, for example, the night auditor who checks a guest into the hotel very late at night. The guest states that he or she only needs the room for a few hours to get some sleep before continuing on their travel. The auditor collects the guest's payment in cash at the time of check-in, but later reduces the day's room revenue by the same amount, stating that the guest was unhappy with the room, left early, and the guest's cash was refunded. Obviously, this could have happened. On the other hand, it is also possible that the guest stayed for the short time indicated at check-in and the auditor has defrauded the hotel of one night's room revenue.

Alternatively, assume that a front desk clerk simply gives the key to a vacant guest room to a friend or relative and collects no room revenue from that individual. The room, of course, must be cleaned the next day by the housekeeping staff. Again in this case, the hotel has been defrauded of its rightful room revenue. The hotel's managers must have systems in place that daily compare rooms cleaned with rooms sold to minimize the chances for employee fraud at the front desk.

Housekeeping

Managers in the housekeeping department must be aware of two distinctly different security issues. The first is the theft of housekeeping supplies, such as in-room amenities, towels, sheets, and the like. Thefts such as these can, of course, be committed either by guests or employees. While it is virtually impossible to stop all theft of minor amenities and in-room items, proper controls and systems should be in place to detect and respond to significant thefts of this type.

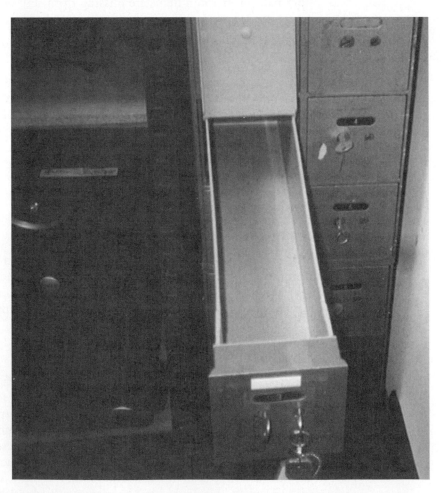

Guests should be encouraged to place valuables in in-room safes or safety-deposit boxes. (*Source:* Joshua D. Hayes)

The second and much more sensitive housekeeping issue involves theft from guest rooms by room attendants or other employees. When guests travel, they often keep valuables in their rooms. This is true despite the recommended use of safety-deposit boxes for such items.

When a guest claims that there has been a room theft, there are at least four possible scenarios:

1. The guest actually is honestly mistaken, and the item(s) reported stolen has simply been misplaced.
2. The guest is attempting to defraud the hotel.
3. The theft was committed, but by another hotel guest.
4. A hotel employee committed the theft.

Obviously, the management of the hotel must be very careful in such situations. If, upon inquiry, management believes a theft has in fact occurred, it is the best policy to report the incident to local law enforcement officials who are trained to investigate the crime.

Food and Beverage

Because food and beverage items can be consumed by virtually everyone, they are a common target for theft. Guests may take silverware and glassware as mementos of their stay, and employees may pilfer the same items for their own homes. More significantly, however, employees who purchase products for the food and beverage department may defraud the hotel by accepting kickbacks from vendors or by purchasing and then stealing food and beverage items intended for the hotel. It is in the development of systems and procedures to reduce the threat of this type of fraud that hotel managers must be extremely vigilant.

Sales and Marketing

Sales and marketing staff are frequently responsible for preventing fraudulent behavior directed at the hotel by unscrupulous individuals. Very often, this takes the form of outside parties billing the hotel for services that were not rendered or were not requested. Typically, this scam takes the form of an official-looking invoice arriving in the sales and marketing department by mail or fax. The invoice states that the hotel owes money for its listing in a published directory of hotels targeted toward a specific group, such as government employees. The invoice will also likely state that the hotel must pay promptly to avoid being dropped from the directory. In fact, however, the directory does not even exist. Those responsible for sending the invoice hope that the hotel will pay the invoice without investigation. This scam and others of a similar nature are common, and hotels that do not have sufficient control of their accounts-payable system may fall prey to them.

It may seem unusual to consider sales and marketing employees themselves as a source of fraud; however, due to the nature of their interaction with clients, threats to asset security do exist. Some of these threats take the form of irregularities with expense accounts. Misstating mileage traveled, clients entertained, or sales trips taken can cause the expense account expenditures of sales staff to be overstated, and as a result their reimbursements will be too high. To combat such potential problems, the hotel must have a good check-and-balance system that requires documentation of sales expenses and routine audits of reimbursements.

Maintenance

A unique problem in the maintenance department relates to the loss of small but sometimes expensive hand tools and supplies. It is important to remember that the types of items typically used in a hotel's repair shop are the same items employees and guests would use to do repairs in their own homes. Thus, portable hand drills, electric saws, wrenches, and the like can easily turn up missing if they are not carefully controlled.

It might seem as if this would be an easy problem to alleviate. In fact, taking an inventory of small hand tools like pliers or screwdrivers on a monthly basis is time-consuming and is often not done. When this is the case, dishonest employees know that they can take small items without much fear of detection. In addition, tools left at a worksite in the hotel during meals or other breaks can, if unsecured, be stolen by guests or others in the hotel. To prevent either of these problems, small hand tools should always be inventoried monthly to determine losses, if any. In addition, hand tools should never be left unattended in a public area of the hotel. The temptation for theft and potential for loss are too great. While it may inconvenience the department, the head of the maintenance department may consider requiring a **sign-in/ sign-out program** for all tools if regular inventories indicate that theft is a significant problem.

LODGING LANGUAGE

Sign-in, Sign-out Program: An arrangement in which individuals taking responsibility for hotel assets (such as hand tools, power equipment, or keys to secured areas) must document their responsibility by placing their signature as well as the date and time on a form developed to identify who last had possession of, and therefore responsibility for, the asset.

■

HOTEL CRISIS-MANAGEMENT PLANS

Hoteliers have the obvious responsibility of protecting employees, guests, and hotel visitors from harm while they are in the hotel and/or on the hotel's property. The best time to determine what procedures to use when a crisis occurs is before, not during, the crisis.

Hotel buildings and the people within them can be confronted with the same types of disasters as a people in any other type of buildingin a community. For example, regardless of where a property is located, potential emergencies include:

- Fires
- Bomb threats
- Robberies
- Explosions

HOTELS AND THE TERRORISM THREAT

The likelihood that a hotel will be terrorism target is small but increases with its size, location, symbolic importance, and other factors. Managers in all properties should be concerned about and reconsider security procedures so as to take practical steps to protect lives in the event of an intentional explosion, fire, or other disaster, possibly even including the use of biological or chemical weapons.

No hotel has an unlimited amount of money to spend on to guarding against a terrorist attack (and it is doubtful, in any case, whether such an attack can be totally prevented). What, then, are practical tactics that all hoteliers can use to address this concern? They include:

- The proper maintenance of existing security and safety equipment/procedures. For example, if surveillance equipment is in current use, it should be properly maintained: information about building-evacuation procedures should be an integral part of new employee training and of coaching activities applicable to longer-term staff members.
- An awareness of the property's potential vulnerability. As the possibility of a terrorist attack increases, so should the precautions taken to address it.
- Controlled access to non-public areas of the property. (Who comes in the back door? Where do they go?)
- The screening (background checks) of employee applicants in accordance with applicable laws.
- Management training that addresses information to yield an awareness of the terrorist threat, the importance of remaining diligent, and the need to be prepared and to keep emergency and disaster plans current.
- The use of practical building-safety tactics, such as plastic film affixed to windows, where applicable, to protect them from bursting and the arrangement of exterior planters that double as barriers in auto drive-up areas.

- Power blackouts

One relatively new and ever-present concern that affects everyone relates to terrorism, especially in the aftermath of the terrorist attacks of September 11, 2001.

Depending upon a hotel's specific location, other disasters may need to be planned for, including:

- Earthquakes
- Hurricanes
- Floods
- Tornados

Wise hoteliers have plans in place that detail what should be done if their property experiences an emergency and, as well, what they can do to help people who flee to their area to escape natural disasters in other locations. *Note:* consider, for example, the fall of 2004, when several hurricanes struck Florida within just a very few weeks. Hoteliers reduced room rates and did everything possible to accommodate as many guests as they could during these very difficult and trying times. No-pet policies were discontinued. (Shelters do not typically accept pets, and many pet owners would not go to shelters because of concern for their pets.) Temporary buffets were set up in properties that did not have electricity, employees slept in offices to provide more sleeping rooms for guests in need of accommodations, and Florida hoteliers were exemplary representatives of their profession in innumerable other ways as they practiced the art of genteel hostmanship.

Plans for managing a crisis should be developed by the hotel's top-level managers with input from other staff members as applicable. Representatives of insurance companies and local fire/police departments can also provide useful information. Large hotels typically have a security department whose personnel would be involved in implementing crisis plans. Managers of small, limited-service properties must include these responsibilities as an integral part of their jobs. Regardless of hotel size, however, plans must be in place that indicate, for every emergency that can reasonably be anticipated, what exactly must be done and who exactly is responsible for doing it.[1]

Since September 11, 2001, the U.S. Congress has enacted many bills related to homeland security. In some cases, these bills affect the hotel industry. It is likely that more hotel-related legislation involving fire safety, crisis planning, and the prevention of terrorist acts will be passed at the federal or even state level. As a result, professionals in the hotel industry should carefully monitor developments in these important areas.

CHAPTER OBJECTIVES REVIEW

If you have successfully studied the material in this chapter, you should be prepared to:

1. Recognize and state the importance of keeping hotel guests and employees safe. (Objective 1)
2. Identify a variety of internal and external resources available to help hoteliers meet their safety and security goals. (Objective 2)
3. Describe at least four special threats to safety that are unique to the hotel industry. (Objective 3)
4. Recognize and state the importance of ensuring property security. (Objective 4)
5. Identify internal, external, and area-specific threats to hotel security. (Objective 5)

[1]Readers desiring more information about crisis management are referred to David Hayes et al., *Front Office Operations: Managing the Hotel's Communication Center* (Upper Saddle River, N. J.: Pearson/Prentice-Hall, forthcoming).

LODGING LANGUAGE

Safety	OSHA	Premiums
Security	Recodable Locking System	Claim (Insurance)
Reasonable Care	Keycards	Incident Report
Damages	Internal Alarm	Embezzlement
Compensatory Damages	Contact Alarm	Bond(ing)
Punitive Damages	Closed-Circuit Television	Fraud
Threat Analysis	(CCTV)	Sign-in/Sign-out Program
Insurer	Emergency Plan	
Safety and Security Committee	Worker's Compensation	

FOR DISCUSSION

1. As we have seen, safety and security are the responsibility of all hotel employees. In some hotels, however, there is a security department with its own full- and part-time employees. List three factors that might cause the management of a hotel to employ security staff on a full-time basis.

2. Guest safety is a primary concern of all effective hotel managers. What steps can you take to ensure that all of the hotel's employees share your concern for guest safety? Identify at least three specific activities.

3. Material Safety Data Sheets are a valuable source of safety-related information for workers. In most cases, however, these documents are provided only in English and Spanish. Increasingly, the hotel industry employs individuals whose native language is neither of these. Assume that your hotel employs 25 such individuals speaking five different languages. How would you help ensure the safety of these workers with regard to handling chemicals and other toxic materials?

4. Good relations with local law enforcement officials are extremely helpful to a hotel. What are two specific activities the managers of a hotel can undertake to build positive relations with the local police?

5. Some hotel managers believe that uniformed security personnel in the hotel increase the comfort level of guests in the same manner as would uniformed police officers. Other managers feel that uniformed security personnel increase guests' concern about security and their own safety and thus have a net negative affect. If it were your decision, would you put your security force in police-style uniforms or uniforms that blend with your clientele? What factors would influence your decision-making?

6. Swimming pool safety is always a concern for hoteliers. Do you believe there should be a hotel policy putting a limit on the number of additional guests a registered guest should be allowed to invite to swim at a hotel pool, or should pools be reserved for registered guests only? What factors would influence your policy decision?

7. Good recordkeeping is an important part of a hotel's safety and security efforts. Identify three reasons why this is so.

8. Guests who are handicapped present special safety concerns for a hotel. This is especially true in times of emergency. What are some steps hoteliers can take to ensure that guests of this type are assisted in case of a hotel emergency, such as a fire or other situation requiring a forced evacuation.

9. Assume that your hotel's housekeeping department is experiencing periodic losses of products that you believe are due to employee theft. What specific steps would you, as the general manager, suggest to address this issue?

10. Pilferage of hotel assets by employees is common in the hotel industry. Would you recommend terminating a good employee proven to have pilfered a bar of soap from a room attendant's cart? Why?

TEAM ACTIVITIES

Team Activity 1

The text indicated that the three major areas of concern for hoteliers seeking to demonstrate that they exercise reasonable care are related to:

- The hotel's physical facilities
- The hotel's staff
- Policies and procedures implemented by the hotel

While all of these are important, which do you believe is *most* important? Why?

Team Activity 2

Terrorism and terrorist acts have become a real concern for hoteliers.
Read the following Associated Press release of 11/12/2003:

> *JAKARTA, Indonesia (AP Online)—Two of Asia's most wanted terrorists are armed with explosives and planning fresh attacks on Western hotels and banks—possibly disguising themselves as beggars and receiving shelter from fellow radicals, officials told The Associated Press.*

> *Malaysians Azahari bin Husin and Noordin Mohammed Top—both alleged leaders of the al-Qaeda-linked Southeast Asian terror network Jemaah Islamiyah and believed to have been key players in last year's Bali bombings that killed 202 people—are the target of a massive manhunt following their narrow escape from a police dragnet in the West Javanese city of Bandung on Oct. 31.*

Assume you are operating a hotel in major metropolitan area. What are three concrete actions you could employ to reduce the threat to your guests and property that would result from your hotel being targeted by terrorists?

15

Careers in the Lodging Industry

Chapter Objectives

1. To provide an overview of career-planning steps.
2. To discuss career considerations applicable to alternative types of lodging organizations.
3. To review fundamental tactics helpful in securing one's first professional position.
4. To explain tactics helpful in succeeding in one's first professional position.
5. To note why some hotel managers want to work for themselves (entrepreneurs) and some (intrapreneurs) desire to work for others.
6. To review opportunities in domestic and global hotel positions.

Chapter Outline

PLANNING PRECEDES CAREER DECISIONS
   Career-Planning Steps
   Assess Personal Interests
LODGING INDUSTRY CAREER ALTERNATIVES
   Independent Hotel or Multi-Unit Organization?
   Large or Small Hotel Company?
   Franchisor or Operating Company?
   Profit or Non-Profit?
OBTAINING THE FIRST PROFESSIONAL POSITION
   Collecting Information
   Important Concerns: Prospective Employers

   Important Concerns: Prospective Employees
SUCCESS IN YOUR FIRST PROFESSIONAL POSITION
   Success Tactics
   First Days on the Job
   Ongoing Professional Development
ENTREPRENEUR OR INTRAPRENEUR?
   Definitions
   Why Hotels Fail
   Tactics of Successful Intrapreneurs
DOMESTIC AND GLOBAL HOTEL POSITIONS
   Working in Another Country
   Success Factors in Global Assignments

Overview: Careers in the Lodging Industry

You have been studying about and, perhaps, working in the lodging industry. These initial experiences may have prompted you to think that a career in the lodging industry would be good for you. How do you plan a career that may last 40 years or longer? Fortunately, there are some basic principles and procedures which are useful in evaluating professional employment alternatives, and you will learn some of them in this chapter.

It will be exciting to accept your first professional position. Where do you obtain the information needed to make this important employment decision? What concerns will prospective employers have? What factors in the employer-selection process should be important to you? We will also answer these questions in this chapter.

After you have obtained your new professional position, it will be necessary to master a number of important competencies. What are they? The first days on the job will be critical, because you will be forming an impression of your new employer, and the organization you have chosen will be learning about you. At this point you will begin to realize what you need to know, and, as well, you are likely to discover that your learning will never end.

Do you want to work for yourself or for someone else? Do you want to work in this country or around the globe? We'll also address these issues in this chapter.

Your future will be exciting. You have already begun preparing for it, and your experiences after graduation will have a significant influence on your career. This chapter should be of extra-special interest to you, so let's begin.

PLANNING PRECEDES CAREER DECISIONS

Many people use a daily schedule to help keep them organized.[1] They prioritize important activities and pay attention to projects with deadlines. Activities can be added, deleted, or changed to help keep the schedule current. While nothing in the future is "cast in stone," schedule planners try to control or, at least, to influence it.

Career planning is similar, in many ways, to planning a daily schedule. The purpose is the same (to keep organized and to manage deadlines). Changes are made to keep the schedule (career plan) current as priorities change. Many things can affect a schedule or plan, but constant efforts are made to retain control over (or, at least, to influence) it.

The recognition that careers should be planned and not left to chance alone is a critical first step in efforts to do all you possibly can to control your professional future.

LODGING ON-LINE

Most, if not all, large hotel and other hospitality organizations have Web sites with an "employment opportunities" (or similar) section. Check out the sites of several organizations for which you might like to work and/or use the Web site addresses of organizations noted throughout this book. What types of positions are most frequently available? What kind of information about the organization is provided to help readers learn about the company?

---

[1]This chapter is loosely based on Chapters 30–34 in Jack Ninemeier and Joe Perdue, *Hospitality Operations: Careers in the World's Most Exciting Industry* (Upper Saddle River, N.J.: Pearson-Education, 2004).

Career-Planning Steps

An overview of the career-planning process is presented in Figure 15.1.

Recognizing the need for career planning is the first step noted above. This should be followed by exploring your personal interests, including skills, values, and even personality, and this analysis should drive the remainder of the career-planning process. Knowledge of as many employment alternatives as possible will help with the ultimate selection of the preferred industry (hospitality), segment (such as lodging), specific organization, and position for the first step in your career. After you have accepted an initial position, it is important to work effectively to attain the goals which prompted you to take the job. Figure 15.1 also illustrates that career progress should be continually evaluated, because the career-planning process evolves as ongoing alternatives are evaluated.

Enrolling in a hospitality management education program is an important first step in career planning. The courses you take, your internships, and your job experiences will all reinforce your initial decision to work in the industry. Then the career-planning priority shifts to issues concerning the desired segment, organization, and position. By contrast, others may be less certain about whether a career in hotels or even the hospitality industry is right for them. Fortunately, the process of answering questions such as "What do I want to do in the hotel industry?" or "In what industry do I wish to work?" utilizes many of the same decision-making elements.

Assess Personal Interests

How can you find a career you will really enjoy? The best way is to carefully consider what you like to do and then to find a career that permits you to do what you like to do.

Can you imagine professional athletes practicing many hours every day to become better at a sporting skill which is not of interest to them? Or how about a chef developing new recipes or a hotel's general manager making important decisions

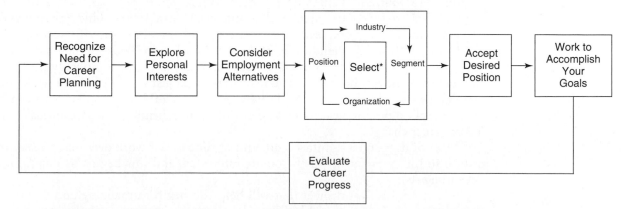

*Note: The process of selecting the area of work is *not* sequential (first industry, then segment, then organization, then position). Rather, it is simultaneous; one considers each of these factors in a personal order of preference. One person, for example, may think first of a position (general manager) and then consider the industry, segment, and organization. Another person may think first about segment (hotel) and then consider the organization and/or the position.

FIGURE 15.1   Steps in Career Planning

Second interviews provide additional opportunities for prospective employers to meet with prospective employees.

about many challenges and opportunities every day? There may be some athletes, chefs, and general managers who do not like what they do. However, their counterparts who continually find pride and joy in their work will be much happier in the part of their life where they will be spending a significant amount of time.

Figure 15.2 summarizes the importance of finding fulfillment on the job. Look at it and ask yourself, "Which do I prefer?" When you have a passion for your job, there is likely to be contentment and an interest in succeeding. This typically yields success in the position and leads to a rewarding career and increased job satisfaction.

Contrast this with the attitude of people doing a job "because they have to." If you have no interest in or, even worse, dislike your job, you will probably not be interested in it and not do it well. You may attempt to just get by by meeting minimal expectations, an attitude which will surely lead to an unfulfilling career. This can become a cyclical process leading to further dislike and disinterest and, eventually, to a job or career change.

Most of us spend a significant amount of time in our work over many years. It is critical to find a career in which you are interested, and this begins by determining your interests.

Figure 15.3 is a worksheet that will help you begin formalizing and organizing thoughts about your personal interests. It allows you to list the things you do well and to consider how your skills, strengths, knowledge, aptitudes, values, and interests have helped you to do well. Emphasizing strengths and identifying personal attributes which complement them is an important tactic to use when planning a career.

This is the lobby of a beautiful hotel. However, recall that you will often be working behind the scenes, where guests do not go.

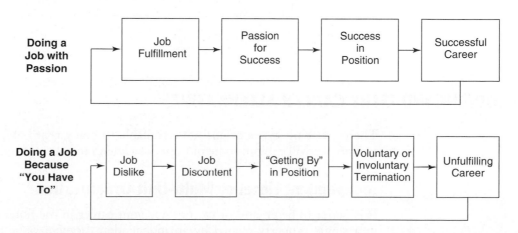

FIGURE 15.2   Find Fulfillment on the Job

PART I

List those things you do well (your strengths):

1. _____

2. _____

3. _____

PART II

Personal Attributes (Characteristics)	How Does This Attribute Help You to Do Well?
What are your greatest skills?	
What are your greatest strengths?	
About what do you have the greatest knowledge?	
For what do you have the greatest aptitudes (natural abilities)?	
What things in life do you most highly value?	
What are your interests? (What do you most like to do?)	

FIGURE 15.3 What Are Your Personal Interests?

LODGING INDUSTRY CAREER ALTERNATIVES

There are many types of positions available in many types of organizations. In this section, we will explore some of these jobs which may be of interest to you.

Independent Hotel or Multi-Unit Organization?

Is it better to begin and/or to continue your career in the hotel industry by working in a single property owned by an independent hotelier or, conversely, by working with a multi-unit hotel organization, such as a contract management company or a

PROFESSIONAL PERCEPTIONS MAY NOT BE REALITY!

Many hospitality students indicate that they are "people persons" and state that this is what excites them about the industry. They want to work in organizations that serve people (guests) and that need people (staff members) to serve them. However, there are many parts of a hotel manager's job that do not relate to people. These include activities relating to financial planning, laws and regulations, insurance and risk management, and technology, to name just a few. If working with people is the highest-priority factor in your career-selection decision, there are some positions in the hotel industry that may not be right for you.

Another stereotype involves thinking about the industry relative to starched white tablecloths and beautiful table appointments (in hotel restaurants) and beautiful atriums and other architectural wonders (in the lobbies of hotels). These amenities are designed into the environment so that guests can enjoy them. However, much of your work will be behind the scenes in offices that look like any other and/or in kitchens, laundry rooms, and other work areas where the environment is usually much less beautiful. As well, you are likely to spend time in corridors, parking lots, meeting rooms, and numerous other spaces as you "manage by walking around."

The hotel industry can be a great business for people who enjoy it. If you learn as much as you can about it before making your employment decisions, your decisions will be good ones.

---

brand organization with company-operated properties? Not surprisingly, the answer is "It depends," and the primary consideration is you and your personal interests.

In this section, we will review a case study of Contina and Ellis as they evaluate the type of employer for whom they want to work. They are both about to graduate from a two-year community college program located in the suburbs of a large city and are interested in the hotel industry. Both have thoughts about the factors that may impact their employment decisions:

Factor	Contina	Ellis
Preferred location	Local area	Anywhere; no preference
Additional hospitality education	No (not now)	Maybe
Good on-job technical training	Yes	Yes
Career which will always have day-to-day operating responsibilities	Yes	No
Access to technical help when working through decisions	No (wants to be "in charge")	Yes (concerned about the impact of a bad decision)
Desired job flexibility	Wants to grow within a position	Wants to "keep options open"
Compensation (salary and benefits)	"Better-than-average"	"Better-than-average"

Let's see what Contina and Ellis think about each factor and use their viewpoints to help them focus on a specific type of hotel employer.

- *Preferred Location.* Contina will probably discover there are several hotels in her metropolitan area that are operated by independents and national, regional, or even local contract management companies. The availability of positions in the area is important because she does not want to relocate. Ellis has no preference about where he goes after graduation. He likes his community but has also traveled enough to know that there are many places around the country where he would enjoy living and working.

- *Additional Hospitality Education.* Both Contina and Ellis recognize the need to become proficient in their first job before exploring the possibilities of additional hospitality education. Contina does not desire further hospitality education now; she may take some classes later. Ellis is potentially interested in additional education sometime. He knows about traditional **distance learning courses** and electronic learning alternatives to continue his education. However, he would like to live and work in a community where a **residential education program** is available.

LODGING LANGUAGE

Distance Learning Courses: Formal education (training) programs that are available to students/trainees in remote locations.

Residential Education Programs: Formal education (training) programs that are available to students/trainees at a specific geographic location.

■

- *Good On-Job Technical Training.* Both Contina and Ellis recognize the need for good technical training in their new position to supplement the very useful and practical knowledge learned in their formal education.

- *Operating Responsibilities.* Contina thinks she would like a job with day-to-day managerial responsibilities involving guests and employees. Ellis knows that he will need to spend several (or more) years in a career of progressively more responsible operating duties. However, at some point he wants to be more removed from the day-to-day operations.

- *Access to Technical Help.* Contina is a "take charge" person who will know when she needs technical help (for example, to improve a guest check-in or housekeeping procedure). She wants a position where she can be fully responsible and accountable. Ellis also likes to make decisions. However, he would like to get all available information from all possible sources before making high-priority decisions.

- *Job Flexibility.* Contina wants to find the right organization, be promoted within it, and enjoy the more structured routine it provides. Ellis wants to keep his options open. A different position in a new organization located in a different city would be a challenge he might accept.

- *Fair Compensation.* Both Contina and Ellis want fair compensation based upon the value they bring to their employer.

Let's consider what we have learned about Contina and Ellis to consider whether an independent or multi-unit hotel organization might be best for them. Figure 15.4 identifies some of the pros and cons of positions in these organizations relative to the factors just discussed.

	Independent Hotel	Multi-Unit Hotel Organization
• Preferred Location	Independent hotels are typically located in only one area.	A multi-unit hotel organization typically has properties in numerous locations.
• Additional Hospitality Education	Must determine whether tuition is a fringe benefit; if residential education is desired, the hotel must be located near a school/college campus.	Large multi unit hotel companies provide educational benefits; if residential hospitality education is desired, it may be possible to transfer to a desired location.
• Wants Good On-Job Technical Training	Training quality depends upon programs established by the hotel and, perhaps, upon whether unforeseen problems arise which reduce training time.	Large multi-unit organizations have structured training programs and resources and may be able to train new employees in units with different challenges.
• Career with Day-to-Day Operating Responsibilities	Top-level managerial positions in independent hotels have daily operating responsibilities.	Higher-level managerial positions often involve multi-unit responsibilities, these managers supervise other managers who are responsible for day-to-day operations in specific hotels.
• Access to Technical Help	The manager in an independent hotel is the "expert." It is only when specialized expertise is needed that external (consulting) help is solicited.	Large multi-unit hotel companies have headquarters-level specialists in many areas of operations that can help managers in individual hotels.
• Job Flexibility (position responsibility)	A career in an independent hotel means working in the same location and building.	A career in numerous locations and in many types of hotel properties is possible.
• Compensation (salary and benefits)	Compensation (starting pay) is typically slightly less than that paid by a multi-unit hotel company.	Compensation (starting pay) from a multi-unit hotel company is typically slightly higher than in independent hotels.

FIGURE 15.4   Pros and Cons of Positions in Independent and Multi-Unit Hotel Organizations

Let's see how Contina and Ellis might personally evaluate the factors in Figure 15.4:

- *Preferred Location.* Employment with an independent hotel dictates the location of employment. Those who desire geographic moves may prefer a contract management company.

- *Additional Hospitality Education.* Tuition assistance is a benefit offered by many independent and multi-unit hotel companies. If a traditional education on a campus is desired, the independent hotel must be close to the campus. By contrast, a multi-unit hotel company has numerous locations.

- *On-Job Technical Training.* The quality of initial orientation and training in an independent hotel depends upon the property. Most multi-unit hotel companies provide structured training and educational opportunities for new managers.

- *Day-to-Day Responsibilities.* Managers in most independent hotels have day-to-day operating responsibilities. Top-level managers are either directly responsible for or supervise managers with direct operating concerns. Higher-level managers in multi-unit hotel companies may supervise hotel managers who, in turn, are responsible for daily operating activities in their properties. While there are many challenges and some stress in all hotel positions, many believe that those who are "one step away from the firing line" (field rather than unit managers) are in preferred positions.

- *Technical Help.* The independent hotel manager is the property's expert on all of the highly specialized and technical fields applicable to property management. By contrast, unit managers in multi-unit companies often have external technical expertise available that can provide additional assistance.
- *Job Flexibility (position responsibility).* Managers with multi-unit hotel companies often have more flexibility in position, industry segment, and location compared to their independent property counterparts.
- *Compensation.* Independent and multi-unit hotel companies are concerned about compensation and recognize it to be an important recruitment incentive. Thus pay for beginning managerial positions must be competitive. However, with exceptions, managers in upper-level positions tend to receive higher compensation in multi-unit organizations because their responsibilities, measured in terms of dollars of business volume, are greater than for their counterparts in independent hotels.

While there are many factors to consider (and we have noted only some of the most important ones in the preceding discussion), it appears that Contina will want to pursue a position with an independent hotel, whereas Ellis will probably seek an initial career position with a multi-unit hotel organization.

Large or Small Hotel Company?

What are the pros and cons of managing in a large or small hotel company?

The advantages to accepting a management position with a large hotel company include:

- *Greater opportunities to advance and relocate.* It may even be possible to transfer to other locations worldwide.
- *Prestige associated with a name.* Large organizations are often better known than their smaller counterparts.
- *Less employment risk.* Many people believe there is greater job security within a larger company.
- *Compensation and benefits.* Managers in larger organizations generally earn more.
- *Legal protection.* Larger companies may provide employees with greater job security because of adherence to written policies and procedures that may include the right to appeal arbitrary decisions related to termination.
- *OSHA and other regulations.* Employees at large companies will be protected by a variety of federal, state, and local regulations.
- *Training.* The training offered in larger Hotel companies is often more structured and effective and is enhanced by dollars allocated specifically for training purposes.

Possible disadvantages to managing in large hotel companies may include:

- *Less control over one's work.* Strategies may be set for the whole organization, and employees may have fewer opportunities to contribute ideas.
- *Anonymity.* Some people believe that they are just a number in a larger organization. (This is similar to how some students feel about colleges or universities with large enrollments.)
- *Less access to senior executives.* When you work for a large organization, you may rarely see the general manager and never see the owners.

There are potential advantages to a managerial position with small hotel companies, such as one owned by an independent with several properties or a management company with just a few accounts in a local or regional area.

- Employees know each other, and there can be a sense of teamwork which may be less common in large companies.
- Employees have a greater variety of duties. They often have more control over their work and can make a greater contribution to the company's short- and long-term strategies.
- Executives in small companies tend to be approachable and available to all employees.
- Employees may have more responsibility, not limited by their job title or job description.
- More company-wide involvement. One is more likely to be involved in the entire organization rather than in a specific department or property.
- Less bureaucracy (rules and regulations).
- The best small companies do not always stay small. Small organizations offer the potential of a job that can grow as the company grows and the chance to be part of building a business.

Disadvantages of management positions in small companies can include:

- Limited benefits. Many small companies do not offer the same benefits as larger organizations.
- Smaller hotel companies often provide less training, and structured training programs are relatively rare.
- Fewer opportunities for promotion. There are, by definition, fewer positions in small companies, which limits one's advancement.

In the United States, most new job growth comes from small businesses. The hotel and hospitality industry readily lends itself to entrepreneurs beginning a new business and enjoying the success that it brings. (We will discuss the world of hospitality entrepreneurs later in this chapter.)

Franchisor or Operating Company?

What are the employment opportunities available from franchisors? As you learned in Chapter 2, franchisors do not usually operate hotels. Franchise companies, however, employ many hospitality professionals. These jobs are often highly paid and are exciting. Among the varied employment opportunities offered by franchisors are positions in:

- *Franchise Sales.* One of the most important positions in a franchise company is that of franchise sales representative. These individuals work with hotel developers, seeking to persuade them to build hotels with the brand name they represent. They also work with the owners of existing hotels to convert these hotels to the brand(s) represented by the salesperson. Franchise sales staff may represent one or more of the franchisor's hotel brands and may oversee regions as small as one state or as large as the entire country. In addition, because many brands are franchised outside of the United States, the opportunity exists for international sales positions.

- *Field Support.* Each franchisor offers consultative support to its franchisees. The franchise services director (FSD) represents the franchisor at the individual hotel level. This person serves an important role as an on-site sales and operations adviser and helper. He or she would normally visit each hotel within the area of responsibility one or more times per month. While employed by the franchisor, the best services directors are strongly committed to the success of the franchisees in their assigned territories, and are knowledgeable and able to provide a real service to those who operate hotels.

- *Marketing Services.* Hotel owners look to their franchise company for assistance in selling hotel rooms. This is the primary responsibility of a franchisor's marketing services department. From designing and implementing national advertising to advising an individual hotelier about a Web site design, employees working in this area of a franchise company are creative, talented marketing specialists. Not surprisingly, these corporate jobs are among a franchisor's highest-paying and most visible ones.

- *Reservation Data Management.* Managing the data required to operate a franchise company is an almost overwhelming task. With thousands of hotels, offering hundreds of different room types at dozens of different rate structures, simply keeping track of which hotel is selling what room at what price is a complex endeavor. Yet, this must be done and done well if rooms are to be marketed over the many distribution channels offering hotel rooms for sale (for example, the Internet, toll-free call centers, and the individual property). The data management department of a franchisor is inevitably very large, and it seeks talented individuals who are detail-oriented. These positions are normally based at a franchisor's corporate headquarters and provide an excellent opportunity for career growth.

- *Training Services.* The top franchisors know that it is in their own best interest to have highly trained staff members working in their branded properties. As a result, each franchisor employs a group responsible for providing this training. These professionals design and deliver training in the form of seminars and workshop sessions. The sessions are held around the country to maximize the number of attendees. The instructors who conduct the franchisor-sponsored seminars and training sessions are among the hotel industry's brightest and most outgoing individuals.

Large franchisors such as Cendant, Hilton, Marriott, Choice Hotels, Best Western, and US Franchise Systems provide individual hoteliers with opportunities for real career growth, even though their employees will not manage hotels. While there are only a few large franchise companies, they all maintain national offices as well as regional offices that must be staffed with skilled employees.

Employees of companies that actually operate franchised hotels will find that they interact often with representatives from the franchise company. In most cases these interactions are positive, but even in the hotel business there are inevitably areas of potential conflict between a franchisor and its franchisees. Franchisors and those working for them provide guidance and assistance to hotel operators, but do not assume financial responsibility for the operating results of franchisees. Interestingly, this is one of the greatest advantages as well as disadvantages of seeking employment with a hotel franchise company.

Profit or Non-Profit?

While the majority of students will go to work in the private or for-profit sector of the lodging industry, there are many hospitality-related jobs in the non-profit sector. Positions in non-profit organizations have traditionally paid less than their for-profit counterparts. Alternatively, however, the non-profit sector has been noted for its job stability and benefit packages as well as the sense of personal achievement many of its jobs provide.

What types of non-profit organizations hire hoteliers? The following partial list will help you understand why individuals with training in the lodging industry are highly valued by non-profit organizations.

- *Convention and Visitors Bureaus.* As you learned in Chapter 8, the goal of a convention and visitors bureau (CVB) is to promote travel to the geographic area represented by the bureau. Review the sample position announcement for a "special events manager" taken from the International Association of Convention and Visitor Bureaus job posting board. Note that the skills needed in this typical position are the same, in many respects, as those required by effective hoteliers. In addition, a thorough knowledge of how the lodging industry works gives CVB staff members an extra edge over bureau employees who do not have a lodging background.

Special Events Manager—[Listed 3/15/2004]
Mammoth Lakes Visitors Bureau

Responsibilities:	Design, plan, and execute the development of new annual events in predetermined designated time periods, concentrating on increasing lodging occupancy percentages in the shoulder seasons. Works with Tourism and Recreation Commission on policy making for department. Establishes and maintains effective working relationships with co-workers, associates, lodging facilities, food and beverage establishments, event venues, stakeholders, and all vendors and suppliers.
Qualifications:	Bachelor's degree and/or equivalent experience. Must have a proven track record of coordinating special events. Effective negotiating skills and superior interpersonal and communication skills.
Compensation:	$44,805–$60,043 annually, negotiable.
Contact:	Mark Bellinger
	Mammoth Lakes Visitors Bureau
	P.O. Box 48
	Mammoth Lakes, CA 93546
	xxx-xxx-xxxx (phone)
	888-GO-MAMMOTH (alt. phone)
	760-934-7066 (fax)
	http://www.visitmammoth.com

- *Chambers of Commerce.* Chambers of commerce, like convention and visitors bureaus, seek to advance the interests of their geographic areas. While CVBs promote tourism, chambers promote their areas as good places to establish and grow businesses. To do so, chambers employee a variety of skilled staff members, including people with a solid understanding of the hospitality industry. These individuals plan and execute special events, may be involved in charitable fund-raising, and use their business skills to help others in the local business community prosper.

- *Association Meeting Planner.* There are over 34,000 trade, professional, charitable, and other non-profit associations in the United States alone. The category of association dictates, in many ways, the goals of the association. Nearly all associations, however, meet on a local, regional, and/or national basis. These meetings may be held to disseminate information, provide training, or simply serve the social interests of the association's membership. For nearly all the meetings held, a representative from the association will secure sleeping rooms, meeting space, and meals from the hoteliers in the location where the meeting will be held. Clearly, a good understanding of how hotels operate provides these professional meeting planners with many of the tools required to be successful in their jobs.

LODGING ON-LINE

The American Society of Association Executives (ASAE) is the professional association for those who manage associations. They provide their members with a variety of services, including information related to job openings. Visit the ASAE Web site at

www.ASAEnet.org

When you arrive, click on "Career Headquarters," then select "Careers in Associations." You will be directed to a job-posting site. Enter the search terms "Meeting and Planning" to see the many meetings planner positions available.

OBTAINING THE FIRST PROFESSIONAL POSITION

Assume you have decided to begin your career in the hotel industry. Where should you start your job search? There are many sources of information about hotel companies where you can obtain background information about potential employers. In addition, you should know about concerns that prospective employers have as they recruit job applicants. You will also have concerns. These are the topics of this section.

Collecting Information

You should obtain as much information as possible about hotel employers for which you might want to work. Methods to do so include:

- *Networking.* There are numerous ways to gain contacts that can provide information about possible hotel employers. Talk with:
  - *Classmates.* Some of your peers may have worked for companies as they completed internships and/or to earn money while in school.

- *Faculty members.* The faculty who teach hospitality-related courses probably have numerous contacts (their own networks) that can help with your job search.
- *Campus recruiters.* Representatives of hotel companies may visit schools and participate in **career fairs** sponsored by educational institutions.
- *School alumni.* Graduates of your school may hold positions in companies in which you are interested.
- *Your family and friends.* In many cases, this is the best source of information about potential employers.

LODGING LANGUAGE

Career Fairs: Trade show–type events which allow prospective job applicants to meet recruiters representing numerous employers in one location during a specified time period.

■

- *Research.* Your own study of the following can help:
  - *The Internet.* Most hotel organizations have Web sites that provide information about their company; increasingly, they also have an "employment opportunities" section on the site. Professional and trade associations also feature employer information and job boards.
  - *Trade publications.* Numerous trade magazines feature articles about current events, prominent organizations, and related information about the hotel industry.
  - *Organization-specific information.* Some companies especially multi-unit lodging companies, have printed information available that reviews important employment information.

LODGING ON-LINE

All of the large-circulation trade journals applicable to the hotel industry have Web sites; here are several:

AAHOA Lodging Business:	www.AAHOA.com
Hotel & Motel Management:	www.hotelmotel.com
Hotel Business	www.hotelbusiness.com
Hotels:	www.hotelsmag.com
Lodging Magazine:	www.lodgingmagazine.com

Check out these Web sites. While reviewing them, note general information that might be helpful when making employment decisions. Also look for employment opportunities advertised on these sites.

- *Other written information.* Annual reports from hotel organizations, recruitment and other brochures, and class handout information can help you learn about prospective employers.
- *Career centers.* Some colleges/universities offer resources to help students learn about prospective employers. They may have written information and may also compile invaluable feedback about positions accepted by past graduates.

WHAT'S THIS ABOUT A STARTING POSITION?

Many students begin their hospitality career as management trainees. They rotate through a planned sequence of positions and begin to master a set of skills that their employer believes are necessary for them to become a manager. They learn basics about responsibilities and tasks in various positions in each department. They also begin to learn about the organizational culture, the relationship of each department to the others, and the managerial challenges and operating procedures of each department.

Many students negotiate an agreement before employment that states they will begin working in a mutually agreeable position after successful completion of the management training program. This will be the beginning of a career track that will take them, at least initially, up the ladder within the organization.

Some students, especially those who have completed internships and/or who have work experience with an employer, may not need to participate in this rotating management training (or, at least, it might be shortened). They can, instead, move more directly and quickly into the managerial position they have negotiated.

Important Concerns: Prospective Employers

Hotel employers look for managers who can "think outside of the box" and have flexible skills. Preferred candidates will possess:

- effective communication skills
- computer aptitude
- leadership and organizational traits
- teamwork abilities
- interpersonal (between-people) skills
- personal accountability
- enthusiasm (enthusiastic personality)
- problem-solving/decision-making skills

ALL IN A DAY'S WORK

The Situation

Recruiters working for hotel organizations typically mention several tactics that hospitality students should avoid as they search for a professional position. These include:

- Developing an overly detailed resume
- Sending a resume to an organization without first learning as much as possible about it
- Being dishonest and/or overstating their experience
- Applying for a management position at a property that is part of a multi-unit or-

ganization without determining whether the resume should be sent to a human resources official at corporate headquarters

A Response

Tactics which should be used when searching for a professional position include:

- Develop a well-prepared resume using facts that will interest prospective employers and sell oneself
- Get to know recruiters representing organizations in which you are inter-

ested. Ask questions and recall that a recruiter can be a good mentor

- Don't utilize a search firm to distribute the resume. E-mail your resume directly to recruiters. (Do your homework; research the company's Web site, and you can probably learn the official's name/Web address.)
- Practice interviewing (and then practice some more!).

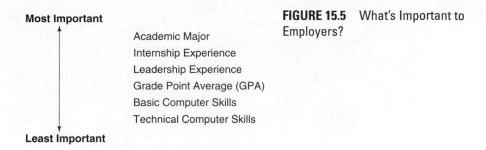

Most Important

Academic Major
Internship Experience
Leadership Experience
Grade Point Average (GPA)
Basic Computer Skills
Technical Computer Skills

Least Important

FIGURE 15.5   What's Important to Employers?

Employers typically state their desire for a total package of knowledge, skills, and aptitudes. They mention critical thinking, intelligence, common sense, and a willingness to learn quickly and continuously. Figure 15.5 shows a ranking of key candidate characteristics which are important to many employers.

Note: These characteristics were suggested by employers responding to a generic survey not focused directly on hospitality. Many in the hospitality industry would agree, however, that one's academic major, leadership (effective use of interpersonal and communication skills), and a basic grasp of technology are very important. They would likewise agree that grade point average (GPA), while somewhat important, is not as important as several of the factors just noted.

Important Concerns: Prospective Employees

Now that you have learned something about the factors that will likely be of concern to employers, let's review some issues that should concern you as a prospective employee.

There are numerous factors to consider as you evaluate professional employment alternatives. Figure 15.6 presents a checklist for assessing employment alternatives that identifies basic concerns likely to be important to you as you consider lodging industry alternatives.

SUCCESS IN THE FIRST PROFESSIONAL POSITION

Your first professional position! The years spent in formal education, the part-time jobs, and the internships are now completed. Most important, you have made important **permanent placement** decisions about the hospitality industry segment, the organization, and the position to begin your career.

LODGING LANGUAGE

Permanent Placement: The first full-time position a student assumes after graduation from a post-secondary school.

■

What's next? The rest of your life—much of which will be spent working. The time to begin thinking about your professional career is now, and many of your thoughts should relate to your first position. In this section, we will discuss success

FACTOR	IMPORTANCE TO ME			
	SIGNIFICANT	VERY	SOMEWHAT	NONE
General				
Relevance of your education	❏	❏	❏	❏
Location	❏	❏	❏	❏
Physical demands	❏	❏	❏	❏
Your aptitude to do required work	❏	❏	❏	❏
Total compensation	❏	❏	❏	❏
Your interest in doing the work	❏	❏	❏	❏
Future of organization	❏	❏	❏	❏
Daily work hours	❏	❏	❏	❏
Weekly work hours	❏	❏	❏	❏
Workplace environment	❏	❏	❏	❏
Location				
Cost of living	❏	❏	❏	❏
Friends/family	❏	❏	❏	❏
Moving expenses	❏	❏	❏	❏
Recreational opportunities	❏	❏	❏	❏
Travel requirements	❏	❏	❏	❏
Position				
Level of responsibility	❏	❏	❏	❏
Quality of training	❏	❏	❏	❏
Challenges	❏	❏	❏	❏
Mentor available	❏	❏	❏	❏
Advancement	❏	❏	❏	❏
Transfer of knowledge/skills to other positions	❏	❏	❏	❏
Company				
Culture	❏	❏	❏	❏
Reputation	❏	❏	❏	❏
Mission	❏	❏	❏	❏
Job security	❏	❏	❏	❏
Management quality	❏	❏	❏	❏
Support for additional education	❏	❏	❏	❏
Compensation				
Salary	❏	❏	❏	❏
Bonus	❏	❏	❏	❏
Health insurance	❏	❏	❏	❏
Life insurance	❏	❏	❏	❏
Vacations/holidays	❏	❏	❏	❏
Sick leave	❏	❏	❏	❏
Pension	❏	❏	❏	❏
Retirement	❏	❏	❏	❏
Profit-sharing	❏	❏	❏	❏
Overtime	❏	❏	❏	❏
Stock options	❏	❏	❏	❏
Pre-tax accounts (health and child care)	❏	❏	❏	❏
Relocation expenses	❏	❏	❏	❏

FIGURE 15.6 Checklist for Evaluating Employment Alternatives

tactics helpful during your first days on the job and the need for ongoing professional development.

Success Tactics

Many hospitality management graduates begin their careers in a management training program. The best training programs identify the **competencies** to be learned, and job descriptions (see Chapter 6) will be available to indicate the tasks a trainee must know and be able to do in the position assigned after the training is completed.

These students have graduated and are ready to go to work full time.

Hotel managers, from entry-level supervisors to those at the highest organizational level, must effectively use basic on-the-job competencies. While the specifics vary by position, Figure 15.7 identifies and provides examples of some basic management competencies. The hospitality industry is a people business; note the emphasis on people with competencies relating to interaction with others, effective communication, and understanding organizations (which, of course, are made up of people). Note also the emphasis on basic managerial competencies, including those relating to making decisions, using technology, managing resources, and utilizing information. Finally, a manager must have appropriate personal qualities to be effective. This is increasingly gaining importance as managers serve more as team leaders and less as people who are simply bossing others around.

Figure 15.8 further illustrates the importance of human relations competencies. Note that supervisors require significant technical skills, while their top-level manager counterparts utilize more conceptual skills. However, human relations skills are an integral part of the job of managers at any organizational level.

First Days on the Job

You have been employed to add value to the organization. What you provide should be worth more to the company than what it must pay for your services. It is your output (work performance), not your input (education and years of experience), that is most important to your employer.

Competency	Example
• Interact with others	• Facilitate the work of employees; interact with guests
• Effective communicator	• Write letters and memos; speak in public; talk with employees, peers, bosses, and guests
• Make decisions	• Solve problems; think creatively; analyze alternatives
• Use technology	• Apply technology to collect/analyze information and to communicate with others
• Manage resources	• Maximize the use of limited resources to attain objectives
• Understand organizations	• Know and use information about how business, social, and political systems work
• Utilize information	• Collect, organize, and study necessary data as needed for effective management
• Basic skills	• Read, write, speak, listen, and use mathematics and science-related abilities
• Personal qualities	• Integrity, time- and self-management, social skills, and respect for oneself and others

FIGURE 15.7   Basic On-Job Management Competencies

You can use a wide range of tactics to help you begin the right relationship with your employer. The good news is that the same tactics should be consistently applied in all positions throughout your career:

- Dress the way you are expected to dress. If there is a uniform requirement, comply with it. (Remember that a clean and pressed uniform will help with your professional attitude.) Managerial positions often require professional business attire that you must provide. Begin to invest in good-quality conservative attire so that you can develop a professional wardrobe over time.

- Develop a system that will help you remember the names of those you meet. You may need to write names down, or perhaps you can use a system which helps you relate a name to something else. Whatever method(s) you choose, the ability to recall the names of those you meet is an important skill.

- Observe your own supervisor and others who are successful in the company. What do they seem to have in common? What can you learn from them to

FIGURE 15.8   Human Relations Competencies Are Important

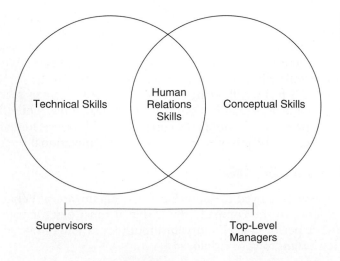

help in your own performance? If it is someone you admire, consider asking him or her to serve as your mentor.

- Use a personal time planner. At the end of the day, think about what you need to accomplish tomorrow. Alternatively, at the beginning of the day, think about your plans for that day. (Make an electronic note or just use pen and paper.)
- Be punctual.
- Don't get into a routine; make sure that you are always doing whatever is the highest priority.
- Be friendly; say "Hello; how are you?" because you are genuinely interested in the person to whom you are speaking.
- Listen much more than you talk!
- Be quick to praise others when they have earned your praise.
- Practice conflict resolution to avoid confrontations. (The other person may be your boss tomorrow.)
- Look for solutions rather than for problems. (Remember the old saying: "If you are not part of the solution, you are part of the problem!")
- Remember that neither life nor your position is always fair. Over time, however, people are likely to be rewarded according to the extent of their efforts.
- Don't get involved in office politics. Stay away from the grapevine, don't complain about your supervisor, and look for opportunities to build up, not tear down, the reputation of your organization.
- Remember that hospitality managers are typically successful because of their team; be a team player and give the members of your team credit for their accomplishments. Contribute your skills and talents freely to help your team be successful.

A WORD ABOUT WORK ETHICS

The concept of **ethics** refers to a person's perception of what is right and wrong. Ethical behavior is influenced by such factors as one's cultural background, religious views, professional training, and personal moral code.

Hotel managers in every position from beginning supervisor to top-level chief executive officer (CEO) must be ethical. When considering alternative courses of action, it is helpful to ask such questions as:

- Is the alternative legal?
- Would the alternative hurt anyone if it were implemented?
- Is the alternative fair?
- Is the alternative the right and honest thing to do?
- How would I feel if I was impacted by the alternative?
- Would I like to publicize the alternative I select?
- Would the organization be improved if everyone utilized the alternative?

Some hospitality organizations have a **code of ethics** which summarizes the acceptable philosophy about ethics and frequently includes policies to be utilized to help ensure that ethical decisions are made.

LODGING LANGUAGE

Ethics: A person's perceptions about what is right or wrong.

Code of Ethics: A statement adopted by an organization which outlines policies developed to guide the making of ethical decisions.

- Solicit feedback. Ask your manager and your peers for advice about your performance. Utilize any improvement suggestions you receive.

- Find a mentor. Some hospitality organizations have formal mentoring programs. Participate if possible. If a formal program doesn't exist, try to identify someone, perhaps even in another department, to provide advice.

- Volunteer for special projects. This will help you to learn more and, at the same time, show your managers that you want to learn as much as possible.

- Recognize that you will likely works extra hours; fifty-hour work weeks are not uncommon, especially early in hospitality careers. Long hours and hard work are typical in many entry-level managerial positions in the hospitality industry.

- Meet fellow employees from outside your department. Networking can be a very effective tactic to learn about an organization and advance in one's career.

- Think about the present and the future. Work hard to succeed in your first position but recognize that it is a first step in what will be, hopefully, a long and rewarding career.

- Keep alert to job openings within your company. Even though you have carefully considered your career, positions may become available that provide educational and professional advancement opportunities. Most companies prefer to **promote from within.** Pay attention to the requirements for these positions and carefully evaluate them for growth potential.

- Have fun at work. Enjoy what you do.

LODGING LANGUAGE

Promote From Within: The concept that a company offers higher-level positions to its existing employees when these positions must be filled.

Ongoing Professional Development

Your first position is the first step in your career. However, **professional development activities** will be necessary as you advance within it.

LODGING LANGUAGE

Professional Development Activities: Formal and informal training and education undertaken to provide the additional knowledge, skills, and experience to prepare one for progressively more responsible positions.

Some hospitality management graduates may think, "My education in the hospitality industry is over; everything else I need to learn will now come from experience." They are partially correct, because experience can be a good teacher. However, in the fast-changing hospitality industry, a mix of additional education along with experience is necessary if you seek to advance up the career ladder. For example, few hotel managers educated even as recently as the 1980s were taught anything about the Internet. Today's hotel managers must be very familiar with the Internet, with high-speed Internet access terminology, and with the technological means required to deliver dependable Internet service to hotel guest rooms, meeting rooms, and administrative offices. Hoteliers who have acquired this type of information have done so through reading and studying.

Figure 15.9 notes some common professional-development opportunities. Some occur on the job as one gains experience in a specific position. Others occur during activities such as group training on specific topics, **job rotation,** and **job enlargement.**

LODGING LANGUAGE

Job Rotation: A systematic plan to move employees into different positions so that they acquire the knowledge/skills required to be effective in these positions.

Job Enlargement: The act of including additional tasks/assignments in one's position to provide more opportunities to learn how the position relates to others.

■

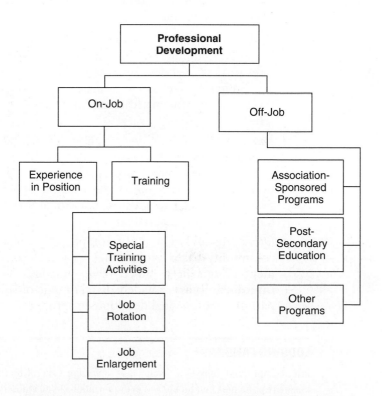

FIGURE 15.9   Professional Development Opportunities

Professional-development activities are important throughout one's career.

Figure 15.9 identifies some professional-development opportunities that arise from off-site job sources.

- *Association-sponsored programs.* Professional associations such as the American Hotel & Lodging Association and the National Restaurant Association consider professional development for members to be a high-priority responsibility. Programs are often available at national and state-level conferences, through independent learning, and from resources available for less formal self-study.

- *Post-secondary educational programs.* Educational institutions frequently offer programs on management topics applicable to the hotel industry. Generic programs may be offered, or programs may be developed for a specific organization. Programs are increasingly available on-line for anyone in any place at any time. If you want to advance, additional formal education may help you to attain a senior managerial position.

- *Other programs.* For-profit companies offer a wide range of programs, as do community-based groups such as local chambers of commerce and governmental agencies. Since the practice of hospitality management is **interdisciplinary,** a widely diverse range of subject matter is useful for study as part of a professional development program.

LODGING LANGUAGE

Interdisciplinary: Between disciplines—involving several domains of knowledge; for example, basic business principles can be applied in organizations in all industries.

SUGGESTIONS FOR SHORT-TERM CAREER PLANNING

- Think about the tasks in your present position you could do better. (You will probably recognize them; in addition, you may receive formal feedback during performance reviews and informal feedback from your own supervisor's coaching comments.) Learn more about the knowledge and skills required to perform these tasks.
- If you have a mentor, he/she can be a ready source of professional-development alternatives.
- Try to objectively assess your strengths and weaknesses relative to your career plans.
- Think about your likes and dislikes. They will influence your career plans and the activities you undertake to move toward career goals.
- Establish professional-development priorities. You may decide to first develop knowledge and skills in areas that will help with promotion. Alternatively, you may focus on your strengths (to become stronger) or weaknesses (to raise them to a par with your other competencies).

Figure 15.10 shows a process for working your professional-development plan:

- Establish learning goals.
- Identify supportive activities that will most help you to attain your learning goals.
- Establish a schedule for completing your learning activity, obtain necessary training resources, if any, and complete the training (work your plan!).

Along the way, success is most certain when you remain motivated and remove any obstacles that hinder your progress.

LODGING ON-LINE

Check out the extensive array of professional-development resources available from the Educational Institute of the American Hotel & Lodging Association (EI of AH&LA) at:

www.ei-ahla.org

You cannot be successful with continuing education activities if you plan to do them "when you have the time." Instead, you must make a commitment, establish a priority, and allocate time (always a precious resource). Some hotel employers provide

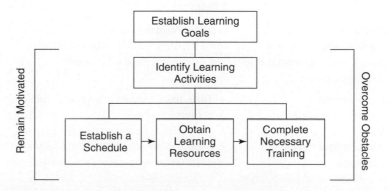

FIGURE 15.10   Working Your Professional Development Plan

compensated time and/or financial assistance to help staff members complete relevant training and education; others do not. Either way, the drive to do better in your position and to move forward in your career is an important prerequisite in an effective professional-development program.

ENTREPRENEUR OR INTRAPRENEUR?

The hotel industry provides lots of examples of people with great ideas who built them into very large and successful businesses. In Chapter 1 you learned about Kemmons Wilson and the Holiday Inns chain. Willard Marriott's small diner in Washington, D.C., was the forerunner of today's Marriott Corporation. The list of success stories could go on and on. Unfortunately, there are also stories about people with many years of hotel industry experience, small (or large) fortunes, and great ideas who were not successful and who lost their life's savings as they pursued their dreams.

Definitions

An **entrepreneur** is a person who assumes the risk of owning and operating a business in exchange for the financial and other rewards it may produce. In the hotel industry, entrepreneurs may be called **independent operators** if they own/operate one or just a few properties. By contrast, an **intrapreneur** is a person employed by an organization whose compensation is based, at least in part, upon the financial success of the unit for which he/she has responsibility.

LODGING LANGUAGE

Entrepreneur: A person who assumes the risk of owning and operating a business in exchange for the financial and other rewards it may produce.

Independent Operator: An entrepreneur who owns/operates one or a very few hospitality properties.

Intrapreneur: A person employed by an organization whose compensation is based, at least in part, upon the financial success of the unit for which he/she has responsibility.

================ **ALL IN A DAY'S WORK** ================

The Situation

Hotel industry recruiters typically note some characteristics shared by new managers who are *not* successful in their first positions. These include:

- They lack commitment.
- They do not take criticism well.
- They lack initiative.
- They have poor follow-through.
- They lack courage.
- They have problems with the life-style of the hotel business.

A Response

Recruiters also note some characteristics that are often shared by new managers who are successful. These include:

- They have initiative; they are self-starters.
- They have the courage to make tough decisions when they are the right ones rather than easy decisions just to avoid conflict.

- They are smart.
- They are mature beyond their years.
- They have a passion for all aspects of the business.
- They have a drive to get better every day.
- They seek additional responsibilities.
- They pay attention to details.

Entrepreneurs start their own businesses. Perhaps, for example, a person has worked in the hotel industry for many years and has also accumulated and/or gained access to the capital resources needed to buy (or lease), equip, and start up a lodging business. Alternatively, a person may have grown up in a family-owned lodging operation and has the opportunity to take it over. Some entrepreneurs are satisfied when their business provides for their immediate wants and needs. Others are challenged to learn whether their success in one (or several) hotels can be extended to still more (and more) hotels. Then, sustained business growth rather than profitability of a single operation becomes a goal.

The concept of intrapreneurship, by contrast, is more difficult to understand. Intrapreneurs are persons with entrepreneurial talent who do not want to start their own business. They work best in organizations that give them responsibility for a specific and defined part of the enterprise. Consider, for example, a general manager of one hotel in a multi-unit organization. The manager may be compensated, in part, by a profit-sharing plan based upon the property's financial success. Within limitations imposed by the organization, the general manager can plan/implement tactics to reduce expenses and to increase revenues. In so doing, he/she can share in the profits generated by the successful business.

In the example cited, the general manager was involved as an intrapreneur in revenue-producing activities. However, this is not always necessary. Managers responsible for housekeeping, the front office, or security may make decisions leading to cost reductions, and their compensation can, at least in part, be based upon their ability to do so.

Why Hotels Fail

New hotel businesses, both those that are franchised with brand recognition and access to proven standard operating procedures and those developed by entrepreneurs, can and do fail. Common reasons include:

- Lack of managerial ability
- Inadequate industry experience
- Lack of financing/funding
- Unrealistic business plans
- Failure to consider realistic goals
- Inability to generate revenues
- Higher-than-necessary costs
- Poor location

DO WHAT YOU LIKE TO DO

Successful entrepreneurs and intrapreneurs have at least one thing in common: they don't consider their job to be work. The goal of having fun at and looking forward to one's job is admirable. As one thinks about the time spent in a career, the old saying "Life is short; be sure to have fun at work!" becomes meaningful.

It is very important to enjoy what you do. Entrepreneurial and intrapreneurial positions in the hotel industry allow this to happen. Positions in the industry become even more meaningful when you consider that while enjoying work, you can also help hotel guests.

Entrepreneurs and intrapreneurs must work hard to be successful.

- Ineffective operating procedures
- Inability to think creatively

Note that the reasons for failure basically focus on two concerns: lack of managerial ability and financial issues (which, in fact, probably relate to the owner's ability to make management-related decisions). The good manager will have hotel industry experience, know how to develop an effective business plan, and develop realistic goals. As well, financial plans will be in place to reasonably estimate revenues and costs, and good managers consider property location, develop effective operating procedures, and think creatively. They also recognize that adequate financial support is critical. Effective managers do not make the all-too-common mistake of believing that the hotel will be successful immediately, and that revenues generated from operations will fund business start-up and ongoing costs.

There is an old saying that "you can't win if you don't play the game." In the context of our present discussion, you can't be a successful entrepreneur unless you start your own business. However, the chances of success increase dramatically when a creative idea is translated into an effective business plan which drives the organization toward its goal.

Tactics of Successful Intrapreneurs

Intrapreneurs use a process of risk-taking and innovation similar to the one utilized by their entrepreneurial counterparts. Some hospitality organizations encourage intrapreneurship, and there are relationships between general managers and **subordinates** in which empowerment allows this to happen. Businesses which encourage intrapreneurs generally have four traits:

- They a realistic vision which is widely understood by and shared with staff members.
- They recruit staff members with entrepreneurial talents and abilities.
- They emphasize teamwork.
- They reward success and do not punish their personnel for creative efforts designed to improve the organization.

LODGING LANGUAGE

Subordinates: Employees whose work is directly supervised or controlled by an individual of higher rank or position.

■

Many managers working for hotel companies have opportunities to think and act like an entrepreneur. They can:

- *Dream/think about ideas to improve the operation.* Questions such as "How would I do this if it were my business?" may provide answers that can be implemented.
- *Obtain ideas from others.* Those performing specific work tasks may have improvement ideas. As these ideas are implemented, feelings of accomplishment like those enjoyed by entrepreneurs can also be enjoyed by the hotel's employees.
- *Take ownership in ideas.* Intrapreneurs can explain and defend why something new should be tried. They should be open for feedback about potential challenges which can arise and why modifications of initial ideas will be helpful.
- *Know what to do when.* They recognize when they need to obtain approval and when they can experiment with existing procedures.
- *Try new ideas.* The fact that something has never been done before or was done yesterday without success doesn't mean that the time isn't right today for another attempt (especially if updated techniques are used).
- *Look for short-term successes.* For example, successful intrapreneurs know the advantage of changing procedures to improve specific products and service tactics.
- *Understand the organization.* They know its expectations and limitations.
- *Encourage open discussions.* They invite discussion with team members, including peers and others within the hotel.
- *Build a coalition supporters.* They seek support from fellow employees who have similar goals.
- *Be persistent.* They recognize that success frequently correlates with revisions to procedures that originally failed.
- *Recognize the importance of teamwork.* They work together with others to create visions of improvement that can involve and inspire others.
- *Keep the boss informed.* The best surprise is no surprise! Input from supervisors with access to "big picture" ideas and information can be helpful as improvement efforts are planned.

SUCCESSFUL INTRAPRENEURS SHARE COMMON TRAITS

- They are driven by a vision for a better way and have the desire to make it happen.
- They consider risks and assess ways to manage them.
- They are consistent and recognize that purposeful change takes time.
- They use careful analysis when information is available, and intuition influenced by knowledge/experience when it is not.
- They are honest and share good and bad results with others.
- They are willing to do any job necessary to further their ideas.
- They ask for suggestions before they ask for financial commitment.
- They share credit with the team.
- They keep the best interests of their hotel and its guests in the forefront of decision-making.
- They stick with their goals but are realistic about the best tactics to attain them.
- They have a clear vision about what must be done.

Is it a surprise that these traits of successful intrapreneurs are very similar to those of successful entrepreneurs?

DOMESTIC AND GLOBAL HOTEL POSITIONS

Living and working in paradise! Always warm weather; close to the ocean; palm trees and beautiful scenery and a lifestyle that will be the envy of your friends and family! Is this what comes to mind when you first think about an island in the North or South Pacific?

Now think about traditional work and a personal life in a city far away in Southeast Asia, South America, or Europe. Each of these locations also offers professional and personal experiences which are vastly different than what you typically experience at home.

You have learned that people from around the world increasingly travel and require lodging and food services as they do so. Since people travel everywhere, hotels need to be everywhere to provide travelers with the services and products they require. Employment opportunities in the hotel industry are available around the world. Positions outside of one's country can be especially rewarding and personally enjoyable. However, they can also lead to professional and personal disaster! A decision to seek employment in the international hotel industry must be the result of careful study.

Working in Another Country

Very large American-owned hotel organizations own and/or operate properties in the United States and throughout the world. Large hotel organizations owned by Asians, Europeans, and people of other nationalities own and/or operate properties in the United States and other regions of the world. It is, therefore, increasingly true that promotions within a multi-unit organization may involve relocating around the country and even to other parts of the world. What should one consider when making a decision about whether to become an **expatriate** hotel manager?

LODGING LANGUAGE

Expatriate: A citizen of one country who is employed in another country. Example: a United States citizen working in Asia would be considered an expatriate by his/her Asian counterparts.

■

LODGING ON-LINE

Hyatt hotels is one of several American hotel companies with properties worldwide. To see where it operates hotels, go to:

www.Hyatt.com

Anyone considering work in a foreign country must take several things into account including:

- *The Political Environment.* The United States is incredibly fortunate to have a stable and long-standing legal and political system. Political evolution is slow, and changes are democratic and well-established. This is not the case everywhere. Governmental structures are much less stable in some countries. This can result in societal turmoil, overnight changes in leadership, laws, and travel restrictions, and the potential for personal harm. The decision about managing a hotel and protecting oneself and one's family in these environments generally signals a "don't go!" for most persons. Fortunately, in many countries, while the legal/political environment is different from that in the United States, opportunities for professional success and personal enjoyment do exist.

- *Economic Issues.* The cost of doing business and living in other countries can be a concern. Diverse tax laws have an obvious effect on business decisions. Currency **exchange rates** and **inflation** impact business and personal decisions. Expatriate hotel managers have an advantage when, for example, they are paid a competitive salary in American dollars but work/live in a country where the dollar (or its equivalent) purchases significantly more than it would in the United States. Living in countries with very high inflation rates (which can be 2000 percent or more annually in some countries!) presents special challenges when purchasing goods/services for business or personal use.

- *Cultural Environment.* People living in a country share a **national culture** of values/attitudes that influences their behavior and shapes their beliefs about what is important. In order to work in another country successfully, it is advisable to learn about and become sensitive to its culture.

LODGING LANGUAGE

Exchange Rate: The rate at which the money of one country is traded (exchanged) for the money of another country.

Inflation: The economic condition which exists when selling prices increase throughout the economy of a country.

National Culture: The values/attitudes shared by citizens of a specific country that impact their behavior and shape their beliefs about what is important.

■

National culture can have a significant impact on how employees view their work and one other. Differences between people from different countries relative to how to they treat each other, behave, compete, and value punctuality (being on time for meetings and appointments) are examples of issues that can significantly affect one's attitudes about and ability to work/live in another country.

Expatriates working in a country with a national culture similar to their own are less likely to suffer from **culture shock** than will their counterparts relocating to a country with a more diverse culture. For example, people from the United States working and living in Western Europe will likely feel more at home than will those working in Asia or in West Africa.

LODGING LANGUAGE

Culture Shock: The feeling of disorientation, confusion, and changes in emotions created when one visits or lives in a different culture.

■

Success Factors in Global Assignments

Figure 15.11 identifies the key factors that influence whether expatriate managers are successful.

Figure 15.11 is a self-test that may be of interest if you are considering a global assignment. Some (but not all) of these factors are easy to assess.

- A person who does not adapt well to change is more likely to have difficulty adjusting to work and living in another culture.

- Someone who desires an expatriate position will be happier than others who take the position only for the sake of career advancement.

- Expatriates with an understanding of the host country's national culture will know what they are getting into; fewer surprises are likely which may detract from their continued interest in living/working there.

- Persons with the knowledge/skills required for successful job performance will feel less stress on the job (and about job security) than those who do not have the necessary job knowledge/skills.

- Interactions with people on and off the job are likely to be a significant factor in whether an expatriate position is successful. Hotel professionals typically think of themselves as people persons; however, they must be effective not only when interacting with fellow workers in their organizations but with their neighbors where they live while in the host country.

WHAT TIME IS IT ANYWAY?

Americans typically value punctuality. For example, if they have an appointment at 11:00 A.M., most of them make every effort to be where they need to be at 11:00 A.M. By contrast, the concept of 11:00 in the morning can mean something entirely different to people in other countries. For example, in some South Pacific Islands, 11:00 in the morning means anytime during the hour of 11:00 in the morning. Therefore, if a person arrives at an 11:00 meeting at 11:50 A.M. or even 11:59 A.M., attendees will be on time for an 11:00 A.M. meeting. (Equally frustrating for the expatriate United States manager, the meeting itself, which is scheduled to convene at 11:00 A.M., may not actually begin until 11:30 A.M., 11:45 A.M., or later!)

Check (√) one box for each factor noted below.

FACTOR	NO	MAYBE (A LITTLE)	YES
You are able to adapt to change.	❏	❏	❏
You want to live in another country.	❏	❏	❏
You understand the country's national culture.	❏	❏	❏
You know the country's language.	❏	❏	❏
You have the knowledge/skill needed for successful job performance.	❏	❏	❏
You have the necessary human relations abilities to manage employees with backgrounds significantly different than yours.	❏	❏	❏
You have previous experience(s) working/ living in another country.	❏	❏	❏
Your family will support the decision to accept a global assignment and to adapt to life in another country.	❏	❏	❏
You have positive reasons (motivations) which influence your interest in a global assignment.	❏	❏	❏
You have reasonable expectations about the experiences you will have.	❏	❏	❏
You are willing to listen to and try to understand the perspectives of others.	❏	❏	❏

FIGURE 15.11   Checklist of Factors Important to Expatriate Success

- Managers with previous experience in another country are likely to know what they are getting into, and their positive attitude and previous professional and personal experiences will be helpful.
- Whether family members are interested in relocating and their general support of the decision are significant concerns that will impact the success of the global assignment.
- One's motivation to accept an international assignment is important. Consider the manager who volunteers for reasons of personal and professional growth and "adventure," and another manager who is told that it is a good career move.
- Expectations about a global assignment must be reasonable. Effective transition training help the manager to realize what working and living in another country will really involve.
- The ability to listen and attempt to understand the beliefs of others is very important. Expatriate managers are likely to experience ideas expressed by co-workers, employees, and others in the host country which are profoundly different than theirs.

Seldom, if ever, is a global hotel management assignment successful by chance alone. Many factors must be in place for an assignment to be acceptable. When these factors work against the international assignment, they can, at best, cause strain and stress, and at worse can yield disastrous professional and/or personal experiences. Figure 15.12 reviews the factors that influence the success of global assignments.

Note that Figure 15.12 first addresses the candidate. The types of personal concerns/factors noted here and discussed above are important considerations. The selection process is also an important factor in the success of a global assignment. Until recently, some hotel organizations made international assignments by doing little more than asking the question "Who wants to go?" or by making the statement "You really should go!" Today, however, a more focused and formalized selection process is generally utilized.

Since expatriate assignments often fail because the employee and/or his or her family cannot adjust, their **cross-cultural adaptability** becomes important. The extent to which one can adapt to a new culture can be assessed by:

- Administering cross-cultural assessment tools to the employee/spouse/family to assess their attitudes and attributes important for adjustment.
- Interviewing/counseling sessions to further explore the potential for cultural adjustment.
- Considering personal cross-cultural development tools of special use to the individual(s).
- Providing detailed information to help the staff member understand the international assignment and adapt to day-day life in the host country.

LODGING LANGUAGE

Cross-cultural Adaptability: The extent to which one can adjust (adapt) to another culture.

■

Figure 15.12 indicates that transitional training is also important. Employees selected for international assignments will, ideally, receive training before they depart. Examples of topics for which training should be provided include:

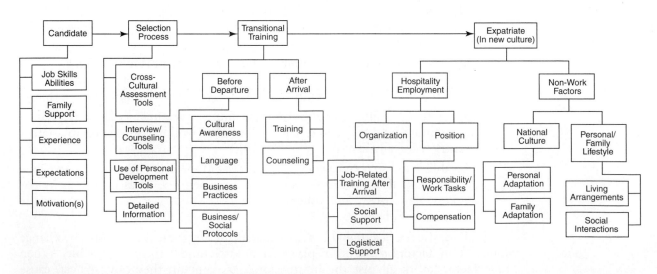

FIGURE 15.12 Factors Influencing Success of Global Assignments

- *Cultural Awareness.* To teach them how the national culture affects work relations, and how teamwork and productivity can be enhanced when working with staff members from that culture.
- *Language Training.* English is widely spoken in many countries (at least in the world of business). However, expatriates must also live in the community and will likely need to acquire basic language fluency to go about their lives off the job.
- *Business Practices.* Changes in basic business practices that will be necessary, including information about applicable laws, tax issues, and the availability of required resources.
- *Business/Social Protocols.* Specific do's and don'ts of business/social practices in the other country must be learned.

Transitional training after arrival is also useful. This can be provided several weeks after the expatriate manager and his/her family arrives. They will have had an opportunity to experience the new environment and to interact with local citizens, and they may be seeking answers to numerous questions. Their beginning efforts at becoming culturally aware can form the foundation for training/counseling that will make their foreign assignment more enjoyable and rewarding.

Several factors influence the success of a global assignment after the expatriate has arrived in the country:

- *Hospitality Employment.* This includes the organization's job-related training after arrival, social support when on and off the job, and logistical support (for example, information about which are the best schools). The position itself (responsibility and work tasks, for example) and compensation are important. *Note:* In addition to a salary and normal benefits, expatriate managers frequently receive extended annual leave, travel costs from/back to the host country, educational expense reimbursements for family members, costs of moving household belongs to/from the host country, and insurance or reimbursements for emergency travel costs.
- *Non-Work Factors.* The expatriate and his/her family must adapt to the host country's culture. The personal and family lifestyle which is (hopefully!) enjoyed will influence the assignment's success. For example, the expatriate's living arrangements, including transportation to/from work and the numerous non-work social interactions, will impact willingness to continue the assignment.

The hotel industry is an exciting one wherever you may work and whatever position you may hold. In the United States or any other part of the world, hoteliers who strive to excel and who continue to learn throughout their careers will meet with great professional and personal success and satisfaction.

LODGING ON-LINE

Those working in the hospitality field can join the professional trade associations located in their own countries but may also consider becoming active in the Paris-based International Hotel and Restaurant Association. To examine an overview of its goals and activities go to:

www.ih-ra.com

CHAPTER OBJECTIVES REVIEW

If you have successfully studied the material in this chapter, you should be prepared:

1. To provide an overview of career-planning steps. (Objective 1)
2. To discuss career considerations applicable to alternative types of lodging organizations. (Objective 2)
3. To review fundamental tactics helpful in securing one's first professional position. (Objective 3)
4. To explain tactics helpful in succeeding in one's first professional position. (Objective 4)
5. To note why some hotel managers want to work for themselves (entrepreneurs) and some (intrapreneurs) desire to work for others. (Objective 5)
6. To review opportunities in domestic and global hotel positions. (Objective 6)

LODGING LANGUAGE

Distance Learning Courses	Professional Development	Subordinates
Residential Education Programs	Activities	Expatriate
Career Fairs	Job Rotation	Exchange Rate
Permanent Placement	Job Enlargement	Inflation
Competency	Interdisciplinary	National Culture
Ethics	Entrepreneur	Culture Shock
Code of Ethics	Independent Operator	Cross-Cultural Adaptability
Promote from Within	Intrapreneur	

FOR DISCUSSION

1. Give three examples (one each) of questions you can ask faculty members, campus recruiters, and school alumni to learn information helpful in identifying alternative hotel employers?
2. What do you see to be the single biggest advantage and disadvantage to working with large and small hotel organizations?
3. If you were a recruiter for a hotel organization, what would be the five most important factors you would consider as you recruited management trainee applicants?
4. What will be your top two most important concerns as you evaluate alternative job offers? Why are these factors most important to you?
5. What competencies required for success in a hotel position do you think are the most difficult to acquire? Why?
6. What risks would be of most concern to you if you were thinking about starting your own business? What else is needed to be a successful entrepreneur besides having a good idea?
7. Assume that you are a department head in a lodging organization that believes in and practices intrapreneurship. What percentage of your total compensation would ideally be based upon your ability to attain predetermined goals? How much discretion would you want in making decisions under this ideal situation?
8. How do you think the national culture of a host country impacts the management of hotels in that country? Give two examples.

9. What would be some of the biggest challenges in your professional and work lives if you were an expatriate managing a hotel in a country whose language you were fluent in? If you were not fluent in the country's language?
10. Would you like to manage a hotel in another country? Why or why not?

TEAM ACTIVITIES

Team Activity 1

The chapter provides examples of competencies that are necessary for job success. Review each of these competencies and:

- cite an additional example of how the competency is used.
- provide an example of a problem that can occur when the competency has not been mastered.

Team Activity 2

Review the section of the chapter that addresses reasons why hotels fail. Are there other factors that can contribute to a hotel's failure? What are some practical tactics that you can use as a hotel manager to make your hotel successful?

Glossary

À la Carte   A food service offering items on an individually priced (by-item) basis, typically in a dining room.

Abandoned Property   Items the owner has intentionally left behind.

Accountability   An obligation created when a person is delegated duties/responsibilities by higher levels of management.

Accounts payable (AP)   The sum total of all invoices owed by the hotel to its vendors for credit purchases made by the hotel. Also called "AP."

Accounts Receivable (AR)   Money owed to the hotel because of sales made on credit. Sometimes referred to as "AR."

Accounts Receivable Aging   A process for determining the average length of time money is owed to a hotel because of a credit sale.

Accrual Accounting System   An accounting system that matches expenses incurred with revenues generated. Revenue is considered to be earned when products/services are provided (not when money is received); expenses are incurred when products, labor, and other costs are expended to generate revenue (not when the expenses are paid for).

Advertising   Information about a hotel that the hotel pays a fee to distribute.

Agitation   Movement of the washing machine resulting in friction as fabrics rub against each other.

Air Handler   The fans and mechanical systems required to move air through ducts and to vents.

Allowances and Adjustments   Reductions in sales revenue credited to guests because of errors in properly recording sales or to satisfy a guest who has experienced property shortcomings.

Amenities   Hotel products and services designed to attract guests. Examples include Internet access and copying services, in-room hair dryers, irons, ironing boards, and microwave ovens, as well as indoor pools, exercise rooms, and in-room movies.

Appreciation   The increase, over time, in the value of an asset. The amount of the increased value is not taxed unless the asset changes hands (is sold).

Asian American Hotel Owners Association (AAHOA)   Association of hotel owners who, through an exchange of ideas, seek to promote professionalism and excellence in hotel ownership.

Atrium   A large, open central space used by some hotels for registration, lobby, retail sales, and food services, among other purposes.

Attitude   The way a person feels about objects, persons, or events.

Attrition   The difference between the original request and the actual pickup of a group. For example, a group might reserve 100 rooms but actually use only 50. Because the room rate quoted to the group was based upon the use of 100 rooms, the hotel's standard group contract may require, in such a case, that the group pay a penalty for its failure to purchase the number of rooms it originally agreed to purchase.

At-Will Employment   The employment relationship that exists when employers can hire any employee they choose and dismiss an employee with or without cause at any time. Employees can also elect to work for the employer or to terminate the relationship anytime they desire to do so.

Audit   An independent verification of financial records.

Authority   The power or right to direct the activities of others and to enforce compliance.

Authorize   To validate. When used in reference to a credit card offered by a guest at the time of check-in, this term refers to the desk agent's validation of the card.

Autocratic Leadership Style   Leadership approach that emphasizes a "do it my way" philosophy.

Average Daily Rate (ADR)   The average (mean) selling price of all guest rooms in a hotel, city, or country for a specific period of time.

Back-door Marketing   The tactic of treating employees, to the extent possible, just as guests would be treated by the hospitality operation.

Back-up Generator   Equipment used to make limited amounts of electricity on-site. Utilized in times of power failure or when the hotel experiences low supply from the usual provider of electricity.

Back-up System   Redundant hardware and/or software operated in parallel to the system it serves. Used in times of failure or power outages, such systems are often operated on batteries. For example, a back-up system to the hotel's telephones would enable outside calling even if the main digital telephone system were to shut down.

Ballast   The device in an electric discharge lamp that starts, stops, and controls the current to the light.

Banquet   A food and/or beverage event held in a hotel's function room.

Banquet   A special and often elaborate meal served (usually in a private dining area) to a select group of guests.

Batch Cooking   Preparing several portions of food at the same time.

Bed and Breakfast Inns   Very small properties (one to several guest rooms) owned or managed by persons living on-site; these businesses typically offer one meal a day; also called B&B.

Benchmark   The search for best practices and an understanding about how they are achieved in efforts to determine how well a hospitality organization is doing.

Bid   An offer by a hotel to supply sleeping rooms, meeting space, food and beverages, or other services to a potential client at a stated price. If the bid is accepted, the hotel will issue the client a contract detailing the agreement made between the hotel and the client.

Biohazard Waste Bag   A specially marked plastic bag used in hotels. Laundry items that are stained with blood or bodily fluids and thus need special handling are put into these bags for transport to the OPL.

Black-out Date Specific day(s) when the hotel is sold out and/or is not accepting normal reservations.

Block Rooms reserved exclusively for members of a specific group. Used as in, "We need to create a block of 50 rooms for May 10th and 11th for the Society of Antique Furniture Appraisers."

Blood-borne Pathogen Any microorganism or virus carried by blood that can cause a disease.

Body Language The concept that one communicates by the way one's arms, hands, and/or legs are positioned during a conversation or presentation.

Bonafide Occupational Qualifications (BOQs) Qualifications to perform a job that are judged reasonably necessary to safely or adequately perform all the tasks required by the job.

Bonding Purchasing an insurance policy to protect against the possibility that an employee will steal.

Booking Hotel jargon for making a confirmed sale. Used as in: "What is the current level of bookings for the month?" or "How many out-of-state tour buses were booked into the hotel last month?"

Brand Standard A hotel service or feature that must be offered by any property entering or remaining in a specific hotel brand. Used, for example, in: "The franchisor has determined that free local telephone calls will become a new brand standard effective January 1."

Brand The name of a specific hotel group. For example, Holiday Inn and Holiday Inn Express are two different brands. Additional examples of brands include Clarion, Comfort Inn, Hampton, Super 8, and Ramada.

Bureaucratic Leadership Style Leadership approach that emphasizes a "do it by the book" philosophy.

Buy-out An arrangement in which both parties to a contract agree to end the contract early as a result of one party paying the other the agreed-upon financial compensation.

C.P.A. Certified public accountant. An individual designated by the American Institute of Certified Public Accountants as competent in the field of accounting.

Calibration The adjustment of equipment to maximize its effectiveness and operational efficiency.

Call Accounting The system within the hotel used to document and charge guests for their use of the telephone.

Call Brand Beverages High-priced and high-quality alcoholic beverages sold by name (such as Johnny Walker Red Scotch) rather than by type of liquor (scotch) only.

Camps/Park Lodges Sleeping facilities in national, state, or other parks and recreational areas that accommodate visitors to these areas.

Cancellation Number A series of numbers and/or letters that serve to identify the cancellation of a specific hotel reservation.

Capital Expenditure The purchase of equipment, land, buildings, or other assets necessary for the operation of a hotel.

Career Fairs Trade show–type events which allow prospective job applicants to meet recruiters representing numerous employers in one location during a specified time period.

Career Ladder A plan that projects successively more responsible positions within an organization or an industry. Career ladders allow one to plan and schedule developmental activities necessary to assume more responsible positions.

Case Goods Non-upholstered furniture, such as guest room dressers, tables, desks, and the like.

Cash Accounting System An accounting system that considers revenue to be earned when it is received and expenses to be incurred when they are paid for.

Casino A business operation that offers table and card games along with (usually) slot operations and other games of skill or chance and amenities that are marketed to customers seeking gaming activities and entertainment. Many casinos offer lodging accommodations for their visitors.

Centralized Accounting A financial management system that collects accounting data from individual hotels, and then combines and analyzes the data at a different (central) site.

Centralized Purchasing A purchasing system in which participating properties develop common purchase requirements and combine purchase quantities. Suppliers frequently lower the price per purchase unit (per pound or per gallon, for example) as the quantities of items to be purchased increases.

CFL Short for "Compact Fluorescent Light."

Chain A group of franchisees who have all franchised the same hotel brand name. Also called "brand" or "flag."

Chained Recipe A recipe for an item (such as a sauce) that is itself an ingredient in another recipe (such as a steak).

Chamber of Commerce An organization whose goal is the advancement of all business interests within a community or larger business region. Sometimes called "the chamber" for short.

Charter A form of transportation rented exclusively for a specific group of travelers. Planes and buses are often chartered for group travel.

Chief Engineer The employee responsible for the management of a hotel's maintenance department. Sometimes referred to as "maintenance chief."

Claim (Insurance) A demand for compensation as the result of loss, injury, or damage.

Closed-Circuit Television (CCTV) A camera and monitor system that displays, in real time, the activity within the camera's field of vision. A CCTV consisting of several cameras and screens showing the camera's fields of vision may be monitored in a single location.

Coaching The process by which a supervisor provides ongoing training and feedback to employees to help them reach their highest levels of performance.

Code of Ethics A statement adopted by an organization which outlines policies developed to guide the making of ethical decisions.

Coding The process of assigning incurred costs to predetermined cost centers or categories.

Cold Calling Making a sales visit/presentation to a potential client without having previously set an appointment to do so.

Communication The transmission of understandable information from one person to another by use of words, numbers, or other common symbols.

Comp Short for "complimentary" or "no-charge" for products or services.

Compensation All the financial and non-financial rewards given to management and non-management employees in return for the work they do for the hotel.

Compensatory Damages A monetary amount intended to compensate injured parties for actual losses or damage they have incurred. This typically includes such items as medical bills and lost wages. Also known as "actual damages."

Competency A requirement that specifies what an individual must know and/or be able to do to be successful in a position.

Competitive Set The group of competing hotels to which an individual hotel's operating performance is compared. Sometimes shortened to "Comp Set."

Competitors Businesses that provide products and services to the same market of guests.

Condiments Salt, pepper, ketchup, mustard, syrups, and related items that guests apply to food to adjust its taste to their personal preference.

Conference Center A specialized hospitality operation specifically designed for and dedicated to the needs of small- and medium-sized meetings of 20 to 100 people.

Confirmation Number A series of numbers and/or letters that serve to identify a specific hotel reservation.

Consortia Groups of hotel service buyers organized for the purpose of reducing their clients' travel-related costs. A single such group is a consortium.

Contact Alarm A warning system that notifies (contacts) an external entity, such as the fire or police department, if the alarm is activated.

Continental Breakfast A simple breakfast consisting of fruit juice or fruit, coffee, and toast or a pastry.

Continuous Quality Improvement (CQI) Ongoing efforts within a hospitality operation to better meet (or exceed) guest expectations and to define ways to perform work with better, less costly, and faster methods.

Controller The individual responsible for recording, classifying, and summarizing a hotel's business transactions. In some hotels, this position is referred to as the comptroller.

Controlling The process of comparing actual results to planned results and taking corrective action as needed.

Convenience Food Food or beverage products that have some labor "built in" that otherwise would have to be added on-site. Alfredo sauce can be purchased in a ready-to-serve form (just heat it), and a Bloody Mary mix can be purchased ready-to-pour.

Convention and Visitor's Bureau (CVB) An organization, generally funded by taxes levied on overnight hotel guests, which seeks to increase the number of visitors to the area it represents. Called the "CVB" for short.

Convention Hotel A lodging property with extensive and flexible meeting and exhibition spaces that markets to associations, corporations, and other groups bringing people together for meetings.

Conversion The changing of a hotel from one brand to another. Also known as "re-flagging."

Cooking Applying heat to a food item.

Corkage Fee A charge assessed when a guest brings a bottle (for example, of a special wine) to the hotel for consumption at a banquet function or in the hotel's dining room.

Corporate Rate The rate a hotel charges to its typical business traveler. This rate is normally 5–20 percent below the hotel's rack rate.

Cost Per Occupied Room Total costs incurred for an item or area, divided by the number of rooms occupied in the hotel for the time period examined.

Critical Incident An activity (outcome) that results in unusual success or unusual failure in some aspect of a job.

Cross-cultural Adaptability   The extent to which one can adjust (adapt) to another culture.

Cross-Functional Team   A group of employees from each department within the hospitality operation who work together to resolve operating problems.

Cruise Ship   A passenger vessel designed to provide leisure experiences for people on vacation.

Culture Shock   The feeling of disorientation, confusion, and changes in emotions created when one visits or lives in a different culture.

Curb Appeal   The initial visual impression the hotel's parking areas, grounds, and external buildings create for an arriving guest.

Damages   The actual amount of losses or costs incurred due to the wrongful act of a liable party.

Decentralized Accounting   A financial management system that collects accounting data from an individual hotel site and combines and analyzes it at the same site.

Deep Cleaning   Intensive cleaning of a guest room. Typically includes thorough cleaning of such items as drapes, lamp shades, carpets, furniture, and walls. Regularly scheduled deep cleaning of guest rooms is one mark of an effective housekeeping department.

Delivery Invoice   A statement from the supplier that accompanies product delivery and provides information to establish the amount of money due to the supplier. This information includes name of product, quantity, and price, and must be signed by a hotel representative to confirm that the products were delivered.

Deluxe Hot Breakfast   A breakfast with hot food choices offered by a limited-service hotel.

Demand Generator   An organization, entity, or location that creates a significant need for hotel services. Examples in a community include large businesses, tourist sites, sports teams, educational facilities, and manufacturing plants.

Democratic Leadership Style   Leadership approach that emphasizes a "let's determine the best way to do it" philosophy.

Demographic Factors   Factors such as age, marital status, gender, ethnicity, and occupation that help to describe a person.

Depreciation   The reduction in the value of an asset as it wears out. This non-cash expense is often termed a "tax write-off" because the decline in the value of the asset is tax deductible.

Depressed Market   A hotel market area where occupancy rates and/or ADRs are far below their historical levels.

Direct Bill   A financial arrangement whereby a guest is allowed to purchase hotel services and products on credit terms.

Direct Mail   The process of sending an advertisement to clients by U.S. mail service. The total cost of a direct mail piece includes the expenditures for the advertisement's design, printing, and mailing.

Direct Report   One's immediate supervisor.

Directing   The process of supervising staff members in the workplace.

Discipline (Negative)   Punishment activities that encourage employees to follow established policies, rules, and regulations.

Discipline (Positive)   Reinforcement activities that encourage employees to continue to follow established policies, rules, and regulations.

Discipline   Activities designed to encourage employees to follow established policies, rules, and regulations.

Distance Learning Courses   Formal education (training) programs that are available to students/trainees in remote locations.

Diversity (Workforce)   The range of differences in attitudes, values, and behaviors of employees relative to gender, race, age, ethnicity, physical ability, and other relevant characteristics.

DOSM   Short for "director of sales and marketing." Variations include DOS (director of sales) and DOM (director of marketing).

Drop In   A potential group buyer of rooms or hotel services who arrives at the hotel without an appointment.

Duct   A passageway, usually built of sheet metal, that allows fresh, cold, or warm air to be directed to various parts of a building.

Electric Discharge Lamp   A lamp in which light is generated by passing electrical current through a space filled with a special combination of gases. Examples include fluorescent, mercury vapor, metal halide, and sodium.

Electronic Cash Register (ECR)   A standalone computer system that includes an input device such as a keyboard, an output device such as a printer, a central processing unit, and some storage (memory) capacity.

Embezzlement   The theft of a company's financial assets by an employee.

Emergency Maintenance   Maintenance activities performed in response to an urgent situation.

Emergency Plan   A document describing a hotel's predetermined, intended response to a safety/security threat it may encounter.

Employee Handbook   Written policies and procedures related to employment at the hotel; sometimes called an "employee manual."

Employee-to-Guest Ratio   The number of employees relative to the number of guests. In the lodging industry, this is typically expressed in terms of employees per room; a 500-room luxury, full-service property may have 500 employees: a 1:1 employee-to-guest ratio. A 100-room limited-service property may have 25 employees: a 1:4 employee-to-guest ratio.

Employer of Choice   The concept that the hospitality operation is a preferred place of employment in the community for applicants who have alternative employment opportunities.

Employment Agreement   Document specifying the terms of the relationship between the employer and the employee and indicating the rights/obligations of both parties.

Empowerment   The act of granting authority to employees to make key decisions within their areas of responsibility.

Energy Management   Specific policies and engineering, maintenance, and facility-design activities intended to control and reduce energy usage.

Engineering   Designing and operating a building to ensure a safe and comfortable atmosphere.

Entrepreneur   A person who assumes the risk of owning and operating a business in exchange for the financial and other rewards it may produce.

Entry-level Employees   Staff members working in positions that require little previous experience or knowledge of job tasks and who do not direct the work of other staff members.

Ethics   A person's perceptions about what is right or wrong.

Exchange Rate   The rate at which the money of one country is traded (exchanged) for the money of another country.

Executive Committee   The group of top-level decision-makers within the hotel, including the manager(s) with property-wide managerial responsibilities and department heads (managers) responsible for specific functions.

Executive Housekeeper   The individual responsible for the management and operation of a hotel's housekeeping department.

Expatriate   A citizen of one country who is employed in another country. Example: a United States citizen working in Asia would be considered an expatriate by his/her Asian counterparts.

Expedite   Facilitating delivery of food, beverage, or other products previously ordered from suppliers.

Extended-Stay Hotel   A mid-priced, limited-service hotel marketing to guests desiring accommodation for extended time periods (generally one week or longer).

External Recruiting   Tactics designed to attract persons who are not current hotel employees for vacant positions at a property.

Federal Trade Commission (FTC)   Government agency that enforces federal antitrust and consumer protection laws. It also seeks to ensure that the nation's business markets function competitively and are free of undue restrictions caused by acts or practices that are unfair or deceptive.

Feedback (Training)   The process by which a trainer informs a trainee about the extent to which a job task has been learned.

FF&E   The furniture, fixtures, and equipment used by a hotel to service its guests.

FF&E Reserve   Funds set aside by ownership today for the future "furniture, fixture, and equipment" replacement needs of a hotel.

Financial Statements   Financial summaries of a hotel's accounting information. Also called the hotel's "financials."

Finger Foods   Small sandwiches, salty snacks, sliced vegetables, and other foods that do not require flatware or other service items for guest consumption.

First-tier   Management companies that operate hotels for owners using the management company's trade name as the hotel brand. Hyatt, Hilton, and Sheraton are examples.

Fiscal Quarter   Any three-month period within the 12-month period that makes up a company's operating year. For example, January, February, and March would make up the first fiscal quarter of an operating year that began on January 1st and ended on December 31st.

Fixed Charges   The expenses incurred in the purchase and occupation of the hotel. These include rent, property taxes, insurance, interest, and depreciation and amortization.

FOC (Franchise Offering Circular)   Franchise disclosure document prepared by a franchisor and registered and filed with the state governmental agency responsible for administering franchise relationships.

Folio   Detailed list of a hotel guest's room charges as well as other charges authorized by the guest or legally imposed by the hotel.

FOM   The hotel industry term for a front office manager.

Food Cost Per Guest   The amount expended for breakfast for each guest. Calculated as: Total Breakfast Food Cost ÷ Number of Guests Served.

Food Items   Food selections that will be available for the guests.

Foot-Candle   A measure of illumination. One foot-candle equals one lumen per square foot.

Franchise Agreement Legal contract between a hotel's owners (the franchisee) and the brand managers (the franchisor) that describes the duties and responsibilities of each in the franchise relationship.

Franchise service director (FSD) The representative of a franchise hotel brand who interacts directly with a hotel franchisee.

Franchise An arrangement whereby one party (the franchisor) allows another party to use its logo, brand name, systems, and resources in exchange for a fee.

Franchisee An individual or company that buys, under specific terms and conditions, the right to use a brand name for a fixed period of time and at an agreed-upon price.

Franchisor An organization that manages a brand and sells the right to use the brand name.

Fraud The intentional use of deceit, trickery, or other dishonest methods to take another's money or property.

Frequent Guest Program A promotional effort administered by a hotel brand which rewards travelers every time they choose to stay at the brand's affiliated hotels. Typical rewards include free-night stays, room upgrades, and complimentary hotel services.

Fringe Benefits Indirect financial compensation, including employer-provided rewards and services other than wages and salaries. Examples include life and health insurance, paid vacation, and employer-provided meals. Sometimes simply called "benefits."

Front Desk The area within the hotel used for guest registration and payment.

Front Office The area within the hotel responsible for guest reservations, registration, service, and payment.

Full-Service Hotel A lodging facility that offers complete food and beverage services.

GAAP Short for "generally accepted accounting principles." Techniques, methods, and procedures utilized by all accountants in the preparation of financial statements.

General Manager (GM) The traditional title of the individual at a hotel property who is responsible for final decision-making regarding property-specific operating policies and procedures. Also, the leader of the hotel's management team.

GFI Outlet Short for "Ground Fault Interrupter." This special electrical outlet is designed to interrupt power ("trip" or "blow") before significant damage can be done to a building's wiring system. These are most commonly installed in the bathroom or vanity areas of a hotel room, where high-voltage usage (hairdryers) or high moisture levels can cause electrical power interruptions.

Global Distribution System (GDS) Commonly referred to as the GDS, this computer system connects travel professionals worldwide who reserve rooms with hotels offering rooms for sale.

GOP Short for "Gross Operating Profit." This popular term is taken from a pre-1990 version of the Uniform System of Accounts for Hotels (USAH) published by the New York Hotel Association. It refers to hotel revenue less those expenses typically controlled at the property level. It is generally expressed on the income statement and in the industry as both a dollar figure and a percentage of total revenue.

Grapevine Informal channels of communication that are not formally developed to disseminate information through an organization but are used for this purpose by employees.

Green Hotel   A lodging property that utilizes environmentally friendly practices in ways that enhance or, at least, do not detract from its guests' experiences.

Group Contract   A legal document used to summarize the agreement between a hotel and its group client.

Group   Individual guests who are part of a larger, multiple-traveler booking. For example, those in a leisure tour bus, wedding party, sports team, and the like.

Guest History   Information related to the past stay(s) of one guest.

Guided Tour   A group tour package that includes the services of one or more tour guides.

Head Table   Special seating at a banquet reserved for special guests.

Health Hazards   Aspects of the workplace that can lead to a decline in an employee's health. Examples include stressful working conditions and exposure to toxic chemicals.

Historical Data   Information related to the stays of past guests. Collectively, this information details the history of all past hotel guests.

Holding   Maintaining food items at proper serving temperature after they are prepared. Holding involves keeping hot foods hot and cold foods cold.

Hospitality Industry   Organizations that provide lodging accommodations and food services for people when they are away from their homes.

Hotel Shuttle   A vehicle used by a hotel to transport guests to and from such destinations as airports, restaurants, and shopping.

Hotel   An establishment that provides sleeping rooms as well as various services to the traveling public.

Hotelier   The owner/manager of one or more hotels.

House Brand Beverages   Alcoholic beverages sold by type (scotch) rather than by brand that are served when a call or premium brand beverage is not requested; also called "speed-rail," "well," or "pour brand."

House Count   An estimate of the number of guests staying in a hotel on a given day.

Houseperson   The employee responsible for the cleaning of public spaces (the house). Also sometimes referred to as a PA (public area cleaner) or porter.

Housepersons   Employee responsible for assisting room attendants with their work.

HR   Short for "human resources." Used for example in "When will the HR department complete the employee turnover study?"

Hub   Typically, a big-city airport within a short driving distance of a very large population center. These mega-airports are used to economically connect travelers with flights to their desired departure and arrival cities.

Human Relations   Skills needed to understand and effectively interact with other people, including employees on the job.

Human Resources Department   The functional area in a hotel with the responsibility to assist managers in other departments with human resources concerns, including recruitment, selection, orientation, training, compensation, legal, safety and health, and a wide range of other specialized tasks.

HVAC   Shorthand term for "heating, ventilating, and air-conditioning."

Incandescent Lamp   A lamp in which a filament inside the lamp's bulb is heated by electrical current to produce light.

Incident Report   A document prepared to record the details of an accident, injury, or disturbance and the hotel's response to it.

Inclusive   A single price that includes all charges.

Independent Operator   An entrepreneur who owns/operates one or a very few hospitality properties.

Induction   The process of informing new employees about matters related to the department in which they will work. This process follows the orientation process.

Inflation   The economic condition which exists when selling prices increase throughout the economy of a country.

Ingredients   Individual components of a food item; for example, flour and sugar are ingredients in bread.

Inspector (Inspectress)   Employee responsible for physically checking the room status of guest rooms and performing other tasks as assigned by the executive housekeeper.

Insurer   The entity providing insurance coverage to a business.

Interdisciplinary   Between disciplines—involving several domains of knowledge; for example, basic business principles can be applied in organizations in all industries.

Interfaced   The process in which one data-generating system shares its data electronically with another system.

Internal Alarm   A warning system that notifies an area within the hotel if the alarm is activated.

Internal Recruiting   Tactics to identify and attract staff members who are currently employed at the hotel for vacancies that represent promotions or transfers to other positions.

Interstate Commerce   Commercial trading or transportation of people or property between/among states.

Intrapreneur   A person employed by an organization whose compensation is based, at least in part, upon the financial success of the unit for which he/she has responsibility.

Issuing   The process of moving products to the place of production.

Job Description   A list of tasks that an employee working in a specific position must be able to effectively perform.

Job Enlargement   The act of including additional tasks/assignments in one's position to provide more opportunities to learn how the position relates to others.

Job Rotation   A systematic plan to move employees into different positions so that they acquire the knowledge/skills required to be effective in these positions.

Job Specification   A list of personal qualities judged necessary for successful job performance.

Job Task   An activity that an employee working in a specific position must know how and be able to do. For example, a front desk clerk in a limited-service hotel must be able to properly check-in a guest.

Keycards   The electromagnetic card used in a recodable locking system.

Laissez-faire Leadership Style   Leadership approach that emphasizes a "do it the way you want to do it" approach.

Last Call   Notice given to guests that service will end at a specified time. For example, guests in a hotel bar may be notified 20 minutes before closing time that last drink orders must be placed, and guests in a lobby breakfast service may be informed that service will end in 10 minutes.

Laundry Par Levels   The amount of laundry in use, in process, and in storage.

Lead   Information about a prospect who is likely to buy products and services from the hotel.

Leadership   Accomplishing goals by working with others while, at the same time, gaining their respect, loyalty, competence, and enthusiastic cooperation.

Liable   Legally bound to compensate for injury or loss.

Licensing   Formal authorization to practice a profession that is granted by a governmental agency.

Limited-Service Hotel   A lodging facility that offers few, if any, food and beverage services.

Line Department   Hotel divisions that are in the "chain of command" and are directly responsible for revenues (such as front office and food/beverage) or for property operations (such as housekeeping and maintenance and engineering).

Line Managers   Managers who work in line ("chain of command") departments within a hotel.

Line of Authority   A direct superior-subordinate relationship in which one person (the superior) is completely responsible for directing (exercising control over) the actions of another (the subordinate).

Line-Level   Employees whose jobs are most often non-supervisory. These are typically positions where the employee is paid a per-hour wage (not a salary) and performs a recurring and specific task for the hotel. Sometimes referred to as an "hourly."

Linen   Generic term for the guest room sheets and pillowcases (and food and beverage department tablecloths and napkins) washed and dried in the laundry area.

Line-Up   A brief informational training session held before the work shift begins.

Link   A relationship between two Web sites. When Web site users select a link at one site, they are taken to another Web site address. An external link leads to a Web page other than the current one; an internal link leads elsewhere on the current Web site.

Linking Pin   The concept that the supervisor links upper levels of management with entry-level employees. Communication flows down and up the organization through the supervisor.

Lobby Food Services   Food services offered by limited-service hotels.

Lodging Industry   The total of all the businesses that provide overnight accommodations for guests.

Long-Range Goals   Goals that are to be achieved over an extended period (usually longer than one year). Sometimes called "long-term."

Lost Property   Items the owner has unintentionally left behind and then forgotten.

Maintenance Chief   The employee responsible for the management of a hotel's maintenance department. Sometimes referred to as "chief engineer."

Maintenance   The activities required to keep a building and its contents in good repair. Also, the department or area of a hotel responsible for these activities.

Make/Buy Analysis   The process of considering quality, costs, and other factors in scratch and convenience food alternatives to determine how products should be purchased for the operation.

Malcolm-Baldridge National Quality Award   Award granted to U.S. businesses that demonstrate successful quality-related strategies relating to leadership, information/analysis, strategic planning, human resource development/management, process management, business results, and customer focus/satisfaction.

Management Company   An organization that operates a hotel(s) for a fee. Also sometimes called a "contract company."

Management contract   An agreement between a hotel's owners and a hotel management company under which, for a fee, the management company operates the hotel. Also sometimes called a "management agreement," or an "operating agreement."

Management   The effective coordination of individual efforts to achieve established goals.

Manager   A staff member who directs the work of supervisors.

Manager's Daily   A re-cap of the previous day's rooms, food and beverage, and other sales. The manager's daily may include additional hotel operating statistics as requested by the hotel's general manager. Sometimes referred to simply as the "daily."

Manager's Reception   A time, usually during the late afternoon/early evening, when complimentary foods and beverages are offered to guests of limited-service properties.

Market Share   The percentage of the total market (typically in dollars spent) captured by a property. For example, a hotel generating $200,000 in business traveler guest room rental annually in a community where business travelers spend $1 million per year will have a 20 percent market share.

Marketing   Activities directly related to increasing a potential guest's awareness of a hotel.

Marketing Plan   A calendar of specific activities designed to meet the hotel's sales goals.

Mark-up   A fee added to a supplier's charges that the hotel bills a guest or group to compensate for value added by the hotel.

Material Safety Data Sheets (MSDS)   Written statements describing the potential hazards of, and best ways to handle, chemicals or toxic substances. An MSDS is provided to the buyer by the manufacturer of the chemical or toxic substance and must be posted and made available in a place where it is easily accessible to those who will actually use the product.

Medicare   Hospital and medical insurance received by persons over 65 years of age who are eligible for Social Security benefits.

Meeting Planner   A professional employed by a group to negotiate its contract with a hotel.

Mentor   To serve as a personal teacher. Also: One who mentors.

Menu Planning   The process of ascertaining which food/beverage items will most please the guests while generating acceptable revenue and/or cost objectives.

Minimum Wage   The lowest amount of compensation that an employer may pay to an employee covered by the FLSA or applicable state law. Most hotel employees are covered by minimum wage provisions; however, exceptions can include youthful employees being paid a training wage for the first 90 days of employment and tipped employees (if reported tips plus wages received at least equal the minimum wage).

Minutes Per Room   The average number of minutes required to clean a guest room.

Mise en Place   French term meaning "everything in its place"; cooks and bartenders must get ready for production; servers must get ready for dining service.

Mislaid Property   Items the owner has unintentionally left behind.

Mission Statement   A planning tool that broadly identifies what a hospitality operation would like to accomplish and how it plans to accomplish it.

MOD   Manager on Duty. The individual on the hotel property responsible for making any managerial decisions required during the period he or she is MOD.

Moments of Truth   Any (and every) time a guest has an opportunity to form an impression about the hospitality organization. Moments of truth can be positive or negative.

Morale   The feelings an employee has about all aspects of the job.

Motivation   An internal force that drives employees to do something to reach a goal.

National Culture   The values/attitudes shared by citizens of a specific country that impact their behavior and shape their beliefs about what is important.

Negotiated Rate   A special room rate offered for a fixed period of time to a specific client of the hotel. As in "What is the negotiated rate we should offer the Travelsavers consortium next year?"

Networking   The development of personal relationships for a business-related purpose. For example, a chamber of commerce–sponsored breakfast open to all community business leaders interested in improving local traffic conditions would be an excellent example of a networking opportunity for a member of a hotel's sales team.

Night Audit   The process of reviewing for accuracy and completeness the accounting transactions from one day to conclude, or "close," that day's sales information in preparation for recording the transactions of the next day.

Night Auditor   The individual who performs the daily review of all the financial transactions with hotel guests recorded by the front office.

Non-yieldable   A discounted room rate that continues to be offered even when a hotel has implemented a yield management strategy. Examples may include corporate or government rates.

No-show   A guest who makes a room reservation but fails to cancel it or does not arrive at the hotel on the date of the confirmed reservation.

Occupancy Rate   The ratio of guest rooms sold (or given away) to the number of guest rooms available for sale in a given time period expressed as a percentage.

Occupational Safety and Health Administration (OSHA)   An agency of the U.S. Department of Labor which administers programs/regulations designed to provide a safe/healthful workplace for employees.

Offer Letter   Document that specifies what the employer is going to give the employee if the job is accepted. Examples include position, compensation and benefits, start date, and employment location.

On-line Distribution   The buying and selling of hotel rooms using the Internet.

Open Bar   A beverage service alternative where the host of a banquet function pays for beverages during all or part of the event; also called "hosted bar."

OPL   Short for "On Premise Laundry."

Organizational Chart   A visual portrayal of the jobs and positions of authority within an organization.

Organizing   Actions designed to bring together and arrange the resources of a group to help it achieve its goals.

Orientation   The process of providing basic information about the hotel which must be known by all of its employees.

OSHA   The Occupational Safety and Health Administration. A federal agency, established in 1970, that is responsible for developing and enforcing regulations to help ensure safe and healthful working conditions.

Outsource   To obtain labor or parts from an outside provider. Typically done to reduce costs or obtain specialized expertise.

Over A situation in which a cashier has more money in the cash drawer than the official sales records indicate. Thus, a cashier with $10 more in the cash drawer than the sales record indicates is said to be $10 over.

Overbooking A situation in which the hotel has more guest reservations for rooms than it has rooms available to lodge those guests. Sometimes referred to as "oversold."

Overload Requiring equipment to produce more than it is reasonably capable of producing.

Overtime The number of hours of work after which an employee must receive a premium pay (generally one and one-half times the base hourly rate).

Owner/Operator A hotel investor who also manages (operates) the hotel.

Ozone System A method of processing laundry that utilizes ozonated cold water rather than hot water to clean and sanitize laundry items.

P&L Short for "Profit and Loss" statement. The P&L records total hotel revenues and expenses for a specific time period. Same as income and expense statement.

Package A group of travel services, such as hotel rooms, meals, and airfare, sold for one price. For example, a Valentine's Day Getaway package to Las Vegas suggested by a travel agent might include airfare, lodging, meals, and show tickets for two people at an all-inclusive price.

Par Inventory System A system of managing purchasing and inventory levels based upon the requirement that a specified quantity of product be available in inventory. For example, if a par of five cases of disposable coffee cups is established, the quantity necessary to bring the inventory level back to five cases is ordered when coffee cups are purchased.

Participative Management A leadership style that emphasizes the solicitation and use of employee input as managers make decisions.

PBX Short for "Private Branch Exchange." The system within the hotel used to process incoming, internal, and outgoing telephone calls.

Peer Pressure Influence from fellow employees in the same position or organizational level to do (or not to do) something.

Per Diem A daily, fixed amount paid for a traveler's food and lodging expenses. Established by companies, government agencies, or other entities, the per diem amount for a traveler will be based upon the costs associated with the area to which the individual travels. For example, the per diem for a traveler spending the night in New York City will be higher than for a traveler spending the night in a less expensive area of the country.

Per Portion A single serving of food; for example, a portioned hamburger patty.

Performance Appraisal A periodic formal evaluation of an employee's job performance, including a discussion of professional development goals; also called "performance evaluation."

Permanent Placement The first full-time position a student assumes after graduation from a postsecondary school.

Pickup The actual number of rooms purchased by a client in a specific time period. Used as in: "What was the Florida Furniture Society's pick-up last week?"

Pilferage Stealing small quantities of something over a period of time; for example, a thief might steal one bottle from a case of liquor.

Pilot Light A small permanent flame used to ignite gas at a burner.

Place Setting The arrangement of plates, glasses, knives, forks, and spoons (flatware), and other service items arranged on a dining table for one guest.

Planning   The process of examining the future and establishing goals for an organization.

PM (Preventive Maintenance) Program   A specific inspection and activities schedule designed to minimize maintenance-related costs and to prolong the life of equipment by preventing small problems before they become larger ones.

PM Checklist   A tool developed to identify all the critical areas that should be inspected during a PM review of a room, area, or piece of equipment.

PMS   The hotel industry term for a "property management system."

Point-Of-Sale Terminal (POS)   A computer system that contains its own input and output components and, perhaps, some memory capacity, but without a central processing unit.

POM   Short for "property operation and maintenance." The term is taken from the Uniform System of Accounts for Hotels and refers to the segment of the income statement that details the costs of operating the maintenance department.

Post   Enter a guest's charges into the PMS in order to create a permanent record of the sale. Used as in "Please post this meeting room charge to Mr. Walker's folio."

Premium Brand Beverages   Highest-priced and highest-quality beverages generally available, such as Johnny Walker Black Scotch; also called "super call."

Premiums   The fees paid for insurance.

Pre-paid Expenses   Expenditures made for items prior to the accounting period in which the item's actual expense is incurred.

Preparing   Steps involved in getting an ingredient ready for cooking or serving.

Pre-shift Training   Training sessions of employees in the same position (such as housekeepers) that last only several minutes and are conducted at the beginning of a work shift.

Preventive Maintenance   Maintenance activities designed to minimize maintenance costs and prolong the life of equipment.

Private Club   Membership organization not open to the public that exists for people enjoying common interests. Examples include country (golf) clubs, city clubs, university clubs, yacht clubs, and military clubs. Some private clubs offer sleeping rooms for members and guests.

Product Usage Report   A report detailing the amount of an inventoried item used by a hotel in a specified time period (week, month, quarter, or year).

Production   The process of readying products for consumption.

Professional Development Activities   Formal and informal training and education undertaken to provide the additional knowledge, skills, and experience to prepare one for progressively more responsible positions.

Professional Development   The process by which hoteliers continue to improve their knowledge and skills.

Professionals   People working in an occupation that requires extensive knowledge and skills in a specialized body of knowledge. Occupations typically involve a common base of information and often require licensing or registration.

Progressive Discipline System   A process of negative discipline in which repeated infractions result in increasingly more severe penalties.

Promote From Within   The concept that a company offers higher-level positions to its existing employees when these positions must be filled.

Public Space   Areas within the hotel that can be freely accessed by guests and visitors. Examples include lobby areas, public restrooms, corridors, and stairwells.

Publicity   Information about a hotel that is distributed for free by the media.

Punitive Damages A monetary amount assessed to punish liable parties and to serve as an example to the liable party as well as others not to commit the wrongful act in the future.

Purchasing The process of determining the right quality and quantity of food products and ingredients to be purchased and of selecting a supplier that can provide these items at the right price and the right time.

Quality Inspection Scores Sometimes called Quality Assurance (QA) scores, these scores are the result of annual (or more frequent) inspections conducted by a franchise company to ensure that franchisor-mandated standards are being met by the franchisee. In some cases, management companies or the property itself may also establish internal inspection systems. In general, however, it is the franchise company's quality inspection score that is used as a measure of the effectiveness of the general manager, the hotel's management team, and the owner's financial commitment to the property.

Quality Suitability for intended use; the closer an item is to being suitable for its intended use, the more appropriate is its quality. Also, the consistent delivery of products and services according to expected standards.

Rack Rate The price at which a hotel sells its rooms when no discounts of any kind are offered to the guest. Often shortened to "rack."

Reasonable Care A legal concept identifying the amount of care a reasonably prudent person would exercise in a specific situation.

Receiving The point at which ownership of products being purchased transfers from the seller (supplier) to the hospitality operation.

Recodable Locking System A hotel guest room locking system designed so that when guests insert their "key" (typically an electromagnetic card) into the guest room lock for the first time, the lock is immediately recoded, canceling entry authorization for the previous guest's key.

Recruitment Activities designed to attract qualified applicants for the hotel's vacant management and non-management positions.

Regional Manager The individual responsible for the operation of multiple hotels in a designated geographic area. In some companies, the person's title may be area or district manager.

Registration (Reg) Card A document that provides details such as guest's name, arrival date, rate to be paid, departure date, and other information related to the guest's stay. In conversation, most often shortened to "reg" card, as in: "Who filed the Reg card for room 417?"

Registration Acceptance for one to work within a profession that is (typically) granted by a nongovernmental agency such as an association.

Reinforcement (Training) Use of words and actions that emphasize the proper way to do a job task.

Remote Printer A unit in a food or beverage preparation area that relays orders entered through an electronic cash register and/or point-of-sale terminal.

Repeat Business Guests who return to the property for additional visits after their first visit. Also, revenues generated from guests returning to a commercial hospitality operation as a result of positive experiences on previous visits.

Replace as Needed A parts or equipment replacement plan that delays installing a new part until the original part fails or is near failure. For example, most chief engineers would use a replace as needed plan in the maintenance of refrigeration compressors or water pumps.

Residential Education Programs   Formal education (training) programs that are available to students/trainees at a specific geographic location.

Resort   A full-service hotel with additional attractions that make it a primary destination for travelers.

Restoration   Returning a hotel to its original (or better than original) condition.

Return on Investment (ROI)   The percentage rate of return achieved on the money invested in a hotel property.

Revenue Management (RM)   The process and procedures used to maximize RevPar. Sometimes referred to as RM for short.

Revenue Manager   An individual whose major task consists of forecasting room demand so that the hotel can maximize RevPar. In larger hotels, this will be a full-time position. In a smaller, limited-service property, the general manager or front office manager will have this responsibility.

Revenue Per Available Room (RevPar)   The average revenue generated by each guest room available during a given time period; the formula for RevPar is: Commonly referred to as "RevPar."

RevPar   "Revenue Per Available Room"; the average revenue generated by each of a hotel's guest rooms during a specific time period.

Role Model   An individual who displays positive personal and professional characteristics that others find desirable.

Room Attendant Cart   A wheeled cart that contains all of the items needed to properly and safely clean and restock a guest room.

Room Attendant   Employee responsible for cleaning guest rooms. Also referred to as "housekeeper." Sometimes called "maids" by guests, but this term is never used by professional hoteliers.

Room Mix   The ratio of room types in a hotel. For example, the number of double-bedded rooms compared to king-bedded rooms, the number of smoking-permitted rooms to no-smoking rooms, and the number of suites compared to standard rooms.

Room Nights   The number of rooms used times the number of nights they are sold. For example, a guest who reserves two rooms for five nights each has made a reservation for 10 ($2 \times 5 = 10$) room nights.

Room Service   Food and beverages are delivered to a hotel guest's sleeping room.

Room Status   The up-to-date (actual) condition of each of the hotel's guest rooms (for example; occupied, vacant, dirty etc.).

Room Type   Specific configurations of guest rooms. For example, smoking vs. non-smoking, king-sized bed vs. double beds, or suite vs. regular sleeping room. Commonly abbreviated (K for king, NS for non-smoking, etc.), the hotel's reserving of the proper room type is often as important to guests as whether the hotel, in fact, has a room available for them.

Routine Maintenance   Maintenance activities that must be performed on a continual (ongoing) basis.

Safety   Protection of an individual's physical well-being and health.

Safety and Security Committee   An interdepartmental task force consisting of hotel managers, supervisors, and hourly employees responsible for monitoring and refining a hotel's safety and security efforts.

Safety Hazards   Conditions in the workplace that can cause immediate harm. Examples include unsafe equipment, accidents, and the improper use of chemicals.

Salary Pay calculated at a weekly, monthly, or annual rate rather than at an hourly rate.

Sales Activities directly related to a client's purchase of hotel rooms or services.

Sales and Marketing Committee The team of employees responsible for coordinating the hotel's sales and marketing effort.

Sales Call A meeting arranged for the purpose of selling the hotel's products and services.

Scratch The use of basic ingredients to make items for sale. A stew may be made on-site with vegetables, meat, and other ingredients, and a Bloody Mary mix can be made on-site with tomato juice and seasonings.

Seasonal Hotel A hotel whose revenue and expenditures vary greatly depending on the time (season) of the year. Examples include hotels near ski resorts, beaches, theme parks, certain tourist areas, sporting venues, and the like.

Second-tier Management companies that operate hotels for owners and do not use the management company name as part of the hotel name. American General Hospitality, Summit Hotel Management, and Winegardner and Hammons are examples.

Security Protection of an individual's or business's property or assets.

Selection The process of evaluating job applicants to determine who is most qualified for and likely to be successful in a vacant position.

Sell-out (1) A situation in which all rooms are sold. A hotel, area, or entire city may, if demand is strong enough, sell out. (2) A period of time in which management must attempt to maximize ADR.

Server Station An area of the dining room with tables/booths assigned to a specific food server.

Service (Guest) The process of helping guests by addressing their wants and needs with respect and dignity and in a timely manner.

Service The process of transferring food and beverage products from service staff to the guests.

Service Areas Non-public areas close to the dining room used to house coffee machines, ice bins, serviceware, and related supplies needed by service staff.

Service Bar A bar where drinks prepared by bartenders are given to personnel who serve them to guests.

Serving The process of moving prepared food or beverage items from production staff to service personnel.

Shift Bank The total amount of currency and coins in a cashier's drawer at the beginning of that cashier's work shift. Used as in: "Let's start the 3:00 P.M. front desk shift with a $750 shift bank."

Short A situation in which a cashier has less money in the cash drawer than the official sales records indicate. Thus, a cashier with $10 less in the cash drawer than the sales record indicates is said to be $10 short.

Short-Range Goals Goals that are to be achieved in the very near future (usually less than one year). Sometimes called "short-term."

Signature Items Food or beverage products produced by a hospitality operation that are unique to the property and/or that the general public associates with it.

Sign-in, Sign-out Program An arrangement in which individuals taking responsibility for hotel assets (such as hand tools, power equipment, or keys to secured areas) must document their responsibility by placing their signature as well as the date and time on a form developed to identify who last had possession of, and therefore responsibility for, the asset.

Sign-off   To verify or approve for accuracy or payment. Used as in: "Ms. Larson, will you sign-off on last night's audit?"

Site Tour   A physical tour of a hotel, hosted by a member of the hotel's staff.

SMERF   Short for "Social, Military, Educational, Religious, or Fraternal groups" and organizations.

Social Security   Retirement benefits paid to primary workers, survivor's benefits, and benefits for the retiree's spouse and children, and disability payments based upon contributions paid by the retiree and the retiree's employer(s).

Sole Investor   A single investor that owns 100 percent of a hotel. A sole investor may be an individual, a company, or some other financial entity.

Solvency   The ability of a hotel to pay its debts as they come due.

Source Reduction   Effort by product manufacturers to design and ship products in a way that minimizes packaging waste resulting from the product's shipment to a hotel.

Staff (Hotel Department)   A department in a hotel employing technical specialists who provide advice to managers and others with operating responsibilities. Large hotels typically have three departments with staff responsibilities: human resources, accounting, and purchasing.

Standard Recipe   A written explanation about how a food or beverage item should be prepared. It lists the quantity of each ingredient, preparation techniques, portion size/portion tools, and other information to ensure that the item is always prepared the same way.

STAR Report   Short for the "Smith Travel Accommodations Report." Produced by Smith Travel Research, this report is used to compare a hotel's sales results to those of its selected competitors.

Stay-over   A guest who is not scheduled to check out of the hotel on the day his or her room status is assessed. That is, the guest will be staying at least one more day.

Stereotype   A common perception (true or untrue) about something; for example, a specific hotel may be perceived in the community as kind or unkind to its employees.

Stockout   The condition that arises when a food/beverage item needed for production is not available on-site.

Storing   The process of holding products under optimal storage conditions until needed.

Subordinates   Employees whose work is directly supervised or controlled by an individual of higher rank or position.

Suggestive Selling   Information suggested by an order taker (in a room service operation) or by a server (in an à la carte dining operation) to encourage guests to purchase items they might otherwise not have ordered.

Supervisor   A staff member who directs the work of line-level employees.

System-wide   Term used to describe a characteristic of all hotels within a given brand. Used, for example, in: "Last year, the system-wide ADR for the brand was $99.50."

Team   A group of individuals who work together and set the goals of the group above their own.

Terry   Generic term for the bath towels, fabric bath mats, hand towels, and wash cloths washed and dried in the laundry area.

Theft   Stealing all of something at one time; for example, a thief might steal a case of liquor.

Threat Analysis   A systematic procedure designed to identify and eliminate identifiable safety risks.

Timeshare   A lodging property that sells its rooms to guests for use during a specific time period each year; also called vacation ownership property.

Total Replacement   A parts or equipment replacement plan that involves installing new or substitute parts based on a predetermined schedule. For example, most chief engineers would use a total replacement approach to the maintenance of light bulbs in high-rise exterior highway signs.

Tour Operator   A company or individual that plans and markets travel packages.

Tourist   An individual who travels for pleasure.

Track   Maintain extensive information on a specific type of traveler. For example, a hotel may wish to track the ADR, rooms used, and arrival patterns of transient military travelers to learn more about this traveler type.

Trade Show   An industry-specific event that allows suppliers to an industry to interact with, educate, and sell to individuals who are part of the industry; also called exhibition.

Traffic   The number of people, such as guests and/or employees, occupying/moving about in a specified area.

Transient   Individual guests who are not part of a group or tour booking. Transient guests can be further subdivided by traveler demographics to obtain more detailed information about the type of guest staying in the hotel (for example, corporate, leisure, and government).

Travel Agent   A professional who assists clients in planning and purchasing travel.

Tri-columned Statement   An income statement that lists (1) actual hotel operating results for a specific time period, (2) budgeted operating estimates for the same time period, and (3) the actual operating results from the same time period in the previous year.

Turnover Rate   A measure of the proportion of a work force that is replaced during a designated time period (month, quarter, or year). It can be calculated as: Number of Employees Separated ÷ Number of Employees in the Workforce = Turnover Rate.

Turnover   The replacement of employees needed in an organization or a position as other staff members leave.

Unemployment Claim   A claim made by an unemployed worker to the appropriate state agency asserting eligibility for unemployment benefits.

Unemployment Insurance   Funds provided by employers to provide temporary financial benefits to employees who have involuntarily lost their jobs.

Unemployment Rate   The number of employable persons who are out of work and looking for jobs (usually expressed as a percentage of the total work force).

Upselling   Tactics used to increase the hotel's average daily rate (ADR) by encouraging guests to reserve higher-priced rooms with better or more amenities than are provided with lower-priced rooms (for example, view, complimentary breakfast and newspaper, increased square footage).

Value (Lodging Accommodations)   The price paid to rent a room relative to the quality of the room and services received.

Value   The guest's perception of the selling price of a menu item relative to the quality of the menu item, service, and dining experience received.

Value   The relationship between price paid and the quality of the products and services received.

Value   The relationship between the price paid and the quality of a product, supplier information, and service received.

Vendors   Those who sell products and services to hoteliers.

Wage   Pay calculated on an hourly basis.

Walked   A situation in which a guest with a reservation is relocated from the reserved hotel to another hotel because no room was available at the reserved hotel.

Walk-in   A guest seeking a room who arrives at the hotel without an advance reservation.

Warm Body Syndrome   An often-used but ineffective selection tactic which involves hiring (almost) anyone who applies for a vacant position without regard to their qualifications for the job.

Word of Mouth Advertising   Favorable or unfavorable comments made when previous guests of a hospitality operation tell others about their experiences.

Work Order   A form used to initiate and document a request for maintenance. Sometimes referred to as a "maintenance request."

Worker's Compensation   An insurance program designed to assist individuals who are victims of a work-related injury or illness.

Wow Factor   The feeling guests have when they receive or experience an unanticipated extra as they interact with the hospitality operation.

Write-off   A guest's direct bill that is considered uncollectible by management and as a result is subtracted from the hotel's accounts receivable total.

Zero Defects   A goal of no guest-related complaints established when guest service processes are implemented.

Zero Tolerance   The total absence of workplace behavior that is objectionable from the perspectives of discrimination or harassment.

Index

À la carte dining, 375, 388
  preparation before guests,
    388–391
  service procedures, 391–393,
    392f
Abandoned property, 295
Accor, 49
Accountability, 70
Accounting department, 248
  budgeting, 251–252
    annual budgets, 253
    long-range budgets,
      252–253
    monthly budgets, 254–255
  expense controls, 269
    accounts payable (AP),
      271–274
    purchasing/receiving,
      270–271
  financial reporting, 274–275
    balance sheet, 277–279
    cash flows statement,
      280–281
    income statement,
      275–277
  income controls, 255
    accounts receivable (AR)
      control, 265–269
    allowances/adjustments,
      262–265
    cash control, 259–262
    operational controls,
      255–259

new issues/procedures (infor-
    mation about), 281
  on-property hotel account-
    ing, 248–249
    centralized accounting sys-
      tems, 249–250
    decentralized accounting
      systems, 250–251
  Uniform System of Accounts
    for Hotels, 276
Accounting systems
    (accrual/cash), 355
Accounts payable (AP), 269
Accounts receivable (AR), 265
  aging, 266, 268f
Administration of Hotel and
    Restaurant Management
    Contracts, 36
ADR (average daily rate), See
    also Hotel performance
    assessment methods
Advertising, 221
  Internet, 69
  word of mouth, 67–68
Agitation, 309
Air handler, 339
Airlines, 15
Alberta Hotel Safety
    Association (ΛHSA),
    412
Allowances/adjustments, 256,
    262–265
Amenities, 14

American Automobile
    Association (AAA),
    225–226
American Hotel and Lodging
    Association (AH&LA),
    23, 87
  certification processes, 74–75
  Educational Institute (E.I.) of,
    23, 235, 299, 414, 465
American Hotel and Motel
    Association. See
    American Hotel and
    Lodging Association
    (AH&LA)
American Hotel Register
    Company, 93
American Institute of Certified
    Public Accountants
    (AICPA), 251
American Society of
    Association Executives
    (ASAE), 454
American Society of Heating,
    Refrigerating, and Air
    Conditioning
    Engineers, 321
Amtrak, 17
Appreciation, 28
Asian American Hotel Owners
    Association (AAHOA),
    23
  and franchise agreement
    change campaign, 47

ASTA (American Society of Travel Agents), 18
At-will employment, 165
Atrium, 348
Attitude, 122–123
Attrition, 216
Audit, 250
 See also Night audit/auditor
Authority, 87
Authorize, 201

Back-up generator, 337
Back-up system, 180
Ballast, 338
Banquet, 376, 399
Banquet event order (BEO), 402–403, 403*f*
Banquet operations, 398–400
 banquet event orders (BEOs) and contracts, 402–403, 403*f*
 menu planning, 401–402
 other concerns, 403
  beverage function control, 405–406
  room set-up, 404
  service styles, 404
 profitability, 400–401
Batch cooking, 387
Bed and breakfast inns (B&B), 9
Benchmark, 60
Best Inn and Suites, 98
Best Western, 41
Bid, 216
Biohazard waste bag, 309
Black-out dates, 197
Block, 216
Blood-borne pathogen, 298, 299
Body language, 121
Bonafide occupational qualifications (BOQs), 162
Bonding, 430
Booking, 213
Brand, 39
 brand affiliation management, 96–98
 brand management, 43
 brand standard, 47
 supervision, 106–107

Breakfasts, 350*f*, 353
 continental, 350
 cost, 354
 deluxe hot, 351
Budgeting information, 220
Bus lines, 15–16
 types, 16
Buy-out, 39

Calibration, 337
Call accounting, 204
Call brand beverages, 405
Camps/park lodges, 9
Cancellation number, 196
Capital expenditure, 253
Careers in lodging industries, 442
 alternatives, 446, 458*f*
  franchisor vs. operating company, 451–453
  independent hotel vs. multi-unit organization, 446–450, 449*f*
  large vs. small hotel company, 450–451
  profit vs. non-profit, 453–454
 career planning, 442–443, 443*f*, 465*f*
  job fulfillment diagram, 446*f*
  personal interest assessment, 443–444, 446*f*
  short-term, 465
 career tracks, 143–145
  career ladder, 144
 domestic and global positions, 470
  international work, 470–472
  success factors (global assignments), 472–475, 473*f*, 474*f*
 entrepreneur vs. intrapreneur, 466–467
  hotel failure (reasons for), 467–468
  intrapreneur success tactics, 468–470

 first professional position (search for), 454
  career fairs, 455
  data collection, 454–456
  employee's concerns, 457
  employer's concerns, 456
  management trainee positions, 456
 first professional position (strategies for success), 457–459
  first impressions, 459–462
  ongoing professional development, 462–466, 463*f*, 465*f*
 on-line information, 442
 trade journals, 455
Carpet and Rug Institute (information), 331
Case goods, 324
Cash bar, 401
Casinos, 10
Catering, 399
Cendant, 40–41, 214
Centralized purchasing, 357
Certification processes, 74
Certified Lodging Security Officer (CLSO), 414
CFL, 339
Chain, 40
Chained recipe, 387
Chamber of Commerce, 224–225
Charter, 16
Chief engineer, 326
Choice Hotels International, 40
Claim (insurance), 424
Clarion, 39
Closed-circuit television (CCTV), 420
Coding, 273
Cold calling, 232
Comfort Inn, 39
Comment cards, 59, 63*f*–64*f*
Communication, 120
"Comp," 95–96
Compensation, 158
 fringe benefits, 160–161, 161*f*
 importance of, 159–160

Competency, 459, 460f
Competitive set, 241
Competitors, 375
Confirmation number, 196
Consortia, 227
Contact alarm, 419
Contribution margin, 401
Controller, 248–249
Controlling, 85
Convenience food, 386
Conversion, 41–52
Cooking, 387
Corkage fee, 406
Corporate rate, 191
Cost per occupied room, 301
C.P.A. (certified public accoun-
    tant), 249, 251
CQI (continuous quality
    improvement), 72–73
Credit/debit cards, and no-
    shows, 190
Critical incidents, and
    performance appraisal,
    134–135
Cross-functional team, 60
Cross-selling, 395
Cruise lines, 10
Culture
    cross-cultural adaptability,
       474
    national, 471
    shock, 472
Curb appeal, 195
CVB (convention and visitor's
    bureau), 217–218
    and hotel marketing, 224

Damages, 411
    compensatory, 411
Deep cleaning, 300
Delivery invoice, 359
Demographic factors, 380
Depreciation, 28
Depressed market, 31
Destination (activity) sites, 13
Direct bill, 103
Direct mail, 233–235
Direct report, 378
Directing, 84

Discipline/positive and
    negative, 136
Diversity (workforce), 171–173
DOSM (director of sales and
    marketing), 213
Drop in, 232
Duct, 339

Electric discharge lamp, 338
Electronic cash register (ECR),
    397
Embezzlement, 429–430
Employee
    employee-to-guest ratio, 56
    handbook, 156
    and management relation-
       ships, 132
    regulations involving, 164
    safety/health issues, 170–171
    See also Entry level employ-
       ees; Staff; Turnover
Employer of choice, 70
Employment agreement, 165
Empowerment, 61
Energy management, 336
Engineering, 320
Entrepreneur, 466
Entry level employees, 114,
    138–139
    expectations from supervi-
       sors, 140
    responsibilities, 139–140
Ethics, 461–462
Exchange rate, 471
Executive Committee, 150
Executive housekeeper, 285,
    290–291
    See also Managing house-
       keeping
Exercise facilities. See Special
    safety-related threats
Expatriate, 471
Expedite, 385
Eyster, James, 36

Fayol, Henri, 83
Federal Trade Commission
    (FTC), and franchise
    fairness, 45–46

Feedback (training), 130
FF&E, 92–93
    reserve, 323
Financial Accounting Standards
    Board (FASB), 281
Financial statements, 274
Finger foods, 351
First-tier (management com-
    pany), 32
Fiscal quarter, 276
Fixed charges, 275
Folio, 182
FOM (front office manager), 179
Food and beverage operations,
    374, 379f
    dining room furniture/sup-
       plies, 393
    food and beverage guests,
       374–376
    food service control points,
       383, 385
       purchasing, 383–385, 384f
       receiving/storing/issuing,
          386–387
       serving and service,
          387–388
    interactions
       housekeeping, 288–289
       maintenance, 325, 332,
          334
    menu design, 383
    menu planning, 378–379,
       380f
       guest concerns, 379–381
       operating concerns,
          381–383, 382f
       operating issues, 396–397
    organization, 376
       large hotels, 377, 377f
       small hotels, 376, 377f
    services, 375f
    and threats, 435
    See also Banquet operations;
       Room service
Food items, 383
Food service and meeting man-
    agement/limited-service
    hotels, 347
    equipment information, 362

Food service and meeting management/limited-service hotels (*cont.*)
food cost per guest, 354
food service trays, 360
food services range, 348–349, 349*f*
breakfast alternatives, 349–351
other food services, 351–352
guest concerns, 365
lobby food services management, 352, 352*f*, 361*f*
clean-up tasks, 362, 364
last call, 363
maintaining breakfast service, 360, 362
menu planning, 352–356, 353*f*
purchasing, 356–358
receiving and storing, 358–359
sanitation, 363
setting up breakfast service, 359–360
managing meetings, 366
meeting food service, 369–370, 369*f*
meeting "procedures," 367–369
small meetings business, 366–367
Foot-candle, 337
Forecasting demand, 183
demand impact on ADR, 183–184
estimating demand, 185
use of PMS in, 185–187
Franchise Offering Circular (FOC), 46
Franchise service director (FSD), 51
Franchising, 39
advantage to franchisor, 41
conversions, 41–42
franchise agreements, 44–48
changes to, 47
importance of, 48
regulation of, 45–47

Franchise Rule, 46
franchise/franchisor/franchisee, 39
franchisor's sales/marketing efforts, 222–224
hotel franchisees, 42–44
advantages to investors/brand name owners, 42–43
brand selection factors, 43–44
hotel franchisors, 39–42
contact list, 44
See also Membership groups
Fraud, 430
Frequent guest program, 223
Fringe benefits, 158, 160–161, 161*f*
Front desk, 178
and housekeeping interaction, 286–288
and maintenance interaction, 324–325
Front office department, 178
information about, 208
responsibilities, 178–179, 179*f*
accounting and data management, 181–183
guest services, 181
property management system (PMS), 179–181
and threats, 433–434
See also Forecasting demand; Guest accounting; Reception and guest service; Reservations; Room rates (establishment of)
Full-service hotel, 7
Function room, 404

GAAP (generally accepted accounting principles), 274
General manager (GM), 30
role, 91–92, 92*f*
brand affiliation management, 96–98
community relations, 98–100
owner relations, 92–93

property management, 94–96
staff development, 93–94
General manager's supervisor, 101
brand supervision, 106
brand-monitored hotels, 106
brand-owned hotels, 106–107
management company supervision, 104–107
owner/investor supervision, 101–103
GFI outlet, 335
Global Distribution System (GDS), 42
and reservations, 197
and Internet booking sites, 197–198
GOP (gross operating profit), 275
Grapevine, 122
"Green" hotel, 314–315
association, 343
and disposable products, 364
Group, 192
contract, 216
travelers, 229–231
Guarantee, 401
Guest accounting, 203–204
data management, 204–207
games, 206
Internet connections, 207
movies, 206
phone charges, 204–206
safes, 207
night audit, 207–208
Guest check average, 396
Guided tour, 21

Hampton, 39
Head table, 404
Health hazards, 170
Hilton, 49
management company, 32, 104
Holding, 387
Holiday Inn, 39, 40
Holiday Inn Express/Express Start Breakfast Bar, 353

Hospitality Financial and Technology Professionals (HFTP), 255
Hospitality industry, 8, 13
  career information, 153
Hospitality Sales and Marketing Association International (HSMAI), 213
Hospitality suite, 395
Hosted bar, 401
Hosted events, 395
Hotel, 3, 6
  classification systems, 2
    services offered, 7
    size, 6–7
  failure (reasons for), 467–465
  "Green," 314–315, 343
  history in U.S. (1900–2000), 3, 4*f*–6*f*
  largest (worldwide), 48*f*
  seasonal, 254
  types, 9–10, 9*f*
    conference center, 10
    convention hotel, 10
    extended-stay hotel, 10
    resort, 10
    timeshare, 11
Hotel brand Web sites, 214
Hotel F&B Executive, 378
Hotel management, 82
  structure, 88–89
    larger hotels, 89, 90*f*
    smaller hotels, 89, 91*f*
  See also General manager (GM)/role; General manager's supervisor; Human resources department; Management companies; Managers' role; Service and hotel management
Hotel Operations Management, 89
Hotel owners, 27–28
  as general manager's supervisor, 101–103
  investors, 28–29
  owner operators, 29

ownership and operational challenges, 50–51
ownership/management alternatives, 48, 50, 50*f*
  multi-unit properties/different brand, 50
  multi-unit properties/management company or brand operation, 50
  multi-unit properties/same brand, 49
  single or multi-unit properties/brand owned, 50
  single-unit property/brand affiliation, 49
  single-unit property/no brand affiliation, 48
  special operational problems, 30
  See also Franchising; Management companies
Hotel performance assessment methods, 2, 10
  average daily rate (ADR), 2, 10–12
  occupancy rate, 2, 12
  revenue per available room (RevPar), 12
Hotel shuttle, 15
Hotel team, 111–114, 115*f*
  and cross-functional teams, 113
  effectiveness factors, 114
  and informal groups, 112
  on-line information about, 113
  See also Career tracks; Entry-level employees; Manager's role; Supervisor
Hoteliers, 3
  interactions with tour operators, 21
  professional development, 22–23
"Hourly," 95
House brand beverages, 405
House count, 258
Housekeeping department, 284
  cleaning responsibilities, 299

employee scheduling, 299–301
guest room cleaning, 301–306
interactions, 286
  food and beverage, 288–289
  front desk, 286–288
  maintenance, 288, 325
laundry operations, 307
managing housekeeping, 289–290
  inventory management, 293–295
  lost and found (management of), 295–296
  staffing, 290–293
  See also Executive housekeeper; Room attendants
responsibilities, 284–286
safety training, 297–299
  and threats, 434–435
  See also Laundry operations
Housepersons, 292, 304
Hub, 15
Human relations, 116
Human resource specialist, preferred background, 151
Human resources department (HR), 148, 151
  activities, 150*f*
    orientation, 154–156
    recruitment, 151–153
    selection, 153–154
    training, 156–157
  background, 149
  challenges, 173–174
  diversity (promotion of), 171–173
  importance of, 148
  priorities, 150
  See also Legal aspects of human resources
HVAC, 321, 339–341
Hyatt
  extended-stay brand, 229
  international opportunities, 471
  management company, 32, 104, 106

Incandescent lamp, 338
Incident report, 427
Inclusive, 219
Independent operator, 466
Induction, 155
Inflation, 471
Ingredients, 384
Inspector/inspectress, 291
Insurer, 413
InterContinental Hotels group, 40
Interdisciplinary, 464
Interfaced, 204
Internal alarm, 419
International Executive Housekeepers Association (IEHA), 291
International Franchise Association (IFA), 46
International Hotel and Restaurant Association (IH&RA), 23
Internet
    booking sites, 197–198
    e-mail effectiveness, 235–236
    See also Web site operators
Interstate commerce, 163
Intrapreneur, 466
    traits, 470
Issuing, 386

Job description, 152
Job specification, 153

Keycards, 418

Laundry operations, 307
    guest-operated laundry, 312–314
    laundry processing, 307–308
        collecting, 308–309
        delivering, 312
        drying, 311
        finishing and folding, 311
        sorting/repairing, 309
        storing, 311–312
        washing, 309–310
    par levels, 312
    PM programs, 334
        task list (sample), 331*f*

Lead, 231
Leadership, 117
    See also Supervisor/leadership style
Legal aspects of human resources, 161
    employee selection, 162–165
    employer-employee relationships, 165
    on-line information, 167, 170
    workplace laws, 165
        compensation, 166
        employee performance, 167–168
        employment records, 169–170
        family and medical leave act (FMLA), 166
        sexual harassment, 165–166
        unemployment issues, 168–169
Liable, 35
Licensing, 74
Limited-service hotel, 7–8, 349
    See also Food service and meeting management/limited-service hotels
Line of authority, 102
Line department, 149
Line-level, 95
Line managers, 149
Linen, 308
Link, 237
Linking pin, 116
Lobby food services, 348
Lodging industry, 9*f*
    common requirements, 3
    history, 2, 3
    other lodging operations, 10
    specific features (segments), 3, 6
    structure, 27
    as travel and hospitality industry component, 2, 8–9, 9*f*
    See also Careers in lodging industry; Management companies; Management of lodging

Long-range goals, 83
Lost property, 295
    documentation, 296

Maintenance, waste management, 342–344
Maintenance chief, 326
Maintenance department, 319–320
    engineering, 320–321
    interactions, 324
        food and beverage, 325
        front desk, 324–325
        housekeeping, 325
    maintenance, 288, 321–323
        emergency, 320, 334–336
        preventive, 320, 330–334, 335
        routine, 320, 327–330
    management, 325
    renovation, 323–324
    staffing, 326
        chief engineer, 326
        maintenance assistants, 326–327
    threats, 436
    utility management, 336–337
        electricity, 337–339
        HVAC, 339–341
        natural gas, 341
        water, 341–342
Make/buy analysis, 386
Malcolm-Baldridge National Quality Award, 75
Management companies, 30
    advantages, 37
    arrangements, 33
        fee for services (standard), 31, 33
        manages hotels it owns, 34–35
        manages hotels it owns and others, 35
        ownership partnership, 33–34
    disadvantages, 37–39
    general manager's supervision, 104–106
    largest, 32*t*
    and management contracts, 35–36

rankings by hotel numbers/revenues, 33
role/structure, 30–31
first/second-tier structure, 32
maintain repossessed properties, 31–32
Manager, 59
See also FOM (front office manager); General manager (GM); Revenue manager
Manager's daily, 255–259
Manager's reception, 351
Managers' role, 82
employee safety/health, 170–171
management functions, 82–83, 83*f*, 85*f*
controlling, 85
directing, 84
organizing, 84
planning, 83–84
management principles, 85–86, 86*f*
management science/art, 87–88
Mark-up, 369
Market. *See* Travelers
Market share, 49
Marketing, 213
back-door, 156
plan, 218
performance comparison to, 240–241
See also Sales and marketing function/activities
Marriott, 49, 106
Material safety data sheet (MSDS), 312
Medicare, 167
Meeting management. *See* Food service and meeting management/limited-service hotels
Meeting planner, 230–231
Meeting Professionals International (MPI), 231
Membership groups, 41

Mentor, 94
and supervisor's role, 132
Microsoft Office products, 187
Minutes per room, 300
Mise en place, 389
Mislaid property, 295
Mission statement, 70–71
Mitel, 205
MOD (Manager on duty), 264
"Moments of truth," 65–67
Morale, 123
Motel, 6, 49
Motivation, 123
and basic human needs, 124–126, 125*f*, 126*f*
on-line information about, 124
Movies, 206

National Restaurant Association, certification processes, 74
Negotiated rate, 227
Networking, 232
Night audit/auditor, 181–182, 207–208
See also Audit
No-show, 190
and credit/debit card issuers, 190
Non-yieldable, 192
Novotel, 49

Occupancy rate, 2, 12
See also Hotel performance assessment methods
Occupational Safety and Health Administration (OSHA), 171, 414–415
Offer letter, 165
On-line distribution, 21
Open bar, 405
OPL (on premise laundry), 289, 307
equipment, 308
Organizational chart, 88, 90*f*–91*f*
Organizing, 84
Orientation, 154
Outsource, 327
Over, 261

Overbooking, 189
Overload, 383
Overtime, 166
Ozone system, 310

P&L (profit and loss), 275
Package, 19
Par inventory system, 357
Parking areas. *See* Special safety-related threats
Participative management, 112–113
PBX (Private Branch Exchange), 205–206
Pellerin Milnor Corporation, 308
Per diem, 228
Per potion, 387
Performace appraisal systems, 133–134, 137*f*
conduct of, 135–136
critical incidents, 1334–1135
on-line resources, 135
special concerns, 134
Permanent placement, 457
Personnel management. *See* Human resources department
Phone systems, 204–206
Pickup, 216
Pilot light, 341
Place settings, 390, 390*f*
Planning, 83–84
PM (preventive maintenance) program, 330
checklist, 332
PMS (property management system), 179–181
effective features, 186–187
use in forecasting demand, 185–187
See also Manager's daily
Point-of-sale terminal (POS), 397
POM (property operation and maintenance), 321
Post, 203–204
Pre-paid expenses, 278
Premium brand beverages, 405
Premiums, 423
Preparing, 387

Private clubs, 10
Product usage report, 294
Production, 386
Professional development, 22
    activities, 462, 463*f*
    job rotation/enlargement, 463
    plan, 465*f*
Professionalism, 73–75
Progressive discipline system,
        167–168, 168*f*
Promote from within, 462
Property protection, 427–429
    area-specific threats, 433
        food and beverage, 435
        front office, 433–434
        housekeeping, 434–435
        maintenance, 436
        sales and marketing,
            435–436
    crisis-management plans,
        436–437
    external threats
        to cash, 432
        to other assets, 432–433
    internal threats, 429
        to cash, 429–430
        to other assets, 430–432
Public space, 293
    PM programs in, 331–332
Publicity, 221
Punitive damages, 412
Purchasing, 384

Quality, 55–56, 384
    Malcolm-Baldridge National
        Quality Award, 75
    Quality Inspection
        Scores/Quality
        Assurance (QA), 97
    See also CQI

Rack rate, 188
Ramada, 39
Re-flagging, 41
Reasonable care, 411
Receiving, 358
Reception and guest service, 198
    arrival and stay, 200–202
    departure, 202–203
    pre-arrival, 199–200

Recruitment, 151
    internal/external, 152
    See also Human resources de-
        partment (HR)
Red Roof Inns, 49
Regional manager, 105–106
Registration, 74
    Registration (Reg) card,
        199
Reinforcement (training), 130
Remote printer, 397
Rental cars, 17–18
Repeat business, 63, 381
Replace as needed/total replace-
        ment, 328
Reservations, 193, 388
    central reservation system,
        195–197
    hotel direct inquiry, 193–195
    Internet booking sites,
        197–198
    See also Global Distribution
        System (GDS)
Restoration, 323
Retail (shopping) stores, 13
Retention issues, 140–143
Return on investment (ROI),
        27–28
Revenue management
        (RM)/manager, 187
RevPar (revenue per available
        room), 12, 183–184
    See also Hotel performance
        assessment methods
Ritz-Carlton Hotel Company
    basics, 77
    corporate mantra, 57
    Credo, 76
    employee promise, 76
    quality emphasis, 75
Role model, 94
Roney Palace, 49
Room attendant, 291–293
    cart, 297
Room mix, 243
Room nights, 196
Room rates (establishment of),
        188
    group rates, 192–193
    transient rates, 190–192

    yield management, 188–190,
        189*f*
Room service, 8, 394
    in-room service, 397–398
    manager, 397
    menu planning, 395–396
    profitability, 394–395
Room status, 286
    terminology, 287*f*
Room type, 183

Safety resources, 416
    external, 422–423
        local law enforcement,
            423
        property insurers, 423–424
    internal, 417
        alarm systems, 419–420
        emergency plans, 421–422
        recodable locks, 417–419
        surveillance systems,
            420–421
Safety and security, 410
    committee, 414
    hotel responsibility/guest
        safety, 412
        facility, 412–413
        policies and procedures,
            416
        staff training, 413–416
    legal liability (guests and em-
        ployees), 410–512
    safety hazards, 170
    terrorism threat, 438
    trade associations, 412
    See also Property protection;
        Safety resources; Special
        safety-related threats
Salary, 158
Sales, 213
    call, 232
    cycle, 215, 215*f*
        post-sales phase, 217
        pre-sales phase, 215
        sales phase, 216–217
Sales and marketing committee,
        218
Sales and marketing
        efforts/evaluation of,
        239–234

performance to plan, 240–241

Smith Travel Accommodations Report (STAR report), 240, 241–244

Sales and marketing function/activities, 212, 215

importance of, 212–214

marketing goal, 214*f*

off-property activities, 222

CVB efforts, 224

frachisor's efforts, 222–224

other efforts, 225–226

on-property activities, 218

sales and marketing budget, 219–220

sales and marketing plan, 220–221

sales and marketing team, 218–219

and threats, 435–436

Sales and marketing function/tools, 231, 233

client-appreciation activities, 238–239

e-mail, 235–236

in-person sales calls, 231–233

print/direct mail, 233–234

telephone, 234–235

Web sites, 236–238

Sarbanes-Oxley Act, 275

Scratch, 386

Second-tier (management company), 32

Selection, 153

Sell-out, 185

Server station, 391

Service, 387

delivery by employees, 68–70

in dining process, 391–393

features of, 74

in Internet advertising, 69

management tactics, service and training articles, 72

See also Room service

Service areas, 391

Service bar, 387

Service and hotel management, 55

evolution of service, 65

"manage by walking around," 59

management tactics, 70

improvement focus, 72–73

orientation/training, 71

recruitment/staff-selection issues, 70

staff empowerment (service authority), 72

supervision/service emphasis, 71–72, 71*f*

"moments of truth," 65–67

on-line resources, 65

professionalism, 73–75

quality (impact of), 55–56

quality service system components (ingredients), 57–58

delivery procedures (development of), 60

evaluate/modify service delivery systems, 62–65

guest profiling, 58

revised systems implementation, 62

staff training/empowerment, 61–62

understanding guest likes/needs, 58–60

service concerns, 57–58

service expectations, 57

word of mouth advertising, 67–68

wow factor, 66

zero defects management, 68, 68*f*

Serving, 387

Sheraton, management company, 32

Shift bank, 260

Shopping service, 60

Short, 260

Short-range goals, 83

Sign-in/out program, 436

Sign-off, 259

Signature items, 354

Small Business Administration, 101

SMERF (social, military, educational, religious, and fraternal groups), 230

Smith Travel Accommodations Report (STAR report), 240, 241–244

Social security, 166

Sofitel, 49

Sole investor, 107

Solvency, 280

Source reduction, 343

South Beach hotels, 99

Spas. *See* Special safety-related threats

Special safety-related threats, 424

exercise facilities, 426

parking areas, 426–427, 428*f*

spas, 425

swimming pools, 424–425

Staff (hotel department), 148

Standard recipe, 386

Stay-over, 287

Stereotype, 151

Storing, 386

Subordinates, 469

Suggestive selling, 396

Super 8, 39

Supervisor, 59

employee retention tactics, 141–142

celebrate successful employees, 143

create hospitable workplace, 143

golden-rule supervision, 142–143

leadership, 141–142

professionalism focus, 142

staff preparation, 142

leadership style, 116–118, 117*f*

autocratic, 118

bureaucratic, 118–119

democratic, 119

laissez-faire, 119

role of, 114, 115*f*

employees' representative, 132

judge, 132

Supervisor (*cont.*)
   mentor, 132
   responsibilities, 115–116, 115*f*
   trainer, 131
   special concerns, 120
   coaching, 130–131
   communication, 120–122
   employee discipline, 136–138
   motivation, 122–126
   performance appraisal systems, 133–136, 137*f*
   training, 126–130
   training of, 120
   See also Hotel team
Swan Inc., 35
Swimming pools. *See* Special safety-related threats
"System-wide" (within brand), 44

Team, 111
Terry, 308
Tharaldson Lodging Company, 103
Theft, 384
Threat analysis, 412
Tour operators, 2, 19–21
   and hoteliers, 21
   National Tour Association (NTA), 21
Tourism industry. *See* Travel/tourism industry
Tourist, 3
Track, 227
Trade associations, 22–23
   international, 475
Trade show, 23
Traffic, 382
Training, 126, 156–157
   benefits of, 127
   distance learning courses, 448

Four-Step Training Method, 128–130, 128*f*, 129*f*
   follow-up, 130*f*
individualized, 127–128
on-line information, 130, 157
residential education programs, 448
and supervisor's role, 131
telephone selling skills, 234–235
Trains, 17
Transient, 192
Transportation services, 13, 14–15
   airlines, 15
   bus lines, 15–16
   rental cars, 17–18
   trains, 17
Travel agents, 2, 14–15, 18–19
   American Society of Travel Agents (ASTA), 18
   Global Distribution System (GDS), 19
Travel/tourism industry, 2, 9*f*
   components, 13, 13*f*
   destination (activity) sites, 13
   hospitality, 13
   retail (shopping) stores, 13
   transportation services, 13
   See also Hospitality industry; Lodging industry
Travelers, 226
   group, 229–231
   reasons, 2, 13
   senior citizens, 194
   transient, 226–228
   long-term stay, 228–229
   types, 14, 212
   business, 14, 227
   government, 228
   leisure, 14, 228

Tri-columned statement, 276–277
Turnover/turnover rate, 70, 141, 151
   managing-turnover information, 143

Unemployment insurance, 168
   unemployment claim, 169
Unemployment rate, 151
Uniform System of Accounts for Hotels, 276
Upselling, 195

Value, 57, 380, 385
Value (lodging accommodations), 6

Wage, 158
   minimum wage, 166
Walk-in, 195
Walked, 189
Warm body syndrome, 153
Web site operators, 2, 15, 21–22, 198
   direct-to-guest model, 22
   merchant model, 22
   opaque rate model, 22
   and sales opportunities, 236–238
   See also Internet booking sites
Wilson, Kemmons, 40
Windows format for hotel-industry software, 187
Wireless waitress system, 391
Word of mouth advertising, 67
Work order, 329
Worker's compensation, 423
Wow factor, 66
Write-off, 269

Zero defects management, 68
Zero tolerance, 165–166